Structured Finance and Collateralized Debt Obligations

New Developments in Cash and Synthetic Securitization

Second Edition

JANET M. TAVAKOLI

Lyons McNamara LLC
Chicago

Published by Lyons McNamara LLC, Chicago, Illinois.

Limits of Liability/Disclaimer of Warranty

This book provides general information only. Neither the information nor any opinion expressed constitutes an offer, or an invitation to make an offer to buy or sell any securities or other investment or any options, futures, or derivatives related to securities or investments. It is not intended to provide personal investment advice and it does not take into account the specific investment objectives, financial situation and particular needs of any specific person or entity. Investors should seek financial advice regarding the appropriateness of investing in any securities, other investment or investment strategies discussed or recommended in this report and should understand that statements regarding future prospects may not be realized. Investors should note that income from such securities or other investments, if any, may fluctuate and that price or value of such securities and investments may rise or fall. Accordingly, investors may receive back less than originally invested. Past performance is not necessarily a guide to future performance.

Under no circumstances will the author or publisher have any liability to any person or entity for (a) loss or damage in whole or in part caused by, resulting from, or relating to, any error (negligent or otherwise) or other circumstance or contingency within or outside the control of the author or publisher in connection with the procurement, collection, compilation, analysis, interpretation, communication, publication or delivery of any such information, or (b) any direct, indirect, special, consequential, compensatory or incidental damages whatsoever (including without limitation, lost profits), resulting from the use of or inability to use, any such information. The financial reporting analysis observations and other observations, if any, constituting part of the information contained herein are, and must be construed solely as, statements of opinion and not statements of fact or recommendations to purchase, sell, or hold any securities. No warranty, express or implied, as to the accuracy, timeliness, completeness, merchantability or fitness for any particular purpose of any opinion or information is given or made by the author or publisher in any form or manner whatsoever. Each opinion must be weighed solely as one factor in any investment decision made by or on behalf of any user of the information contained herein, and each user must accordingly make its own study and evaluation of each security and of each issuer and guarantor of, and each provider of credit support for, each security that it may consider purchasing, holding, or selling.

Library of Congress Cataloging-in-Publication Data (Previous via Wiley Finance):
Tavakoli, Janet M.
[Collateralized Debt Obligations and Structured Finance]
Structured Finance and Collateralized Debt Obligations: New Developments in Cash and Synthetic Securitization – 2nd ed.
Originally published in 2003 under title: Collateralized Debt Obligations and Structured Finance]
Wiley Finance
Includes biographical references and index
1.Asset-backed financing—United States. 2. Mortgage-backed securities—United States. I. Title.

Hardcover Edition. 2019 reprint of the 2008 Second Edition

ISBN-10: 1-943543-31-3

ISBN-13: 978-1-943543-31-1

Books by Janet Tavakoli

NONFICTION

Risk

Decisions: Life and Death on Wall Street

Unveiled Threat: A Personal Experience of Fundamentalist Islam and the Roots of Terrorism

Structured Finance and Collateralized Debt Obligations

Dear Mr. Buffett

Credit Derivatives and Securitization (3rd Edition)

The New Robber Barons

FICTION - MYSTERY

Archangels: Rise of the Jesuits

"Conspiracies within conspiracies, a fast-paced thriller."
—*Publishers Weekly*

Finance Classics

Fifty Years in Wall Street
Parts One and Two

By Henry Clews
Contributions by Janet Tavakoli

The Wall Street Point of View

By Henry Clews
Foreword by Janet Tavakoli

Twenty Years of Inside Life in Wall Street
or
Revelations of the Personal Experience of a Speculator

By William Worthington Fowler
Foreword by Janet Tavakoli

Contents

Preface

What's new in structured finance? Since the first edition of this book came out in 2003, the structured finance landscape has sustained several seismic shifts, particularly in the collateralized debt obligation (CDO) market. New technologies blossomed along with problems of transparency and application. Rapid growth became explosive growth peaking in the second half of 2007. Abuse led to a rapid decline in new CDO issuance in 2008, and future deals will employ more tested tradecraft and fewer opaque financial engineering techniques

Post-Enron accounting changes have made CDO equity a hot potato for former investors who do not want to consolidate entire deals on their balance sheets. This has opened the door to the rise of inexperienced CDO managers, new and unknown offshore entities, hedge fund investors, and private equity investors.

CDO managers of all types—from the savvy to the naïve—waded into the global securitization market. Even former stints at SEC-alleged Ponzi schemes or fines paid after SEC-alleged accounting fraud were not deterrents for investment banks doing business with reinvented CDO managers. CDO managers giving the appearance—if not the reality—of investing in CDO equity were pushed through internal approval committees of investment banks.

Not-so-savvy hedge funds purchased the sucker tranches of CDOs. Savvy hedge funds became CDO managers recognizing the benefits of being on the right side of a cash flow engineering windfall. Some hedge funds became major participants in the CDO market, embracing the leverage afforded by synthetic technologies, financial engineering, and the fees to be earned by managing CDOs. Other hedge funds became independent speculators in the CDO markets, using hedging techniques such as shorting the ABX indexes as tools for wildly profitable speculation.

Single-tranche CDOs rose and waned to be overshadowed by constant proportion debt obligations (CPDOs), constant proportion portfolio insurance (CPPI), and other highly structured leveraged products.

Cash securitizations explored novel asset classes. Belts and braces sometimes gave way under the strain of unrealized cash flow. Investment banks have become major lenders to originators of products with unprecedentedly low underwriting standards combined with unprecedentedly risky products.

Retail investors are being solicited through products that employ form-over-substance sleight of hand. Products that could not be sold to retail investors through the debt markets in the United States due to Securities and Exchange Commission (SEC) restrictions are being sold through the stock markets, through structured notes, through mutual funds, and through pension funds.

New products require another look at credit default swaps (CDSs) and total rate of return swaps in the context of synthetic securitizations. Synthetics introduce unique structural risks to CDOs and structured finance products. We will look at recent changes in the CDS market posed by CDSs on asset-backed securities (CDSs of ABSs). We will also look at synthetic indexes.

Securitization groups continue to use their financial institutions' balance sheets. Securitization technology originally moved mortgage-backed securities, consumer loans, and other loans off financial institutions' balance sheets so they could reduce balance sheet risk and do more business. In recent years, securitization groups are added risk to a variety of financial institutions' balance sheets, added invisible risk to trading books, or placed risk in stagnant conduits in order to earn fee income. As a result, banks, investment banks, hedge funds, insurance companies, and conduit investors were more exposed to concentration risk and losses due to fraud.

The Sarbanes-Oxley Act of 2002 (Sarbox) was meant to combat fraud on a corporate level for firms regulated by the SEC. Whatever its value at the corporate level, it has not hampered structured financing as many feared, nor has it affected the evolution both positive and negative of structured finance in a significant way. In fact, evidence is presented later in this book that suggests securitization professionals feel free to ignore the beneficial intent of Sarbox.

Fraud has been an ongoing concern, particularly in the way we originate assets. Even when fraud is absent, markets have been plagued by poor underwriting standards combined with risky assets. The current market has seen a surge in problematic loans. The subprime and Alt-A mortgage loan markets in several countries provide handy examples. This book focuses primarily on the dynamics of the U.S. mortgage market because it is the largest of the affected markets and the most egregious offender. The role of financial institutions that provided credit to mortgage bankers is examined in Chapter 8. While the mortgage market is one example, it is not the only one. Other asset classes present their unique problems: commercial real estate, project loans, corporate receivables, and more.

As we are all aware, fraud can be internal to an arranger securitizing a deal; fraud can be external, as when a corporation fudges its accounting; and fraud can take the form of a conspiracy when both external parties and internal deal makers agree to hide relevant facts. We shouldn't be surprised by fraud; we should expect to deal with it and can take steps to guard against it.

For instance, we know that in the United States one-third of small businesses that lose money do so not because of utility cost increases, not because of rent increases, not because big companies take their business, but *because of employee fraud.* We've also discovered that fraud isn't committed by petty thieves or uneducated thugs. Eighty percent of fraudulent employees are white; they are 16 times as likely to be managers or executives, 4 times as likely to be men, and 5 times as likely to have postgraduate degrees. We also know that many employees will commit fraud given the right circumstances. These "right circumstances" are known as the fraud triangle: need, opportunity, and the ability to rationalize one's behavior.

Knowing human nature, we can't expect it to change in large corporations, in commercial banks, in investment banks, in insurance companies, in hedge funds or in other financial institutions. We can expect the individual to feel his own needs are greater than those of the whole. The need for a Rolex, the need for an estate in Florida, the need for a castle in the South of France, the need for an enormous annual bonus—all of these so-called needs seem to be greater in the finance business. Given the keen intelligence of the players and the complexity of structured financial products, opportunity, and the ability to rationalize behavior may be greater as well. Decreasing opportunity increases sound business.

While we look at some instances of fraud in this book, we also look at instances of gray-area opportunities presented by structured products. And we look at opportunity costs due to both ignorance and intent.

One would think that in an efficient market, the deterrents in place would stop this behavior. Even in the absence of legal remedies, censure by other firms can be costly. Yet even with predetermined sanctions, the market is not always efficient about routing out this behavior, and we shouldn't expect it to be.

In isolated incidents we see financial institutions and individuals blackballed for pulling a fast one, but increasingly it is also true that we see people relying on the depth and breadth of the market to move on to a new set of unaware market players.

Synthetic CDOs—namely, securitizations incorporating credit derivatives technology to transfer asset risks and cash flows—make up most of the CDO market. This is due to the seeming arbitrage advantage of synthetic versus cash assets caused by creation of a super senior tranche, and the increased leverage of the equity tranche. The ability to sell synthetic CDOs backed by investment-grade collateral is another huge advantage over cash CDOs in the current credit environment.

Cash CDO issuance has also ballooned, as financial institutions rushed to securitize everything from mortgage loans to the value of intellectual capital. The availability of credit derivatives to hedge cash CDOs has contributed to the unprecedented growth of this market.

CDOs are still an evolving product, especially in Europe where special venue considerations introduce technological challenges. This market has enthusiastically embraced credit derivatives since synthetic structures solve certain venue issues for risk transfer. Credit derivatives also often allow special gimmicks to be employed which can produce certain regulatory advantages.

The purpose of this book is to point out key issues in valuing structured financial products. I review the basics of the market so that any reader with some knowledge of the capital markets will understand the components required to evaluate structured products. Readers looking for a book on models should go elsewhere.

The irony of the complex CDO market is that the basic principles of sound finance are often violated in ways the models cannot capture. Models are a secondary overlay in determining fundamental value. Therefore, this book focuses on preserving fundamental value, and it does not focus on mechanical models. Yet model building is in vogue, particularly the building of inferior correlation models, and the industry has produced many "model monkeys." They produce encyclopedias of code, but even if the code is correct, it is often of little practical value.

Richard Feynman once pointed out that students in Brazil memorized the definition and formulas for *triboluminescence*, but they had no idea what they meant. While they could spout the theory of the production of light in the destruction of a crystalline lattice, the students had no idea which crystals produce light when crushed or why they produce light. Feynman wanted to send them into a closet with a sugar cube and a pair of pliers to observe the faint blue flash of light produced by crushing the crystals.

I'm not saying models have no value; I use models. I'm simply pointing out that if you don't know where you are going, writing a model isn't going to get you there.

Quality control in CDOs and structured credit products is uneven. A small number of firms have built sound business models with strong professional teams, but they are the exceptions. Many structurers and credit derivatives professionals are inadequately trained in the capital markets to be competent in their jobs, and the investor community is suffering the results. A major problem in today's markets is lack of cross training. The result is poor understanding of the basic mechanics of the products of the global financial markets. The problem is exacerbated by the fact that securitizations have recently become a lot more global.

Credit derivatives professionals often have never traded cash products or traded an interest rate swap. Some have no exposure to the bond markets, or even the currency or swap markets. Many cannot explain how to construct a par asset swap, one of the benchmark relative-value instruments for their market. Some have no exposure to repurchase agreements. This lack of general knowledge has caused dangerous misunderstandings.

I believe the reason this problem falls below the radar screen is that financial institutions rapidly grow these departments and need to dub ad hoc "experts" to satisfy a need. The growth in business of managing CDOs, and the influx of new participants such as hedge funds and pension funds, has made what was formerly a big problem into a critical one. The required qualifications and training take a back seat to representing to upper management that departments are in place. Upper management is often confused by the complexity of these products and, as a result, many institutions are going through growing pains, and some may not make it to full maturity.

Another reason this problem hasn't been solved is that upper management often has difficulty assessing true performance. If a group has lost money, there seems to be a ready reasonable excuse. Many groups have no clear idea why they lose money or why they make money. They make a bet and it either wins or it loses. There is no business model in place to support consistent revenue growth. If they make a little money, they persuade management that a hockey stick profit projection profile depicts the future of their fledgling department. The philosophy is to tell management what they want to hear, even if it isn't close to the truth. Don't tell management the department is nothing more than just a few guys taking bets. Opportunity cost is invisible.

In Europe in particular, where synthetic securitizations often seem to pose a solution to sticky venue issues, there is a dearth of capital markets experience in the structuring community. Virtually any asset can be securitized, and virtually anyone thinks he can do it.

One securitization professional told me he'd been an unsuccessful emerging markets trader, but now he felt he'd found his niche. Lack of experience was no impediment. He informed me he was a native Italian, and the language skill was more valuable. He cloned mandate letters of his more experienced colleagues and sent them to banks to ask them to allow him to do their balance sheet securitizations. When that strategy wasn't successful, he simply lowered his costs. In his mind, that was all it took. The ability to offer creative structural solutions or value added wasn't a chief concern for him. This attitude has the potential to hurt this growing market.

Cash flows can be manipulated to solve almost any problem; they can also be manipulated to *hide* almost any problem. Much of what we consider unethical practice is a matter of custom, legislation, and the time in which we live. That applies as much to financial practices as it does to sexual practices. Giving kickbacks in Europe was almost standard operating procedure until the Lockheed scandal caused vilification in the United States of the U.S. participants. Many Europeans were initially confused by the uproar, but in the end, the negative publicity caused the European business community to rethink this practice. Determining what is unethical is sometimes a difficult call, and opinions are divided. Nonetheless, I attempt to address this issue where applicable.

I do not delve deeply into tax products or accounting issues, because it would require an additional book to do them justice. Furthermore, these issues change and they vary by venue. One should always refresh the relevant rules when doing a securitization. Structured finance tax products have long hangovers. Investors may need to produce documentation for accounting and tax-related transactions years after the product matures. One Cayman Islands–based investor received calls from the U.S. Department of the Treasury for 15 years after a tax-related product matured. Tax laws are constantly changing. Single-venue tax code interpretation is complex, and cross-border tax code interpretation adds another layer of complexity.

Despite the caveats, I'm an enthusiastic proponent of structured financial products and welcome the growth of new products in the market. Wherever possible, I've tried to point out how existing structuring technology has benefited new markets and has the potential to create even better products. It is my intent to facilitate a clearer understanding of these products that will encourage investors to confidently participate in this fascinating market.

Acronym Key

ABS	asset-backed securities
ACH	checking transfers
AFC	available funds cap
AIG	American International Group
ALT-A	Alternative-A mortgage loans (just above subprime)
ARM	adjustable-rate mortgage (see also hybrid ARM)
BaCa	Bank Austria Credit Anstalt
BAFin	Bundesanstalt für Finanzdienst-leistungsaufsicht (Bundesbank Regulations and Guidance)
BofA	Bank of America, N.A. (successor by merger to NationsBank, N.A.)
BofA Sec	Bank of America Securities LLC (successor by merger to NationsBanc Montgomery Securities LLC, or NMS)
Bank One	Bank One Capital Markets (successor by merger to BancOne)
BBVA	Banco Bilbao Vizcaya Argentaria S.A.
BBA	British Banker's Association
BEY	bond equivalent yield
BIS	Bank for International Settlements
BISTRO	broad index secured trust offering
BofA	Bank of America, N.A. (successor by merger to NationsBank, N.A.)
BofA Sec	Bank of America Securities LLC (successor by merger to NationsBanc Montgomery Securities LLC, or NMS)
BOJ	Bank of Japan
BP	basis point
C&I	commercial and industrial
CAG	cash against goods
CBO	collateralized bond obligation
CBOE	Chicago Board Options Exchange
CBOT	Chicago Board of Trade

CBT	Chicago Board of Trade
CDO	collateralized debt obligation
CDPC	credit derivative product companies
CPDO	constant proportion debt obligation
CDS	credit default swap
CEO	chief executive officer
CFO	collateralized fund obligation; chief financial officer
CFTC	Commodities Futures Trading Commission
Chase Sec	Chase Securities, Inc. (successor by merger to Chemical Securities, Inc.)
Chase Bank	The Chase Manhattan Bank (successor by merger to Chemical Banking Corp.)
Chase USA	Chase USA, N.A.
CJE	Calamity Jones Entertainment
CLN	credit-linked note
CLO	collateralized loan obligation
CMO	collateralized mortgage obligation
CN	combination note
CP	commercial paper
CPA	certified public accountant
CPDO	constant proportion debt obligations
CPPI	constant proportion portfolio insurance
CQT	collateral quality test
CSFB	Credit Suisse First Boston
CSFP	Credit Suisse Financial Products
CSLT	Chase Secured Loan Trust
CSO	credit spread option
CUSIP	Committee on Uniform Securities Identification Procedures
DBA	doing business as
Dimat	Dimat Corporation (succeeded by J.L.J., Inc.)
DSCR	debt service coverage ratio
DTC	Depository Trust Company
EC	European Community
ECB	European Central Bank
ECR	estimated cash recovery, the same as credit card grading model score

EFC	Enterprise Funding Corporation (multiseller conduit)
EMCC	East Mississippi Collection Corporation
EMTN	Euro Medium Term Note
EOD	event of default
FASB	Financial Accounting Standards Board
FASIT	Financial Asset Securitization Investment Trust
FED	Federal Reserve Board and the Federal Reserve System
FDCPA	Fair Debt Collection Practices Act
FDIC	Federal Deposit Insurance Corporation
FHLB	Federal Home Loan Bank
FNMA	Federal National Mortgage Association (Fannie Mae)
FHLMC	Federal Home Loan Mortgage Corporation (Freddie Mac)
FRN	floating-rate note
FSA	Financial Services Authority (UK)
FTP	failure to pay
GAAP	generally accepted accounting principles
GARP	Global Association of Risk Professionals
GBP	Great Britain Pound (Sterling currency)
GLPC	Guaranteed Loan Pools Certificate
GmbH	Gesellschaft mit beschränkter Haftung (limited liability company)
GNMA	Government National Mortgage Association (Ginnie Mae)
GREAT	Global Rated Eligible Asset Trust
HLT	highly leveraged transactions
Hybrid ARM	an ARM that is fixed for a set period and then becomes adjustable
IA	investment adviser
ICO	Instituto de Credito Oficial
IMF	International Monetary Fund
IO	interest only (tranche)
IOR	Istituto per le Opere di Religione (The Institute of Religious Work, also known as the Vatican Bank)

IPO	initial public offering
IRB	internal ratings-based approach
IRR	internal rate of return
IRS	Internal Revenue Service (U.S. Tax Department)
ISDA	International Swaps and Derivatives Association, Inc.
ISP	interest subparticipation piece
J.L.J., Inc.	Successor by merger to Dimat Corporation.
KfW	Kreditanstalt für Wiederaufbau
KHFC	Kitty Hawk Funding Corp. (multiseller conduit)
LIBOR	London Interbank Offered Rate
LOC	letter of credit (also LC)
LPFC	limited purpose finance corporation
LSS	leveraged super senior
LSTA	Loan Syndications and Trading Association
LTCM	Long Term Capital Management
M&A	mergers and acquisitions
Mayer Brown	Mayer Brown Rowe & Maw, P.A. (the successor to Mayer Brown Rowe & Platt)
MBS	mortgage-backed security
MIE	multi-issuance vehicle
MLEC	master liquidity enhancement conduit
MTN	medium-term note
N/A	not applicable; not available
NAIC	National Association of Insurance Commissioners
NASD	National Association of Securities Dealers
NAV	net asset value
NER	noneconomic residual
NPF	note purchase facility
NPV	net present value
OCC	Office of the Comptroller of the Currency
OECD	Organization for Economic Cooperation and Development
OPM	other people's money
OSFI	Office of the Superintendent of Financial Institutions
OTC	over-the-counter

P&L	profit and loss statement
PAC	planned amortization class
PAUG	pay-as-you-go
PCAOB	Public Company Accounting Oversight Board
PIK	pay-in-kind; payment-in-kind
PN	participation note
PO	principal only
PPM	private placement memorandum
PPN	principal-protected note
PPS	principal-protected Schuldschein
QIB	qualified institutional buyer
QSPE	qualifying special purpose entity
RBA	ratings-based approach
REIT	real estate investment trust
REMIC	real estate mortgage investment conduit
ROSE	repeat offering securitization entity
RP	repurchase agreement or repo
S&L	savings and loan
S&P	Standard & Poor's
Sarbox	Sarbanes-Oxley Act of 2002
SCB	specified correspondent bank
SDA	specified deposit account
SEC	Securities and Exchange Commission
SFA	supervisory formula approach
SIV	structured investment vehicle
SLMA	Student Loan Marketing Association (Sallie Mae)
SLT	secured loan trust
SMART	securitized multiple assets related trust
SME	small to medium-size enterprise
SPAC	special purpose acquisition company
SPC	special purpose corporation
SPE	special purpose entity
SPV	special purpose vehicle
STCDO	Single tranche collateralized debt obligation aka bespoke tranche
STRIPS	separate trading of registered interest and principal of securities

SWIFT	Society for Worldwide Interbank Financial Telecommunications
T-bill	Treasury bill
T-bond	Treasury bond
TRORS	total rate of return swap (also TRS or total return swap)
USD	U.S. dollar
UST	U.S. Technologies, Inc.; U.S. Treasury; U.S. Treasuries (bonds)
VAT	value-added tax
WAC	weighted average coupon
WARF	weighted average risk factor
YTM	yield to maturity

Structured Finance and Collateralized Debt Obligations

Chapter 1

Securitization Terminology

Structured finance is a generic term referring to financings more complicated than traditional loans, generic bonds, and common equity. Relatively simple transactions that lower corporations' funding costs by converting floating rate obligations to fixed rate obligations (or the opposite) through the use of interest rate swaps are traditionally considered structured finance transactions. Financial engineering involving special purpose entities is also considered a part of structured finance. Extremely complicated leveraged products such as constant proportion debt obligations (CPDOs) and complicated securitizations such as collateralized debt obligations *of* collateralized debt obligations (CDO^n) are also included in the definition of structured finance.

Key motivations for using structured finance include lowering funding costs, changes in debt and equity composition of the balance sheet, taking companies public or private, freeing up balance sheet capacity, monetizing balance sheet assets, financing assets, regulatory capital arbitrage, sheltering corporations from operating liabilities, tax management, financing leveraged buyouts, poison pill takeover defenses, hedge fund speculation, accounting rule compliance and leverage. The structures may address several issues at once including risk transfer, accounting, taxation, bankruptcy, and credit enhancement.

Securitization is a generic term for a subset of structured finance. A securitization is simply the creation and issuance of securities backed by a pool of assets, also called the portfolio, usually with multiple obligors. A *synthetic securitization* employs credit derivatives technology to transfer asset risk (see also Chapter 3, "Credit Derivatives and Total Rate of Return Swaps"). Securitization offers the possibility of portfolio diversification, even when it doesn't always deliver on this promise. Virtually any combination of financial assets or stream of cash flows can be securitized. In the early 1990s Prudential brought so-called death bonds to the market. These were securitizations of the life insurance premiums owed to Prudential. The firm provided actuarial information showing dropout rates and potential death rates of the premium payers so investors could get an idea of the future cash flows. Investors learned a new meaning for the term *deadbeat*. This structure was one of the early *future flows* deals. The risk was in whether the projected future cash flows would be realized, due to the ultimate lack of future of the premium payers.

Collateralized debt obligation (CDO) is a generic term for a subset of securitizations. Collateralized debt obligations can be backed by any type or combination of types of debt: tranches of other collateralized debt obligations, asset backed bonds, notes issued by a special purchase entity that purchases other underlying assets, which are used as collateral to back the notes, hedge fund obligations, bonds, loans, future receivables, or any other type of debt.

The term *collateralized debt obligation* encompasses collateralized bond obligations (CBOs), collateralized mortgage obligations (CMOs), collateralized fund obligations (CFOs), asset-backed securities (ABS), synthetic credit structures and more. In the U.S. capital markets, the term *asset-backed securities* was originally used to describe deals backed by credit card receivables and auto loans. In recent years, this term has also been used to describe residential mortgage-backed securities (RMBS) and commercial mortgage-backed securities (CMBS).

Terms used in the mortgage market are sometimes difficult to interpret. Collateralized mortgage obligations usually refer to mortgage-backed securities with strict underwriting standards, where risk is primarily defined by the allocation of principal and interest payments. RMBS and CMBS are terms usually reserved for deals backed by a portfolio of mortgage loans tranched into various classes of credit risk. Similarly, *mortgage-backed CDO* is a term usually reserved for deals backed by a portfolio of mortgage-backed *bonds* that are tranched into various classes of credit risk.

Credit derivative is the generic term for any derivative contract used to transfer credit risk on a reference entity or reference obligor between a credit protection seller that is long the credit risk, and a credit protection buyer that is short the credit risk. A *credit default swap* is a bilateral contract between the protection buyer that is short the credit risk and the protection seller that is long the credit risk.

A *total return swap* (TRS), also known as a *total rate of return swap* (TRORS), is considered a type of credit derivative, and it is fundamentally a form of financing. An investor uses financing (i.e., leverage) and obtains the economic benefits of an asset (or assets) without owning the asset or ballooning its balance sheet. The investor is the receiver of the total return on a reference asset or assets, including interest, capital gains/losses, or other economic benefits during the predefined payment period. The investor's counterparty finances the transaction and receives a specified fixed or floating cash flow usually related to the creditworthiness of the investor. The reference asset may be virtually any financial obligation.

Special purpose entities (SPEs) are powerful structured finance tools frequently used in securitizations and CDOs. *Special purpose entity* is a global term and is used interchangeably with the term *special purpose vehicle* (SPV) and *special purpose corporation* (SPC). Special purpose entities can be trusts or companies. They house asset risk either through the purchase of the assets or in synthetic form. The assets are then used as collateral for notes or other forms of risk transfer (see also Chapter 2).

Market professionals agree all CDOs are structured products, but total agreement usually ends there. Market professionals often disagree on the definitions, so I attempt to be clear at all times how I am using terminology in specific examples throughout this book. Some market definitions are confusing and redundant. We deal in a global market with people with a wide variety of professional backgrounds and ethnic origins. It is always best to agree on definitions of terms before engaging in any new transaction.

Structured finance benefits participants in various ways:

- Securitization may provide funding and liquidity by converting illiquid assets into cash.
- Structured finance can reduce borrowing costs. Often captive finance companies and independent companies can obtain capital at rates better than those obtainable for the originator of the securitized assets.
- Securitization may transfer the risk of assets or liabilities to allow an asset originator to do additional business without ballooning its balance sheet. Corporations use structured finance vehicles to finance assets used in the course of their business.
- Securitization can enable a financial institution to exploit regulatory capital arbitrage. At times, both banks and insurance companies engage in regulatory capital arbitrage as a prime motivation for securitization of assets that offer a low return on regulatory capital.
- Structured finance vehicles can be used to shelter corporations from potential operating liabilities.
- Securitizations and structured finance vehicles can be used for tax management.

To do all of these things, structures must address issues of bankruptcy, accounting issues, tax issues, and credit enhancement.

Traditionally securitization has been a means for financial institutions to reduce the size of their balance sheets and to reduce the risk on their balance sheets. This allowed them to do more business and allowed investors access to diversified pools of assets to which they otherwise would not have had access. Securitization was a good deal for almost everyone.

SIMPLIFIED CASH CDO

A simple cash collateralized debt obligation is based on a portfolio of corporate bonds. The bonds throw off coupon income and are redeemed at par at maturity. In practice, cash CDOs have a target average life and target final maturity due to the varied maturities of the underlying bonds. At the final maturity, the bonds are redeemed at par. Figure 1.1 shows the basic CDO structure.

A CDO backed by the portfolio of bonds might be tranched into four classes of risk with the following ratings: a senior ("AAA") tranche, two mezzanine tranches (rated "A" and "BBB" respectively and shown in the figure as one block), and one unrated first-loss or equity tranche. First-loss risk is also called *equity*, or *preferred shares*, or *residual*, or *junior tranche* (especially used for the highly leveraged first-loss slice of a portfolio of highly rated assets), or by other names, but it is not to be confused with common equity or preferred shares issued by corporations with ongoing businesses.

A special purpose entity usually houses the collateral pool and becomes the issuer of the various classes of debt. By this means, the deal arranger/structurer isolates the risks and opportunities. Investors want to have exposure to a specific pool of assets, but they have various appetites for risk.

The deal arranger is typically the underwriter selling or retaining all of the tranches at market prices. The difference between the income from the

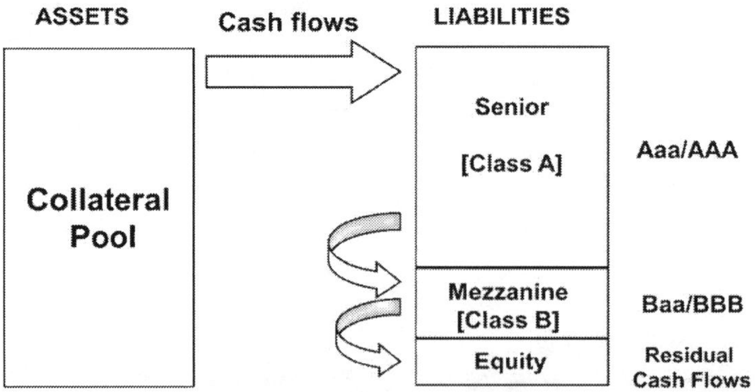

FIGURE 1.1 Basic CDO Structure

portfolio and the cash owed to the investors (the liabilities), less the deal expenses (legal, rating agencies, structuring fees, and more), is known as the *CDO arbitrage*. In particular, the investment bank arranger will normally presell the first-loss tranche, the riskiest tranche, also called the equity. The implied internal rate of return at which this equity risk can be sold to an outside investor is a key determinant of the CDO arbitrage.

THE CDO ARBITRAGE

In practice, there is actually no such thing as a CDO arbitrage. An *arbitrage* is a money pump. A true arbitrage guarantees a positive payoff in some scenario, with no possibility of a negative payoff and with no net investment. The opportunity to borrow and lend at two different fixed rates of interest, leading to an assured profit, is an arbitrage. Another example is the ability to *simultaneously* buy and sell the *same* security in different marketplaces and earn a profit at no cost and with no risk. The efficient market hypothesis asserts that the market will take into account all relevant information and price risk accordingly. Therefore, arbitrageurs will force the rates to converge and drive the arbitrage out of the market. In other words, it shouldn't be possible to make a guaranteed risk-free profit.

Note that the process of buying bonds on the bid side of the market for later resale to customers at the offer side of the market is called *trading*. Often both sides of the trade do not occur simultaneously; traders must assume market risk, and so trading isn't considered an arbitrage. Profits are not guaranteed. We often loosely and incorrectly use the word *arbitrage* to describe a hedged position that made money. For instance, we might say that a long bond position was arbitraged by a short sale.

Structurers of CDOs buy collateral and resell the collateral risk in another form at a lower all-in cost. As we shall see later, sometimes the risk is not completely sold and is held in a trading book due to distribution challenges. Sometimes the risk represented in the CDO tranches (the notes or liabilities issued by the CDO) is not the same risk represented by the collateral of the CDO. Sometimes the residual risk is deliberately held in a trading book and *dynamically hedged*. Sometimes an entire tranche, usually the super senior tranche, is held in the trading book with no hedge whatsoever, and is *marked-to-market* in theory, but not in actual practice.

Structuring groups that have separate profit and loss statements (P&Ls) from trading desks can with some truth claim that they benefit from a CDO arbitrage, but their financial institution does not. The structuring group means that they put together a deal, pay themselves a structuring fee, pass the risk of distribution and management of the tranches to the trading desk, and declare victory for the structuring group. They have acted as middlemen, taken out a fee, and washed their hands of the risk management and distribution challenges. Many deal arrangers are set up this way. They recognize this moral hazard, link structuring and trading P&L, and track CDO profitability throughout the deal life, but many deal arrangers do not.

Financial institutions that structure CDOs come closest to approaching an arbitrage when they buy the collateral, tranche the exact risk represented by the collateral, and sell every tranche of the collateral through their distribution network. Time elapses between the accumulation of collateral and the closing of the transaction, especially in a cash asset-backed deal. During this warehouse period, there may be significant market and credit risk that must be hedged, if possible. The hedge may generate gains or losses, and this risk (or reward) is usually borne by the deal arranger—usually an investment bank or commercial bank, but it may be borne by the equity investor(s) if it is pre-agreed. Once the deal closes, there may be further risk to the bank arranger due to holding tranches in trading book inventory before the deal is entirely sold.

Financial institutions also make a secondary market in the CDO tranches, and these positions are usually hedged. Reserves are held as a cushion for the residual risk of ongoing trading and risk management. The financial institutions that use this business model have the cleanest type of transaction management from the arbitrage point of view, but it is still not strictly an arbitrage.

It is more correct to call the cash calculation of the CDO the *economics* rather than the *arbitrage*. The economics of a typical CDO are calculated as follows:

> *Cash thrown off by the collateral plus interest on collateral, if any, minus structuring fees; plus/minus hedging gains/losses; minus underwriting fees or sales fees (of the tranches or liabilities); minus legal fees, trustee fees, and management fees, if any; minus administration fees, special purpose vehicle fees, rating agency fees, and listing fees; minus the payments due on the CDO notes (the tranches, which are the liabilities, of the CDO), equals profit.*

Later we look at the CDO economics in more detail. We examine the failure of arbitrage terminology to describe the fluctuating profitability, and sometimes the loss, in these transactions, especially for financial institutions that do not distribute all of the liabilities of the CDO.

Chapter 2

Structured Finance and Special Purpose Entities

Special purpose entity (SPE) is a global term and is used interchangeably with the term *special purpose vehicle* (SPV). An SPE is either a trust or a company. Special purpose corporations (SPCs) are used for a variety of purposes, including structured risk management solutions. In securitizations, the SPE houses the asset risk either through the purchase of the assets or in synthetic form. The assets are then used as collateral for notes issued by the SPE.

Special purpose entities are powerful structured finance tools. They can be either on shore or offshore. Because of their normally off-balance-sheet, bankruptcy-remote, and private nature, SPEs can be used for both legitimate and illegitimate uses. Most of the structures discussed in this book are legitimate uses of SPEs. I point out several structures along the way that lend themselves to money laundering, disguising loans as revenue to misstate earnings through wash trades, concealment of losses, embezzlement, and accounting improprieties. Even when used legitimately, the way the issuance of SPEs is represented is sometimes ethically marginal.

All of the following are examples of SPEs: SPCs that may or may not be special purpose subsidiaries or *captives*; master trusts; owner's trusts; grantor trusts; real estate mortgage investment conduits (REMICs); financial asset securitization investment trusts (FASITs); multiseller conduits; single-seller conduits; and certain domestically domiciled corporations.

Special purpose entities are often classified as either *pass-through* or *pay-through* structures. Pass-through structures pass all of the principal and interest payments of assets through to the investors. Pass-through structures are therefore generally passive tax vehicles and do not attract tax at the entity level. Pay-through structures allow for reinvestment of cash flows, restructuring of cash flows, and purchase of additional assets. For example, credit card receivable transactions use pay-through structures to allow reinvestment in new receivables so bonds of a longer average life can be issued.

For securitization of cash assets, the key focus is on nonrecourse financing (i.e., nonrecourse to the originator/seller). The structures are bankruptcy-remote so that the possible bankruptcy or insolvency of an originator does not affect the investors' right to the cash flows of the vehicle's assets. The originator is concerned about accounting issues, especially that the structure meets requirements for off-balance-sheet treatment of the assets, and that the assets will not be consolidated on the originator/seller's balance sheet for accounting purposes. For bankruptcy and accounting purposes, the structure should be considered a sale. This is represented in the documentation as a *true sale at law* opinion. The sale is also known as a *conveyance.*

The structure should be a debt financing for tax purposes, also known as a debt-for-tax structure. Tax treatment is independent of the accounting treatment and bankruptcy treatment. An originator selling assets to an SPE will want to ensure that the sale of assets does not constitute a taxable event for the originator. The securitization should be treated as a financing for tax purposes, that is, treated as debt of the originator for tax purposes. This is represented in the documentation in the form of a tax opinion.

The structured solution to the bankruptcy, true sale, and debt-for-tax issues varies by venue. The deal arranger may be a bank, insurance company, hedge fund, CDO manager, independent asset originator, or other entity that has the ability to accumulate assets. For example, if a U.S. arranger wants to securitize receivables, the structure requires two SPEs to avoid a federally taxable asset sale and to achieve off-balance-sheet financing and a bankruptcy-remote structure. In the United States, SPEs are usually organized as trusts (for tax reasons) under the laws of the state of Delaware or of New York. The first SPE is a wholly owned, bankruptcy-remote subsidiary of the originator/seller, and the SPE buys the assets in a true sale. The assets are now beyond the reach of both the originator/seller and its creditors. Wholly owned subsidiaries are consolidated with the originator/seller for U.S. federal tax purposes, so this achieves the debt-for-tax objective. The second SPE is the issuer of the debt (or asset-backed security, ABS) and is entirely independent of the originator/seller. It is a bankruptcy-remote entity. The second SPE buys the assets of the first SPE as a true sale for accounting purposes, and a financing for tax purposes. A schematic of this structure appears in Figure 2.1.

Other venues are more problematic, and the regulations with respect to the local equivalent of the U.S. Bankruptcy Court's automatic stay procedures, accounting rules, and tax laws must be verified with experts who have local expertise.

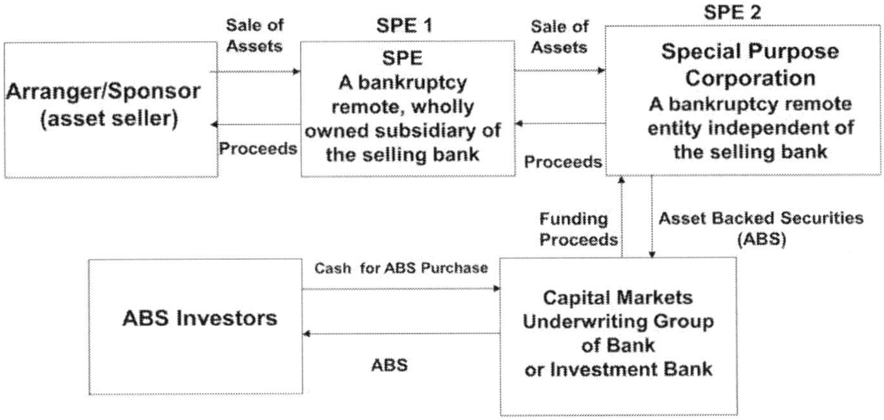

FIGURE 2.1 Double SPE Structure for U.S. Accounting and Tax Regulations

For example, two entities are required for Italian securitizations. The first entity can be onshore and purchases the assets. The onshore entity cannot issue bonds, or it will attract heavy Italian taxes. The second entity is offshore, and it issues the bonds.

Synthetic securitizations do not get true sale treatment for accounting purposes, since no asset has been sold. This is true whether the vehicle is an SPE or a credit-linked note. Bank arrangers usually do these deals to reduce regulatory capital according to regulatory accounting principles, for credit risk relief, and to free up balance sheet capacity. Hedge funds, investment banks, and other entities do these deals for risk transfer, balance sheet management, and for profit. Partial funding is feasible with a hybrid structure. We compare and contrast synthetic and true sale structures in Chapter 12.

Investors in CDOs want to invest in a risk class of a pool of receivables and want the asset to be bankruptcy-remote so the supplier of the assets has no further claim on the assets. It is also usually important that the deal is structured in such a way so that the equity class investor does not have to consolidate the entire special purpose entity on its balance sheet.

In the United States, before Enron's collapse, the minimum outside investment for an off-balance-sheet special purpose entity was 3 percent. In reaction to Enron's collapse and the revelations of its massive abuse, accounting rules regarding SPEs changed. The following summary of changes in U.S. accounting reflects changes post-Enron and is subject to interpretation and change. It also varies by venue. Anytime a securitization is done, the rules must be revisited and reinterpreted, because they are subject to change.

Nonetheless, the following summary gives an idea of the changeable nature of the rules. Changes can present both problems and opportunities.

A qualifying SPE (QSPE) does not have to be consolidated on the balance sheet of an issuer or equity investor, but it is more difficult to claim that status.

If the SPE is not a QSPE, it may or may not be a *variable interest entity* (VIE). If it is a VIE, then you have to determine the primary beneficiary for consolidation purposes. The primary beneficiary records the assets on the balance sheet at fair value or, if the assets are transferred to the primary beneficiary, they may be recorded at book value while recording the fair value of the liabilities and the fair value of the minority interests in the VIE.

The SPE is not a VIE if the total equity investment is sufficient to finance activities without additional financial support, and that is not necessarily 10 percent; it might actually even be less. If the equity is adequate and if it is well dispersed the SPE may not be deemed to be a VIE. But this is subject to interpretation. In addition, it is not a VIE if equity investors have a direct or indirect ability to make decisions through voting or similar rights, or they have an obligation to absorb expected losses and the right to receive residual returns. If it is not a VIE, then special consolidation applies.

A number of proprietary solutions are employed to avoid consolidation of an SPE in the United States and in some European venues.

SPCS AND HISTORICAL ABUSE

Special purpose corporations, also known as *shell corporations*, have been around in various forms for decades. They have been used and abused throughout their history. Later chapters detail legitimate uses of SPEs, but recent U.S. corporate scandals threaten to give them a bad name, so it is worthwhile to spend some time discussing abuses.

Special purpose entities are a convenient tool for criminals. They are often offshore, usually bankruptcy-remote, and the ownership structure is undisclosed. The board seemingly makes investment decisions, but these are virtually dictated by the entity that structured the SPE in the first place. The entity that paid the original setup costs is the puppet-master, or the actual driver of the vehicle.

There is nothing wrong with SPEs in and of themselves, just as there is nothing wrong with any other tool. A hammer can be used to build a house or used like “Maxwell’s silver hammer” to kill someone. A car can be a vehicle for driving children to school, or it can be the vehicle used as a getaway car in a bank robbery.

Enron used SPEs to indulge in creative accounting, but they weren't the first and they weren't even the boldest. Enron was a surprise only to those who had forgotten financial history.

In the mid-1970s through the early 1980s, the august hierarchy of the Catholic Church participated in a financial game of shells and shills. In 1974, the crash of Franklin National Bank was the largest bank crash in the history of the United States up to that time. Michela Sindona was sentenced to 25 years in the Otisville U.S. Federal prison for his role in the collapse. He ran a money laundering operation for the Sicilian and U.S. Mafias. A United States Comptroller of the Currency's report showed that Big Paul Castellano, among others, had a secret account at Franklin National Bank. (Castellano was gunned down outside New York's Sparks Steak House on East 46th Street in an unrelated mob hit in December 1985.) Few people in the securitization business remember Sindona's name, but at the time he was internationally famous for his bold financial crimes.

Sindona hated prison and sought revenge when his longtime friend Roberto Calvi, the chairman of Banco Ambrosiano (also known as "the priests' bank"), turned his back on him. Sindona told Italian banking authorities to start investigating Calvi, Calvi's foreign special purpose corporations, and Calvi's links to the Vatican Bank. Sindona was later turned over to Italian authorities. The Vatican Bank lost $55 million when Franklin collapsed. Archbishop Paul Marcinkus was also a suspect when it was revealed Sindona paid a total $6.5 million to him and to Roberto Calvi. The payment was allegedly for a stock price-inflating scheme involving three banks: Franklin, Ambrosiano, and the Vatican. In March 1986, Sindona was found poisoned to death after drinking a cup of coffee in an Italian prison where he served a sentence for ordering the death of investigator Giorgio Ambrosioli.

Archbishop Paul Casimir Marcinkus was a huge, charming American of Lithuanian heritage, born in 1922 in Cicero, Illinois—Al Capone's neighborhood. He got his big break in the early 1970s when a knife-wielding assassin lunged at Pope Paul VI during a papal tour in the Philippines. Marcinkus tackled the assassin, saved the pope's life, and instantly became a star in the Vatican. Pope Paul VI gratefully made him head of Vatican Intelligence and Security. Then, with Cardinal Spellman's backing, Marcinkus became Chairman of the Istituto per le Opere di Religione (the Institute of Religious Work, known in Europe as the IOR), better known in the United States as the Vatican Bank.

Marcinkus was now bishop of Orta, chairman of the Vatican Bank, chief of Vatican intelligence, and mayor of Vatican City. The Vatican is a sovereign state surrounded by Italy. Archbishop Marcinkus headed both the bank and the intelligence service. That seems a bit like allowing the CIA to run the Federal Reserve Bank. Who watches the watchers? Such concentration of power can speed up a due diligence meeting, and the charming archbishop liked his spare time; he was an avid golfer.

Among other functions, the Vatican Bank administered some of the tithe, also called "Peter's pence," that the global congregation of the faithful contributed to the collection basket during the ceremony of the Mass. The faithful give their hard-earned after-tax money with the trust that it is being used to spread the word of the gospel and to do good works.

When Pope Paul VI died in 1978, the College of Cardinals elected Albino Luciani, the cardinal of Venice. He ascended to the papal throne as Pope John Paul I. The new pope was furious with Marcinkus, who had sold the profitable Venetian Bank, Banco Cattolica del Veneto, to Roberto Calvi over the then Cardinal Luciani's vehement objections. He vowed if he became pope, he would put an end to Archbishop Marcinkus's power and influence over Vatican affairs.

Pope John Paul I didn't have a chance to implement his plan. He reigned only 33 days. Vatican intelligence said Pope John Paul I died of natural causes, albeit he was reputed to be in good health. Speculation over the cause of his death inspired a scene in the movie *The Godfather Part III*, depicting the Mafia-directed murder of a fictitious pope.

Pope John Paul II's election was a stroke of luck for Marcinkus. The Polish pope was initially an outsider in the Vatican power structure. He was the first non-Italian pope since Hadrian VI in 1522, almost 500 years earlier (the current pope, Benedict XVI, is the second). Marcinkus and the new pope became fast friends; both were hulking Slavic men, and they instantly hit it off. The traditional Italian Vatican power structure gradually lost its control. Marcinkus helped the pope find his power base and reported directly to him.

The Vatican Bank (IOR) controlled several offshore shell companies involved in the embezzlement of funds from Banco Ambrosiano. For example, the IOR accepted time deposits from Banco Ambrosiano's Lima, Peru, operation. The IOR lent the money to a Panama shell company. At maturity, the IOR refused to pay, claiming the Panama company owed the money, but the Vatican Bank held the share certificates for the company as controlling fiduciary for Banco Ambrosiano.

In 1982, Banco Ambrosiano collapsed. Roberto Calvi was alleged to have looted $1.3 billion from Banco Ambrosiano. The Vatican Bank paid a $250 million settlement to the defrauded depositors of Banco Ambrosiano, but the Vatican Bank admitted nothing. Calvi had turned to the Catholic Church in his hour of greed, and the worldwide Catholic community unknowingly gave a large donation to help cover his malfeasance. Catholic priests take a vow of poverty. Members of the congregation sometimes wonder just whom it is the priests have vowed to impoverish.

Marcinkus used the Alzheimer's defense: "I'm not a crook, I just can't help it if I don't have all my wits." He claimed he didn't know what he was signing. He had studied law in Rome and was chairman of the Vatican Bank for 10 years, yet he claimed he'd never read or didn't understand the documents he signed. He said he trusted Calvi and claimed Calvi took advantage of his naiveté.

At the time of Banco Ambrosiano's collapse in 1982, Roberto Calvi was serving time for illegal foreign money transfers. After being released on appeal, Calvi fled to London, carrying a briefcase stuffed with incriminating documents. Flavio Carboni, another bank officer, joined him. Shortly after his arrival in London, Roberto Calvi's corpse was found hanging under Blackfriar's Bridge. His pockets were stuffed with rocks, and it was rumored his wrists looked as if they had been bound with rope that was later removed. Carboni and the documents were missing.

After his side trip to London with Calvi, Carboni resurfaced. Italian officials arrested him attempting to extort $900,000 from Vatican officials in exchange for Calvi's stolen documents. Bishop Pavel Hnilica, a key member of Marcinkus's inner circle, was arrested trying to buy back the incriminating documents.

Archbishop Paul Marcinkus was indicted and sought for questioning by Italian authorities during the investigation of Banco Ambrosiano's collapse. He lived in the Vatican for six years during the papacy of John Paul II, never stepping foot in Italy, where he would have faced arrest. Eventually the Vatican came to an agreement with Italy to drop the matter. Marcinkus did not step aside as head of the Vatican Bank until 1989, and he remained pro-president of Vatican City until his retirement in 1990. He retired to the United States and lived as a parish priest in Sun City, Arizona, where he enjoyed his favorite pastime, golf.

Roberto Calvi's death was officially deemed a suicide in 1982, after a hasty investigation by London authorities. In 2002, 20 years after Calvi's death, Italy performed a new postmortem examination of his remains using modern forensic techniques. The examiners concluded that Calvi's murder was staged to appear to be a suicide. He had been strangled and then strung up to the scaffolding under London's Blackfriar's Bridge. Licio Gelli, a former grand master of the illegal P2 Masonic lodge, serving a prison sentence for his role in the Banco Ambrosiano fraud, was investigated. Four others were indicted in 2005: Flavio Carboni, who had fled with Calvi to London; Manuela Kleinszig, Carboni's Austrian girlfriend; Ernesto Diotavelli, an underworld figure from Rome; and Pippo Calo, a boss of the Cosa Nostra, who is already in prison for other crimes. Prosecutors suspected Calvi knew too much about Mafia money being laundered through the Vatican Bank and through Banco Ambrosiano. All of the suspects were found not guilty in June 2007.

Marcinkus died on February 20, 2006, at the age of 84, without ever volunteering any information—despite the ongoing trial—that might have helped solve the murder of Roberto Calvi. In the face of murder and suspicious financial transactions, the Catholic Church has remained silent. The Vatican is still a sovereign state, and it is still a popular offshore venue with a unique approach to nonregulation.

If you can't trust the Vatican Bank to safeguard your money, whom can you trust? The answer is no one. At least, you can't just accept things at face value without doing independent verification.

That's why the financial markets are pushing for greater transparency. One should know one's customer. Suspicious transactions must be reported. The trouble is that many of these transactions appear legitimate on the surface. At the time of Calvi's creative workmanship, it would have been extremely difficult to untangle the ownership structure of the shell corporations, especially with bank officers involved in the deception.

As an example of how a web of shell corporations obscures ownership, let's suppose I'm a drug lord with lots of cash. My circle of friends seems to have the same problem I do. We want to spend our money to buy nice things, but people don't want to do business with us if they can trace the money back to our enterprises. We might begin by using couriers to carry currency out of our home countries. We might even buy gems and jewelry and smuggle them out. I might make a very generous donation to my church in my home country, which later shows up as a bank balance in my name in another country. The money is transferred directly from the church account to the account of several shell companies to disguise its true ownership. I'd use some corporate-friendly venues to set up the phony corporations.

Now suppose you are investigating me and find an account set up in the name of RANA Corporation, and you suspect this account has links to my drug money. The only reason you suspect this is because you got a tip-off. Apollo Corporation owns 60 percent of RANA, and Delphi Corporation owns 40 percent. Tech Corporation owns 30 percent of Apollo, and Mark Corporation owns 70 percent. Lana Corporation owns 50 percent of Delphi, and Capa Corporation owns 50 percent. Are you still with me? Or have you fallen asleep after wading through a stack of documents that could sink a ship?

I own Tech Corporation. RANA Corporation's only assets are a $1.2 billion cash account in a Basel bank. That means that of the $1.2 billion, my share is 30 percent of 60 percent of $1.2 billion, or $216 million.

And that's just in the RANA account. Tech Corporation also has part ownership in a few other corporations.

These are private corporations. They don't have to disclose anything. It is extremely difficult—if not impossible—for you to discover that I'm the true owner of Tech. It's also difficult for you to discover the true owners and ownership interests in the other corporations.

This is what all the fuss is about. Legitimate means can always be twisted to serve illegitimate purposes. The legitimate international banking community is doing it is best to crack down on money laundering and suspicious movement of money across borders.

Yet chicanery continues. Long after the Banco Ambrosiano scandal, Enron's former officers set up corporations with complex ownership structures. Loans were made; interests were conflicted; pockets were lined; officers were indicted and jailed. RBG Resources PLC, Allied Deals Inc., Hampton Lane Inc., and SAI Commodity Inc. allegedly used shell corporations to falsify transactions and fraudulently secured cashable letters of credit.

American Tissue was the fourth largest tissue company in the United States before its bankruptcy in 2001. Several lawsuits include the following allegations. The owners allegedly borrowed hundreds of millions and diverted the money through a network of affiliated corporations. American Tissue was owned by Middle American Tissue as its sole asset, which was owned by Super American Tissue. It's estimated American Tissue had more than 25 subsidiaries. One of the owners set up around 45 companies, which were affiliates of American Tissue. American Tissue lent money to the affiliates, and the loans required no interest payments and had no maturity. American Tissue bought machinery for several million dollars and sold it to one of the owners for one dollar just two months later. Arthur Andersen, American Tissue's auditor, is being investigated by the U.S. Department of Justice for allegedly taking a role in shredding American Tissue documents.

Some applications of SPEs are not currently illegal but may come under closer public policy scrutiny in future. In an example of art imitating life, the U.S. television show *West Wing,* about the internal workings of the White House, offers a typical example. One of the president's staff formerly worked for a law firm that created SPCs for each oil tanker the oil company proposed to purchase. To keep costs low, the oil company chose old clunkers that probably should have been junked. The SPCs financed the tankers 100 percent. If there were an event such as an oil tanker leak, the individual SPCs acted as a liability shield. But if litigation penetrated the liability shield, the SPCs would have no real assets, only debt. The oil company was judgment proof.

The fictional account is very close to actual transactions using SPEs. These transactions are not illegal, merely sleazy. But what we consider clever finance today may be viewed as fraud tomorrow, and vice versa. Tax avoidance is legal; tax evasion is illegal. Tax avoidance today may become tax evasion under tomorrow's public policy. Today's clever liability shields may be deemed fraud tomorrow.

Game theory is the study of conflict between thoughtful and potentially deceitful opponents. In his *minimax theorem* John von Neumann mathematically proved there is always a rational solution to a precisely defined conflict between two players whose interests are completely opposed. In structured finance the various interests of investors, deal managers, issuers, regulators, tax authorities and deal arrangers may be opposed. Before others make their move, you have to understand the cash flows and the documentation to see if you can counter potential moves in advance.

Abuse won't disappear. People with a mind-set to pull a fast one assume that those who don't, just don't know how to pull it off; or if they do know how, they don't have the guts to do it. Given that it is so easy to pull off a shell game, it is a credit to the ethics of the financial community that it doesn't happen more often. What makes the capital markets work—and for the most part they do work—is that at its core are people whose word is their bond. Nice guys may not always finish first, but they last, and they finish.

SPES AND SPVS

As we've discovered, both special purpose companies and special purpose trusts are called special purpose vehicles (SPVs) or special purpose entities (SPEs). The terms *special purpose entity* and *special purpose vehicle* can be used interchangeably, but it is important to distinguish between the corporate and trust structures. Special purpose entities support various customer-and investment-oriented activities for banks, investment banks, insurance companies, and corporations. They have been used for years as a tool to support securitization assets. They can be onshore, domiciled in the home country of the deal arranger, or offshore.

There are a multitude of considerations and choices in setting up an SPE. Setup time can vary from four weeks to three months. To illustrate key points, I offer the following observations about some of today's issues in setting up an SPE. One must research current information, because tax issues, accounting issues, bank regulatory issues, and other structural issues are always in flux.

There is no easy answer to the question, "Where is the best place to set up an SPE?" It depends on the structured finance application, among other considerations. SPEs are currently set up in a variety of tax-friendly venues including Delaware, New York, Luxembourg, the Netherlands, the Caymans, the Bahamas, Ireland, Jersey, Guernsey, and Gibraltar.

While SPEs in the United States are often, but not always, set up as trusts for tax reasons, in non-U.S. venues the SPC is a common structure. Venues can be chosen wherever an SPE structure is allowable, but as a rule, only tax-friendly venues for the specific structured finance application are chosen.

While choice of venue usually revolves around tax issues, other considerations can be important. For example, many investors in Germany will buy notes issued by SPEs, but often require an Organization for Economic Development (OECD) issuer. Therefore, the SPE must be set up in an OECD country. Among the OECD countries, the Netherlands, Luxembourg, and Ireland are currently the most commonly used tax-friendly venues.

In tax terms, we want the SPE to pay zero tax on payments flowing in and flowing out. We want to avoid corporate income tax at the venue of the SPE and the deal sponsor. There are two withholding tax issues: (1) withholding tax at the source, the venue of the incorporation of the SPE, on Euro Medium-Term Notes (EMTNs) issued by the SPEs; and (2) withholding tax imposed on the underlying assets purchased by the SPEs by the country in which the assets were originated. The goal is that neither interest nor dividends paid by the SPEs is subject to withholding tax, so an ideal venue does not impose this tax.

If we choose a venue such as the Cayman Islands that does not have tax treaties in place with most jurisdictions, there is no mechanism for reclaiming tax withheld (if any) on the underlying asset income from the country of origination. The SPE will purchase assets that are not subject to withholding at the country of the assets' origination so that investors will not suffer a reduced return.

If instead we choose a venue with tax treaties in place, assets that suffer withholding tax may specifically be chosen so the withholding tax can be reclaimed. Several years ago it was popular to purchase Italian government bonds and repackage them in a Luxembourg-domiciled SPE. Luxembourg had a double tax treaty with Italy, the withholding tax was reclaimed, and repackaged notes backed by the Italian government bonds were sold to investors in venues without Italian tax treaties. The investors enjoyed the gross coupon effect of the Italian government bonds that was otherwise unavailable to them. Figure 2.2 shows a simplified example.

This is a legitimate use of an SPE. Tax evasion is illegal; tax avoidance is legal. In this instance, German investors realized the full benefit of the gross income from the Italian government bonds.

We do not want to suffer tax on the SPE's income. In Europe, we also want to avoid value-added tax (VAT) and stamp duties. The goal is

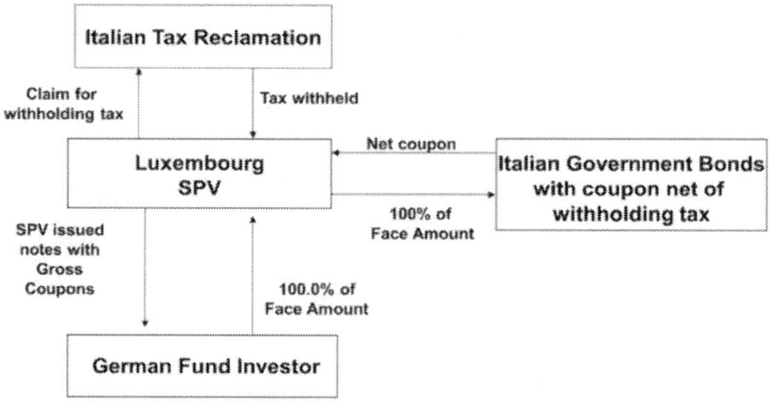

FIGURE 2.2 Luxembourg Domiciled SPV with Italian Government Bond Collateral

to have zero tax leakage, if possible. Venues such as the Caymans, Jersey, and Guernsey offer this advantage, but may not enjoy ready investor acceptability.

Other venues such as the Netherlands, Luxembourg, and Ireland also offer several tax advantages. There is no withholding tax on note interest. There is no stamp duty. There may be a very small value-added tax on servicing and administration for the SPE. There is no withholding tax on deposits.

Among these three venues, there are other considerations that may affect the final choice. The Netherlands seems to take several weeks longer to provide tax rulings for SPEs compared to Ireland and Luxembourg. In the Netherlands, there seems to be a turf war between Amsterdam and Rotterdam. Most SPEs are set up in Amsterdam. For speed, one might choose Ireland or Luxembourg. In Ireland, the SPE must fit within the Irish tax securitization code. This may drive up the cost slightly relative to Luxembourg. United Kingdom–based deal arrangers might find it more convenient to deal with Ireland, since Ireland uses an English law–based system. Lately, Ireland has been the fastest of the three venues in actual setup time, usually two to three weeks once the paperwork is in order.

DOCUMENTATION

The documentation for SPEs and SPVs varies somewhat by venue. Program documents may include an offering circular, a master trust deed (a structure not usually recognized in the Netherlands), a program agreement, an agency agreement, a master swap agreement or International Swap and Derivatives Association (ISDA) agreement, various legal opinions, tax rulings, a trustee agreement, custody agreement, letter of appointment for the process agent, and board resolutions. SPE documents include a memorandum and articles of association, a declaration of trust of shares in the SPE, and a management or administration agreement. Each EMTN has a pricing supplement and may have a supplemental trust deed, a local legal opinion for the investor, swap documentation, SPE venue legal opinion, board resolution, or other additional documents. Rated EMTNs may have even more additional documents including corporate authority, a declaration the notes are legal and binding, a true sale opinion, or wrap documentation.

SETUP COSTS

The SPE setup requires some sunk costs as well as ongoing fixed costs, variable costs, and semivariable costs. The up-front setup costs are sunk costs and are usually between $250,000 and $500,000. Rated programs may incur further charges. The cost will depend on the complexity of the structure and the number of changes the arranger inevitably requires during the setup process. There is also an annual fixed cost for the maintenance of the SPEs. Each time the SPE issues an EMTN, it will incur a variable cost. Each tranche may incur incremental costs as necessary depending on specific investor requirements. Listing, rating agency fees, UK tax and legal opinions, Cayman legal opinions required for rating agencies, other venue legal opinions required by rating agencies, pledge opinions, true sale legal opinion, U.S. 144a opinion, and investor tax opinions can be among the causes of additional costs to issue a particular EMTN.

The cost of setting up the second of two SPEs, one for rated tranches and one for unrated tranches, can be as low as $50,000 to $100,000. The documents required for both programs are very similar, which reduces the cost of the second entity. The benefit of setting up separate issuing entities is that it will be possible to issue unrated tranches quickly, cheaply, and with flexibility. Separate legal opinions per tranche are required by the rating agencies for all tranches issued by SPEs with any outstanding rated tranche. These costs are avoided by dedicating one of the SPEs to issuing only unrated product.

EXAMPLE OF A MULTIPLE ISSUANCE ENTITY

The following example illustrates typical issues one might address in the establishment of SPEs used for repackaging. Later in this chapter we look at repackaging SPEs used to create credit-linked notes (CLNs) linked to tranches of synthetic transactions and prespecified underlying collateral. That is a popular use of an SPE. One possibility is to issue the notes from an SPE that uses a pool of underlying collateral. Another possibility is a structure used for synthetic collateralized debt obligations (CDOs) that requires the notes be issued as limited recourse notes from a multiple issuance entity (MIE), which we review in Chapter 12.

In this example, a U.S.-based investment banking arranger (in practice, the arranger can be any of a variety of entities including private equity groups and hedge funds) sets up two independent Cayman Islands–incorporated SPEs that are SPCs to support various customer-oriented activities of its London branch. English law governs the EMTN programs of the SPEs. These non-U.S. vehicles target non-U.S. investors, but they allow for the possibility of occasional sales to U.S. investors. The SPEs' legal structure ensures the cash flow integrity of the SPE. It ensures the transaction is treated in a tax-efficient manner. It ensures specific types of investors will not be precluded from investing in the EMTNs of the SPEs by country laws, adverse tax consequences, or regulations applicable to them. It ensures that offerings and sales of securities comply with applicable securities laws of the relevant jurisdictions. Finally, it ensures any issues sold to U.S. investors are private placements exempt from SEC registration. For U.S. sales, the exemption is provided by Rule 144A of the Securities Act for sales to qualified institutional buyers (QIBs).

The Cayman Islands are a tax haven. The SPCs are exempt from all corporate tax, both United States and foreign. The choice of the Cayman Islands may limit the investment bank's ability to distribute repackaged product to European investors who prefer an OECD issuer. Sales to the SPE from the arranger's trading book, or other source's trading book, are treated as any other trading asset.

If assets are sold to the SPE from the arranger's balance sheet, however, the dual SPE structure outlined earlier might have to be utilized for tax purposes. That is not the primary purpose of this SPE, so that circumstance should be a rare event, and applicable only to that specific transaction.

The vehicles are qualifying special purpose entities (QSPEs) for Financial Accounting Standards Board (FASB) purposes. By definition, they are off-balance-sheet, bankruptcy-remote entities. The assets are put presumptively beyond the reach of the arranger's creditors through a *true sale at law*. Furthermore, the arranger is not obligated to repurchase the transferred assets. Setting up the SPE in this way insulates the customers from the arranger's credit risk and ensures the assets don't re-emerge on the bank's balance sheet, even though the SPE may often purchase assets from the arranger's books.

Accounting rules are always subject to change. The FASB continually reviews the conditions to be imposed on active SPE assets through equity ownership, management agreements, or other means. They have regular meetings on SPEs, sale criteria, transfers of financial instruments, and modification of the definition of a QSPE.

The SPEs are multiple issuance entities. The MIEs issue notes that reference only the underlying collateral specific to each note (unlike the structure in which the collateral for all the EMTNs is a reference pool of assets). The noteholders do not have a claim to any other asset owned by the SPE. Each set of assets is funded separately with its own EMTN tranche combining the risk characteristics of the underlying assets and/or derivatives. The derivatives may be hedges or may actually be an underlying asset, such as a credit derivative.

Banks, insurance companies, hedge funds, and other financial entities often have vehicles that are rated and funded, customarily with U.S. commercial paper (CP), and the vehicles issue indivisible obligations with identical risks for each investor. They cannot be used for the purpose under discussion. They are unsuitable for issuing discrete-risk, ring-fenced notes (defined shortly) linked to a specific asset.

With the MIE structure, each EMTN tranche has its own unique risks, which are passed directly to the investor. Each tranche remains unaffected by credit or market events that may affect other tranches. Each tranche will have its own swap transaction and unwind trigger events, if applicable. This is known as *ring fencing* and is a critical feature of MIEs. Ring fencing ensures that assets are secured for the benefit of the swap counterparty and noteholders of a particular tranche; the underlying assets are unavailable to any other creditors. No other assets of the SPE are available to a noteholder and/or the swap counterparty except those relevant to their specific note.

Ring fencing is achieved in the following manner. The documentation specifies appropriate ranking security interests for the relevant noteholders and the counterparties. The noteholders' and swap counterparty's claims are limited recourse. This means the claims are satisfied by the note's underlying collateral only, not any other collateral in the SPE dedicated to other notes. The documentation ensures that default under one issue will not trigger a default in another issue of the SPE. This is known as *no cross-default*. The SPE signs a new swap confirmation, if any is required, for each issue. The single-agreement contractual netting provisions of the ISDA master agreement are not applicable for other tranches issued by the SPEs.

It is the legal counsel's responsibility to ensure the creation, perfection, and priority of all security interests. This is especially important in nontraditional asset classes such as CDOs, high-yield obligations, and emerging markets obligations. The obligations are held by a foreign depository (from the

U.S. perspective), and the foreign depository laws must not conflict with the interests of the noteholders and derivative contract counterparties of the SPE.

The SPE gives the security trustee a security interest over the underlying asset(s) for the benefit of the swap counterparty and the investor. The relative ranking of the noteholder and swap counterparty varies. Often derivatives traders will provide a swap to the SPE and attempt to hold a senior position to the noteholders. Many investors are unaware this occurs. Other investors are aware of the distinction and often will not tolerate this. They insist the swap provider hold a *pari passu* position to the noteholder, and sometimes request a subordinate position to the noteholder, albeit this may not be acceptable to the swap provider.

In the case of credit derivatives, the underlying collateral must be reserved first for the settlement of the credit derivative contract and must be senior to the interests of the investor. This isn't in conflict with appropriate seniority, however, since this credit risk is the risk the investor set out to take.

Limited recourse means that payments are owed by the SPE only to the extent that equivalent amounts are received on the underlying assets. To the extent that there is a shortfall, claims are extinguished. After enforcement of the security, no further action may be taken against the SPEs, and no winding up proceedings may be taken. Limited recourse provisions exist with respect to the noteholders, swap counterparty, security trustee, charitable trust directors, paying agents, administrator, and any other parties involved in the transaction.

CAYMAN-DOMICILED SPES

A Cayman-domiciled charitable (not-for-profit) trust owns the shares of the SPE. Share capital, also called equity capital, for each SPE is nominal, usually around $1,000. Cayman counsel will recommend the board of directors, who are independent of the arranger setting up the SPE. The board must be comprised of Cayman residents. The board's purpose is to make decisions on whether to enter into transactions brought to it by the arranger. If the initial proposal allows the Board to consider deal proposals from entities other than the arranger, they may do that, too. The SPE will purchase assets and will have the power to execute derivative transactions. The SPE receives a small fee for each transaction accepted by the board. In practice the board ratifies every deal brought to it by the arranger, provided it meets the criteria specified in the SPE's documentation. That is usually all of the deals.

The SPE purchases separately funded dedicated assets for each note. Each set of assets (or single asset) has its own EMTN tranche combining the risk characteristics of the underlying assets and derivatives. The structure of each issuance is driven by each investor's risk appetite. There is no restriction on the final maturity of the EMTNs other than the initial 20-year corporate tax hiatus in the Cayman Islands, which shortens in direct proportion as the SPEs age. The structurer may specify the volume of issuance for internal arranger approvals, but the SPEs will each have the ability to issue up to $10 billion of EMTNs per the articles of incorporation.

The structurer anticipates and specifies eligible assets at the inception of the SPE. The SPE may only purchase these prespecified assets. Eligible assets usually include investment-grade debt, non-investment-grade debt, unrated debt securities, assignable loans, equities, leases, receivables, and loan participations of non-arranger-affiliated entities. The proposed SPEs will not engage in participations of loans on the arranger's balance sheet due to FASB considerations. In this example, the SPEs can purchase receivables and leases. These will probably be rare securitizations, and the SPEs pass through the cash flows and risks of these underlying assets directly to the EMTN investors. The SPEs may also hold credit derivatives and other derivative instruments as assets.

Notice that eligible assets include assets on which withholding tax has been levied by the country of origination, even though withholding tax cannot be reclaimed by the Cayman Islands. On a net revenue basis, these assets are normally noncompetitive with structures that are able to capture gross revenues on assets. There is usually no specific prohibition of the purchase of these assets, however.

Figure 2.3 shows a typical generic repackaging. The SPE purchases assets. The assets are prefunded from proceeds of an EMTN issued by the SPE and underwritten or sold by the arranger's capital markets group. The SPE

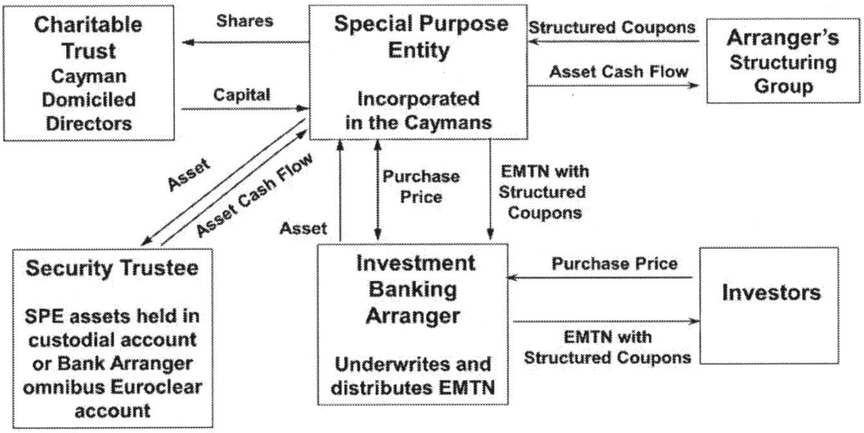

Note: **EMTN has structured coupons backed by single asset**

FIGURE 2.3 Cayman Domicile SPE Cash Flows

pays the asset cash flows to the arranger's swap desk as one leg of a swap payment. The arranger provides the structured coupons due to the investors under the EMTN issue.

Cayman SPEs do not require audited accounts. No financial or managerial reporting is required in the Caymans. The arranger or a third party acceptable to the EMTN investor is the swap counterparty to all derivatives transactions with the SPEs. The arranger may handle the back office for the SPEs, leaving nothing for the SPEs to administer. The arranger is the calculation agent and issuing and paying agent for the EMTNs issued by the SPEs. The SPEs receive the swap confirms, but do not generate confirms or negotiate terms. The arranger in the role of paying agent makes the payments on the SPE-issued EMTNs.

The security trustee, on behalf of the SPE, administers the security interest over the underlying asset(s) for benefit of the swap counterparty and the EMTN investor. To keep this at arm's length, especially if an early termination event is triggered, an institution separate from the arranger acts as security trustee.

REPACKAGINGS TO SATISFY INVESTOR DEMAND

A diverse group of investors will probably purchase EMTNs issued by these SPEs. These include hedge funds, pension funds, insurance company portfolios, mutual funds, bank-sponsored funds, corporations, insurance company investment funds, commercial banks, merchant banks, investment banks, savings banks, regional banks, and U.S. investors eligible to purchase 144A assets.

The reason the bank arranger sets up the vehicles is to satisfy various investor needs. The SPE offers more competitive note issuance because it can take advantage of a more advantageous funding cost relative to the bank's funding cost. The following are some of the repackaging uses of an SPE:

- The SPE repackages asset swaps and issues floating-rate EMTNs.
- The SPE can issue repackaged tranches of synthetic CDOs in note form.
- The SPE can issue notes linked to individual loans or clusters of loans for investors who cannot service loans or purchase loans outright.
- The SPE can issue freely transferable notes even if the underlying asset is a securitization of funding agreements with limited tradability.
- The SPE can issue notes linked to a portfolio of trade receivables.
- The SPE can buy an asset denominated in one currency and issue an asset denominated in the investor's preferred currency.

- The SPE-issued note can imbed derivatives in the note for investors with regulatory restrictions, or who lack capacity to enter into derivatives transactions.
- Investors can do business even if they do not have ISDA documentation in place with the arranger and may prefer the simpler MTN documentation.
- The SPE-issued note can imbed derivatives for investors for whom the arranger doesn't have credit lines or for which it doesn't want to use up credit lines. This is particularly useful for transactions that imbed a high degree of counterparty exposure. Examples include long-dated transactions and highly leveraged transactions.
- From the investor's point of view, the SPE-issued note is different from a credit-linked note (CLN) issued by the arranger, since the investor has no exposure to the arranger (assuming that the arranger's collateral is not used for synthetic repackagings). The note is securitized by collateral purchased by the SPE and frequently, but not always, selected by the investor.
- If the arranger happens to be a bank and it enters into a credit default swap agreement with the SPE, the SPE can purchase 0 percent or 20 percent Bank for International Settlements (BIS) risk-weighted highly rated collateral, which will satisfy the required CDS payments if a credit event occurs.

CREDIT-LINKED NOTES AND FUNDING COSTS

The collateral used in the SPE can generate more implied income on the EMTN issue. This income may be passed on to the investor, but it is sometimes retained by the arranger, even though the collateral can introduce extra risk. Eligible collateral is any collateral that can be held by the SPE and is also specified in the EMTN documentation.

An unwary investor may agree to any highly rated underlying collateral but may not be sensitive to the nuances. SPEs can purchase an asset of high credit quality that generates coupon income of LIBOR plus 50 basis points (bps). For example, combining the AAA tranche of a synthetic CDO paying 50 bps with an AA-rated bank deposit at LIBOR flat creates hybrid underlying collateral with a coupon of LIBOR plus 50 bps. This coupon is then used as the floating payment in a structured swap or to enhance the coupon of a further CLN repackaging. For instance, the hybrid collateral can now be combined with a credit default swap referencing the BBB tranche of another synthetic CDO. If the credit default swap referencing the BBB tranche pays a premium of 650 bps for credit protection, one would think a repackaging with this hybrid collateral would pay somewhere around LIBOR plus 700 bps. It seems logical that at least part of the benefit of using hybrid collateral would be passed on to the investor. This isn't necessarily the case. Some bank arrangers pocket all of the additional spread, if the investor is unaware, and the investors will only receive a coupon of LIBOR plus 650 basis points. The investor may have assumed that a bank deposit returning only LIBOR flat was used as collateral. Figure 2.4 shows a schematic of the cash flows where the bank arranger captures the excess spread.

Investors should not be indifferent to the difference in risk of an AAA-rated bank deposit versus the risk of that deposit combined with the risk of an AAA-rated tranche of a CDO. Even the shorter-form documentation used for these transactions can be daunting. Yet the tedium can be worth it, since investors can demand more income when hybrid collateral is used.

The documentation might state that eligible collateral is rated single A or higher, or it may state that eligible collateral must be rated AA or higher. It may specify that securitized assets and ABSs, among other types of collateral, are eligible. How many types of assets can you squeeze into those innocuous-sounding definitions?

Investors have control of the process when the SPE is an MIE. The collateral is not a blind pool. The investor can negotiate the type of collateral and the compensation for the collateral. Investors should ask detailed questions; doing so pays economic rewards. To remove all doubt, an investor

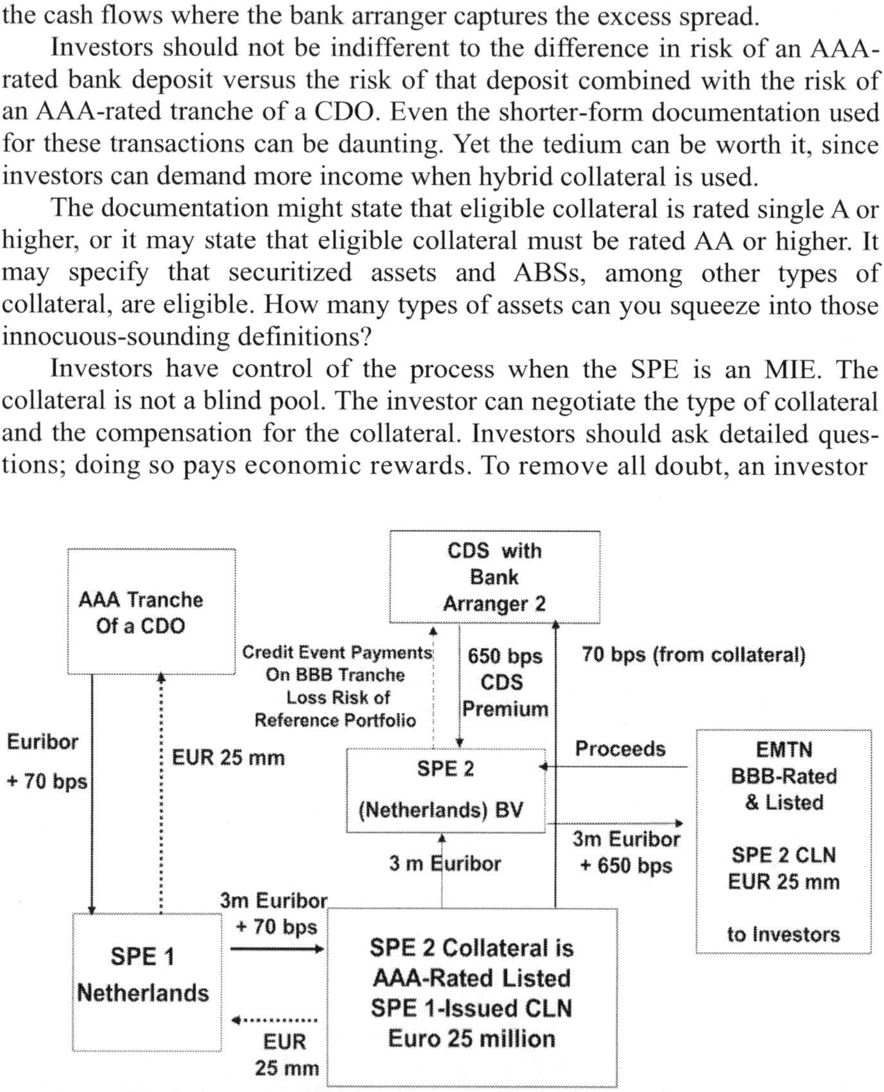

FIGURE 2.4 Synthetic Repackaging with Synthetic Repackaged Collateral

can specify that the underlying collateral for his note be restricted to specific types of collateral, or even a specific bond with a specific Committee on Uniform Securities Identification Procedures (CUSIP) number.

If an investor is happy with having a hybrid asset as the underlying collateral, that is fine. The idea is that the investor should be aware that this is the case, and aware of the risks. Furthermore, it seems reasonable that any aware investor happy with this collateral would attribute part of that happiness to a higher spread earned on the EMTN. Investors usually ask a price for taking additional risk, and it usually isn't zero.

STRUCTURED FINANCE FLOATERS

Some investors cannot engage in interest rate swaps, caps, or floors and thus cannot normally buy asset swap packages. These investors can often buy a floating-rate note issued by an SPE with an asset swap package as the underlying asset. The coupons on these EMTN issues are usually generic floating-rate coupons. Extra income can be created in number of ways. For instance, if the investor can accept an interest rate cap, the deal arranger can create more current income for the investor versus a generic floating-rate note by creating a capped floating-rate note, as shown in Figure 2.5.

PRINCIPAL-PROTECTED NOTES

Bank sponsors may use SPEs to enhance the distribution of non-investment-grade CDO tranches. SPEs are used to repackage equity tranches of

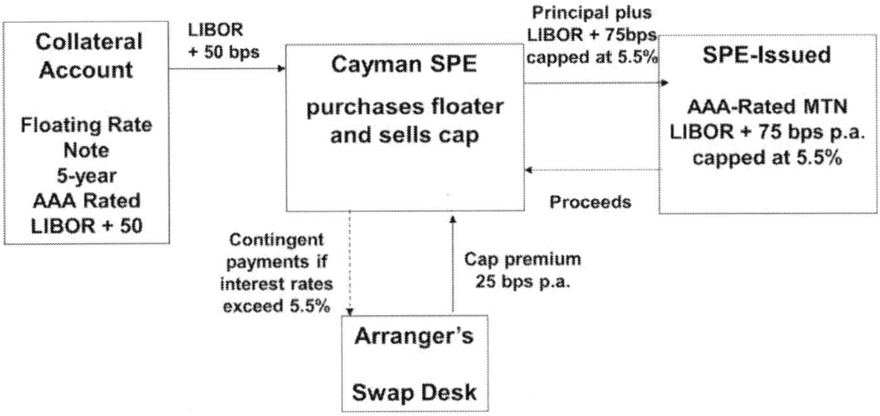

FIGURE 2.5 Capped FRN

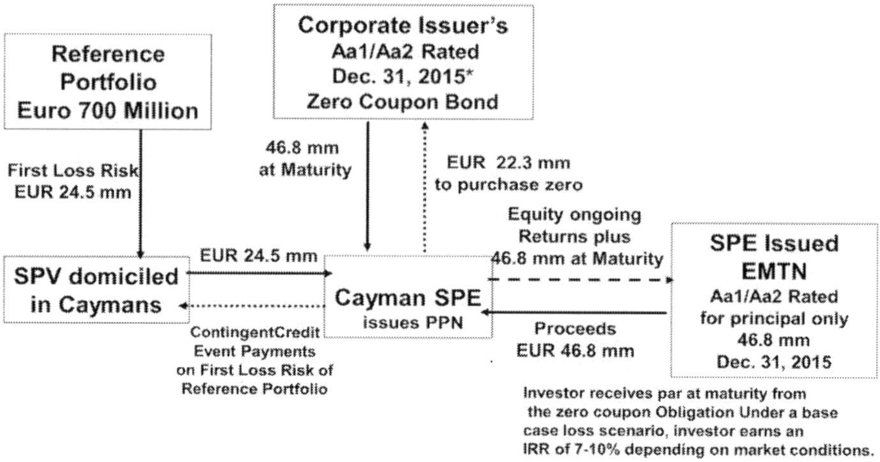

FIGURE 2.6 Principal Protected Rated EMTN: Zero plus Equity

collateralized loan obligations (CLOs) or collateralized bond obligations (CBOs) combined with highly rated zero-coupon bonds to create principal-protected EMTNs. Often the principal portion only of these notes will be rated. This structure is popular in Europe. If 144A tranches are issued, U.S. investors can also participate. Figure 2.6 illustrates this application.

LOAN REPACKAGINGS

Some investors cannot buy loans but can purchase securities. Loans can be repackaged and sold to investors in note form. Another variation is to repackage a credit derivative referencing the loan with underlying collateral purchased by the SPE to create a CLN.

European investors often want access to loans to leveraged borrowers. Leveraged loans are usually defined as loans with coupons in excess of LIBOR plus 250 bps. Many funds cannot directly purchase loans but can purchase them when they are repackaged in the form of an EMTN. The EMTN's underlying assets would be leveraged loans, and the EMTN passes all the risk of the underlying asset to the investors. Historically, leveraged loans had high recovery rates, making them a desirable alternative to high-yield bonds, but in the past few years, excessive leverage suggests that recovery rate assumptions should be adjusted. Some of these leveraged loans are not traditional bank underwritings but may be the result of private equity firms' or hedge funds' leveraged acquisitions. The arranger usually marks the EMTN to market for the trustee and for the fund and services

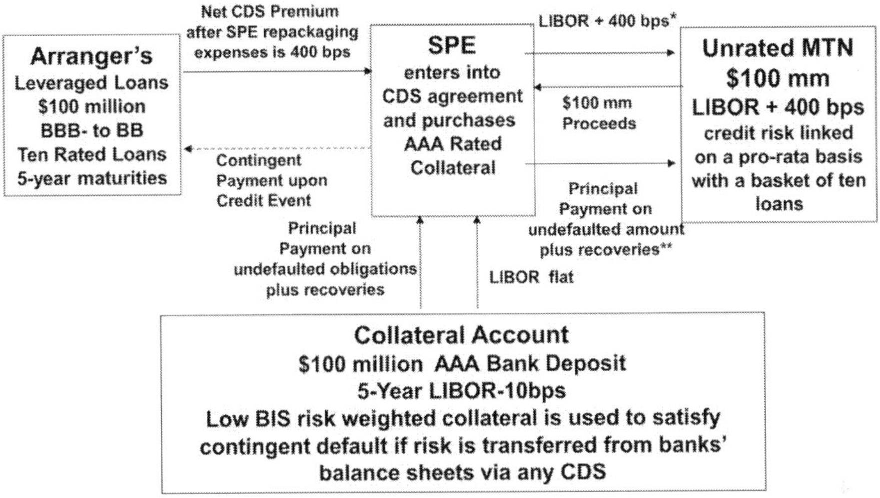

- Investor receives coupon payment on the remaining principal balance of undefaulted bank loans in the reference portfolio.

**Investor receives $100 million at maturity (plus coupon) if there are no defaults in the reference portfolio.

FIGURE 2.7 MTN Collateralized with Leveraged Loans

the loan. Of course, the loan credit risk can also be transferred in the form of a credit default swap or a total return swap (TRS). Figure 2.7 shows an example using credit default swaps to transfer the credit risk.

LIQUIDITY

The liquidity of the EMTN varies. The investor has the right to sell an EMTN at any time. The secondary market for many of the issues of an SPE may be limited, so the SPE may seek the help of the bank sponsor, as market maker, to unwind the transaction. In absence of a default of the underlying asset, the investor typically solicits bids from dealers for the asset and derivatives transactions (if any) and compares this with the bank sponsor–provided mark-to-market. If the investor finds a more favorable price in the dealer market for the underlying asset, this price is used for the unwind.

MISMATCHED MATURITIES

Funds, banks, and other investors may have a maturity restriction on investments. If these investors can accept price and principal risk at maturity of the EMTN, a longer-dated asset can be imbedded in an EMTN, which meets

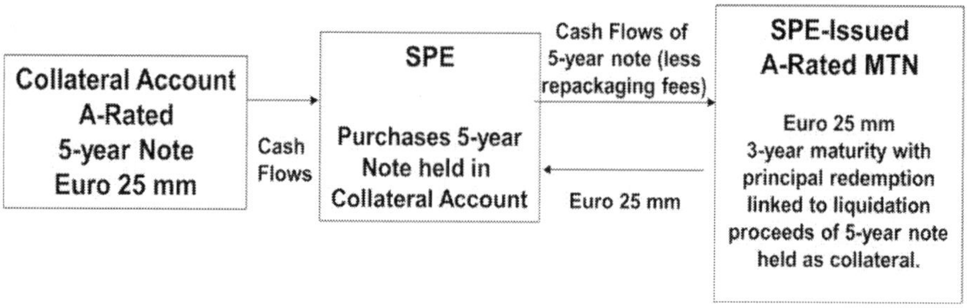

FIGURE 2.8 Mismatched Maturity Transaction

the investor's maturity requirement. This is especially useful for amortizing assets with a short average life, but long-dated legal final maturity. For example, many funds with a maturity constraint of three years are willing to buy five-year maturity assets repackaged to a three-year maturity, provided the yield of the assets is sufficiently high and provided they have a positive view of the underlying credits. The SPE purchases a five-year maturity asset and issues an EMTN with a three-year maturity. The SPE passes all of the benefits and risks of the asset through to the investor. At the three-year maturity of the SPE, the underlying asset is sold at market, and the proceeds are paid to the EMTN investor. Any price change is knowingly borne by the investor, as in Figure 2.8.

Sometimes a repackaging is not driven by investor demand but is driven by the arranger's need to lay off risk in the form of a repackaging. The arranger will repackage risk on its own balance sheet, underwrite the EMTN, and distribute the EMTN through its own sales force (if it is a commercial bank or investment bank) or through that of its investment banker's balance sheet (if it is an entity that originates loans or other assets). For instance, it is sometimes cheaper to lay off credit risk in the form of a credit-linked note than it is to buy credit default protection in the credit derivatives market. Theoretically, the arranger could sell the underlying asset outright, but that may not be a politically acceptable alternative. For instance, the arranger may prefer not to sell the asset outright for confidentiality reasons. This usually happens when the asset is a loan.

UNWIND TRIGGERS LINKED TO DERIVATIVES TRANSACTIONS

The following refers to non-credit-default derivative contracts such as interest rate and currency swaps and options. The swap provider has potential market risk exposure due to the fact that it is providing a hedge to the

SPE. This exposure is the sum of the mark-to-market exposure on the swap plus the potential value move of both the underlying asset price and the swap mark-to-market between notice of liquidation and closeout. The swap provider will often attempt to cause its payment obligation to the SPE under the swap agreement to be conditional upon the performance of the underlying assets dedicated to the specific EMTN.

A default of the underlying assets triggers an early redemption event for the EMTN. The underlying assets secure the EMTNs and the swap and are held in either a bank custodial account (for non-Euroclear eligible assets) or a custodial omnibus Euroclear account. If the unwind is triggered (explained shortly), the security trustee sells the assets at prevailing market prices and the proceeds are passed to the EMTN investors and to the swap provider in order of the seniority set up in the note agreement. Other unwind triggers are possible.

In the event of default of the underlying asset, the security trustee liquidates the underlying asset by soliciting dealer bids from a prespecified set of derivatives dealers and provides the mark-to-market on the derivatives transaction. The security trustee pays in order of seniority. For instance, if the seniority is *pari passu*, the EMTN investor and the swap provider will get a pro rata payment based on the par value of the EMTN and the positive mark-to-market on the swap. If there is a negative mark-to-market on the swap, the proceeds usually remit to the swap provider, although the disposition of this payment is sometimes negotiable.

The bank swap provider often has the option (but not the obligation) to trigger liquidation of the underlying asset and unwind the swap once prespecified conditions are met. These conditions are known as the *unwind triggers*. The unwind trigger will ensure the early termination of the EMTN, to prevent the possibility that a combination of market movement and price decline of the underlying asset might fail to cover the positive mark-to-market value (if any) to the swap provider. As mentioned before, the security trustee administers the unwind of the EMTN, which includes liquidation of the underlying asset and payment of any positive mark-to-market.

Unwind triggers may vary by repackaging. Unwind triggers are set to liquidate the underlying assets to cover the expected potential market risk exposure of the swap provider. A dynamic trigger is the most common type, but riskier transactions may have multiple unwind triggers. A key factor in determining unwind triggers is the degree of liquidity of the underlying asset. Illiquid assets may require different trigger strategies and trigger levels. The documentation of each EMTN series provides full disclosure of all unwind triggers.

A dynamic trigger comes into effect when the mark-to-market of the swap reaches a prespecified percent of the market price of the asset. This prespecified trigger is usually set at 80 to 90 percent of the market price of the asset for liquid investment grade assets since this is the usual worst-case overnight move in underlying assets. This is known as the *gap margin*. This trigger will be set based on several factors: credit quality of the underlying asset, maturity of the transaction, size of the transaction, price volatility of the asset and derivatives transaction, and perhaps even endogenous and exogenous factors related to the quality of the underlying asset and swap. As an added fail-safe feature, this dynamic trigger can be scaled to decline as the public credit rating of the underlying asset declines.

Static triggers come into effect when a prespecified boundary condition is met. These are also called *knock-in* unwinds. Default of the underlying asset, regardless of price, is an unwind trigger. Another type of static trigger may be used in which the unwind trigger is set for the condition when the underlying asset price equals a prespecified estimated recovery value of the underlying asset in the event of default.

DAX-LINKED NOTE WITH TRIGGERS

The following is an example of a note with triggers. A UK corporation's fixed-rate generic secondary paper with a one-year remaining life trades at par. The SPE purchases the UK corporation's secondary paper and restructures the coupon cash flows via a swap with an arranger. The arranger receives the fixed sterling cash flows and pays euros linked to the Deutsche Aktienindex, or German stock index (DAX), for one year.

The arranger has risk when there is a major price decline in the underlying secondary paper *and* when the euro depreciates sharply against sterling. For purposes of assessing mark-to-market movements, the interest rate risk of the one-year underlying UK corporate paper is a minor effect relative to the currency effect.

The arranger estimates the underlying UK corporate asset will not decline by more than 20 percent during a five-day liquidation period. Furthermore, the arranger believes that downward moves in the euro will be orderly declines rather than extreme overnight gaps. The arranger chooses a dynamic trigger based on this assumed maximum market price decline during the liquidation period. Since it believes 20 percent is a safe gap margin for this asset, it sets the trigger so an unwind will occur if the positive mark-to-market of the swap reaches 80 percent of the asset market bid price. The asset and swap are marked to market daily and compared with the trigger.

The arranger also makes the gap margin dynamic. The gap margin is scaled to change with the rating of the underlying security. The UK corporation is rated A2 at the outset of the transaction. The gap margin is 80 percent of the asset market bid price at the current rating but scales down to 60 percent of the asset market price if the rating drops to BBB+ or BBB flat. If the rating drops below BBB flat, it is an automatic unwind trigger.

The arranger also sets static triggers. The arranger's estimated recovery rate for the UK corporation's senior debt is 40 percent, so it sets a static trigger condition when the underlying bond price declines to 40 percent of the original par value. Another static trigger condition is met if there is a credit event, defined as the UK corporation failing to pay any debt obligation, being declared bankrupt, or having its debt rescheduled. Because of the automatic unwind trigger if the UK corporate credit rating drops below BBB flat, the bank is willing to take the risk of the remote (in its view) possibility that the asset would default before this trigger is met and, if it did, that the positive mark-to-market on the swap would exceed 40 percent of the par value of the asset. Figure 2.9 summarizes the cash flows and triggers.

When dealing with emerging market securities, or when dealing with soft currencies, certain considerations need to be emphasized. When determining mark-to-market exposure, correlation between the mark-to-market of the swap and the underlying asset is a factor.

Right-way-around swaps are those in which an arranger receives the soft currency and pays a hard currency. The arranger exposure is likely to be very low. The soft currency is unlikely to appreciate after a default of the underlying sovereign asset. In the event of a default of the underlying sovereign asset, the swap will probably have a negative mark-to-market to

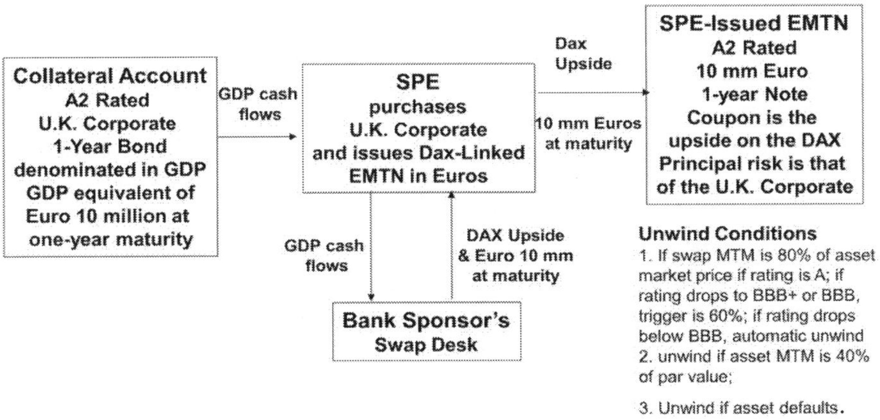

FIGURE 2.9 Dax-Linked Note with Triggers

the arranger. This means the arranger will not *be owed* money under the swap agreement; rather, it *will owe* money under the swap agreement. This is a mitigating risk factor for sovereign assets.

Wrong-way-around-swaps are those in which the arranger receives a hard currency and pay a soft currency. The arranger is likely to have more exposure, and the liquidity and the credit quality of the underlying asset are of much more concern. Not all assets will be sovereign assets, however. Single-currency swaps in hard currency have less exposure than the same type of swap in a soft currency, and there is often little correlation between the swap mark-to-market and the underlying asset quality.

RATINGS

One of the SPEs in the preceding example will issue rated EMTNs. The rating agencies review all new rated issues to ensure the new issues will not impact the rating on existing securities. The rating agencies typically require that such language be embodied in the rated SPE's articles of incorporation. If the swap provider holds a senior position to the noteholders, the rating agencies will usually not allow an EMTN issue to have a rating higher than that of the swap provider. There are a few exceptions, such as when the cash flow stream is relatively negligible and there are strict substitution clauses (should the swap provider's rating deteriorate) in the documentation.

A deal arranger may employ a credit wrap on either the swap or the underlying assets to enhance the overall rating of an EMTN series. Reinsurance companies and highly rated banks are all providers of credit wraps, for a fee.

MASTER TRUSTS

Master trusts are the most important asset-backed trust structure developed in the 1990s. This innovation enhanced investor appeal of securitizations of short-dated assets such as credit card receivables, and long-dated assets such as European MBSs. Credit card receivables have been the dominant asset for master trusts, but others are gaining popularity. The master trust can issue multiple series from the same trust, and each series is backed by the trust's entire asset pool. The advantage is that if a series has a target maturity date, principal payments can be made from any asset in the trust.

Besides allowing synergies in legal and administrative costs, the master trust structure allows the creation of a variety of cash flow structures.

Inevitably some new terminology was developed along with the master trust structure:

- The pass-through structure simply passes through principal and interest payments. This is also known as an *uncontrolled amortization* or *fast pay* structure.
- A *controlled amortization* prespecifies the amount of collected principal that will be passed through on a payment date.
- *Revolving term securitizations* have a *revolving period* followed by a controlled amortization period also known as the *payout period.* At the end of the preset revolving period, the excess cash flow is used to amortize or retire debt, and the principal is repaid in equal scheduled repayments. During the revolving period, net excess cash flow after meeting interest and other liabilities is used for the purchase of new receivables. The nonamortizing revolving period followed by an amortization period is used most frequently for credit card receivables, although the next structure is more popular.
- A *soft bullet* structure aims to pay back principal on an expected maturity date. There is an initial revolving period, but principal payments after the revolving period are collected in a principal funding account and reinvested to be paid back in a lump sum at an expected, but not guaranteed, maturity date. For securitization of short-term assets such as credit card receivables and trade receivables, the soft bullet is currently the most elegant and popular solution available.
- The *hard bullet* or *bullet* structure has a guaranteed principal repayment at a preset maturity date. The guarantee is usually accomplished by purchasing third-party liquidity enhancement. The added certainty, with its added cost, is not deemed necessary by most investors.

The UK has adopted the master trust structure as an elegant solution for residential mortgage-backed securities (RMBS) and CLOs in the European market. Investors like the soft bullet structure. Originators like the economies of scale in the legal and administrative costs and the flexibility provided by the revolving period.

OWNER TRUSTS

Owner trusts are used to securitize nonmortgage, nonrevolving assets and provide more cash flow flexibility than grantor trusts. As a result, they are gaining in popularity, even for auto, student, and equipment loan securitizations. This structure allows seniority tranching and different maturities for bonds.

In securitizations of assets where a residual value of the asset is involved, such as auto lease receivables, it is more difficult to achieve debt-for-tax treatment with the owner trust structure than with a revolving structure. For tax purposes, the equity piece is structured to look like a bond. The tax benefits all devolve to the equity piece. The tax benefits can therefore either be retained by the originator/seller or sold to an outside investor, who can also realize the tax benefits. The documentation states that if somehow the entity becomes taxable, it would convert to a partnership and pass income and expenses through to the partners, thus avoiding the entity level tax.

GRANTOR TRUSTS

Grantor trusts issue senior and subordinated interests in pass-through certificates and are pass-through structures. As such, they do not attract entity-level taxes. In other words, they are passive tax vehicles.

The grantor trust's limited ability to reinvest cash flows or purchase additional receivables is a drawback for short-dated receivables such as credit cards and long-dated receivables such as RMBSs, but these are usually not severe drawbacks for auto, student, and equipment loan securitizations.

Grantor trusts have other general drawbacks. Investors receive principal and interest on a pro rata basis. No time tranching is allowed, albeit the trust can tranche senior and subordinated bonds. Since the payments occur over the life of the transaction, the wide payment window of the grantor trust structure has limited appeal to many investors. The owner trust structure has the ability to create greater cash flow certainty and is gaining in popularity versus the grantor trust structure, especially for auto loan receivables.

REAL ESTATE MORTGAGE INVESTMENT CONDUITS

Real estate mortgage investment conduits (REMICs) are a U.S. phenomenon allowed by part of the Internal Revenue Code of 1986. Only assets secured by real assets can be used in a REMIC structure. These are term transactions and allow all of the flexibility of collateralized mortgage obligation (CMO) tranching technology, including tranching of the cash flow payments and timing of cash flows. This structure avoids entity level taxation. A REMIC has the tax certainty of a pass-through entity, and the investor classes are treated as debt for U.S. federal income tax purposes.

The equity class of the REMIC is the residual interest, more commonly called the *residual*. The residual must be owned by a taxpaying entity. The transfer must be done in such a way to ensure that taxes associated with the residual interest will be paid. Due to projected cash flows of the REMIC, at some time during the REMIC life, one can expect the residual to become a noneconomic residual interest (NER). The NER's present value of net expected tax liabilities is greater than the present value of expected distributions. To transfer this asset, the owner makes a payment for the tax loss along with the transfer of the asset. Another investor with a tax loss offset could become the low bidder and avoid paying tax on the residual interest.

If the transfer is not done correctly, it may be disregarded for tax purposes, and the original owner becomes responsible for the residual interest tax liabilities. To be absolutely sure that the transfer won't be disregarded, the transferor should comply with the regulations of 1992 and further regulations added in 2002 that ensure *safe harbor* against disregard of the transfer. Since these regulations are subject to change, they should be rechecked at the time of the transaction.

Financial asset securitization investment trusts (FASITs) are another U.S. structural phenomenon and are similar to REMICs. They are rarely used because gains, if any, on the sale of assets to a FASIT are taxable at the time of the sale.

MULTISELLER AND SINGLE SELLER CONDUITS

Conduits are SPCs set up so that the entire vehicle is funded and rated. *Multiseller* conduits buy interests in pools of assets (mainly receivables) from a number of different sellers and issue indivisible obligations, usually asset-backed commercial paper (ABCP), but they may also issue notes. Banks or finance companies that generate a large number of receivables—bank-sponsored credit card programs, for instance—sometimes set up *single-seller* conduits but are cost-effective only for generators of high volumes of assets. Banks set up most conduits, although a few fund groups have also set up conduits. These SPCs are more numerous in the United States but are now growing in use in Europe.

Unlike the MIE we examined earlier, conduits primarily use short-term funding with a claim against the entire pool of assets owned by the conduit. *Mind the gap*. Even though short-term funding rates for the diversified pool of assets is usually lower than for the longer-term assets in the pool, that may not always be the case. Conduits use an interest rate hedge overlay for the entire program life to minimize gap risk.

Assets must meet the credit requirements of the conduit. If the assets do not meet them on their own, the conduit may require seller-level enhancement, which applies only to that specific seller's sold assets. The seller might be asked to overcollateralize, to sell a senior portion and retain the subordinated piece, or to allow limited recourse back to the seller. The good news from the seller's point of view is that the credit requirements of the conduit are usually only the equivalent of a low investment-grade rating. An explicit rating usually isn't required, so the seller can avoid rating agency costs.

Unlike the other long-term structures we've examined, the sponsor banks usually administer conduits, but that is not always the case, especially if a large originator of receivables is setting up its own conduits. A trustee is required only if the SPE selling the ABCP is set up as a trust. Since bank employees are often administering the conduits, they often have influence over the sponsor bank's willingness to provide liquidity. They often receive pressure to introduce assets of bank customers into the conduit. The asset securitization groups of banks with poor capital markets underwriting and distribution capabilities sometimes set up conduits to pool unsold assets. Diversification depends on what the group is securitizing. Investment banks with strong distribution capabilities frown on the use of conduits for this purpose.

From a commonsense standpoint, one would want to minimize the influence an internal group can exert on the assets purchased by the conduit administrator. As a practical matter, it is often difficult to ensure objectivity. Investors in conduit ABCP should take this into account when evaluating various conduits.

Conduits also use program-level credit enhancement, which applies to the entire asset pool. This includes credit wraps in the form of surety bonds and a letter of credit from the sponsoring bank. Credit enhancement providers must have ratings at least as high as that of the conduit's commercial paper.

Liquidity facilities are employed to bridge the gap between timing of asset cash flows and the commercial paper cash flows. There is often more than one source of liquidity, and liquidity providers must have a short-term rating equal to or higher than the conduit's rating. Since banks are currently not required to hold risk-based capital against obligations shorter than 365 days, these facilities are usually 364 days long. These have to be renewed, and the renewal cost, or *repricing risk,* is always a factor.

Conduit sponsors sometimes represent that liquidity lines are virtually risk-free. They aren't meant to be an additional means of credit enhancement and are not meant to cover defaulted assets. The lines are not risk-free to the providers, however. A commercial paper market disaster could result in drawn liquidity lines without immediate means of repayment. Changing capital regulations often threaten to make liquidity lines too expensive for banks to supply. Bank managers have noticed that the lines are not risk-free and seesaw in their willingness to provide them. Some banks will not provide liquidity lines for outside conduits.

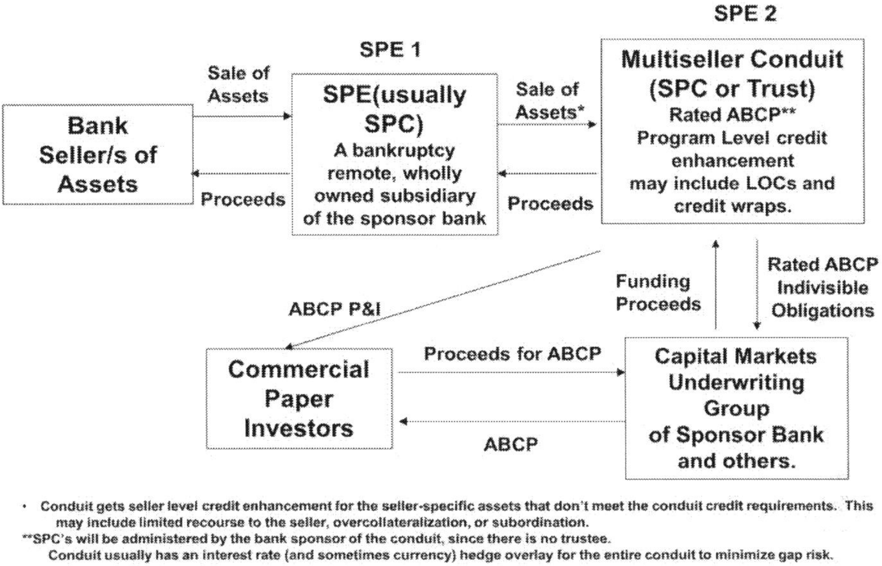

FIGURE 2.10 Multiseller Conduit

Figure 2.10 shows the cash flows and credit enhancement for a multiseller conduit. The size of the program varies depending on the timing and volume of the receivables of the various sellers.

DOMESTICALLY DOMICILED CORPORATIONS

Special purpose corporations can be set up onshore in certain venues. Some corporations are not meant to issue bonds but provide a means for investors to take degrees of credit risk through either equity shares or loans.

For example, in the German market, a *Gesellschaft mit beschränkter Haftung* (GmbH) corporate structure is sometimes employed. The GmbH issues obligations, which are backed by a diversified portfolio of non-investment-grade corporate bonds. The GmbH has both lenders and shareholder(s). The investors who are lenders are limited partners (Kommanditists) and are only liable to the extent of their capital investment. The shareholders (Komplementär) are fully liable partners. The shareholder is often the bank arranger. Figure 2.11 shows a typical GmbH securitization.

An arranger-affiliated asset manager usually handles portfolio management and credit research for a fee of around 50 bps per annum. An arranger-affiliated trustee usually handles administration services for the GmbH for a fee of around 5 bps per annum. The costs of setting up the structure are

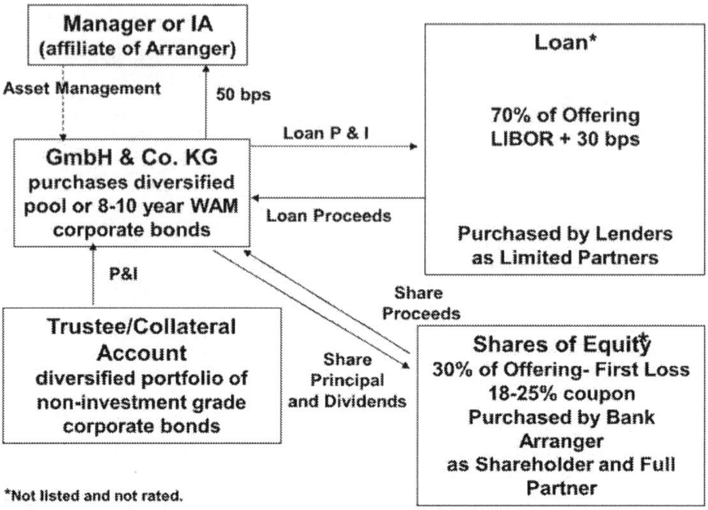

FIGURE 2.11 GmbH Securitization

usually cheaper than for an offshore SPE, but the applications are more limited and the first-loss piece is generally larger, resulting in a higher regulatory capital charge relative to other structures, if the bank arranger retains this piece.

The lenders loan money to the corporation and have a higher credit quality risk than the shareholders. The credit risk of the loan is investment-grade equivalent risk. The shareholders in the corporation are analogous to equity investors and take the equivalent of non-investment-grade first-loss risk.

These investments are not listed and are not rated. Listing is a requirement for debt investment in Germany, but that doesn't apply to shares. There is also no need for an offshore securitization vehicle. Local corporate tax regulations apply, and from this point of view, the transaction may appear more transparent to German participants.

BANKRUPTCY-REMOTE

In order for investors to have the highest-priority claim against the assets in a securitization, they must have protection from bankruptcy of the original owner of the assets or the seller, or from any creditor lien including a government lien involving taxes. If a bank is the seller of the assets, then protection from bankruptcy of the original owner is usually not an issue, at least in the United States. We're already aware that this protection is usually accomplished via a *true sale at law* of the assets to an SPE. The SPE is a specially created corporation or trust that is *bankruptcy-remote* from the original seller of the assets.

Accountants usually verify that the financing gets off-balance-sheet treatment. Usually this means that the SPE must be legally independent of the seller. For instance, the SPE cannot be a wholly owned subsidiary of the seller, or the assets of the SPE would have to be consolidated on the seller's balance sheet under U.S. general accepted accounting principles (GAAP).

Sellers want to avoid creating a taxable event by the sale of assets. For tax purposes, the seller wants to characterize this transaction as a financing. Tax laws are independent of bankruptcy treatment and accounting treatment. The securitization is usually structured as seller debt for tax purposes, but as a sale for bankruptcy purposes.

While the afore-noted conditions are opinions issued by accountants and lawyers, they may not protect the investor's economic interests. The financial institution sponsoring an asset-backed transaction has made representations and warranties. In the event of bankruptcy, the investor may find these representations are in breach. After all, the financial institution didn't go bankrupt because it was well managed, did it?

If the financial institution is also the servicer of the transaction, the bankruptcy court may not want you to replace the servicer, and yet the rating agencies may view this as a potential credit event. Collateralized debt obligations attempt to account for this by documenting that a servicer must be replaced if the servicer's rating declines below a certain credit rating, but if the deterioration is very swift, there may not be time for replacement before the bankruptcy court gets involved.

Different countries take different positions on bankruptcy law. It is important to review the price at which the assets are sold to an SPE under *true sale at law*. In some venues, if a financial institution is in a shaky state, and if it sells assets at a discount, the sale could be voided if the financial institution goes bankrupt. For example, in the United States, this might be viewed as a *fraudulent conveyance*, and the sale could be voided. Of course, rated deals will have opinions as to the legality of the transfer of assets and the fair price transfer of the assets. These are only opinions, however. Sound financial institutions usually don't cut corners. It is usually when a financial institution isn't doing well that it cuts corners or is tempted to engage in transactions that are in the grey zone. Opinions can be overruled.

Many venues have rules against *preferential payments*. In the personal finance arena, the equivalent would be paying off your Rolls Royce just before declaring bankruptcy. If you received deal payments from an issuer, or if you received support agreement payments from a credit wrap provider who subsequently declares bankruptcy, these payments might be deemed to be preferential. Payments made in the *ordinary course* of business are exempt from preferential status, and a legal opinion can be issued showing that the payments satisfy a series of conditions. That is only a legal opinion, however, and if something goes amiss with the deal or the financial institution, all of the deal documentation will be reviewed.

In the United States, banks and thrifts are not subject to the bankruptcy code and are not subject to the same preference risk, at least theoretically. In the case of proven fraud, however, the Federal Reserve could potentially step in and reverse the transaction. Their mandate is to protect the banking system, not investors in fraudulent transactions. The Federal Reserve would be reluctant to do this, since securitization is a key tool of U.S. banks, but it doesn't pay to get complacent if it appears something is amiss in the documentation of a deal for which a bank is a sponsor. In any case, under financial duress, a bank sponsor would be asked to stop making payments that might be viewed as favorable to a creditor's interest at the expense of another once the financial difficulty is known.

Structural protections work for many of the payments due to investors. As we saw earlier, first perfection of collateral security interest protects investors from preferential treatment of collateral cash flows. Some conduit structures will have a *clawback* letter of credit that allows investors to claim reimbursements if any of their payments are reversed because they are ruled preferential.

Rules may change, so there is no substitute for checking with lawyers in each venue to maximize the probability that a deal will always be viewed as bankruptcy-remote from the sponsoring entity.

Even when a deal is bankruptcy-remote, the investor may make decisions that result in bankruptcy risk. One obvious trap is to invest proceeds in the collateral of the sponsoring entity. The collateral is subject to bankruptcy risk of the arranger/sponsor.

JPMorgan estimated it had about $100 million in unsecured exposure to Enron, who acted as servicer of a supposedly bankruptcy-remote SPE for which JPMorgan acted as administrative agent. Enron sold receivables to the bankruptcy-remote SPE but invested the cash in Enron commercial paper. JPMorgan claims Enron didn't inform it of the composition of the assets in the SPE. It's hard to be sympathetic if the documentation didn't exclude investment of cash from receivables in Enron paper in the first place.

Investors can protect themselves by insisting the documentation specifies nonsponsor collateral.

ENRON, JPMORGAN CHASE, AND SURETIES

Enron used JPMorgan Chase's special purpose corporations to transform a loan liability into revenues for accounting purposes. The special purpose corporations, Mahonia and Stoneville, had the same board of directors and the same address in Jersey, in the UK Channel Islands. They received loan money from JPMorgan Chase by way of two special purpose vehicles. They agreed to pay back the loan over time via the same set of special purpose vehicles. Figure 2.12 shows a schematic of the transactions.

Enron and JPMorgan Chase's special purpose corporations also engaged in a gas trade with the same vehicles. The gas trade was a wash transaction. One leg of the gas transaction allowed Enron to receive the up-front payment of the loan monies. Another leg of the gas transaction allowed Enron to repay the loan.

JPMorgan Chase had a small problem. It already had a lot of Enron exposure. The special purpose vehicle that was paying back the loan had assets that could be directly tied to Enron and had no other assets of its own. JPMorgan Chase had to hedge its Enron exposure.

A credit derivative would have been more expensive than JPMorgan Chase's ultimate structural decision. The credit derivative would also have explicitly documented that the underlying revenues and credit risk were Enron's, which would have made it difficult for Enron to disguise its liability and book the loan as revenue.

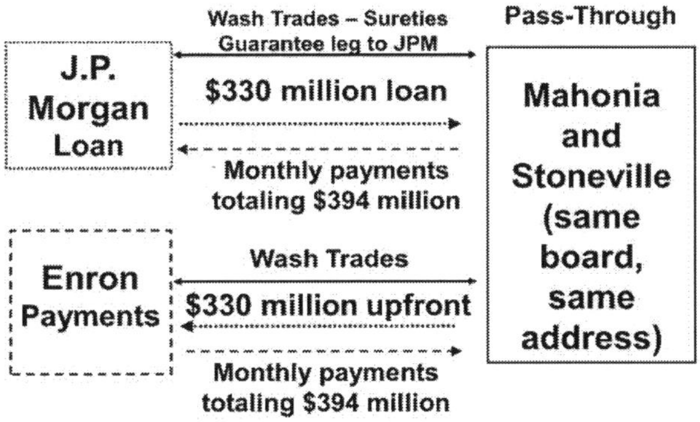

FIGURE 2.12 Disguised Loan

Since loan payments cannot be insured, JPMorgan Chase used surety bonds to protect the series of gas deliveries Enron was to make to Mahonia. Surety bonds are a form of insurance and protect against losses on specific assets. The insurance companies or *sureties* included Citigroup's Traveler's Property Casualty, Liberty Mutual Insurance, and St. Paul companies, among others. The value of the gas deliveries was equal to the loan payments.

When Enron declared bankruptcy on December 2, 2001, JPMorgan Chase had $965 million in losses from payments due on oil and gas contracts with Enron. The insurers claimed JPMorgan Chase and Enron used fraudulent inducement to cause them to enter into the contracts. They used this as a defense against not making immediate payments under the terms of the surety bonds. JPMorgan Chase sued in an attempt to recover payments.

The judge, Jed Rakoff, ruled that a senior JPMorgan Chase official's e-mail describing the transactions as "disguised loans" could be used in the trial, but he dismissed claims that JPMorgan Chase aided in Enron's financial fraud.

JPMorgan Chase and the insurers agreed to a settlement just before the case was due to go to jury trial in January 2003. Instead of $965 million, JPMorgan Chase received around $600 million and took a fourth quarter 2002 pretax charge of about $400 million to recognize the net loss.

This was poetic justice. The insurers wanted to claim they were innocent of the details of the disguised loan transaction. JPMorgan wanted to claim it was ignorant of Enron's accounting intentions, albeit it transpired that the accounting treatment was compliant with generally accepted accounting principles (GAAP). In the end, both JPMorgan and the insurers suffered economic loss for trying to earn riskless fees on what was a structural obfuscation.

What would have been the outcome had the case gone to trial? We may never know, but it is possible that since the transaction was GAAP compliant, JPMorgan Chase may have suffered no loss.

Were these transactions a good idea in the first place? What we consider clever finance today may be viewed as fraud tomorrow, and vice versa. Tax avoidance is legal; tax evasion is illegal. Tax avoidance today may become tax evasion under tomorrow's public policy. Whenever someone is getting something for nothing, there is always that added risk. Anytime we use offshore vehicles to legally translate the character of cash flows, we need to be aware of public policy risk.

Chapter 3

Credit Derivatives and Total Rate of Return Swaps

RISK TO PORTFOLIO VALUE

There are three types of credit risk. The first is risk of a downgrade in credit quality of an asset. On a purely statistical basis, the rating agencies each publish their own *transition matrices*. This shows the probability of a single asset being upgraded or downgraded based on historical corporate data.

With these probabilities, we could use a simple binomial tree to calculate a horizon price in one year. This would then allow us to calculate a horizon value and an expected return for the asset. Similarly, we could do this analysis for a portfolio of assets. Figure 3.1 gives an example of the ratings migration and price change of a hypothetical BBB-rated corporate bond.

The second risk is a general widening in credit spreads, which will cause the price of the asset to decline. The third risk is the risk of default by the obligor. Rating agencies publish data on the cumulative default rates based on historical corporate and CDO data. The data varies depending upon which time period one examines. Just after the turn of the century through 2004, many CDOs backed by investment-grade corporate debt experienced downgrades due to faulty recovery rate and default probability assumptions. In recent years, rating agency data has become unreliable for new collateral—such as risky subprime mortgage loans, subprime auto loans, and highly leveraged loans. Recovery rates are lower, and probability of default is much higher than those reflected by the rating agencies at the time these deals were rated. This applies in particular (but is not limited) to deals rated in 2005, 2006, and the first half of 2007.

The market demands a premium, or more compensation, for highly structured products, because they are harder to analyze. This phenomenon is known as the *liquidity premium* or *risk premium*. When the underlying collateral of a CDO becomes questionable, as it did in the subprime

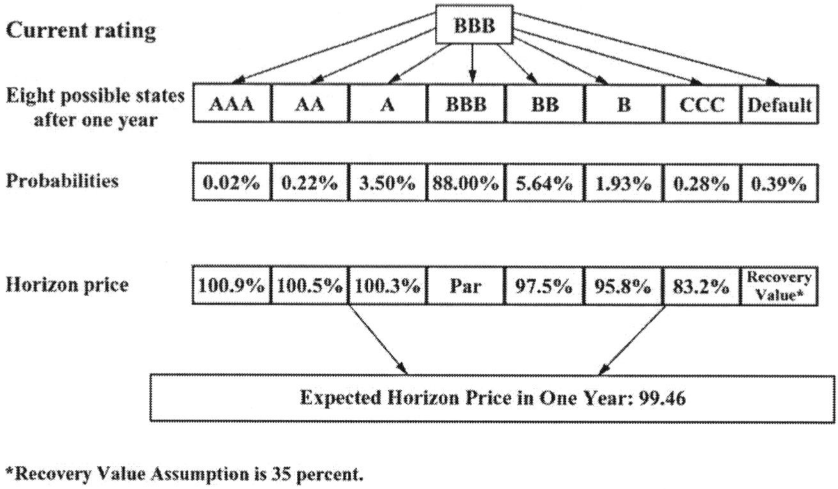

FIGURE 3.1 Price Change of BBB Bond due to Rating Migration

mortgage loan market in 2005, 2006, and the early part of 2007, and when the recovery value assumptions decline due to structural issues in regions hardest hit by subprime defaults, the market penalizes securities not only for a perceived higher risk, but also for perceived lower liquidity. What was formerly a par coupon for BBB securities may rise due to general credit spread widening for BBB tranches. Additionally, legacy BBB tranches are now perceived as much lower credit quality because the rating agencies awarded a BBB rating when it was undeserved in the first place. Added to that were concerns about allegations of fraud levied against subprime mortgage lenders that had sold mortgage loans that ended up in RMBS, subprime-backed mortgage bonds, and CDOs backed by subprime mortgage bonds.

At one point, derivatives indexes traded down in price to the low 50s, reflecting concern that losses due to defaults would touch the BBB-rated tranches. Figure 3.2 shows an example of the change in sentiment for the market price of a BBB tranche of a CDO backed by risky subprime mortgage collateral. Prices for individual BBB-rated tranches varied depending on a thorough analysis of the state of the underlying collateral. A rigorous analysis is an expensive and time-consuming process.

Portfolios also have market risk. If the general market level of interest rates increases, the price of a fixed-rate bond will decline. If the general market level of interest rates decreases, the price of a fixed-rate bond will increase. If the portfolio is a multicurrency portfolio, the portfolio may also have currency risk relative to the investor's benchmark currency.

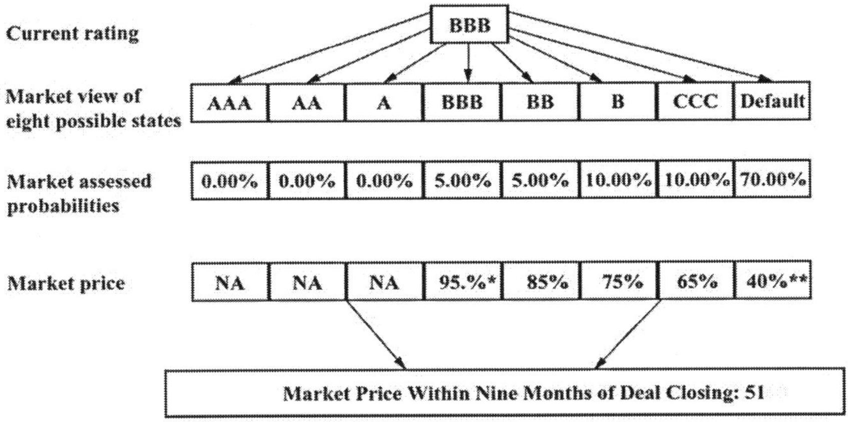

NA means not applicable.
*BBC tranches suffer general credit spread widening and par coupons are higher, resulting in implied lower price.
**Recovery value due to depressed subprime home prices is revised downword to 40 percent.

FIGURE 3.2 Price Change of BBB Tranche of CDO Backed by 2006 Vintage Subprime-Backed Mortgage Bonds

Of course, it is possible that an asset can be upgraded or that credit spreads can tighten. It is also possible that interest rates and currency rates move in a direction that enhances portfolio value.

Just as we looked at the horizon value of a bond due to rating transition, we can incorporate all of the preceding factors, taking into account the corresponding estimates of volatility, to model the horizon value of a portfolio.

Synthetics such as credit default swaps, total rate of return swaps, and credit spread options can mitigate risk in a portfolio or can add risk to a portfolio.

CREDIT DERIVATIVES AND CREDIT DEFAULT SWAPS

A credit default swap (CDS) is a transaction in which the credit protection buyer pays a fee, usually called a *premium*, to a credit protection provider (the seller) in exchange for a payment if a credit default event of a reference asset(s) occurs. The *buyer of a credit default swap* is the credit protection buyer, the premium payer, and is short credit risk. Put another way, the protection buyer is the seller of default risk similar to the seller of a bond. The *seller of the credit default swap* is the credit protection seller (also called the protection provider), the receiver of the premium, and is a buyer of credit

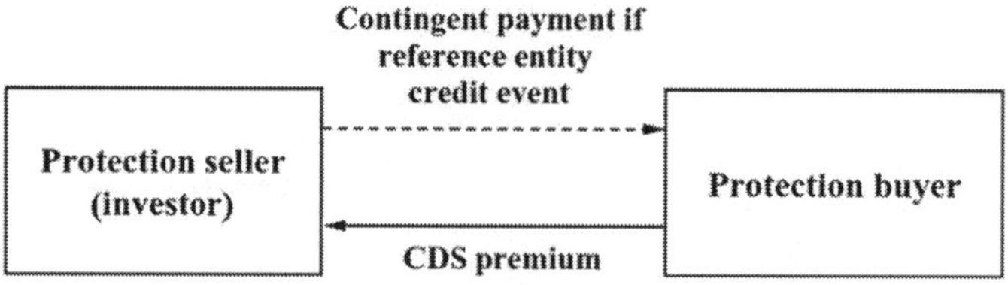

The protection seller receives a periodic premium from the protection buyer in exchange for a contingent payment if there is a credit event of the reference entity. The contingent payment is determined based on prespecified settlement terms.

FIGURE 3.3 Generic Credit Default Swap (CDS)

risk. The protection seller is *long* credit risk similar to the buyer of a bond. The protection seller is often called the *investor* and makes no payment unless a credit default event occurs.

The protection seller and the protection buyers are called credit default swap *counterparties*. Credit default swaps are sometimes called credit default options, but market professionals usually use the former terminology. Figure 3.3 shows a generic credit default swap.

A key feature of a credit derivatives contract—unlike an insurance contract—is that the protection buyer does not have to suffer loss as a result of a credit event in order to get paid under the terms of a credit derivatives contract. In the United Kingdom, this feature exempts credit derivatives from the necessity to get authorization under the Insurance Companies Act of 1982, because a credit protection buyer under a credit derivative does not have to hold an underlying obligation in order to get paid. In some venues, insurance companies can raise other issues as a defense against paying out under the terms of an insurance contract. It is usually more difficult to raise a defense against payment under a credit derivatives contract than an insurance contract, except when ambiguities in the original credit default swap contract are disputed.

Investing in a CDS is similar to going long the credit risk of a cash asset, except that a CDS isn't funded, it is purely synthetic. These are over-the-counter (private, confidential dealing) negotiated contracts. The terms and conditions can be modified.

Credit derivatives are bilateral financial contracts that isolate credit risk from financial instruments. A financial institution can transfer or take on credit risk in a trading book. When trading books are used, credit derivatives are off-balance-sheet transactions. Even if one isn't transferring risk from a trading book, one can transfer credit risks without transferring underlying reference assets. For instance, a lender (bank, investment bank, hedge fund, private equity firm) can use a CDS to transfer credit risk of a loan and does not need to notify the borrower. The lender retains legal ownership of assets while hedging default risk. This is particularly useful when assets are underwater (below their initial book value), because a sale of the loan would require the lender to recognize a loss.

NEGOTIATED LANGUAGE

A structurer can use a CDS to transfer an assets credit event risk to a CDO and can negotiate features rather than use ISDA or "market template" documentation. The United States, Europe, Asia, and the Middle East often use different language in generic CDS contracts. CDO structurers and synthetic deal managers should use the flexibility of this market to their advantage. Structurers can tailor credit risk in terms not available in cash markets. Structurers can also create arbitrage opportunities not available in cash markets. Finally, structurers can hedge any type of credit exposure, even anticipated exposure.

BASIS RISK: PERSISTENT CDS LANGUAGE ISSUES

Just about any contract imaginable can be created. ISDA has attempted to keep up, but individuals need not rely on ISDA language. ISDA has had to modify its language regarding a variety of issues since the inception of the CDS market. Since 2003, there have been a variety of alterations and disputes:

- Bankruptcy, repudiation/moratorium.
- Restructuring—none, full, modified, mod-mod.
- Binding notice of physical settlement.
- Reference entity obligations: direct, downstream.
- Successor upon merger definitions.
- Definition of qualifying affiliate.
- Novations—assignment of contracts.
- ABS confirms.
- Settlement issues: cash, physical, pre-agreed amount.

The key issues in the credit default swap market revolve around pricing and contract language:

- Credit event triggers (potential source of basis risk).
- Determination of the default protection fee.
- Reference obligations.

- Settlement: cash and/or physical settlement and satisfaction thereof.
- Recovery values: Calculation of the default payment for cash settlement is a potential source of basis risk.
- Deliverables and delivery: Allowable deliverables are a potential source of basis risk.

In the current market, fees are usually paid like swap payments—quarterly in arrears—but any negotiated payment structure is feasible. The premium can be thought of as the credit spread that an investor would demand to take the default risk of a par asset swap package or a par floating-rate note (FRN)

PHYSICAL SETTLEMENT AND CASH SETTLEMENT NEGOTIATIONS

The notional amount of credit default swaps can exceed the actual par value of outstanding financial obligations of a reference entity. Since the beginning of the CDS market, I have recommended that cash settlement should be written into the agreement as an option to physical settlement. This is not always possible with some specialized contracts, but it is usually possible. The calculation agent determines the final cash settlement. Typically a swap contract calls for three to five dealers (it is not always possible to find five dealers willing to provide a market price for illiquid products) and takes the average price. The calculation agent determining the final cash settlement is often one of the dealers offering a price.

Due to recent market squeezes in defaults such as Delphi and Collins & Aikman, the market has come up with a negotiated settlement process, but it is a voluntary process. Individual investors can write their own language and head off this problem. The individual solution may be better than that offered by the voluntary process. In fact, the voluntary process was practically an admission by ISDA of the failure of its so-called standard language. Very illiquid assets may require other measures than a dealer poll. High-yield assets in the United States, for instance, can be very difficult to price. Many securities do not trade often, and dealers do not stand ready to help out competitors by providing pricing.

For cases like this, an auction method is preferable. The deal confirmation may call for an auction set at the maturity of a total rate of return swap (TRORS) for a total rate of return transaction, or after a credit event in the case of a credit default option. If the receiver of the TRORS or if the seller of credit default protection is not happy with the results of the auction, they retain the right to take physical delivery of the reference asset.

Default protection can be purchased on any notional stream of cash flows. For instance, it can be purchased on an asset swap package, a loan, a bond, receivables, tranches of CDOs, sovereign risk due to cross border commercial transactions, or even on credit exposure due to a derivative contract such as counterparty credit exposure in a cross-currency swap transaction. Credit protection can be linked to an individual credit or to a basket of credits.

By *notional*, I mean a counterparty doesn't have to own—or ever intend to own—the underlying reference asset in order to buy protection. Suppose an investor wants to own the risk of a corporate loan, but the investor is not allowed to buy loans. The investor can sell credit protection (buy credit risk) on the loan and use cash settlement. The credit protection buyer can even buy credit protection on a notional exposure, such as the exposure an interest rate swap desk might have to a counterparty in an interest rate swap. Conversely, a protection seller does not ever have to take delivery on a defaulted asset. The settlement can be a cash settlement referencing the loss on an asset or on a notional exposure.

Figures 3.4 and 3.5 show the cash flows of investment in a par floating-rate note versus a generic CDS, which provides credit default protection for the protection buyer, who owns a par floater, the reference asset. In this example, the CDS uses physical settlement if a credit default occurs. In physical settlement, the protection seller purchases the floater at par and takes delivery of the floater, which is now only worth its current market price, or recovery value. In cash settlement, the protection seller does not take delivery of the asset but makes a net contingent payment equal to par minus the market price.

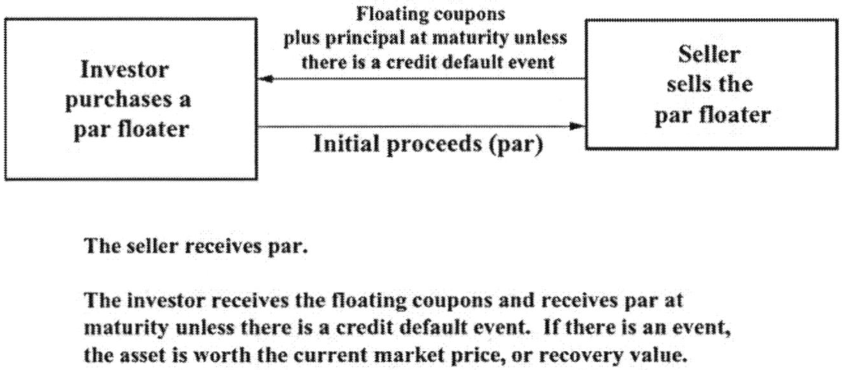

FIGURE 3.4 Par Floating-Rate Bond Purchase

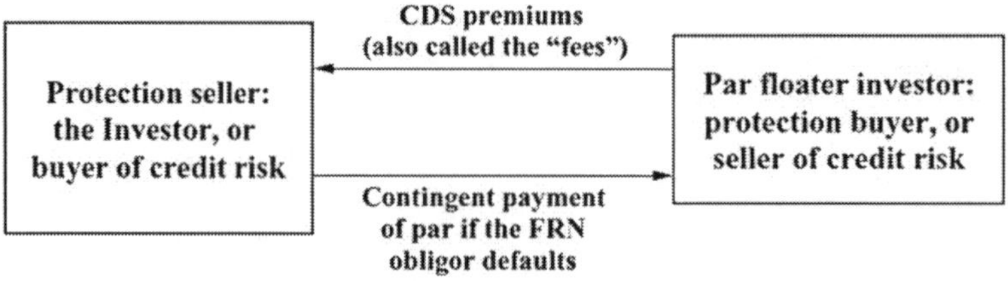

The protection seller (investor) receives a periodic premium from the protection buyer.

If the FRN obligor defaults, the protection seller pays par for the floater and takes delivery of the FRN, which is worth only the current market value, or recovery value.

FIGURE 3.5 Par Floating-Rate Note Investor Buys Credit Default Protection

The *market price* is the post-default price, or the *recovery value*, of the reference asset. Par minus the market price equals the loss on the reference asset, so the protection buyer is made whole on the initial value of par. Notice that either one of these counterparties can be called an investor, so it is safer to identify a counterparty as either the *protection buyer* or the *protection seller.*

The credit default option or swap is a contingent option. The protection seller makes a termination payment only if a credit event occurs. If the credit event does not occur, the default protection seller has no obligation.

The credit default swap premium may increase, but it is never actually in-the-money until a credit default event, as defined by the confirm language, occurs, as defined by the contract language. That seems like a knock-in option or a knock-in swap, which is a type of barrier option. The *knock-in* is triggered by either a credit default or a *credit event*. If the option knocks in, then and only then is the option in the money.

Any negotiated payout in the event of default is feasible. However, the most common market structure is the *par value minus market price* structure (also called the "100 minus market value times notional" structure). It can leave a position of premium bonds partially unhedged or can overhedge a position of bonds trading below par.

DIGITAL, BINARY, ZERO-ONE, OR ALL-OR-NOTHING CASH SETTLEMENT

A *digital* or *binary* termination payment is a fixed percentage of the notional principal. Settlement is usually cash. There are two types of digital payouts.

The *all-or-nothing* (also known as the *zero-one*) payment is equal to the entire notional amount. The investor loses the entire notional amount—not merely coupon and some principal loss—if there is a default event. I believe there is no need to offer credit protection on the entire notional amount for a CDO, since recovery rates are usually greater than zero. Using this payout structure for most corporate credit introduces significant basis risk into a CDS. For other structured finance products, however, the digital payout may be a useful tool. For instance, if the underlying obligations are trade receivables, the structurer may feel that if payment isn't made within an allowable grace period, none will be made at all.

The second type of digital payment is *fixed recovery settlement*, a pre-agreed cash payment in the event of default. For instance, in 1997, the Union Bank of Switzerland (UBS), successor by merger to the deal originator, Swiss Bank Corporation (SBC), launched a watershed deal, Glacier Finance Ltd. Some payouts were set at 51 percent of par, the average recovery value for senior unsecured obligations according to the Moody's standard at the time. UBS used this termination device when there was no specific reference asset. For example, this might occur if the credit exposure is due to a cross-currency swap with a reference obligor. The reference was the notional exposure of the cross-currency swap. The reference could also be imaginary risk, a means for UBS to create capacity to take on the reference credit risk at a later date.

Pre-agreed fixed cash payments also make sense in other scenarios. If a credit event occurs, daily price volatility can be enormous. Emerging market debt spreads are often highly volatile. As most credit default contracts look for settlement within a month of an event, a daily price fluctuation can work against the default protection buyer. If the protection buyer wants to protect itself against this possibility, it may make sense to agree in advance on a fair default payment.

Another scenario is one in which the protection seller doesn't want to get tagged with the exercise of a cheapest-to-deliver option. From the protection seller's point of view, the pre-agreed payment completely avoids this risk, but also closes out the possibility of a recovery value higher than the pre-agreed payment.

INITIAL VALUE X (PAR – MARKET VALUE)

Another termination payment calculation used in the market today is the following formula:

$$\text{Initial Value} \times (\text{Par} - \text{Market Value})$$

This may be particularly useful for arbitrage CDOs that use both cash and synthetic securities. The CDO can sell credit default protection on a specific bond or loan. The initial value is equal to the full value or total cost of the specific reference asset. When the reference asset is trading well above or well below par, this settlement calculation is a better option. When assembling a portfolio, a CDO structurer or CDO manager should try to incorporate this language when a reference asset is trading below par (i.e., the CDO portfolio is long the credit protection seller and receives the fee).

When a desired reference asset is trading well above par, and when other assets of the same reference obligor trade well above par, it may be useful to employ a different strategy. It might be worthwhile to execute a standard CDS and agree to pay only par minus market value on an allowable set of deliverables. Investors should look at the language of deals to see if an attempt was made to get the most favorable terms on synthetic exposures.

If a bond trades above par, and if the generic contract isn't available, the calculation amount should decrease to the equivalent of a par price over time. Most credit derivatives desks feel this is too complicated. Rather, they adjust the calculation amount of the transaction in an attempt to compensate the default protection seller for the potential additional termination payment. The default protection buyer pays a fee based on a higher calculation amount adjusted to reflect the initial price of the bond. For instance, for a bond with a $10 million face amount trading at 105, the calculation amount would be $10.5 million instead of $10 million.

NORMALIZED PRICE METHOD—ALTERNATE TERMINATION PAYMENT

To be fair to both the default protection buyer and seller, one should account for the initial price of the reference asset and recognize that the price will change over time. The price *decreases* to par if the reference asset initially trades *above* par; the price *increases* to par if the reference asset initially trades *below* par. The reflected price should be adjusted to screen out price changes due to market moves and changes in the term structure of credit spreads.

Creating a fictitious asset with the same maturity and coupon as the reference asset can normalize the price of the reference asset. The spread of the reference asset to a risk-free asset, such as an AAA Treasury security, is input into a bond pricing calculator. That way, as the reference asset approaches maturity, the price of the shorter maturity proxy bond can be used as the reference price to calculate the termination payment.

This method is rarely used, because most practitioners don't want to draft the language, but there may be times when it pays to do this.

HEDGE COSTS IN CASH AND SYNTHETIC CDOS

Synthetic structures sometimes fold hedge costs into termination payments. Suppose a buyer of protection asks for credit default protection on a par asset swap package. The buyer may ask for a par minus market value payment, plus accrued interest, plus hedge costs. The hedge costs are the costs of unwinding the swap in the asset swap package. Since the reference asset may not be priced at par, the price difference from par is reflected in the hedge cost.

It is important to note that the seller of protection does not usually get a rebate if there is a net market gain in the hedge. If there is a net market loss, however, the hedge cost will most likely reflect all costs to make sure the buyer is made completely whole.

In credit-linked note (CLN) structures, issuers often incorporate the hedge costs of a swap from fixed to floating coupons as part of the termination payment. This is tricky for the seller, since the theory is that the hedge costs make up for any price difference from par of the reference asset. This practice is even used in multicurrency structures in which an issuer may hedge a nondollar asset to dollars. This is fine if the intention of the default protection seller is to hedge all of the risks for the buyer on a dollar basis, but that cost should be factored into the seller's price of protection.

CDOs of cash assets often require currency hedges. For example, a bond denominated in U.S. dollars with a fixed coupon may have to be swapped to euros with a floating coupon. Sometimes a manager will ask a deal arranger to provide a hedge so that if the underlying reference asset defaults, the arranger will unwind the hedge at no cost to the deal. If the arranger agrees, it has written a credit contingent option to unwind a cross currency swap at no cost to the deal. Often this isn't effectively priced into the overall deal cost, which is, quite simply, a mistake.

DELIVERABLES: CDOS AND THE CHEAPEST-TO-DELIVER OPTION

Structurers at banks and investment banks attempt to exploit the cheapest-to-deliver option at the expense of CDO investors whenever possible. Synthetic arbitrage CDOs, for example, provide credit protection to the structuring bank or structuring investment bank that arranges the deal. The arranger will attempt to incorporate the broadest delivery language possible into a synthetic CDO or synthetic first-to-default baskets. When the arranger sells protection, however, the arranger will attempt to limit deliverables to the most expensive-to-deliver ones possible. As you've probably deduced, the arranger keeps the difference in value whenever possible.

It's reasonable for CDO investors either to insist on limiting deliverables or ask for a higher spread for each tranche to reflect the added risk of the cheapest-to-deliver option.

In the preceding example, we calculated the termination payment referencing a single specific reference asset, but a financial institution may have a variety of credit exposures from a given reference obligor. The reference obligor is also known as the reference entity. We call this cluster of exposures *reference obligations.* In the current market, it is popular to reference *borrowed money,* usually meaning bonds and loans. Many dealers will try to say this is the standard contract and therefore more liquid. So what? In times of high volatility in a given credit sector, the contract may be easier to trade, but you won't necessarily like your execution.

If you sell a bank credit protection on a loan, you don't want undue basis. The basis risk results from the option of the credit protection buyer to produce the *cheapest to deliver.* The credit protection buyer may own a loan but, under the terms of the contract, can buy a discounted bond in the marketplace and deliver this instrument, thus getting a higher payout under the CDS.

The seller of credit protection does not have to accept whatever the market wishes to dish out. In fact, I would encourage protection sellers to differentiate between types of deliverable assets, and price the fee for the credit protection differently depending on the reference asset.

Convertible bonds pose a unique set of challenges to delivery in the credit derivatives market since investors can purchase them as convertibles or can buy strips of the risk of the convertible bonds.

CONVERTIBLE BONDS AND ASSET SWAPS

Convertible bonds or *converts* are corporate securities that can be exchanged for a fixed number of common equity shares at a prespecified price at prespecified times at the bondholder's option. Many convertible bonds issued today are combinations of zero-coupon bonds and warrants, but the debt portion does not necessarily have to be a zero-coupon bond. The shares are usually the shares of the issuer of the convertible, but not always. In general, convertibles can be either debentures or preferred shares (convertible into common shares), but we focus here on convertible bonds.

If the stock price rises, convertibles behave like equity and their price move is almost the same as the equity. The embedded option to convert into shares of stock is deep in-the-money and the price movement of the convertibles approaches one-to-one with the stock. When the stock price plummets, the option moves out-of-the-money and has less value. The fixed-income characteristics of the convertible dominate its price behavior.

The issuer has the right to call most convertibles. If the convertible has a *conversion price* above par, the issuer will try to minimize the value of the bond and call the issue at par. The investor, however, wants to maximize the value of the bond, and has an economic imperative to convert the bonds to shares and capture the value above par, rather than receive only par on the call date. This is a *forced conversion*.

The *conversion ratio* allows the investor to calculate the number of common equity shares into which the bond is convertible. For instance, a bond with a face value of $1000 is convertible into 25 shares of common stock in the same company. The theoretical *conversion price* for the common stock is represented by X in the calculation below and is calculated as follows:

$$\frac{25 \text{ Shares}}{1 \text{ Bond}} = \frac{\$1{,}000}{X}$$

$$X = \$40$$

The conversion price is $40. An investment of $10 million face value in bonds of this corporation's convertible bonds would be convertible into 250,000 shares of stock at the conversion price of $40. If the price of the stock is only $30, the *conversion parity* is 25 shares times $30, or $750 per $1,000 face value investment. For a $10 million face value investment, the conversion parity is $7.5 million.

For instance, convertible bonds with a face value of $10 million that trade at $9.5 million but have a conversion parity of $7.5 million trade at a high conversion premium. The conversion premium is $9.5 million minus $7.5 million, or $2 million. The *percent of conversion premium* is calculated as follows:

$$\text{Percent of Conversion Premium} = \frac{\$9{,}500{,}000 - \$7{,}500{,}000}{\$7{,}500{,}000} \times 100$$

$$= 26.67\ \%$$

This is the percent conversion premium over conversion parity. Notice that this is a high percentage. When convertible bonds trade at a premium to conversion parity, they trade at a *conversion premium*. A low conversion premium means that the convertible's price behavior will track the market value of the underlying stock. A high conversion premium means the convertible price behavior will be similar to that of comparable fixed-income bonds.

Convertibles may have a variety of other features that make them challenging to price. The following is a summary of some of the variations:

- If the convertible is callable at a certain date at certain prices, the call is an *unprotected call.*
- If the convertible can only be called if the stock price is above a certain barrier, the call is a *barrier option*, and the call is a *protected call.*
- Convertibles may be capable of being put by the investor, and this increases their value.
- Conversion is sometimes into a combination of shares and cash instead of shares only.
- *Conversion numbers*, the number of shares and/or amount of cash into which the bond can convert, may vary over time.
- Convertibles may have *step-up coupons,* which are prespecified increases in coupons.

Convertibles may be convertible into shares of different issuers in different countries, thus exposing the investor to currency risk.

Dividends and dilution are other considerations. Stock dividends affect the price of convertible bonds because they affect the price of the shares into which the convertible may convert. If an investor converts and receives newly printed shares, the company now has more shares for the debt-adjusted capital base, thus creating a *dilution effect.*

All of these considerations will determine when it is financially advantageous for an investor to convert to stock. Nonetheless, sometimes investors fail to convert. Sometimes this is *rational* behavior and sometimes it is *irrational* behavior. Rational behavior includes tax considerations, or perhaps the investor was attending to more attractive financial opportunities and had conversion further down the list of things to do. Irrational behavior usually occurs because someone miscalculated, or because someone simply forgot.

Efficient market theory suggests that options should never be irrationally exercised or remain irrationally unexercised. But it happens all the time. The philosophical camp says that forgetting, or making cognitive errors, is a part of human nature, and therefore is consistent with efficient market theory. In other words, the market is as efficient as human beings. For my part, I simply view this as irrational behavior. Pricing models are easy to construct in comparison to trying to understand the complications of human nature, at least for me. Others may be able to incorporate this feature into their models, and if so, I look forward to learning more about myself.

Convertibles are deliverable obligations in many credit derivatives contracts. Many CDOs limit the percentage of the original portfolio against which convertibles would be deliverable in the event of default. The rating agencies pay attention to the ability to allow the delivery of convertibles as well. Moody's, for instance, will add stress tests to the cash flow model of a CDO that allows convertibles as deliverables.

Convertible arbitrageurs consist of hedge funds and specialized structurers at banks and investment banks. It is estimated that arbitrageurs buy more than 50 percent of new issue convertibles. New issues tend to imbed cheap equity call options. These long-dated call options are known as *warrants* and are a source of cheap equity volatility.

The arbitrageurs sometimes purchase the convertible and hedge the credit risk by buying credit protection in the form of a credit derivative. The characteristics of convertibles in their whole form shouldn't be confused with *stripped convertibles*, however. Alternatively, the arbitrageur strips out the option to convert into the equity shares. The arbitrageur is left with an inexpensive equity warrant, and a deeply discounted zero-coupon bond. They repackage and sell the bond as a *callable par asset swap*.

Normally, when the equity warrant is stripped from the convertible bond, the right to force conversion is also purchased by the arbitrageur, the holder of the equity warrant portion of the convertible bond. Investors in the callable asset swap should anticipate efficient exercise of the option by the arbitrageur. The par asset swap investor has sold the arbitrageur a call option on the bond at any time before the maturity or put date of the contract. The convertible asset swap either matures on the first put date, if any, of the underlying convertible or on the maturity date of the original convertible bond.

Since the arbitrageur can call the asset swap package immediately, the structure usually includes a six-month *clawback* so the buyer of the convertible asset swap package is guaranteed to receive the spread for at least the minimum equivalent of a six-month period. The clawback includes a compensation for the break funding costs, if any. The clawback is also called a *make whole provision*. The specified period—six months in our example—is more commonly called the *lockout period*. The lockout period is negotiable. Most of the early convertible asset swap packages were sold without this feature, but most investors currently demand a lockout of at least six months.

The option to call back the bond is a *credit spread option* (CSO). The call option on the bond is the same as a put option on the spread. As the spread decreases, the bond trades at a higher theoretical price, and the right to call the bond becomes more valuable.

Many banks buy the stripped convertible par asset swap and buy a credit default swap as a hedge against the company's credit risk. Since the bonds are callable, there is a potential mismatch between the credit default swap protection and the par asset swap.

In a par asset swap package that includes a credit default swap, the convertible bond's fixed-income strip value is calculated by netting out the value of the credit spread option. Many banks use a forward-starting duration-weighted option to value the bond portion using bond spreads. Binomial models are simpler and more transparent than more complicated models, and a model with simplifying assumptions can be constructed in a short time frame.

Credit spread options (CSOs) are used to hedge against or make a bet on credit spread changes. A generic credit spread option contract specifies a reference asset, or even an index. It will also specify a strike spread at each payoff period. Often the payoff period will be the maturity date of the option. The gross spread is the difference between the credit spread and the strike price.

Convertible asset swaps have an imbedded American credit spread option. The investor pays an up-front premium. The option payoff profile is asymmetric with changes in the credit spread.

Credit spread options can be puts or calls. The payoff for the put occurs when credit spreads tighten and is represented by the following formula:

$$P_i = \text{Notional} \times \text{Max}(\text{DWOE}(S - \text{FCDS}), 0)$$

where P_i = the put payoff at time i, which is just at the end of the lockout period.

Notional = the notional amount of the par asset swap

DWOE = the duration weighted optimal exercise

S = the strike spread or recall level

FCDS = the Forward Credit Default Swap at optimal exercise.

Since the put option is priced at the end of the lockout period, the value can be discounted to the present using the following formula:

$$P_0 = P_i \times e^{-r \times t1}$$

where P_0 = the put payoff at time 0 (now)

r = the risk free rate

t_1 = the number of time increments in the period (e.g., 260 trading days)

Duration, a first-order derivative, is not sufficient to describe the price behavior of bonds. Second-order terms such as convexity, and even higher-order terms, are often necessary to model bond price behavior. I ignore convexity and higher-order terms here to make the example easier to follow. In this case, ignoring convexity understates the option value. If the credit spread tightens, the present value is greater than expected, since the underlying CDS has negative convexity and the option's value will increase more than the option model predicts.

Furthermore, CDS prices tend to track bond prices, but not always, as we've seen earlier when demand causes pricing distortions. However, the CDS price change is included in this formula as if it is proportional to the duration of the bonds. I've made a further simplifying assumption that the duration of the bonds doesn't change at exercise. I've also ignored the change in duration of the bonds at optimal exercise. I've assumed optimal exercise occurs when one-third of the time to maturity elapses. In actual practice, this is often the case. Now we can restate duration-weighted optimal exercise as follows:

$$DWOE = (1 + r) \times (t_e / t_t) \times 3$$

where: r = the risk-free rate

t_e = the time to exercise or one-third of elapsed time to maturity beyond the lockout period (e.g., one-third of the number of trading days left to maturity at the end of the lockout period)

t_t = the number of time increments in the period (e.g., 260 trading days)

Rating agencies are often concerned about delivery of the stripped portion of the convertible. Recent history shows that the amount paid in the event of default on a deeply discounted convertible is comparable to the net liability on a generic par bond in the event of default. When Enron defaulted, the deeply discounted stripped convertible recovery value was calculated from the implied accreted price for the deeply discounted bond, and protection providers paid amounts only slightly higher than did protection providers that made the calculation from bonds that were originally par generic bonds. Nonetheless, the rating agencies are still cautious about the potential for calculation differences and view these deliverables as potentially creating a higher liability in the event of default.

NEGATIVE BASIS TRADES

Supply and demand often drive credit default swap prices, and even the best models cannot accurately predict the effects. For example, we know that new issuance of convertible bonds creates demand for credit default protection on the issuer. In December 2001, Fiat brought a $2.2 billion convertible bond issue to market. The bonds paid a coupon of 3.25 percent and were convertible into common shares of General Motors (GM). Arbitrageurs bought protection in anticipation of this issuance, and the price of protection in the form of credit default swaps increased from about 130 basis points to about 190 basis points in just over one week. Cash instruments were locked up in buy-and-hold portfolios, and their spreads remained the same. This caused a dramatic widening in the spread between credit default swap levels and the spread of Fiat fixed-income securities in the same maturity, such as the benchmark euro Fiat issue maturing in 2006. The *positive basis* widened.

The effects are not wholly predictable, however. As we saw earlier, convertibles often have short-dated puts or maturities sooner than five years. The most actively traded and most liquid credit default swaps have five-year maturities. When arbitrageurs buy large amounts of protection in the short end of the curve (for example, the two-year area), the credit default swap curve tends to invert for this reference credit. Furthermore, it is often possible to buy a normal five-year par asset swap, purchase five-year credit default protection, and lock in a positive spread. In other words, one can put on a *negative basis trade*.

DEFAULT AND RECOVERY RATE

Two of the key determinants of value of a credit derivatives contract are the probability of default and the recovery rate. These are based on historical data, and estimates are available from databases kept in the public market as well as proprietary databases. We'll see later how historical data—particularly rating agency data—can let us down, but for now, we'll examine how the market employs this data. In practice, investors are better off performing due diligence on the underlying collateral and assessing their own probabilities of default and potential recovery in the event of a default.

The major rating agencies maintain tables that show the probability of default for bonds with given ratings. This data includes mainly U.S. and European credits. It is often used to estimate default probabilities for any bond with the same rating.

Data is limited especially for Asian markets and sovereign bonds. Sovereign defaults tend to be both event- and credit-related. Sovereign risk requires a macroeconomics analytical approach, and one must pay attention to global economic and political events.

Default risk may vary over time. Rating agencies keep data that measures the cumulative risk of issuer default over the term of an obligation. For discrete time periods within the term of an obligation, rating agencies also measure the marginal risk of default, which shows the change in the default probability of the issuer over time. During the term of an obligation, it is wise to refresh this data to incorporate current data and revised predictions on the credit prospects of an issuer.

Recovery rates pose another problem. The major rating agencies also compile data on public and rated securities and their recovery rates, but the data isn't always available. For instance, in Europe, where recovery rate data is sparse, rating agencies may arbitrarily assign a percentage recovery rate to the corporate obligations of an entire country. In 2002, about 60 percent of Moody's revenues in Europe came from rating CDOs, yet this crude method is what the rating agencies use. Recovery rates in the United States show a wide variance.

Credit officers at many institutions may do individual name analysis based on their experience and on the fundamentals of the company. A bank, hedge fund, or private equity firm with a lending relationship may have access to data that is difficult to obtain in the public market and may be the best source of a recovery value estimate.

Relative recovery rates—even if one doesn't successfully guess the absolute recovery rate—among reference assets of the same reference obligor are very important to a seller of credit default protection. Seniority of the obligation and the capital structure of the issuers (reference obligors) are key factors in recovery rate estimates.

Secured loans usually have a higher recovery rate than bonds. Senior secured debt usually has a much higher average recovery rate than even senior subordinated debt. Recent history has varied widely, however. Risk introduced into the mortgage markets and leveraged loan markets suggests that recovery rates may be much lower on corporations and on loans that have employed overly leveraged financing and unsecured financing.

Due to the high volatility of the recovery values, there is a lot of overlap in the recovery values among these categories as well as all the classes of debt. In normal trading, loans are more price robust than fixed-rate bonds because loans have a floating-rate coupon. If the coupon could adjust instantaneously, and if credit spreads remained the same as at the beginning of the loan agreement, the loan would always trade at par. As market rates moved, the loan's coupon would instantly readjust. In reality, there is some lag in the loan coupon, but this market readjustment tends to help even in a default situation where the market coupon readjustment of defaulted bonds adds another element of confusion to the price of defaulted bonds.

A notable exception is corporate bonds with coupons that step up if the credit of the reference obligor deteriorates, usually reflected by a rating downgrade. This is especially true if the coupon is floating.

The major advantage for the price robustness of loans is that loans are negotiated agreements between banks and the borrower. Loans have a hierarchy. Loans secured by current assets have higher average recovery values than loans secured by plant and equipment. The bank may have a long-standing business relationship with the borrower and have access to extensive financial data. Often banks are advisers, and bank officers may be on the board of directors of the borrowing institution. Loans are often restructured and have customized workout periods. Loans have an inside nature.

Once you've guesstimated the default probability and loss in the event of default (or its complement, the recovery value), the next step is to calculate the expected loss for the issuer. In its simplest form, expected loss is defined by the following formula:

$$\text{Expected Loss} = [\text{Default Probability} \times (1 - \text{Recovery Rate})] \times \text{Loss Exposure}$$

This is an average number, an average expected credit loss. If one wanted to examine a worst-case scenario, one could look at the worst-case default probability and worst-case recovery rate for a given loss exposure to calculate an expected loss.

ISDA has incorporated new successor definitions for bonds that can be substituted into a reference entity pool. There are threshold tests on the size of the issuance to address liquidity issues and rules for substitution.

Moody's will penalize a synthetic CDO deal, which allows for unlimited delivery of convertible bonds, even though they agree owners of Enron convertible bonds had about the same loss experience as generic bondholders. They envision a scenario in which delivery of convertible bonds will cause a credit protection provider to suffer a greater loss. Zero-coupon bonds can also be problematic. The solution is to modify the CDS to eliminate the possibility of delivery of a convertible, but this isn't always possible. An alternative is to allow a fixed percentage, usually 10 percent, into the potential deal pool.

From the rating agency perspective, a CDS can be structured to fit their recovery assumptions. Moody's defines the loss severity as the difference between par and recovery rate. Moody's uses the market value of defaulted instruments about 30 days after default for the recovery rate estimate.

THE DEFAULT PROTECTION SELLER: COUNTERPARTY CREDIT AND CORRELATION

Who is the most desirable credit default protection seller? If prices were the same, a default protection seller with a triple-A credit rating—if you can find one—and negative correlation with the asset the credit protection buyer is trying to hedge would be the most desirable. A default protection seller with these characteristics should be the high-cost provider, but the current market is inefficient. You'd be hard-pressed to find a highly rated entity with the exact criteria you desire, but you'll probably find several suitable providers. However, there are also unsuitable providers.

Theoretically, the premium paid on a CDS should be sensitive to the credit quality of the credit default protection provider. The premium should also be sensitive to the correlation between the protection provider and the reference obligor on which one is buying the credit default protection.

DEFAULT LANGUAGE FOR SOVEREIGN DEBT

The generic credit default market ceases to appear generic after we deviate from the most basic definition of credit default. The market now differentiates between suitable language for a sovereign credit risk versus a corporate credit risk.

For sovereign debt, one reasonable way to define the default event is to use language similar to that in the prospectus for the reference obligations one is trying to hedge. For example, for non-U.S. sovereign dollar-denominated bonds, the default is usually defined with some minimum standards to objectively determine default. Conditions usually include the following: materially prejudicial to the bondholders' interests; an acceleration in excess of a high preset amount (for instance, $25 million or equivalent); failure to make payment on public external debt in excess of a high preset amount; declaration of a moratorium of payment of principal or interest on public external debt; or the sovereign's denial of its obligations

If you are trying to hedge a different sort of sovereign risk, you and your counterparty may want to create your own language. You may wish to include war or coup d'état as a credit event.

DEFAULT LANGUAGE FOR NONSOVEREIGN DEBT: CONTROVERSY AND CDOS

In the fourth quarter of 2000, the credit derivatives dealer community was up in arms about settlement of termination payments on Conseco credit default swaps. The banking community restructured Conseco loans and triggered a credit event under the ISDA restructuring definition. Delivery in the event of a credit event could be either a bond or a loan. This was common language in credit derivatives documentation.

The credit event was the deferral of the loan's maturity by three months, and this was an allowable event according to ISDA's restructuring definition. The slight extension may have been disadvantageous to the banks in a very minor way, but the restructuring also included features very advantageous to the banks: an increased coupon, a new corporate guarantee, and additional covenants in favor of the lenders. The senior unsecured rating was only downgraded to B1, which is not the rating of debt in default or bankruptcy. This is now known as a *soft default.* Moody's did not consider this to be a *diminished financial obligation* or a *distressed exchange* default. The market didn't seem to think that there was any harm done, either. In fact, just the opposite: The restructured loan prices *increased.*

Protection buyers delivered long-dated, deeply discounted bonds—instead of the robustly priced loans—to the credit default protection providers. The long-dated bonds were susceptible to both market risk and credit risk. Furthermore, as we discussed earlier, long-dated bonds often trade at drastically reduced prices to short-dated bonds under workout situations. The price disparity between long-dated bonds and loans was pronounced. The credit default protection providers had to pay the difference between par and the market price of the discounted bonds.

Protection sellers felt burned two ways. They felt the banking community was closer to the Conseco situation. After all, the banks were the loan underwriters. Protection sellers also knew that the banks had significant control over the restructuring. Second, protection sellers felt that by delivering the deeply discounted bonds, banks that were protection buyers were not acting in good faith.

If counterparties imbed a cheapest-to-deliver option into credit default documentation, the protection seller should get paid for the imbedded option. Granted, this is difficult to price, but the protection seller should at least attempt to value this. In the Conseco transactions, most protection sellers were caught completely unaware of their additional basis risk.

Some credit default contracts—including many credit derivative indexes—are now written excluding restructuring as a credit event. Banks hedging loans cannot use those credit default options, however. When banks buy credit default protection against their loan portfolios, restructuring must be specified in the credit default protection contract; otherwise the banks cannot get regulatory capital relief. The banks in the Conseco transaction that took the short-term opportunity nearly closed the door for themselves for future credit-hedging transactions.

To eliminate gaming from the settlement procedure, counterparties can craft their own language for allowable deliverables. Language changes in ISDA contracts have already occurred in response to the Conseco controversy. The Loan Syndications and Trading Association (LSTA) and ISDA have formed a joint working group to advise ISDA's credit derivative documentation group on issues that arise in connection with the physical delivery of a loan as settlement for a credit derivatives transaction.

ISDA introduced new *modified restructuring* language that is used in most U.S. CDS contracts, but not in Europe. (ISDA confirmation language is available from the ISDA web site: www .isda.org.) ISDA introduced language to limit the maturity of deliverable obligations for physically settled swaps after the occurrence of a restructuring event triggered by the credit protection buyer. The maturity of the deliverables is limited to the earlier of 30 months after the restructuring date or the latest final maturity date of any restructured bond or loan. Furthermore, if the restructuring event occurs on a five-year default swap in the first year of the contract, protection buyers would be able to deliver physical securities with maturity dates equivalent to the termination of the swap date, but the limitation cannot be set earlier than the swap termination date. The obligations must be fully transferable, and no bilateral loans can be used to trigger a credit event. The obligations must be *multiholder obligations*.

When the reference obligations are bonds, modified restructuring is fine. It's trickier when loans are included as reference obligations. The proposed Basel Accord on capital adequacy standards calls for some form of restructuring to be recognized in a CDS in order for banks to get regulatory capital relief, and there is no clarity on just how far the language must go to satisfy this requirement.

Moody's has been very vocal about how this rating agency views non-credit-related risk introduced by ISDA language. Moody's is clear that it cannot account for this in rating CDO transactions. Its data was never meant to capture this kind of risk. Moody's feels this is a potential conflict of interest or moral hazard risk. The sponsoring bank determines when a loss event has occurred, and the bank can control the payout by manipulating the deliverable.

Obligation acceleration is another credit event prone to abuse. Whenever the protection buyer has the right to accelerate, there is the potential for moral hazard. Suppose a bank purchases protection on a loan. Suppose further that the borrower has suffered some credit deterioration, or violated some covenants, but is not in immediate danger of defaulting on any payments. The bank knows it will get all of its money back if it accelerates the loan. The bank accelerates the loan and declares a credit event. Then the bank gets bids on the remaining outstanding debt and produces the cheapest-to-deliver (the bond trading at the lowest price) under a credit default swap in which the bank has bought credit default protection on the borrower. If bonds trade at 80 percent, the bank gets 20 percent of the contract notional amount in loss compensation, but the bank has suffered no loss whatsoever.

Repudiation and *moratorium* were included in many corporate CDSs, and now are usually dropped. These terms apply to sovereign risk and shouldn't be included in a corporate CDS.

CDO structurers often need deals rated, and Moody's prefers language that differs from ISDA documentation. Particularly in arbitrage CDOs meant to mirror the bond market, rating agency language protects investors in the tranches of CDOs. Wherever possible, it is a good idea for investors in arbitrage CDOs to ask for deals that match Moody's preferences as closely as possible. Buyers of CDO tranches should be especially wary of unrated deals. CDOs that include only bankruptcy, failure to pay, and modified restructuring give the best protection, but even then, there are differences in Moody's' preferred language and in language proposed by ISDA. The following are examples:

- *Bankruptcy.* ISDA allows swap counterparties to terminate early due to credit problems with a counterparty, even before a default occurs. Planning for or considering a bankruptcy filing might be in furtherance of bankruptcy, and can trigger an ISDA default, but would not generally be considered a bankruptcy event by Moody's. This is because ISDA originally meant to protect counterparties in interest rate swaps in which a payment failure can occur even when the counterparty is a worthy credit risk. Here's a scary thought. If you check with the back office of any interest rate swap desk, you will find several counterparties who have failed to make payments on their swaps. Sometimes the amounts owed are very large. This is usually due to a counterparty back office problem or a miscalculation. This could potentially be viewed as a credit event. Why should an investor in a CDO accept this condition as a potential credit event?
- *Failure to pay.* ISDA allows a broader category of reference obligations than Moody's recommends. Moody's also recommends higher payment thresholds.
- *Restructuring.* Moody's prefers restructuring to be defined as the result of deterioration of the obligor's creditworthiness or financial

TABLE 3.1 Credit Event Definitions for Rated Arbitrage CDOs

Old Paradigm	New Paradigm
Old Standard ISDA Swap Confirmation • Bankruptcy • Failure to pay • Obligation acceleration* • Repudiation or moratorium* • Restructuring **Menu of additional events** • Downgrade • Credit Event Upon Merger • War • Coup d'état • Obligor is past due for more than 90 days on any credit obligation (Basel proposal)	**Recommended CDO Credit Events** • Bankruptcy • Failure to pay • Modified or no restructuring • Additional events for sovereigns including repudiation and moratorium • Special definitions for ABSs

*Contracts entered into after 2002 usually exclude these definitions.

condition. Distressed exchange involves a *diminished financial obligation* or exchange that helps the borrower avoid default. Moody's does not consider some voluntary restructurings credit events.

There are broad implications to the CDO market. Synthetic collateralized loan obligations (CLOs) that have this imbedded language risk in the credit default documentation may have to be reexamined. Newly structured arbitrage CDOs should incorporate language that serves the interest of potential investors. Table 3.1 tracks some of the recent language changes with respect to credit events.

When the deal is a CDO of CDOs with ABS underlyings, special language is required. When does a default occur, what is deliverable, and how is the loss given default determined? The definitions may vary depending on the underlying assets.

CDS PRICING ISSUES

Credit default protection should logically trade near the spread of the reference security to a risk-free asset. For instance, if a 10-year maturity bond trades at a spread of 100 basis points (bps) to the 10-year U.S. Treasury, the amount of spread due to credit risk is about 100 bps. Some of the 100 bps may be due to liquidity. Credit default swaps, however, tend to trade at a level that is benchmarked to the asset swap market. This is because most banks benchmark their funding costs based on a spread to the London InterBank Offered Rate (LIBOR) and look at the net spread they can earn on a given credit relative to their funding costs.

Most modelers of credit derivatives build models to predict the possible payoffs. The simplest model is little more than a binomial tree with a few key variables to predict the potential payoff under preset scenarios. The result will be modified for soft variables including supply and demand.

Key inputs include the following:

- Credit quality of the obligor (or obligors, in the case of baskets).
- Credit quality of the default protection provider.
- Correlation among the obligors.
- Correlation of the obligor(s) with the credit protection provider in the CDS contract.
- Probability of default (and volatility of the data) of the obligor(s).
- Probability of default (and volatility of the data) of the credit default protection provider.
- Joint probabilities of default in the event that the obligor(s) and credit default protection provider are correlated.
- Recovery rate in the event of default of an obligor.
- Recovery rate in the event of default of the credit protection provider (replacement value of the CDS).
- The leverage of the structure.
- Maturity of the deal.
- Settlement provisions in the event of default.
- Supply and demand for the credit default protection.
- Economic research that may change my view of the credit quality.
- Urgency of the need to reduce my credit exposure.
- Special documentation considerations.
- If applicable, BIS risk weighting of the default protection seller.

SYNTHETIC CDOS

Financial engineers have tremendous flexibility when using credit default swaps. In the past, a typical collateralized debt obligation required the accumulation of a portfolio of cash assets. Figure 3.6 shows an example of a vanilla collateralized bond obligation. An underwriter would typically accumulate, warehouse, fund, and hedge a portfolio in anticipation of securitizing the assets in a bond portfolio. Reinvestment and cash flows of a

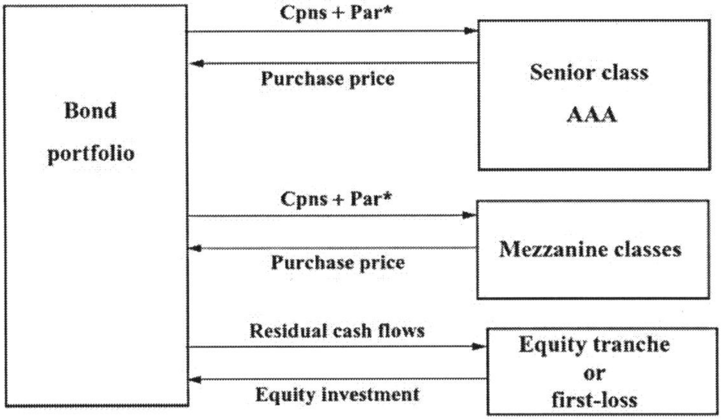

* Par at maturity if defaults do not affect the principal of this tranche.

FIGURE 3.6 Cash Collateralized Bond Obligation

variety of bond maturities would have to be dealt with. Credit derivatives allow a deal with a specific maturity to be issued referencing virtually any class of reference assets one desires. Figure 3.7 shows a generic structure for a static (nonmanaged) synthetic arbitrage CDO. We discuss variations on this structure in more detail in Chapters 9 through 14.

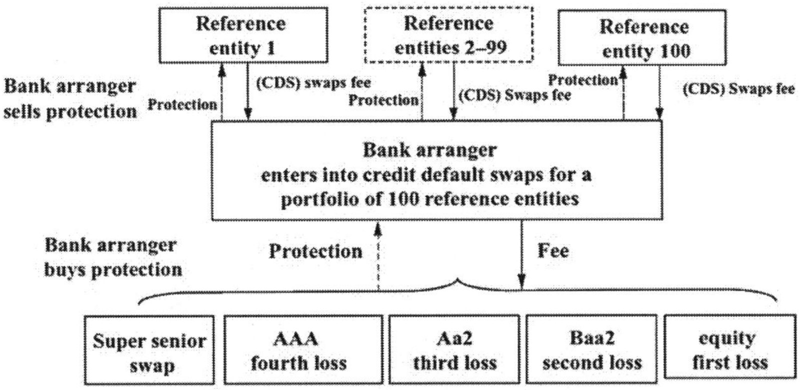

Losses are first absorbed by the junior-most investors up the line to the senior-most investors: the equity, the mezzanine tranches, and finally the super senior tranche.

FIGURE 3.7 Synthetic Static Arbitrage CDO

TOTAL RATE OF RETURN SWAPS (TOTAL RETURN SWAPS)

A *total rate of return swap* (TRORS) is also called a *total return swap* (TRS). I usually refer to these transactions in the former way to highlight a minor distinction that may occur in the cash flows of these transactions, which I will discuss in a minute. For now, let's define a TRORS.

A TRORS is primarily used as a financing tool, but it is also a complete hedge of market and credit risk of an asset. A TRORS is a bilateral financial contract between a total return payer and a total return receiver. The total return payer pays the total rate of return of a reference security and receives a form of payment from the receiver of the total rate of return. The receiver's payment is usually a floating-rate payment. The payment is usually a spread to a floating-rate index such as USD LIBOR or Euribor, but any index can be used, including a fixed-rate index, an equity index, or a bond performance index. The reference assets can themselves be indexes, corporate bonds, sovereign debt, bank debt, mortgage-backed securities (MBS), asset-backed securities (ABS), loans (term or revolver), leveraged loans, equities, real estate receivables, lease receivables, or commodities. Virtually any asset can be a reference asset in a TRORS.

Figure 3.8 shows a generic schematic of the cash flows of a TRORS.

Total return swaps and repurchase agreements are popular with hedge funds due to the leverage they provide. Banks and investment banks with lower funding costs usually require up-front collateral from hedge funds that is a fraction of the initial asset value, often allowing hedge funds 20:1 leverage.

Notice that the timing of the reference asset(s) cash flows does not have to match the payment of the total rate of return to the total rate of return receiver. For instance, a particular reference asset may have a monthly coupon, but the payments on the TRORS may be set for quarterly periods or even annual payments. This means that the coupons must be reinvested according to a pre-agreement between the receiver and payer. There may be some reinvestment risk of the cash flows. Likewise, settlement structure in the event of default may introduce some cash flow mismatch. To highlight this point, I refer to these transactions as total rate of return swaps. Others may prefer to say TRS. Use whichever terminology resonates best for you, as long as you are clear about the terms of the transaction.

The *total rate of return payer* is the legal owner of the reference as-set(s) and holds the reference asset(s) on balance sheet. The total rate of return payer has created a short position in the market risk and a short position in the credit risk of the reference asset(s) until the maturity of the swap.

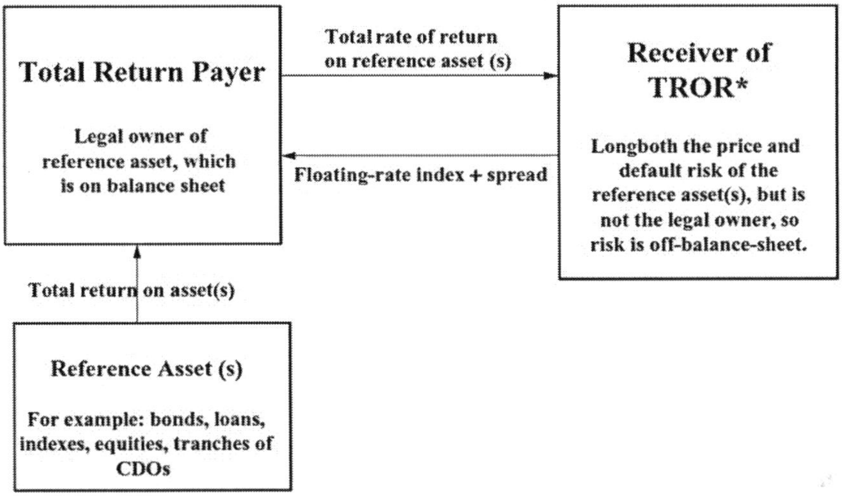

*Receiver of the TROR hedges both the price and default risk of the reference asset for the legal owner. Price risk can be due to credit spread widening, credit downgrade, or changes in market levels of interest rates.

FIGURE 3.8 Generic Total Rate of Return Swap (TRORS)

The *total rate of return receiver*, also called the *investor*, is not the legal owner of the reference asset(s). The TRORS is an off-balance-sheet transaction for the receiver, who has a synthetic long position in the market risk and a synthetic long position in the credit risk of the reference asset(s). The TRORS documentation is negotiable, and often the total rate of return receiver will want the option to purchase the reference asset at the then prevailing market price at the maturity of the swap. Note that this feature is independent of settlement structure in the event that there is a default of the reference asset(s).

In the event of a reference asset(s) default, the total rate of return receiver makes the total rate of return payer *whole* for the market risk and credit risk of the reference asset. The total rate of return receiver makes a net payment of the difference between the price of the reference asset(s) at the beginning of the transaction (or at the latest price reset if this comes later) and the price of the reference asset(s) at the time of default. Alternatively, the total rate of return receiver may take delivery of the defaulted reference asset and pay the initial price or last reset price, if later, of the reference asset(s) to the total rate of return payer. This settlement terminates any obligation to the other party, and the TRORS for the relevant reference asset(s) terminates.

Just like CDSs, the documentation for a TRORS is negotiable. The observations we made earlier regarding ISDA documentation with respect to rated CDOs applies for TRORS. We want to be careful how we specify credit default events if we want to use a TRORS in a rated CDO.

PRICING TRORS ON LEVERED CDO TRANCHES

There is no standard method for pricing total rate of return swaps. Let's focus on the pricing from the point of view of a bank that is providing financing for a counterparty. The bank buys an asset and pays the total rate of return to the counterparty in exchange for periodic payments of a spread over LIBOR on the notional amount of the asset.

One reasonable lower bound for pricing is the rate the bank would charge to provide an unfunded revolver of the same maturity to this counterparty. This seems to be the absolute lower bound, however. An unfunded revolver is essentially a standby loan. The loan will probably have a lower expected loss than the asset used as the reference obligation in the total rate of return swap. Furthermore, a revolver will usually reflect pricing that may be negotiated based on the relationship of the lender to the borrower.

The upper bound is *whatever the market will bear*. Generic TRORS tend to trade at a level that allows the bank providing the financing to earn a positive spread to its funding costs and an adequate return on economic and regulatory capital. The counterparty receiving the financing will compare the offered level for the financing to calculate the all-in return on the transaction. The total rate of return swap should be comparable with the return on floating assets or asset swaps of similar credits (although funded obligations should trade at a premium since the counterparty is using much less capital and getting an off-balance-sheet transaction and a leveraged return). Total rate of return swaps have been done on high-credit-quality MBSs, for instance, in the range of LIBOR plus 10 to LIBOR plus 25 bps in maturities of three months to five years. Assets rated BBB have been financed at rates from LIBOR plus 25 to LIBOR plus 50 bps for maturities under three years. It is difficult to generalize.

Pricing varies with supply and demand factors. Total rate of return swaps for low spreads must be done in large size to make the documentation and capital considerations work for the bank providing the financing. Often outside counterparties will attempt to arbitrage the bank's various financing desks: the total return swap desk and the traditional financing desk.

Again, the upper bound is whatever the market will bear. Prime brokers aggressively competed for hedge fund business in 2006 and the early part of 2007, but by mid-2007 they were reconsidering the generous terms and relaxed mark-to-market protocols in the wake of the implosion of formerly well-regarded, overleveraged hedge funds.

When there are a limited number of counterparties offering financing, there may be few options for the total return receiver to reduce the funding cost. The best one can do is prepare to negotiate if possible.

To get a lower funding cost, the first step is to try to determine where the market is in general for the type of transaction you want to do. Mezzanine tranches of CDOs can be structure specific, but at least try to determine the market for mezzanine tranches of the same underlying collateral. There will be a limited number of suppliers, and it is useful to get to know them all. If the suppliers will not supply information on pricing in the absence of a live transaction, then it is time to consider how one would look at the upper bound of a more generic TRORS.

To determine the market value of any security, there are certain rules of value. Everything trades off of the next most certain bond or asset. For a TRORS, one would look at floating assets or assets of a similar credit. Compare the potential return on unfunded equity transactions relative to the TRORS on the next most senior mezzanine tranche. Also compare the potential return on the unfunded equity transaction with one in which a hedge fund posts Treasury collateral and earns the excess spread on a portfolio of high-yield bonds overcollateralized with the injection of Treasury collateral. We discuss these equity transactions in Chapter 10.

This is still a touchy market for mezzanine TRORS pricing, so in the end, the hedge fund will have to decide whether the return for the credit risk is worth it relative to its traditional investments.

TRORS VS REPOS

Both TRORS and repurchase agreements are used as CDO structuring tools. Why would one do a TRORS instead of buying an asset? The reason is that the receiver of the TRORS gets *leverage*. Because of leverage, hedge funds like to be the receivers in TRORS.

Repurchase agreements are also a type of financing. What is the difference between a TRORS and a repurchase agreement? In a repurchase agreement, also called a *repo,* the owner of an asset, the seller, sells the asset to a buyer and agrees to repurchase the asset at a fixed price on a fixed date. The asset seller agrees to pay the buyer a prenegotiated rate of interest, the repurchase rate, also called the *repo rate*. The buyer lends the seller money for the period of the agreement at the repo rate implied by the difference between the asset sell price and the asset repurchase price. At the maturity of the agreement, the seller is obligated to repurchase the securities at the prespecified repurchase price.

In a TRORS, the total rate of return receiver is not obligated to purchase the reference asset at the maturity of the transaction, nor is there a pre-agreed fixed price for the reference asset at the maturity of the transaction. The TRORS receiver is obligated only to exchange payments based on the market value of the reference asset at the maturity of the transaction.

When the maturity of the TROR is much less than that of the reference asset(s), the price risk due to market value fluctuations in the absence of default can be substantial. Some TRORS receivers, the protection sellers, will not participate in mismatched maturity transactions. TRORS receivers who do engage in these transactions like the ability to invest in a reference asset for a shorter period of time than is available in the market, and they are happy to take the additional element of market risk.

How do we determine market price? In between the inception and the maturity—due to default or expiration—of the TRORS, the receiver may be content with prices provided by the seller. In the event of default of the reference asset, or if the TRORS matures before the reference asset, market value is often determined by a dealer poll. The calculation agent calls three to five market makers—the names are often prespecified in the documentation—in the reference asset and takes the average price. The calculation agent may be one of the dealers offering a price. An auction method is preferable for very illiquid assets that are difficult to price. Because of the market value risk, the receiver of the TRORS usually retains the option to take physical delivery of the reference asset and pay the difference between the initial price (or last reset price, if later) and the dealer poll price or auction price.

EQUITY TRORS: CORPORATE LOANS DISGUISED AS CAPITAL INJECTIONS

Disguising a corporate loan as a capital injection is accomplished by several banks by entering into an equity total return swap with a corporation desiring cash. (U.S. banks used to book this transaction in a foreign entity to avoid Glass-Steagall Act restrictions against banks trading equity, although the restrictions are changing.)

The bank buys the corporation's equity, receives LIBOR plus a spread, and pays the corporation the total return on the equity. The cash is on balance sheet as a capital injection, and the TRORS is off balance sheet. The corporation usually enjoys a per annum spread to LIBOR of only 50 bps. A BBB-rated corporation could raise cash at a cost of only 50 bps per annum over LIBOR versus a cost of around 250 bps more in the loan market. Of course, if the stock price goes down, the corporation is asked to put up more stock as collateral for the mark-to-market changes in the stock price that is owed by the corporation to the bank.

The bank gets equity as collateral, and the corporation gets a low-cost loan. What could be the problem?

Given that credit-risky corporations are eager to enter into this transaction since the cost of raising cash is lower than taking out a loan, the transaction raises several unpleasant issues. The opportunity to account for the cash paid for the equity as a capital injection raises an accounting red flag that only an Arthur Andersen auditor could ignore. As we saw earlier, a TRORS is a financing tool. From the bank's point of view, if the price of the stock goes down either due to a weakness in the corporation balance sheet, due to the economy, or due to a general depression in stock prices, the bank receives additional stock. This additional equity delivered to the bank may dilute the corporation's shareholder value at a time when the corporation can least afford it. Right about now it should occur to the bank that the floor price for equity is zero, especially if the bank is being delivered start-up technology stocks. In the past couple of years, many of the corporations that engaged in this activity saw their stock prices plummet.

This activity is a sweet deal for the heads of total return trading desks. Often banks recognize the price risk of the equity collateral by asking for initial overcollateralization of the transaction, and corporations are happy to oblige by handing over more equity. Is it hard to find takers for this transaction? It's like waving a bankroll over your head in a Turkish bazaar: A lot of takers will be delighted do business with you. The TRORS trading book earns fee income that is often recognized on an accrual basis. The traders have an incentive to put on as many trades as possible for as long as possible. Their bonuses are tied to the revenue generated on the trading desk.

Banks might want to ask themselves how they prefer to engage in lending activity. Does the bank prefer to perform lending activities from traditional lending groups that may ask for hard assets against a secured lending and get a higher fee? Does the bank prefer to participate in potential accounting games by lending money to corporations in the form of a financing from the total return trading book and earn less money in the process?

Ironically, hedge funds that lend money for stock are vilified for engaging in *toxic convertibles*. If stock prices decline enough, the amount of stock required to repay the loan may actually cause the control of the corporation to change hands. When banks do the same thing, they claim they're performing a public service.

INFORMATION ASYMMETRY AND MORAL HAZARD

Total rate of return swaps have the same moral hazard risk as credit default swaps when it comes to loans. If a financial institution originates a loan and is paying the total return of an on-balance-sheet loan, how much financial information is it required to disclose to its protection seller counterparties? Does the financial institution have an obligation to the original borrower to keep confidential its knowledge of the corporation's non–publicly disclosed financial information? Does the lender have insider information, an unfair advantage over its counterparties? Does the lender bank have control over the credit event trigger?

The lender, as legal owner of the loan, retains voting rights when it pays the total rate of return on a loan or when it buys credit default protection on a loan. There is usually a gentleman's agreement that the lender will vote according to the wishes of the total rate of return receiver, or the credit default protection provider. If the lender cannot contact the counterparty, however, it is usually assumed that the lender will vote with the majority of the other lenders, if any. This may or may not be in the best interests of the lender's counterparty. There is the further issue that the lenders may have better information than the counterparty, which may influence the majority vote. This moral hazard can be substantial.

Likewise, if an underwriter is accumulating assets in a warehouse and knows or has reason to know that there is a material change in the status of the assets, that information must be disclosed. If the final deal is a private placement and risk disclosures include caveats about new asset classes or exceptions to past debt (or loan) underwriting practices, investors should ask for proof of adequate due diligence on the probability of default and potential recovery in the event of default on the underlying collateral. If that information is not available, a sophisticated investor should not buy the final deal until it performs adequate due diligence.

CDS VERSUS TRORS

Besides the difference in applications previously described, it seems the chief difference between a CDS and a TRORS is that in addition to default risk, a TRORS also hedges market risk. Some regulators have correctly pointed out that while a CDS will hedge credit default risk, it will not exactly hedge credit spread widening risk, completely confer the benefits of credit spread narrowing, completely hedge credit quality deterioration, completely confer the benefit of credit quality improvement, or hedge other changes in value due to other market risk factors. For this reason, some regulators will give only partial regulatory capital relief, if any, for bonds and loans hedged with a CDS.

It seems reasonable to hedge the credit risk of investments held to maturity with a CDS. It also seems reasonable to recognize that the CDS provides at least a partial hedge of credit migration and credit spread moves, since CDS spreads tend to move in tandem with these events. There is no current consensus on regulatory relief across venues.

PAY-AS-YOU-GO (PAUG)

ISDA introduced the pay-as-you-go (PAUG) template in 2005 for RMBS and CMBS securities, and for CDOs in June 2006. The ISDA PAUG standard template is an attempt to replicate the cash flow profile of the cash bond with a CDS contract. One can modify these terms, and that may make the contract less liquid, but as many investors have pointed out, the ISDA contract can be problematic when it comes to asset-backed securities (ABSs).

Asset-backed securities present special issues. For example, in RMBS deals with tranche risk backed by mortgage loans, interest is paid sequentially to the most senior bond in the deal first, and so on down the line. The ultimate amount of interest paid is capped at the weighted-average mortgage rate net of expenses. This is also known as the net WAC, or the available funds cap (AFC).

Unlike other CDS contracts, the protection seller makes floating payments if there is an RMBS reference obligation interest shortfall, called the AFC shortfall; or if there is a CMBS reference obligation interest shortfall, called a WAC shortfall; or, if the reference obligations are CDOs, the interest shortfalls are called pay-in-kind (PIK-ing) shortfalls. The protection buyer may reimburse these payments if the interest shortfall is ultimately recovered. Protection buyers usually have an option whether to call a credit event or a floating amount event.

Some investors are not satisfied with this contract, in particular PIK-ing, and prefer to rewrite the language depending on the assets and the structure. Language that allows restructuring of mortgages is problematic because it is difficult to determine whether the restructuring is noneconomic and simply a delaying tactic to avoid recognizing losses. Furthermore, the PAUG introduces substantial basis risk, and the market may demand further changes.

PAUG credit events for pay-as-you-go contracts are defined as follows:

- Failure to pay (FTP) principal.
- Write-down.
- Distressed rating downgrade (CCC or below).
- Failure to pay (FTP) interest for CDO reference obligations only.

PAUG floating amount events are:

- Interest shortfalls.
- Principal shortfalls.
- Write-down amounts.

PAUG settlements are trickier than for other CDSs. Since the secondary market for structured finance securities is illiquid, it is difficult to obtain objective valuations. Floating payments are designed to replicate the actual loss amounts, but as we shall see later, it is possible to manipulate those amounts, and that is becoming an issue in the subprime market and its related CDS indexes in particular. If a credit event occurs—or, more accurately, is *deemed* to occur—then the protection buyer has the option to physically deliver all or part of the notional amount to the seller. If the entire notional is physically settled then the CDS is terminated. If a portion of the notional is settled, then the CDS continues on the remaining amount.

There are several interest shortfall cap options:

- *Fixed cap*. Floating payments are limited to the amount of the CDS premium.
- *Variable cap*. Floating payments are limited to LIBOR plus premium.
- *No cap*. No limit to the floating rate payments. This option completely replicates the payments of the cash bond or total return swap; it may require principal to be liquidated to pay interest shortfall.

REMIC law limits a floating rate RMBS bond pass-through rate to the lesser of the bond spread plus a predefined index—one-month or three-month LIBOR, for example—or the net WAC, the underlying mortgage collateral pool's weighted average coupon, net of expenses. Whether the cap is reached depends on the actual prepayment speeds of underlying mortgages, the effectiveness of interest rate hedges in the RMBS structure, and the short-term interest rate increases before hybrid ARM mortgages switch to floating interest rate payments.

The unrecovered AFC interest shortfalls for lower-rated RMBS bonds in the 2005 and 2006 vintages—rated BBB and lower—are substantial and climbing. While the overall amounts are small, they are concentrated in these vintages, and we can expect more of the same for some of the bonds backed by mortgages in the first half of 2007 in subprime and Alt-A loans.

INDEXES

Indexes on any cluster of CDSs and even structures made from clusters of CDSs, including CDOs, have sprung up to suit market needs. Some of these indexes have been more successful than others, and most of them are tracked by Mark-it Partners. For example, in early 2006, the ABX.HE Index (asset-backed home equity index) was launched, linked to rated slices of subprime residential mortgage loans. The next best thing was the ABX-HE-BBB 06-2, linked to subprime residential mortgage loans (see also Chapter 8). If one wants to buy protection on the index, one shorts the index. As the level of this index declines, it reflects a decline in the price of the underlying rated product, and the value of the position increases. Due to demand for subprime market hedge indexes, the TABX was launched on February 14, 2007. It is composed of standard tranches on the ABX.HE Index.

Corporate bond indexes have been used as reference portfolios to create bespoke tranches of CDOs and as a reference for other new products which are discussed later in this book.

Chapter 4

CDOs and the Global Capital Markets

Credit derivatives have been the most powerful driving force for change in the structured finance market. In 1996, the global credit default swap market was only $100 billion to $200 billion in size. Morgan Stanley estimated the credit default swap market grew to $2.4 trillion in 2002. The British Banker's Association (BBA) estimates that credit default swap volume was close to $1.2 trillion in 2001 and grew to $1.9 trillion in 2002. These figures do not include asset swaps or total return swaps. By 2004, London had captured more than 50 percent of the global credit default swap trading business. ISDA estimated the market size as $8.42 trillion in 2004 and more than double that at $17.3 trillion in 2005. In 2006, ISDA estimated the market size at $34.5 trillion, while the BBA's estimate was $20 trillion. For year-end 2007, ISDA estimated outstanding credit derivatives contracts at more than $62.2 trillion. Market size may reach more than $80 trillion outstanding contracts by the end of 2008. While growth has slowed in the CDO market, credit derivatives seem more robust—but 2008 year-end numbers have not yet been tallied. This over-the-counter (OTC) market is difficult to estimate since transactions are private and off balance sheet. It isn't surprising that different sources have different estimates of market size.

Credit derivatives drove the explosive growth of the global CDO market through the first half of 2007, but cynical use of this technology is partially responsible for the rapid decline in mortgage-backed CDO issuance during the end of 2007 and the beginning of 2008. Synthetic securitizations, CDOs using credit derivatives technology, have further muddied the waters, making it even more difficult to estimate market size.

EVOLUTION OF THE CDO MARKET

The collateralized bond obligation (CBO) market (not including collateralized mortgage obligations), the precursor to the current new collateralized debt obligation (CDO) products, began in the late 1980s when high-yield or junk bonds had yields of about 13 to 20 percent.

In the United States, the Resolution Trust Corporation (RTC) was charged with liquidating positions held by savings and loan (S&L) associations. Prior to this, S&Ls essentially enjoyed a put to the U.S. government. They realized they could buy highly leveraged residuals from CMO transactions and could buy high-yield bonds for yield. If there were no losses, they were heroes. If their positions didn't do well, they could put the S&L to the government and walk away. There was more to the crisis than that, such as fraudulent real estate loans, but this was a contributing factor to the S&L crisis in the United States. The fall of Drexel added further cheap high-yield supply to the market, and changes in U.S. insurance capital regulations squelched demand for high-yield product.

The beneficiaries were investors interested in diversified pools of cheap high-yield bonds. Arbitrage CBOs were the answer. These deals were actively managed cash arbitrage CDOs. These early deals were exclusively leveraged market value deals. The supply glut of high-yield bonds declined drastically in the 1990s, and the prices of high-yield bonds rose with a corresponding decline in yield. Deal volume declined in the early 1990s. The emergence of the simpler cash flow CDO structure rekindled investor demand after 1995. This was the old paradigm.

By the late 1990s there was a paradigm shift in the CDO market. A look at the reasons for almost nonexistent growth in the European market versus the U.S. market illustrates the sea change in CDOs and the causes for the paradigm shift.

By 1999, the U.S. bond market was approaching $600 billion in size. In contrast, the European bond market was only about $35 billion in size. For more than a decade, the capital markets believed that this anemic issuance, combined with the multicurrency nature of the European issuance and investor market, would guarantee that Europe was never a significant factor in CDOs. The lack of supply of high-yield bonds in Asia and Australia also inhibited their participation in CDO issuance.

Before 1995, virtually all CDOs were cash deals. Figure 4.1 shows a change in the growth pattern beginning after 1995.

The way the figures are presented depends very much on who's reporting them. Figure 4.1 primarily represents CBOs and CLOs but does not necessarily include the broad range of assets that can be securitized. It is

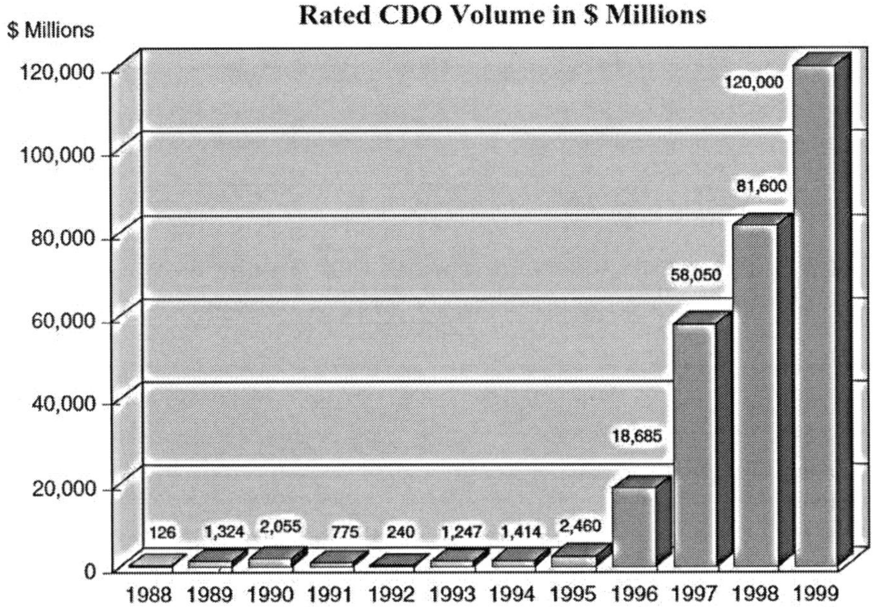

FIGURE 4.1 CBO/CLO Market Size—The Old Paradigm
Note: Figures represent explicitly rated tranches of CBO/CLO transactions only.
Sources: Bank of America and Moody's Investors Service.

also important to note that these numbers represent outstanding volume, not annual volume of deals.

Going back to the CBO/CLO market, we discover a pattern shift that was mainly due to the introduction of *synthetics*. Structurers use credit default swaps and total return swaps to transfer the risk of assets, instead of selling cash (or physical) assets. As we will see later, the creation of a new tranche, the super senior tranche, gave an enormous boost to the deal arbitrage. It also created greater flexibility and allowed for easier transfer of risk. In 1995 the CBO/CLO market was about $2.5 billion in size; by 1999, it was around $120 billion.

The growth spurt was chiefly due to the introduction of synthetic CDOs. Synthetics facilitate more efficient portfolio ramp up and diversification; they also facilitate getting a higher average credit rating. The synthetic arbitrage is facilitated by the feasibility of a smaller equity tranche, which creates more leverage. The synthetic arbitrage gets a further huge boost from the large, inexpensive super senior tranche which makes up the bulk of the synthetic deal.

Another key shift in the market is the unprecedented number of credit downgrades and defaults in the early part of the twenty-first century. Defaults in 2001 and 2002 exceeded $180 billion. The high-yield market was particularly hard hit, but investment-grade credits were not immune. Defaults in investment-grade bonds during that period exceeded the cumulative total of the previous 20 years. The increase in defaults and credit downgrades contributed to a growth rate in CDO downgrades of 318 percent in 2002. Most of the downgrades, about 74 percent, were in the high-yield sector. The fact that the synthetic CDO arbitrage was viable using exclusively investment-grade credits was a clear advantage for the synthetic CDO market, but it also led to lax practices as many CDOs were stuffed with identical "investment-grade" names that defaulted, such as Enron and Worldcom.

The introduction of the euro created a wider base of single-currency reference assets in Europe. In addition, a wider investor base could participate in the deal when it was brought to market, because they were all purchasers of euro assets. This helped boost issuance to about $200 billion in 2001, or $325 billion counting the full notional of bespoke tranches also known as single-tranche CDOs (STCDOs). Issuance in 2002 was more than $250 billion, or $600 billion if one counted the full notional of STCDOs. The percentage of the overall CDO market made up of synthetics varied by venue. The U.S. market is made up of only about 25 percent synthetic CDOs, probably due to the greater volume of high-yield bond and loan issuance that allowed the U.S. market to bring more cash deals to market. In Europe and Asia, about 80 to 90 percent of the CDO market is made up of synthetics. Whereas all of a deal's assets were cash assets in 1995, by 2002, synthetics made up more than 75 percent of the CDO market.

Collateralized debt obligations employ credit derivatives technology, and the size of the market is difficult to quantify, especially with the rise of unrated bespoke tranches. Credit derivatives give to the CDO arbitrage, as it's called. While credit derivatives add flexibility, they also challenge investors to invest time in education, lest they invest money for insufficient value. Potential confusion isn't unique to investors, however. Bank managers often do not know how to quantify the value of single-tranche CDO trading books. These books grew in size, because banks didn't invest in the resources to effectively market all of the CDO tranches. As a result, banks often unwittingly hold equity risk—as well as the senior tranches—in their trading books (see also Chapter 14).

If a bank arranger sold each tranche and then sold protection in the credit derivatives market on each portfolio position, it would be fully hedged. Since single-tranche trading books usually sell only the mezzanine (the middle) tranche and then delta-hedge, they are riskier than fully hedged positions. Theoretically, one should make more money than the fully hedged position because one has more risk. Often, however, the single-tranche books make even less money for greater risk, because traders make additional credit bets or make a bet on hedge ratios. Traders must take risk, but when a trader loses money on the bets relative to a fully hedged position, the trader isn't very good at the craft. Since these books usually report positive income, even if it is insufficient income, bank managers are challenged to figure out whether the bank's risk is properly rewarded.

Risk is not measured in billions or in trillions of notional amounts. Risk is measured as value at risk (in simplified terms). The sold tranches of synthetic CDOs are horizontal slices of a much larger CDO, which is referenced in the deal documentation. The equivalent risk of the unsold CDO tranches remains on the arrangers' books. From a risk perspective, it is more correct to report the size of the single-tranche synthetic CDO market in terms of total notional portfolio size, and the current practice of reporting only the sold tranche is misleading.

A sold tranche represents a horizontal slice of the risk of the entire CDO. The typical hedge is to sell credit default protection—creating income—on a vertical slice of the CDO. The hedge ratio is a best guess derived from debatable data.

At the outset, it appears as if the single-tranche deal arranger is making more income than if it had sold credit default protection on the full notional amount (in the trillions of dollars for 2005) and fully hedged its position by selling all of the tranches of the synthetic CDO. But the net income has often proved over time to be lower for this riskier position.

When credit spreads have been tight in recent years, the return on the implied equity risk remaining with the arranger was less than 10 percent, versus 60 percent and higher when credit spreads have been very wide. If one considers the full notional amount of the CDO, it is easy to figure this out, but if one is misled by reporting only the sold tranche of the CDO, this risk and this insufficient reward is obscured. My estimates of the outstanding size of the market based on notional amount through 2006 are shown in Figure 4.2. Based on the write-downs announced in 2007 and 2008 related to deals that were issued in 2006, this seems the more sensible way to view the market risk. Issuance peaked in 2007 and has declined as a result of the mortgage lending debacle.

Rating agency data is markedly different. Rating agencies track the tranches they actually rate, but do not track the full notional amounts or unrated STCDOs. Rating agencies typically divide CDOs into two major sectors: asset-backed CDOs and corporate credit CDOs and CLOs; they lump everything else into subsectors. Moody's data shows that CDO

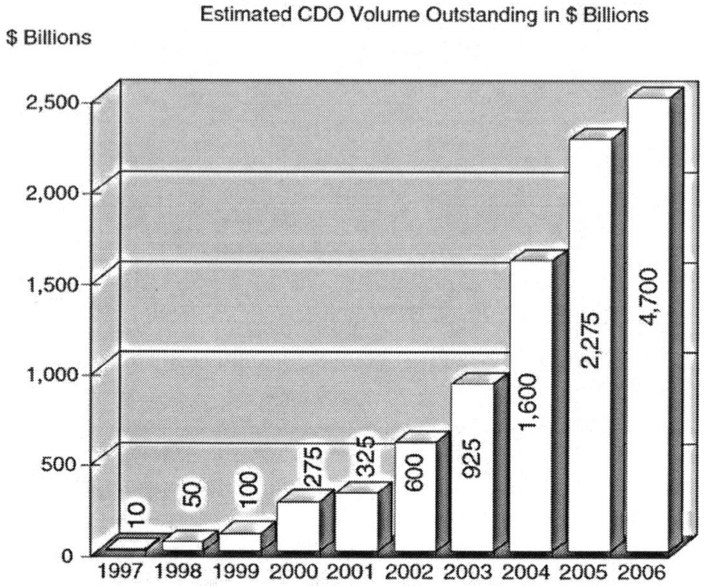

FIGURE 4.2 CDO Market Size—The New Paradigm
Sources: Tavakoli Structured Finance.

issuance grew at a constant annual growth rate of around 27 percent from $14 billion in 1996 to $158 billion in 2006, for total issuance volume of only $329.3 billion in 2006. Moody's is missing data from the issuance of bespoke tranches and from tranches based on CDS indexes, which are usually unrated.

Traditional CDOs were bankruptcy-remote special purpose entities. The market changed drastically, leaving investment banks to manage huge risk positions, often unbeknownst to senior managers.

Synthetic CDOs usually fall into one of three categories: balance-sheet CDOs, static synthetic arbitrage CDOs, and managed synthetic arbitrage CDOs.

Most balance-sheet CDOs are regulatory capital driven. Recently, several arbitrage-driven multisector balance-sheet CDOs have come to market when banks used portfolios of mezzanine (BBB average rated) tranches of multisector CDOs from their investment portfolios as the reference collateral.

The figures previously cited understate the size of the synthetic market, because CDO statistics capture only a portion of CDO-related synthetic activity. Many cash deals employ synthetics to make up a portion of the total portfolio. Many synthetic arbitrage CDOs brought to market were *unrated*, as were many of the single tranche CDOs sold in recent years. We rely on rating agencies to compile most of the statistics. If a deal isn't rated, and if a deal is privately placed, we rely on word of mouth to compile deal data. Some portfolio swaps are privately placed, and some are untranched. Intermediations of synthetic product are not reported in CDO statistics. Neither are basket swaps, a separate but related category of synthetic activity.

How did banks and investment banks manage to sell such a huge volume of new issuance to traditional CDO investors (mutual funds, bank portfolios, pension funds, insurance company portfolios, hedge funds) in such a short period of time?

The answer is that most of the synthetic volume is not going to traditional CDO investors. The super senior tranche makes up a large percentage of synthetic CDOs. This tranche is often retained by the banks structuring the deals and/or is protected by monoline insurance companies. Products such as leveraged super seniors, constant proportion portfolio insurance, and structured investment vehicles for junior super senior tranches and mezzanine triple-A tranches also provided liquidity to this market.

As we will see later, hedge funds also became a driving force for CDOs. Often they could initially employ massive amounts of leverage, putting very little money down to take an interest in the highly leveraged equity tranche of a CDO. When an investment bank does this kind of transaction with an opaque hedge fund or a thinly capitalized CDO manager, the only thing the investment bank should count on is the up-front collateral, and that could range from only 5 to 15 percent of the notional amount of the transaction. Synthetics allowed the CDO market to increasingly rely on leverage throughout the capital structure, and this contributed to the global credit crunch of 2007 and 2008.

Chapter 5

Risk and Valuation Issues

THE PORTFOLIO DIVERSIFICATION MYTH

The least useful finance nursery rhyme for CDO investors is "Diversification reduces risk." Diversification is often an illusion, and diversifying simply for the sake of it can add risk to an investor's portfolio or lull an investor into a false sense of prudence so that the investor ignores discrete risks in the portfolio.

Unskilled investors often diversify for the sake of diversification, and CDOs can "help" them diversify into their areas of incompetence. Diversification doesn't guarantee you won't lose money; it only guarantees that it is unlikely you will lose it all at once. Diversification is a defensive strategy, and like all defensive strategies, it is most effective if you know what you are defending against.

There is no point in diversifying just for the sake of it; only diversify into assets you understand well. The best investment managers diversify into businesses they understand, businesses that throw off tremendous cash flows, and businesses that have high growth potential. At least, they do that most of the time. Highly skilled investors often diversify less and perform better than less skilled managers.

Lack of due diligence on the collateral in portfolios, CDO cash flow structures, and the background of the CDO manager have been the key reasons that investment-grade CDOs have performed poorly. This chapter primarily deals with the first of those issues.

While investors need to consider the degree of portfolio diversification, it is much more important to look at the type of risk in the portfolio, and the individual names in a portfolio. It is possible to diversify into uncharted territory and actually introduce imprudent risk in the name of diversification.

Since the turn of the century, major defaults have included Adelphia Communications, American Tissue, Argentina, Armstrong, Crown Cork & Seal, Enron, Global Crossing Ltd., Kmart, Marconi, National Century

Financial Enterprise Inc., Railtrack, Swiss Air, RBG Resources et al., UAL Corp. (the parent of United Airlines), US Airways Group, WorldCom, Collins & Aikman, Delphi, and others. The first half of the decade was plagued by downgrades of CDOs backed by investment-grade corporate debt in unprecedentedly large numbers. The latter half of the decade will be plagued by the downgrade of CDOs backed by subprime and Alt-A mortgage-backed securities (see Chapter 8). Other portfolios and structures that were not well crafted will see problems, too.

Models that rely only on parametric analysis by manipulating defaults, recovery rates, and correlations will not uncover the problems that due diligence will uncover. We will explore this in more detail in later chapters.

MODERN PORTFOLIO THEORY: BANE OF CDOS

Assume portfolio returns are normally distributed—a very bad assumption. Now that we've assumed a distribution of returns, we can use historical data to calculate the mean, variance, and correlation of the assets. A standard approach is to weight portfolio assets with fractions that add up to one and then calculate the portfolio standard deviation (volatility) and expected return. The standard deviation of the portfolio, σ_p, is simply the square root of the portfolio variance, expressed as follows using matrix notation:

$$\text{Risk} = \sigma_p = \sqrt{\sum_{i=1}^{n} w_i^2 \sigma_i^2 + \sum_{\substack{i=1 \\ i \neq j}}^{n} \sum_{j=1}^{n} w_i w_j \sigma_{i,j}}$$

where: ω = the asset weighting;
n = the number of assets in the portfolio;
σ = the standard deviation of the asset

A simple example for a two-asset portfolio is as follows. If ω is the weight of the first asset, the weight of the second asset will be $(1-\omega)$. The portfolio expected return is:

$$\omega r_1 + (1-\omega) r_2$$

where r = return on the assets.

$$\text{Variance} = \omega^2 \sigma_1^2 + (1-\omega)^2 \sigma_2^2 + 2\,\omega\,(1-\omega)\,\mathrm{Cov}_{12}$$

where Variance = volatility of the portfolio

σ_1^2 = variance of asset 1;
σ_2^2 = variance of asset 2;
Cov_{12} = covariance of assets 1 and 2

For a two asset portfolio of equal weights, let's assume asset 1 has an expected return of 20 percent with a variance of 0.04, and asset 2 has an expected return of 12 percent and a variance of 0.03. I'll further give you data that the covariance of the assets is 0.02.

The expected return of the portfolio is:

$$(0.5 \times 0.20) + (0.5 \times 0.12) = 0.16 \text{ or } 16 \text{ percent}$$

The portfolio variance is:

$$(0.5^2 \times 0.04) + 0.5^2 \times 0.03 + 2(0.5)(0.5)0.02 = 0.0275$$

The standard deviation of the portfolio return is:

$$(0.0275)^{1/2} = 0.1658$$

or the volatility is 16.58 percent

If I want to calculate my value-at-risk (VAR) at the 99% confidence level, there is a 1% chance the portfolio will lose more than 26.8%*.

What happens when we add an asset? Let's assume we now have a three-asset portfolio of equal weighting. The third asset has a return of 16%, and its variance is the same as that of asset two or 0.03. The covariance of the assets is 0.1. The covariance is lower than for the two-asset portfolio, because the portfolio is now more diversified (more on this later).

The expected return of the portfolio is:

$$(0.33 \times 0.20) + (0.33 \times 0.12) + (0.33 \times 0.16) = 0.16 \text{ or } 16\%$$

$$\text{Variance} = (\omega_1^2 \times \sigma_1^2) + (\omega_2^2 \times \sigma_2^2) + (\omega_3^2 \times \sigma_3^2) + 3 \times (\omega_1 \times \omega_2) \times (\omega_3 \times Cov_{123})$$

**Note*: The 1% tail is 2.58 x 0.1658 = 0.428 away from the mean. The level of VAR is 0.16 – 0.428 = –0.268

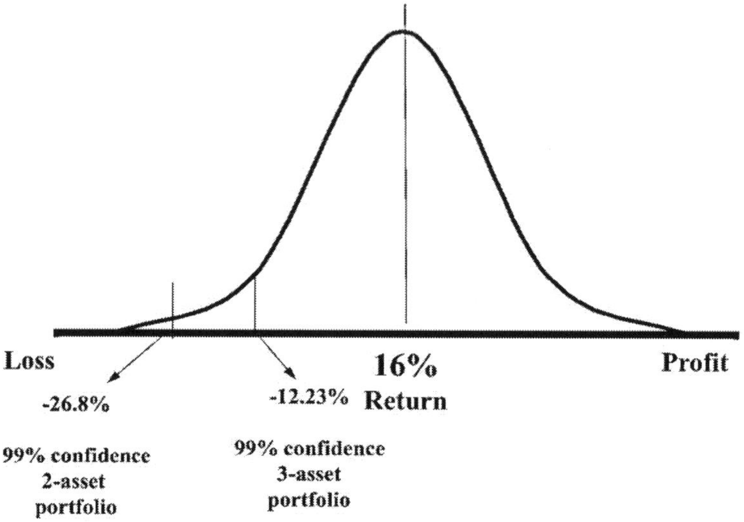

FIGURE 5.1 Value at Risk

The portfolio variance is:

$$[(0.33)^2 \times 0.04] + [(0.33)^2 \times 0.03] + [(0.33)^2 \times 0.03] + [(3 \times (0.33) \times (0.33) \times (0.33) \times 0.01) = 0.011968.$$

The volatility of the portfolio is the square root of the variance or 0.1094 and it is expressed as in percentage terms as 10.94 percent.

At the 99 percent confidence level, there is a 1 percent chance the portfolio will lose more than 12.23 percent.[2]

According to the theory, although the expected return of both the two-asset and three-asset portfolios is the same, the volatility of the three-asset portfolio is lower and the probability of sustaining the same magnitude of loss as the two-asset portfolio is also lower. We want to minimize the volatility of the losses to minimize the volatility of the expected return. Figure 5.1 shows the benefit of reducing the value at risk in the portfolio.

Another way of looking at this is to say that if I take into account my expected losses, I get my expected return. If I don't get my expected return,

Note: The 1 percent tail is $2.58 \times 0.1094 = 0.2823$ away from the mean. The level of VAR is $0.16 - 0.2823 = -0.1223$.

it is due to the fact that I experienced *unexpected losses*. Unexpected loss is a measure of the volatility of the expected loss. Most market professionals are familiar with the following formula for calculating unexpected losses due to credit events:

$$UL_{(u,c)} = \sqrt{\sum \rho_{ij} n_i n_j \sqrt{\frac{(P_{(ui \mid c)})(1 - P_{(ui,c)})(P_{(uj \mid c)})(1 - P_{(uj,c)})}{(1 - P_{(c)})}}}$$

where $UL(u,c)$ = unexpected loss or credit event risk (default)
$P(ui|c)$ = probability of default of asset i
$P(uj|c)$ = probability of default of asset j
$P(ui, c)$ = joint probability of default of asset i and counterparty
$P(uj, c)$ = joint probability of default of asset j and counterparty
$P(c)$ = probability of default of counterparty
$\rho i,j$ = correlation of default between asset i and asset j
ni = asset i's weight in the portfolio
nj = asset j's weight in the portfolio

Portfolios with only market risk tend to have normal returns because losses due to market risk are often normally distributed (also known as a Gaussian distribution) and have the familiar bell-curve shape (even that assumption often goes awry, however). The distribution of credit losses, and therefore expected returns in a portfolio that has credit risk, is *not* normally distributed. As one risk manager said after looking at the lopsided shape of the returns, "I've been skewed." Credit returns are skewed, or lopsided, with a long fat tail, as shown in Figure 5.2.

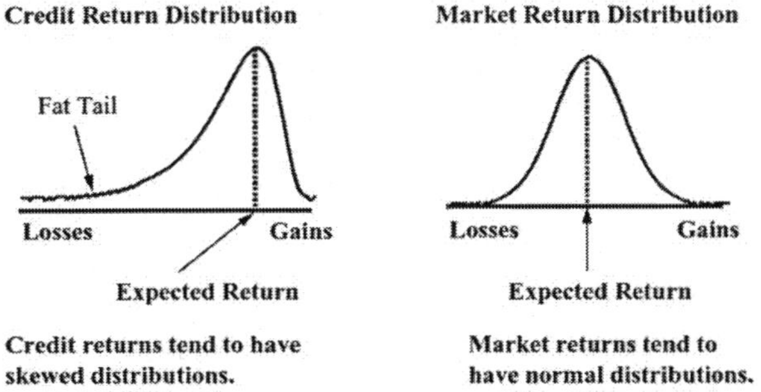

FIGURE 5.2 Credit Return versus Market Return Distributions

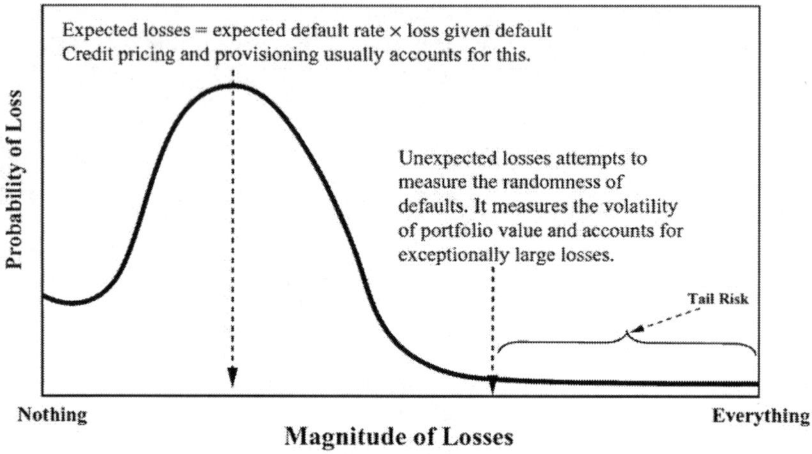

FIGURE 5.3 Expected and Unexpected Losses

Mean and standard deviation calculated assuming a normal distribution do not adequately describe credit risk. Most portfolio managers use a horizon analysis. They assume a future time period and measure value at risk due to upgrades, downgrades, and defaults; then they estimate a distribution of portfolio value. Figure 5.3 shows how a portfolio manager might view expected and unexpected losses on a portfolio. The portfolio manager might use these estimates of expected and unexpected losses to determine how much capital or reserves to set aside to account for these credit risks.

So is that it? If we estimate expected and unexpected losses, what else could there be? One would think the term *unexpected losses* would cover everything we didn't cover when we estimated expected losses. Unfortunately, there is more. Unexpected losses are only an estimate of how bad it can get most of the time. Anything not captured up to the point we measure unexpected loss is called *tail risk*. That's just another way of saying it's the variance of risk (or the variance of return) due to everything else we didn't think about. We might experience an extraordinary loss due to fraud, for instance.

ABNORMAL IS NORMAL

If we use the model for a normal distribution, a five standard deviation credit event should only happen once in every 7,000 years. But in the marketplace, we see this happen once or twice in a decade. Banks that held large concentrations of Enron, RBG metals, Global Crossing, or WorldCom credit risk might argue that it happens even more frequently than that.

We want to maximize expected return. We want to minimize variance of return. Diversification is the Kevlar vest we wear to avoid taking a fatal shot from variance of return. Since the torso is the largest surface area, it is less likely an extremity will get hit. At least, that's the theory. We're still exposed in areas not protected by the vest, but the best protection is to avoid getting shot at in the first place. Unfortunately, using the wrong assumptions about your distribution, using incorrect assumptions about the likelihood of extreme events, combined with leverage, almost guarantees that you will take a head shot sooner rather than later.

For decades, the traditional value-at-risk paradigm using a normal or Gaussian distribution to describe risk has been recognized as seriously flawed. Using a lognormal distribution or an otherwise skewed distribution is a better idea, but it is still a compromise. It is shorthand for not having a complete understanding of the actual shape of the distribution that accurately describes the behavior of the underlying collateral, and it doesn't take into account that the shape of the distribution may radically warp as circumstances change. Assuming a distribution shape blinds us to extraordinary, unexpected events.

Monte Carlo models do not help with this problem. Another finance fairy tale is that Monte Carlo models improve your ability to manage risk. They do nothing to improve your ability to manage risk if you use flawed assumptions. They are only as good as the scenarios we imagine when we employ them. In fact, some investors manage risk much better than those using Monte Carlo models.

There is no substitute for understanding the fundamentals of risk—for example, the corporate balance sheet, if one is considering corporate credit risk—and then stressing our assumptions for highly improbable events. Unfortunately, this rigor is usually not applied to probable events, much less improbable events.

The capital markets seek to get the maximum value out of any asset class. Collateralized debt obligations incorporate powerful technologies to customize risks and returns for any investor appetite. Expertise is required to make the most of the technology.

Large investment banks often take advantage of less sophisticated investors, and even sophisticated investors must avoid a variety of hazards when transacting CDOs. For years investment banks have claimed that today's challenges are the hangover of past years' flawed deals. Pick a year and pick a past. While it is true that some past years' flawed deals are giving us a collective hangover, this year's flawed deals promise tomorrow's headache to the unwary investor. Investment banks themselves are often unintentional investors when unwary management is oblivious to the fact that its portfolios and trading books are becoming passive investors in the remaining risk of structured finance deals that are only partially sold. This opaque market is even cloudier today than at its inception.

MARK-TO-MARKET HAZARD

One key moral hazard stems from the fact that managers are often paid based on their performance. The managers report their own performance and investors do not have the ability to check the accuracy of the performance report. Many cash assets such as distressed loans are difficult to mark to market, and the investor must rely on the manager for pricing of the underlying assets. If the deal is a market value deal and the manager earns fees based on the fund performance, there will be a temptation to mark up the prices of the underlying portfolio of assets. There is no mechanism for the investors to verify the pricing.

The SEC alleged that the managers of Beacon Hill, a hedge fund, artificially marked up the prices of the fund's mortgage-backed securities shortly after renegotiating their management contract, increasing their performance fees. The prices of assets in the portfolio were rising, but market prices were dropping.

Recently a top tier investment bank and a large hedge fund have been marketing a market-value CDO fund product for which the underlying assets are even less transparent and for which market pricing is even less available than for the assets in the Beacon Hill fund. The proposed final maturity is 10 years. The underlying assets are high-yield mezzanine investments, distressed debt, bank loans, and equities. The equity tranche, sold as common shares, is half of the proposed $1 billion deal, or $500 million. This is the hedge fund's first foray into managed CDOs. The targeted investors are high net worth individuals and financial institutions who can buy in minimum increments of $10 million. Expenses are 20 bps on the total collateral or $2 million per year. Management fees are a further 1 percent or $10 million per year, and the manager earns an additional 20 percent on any return above 8 percent. This structure is ripe for abuse, since the investors have no way of verifying if the prices are accurate, or whether they are being paid so-called returns with their own initial investment money.

This deal is a private placement. SEC regulations do not allow the advertisement of private placements, and it is not customary to make cold calls on these products, since they should only be sold to investors capable of analyzing the risks. Yet I received a cold call from one of the hedge fund's managing directors trying to sell this product to new and unknown investors.

CASH FLOW HAZARD

Another moral hazard involves the claim to the deal cash flows. If a deal manager has a claim on the equity cash flows, there is a conflict of interest between the manager and more senior noteholders. Investors should be particularly wary of deals in which four structural conditions are met, which can tempt managers to behave against the interest of the noteholders. The first condition is that losses are allocated in reverse order of seniority, and loss deductions are limited to the initial investment of each tranche investor. The second condition is that excess spread does not accrue to the benefit of any of the noteholders and is not available to absorb losses. The third condition is that the manager does not have adequate restraints on his ability to cause a deterioration in the quality of the underlying portfolio. And the fourth condition is that the manager has a claim on the excess spread.

Once the equity is gone, the next most senior noteholder bears additional losses. When losses exceed the initial equity investment, all of the residual cash flows are diverted to the benefit of the manager. The manager now has an incentive to trade out of good credits into credits on negative credit watch, or even into lower-rated but higher-spread credits—if there are no constraints prohibiting this.

This recently happened in a cash CDO deal in which even the integrity of the single-A tranche of the CDO was compromised. The portfolio was originally investment grade, but due to aggressive trading to create excess spread, the portfolio ended up with a junk rating. The single-A investor threatened litigation, and the manager reached a settlement agreement with the investor.

Other hazards for investors include but are not limited to the following issues:

- Arrangers sometimes optimize portfolio selection to have the riskiest portfolio allowable given the credit constraints, to maximize spread.
- Arrangers sometimes play games with the tranching and erode investors' protection with less subordination than the deal warrants. Arrangers have included names like Ford Motor Credit and GMAC in the finance risk bucket, while simultaneously filling up the automotive risk bucket. These and similar examples concentrate credit risk and artificially increase the diversity score.

- Arrangers sometimes arbitrage the credit default swap contract documentation, the ISDA language, so that the arranger gets the most favorable language and the CDO investor gets the least favorable language.
- Arrangers may provide inadequate cash flow structural protections for the CDO investor.
- Investors are often unaware that the ratings across rating agencies are not comparable for CDOs. They fail to negotiate for more income when their particular rating is disadvantageous relative to that of another rating agency.
- Naïve investors often fail to participate in all available cash flows, such as collateral coupon spreads.
- For synthetic single-tranche CDOs (also known as bespoke tranches, STCDOs, or custom CDOs), the investor and the arranger often have a conflict of interest. The portfolio choice—including credit and correlation—is to the advantage of the arranger.
- Investors may fail to limit trading by arrangers and CDO managers by writing criteria on the number of trades, trading volume, credit protection, cash flow protection, and hedging into the documentation.

A securitization is a subset of structured finance. A securitization is simply the creation and issuance of securities backed by a pool of loans, bonds, receivables, or future flows. The securities may be asset-backed bonds or notes issued by a special purchase entity which purchases the underlying assets used as collateral to back the notes. In either case, the securities are backed by a pool of assets, and there are multiple obligors. The pool offers the possibility of portfolio diversification, even when it doesn't always deliver on this possibility. In many asset securitizations the pool of assets is called the portfolio.

GLOBAL DERIVATIVES RISK

In 1995 the Bank for International Settlements (BIS) estimated that the global notional value of all derivatives was about $41 trillion, but the loss to creditors if everyone stopped paying at once was only about $1.7 trillion, or 4.3 percent of the notional value if you adjusted for legally enforceable bilateral netting and risk reduction. By the end of 2006, total outstanding contracts had grown nine fold to $386 trillion (tenfold to $416 trillion if you include credit default swaps but not total return swaps), or around $16.5 trillion—not counting credit derivatives—if you adjust for legally enforceable bilateral netting and risk reduction.

Credit default swaps were insignificant in 1995, but had grown to nearly $29 trillion by the end of 2006, according to BIS. ISDA counted credit derivatives at almost $35 trillion at the end of 2006, but it is not clear how much it captures in total return swaps. By either count, credit derivatives were on track to double in 2007. At first credit derivatives seem a drop in the bucket compared to other global derivatives business, but the net exposure in credit derivatives may be as much as $9 trillion in 2006, and on an institution by institution basis, the credit exposure varies radically. An institution may have massive exposure to a single-name underlying or to a basket of names, while most of its remaining exposure is netted out. Net exposure due to credit derivatives and other derivatives exposure can be securitized, and this risk has found its way into synthetic securitizations, which further muddies the waters when it comes to assessing global risk.

LOANS AND LEVERAGED LOANS

Private equity firms, certain hedge funds, and bank balance sheets tend to concentrate credit risk in the form of loans. If I had $1 billion in interest rate swaps with Enron, I might have had only around $43 million of net credit exposure to Enron. If I had a $1 billion loan to Enron, I'd have had $1 billion in exposure to Enron. Which exposure should concern me more? Banks—other than perhaps JPMorgan Chase—don't mark their balance sheets to market (trading books, however, are marked to market). Private equity firms and hedge funds have difficulty marking loans and leveraged loans to market, because they do not often trade. They sometimes remain in denial until either the newspapers advertise a critical problem, or an obligor actually defaults.

Securitization has recently introduced new credit risks to bank balance sheets, and this could affect the future growth of the securitization business.

A traditional source of risk is the concentration risk that loan officers introduce to the balance sheet through large unsyndicated loans. So-called low-risk, high-concentration exposures are the bane of the banking industry. Loan officers often argue it is fine to take the exposure because of the importance of the relationship and the supposedly low risk of default. A few years ago credit officers made this argument for a then perceived AAA credit risk, Long Term Capital Management. Afterwards, loan officers made that argument for Enron, Worldcom, and large concentrations of technology company exposures. New business development and the ensuing tech fever led to huge exposures in Marconi, Adelphia Communications, Global Crossing, and WorldCom. The latter weren't even viewed as stel -lar credits. They were viewed as fast-moving trains and banks needed to jump on board—that is, until they crashed. Many banks had exposures of

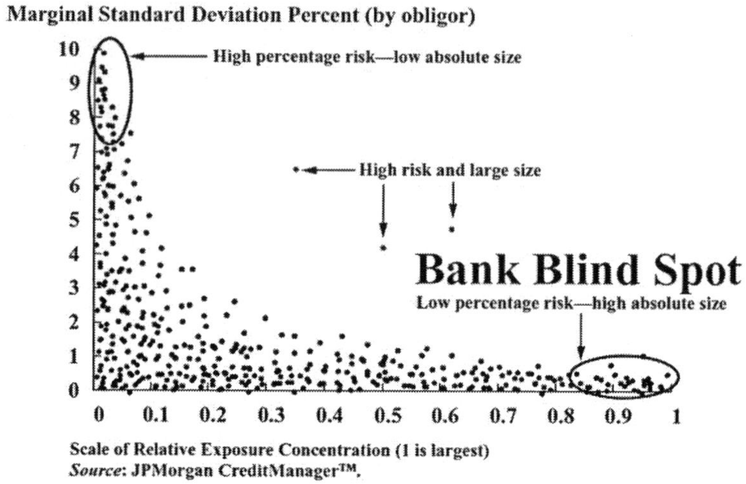

FIGURE 5.4 Exposure Size versus Risk

$500 million to close to $1 billion. Today, loan officers make that argument for bridge loans for highly leveraged takeovers. Even if one loves a given risk, too much of a good thing can still produce an unacceptable expected loss.

Figure 5.4 shows areas of exposure that should be of particular concern to bank managers, along with what I like to call the "blind spot." Usually credits that are known to be in trouble—even when the exposures are very small—are the subject of lengthy meetings, discussions, reports, and risk analysis presentations.

Enormous credit exposures that are deemed to be solid or deemed to be good for business growth are not examined with the same jaundiced eye. This is true even when the exposure is $1 billion or more. These exposures do not get the scrutiny they deserve. In fact, the possibility of risk is often strenuously denied.

Syndication is a prudent way to spread the risk of a given obligor among a number of banks, but it isn't the final answer to diversifying risk. Its very prudence can disguise another credit trap. Banks tend to overconcentrate in an industry by being lulled into thinking that having a number of shaky obligors in a developing technology sector is less risky than concentrating the risk in only one shaky obligor. Unless the correlation between obligors is perfect, this is true, but the high correlation among the obligors in a developing industry sector may amount to nearly the same exposure risk as taking on an enormous loan to one obligor. When a bank has made a commitment to develop business in a sector such as telecommunications, examining the risks of each obligor and the correlation of the risky elements is very unpopular.

Raising a concern about these risks when everyone else is hell-bent on lending more money to one of these corporations is a career-cratering event for a middle manager. The top of the house has to take the reins to control the stampeding horses, but that's impossible when they are among the herd.

In the equity markets, it is sometimes possible to take on large concentrations of risk and get rewarded for it. The debt markets are different. A lender cannot expect to be rewarded for taking on large concentrations of risk. Debt has no upside potential.

In the 2001 and 2002 debt markets, and again in the current mortgage markets, the markets cruelly drove home this point. Some investors had large pockets of highly concentrated risk. Recovery rates were inversely correlated with annual default rates, and defaults reached highs that hadn't been seen in many decades. Not only were there more defaults on highly concentrated risk, but when defaults occurred, the banks recovered a lower percentage than historical data would have indicated.

THE LEVERAGE PARADOX

Given that debt has little or no upside, many banks and hedge funds have overlooked the irreversible problems presented by extending credit lines to hedge funds that invest primarily in debt.

Traditionally, hedge funds borrowed to lever up in the equity and commodities markets. While equity prices can be volatile, downward swings could be offset by upside gains. Companies that had done poorly could earn it back in good times as their fortunes improved.

Borrowing to lever the equity of solid companies with growth potential sometimes paid off handsomely, since underperforming companies could recover. It made less sense to leverage an equity position in a mature company, since a slump could persist. Leveraging against a position in commodities such as oil, gold, and so forth, was simply a way to lever up a bet on future prices, but underpriced commodities could rise substantially in value. Some distressed debt has a high potential for recovery and trades at deeply discounted prices, so levering against vetted positions also had a high upside potential. But it makes much less sense to lend money to someone to lever up a position in nondistressed debt securities. The reason is that if the debt is originally purchased at full market value, it has very little upside potential. If the debt price drops due to a permanent and irreversible problem, such as fraud or the systemic issues in the subprime mortgage market, the value.

destruction is permanent. There is no upside potential to bail out the leveraged position. Funds that leveraged against these assets without sufficient liquidity are doomed to collapse.

Yet, time and again, bankers have extended credit lines to funds using fully priced tranches of collateralized debt obligations, turning a blind eye to the unwind potential. It is important to note that even CDO equity behaves much more like a debt instrument than a corporate stock, since it does not have the potential to create new products or generate significant revenue growth.

NEW STRUCTURED FINANCE DEALS

Large loans aren't the only source of risk, however. Finance and securitization groups sometimes use the bank balance sheet as a dumping ground for deals they can't distribute through the bank's capital markets group. *Marquee deals* often make their way onto the bank's balance sheet.

This phenomenon is a perversion of the reasons securitization became popular in the first place. Banks used securitization as a balance sheet tool. Banks securitized credit card receivables and MBSs, and in the process reduced their balance sheet exposure and gave investors worthwhile products. Banks then originated more MBS and credit card receivables and didn't balloon the balance sheet.

Today, some finance groups securitize receivables, stuff them onto the bank balance sheet, and declare victory. Why not just call this activity what it is—secured lending—and pay the group the way the bank pays loan officers: a lot less? This may sound harsh, but it is probably not harsh enough. Banks must create disincentives for this behavior. At the very least, the bank should insist on prudent reserves that dent the group's perceived profitability, and thus bonuses.

FRAUD

Expect fraud.

We transact with human beings, and some of them weren't brought up with our stellar values. Even when we expect fraud, we're capable of being stunned. Lenders were stunned when it was discovered that WorldCom, Global Crossing, and Enron cooked their books. Fraud on that scale is difficult to grasp, especially when a bank's individual exposure is in the high hundreds of millions or more. In the United States mortgage market, allegations of fraud by borrowers and on borrowers makes it difficult to assess the value of CDOs without doing due diligence on the remaining loans in large portfolios, and most investors are not prepared for this expense.

Steve Martin's character in *The Spanish Prisoner*, a movie about a confidence game, advised his mark: "Always do business as if the other person is trying to screw you, because most likely they are, and if they're not, you can be pleasantly surprised."

While I don't recommend that cynical view of the world, I do recommend that you at least consider the possibility that people and firms aren't necessarily what they seem. It's easy to believe something when we wish it to be true, because we're lured by the thought of a huge fee. That's why I believe a fraud analysis should be part of the analysis of any deal.

In the mid-1970s Paul Erdman wrote an entertaining fiction book called *Silver Bears,* in which a scam involved spreading rumors about a large silver discovery in the ancient Persian silver mines of Susa. No one actually checked the mines to see whether the alleged new silver supply actually existed. The limited amount of silver that was produced as evidence of the find came from trading contraband gold for legal silver to sources on the Indian subcontinent. The scammers shorted silver just before leaking rumors of the find and covered their shorts when the price of silver plummeted. Then the scammers went long silver just before they leaked news of the deception. The price of silver soared. They made a killing. The point of the story was that *no one checked out the story*. Well-dressed educated people with a plausible story manipulated the market using little more than their vocal cords and a smart suit to pull it off.

Appearances can deceive. One of the wealthiest people I know drives a secondhand car. He doesn't tie up cash in depreciating metals inventory. He dresses modestly. He doesn't fit the American preconception of a multimillionaire. He puts it this way: "It is a lot easier to get rich than to stay rich." He doesn't feel the need to impress people with his wealth but uses his wealth to do really amazing things when he feels like doing them. As a result, he probably wouldn't get the best table at an L.A. restaurant if he decided to negotiate a deal to buy a major film studio over dinner, but he doesn't care.

Robert Cialdini, Ph.D., wrote about how con men work in his book *Influence*. Bunco artists know that titles and trappings work forcefully on us, and they do so unexpectedly. A study in the San Francisco Bay area showed that owners (or even renters!) of prestige autos receive a special kind of deference from us. Furthermore, the tendency to lend money just because another bank has lent money is a phenomenon known as *pluralistic ignorance*. We look at what everyone else is doing to assess a situation, and if everyone else is okay with it, we go ahead. The trouble is, everyone else may also be assessing the situation and, noting our apparent calm, they, too, think everything's okay. One by one we keep lending. Even worse, we tend not to like people who give us bad news such as "Stop! Don't throw away more money!"

Fortunately, Dr. Cialdini gives us a simple antidote. All that is required is that we make a conscious decision to be alert to counterfeit social evidence. Question your preconceptions before they question you. By the way, did you even ask yourself in what field of study Robert Cialdini got his Ph.D.? It's in psychology. But if it had been in interior decorating, you'd be justifiably upset with me. It pays to question.

The head of RBG dressed well, drove expensive cars, wore expensive accessories, sat in plush offices, and lived in a mansion at a fancy address. Most of the veneer was rented, but it fooled a lot of people, including at least one bank that was introduced to RBG through a broker, the financial equivalent of a blind date. Where was the due diligence? A large group of international banks including JPMorgan Chase, FleetBoston, Westdeutsche Landesbank, Hypovereinsbank, and Chinatrust Commercial Bank, among others, were ensnared in the alleged RBG metals fraud.

A network of related metals companies duped the banks: RBG Resources, Hampton Lane, Allied Deals, and SAI Commodity. Initially it appears the metals firms traded nickel and cobalt at a wash. For a few years, they bought the metals and sold them again at the same price or at a tiny profit. In this way they generated volume to continually increase credit lines in preparation for pulling off a large scam.

RBG wasn't what it seemed, either. Allegedly, affiliated companies used shell corporations that issued bills of lading and other papers for nonexistent metals. On the strength of this paperwork, banks authorized letters of credit to be drawn against trading credit lines. But the metal didn't exist, and the banks couldn't collect on their letters of credit.

Most banks that had been roped into this scam immediately wrote off their entire exposure. They felt if they were lucky enough to recover anything, it would be serendipity. One European bank did a postmortem analysis on the deal. It felt it could not blame the individual in the principal finance department who had arranged the deal, because it was fraud. The employee had, after all, played by the bank's rules, or lack of them.

The bank's solution was to suggest that reserves be held against the principal finance group's positions. It reasoned that the principal finance group's asset securitization business was a paper business. If the papers were in order, the bank went ahead with the deal. It accepted that people weren't going to perform due diligence, no one was going to check the facts, so it would be prudent to take reserves against transactions.

The bank's solution reminds me of what ice hockey players said after Teddy Green suffered a severe head injury in 1969. Players thought it was foolish not to wear a helmet; but they still didn't, because the other guys didn't. They said if the league made them do it, they would, and nobody would mind. Individuals will often behave suboptimally and foolishly due to peer pressure or fear of ridicule. The only reason things changed is because the hockey league eventually made helmets mandatory.

The bank only got it half right. Reserves are a good idea. Due diligence is a good idea. Due diligence combined with reserves is a *better* idea. In fact, it's a plan.

Due diligence isn't a cure; it's only a defense. Even with due diligence, we can be fooled. Years ago Bernie Cornfeld thwarted lenders performing due diligence on his oil tank inventory. He simply poured a layer of oil over a tank full of water. When investigators plunged their dip sticks into the tanks to check the liquid level, the sticks emerged coated with a film of oil. They assumed the tanks were full of oil and signed off on the loans. Bernie gave new meaning to corn oil.

If people work hard enough to deceive us, they will. To do any kind of business, there must be a certain level of trust, and that trust can leave us vulnerable to exploitation. We have a responsibility to make it difficult for people to exploit that trust. But for the times they are successful, we need fraud reserves.

HEDGE FUNDS: A NEW INVESTOR CLASS

Hedge funds are important players in structured finance products and are key investors in the leveraged tranches of CDOs. The potential for high returns, leverage, and funding attracts hedge funds. The key to doing business with hedge funds is to ask for full financial disclosure and to require adequate collateral. Banks that don't insist on this are adding risk to their balance sheets. As we already know, many bank structuring groups are themselves hedge funds, whether their employers are aware of it or not.

Taking on credit risk allows hedge funds to diversify their leveraged strategies. Many hedge funds rely on prime brokers for financing. CDO managers can lever tranches of CDOs at cheaper rates, and usually constant rates over the life of the CDO. The ultimate leverage is an unfunded investment in a synthetic CDO.

Hedge funds are private funds. Some make limited disclosure filings with the Commodity Futures Trading Commission (CFTC), but that only applies to hedge funds that invest in products regulated by the CFTC. Some venues outside the United States require principal-guaranteed structures. The only other regulation is that they must either have fewer than 99 investors worth at least $1 million each, or they can sign up to 500 investors worth at least $5 million each. These thresholds may be increased in the near future. Some hedge funds have minimum net worth requirements greater than these guidelines, however.

Almost any fund that hedges risk can call itself a hedge fund, and anyone can start a hedge fund. Most financial professionals feel the defining characteristic of a hedge fund is the heavy use of leverage. Estimates about the number of hedge funds vary, but there are probably about 4,000 to 7,000 globally depending on who is counting, although the majority are in the United States. About 10 percent of them will fail this year.

Many hedge funds perform as expected for their investors. Traditionally these were long/short equity managers with little or no leverage with less risk than many equity mutual funds. They are often high risk, with hedged risk, and in many years they offer high returns. Some quarters, or even some years, performance may be disappointing, but overall the return on investment can be high for long-term investors in well-managed funds. Several funds have long successful track records. Some well-respected funds, such as Gotham and Long Term Capital Management (LTCM), go under after a few successful years. Others are new and untested. Hedge funds resist disclosing balance sheet information. A hedge fund can have less than $10 million under management or can have several billion dollars under management.

Why are individuals and financial institutions so keen to start hedge funds? It's because hedge fund managers usually charge high fees. For instance, a manager may charge a 2 percent (or more) per annum management fee plus an incentive fee of 20 percent (or more) of the upside of the investment strategy. Managers don't offer to refund 20 percent of the downside in a bad year, however. It's a great job. You use other people's money (OPM), you get paid a fee to risk that money, you get paid if you win money on your bets, and you don't refund money if your bets lose.

Managers of smaller hedge funds may not be able to live off of the management fee, so they have to take leverage risk in an attempt to capture incentive fees. Leverage can make even a mediocre manager look good in the short run, if the manager is lucky.

In September 1997 I wrote about hedge funds for *Credit Derivatives: A Guide to Instruments and Applications* (John Wiley & Sons, 1998) *before* the collapse of LTCM:

> *. . .the credit manager has no way to determine how much leverage the hedge fund employs.... A hedge fund Counterparty seems to be a perversion of the concept of credit derivatives.... If I want to lay off risk in the portfolio, to what degree am I hedged when the Counterparty is a hedge fund?...*

> *The protection provided by the hedge fund is phantom protection. The only benefit is from the up-front collateral, which may reduce my exposure in the event of a default on the underlying asset. . . . The question remains whether the enhanced spread income of LIBOR +75 and more which hedge funds are willing to pay as a funding cost is enough to compensate banks for the credit risk.*

In August 1998, the Soros Quantum Fund lost $2 billion after Russia defaulted on short-term government debt obligations and the ruble was devalued. Long Term Capital Management (LTCM), founded in 1993, also lost around $2 billion.

The managers at LTCM were meant to be among the best financial minds in the business, and they probably were. Myron Scholes and Robert Merton, co-winners of the 1998 Nobel Prize in Economics, pioneered equity option model pricing. John Meriwether, former head of Salomon's arbitrage group, and David Mullins, a former Federal Reserve Bank vice chairman, were also partners.

Among other strategies, LTCM leveraged investments using total return swaps. LTCM managers refused to disclose positions or trades. They claimed they had to keep their transactions proprietary to protect their trading positions. In the end, others were probably grateful they couldn't copy LTCM's strategies. After several years of 40 percent-plus returns, and shortly after the Russia crisis, LTCM's net asset value (NAV) was down about 44 percent, meaning investors had lost about 44 percent of their money if they were original investors.

UBS chairman Mathis Cabiallavetta and three other UBS executives lost their jobs after UBS disclosed it lost $700 million. Earlier, UBS had sold a seven-year call option on LTCM shares to LTCM's partners. They received a premium of $293 million, invested the majority of the call premium in LTCM, and hedged the call option by purchasing $800 million of LTCM fund shares. Unfortunately for UBS, the value of the shares plummeted.

Leverage is a very useful financial tool. Most of us use high degrees of leverage when we buy a home. But there is a difference between the way a bank treats you when you ask for a high degree of leverage and the way many banks have treated hedge funds that ask for a high degree of leverage. Would you have been able to get a mortgage—even though you pledged your home as loan collateral—if you refused to disclose your financial details, including other debt, to the lending bank? Why should a hedge fund, which admittedly plans to employ high-risk strategies in a gambit to get high rewards, be treated with unqualified faith?

Given that hedge funds can invest in any sector of the capital markets, and can have any type of concentration risk they choose, indexes designed to track hedge fund performance cannot be relied upon as indicators of value for a specific fund. Many hedge funds invest in leveraged tranches of CDOs and further lever the investment through total return swaps or other funding. This asset class is not tracked by an index.

TAVAKOLI'S LAW, HEDGE FUNDS, AND THE GREAT UNWIND

Hedge funds have become huge investors in CDOs. They purchase already leveraged tranches and lever their positions even further. Nonrecourse off-balance-sheet financing is a huge motivator for hedge funds. The prime brokers (investment banks and others) that lend money to hedge funds have no recourse to the managers of the hedge funds—meaning they cannot look to the managers to pay off the loans; they can only look to the funds' assets. Furthermore, much of the funding is off-balance-sheet through synthetic financings or other means, and it is difficult for fund investors to assess the true leverage and risk of the hedge funds. Meanwhile, the managers earn hefty fees whether the hedge funds perform or fail. Some hedge fund managers invest in the funds they manage, but some invest only to a small degree, and some do not invest at all.

In an April 30, 2007, *Wall Street Journal* article by Randall Smith and Susan Pulliam, titled "As Funds Leverage Up, Fears of Reckoning Rise," I noted that investment banks do not disclose the amount of total return swaps (among other credit derivatives and leveraged products) on their books and it is "trouble in the making." I also noted that the collateral provided by hedge funds to secure swaps could be difficult to trade. In a market downturn, attempts to unwind such positions could lead to a vicious cycle of selling that would feed on itself. Since then, mini-unwinds have occurred as hedge funds needed to liquidate CDO positions worth billions of dollars to meet margin calls and redemptions from investors. Perhaps this book will help contain the problem so that the extreme liquidation scenario experienced by individual funds does not become a more widespread problem affecting global markets.

In 2007, the Financial Services Authority (FSA) claimed that hedge fund gearing had decreased, and the Federal Reserve Bank of New York suggested the current situation with hedge funds is less alarming than in the past. Winston Churchill said we must alert somnolent authority to novel dangers; but in this matter authority seems complacent, and the dangers are not novel.

The FSA produced numbers from a partial survey of hedge funds and discussed "average" leverage, thus highlighting the well-known *flaw of averages*, a term coined and popularized by Dr. Sam Savage. If a swimming pool's average depth is four feet, but the deep end of the pool is eight feet, nonswimmers are presented with unacceptable risk. The average would suggest nonswimmers can safely use the pool, but a drowning man finds out the hard way that the average doesn't contain information descriptive of the risk.

The New York Fed uses data to examine volatility and correlations, both of which are not of much use in a crisis when correlations deviate from historical measures and even approach one. Indeed, even today, one should consider that hedge fund returns are anything but independent. Hedge funds are often called *alternative* assets, but they have not created new asset classes. Hedge funds invest in the global markets along with other investors, albeit hedge funds may be more creative, more illiquid, and may employ more leverage.

Tavakoli's Law states: *If some hedge funds soar above market averages, others must crash and burn.*

If one accepts that passive investors are indexed and reap average market returns, then active investors that reap extraordinary returns above the market average are offset by active investors who experience extraordinary losses in aggregate.

The current situation may indeed be different from that presented by Long Term Capital Management, but it may be even more alarming, not less alarming. Due to the use of structured products and derivatives, hedge funds can take on hidden leverage above and beyond that which can be explained by polling prime brokers. Furthermore, illiquid structured products will experience a classic collateral crash when hedge funds try to liquidate these assets to meet margin calls or collateral cures.

Since 2000, assets invested in hedge funds have more than tripled to around $1.5 trillion. While on average leverage may appear manageable, some hedge funds employ high degrees of leverage. A potential source of a great unwind arises from a trigger event affecting highly leveraged hedge funds, and another potential source is systemic risk that affects a larger cohort of hedge funds.

Many hedge funds are not highly leveraged, and they will weather the storm. But the explosion of hedge fund investments in illiquid assets combined with leverage currently pose a greater risk to the global financial markets than we experienced at the time of the LTCM debacle.

Amaranth and the Bear Stearns High-Grade Structured Credit Strategies Enhanced Leverage Fund are recent examples of funds overleveraged in illiquid positions. Amaranth was undone by overleveraged illiquid positions in natural gas futures. The Bear Stearns fund was undone by leveraged positions chiefly in so-called high-grade CDO tranches backed by subprime mortgages and other leveraged loans. Bear Stearns Asset Management characterized the fund's investments as "liquid," but when it tried to sell assets to raise cash, it pulled back its bid lists in the face of plummeting prices. That experience is virtually the definition of illiquidity.

As long as hedge funds employ similar strategies, we are destined to relive mini-LTCMs fund by fund. The failure of a few funds may not affect the market or cause a great unwind in the broader capital markets, but if it happens to a fund you run or a fund in which you've invested, it will feel like the great unwind to you. This extreme liquidation scenario has driven investors to seek out comforting liquids.

The underlying assumptions of the models were not justified. Mathematics is a universal language, but any language can be used to spout sophisticated-sounding gibberish. We occasionally award prizes for it. Logic—not mathematics—is the universal language that always strives to make sense. An understanding of mathematics is a necessary but not always sufficient requirement to succeed in the global financial markets, and a fascination with higher math may actually cause one to fail.

Even the simplest financial models have huge flaws. All financial models require us to make assumptions, and when the models themselves are not flawed, the assumptions we use can be flawed. There can be flaws of design, flaws in application, or both. Although financial models are a form of shorthand to help us understand the complexities of the market, they are no substitute for common sense, experience, and good judgment. Moreover, correct mathematical equations are frequently misapplied. Anyone can compute the wrong answer to nine decimal places. We can be astonishingly precise when we are frighteningly inaccurate.

There is an alternative to blind reliance on flawed models, but before we get to that, it may be useful to take a detour and explore a flawed theory.

BRAIN DAMAGE THEORY

Let's hear it for brain damage. The *Journal of Economic Literature* reported that with regard to investments, "frontal damage can result in superior decisions," in the article "Neuroeconomics: How Neuroscience Can Inform Economics" in its March 2005 issue.

At least that is what the authors—Colin Camerer of the California Institute of Technology's Division of the Humanities and Social Sciences, George Loewenstein of Carnegie Mellon's Department of Social and Decision Sciences, and Drazen Prelec of the Massachusetts Institute of Technology's Sloane School of Management—believe, even though such damage results in poorer overall decision-making ability.

The idea is that frontal damage makes one more willing to accept reasonable risk than those of us without brain damage. For example, those with frontal damage will accept a 50–50 bet in which they will either win $300 or lose $200; whereas most people of sound mind will not accept the bet until they have the possibility of winning twice as much as they may lose: the 50–50 chance of winning $400 versus losing $200.

The authors use this example of aversion to loss to suggest that those with brain damage might be better investors.

I am not making this up.

To try to infer these people will make better investors is simply a false analogy, because the market does not present us with certain outcomes. We do not know the probabilities in advance, and we may not even have a precisely defined outcome. The reality is that this isn't a superior decision; it is simply a greater willingness to accept a lower margin of safety. In fact, this behavior is labeled an inferior decision when the market tanks and one hasn't managed the risk.

What the authors failed to take into account is that taking more risk when upside is skewed—for instance, by buying on margin in a bull market—will usually produce better results. The true test of a good investor is when there is the possibility of unacceptable loss or when one is dealing with a market in which outcomes are uncertain. In fact, we usually grapple with unknown probabilities and variable outcomes. Brain damage is most unhelpful in these circumstances, since what seems like a certain upside is merely an illusion.

Amaranth Advisors provides an object lesson. In August 2006, Nick Maounis, Amaranth Advisors' founder and chief executive, claimed that Brian Hunter, his star natural gas trader, was very good at taking controlled risks. The reality was very different, even though the Amaranth trades seemed logical on the surface. Treasury traders often go long the current long bond (the 30-year, now the 29.5-year) and short the penultimate, off-the-run long bond. Inferring from publicly available information on the fund's losses, Amaranth held positions that were highly correlated to long winter natural gas futures contracts while simultaneously being short fall and spring contracts in sequential years from 2007 through 2011, according to an EDHEC-Riskstudy by Hilary Till in the January 2007 issue of *Hedge Funds Review*.

DEAD MAN'S CURVE AND LEVERAGED FUNDS

Just as too much money flowing into these trades can collapse spreads in the Treasury market, too much leveraged money flowing into the much thinner commodities market undid Amaranth's trades. Spreads tightened by five to ten standard deviations in the September/December natural gas spreads, depending on which time period you use for your data. Assuming a normal distribution is simply incorrect. Furthermore, the pain deepened as the market realized Amaranth was suffering an extreme liquidity event. It needed to sell price-depressed illiquid assets to meet the demands of its nervous lenders.

In September 2006, the *Wall Street Journal* reported that Amaranth had lost half of its value, skidding from $9 billion to only $3 billion in assets, having put on the classic "Dead Man's Curve" trade ("The last thing I remember, Doc, the market started to swerve.. ."). These trades stubbornly refuse to follow history's pattern.

Nick Maounis is an alumnus of Paloma Partners. Another Paloma alumnus, Nassim Taleb, wrote a book called *Fooled by Randomness* (W. W. Norton & Co., 2001), which offers a new approach to the well-worn territory that human beings are not good at assessing probabilities without formal training. We have a tendency to explain random events as if we had foreknowledge of the outcomes. Many hedge funds' success (or failure) in the market is the product of lucky (or unlucky) bets. If the bets randomly pay off, the lucky fund manager incorrectly believes he is a genius. This may explain Maounis's willingness to give his star trader so much rope.

MARGIN OF SAFETY VERSUS ONE-SIDED ILLIQUID LEVERAGED BETS

Ironically, both Taleb and Maounis misapply probability theory. They both ignore *conditional* probabilities. Taleb suggests that we give undeserved accolades to the lucky Warren Buffett, and he damns Mr. Buffett with faint praise: "I am not saying that Warren Buffett is not skilled; only that a large population of random investors will almost necessarily produce someone with his track records."

But Taleb's example is not apt. Mr. Buffett works hard to uncover a margin of safety whenever possible. The second edition of Taleb's book was published well after Amaranth was founded, and its apparent success was an excellent example of success due to random luck. Mr. Taleb e-mailed me, suggesting I have "hindsight bias"—another misapplication on his part. Amaranth's implosion was foreseen by Christopher Fawcett—albeit Mr. Taleb couldn't see it—and its prior ephemeral success was precarious. If not Amaranth, Mr. Taleb could have chosen among dozens of other examples much more apt than Mr. Buffett.

We have a responsibility to try to figure things out and to avoid foreseeable risks. For years I have consistently asserted (see the 1997 edition of my book *Credit Derivatives and Synthetic Structur*es, published by John Wiley & Sons) that hedge funds exhibiting Amaranth's characteristics are accidents waiting to happen.

Christopher Fawcett, head of Fauchier, specifically forecasted Amaranth's implosion. He listed the reasons that he dumped his holding in Amaranth in September of 2005. He mentioned the poor liquidity terms, seeming lack of sufficient controls, poor transparency, high leverage, performance dominated by a single strategy, uncapped expenses on top of management and performance fees, lack of independent verification of returns, an annual reset on the high watermark on performance fees not in favor of the investor, an in-house broker-dealer so that returns might be smoothed, noninvestment by traders in their own books, and management team hubris.

What is the probability of a successful investment, given that one has a sound method for analyzing a business as Warren Buffett has? It is much better than the probability of success without the sound methodology, and the probability of disaster is very low.

In contrast, a one-sided hedge fund bet presents an altogether different conditional probability. What is the probability of a disaster, given that one has merely leveraged a market bet based on historical relationships as Amaranth did? If one is lucky one will do well, but if one is unlucky, the probability of disaster is about 100 percent. Taleb is correct that one can be fooled by randomness, but do not be a fool for randomness.

CDOs include highly leveraged products. Equity investments are highly leveraged, and leverage usually increases as portfolio quality appears to improve. Furthermore, hedge funds and other investors further leverage these products through financings, often employing total returns swaps or other forms of synthetic financing.

Since hedge funds and other leveraged CDO investors often apply further leverage on already leveraged investments, the lesson of not relying on results derived from a seemingly normal distribution are highly applicable. As we shall see later, a key determinant of success is getting a handle on the default probability of the individual portfolio assets and understanding the various structural and documentation features of a structured financing.

Chapter 6

Early CDO Technology

A collateralized debt obligation (CDO) is backed by portfolios of assets that may include a combination of bonds, loans, securitized receivables, asset-backed securities, tranches of other CDOs, or credit derivatives referencing any of the former. Some market practitioners define a CDO as being backed by a portfolio including only bonds and/or loans, but most market practitioners use the former definition. I'll use CDO as an umbrella term for asset securitizations.

Up to the end of the 1990s, CDOs all used special purpose entities (SPEs), also known as special purpose vehicles (SPVs), that purchased the portfolio of assets and issued tranches of debt and equity. The SPE purchased the assets from a bank's balance sheet and/or trading books. These are known as *true sale* structures.

Special purpose entities are usually bankruptcy-remote, meaning they are *delinked* from the credit risk of the bank arranger, also known as the originator. The bank arranger can earn servicing fees, administration fees, and hedging fees from the SPV, but otherwise has no claim on the cash flows of the assets in the SPV.

Formerly, banks and investment banks underwrote the CDO tranches to provide the funds—often along with bridge financing—for the purchase of the portfolio assets, which backed the tranches. This is no longer always the case. Synthetic securitizations eliminate the need for a special purpose entity, albeit they may also use an SPE to issue limited recourse notes linked to a CDO's tranched credit risk. We'll examine these structures later.

TRUE SALE HYBRID AND SYNTHETIC STRUCTURES

Figures 6.1 and 6.2 show simplified versions of the true sale structure and a purely synthetic structure. Notice that the true sale structure doesn't have one of the tranches found in the synthetic structure: the super senior tranche.

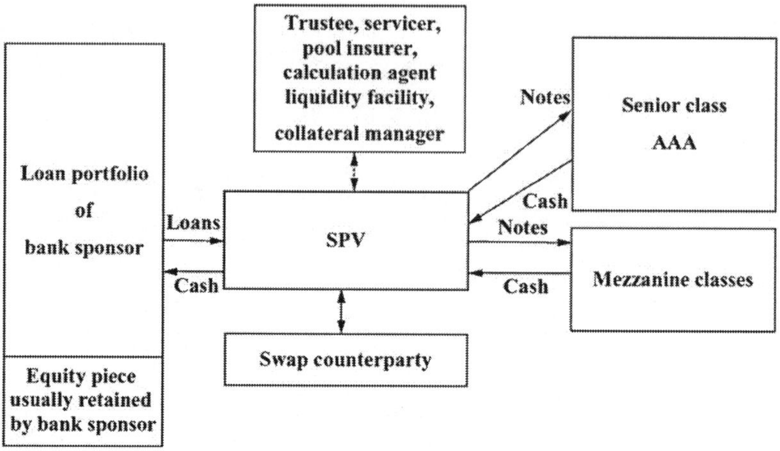

FIGURE 6.1 Simplified True Sale Balance-Sheet CLO

We'll talk about the advantages of this tranche in detail later. We'll also discuss the applications of true sale and synthetic structures with respect to arbitrage and balance sheet deals.

Choice of the type of structure will take into account tax, accounting, and regulatory constraints. It will also take into account the types of assets the vehicle can issue, as well as investor preferences for the types of product the vehicle can issue. We'll examine these issues in the section on SPEs later in this book, and I cover the terminology of SPEs in that section.

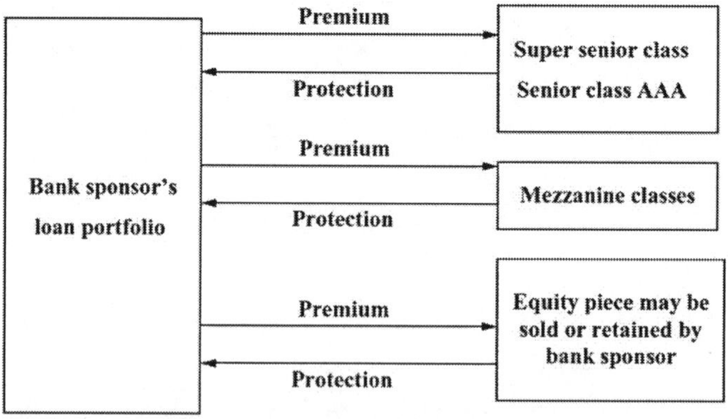

FIGURE 6.2 Simplified Synthetic Balance-Sheet CLO

Credit enhancement comes in a variety of forms, and several types of credit enhancement are usually structured into a single transaction. Popular forms of credit enhancement include the following:

- Initial overcollateralization.
- Subordination in the form of an equity piece.
- Junior lenders to the securitization vehicle.
- Credit wraps.
- Surety bonds.
- Government guarantees.
- Reserve accounts of excess coupon spread not required for immediate payment of liabilities.
- Reserve accounts of excess cash.
- Credit derivatives.
- Cash flow diversion once prespecified conditions or *triggers* are met.

Conduits may employ letters of credit (LOCs) and liquidity lines to ensure cash flow requirements, and may also add a *clawback* LOC to protect against payments being reclassified as preferential in the event of bankruptcy.

Several years ago, LOCs were a common form of credit enhancement for credit card securitizations. Recently, a structurer asked me what happened to all the LOCs—were they too expensive? It isn't that the cost is prohibitive—although it may become prohibitive under Basel II—but rather that an LOC has less value as credit enhancement, because so many banks have been downgraded.

MONOLINE AND MULTILINE INSURANCE

Monoline insurance companies provide *credit wraps,* which are *financial guarantees.* Monoline insurance companies are the only entities allowed to provide financial guarantees under New York law, where most securitizations are closed. Seven monolines were rated AAA at the time of this writing, but several were in peril of losing that rating. Historically, MBIA, Ambac, and FSA dominated market share for structured finance wrapping, although other monolines are active in this business, and the former two may lose their ratings (see also the section titled "Monoline Meltdown" in Chapter 17). Monoline insurance companies started out providing wraps for U.S. municipal finance, but branched out into structured finance to diversify the risk in their portfolios. Ambac, FSA, and MBIA in particular have made a concerted effort to judiciously diversify into global risks.

The highest rating possible on a wrapped tranche is the rating of the credit wrap provider. The amount of credit enhancement, which depends on the deal structure, is expressed as a multiple of the expected loss level. For instance, to get a triple-A rating, a general rule is that the credit enhancement must equal five times the expected loss level. The amount of enhancement required declines for lower rating requirements. Against this, monolines must maintain capital. Moody's requires capital to cover 130 percent of losses in its base-case scenario and 100 percent of losses in its stress scenario for a monoline to keep a triple-A rating.

Investor satisfaction with the performance of wraps under duress has been very high, so disruptions to the monolines may rattle investor confidence. The view of investors and rating agencies is that the wrap providers guarantee uninterrupted cash flows. The credit wrap also serves to preserve the rating of tranches in jeopardy of downgrade. Some triple-A tranches of CDO would have been downgraded by the rating agencies in the recent past, but they maintained their triple-A ratings only by virtue of the credit wraps supplied by AAA-rated monolines.

Multiline insurance companies, or *sureties,* may provide surety bonds or performance bonds. The surety bond guarantees the principal or obligor will perform its obligations under a contract. This is different from a financial guarantee. For instance, a commercial surety bond can be an advance payment bond that indemnifies against default on prepaid supply transactions involving the delivery of physical commodities.

The difference between a *financial guarantee* and a *credit derivative* is that the buyer of protection in a credit derivative contract does not have to own the underlying security or actually suffer a loss, as we saw in Chapter 3. In the recent past, protection bought in the form of credit derivatives has outperformed protection bought as surety bonds in non-CDO structured finance products. We looked at one example involving Enron and JPMorgan in Chapter 2. This has important implications for future use of surety bonds.

Overcollateralization is achieved through investment in more collateral than is required to meet the CDO's static cash flow requirements. The SPE may invest in more physical assets, or equity investors may inject additional cash into the deal. Cash injections are usually invested in virtually risk-free assets such as short-term government assets.

Tranching creates more than one class of debt within a given structure. Junior investors provide credit enhancement for senior investors. Investors in subordinated classes earn a higher coupon but have higher risk to their initial principal investment. The subordinated debt holders agree to absorb losses before the senior debt holders. Several tranches may exist in one deal, and the payments due to each tranche holder are defined in the prospectus according to the tranche payment priority. The more certain the payment, the higher the credit rating and the lower the nominal return. The less certain the payment, the lower the credit rating and the higher the nominal return.

Issuers may deposit cash in a reserve account or a trust account, and these funds can be used to meet principal and interest payments as needed. Excess spread may also be trapped in a reserve account. Excess spread is the current cash flow remaining after payment of investor coupons and fees. The excess spread account may be used for the benefit of all of the tranche investors to offset loss in value from nonperforming assets with remaining funds reverting to the deal manager or the first-loss investor at maturity, but this is not necessarily the case. In many structures, the reserve account is for the benefit of the first-loss investor only.

CDO CLASSIFICATION

Any potential future stream of payments or future value can be securitized. Table 6.1 shows a partial list of the types of assets that can be securitized, but one should not let a list limit one's imagination. Tranches of CDOs are included in securitizations, and tranches of those CDOs have been included in subsequent securitizations.

The following summary shows broad classifications one should be on the alert for in evaluating reported CDO data. Statistics on CDO issuance are often reported according to type of collateral classification. Many CDOs

TABLE 6.1 Partial List of Conventional Asset Classes

• MBS	• Future export receivables
• Corporate Loans	• Home improvement loans
• Auto Loans, leases	• Insurance premium loan receivables
• Aircraft Leases	• Manufactured housing loans
• Credit Card Receivables	• Marine loans
• Computer leases, service contracts	• Oil and gas contract receivables
• Consumer loans – unsecured	• Property rental and income streams
• Commercial Ofce & equipment leases	• Railcar leases
• Commercial MBS	• Small business loans
• Franchise Loans	• Student loans
• Healthcare receivables	• Timeshare loans
• Home equity loans	• Toll road receivables
• Second residential mortgages	• Utility receivables

securitize assets from more than one asset class, so it is difficult to generalize. Different reports may use different definitions and benchmarks, so it is important to read the classification criteria to understand reported data.

One important class is consumer receivables, which include auto loans, auto leases, home equity loans, and credit card receivables. Student loans have unique characteristics and are grouped into their own category.

Mortgage-backed securities are usually categorized as residential mortgage loans (single-family, multifamily, condominium, cooperatives) or commercial mortgage loans. Manufactured housing loans are often grouped into a separate category due to unique homeowner profiles.

Commercial and industrial loans include investment-grade corporate loans and high-yield corporate loans. Small business loans in the United States have their own category due to the government guarantee and unique structural features. In Europe, small to medium-size enterprise loans are grouped into a multicountry category. These loans are smaller in size than usual commercial and industrial loans, and the obligors are often not publicly rated. Investment-grade corporate bonds and high-yield corporate bonds are often viewed as separate categories.

Receivables such as computer leases, aircraft leases, marine leases, and equipment leases are usually grouped separately. Utility stranded costs have been securitized for years and have their own separate category. Equipment loans and equipment leases are considered a separate small to medium-size loan category. Expectations of payments, such as delinquent tax liens, have a separate category. Future flows deals have another separate category and are sometimes included in emerging markets statistics.

Bonds backed by receivables such as the right to televise Formula One sporting events, or cable subscriptions, are also sometimes classified as CDOs, although they are usually lumped into the broader category of structured finance.

Private equity and hedge fund of fund securitizations are in separate categories. Nonperforming loans also have a separate category. Investment-grade sovereign debt may be included in bond obligations, but emerging market debt is usually considered separately, albeit this debt is often found in high-yield bond obligations.

I just mentioned assets that can be used in the CDO portfolio, but even the asset definitions are subject to debate. For instance, asset-backed securities are structured securities in which the underlying collateral is itself a pool of loans or receivables.

A *collateralized loan obligation* (CLO) is a type of CDO and is backed by a portfolio of loans. The term is reserved for a securitization that is exclusively backed by loans. In 1990, the first rated CLO backed by U.S. bank loans was brought to market.

A *collateralized bond obligation* (CBO) is another type of CDO. In 1988, the first rated CBO backed by high-yield bonds was brought to market. CBOs are backed by a portfolio of secured or unsecured senior or junior bonds issued by a variety of corporate or sovereign obligors. Often a CBO will include loans in the portfolio, but the majority of the collateral usually consists of bonds. CBO transactions realize the positive spread between a portfolio of higher-return, higher-risk assets, often rated below BBB; and lower-cost, highly rated CBO securities issued to purchase the portfolio of bonds backing the CBO.

A collateralized mortgage obligation (CMO) is backed by mortgage-backed securities (MBSs), also called mortgage pass-through securities. CMOs and the individual tranches of CMOs are also called mortgage-backed securities. This terminology is usually reserved for the U.S. market, and we'll briefly look at this later in this chapter. Ironically, CMOs, the CDO precursors, are usually excluded from CDO reports and are not considered in the definition of CDOs by many market professionals.

Structural differences in the European market did not lend themselves to the same type of cash flow tranching as the U.S. market. Often European mortgages do not enjoy government support. A look at the German market illustrates just some of the differences between the U.S. and European mortgage-backed securities market. The German Pfandbriefe market has been in existence for more than 200 years. The underlying mortgage loans must have a loan-to-value ratio of less than 60 percent, so the overall credit quality is deemed to be triple-A. In the U.S. market, mortgage-backed securities are a balance sheet management tool. In the German market, however, Pfandbriefe cannot be prepaid and are kept on the bank's balance sheet, albeit they may be pledged as collateral. Securitization of other types of mortgage-backed securities as a balance sheet management tool has gained momentum only in the past three years after a very slow start.

CDOs are further classified as synthetic (credit derivatives) or cash. Some CDOs are backed by combinations of cash and synthetic securities.

CDOs are either arbitrage deals, balance-sheet deals, or both. Both can have any combination of cash and synthetic underlyings. Arbitrage CDOs take advantage of greater market prices for the underlying obligations versus the price at which the combined liabilities can be sold. Balance-sheet CDOs are normally used for regulatory capital relief, albeit funding may be another motive for a balance-sheet deal.

Arbitrage CDOs are either market value CDOs or cash flow CDOs. They can be backed by either cash assets, synthetic assets, or a combination of both. Cash flow CDOs make up 85 to 90 percent of the arbitrage market and are growing at a much faster rate than market value CDOs.

MARKET VALUE CDOS

Market value CDOs make up approximately 10 to 15 percent of the arbitrage CDO market. In market value deals, like most CDOs, either (1) assets are pledged to a trustee to back debt for the benefit of the investors, or (2) a bankruptcy-remote SPV buys the assets and pledges the collateral to back debt or equity (or preferred stock) for the benefit of the investors. Market value deals may also use a third, less common, structure. Investors have a claim on all of the assets in the fund and the seniority of their claim depends on the class of debt or equity (preference shares or preferred stock) they own.

Market value structures meet principal (if applicable) and interest liabilities by generating cash from trading assets, and from interest on invested assets. If a collateral pool consists of defaulted bonds or loans, the market value structure is usually used, since these assets do not generate predictable cash flow streams, but have significant market value upside potential. Managers who have good track records trading investment-grade debt and high-yield debt often prefer market value deals.

Market value deal managers trade actively and aggressively and usually employ leverage. Of course, not every trade results in a gain. Both credit and market considerations are important to market value deal managers. Investors who must mark their assets to market might prefer market value structures, since market value CDO managers must mark the portfolio of CDOs to market.

The ratio of the market value of assets to the face value of liabilities is the focus of a market value CLO. Market value deals require overcollateralization or a "haircut." The overcollateralization protects investors from asset price volatility due to changes in general interest rate movements, general credit spread movements, or other general market movements. Market value CDOs require maintenance of a minimum overcollateralization level. If this level is breached, the assets must be sold to pay down liabilities or the assets must be sold and exchanged for highly rated liquid instruments. This is known as a *trigger event.* The rating agencies monitor the debt coverage ratios. The performance of a market value CDO depends upon the manager's trading ability.

CASH FLOW CDOS

Nonsynthetic *cash flow* CDOs invest in cash assets as collateral. The structure passes principal and interest payments generated by cash flows of the underlying collateral through to the investors. For a deal to be successful, the cash flow from the collateral pool must meet all deal liabilities including the interest and principal obligations from the notes issued by the CDO. The cash flows are hedged, reinvested, and tranched by time and seniority. The rating of a note depends on the probability of cash flow sufficiency to service that particular note. If the cash flow deal is properly structured, investors only experience a loss if there are defaults in the collateral pool.

Cash flow CDOs backed by a pool of cash obligations require a manager, whereas synthetic cash flow deals may or may not have a manager. For the cash asset-backed CDO, the manager's role is more limited than that of a market value CDO manager. The manager is carefully chosen for credit expertise rather than trading expertise. The cash flow CDO manager of a cash instrument–backed deal chooses the initial diversified portfolio of cash instruments and chooses credits to purchase during the reinvestment period. The manager may also participate in a workout in the event of default to maximize recovery. We examine these structural details when we compare cash and synthetic CDOs in Chapter 9.

Deals can be managed or unmanaged. Only deals that reference a static pool of assets can dispense with a manager. This is most common with arbitrage synthetic CDOs, or cash CDOs where a fixed pool of assets is used in a pass-through type structure.

Cash CDOs are usually broken into broad categories that represent the bulk of the issuance:

- High-yield loans.
- Multisector.
- Investment-grade corporate (which normally includes one-quarter to one-third high-yield collateral).
- High-yield bonds.

Synthetic CDOs are backed by credit default swaps on a diversified pool of reference obligors. The credit default swaps can reference any type of cash obligation. They can be either balance-sheet deals or arbitrage deals and are often classified into three categories: (1) managed CDOs, (2) CDOs with right of substitution, and (3) static CDOs. Managed CDOs will have an actively involved manager and may look similar to a market value CDO in that the underlying pool of assets is actively traded in an attempt to add value. Some managers are more passive and trade only to avoid losses. CDOs with the right of substitution have managers that may not be arms-length managers. The bank arranger's structuring group may handle management activities that allow them to trade out of credits according to preset rules. The object is to trade out of deteriorating credit before default and trade into a higher credit quality obligation.

Static pools of credit default swaps back a static CDO. No trading is allowed. By definition, this is a cash flow CDO. Synthetic static arbitrage CDOs differ from cash CDOs that are also cash flow CDOs because the synthetic deal normally has no preplanned reinvestment period. Since the CDS market allows cash flow maturities to be defined at the deal inception, there is no need for reinvestment, other than possibly to reinvest recovered amounts after a default, if any. We examine the advantages and disadvantages of managed versus static CDOs in Chapter 9.

This menu of different products may seem confusing at first. The structural details are indeed important, and we'll review various structural features later. As we've already seen, the key is to avoid getting shot in the first place. The place to start evaluating the fundamental value of any securitization is with the pool or portfolio. If an investor doesn't like the names in the portfolio, no structure can make up for it. If the investor likes the names in the initial portfolio, then the negotiation begins for the best possible structural protections.

THE ORIGINS OF U.S. SECURITIZATIONS

Most of today's securitization technology originated in the U.S. financial markets. The origins teach us about structural features that can be applied to today's markets. Finally, the origins teach us about how resistant we are to learning the hard lessons experience has to offer. A quick look at the U.S. mortgage-backed securities (MBS) and collateralized mortgage obligation (CMO) markets allows us to isolate the cash flow risk without worrying about credit risk for the moment.

In the U.S. market, mortgage-backed securities are not included in the definition of asset-backed securities, but the European market includes mortgage-backed securities in this definition. In the United States, the term *asset-backed security* is reserved for securitizations backed by credit card receivables, auto loans, auto leases, student loans, home equity loans, and manufactured housing loans. This list doesn't include other even more obscure receivables that are securitized in the U.S. market. The fact that MBS is not included in the definition of asset-backed securities in the U.S. is an artifact. MBS securitization so completely dominated the U.S. structured market at its inception that it required a name of its own.

The Government National Mortgage Association (GNMA, or Ginnie Mae), the Federal Home Loan Mortgage Corporation (FHLMC, or Freddie Mac), and the Federal National Mortgage Association (FNMA, or

Fannie Mae) are the three entities that caused a major leap forward in U.S. securitization. These three entities set guidelines and created pools of residential mortgages. These mortgage pools then backed pass-through securities issued by GNMA, FNMA, and FHLMC. Each of these pass-throughs pays both a coupon and pass-through principal prepayments. Interest payments have a delay to account for collections.

The U.S. market views the issuance from these entities as risk-free, or as good as an obligation of the U.S. government, but that isn't strictly true. GNMA is a government agency, and GNMA pass-throughs, also known as agency pass-throughs, are backed by the full faith and credit of the U.S. government. Fannie Mae (FNMA) and Freddie Mac (FHLMC), the privately chartered United States mortgage giants which are overseen by the department of Housing and Urban Development (HUD), issue conventional pass-throughs. Although FNMA and FHLMC issued securities are not guaranteed, there is an implied moral obligation. The U.S. market perception is that the government would never allow FHMLC or FNMA to default because it would shake the investment community to the core. The credit risk is viewed as negligible.

This perception of safety for FHLMC and FNMA is not always shared in the European market, and this initially made marketing of these securities in Europe more problematic. When U.S. deal arrangers first tried to sell floating-rate mortgage-backed securities in the European market, they met with resistance. Investors were initially even suspicious of the creditworthiness of GNMA. As investors learned more about the entities, the resistance to investment abated. In much of Europe, GNMA is usually assigned a 0 percent BIS risk weight, whereas FHLMC and FNMA are assigned a 50 percent BIS risk weight, as they are in the United States.

It was this perception of lack of credit risk in the United States that made reward for the cash flow risk of these securities all the more appealing. Many institutions that could not invest in options or take high degrees of interest rate risk could purchase these securities because of the sterling creditworthiness of the issuers. Life just got a lot more interesting for wide classes of investors in the United States. This is because when an investor bought these securities, they were short an imbedded call option, the right of the U.S. homeowner to prepay his mortgage.

How did this work? Suppose a mortgage pass-through traded at a discount. Securities of an issuer without credit risk trade at a discount if the coupon is lower than the issuer's coupon of a new issuance at par. One can see this in the U.S. Treasury market as interest rates fluctuate. Since interest rates had been volatile, by 1986 there were a variety of outstanding issues with a variety of coupons. For a discounted issue trading at a price of 99, one received a lower coupon than a current issue would offer, but if interest rates declined, it was likely that mortgage prepayments would speed up. Then one would get repayments of principal at 100. If one bought a premium security, one could enjoy a high coupon, but the investor hoped that prepayments declined. Then the high coupon could be earned for a longer period of time. Since there was apparently no credit risk, investors could place bets that weren't obvious to their constituencies.

Travelers, for instance, bought GNMAs with double-digit coupons at high premiums in the mid-1980s. This allowed Travelers to report extremely high current income—at least for a while. Unfortunately, interest rates were both volatile and dropping. Prepayments sped up—a lot. Those high-premium securities began prepaying at par or 100. Travelers took a mark-to-market loss while simultaneously losing a large portion of the cash flow stream of those high coupons.

The lower interest rates rubbed even more salt in the wound. The prepayments and remaining coupons had to be reinvested at lower rates. Suddenly GNMAs were no fun anymore. It was a debacle. Too late to staunch hundreds of millions in losses, but early enough to avoid further major losses, Travelers bought long-dated U.S. Treasury (UST) zeros as a hedge. Zeros have the property of popping up in price for large declines in interest rates. Travelers chose 20-year UST zeros since these were trading cheap relative to the UST interest rate curve. This partially offset the loss on the GNMAs. The hedge provided no current income, however.

This example may seem unrelated to current events, but it actually exemplifies pivotal concepts. It is a theme that gets replayed with variations many times over the course of the ensuing years. Let's take a moment to dissect some of the components. We'll see these ideas again in various forms in other structures. Today we still combine high cash flow equity with zero-coupon bonds in principal-protected structures.

Suppose for a moment that Travelers had owned high coupon premium bonds that had no prepayment risk, and no credit risk. The duration of those bonds would initially be shorter than current coupon bonds in the market due to their high coupons. These coupons have to be reinvested at lower interest rates. These bond prices would move inversely with interest rates, so as rates dropped, the price of the bonds would rise, but not as much as a bond with a lower coupon.

Which of the bonds below will have the greatest effective yield to a six-month horizon if rates decline by 100 basis points?

Bond A 7 percent coupon 30-year maturity 10 percent yield

Bond B 12 percent coupon 30-year maturity 10 percent yield

Bond A has the longer duration and will therefore have a larger increase in price if rates decline 100 bp. Bond A's effective yield and its total rate of return to the six-month time horizon will therefore be greater than Bond B.

Travelers was already behind the eight ball when interest rates dropped. Being short the imbedded call option only made a bad situation worse. It was as if Travelers had bought a bond and then sold a structured call option, which is only partially exercised when prepayments speed up. The selling of the call option yielded more income initially, but it resulted in even more pain than Travelers would otherwise have experienced.

During which of the following scenarios will the implied option premium of the imbedded call option be highest?

- Low volatility with rates falling.
- Low volatility with rates rising.
- High volatility with rates falling.
- High volatility with rates rising.

The premium will be highest when volatility is high, and rates are falling. This is the scenario Travelers experienced. Since it was short the option, the higher implied option premium meant that the price of the bond would decline rapidly. These bonds were highly negatively convex, which means the duration of the bonds fell rapidly. In fact, instead of rising, the price of these bonds started falling when interest rates fell.

The managers at Travelers searched for a hedge. Initially, they couldn't find anything at a price they were willing to pay. Treasury zeros seemed to be the answer, albeit they would have been happier to stumble on the solution earlier. Since Travelers owned securities that were negatively convex due to a short call option, they wanted something that had a high degree of positive convexity and would have characteristics similar to a call option. At the time, 20-year maturity Treasury zeros seemed to provide an answer to a part of their problem.

I once heard a professor tell his class that zero-coupon bonds have zero convexity, but it isn't true. Formulas and academic definitions can obscure the utility of a financial instrument, its value as a tool. Forget the labels. Cash flows are what matter. The definitions of *duration* and *convexity* in the bond markets are linked to price performance. *Modified duration* is conventionally defined as the percentage price change in the full price of a bond for a 100 bp movement in rates. *Convexity* is a second-order term helpful in describing how far off duration's predictive power can be in a nonstatic world. The following shows the change in the price behavior (Delta P) of a 20-year zero-coupon bond with a bond equivalent yield (BEY) of 6 percent for increments of 25 basis points as rates move in a range from 5 to 7 percent:

BEY	Price	DP
7.00	$25.26	($1.25)
6.75	$26.51	($1.31)
6.50	$27.82	($1.38)
6.25	$29.20	($1.45)
6.00	$30.66	0
5.75	$32.18	$1.53
5.50	$33.79	$1.60
5.25	$35.47	$1.69

$$100 \times [1 / (1 + .06/2)^{40}] = 30.6556.$$

You'll recall that you price a 20-year zero with a semiannual BEY of 6 percent as follows:

I rounded to 30.66 for the preceding BEY table. As interest rates move and the bond is repriced, the drop in price when rates rise is less than the increase in price when rates decline. This is due to the fact that the zero-coupon bond has positive convexity. As one can see from the pricing formula, longer-dated zeros have the most convexity. The long-dated zeros have about three times the convexity of a similar maturity current coupon bullet bond. The highly positively convex zeros can be combined with negatively convex securities to create a price performance hedge.

How did Travelers determine a hedge ratio? They guesstimated. This was a time when no one had a good handle on how to value the imbedded prepayment option. Prepayment data was just in the process of being loaded into large databases. The models seemed to have more code than the Cray computer in the Pentagon at the time. Even after better data and better pricing models existed, a hedge ratio for a security like this is still a guesstimate. The uncertainty of prepayments makes the option, and therefore the price behavior of the security, an educated guess. Even if the price behavior could be exactly determined, the hedge is imperfect because the price behavior of Treasury zeros differs from that of mortgage-backed securities. Duration and convexity are known as first- and second-order terms, respectively, in a differential equation that attempts to model the performance of these bonds. We require even more terms than that to model the performance of mortgage-backed securities.

A popular method at the time was to use a minimum variance hedge ratio. Suppose you had a series of prices of a security X, and a series of prices for a security Y, for a range of parallel shifts in interest rates. Security X behaves like a GNMA pass-through, similar to the security purchased by Travelers. Security Y behaves like a long-maturity U.S. Treasury zero. Let scenario 5 in the following table be today's base-case rate. Scenario 1 is the lowest rate scenario, and scenario 10 is the highest interest rate scenario. The other numbers denote equal gradations in between. The prices under a series of rate scenarios might look as follows:

Rate Scenario	**1**	**2**	**3**	**4**	**5**	**6**	**7**	**8**	**9**	**10**
X	102.00	102.50	103.00	105.50	105.30	105.20	105.10	104.80	104.70	104.60
Y	39.11	35.47	33.79	32.18	30.66	29.2	27.82	26.51	25.26	24.07

Denote the mean of each of the series of prices and calculate differences from the mean, and the square of the differences from the mean:

Mean of X = 104.27
Mean of Y =30.407
n = 10

Rate Scenario	1	2	3	4	5	6	7	8	9	10
Xi – X = a	-2.27	-1.77	-1.27	1.23	1.03	0.93	0.83	0.53	0.43	0.33
Yi – Y = b	8.70	5.06	3.38	1.77	0.25	-1.21	-2.59	-3.90	-5.15	-6.34
$(Xi – X)^2$	5.15	3.13	1.61	1.51	1.06	0.86	0.69	0.28	0.18	0.11
$(Yi – Y)^2$	75.74	25.63	11.44	3.14	0.06	1.46	6.69	15.19	26.49	40.16
a x b	-19.76	-8.96	-4.30	2.18	0.26	-1.12	-2.15	-2.07	-2.21	-2.09

We can easily calculate the variances and standard deviations of the price series as follows:

Variance of X = $(X – Xi)^2 / n$ = 1.4601
Std Dev of X = $(\text{VarianceX})^{½}$ = 1.21

Variance of Y = $(Y – Yi)^2 / n$ = 20.60136
Std Dev of Y = $(\text{VarianceY})^{1/2}$ = 4.54

The covariance is calculated as follows:

Covariance = Sum {(X-Xi) x (Y-Yi)} / n = −4.02119

The covariance is also known as the *moment of the joint distribution* and is a measure of the direction of the relationship between these two series of data. If the relationship of the price changes as interest rates shifted was independent, the covariance would be zero. A positive number would indicate that the prices were positively related, so a higher price of the GNMA would tend to correspond to a higher price of the UST zero. That doesn't seem to be the case, since the number is negative. This suggests that a higher price of the GNMA tends to correspond to a *lower* price of the UST zero. The direction of the relationship tends to be negative.

How would I compare the strength of this relationship with the strength of other relationships? In order to do that, we've developed yet another term. This was necessary because sometimes we might want to look at other types of relationships and compare strengths. For instance, we might want to look at bonus compensation compared with the number of years of service of an investment banker. The problem is that the units are not the same. The units of the covariance are dollars and years. We create a unitless measure of the strength of the relationship by dividing the covariance by the product of the standard deviations of the two series.

The Greek letter ρ is often used to denote the correlation coefficient. In the case of our two price series:

$$\rho = -4.02119 / (1.21 \times 4.54) = -0.73$$

In this case, the prices are negatively correlated. If the correlation co efficient were zero, the two price series would be uncorrelated. If it were a positive 1, the prices would have a perfect positive correlation, and the volatility of the portfolio would be the sum of the individual asset volatilities. If it were a negative 1, the prices would be perfectly negatively correlated. The volatility of the portfolio would be the difference of the individual asset volatilities, and the risk would be minimized. The correlation coefficient is always between + 1 and −1, but not zero.

Correlation has the drawback of being the measurement of a linear relationship. As we shall see when we are looking at credit risk, we can't just assume the relationship is linear. We could do more statistical work and try to determine the amount of the variance accounted for by this linear regression, but we can put this aside and employ other techniques as well.

Continuing with this example, I'll suggest an approach, which will serve us through a variety of correlation problems.

The minimum variance hedge ratio is calculated as follows:

$$\rho_{xy}\left(\sigma_y / \sigma_x\right) = -2.75$$

This means I can own 2.75 of the GNMAs for one of the Treasury zeros. Or, put another way, I buy 0.36 zeros for every GNMA I own.

I might want to buy fewer of the zeros, however, and just hedge for extreme price moves. Figure 6.3 depicts what a profile of the two securities might look like.

Notice the price behavior of the two securities. They are nonlinear. We saw this effect already for the zero. We can see why it must also be so for the GNMA. An intuitive way to think of this is that although these premium-priced high-coupon mortgage-backed securities are now dropping toward par in price as interest rates fall, this cannot continue forever. As the price approaches par, the price drop will slow down. Convexity is a second-order effect. Duration can still be negative, yet convexity can become positive. When duration is negative, convexity can be either positive or negative. For instance, if I'm driving and I'm accelerating, my velocity is positive, and my acceleration is positive (positive duration and convexity). If I take the foot off of the gas pedal, I decelerate, albeit my velocity is still positive and dropping (positive duration, negative convexity).

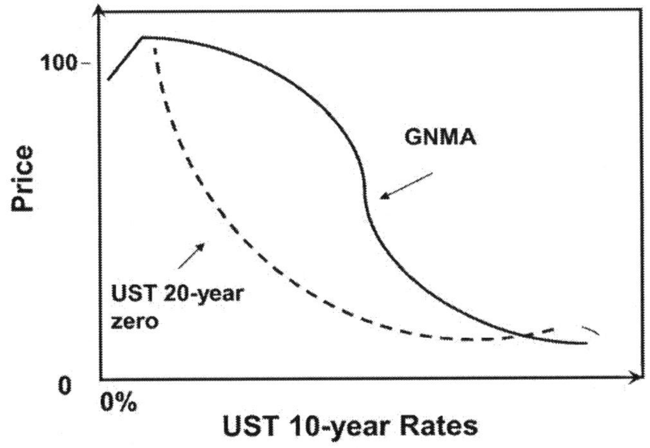

FIGURE 6.3 GNMA vs UST Zero Hedge Pattern of Price Behavior

Consider that the formula for duration is defined as follows:

$$D = -100/P \times dP/dY$$

then convexity is simply

$$100/P \times d^2P/dY^2$$

where

C = convexity
D = duration
P = price of the bond
Y = yield of the bond

Convexity can be written as the following expression:

$$C = -dD/dY + D^2/100$$

How did I get that? I did it as follows:

$$C = 100/P \times d^2P/dY^2 = 100/P \times d/dY\ (dP/dY)$$

We know that

$$D = -100/P \times dP/dY$$

and therefore

$$dP/dY = (-D) \times P/100$$

Substituting, we get:

$$C = 100/P \times d/dY\ (-D \times P/100)$$

$$= -100/P \times dD/dY \times P/100 + 100/P \times (-D) \times dP/100 \times dY$$

Substituting and canceling terms, we get:

$$C = -dD/dY + D^2/100$$

One could calculate a hedge and try to keep rebalancing it as conditions change. This is known as *dynamic hedging*. I define dynamic hedging as dynamically recognizing your losses. Death by one thousand cuts.

The challenge is that most of the assets we examine will exhibit nonlinear behavior for the variables we wish to examine. For this reason, I prefer to do scenario analysis. This allows you to create a hedge that performs well in the scenarios you find most unpalatable. The hedge may let you down in scenarios in which you can afford to take a loss. It may also let you down in scenarios in which you have an offset somewhere else in your holdings. But the hedge will perform in the scenarios in which you can't take a loss and in which you don't have an offset somewhere else in your portfolio. This approach has an added advantage of making one clearly think through the performance of one's holdings as well as the objective of keeping those holdings.

Scenario analysis has the added plus of forcing an investor to think about appropriate stress tests for a portfolio. Historical knowledge coupled with imagination of future possible scenarios helps in the management of any portfolio. Imagination is important because it helps us create scenarios that may not be reflected in historical data. For instance, in evaluating corporate exposure, it may be useful to imagine a worst-case scenario of fraud.

When it comes to hedging, there is more than one answer to the problem, and all of them are imperfect, which is the definition of a hedge. If a hedge were perfect, and if one could still make money after paying for perfection, it wouldn't be called a hedge; it would be called an arbitrage.

COLLATERALIZED MORTGAGE OBLIGATIONS

Investor demand for more perceived safety combined with investor demand for even more structural choices spurred investment banks to create collateralized mortgage obligations (CMOs). The CMOs were mainly backed by GNMA, FHLMC, and FNMA pass-throughs. Some CMOs used nonagency collateral, and these traded at wider spreads due to additional perceived credit risk. These securitizations took cash flow technology to unprecedented heights. The imagination is the only limit to the number of ways one can carve up these cash flows. Collateralized mortgage obligations were issued by special purpose corporations (SPCs), real estate mortgage investment conduits (REMICs), trusts, finance subsidiaries, and real estate investment trusts (REITs). Today the REMIC structure dominates the market due to tax considerations.

The first CMOs had only four sequential pay slices, or tranches. The first three tranches received interest or coupon payments and the fourth tranche accrued coupon payments. Sequential pay meant the first tranche paid down with a portion of the remaining cash flows. Once this was fully amortized, the second tranche received principal payments until it, too, was retired; then the third tranche began receiving principal payments; then the fourth tranche received payments. The goal was to have enough cash flow from the pool to retire all tranches by the stated maturity even when one assumed low reinvestment rates and zero prepayment rates. Figure 6.4 is a simplified sequential-pay CMO with fixed-rate tranches, a floating-rate

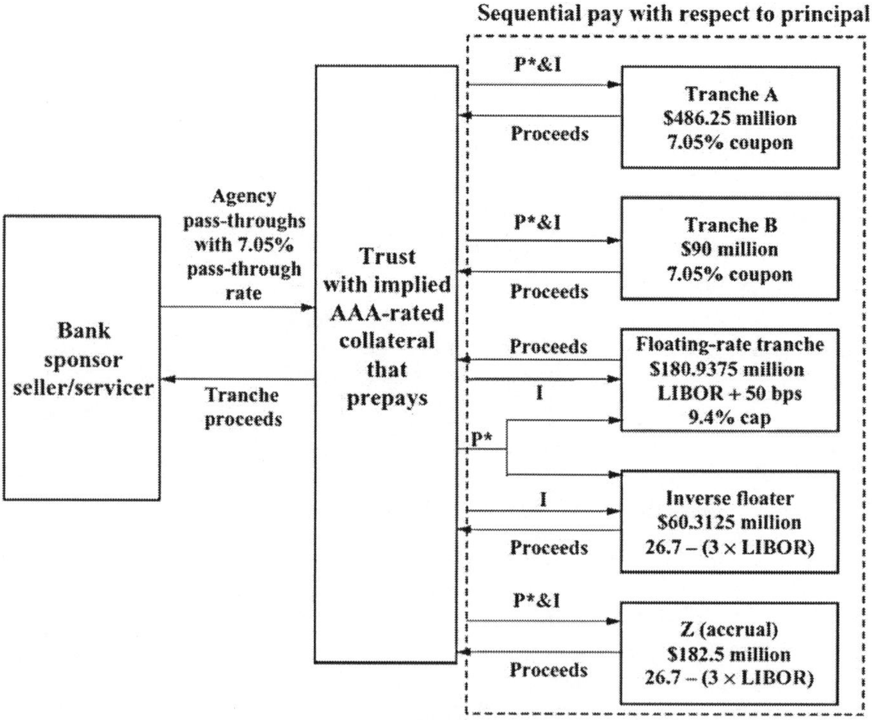

*Principal payments are allocated to each tranche in sequence. The floater and inverse floater receive a pro-rata share of principal from the original tranche which was third in the sequence.

FIGURE 6.4 Simplified CMO Structure

tranche, an inverse floating-rate tranche, and an accrual bond, also called the *Z* tranche.

The collateral has a 7.05 percent pass-through rate and a weighted average coupon (WAC) of 7.675 percent. The weighted average maturity (WAM) is 357 months. I took one of the tranches and created a capped floating-rate note and an inverse floater. Every floater must have an inverse floater when the collateral consists of pass-throughs that pay fixed coupons. The floater and inverse floater can have an infinite number of combinations, but the sum of the interest paid on the pair must equal the interest available on the original fixed-coupon tranche.

In this example, I created the floater and inverse floater out of a tranche that was originally $241,250,000 in size with a 7.05 percent coupon. It was the third tranche in the sequential pay sequence. Seventy-five percent of the tranche is a floater, and 25 percent is an inverse floater. The floater pays LIBOR plus 50 bps and has a 9.4 percent cap. The inverse floater has three times leverage with respect to LIBOR. This means that as LIBOR decreases, the inverse floater coupon increases threefold. The generic formula for an inverse floater of this type is given as follows:

$$C - (\text{Leverage Factor} \times \text{LIBOR})$$

where

C = a constant, the cap on the inverse floater coupon

Leverage Factor = the amount of leverage with respect to the last LIBOR fixing

LIBOR = the last LIBOR fixing for the CMO

The inverse floater for my CMO has a cap of 26.7 percent. This inverse floater does not have a floor coupon, albeit some CMOs have inverse floaters with a minimum coupon in addition to a cap. The leverage factor is three. The inverse floater coupon is calculated at any given time as follows:

$$26.7\% - (3 \times \text{LIBOR})$$

where LIBOR is the fixing at the last coupon reset period.

The Z or accrual tranche is the only tranche that does not receive interest each month. The interest accrues and is added to the principal balance. The foregone interest is used to pay down the tranches ahead of it in the sequential pay structure, each in their turn. Investors who are concerned with reinvestment risk can reduce that risk, since this tranche has no reinvestment risk until all of the other tranches are paid off.

The interest payments on the deal are disbursed to the A, B, floater, and inverse floater each month based on the amount of principal outstanding (the amount not prepaid, if any) at the beginning of the period. The Z tranche accrues interest based on the principal plus accrued interest in the previous period, and the Z tranche current interest is used to pay down the outstanding previous tranches in sequence.

Tranche A receives principal payments until it is completely paid off. Next, tranche B receives principal payments until it is paid off. Next the floater and inverse floater receive pro-rata principal payments until they are paid off. After all of the other tranches are paid off, the Z tranche receives principal payments until the original principal balance plus accrued interest is totally paid off.

The servicer, the entity that collects cash flows and pays monthly principal and interest to the CMO's trustee, receives a fee. The right to service the CMO is traded in an active secondary market. The price of servicing behaves like that of an interest-only (IO) tranche. The longer the CBO tranches are outstanding, the longer the servicer earns fees. As the CMO prepays, the amount of servicing fees declines.

Residual cash flows are what is left over after all obligations are met. These cash flows come from a number of sources. One source is the difference between the weighted average coupon (WAC) on the pass-throughs and the lower weighted average coupon on the combined CMO tranches. Deals are sometimes overcollateralized (especially nonagency issues), and another source of residual cash flow is from the higher principal amount of the underlying collateral and the lower combined principal amount of the CMO tranches. When excess reserve funds are reduced due to lower maintenance requirements as the deal prepays, this is an added source of residual cash flows. If market rates are higher than the low cash flow reinvestment rate assumption used in structuring the deal, the excess cash may be paid out as residual income.

Investors asked for even more complicated structures. For instance, bonds with planned amortization classes (PACs) allow investors to enjoy a predetermined amortization as long as prepayments stayed within a predefined range. Traditional corporate bond investors were encouraged by the perceived lack of credit risk, greater certainty of cash flows compared to an MBS pass-through, shorter maturity, and competitive coupon compared with lower-rated corporate bonds. If prepayments strayed outside the range, it could be a problem, so investors learned more about prepayment data and trends.

Floating-rate tranches satisfy demand of banks and other entities that fund versus LIBOR (London interbank offered rate), and the floaters have caps. For every floater, there is an inverse floater. These can be offered in a separate tranche or imbedded in residual cash flows. We'll talk more about residuals later in this book. In early deals, the buyer had to look closely at the way the floating-rate coupon was calculated. Some initial floating-rate tranches paid on a 30/360 day-count (bond basis), and some on an actual/360 basis (money market basis). As we will see later, this is a material economic difference, and unwary investors were sometimes exploited. Some CMOs paid monthly, some quarterly, and some semiannually. All had delay days, which sometimes varied by deal. Added choices came with added complications.

Some deals had tranches that could receive only interest, called *IOs* or *interest-only* tranches. Other tranches received only principal and were called *POs* or *principal-only* tranches. These and even more volatile combinations were created. One's view on prepayments became very important.

Wall Street invested millions of dollars and man-hours developing prepayment models. A slavish religious-like belief in the model outputs developed, and I could almost hear the chanting on the streets of New York.

Models are wonderful tools, but they are just that. They have their limitations. Chief among them are the data and the assumptions we make about the continued reliability of the data. The problem with data is that it is an observation of something that has already happened. By definition, it is history. It's a good idea to leave a margin around the edges of model dogma to make room for otherwise. If you put too much at stake in a model's ability to predict future prepayment rates, or anything else, for that matter, you are asking for trouble.

Still, we celebrate the model du jour, the genius du jour, and the trader du jour. If a trader says he can predict the market, stay away from him. Most traders aren't clear on why they make or lose money in a wild market swing.

If you have 64 people in a room, each tossing a coin, the chances are 50–50 that each person will toss heads on the first flip. Thirty-two people will toss heads on the first try. Thirty-two people begin thinking they control the outcome. On the next toss, 16 people will toss heads two times in a row. Sixteen people become very cocky.

The law of probabilities being what it is, *one* person will flip heads *six* times in a row. This person will be dubbed a genius. What genius? What cockamamie twaddle!

The next thing you know, another firm has signed the lucky person to a two-year contract at a minimum of $1 million per year. Who knows? Maybe that lucky person will toss heads seven times in a row.

When the coin stops coming up heads, and the formerly lucky person loses a pile of money, he can't figure out what went wrong. His ability to predict the market deserted him.

In 1993, I had the opportunity to talk at length with a Morgan Stanley trader of very volatile tranches after she'd had a profitable week. I said I was nervous about the size and hedges of one of the positions she traded, because no one could predict homeowner prepayments. One could get a fair idea of the boundaries with a model, but one couldn't predict an exact number. Prepayment behavior sometimes gave one a nasty surprise. It was an unknowable unknown. Perhaps finding more investors and lightening up the holdings would be prudent.

I knew the trouble with this recommendation was that there weren't enough buyers, so a trader's willingness to position these tranches allowed Morgan Stanley to bring more deals, which led to more fee income, which led to higher bonuses. . . you get the idea.

She eyed me aggressively. I persisted, and she began squirming. She started to look uncomfortable. I recognized the feeling. It's the feeling I get right before I face an unpalatable truth that I've worked hard to avoid. She suddenly got up and strutted to the trading floor. She barked an order to a trading assistant. She returned relaxed, having asserted some control. I recognized that, too. Push that unpalatable truth right back in the closet where it belongs.

She asserted that *she* knew how to predict homeowner prepayments, and thus she knew how to predict the behavior of her market. She used Morgan Stanley's prepayment model! It was the best in the business. *She knew the unknowable unknown.*

She made only one error: She forgot to share her insight with American homeowners. Interest rates went down, and homeowners rushed to refinance at unprecedented rates. The price of those volatile securities plummeted like an eagle shot from the sky. Before the year was out, Morgan Stanley lost a lot of money in that trading book. It was enough to get her fired, along with her boss, who also knew how to predict homeowner prepayments.

There is nothing wrong with taking on a lot of risk. Investment banks expect to take occasional losses. The only thing they cannot forgive is if you fool yourself, and consequently your managers, about the amount of risk you are taking.

Many yield-hungry investors also lost a lot of money. I'll digress with an example. One of my colleagues at PaineWebber dubbed one of my customers "the Hammer." The Hammer worked for the New York subsidiary of a Japanese trading company. The trading company leveraged its investment portfolios. In fact, these weren't investment portfolios; they were *hedge funds*. The Hammer was on the Tokyo board of directors and had a secure lifetime job. He also had a high-stakes gambler's appetite for risk. His firm was famous in Japan for making hundreds of millions of dollars in the currency exchange market, angering Japanese banks by making money in yen/dollar arbitrage at their expense. Although he could not speculate in currencies as head of the New York office, he found other ways to indulge this passion. He was lucky. So far, this strategy had paid off, but if one relies only on luck, there is nothing to fall back on when it runs out.

I showed the Hammer two deals. Each deal was a combination of two securities: an inverse floater, and an interest-only piece. One of the combinations had a yield of 14 percent, the other had a yield of 15.25 percent. Not bad in 1991, when 30-year Treasury bonds were yielding less than 8 percent.

There was just one catch: The effect of the prepayment rate was highly leveraged for the combination with the 15.25 percent yield. (The cash flows were path dependent and highly sensitive to the path.) If interest rates declined and prepayments sped up, future cash flow from these securities disappeared faster than the bullet train. Forever.

I explained: "The combination with 15.25 percent yield is much riskier than the other deal. If interest rates go down, the security *vaporizes*, along with the money you paid for it. I recommend the other deal, which isn't nearly as sensitive."

The Hammer glared at me, as if he was a Hell's Angel and I was a meter maid.

"Thank you for your advice, Tavakoli-san," he said dismissively. "Our Tokyo office thinks that interest rates are going *up*, not down, so your warning is not needed."

"While that may be true," I continued, "for just a *little* less return, you can eliminate a *lot* of the risk. The deal with the 15.25 percent base-case yield requires a big bet that interest rates will stay constant or only rise slightly. Even if you are right in the short term, if interest rates later drop below today's levels, you will rapidly lose value."

"The guy from Kidder Peabody never talks to me like that!" The Hammer now looked at me as if I had just told him not to go out without condoms. I was no fun at all. He looked angry enough to reject *both* proposals.

He looked down at the proposals and made me wait. Finally, he sat up from the papers and sat back with a slow but fluid movement.

"Tavakoli-san, is there a special *discount* on price?"

"No, I'm afraid that isn't possible," I said evenly. Then I went for the close. "May I have your order on the deal with 15.25 percent in the base case?" I believe in an informed adult's freedom to choose.

The Hammer actually smiled! I had learned my lesson. No more depressing talk of risk.

"Yes," the Hammer chuckled, still smiling. "*I'll take it.*"

And that was that.

But what happened to the trade, you ask?

Oh, yes, the trade. Interest rates kept declining, and prepayments kept speeding up. A few years later, the Hammer called me. His mortgage-backed holdings sustained several years of losses. For fiscal year-end March 1995, the losses were $200 million. He lost his lifetime job.

I offer these examples to show there is a way to carve up cash flows to meet any investor desire. Many Japanese banks benefited from the purchase of floating-rate tranches with high caps. Many global investors earned income unavailable to them with other investment alternatives. Some investors crave certainty and predictable income; others crave risky income. Human nature hasn't changed. We'll see the same pattern of risk profiles recreated with different instruments as this book describes the evolution of structured products.

Chapter 7

Early Warning Commercial Financial Services

RATING AGENCIES' FAILED MODELS

The proceedings of the criminal trial of Bill Bartmann (*United States of America v. William R. Bartmann*), after which he was acquitted, gives a textbook example of what securitization professionals, rating agencies, regulators, investors, and the management of investment banks should consider when performing due diligence. Yet, the same mistakes would be repeated in future asset-backed securitizations, particularly in the subprime mortgage market.

On October 21, 1998, Duff & Phelps Credit Rating Co. (DCR, now a part of Fitch) downgraded Commercial Financial Services' (CFS) securitizations six notches from single A to BB—from solidly investment grade to well below investment grade. DCR cited CFS's reliance on sales of the securitizations' assets to make payments due to investors. DCR suddenly had serious concerns about CFS's assumptions to make its cash flow payments. A couple of days later, Fitch IBCA lowered the rating of CFS's securitized transactions to CC, 10 notches below investment grade. It claimed it relied on CFS's representations that assets sales did not represent a significant amount of monthly collections, and it did no independent investigation of sales of which it was already aware. Moody's and S&P also downgraded the transactions below investment grade. Shortly thereafter, all of the rating agencies stopped rating CFS's securitizations.

The rating agencies were not reacting to their own initiative, even though the facts hid in plain sight. Instead they relied on the kindness of a stranger: a tip-off. In the early fall of 1998, the rating agencies received an anonymous letter concerning the cash flows of the securitizations issued by CFS. The letter alleged that about 20 percent of cash collections on assets for the securitizations came from asset sales, even though the securitizations were supposed to be static pools from which only assets on which collections were zero or not cost effective could be sold. Furthermore, the sales were made to a newly incorporated company called DIMAT Inc. and the officers of the company were unknown.

DIMAT seemed happy to pay two or three times the market rate for the assets, which were charged-off credit card receivables having little or no recovery value. The letter alleged that delinquent assets were reclassified as current by a single CFS officer during weekends. Yet DIMAT paid these high prices without performing any due diligence. The sales usually occurred on the last day of the month, just in the nick of time for CFS to meet the cash collection requirements for its securitizations. DIMAT was also happy to continue to pay fees to have CFS service these dead assets.

The fundamental basis for value in CDOs is the cash flow. The timing, frequency, magnitude, and probability of receipt of the cash flows are affected by a variety of factors. Just as in any financial transaction, common sense about who one is doing business with and one's ability to grasp the fundamentals of what is happening with the cash flows is key. Yet, time and again, deal sponsors/arrangers, rating agencies, regulators, and investors make the same mistakes. Cases related to CFS were litigated for years in the U.S. courts, and details were widely reported. To securitization professionals and rating agencies, CFS's securitization and rating problems are public knowledge.

Despite the lessons that should have been learned by the alleged fraud—and by earlier CDO problems—strikingly similar industry failures cropped up again in subsequent years with respect to securitizations by Enron, Parmalat, manufactured housing loans, metals receivables, furniture receivables, subprime and Alt-A deal arrangers, and a host of new deals currently in the market.

ANATOMY OF A FLAWED PROCESS

In 1986, Jay Jones co-founded Tulsa, Oklahoma–headquartered Commercial Financial Services, Inc. along with William R. Bartmann, the diminutive chairman and chief executive officer of CFS. Jones owned 20 percent of the company and Bartmann owned 80 percent.

During CFS's brief heyday, Bartmann was rumored to be one of the world's richest men, with estimates of his net worth ranging from $4 billion to $7 billion. It was flimsy paper wealth, yet Bartmann himself seemed to encourage the reports. He replicated a pattern of lavish excess, copied subsequently by others who would rise and fall in future financial debacles: Enron, RBG metals, Tyco, and more. Bartmann flew in the company's

Gulfstream G-IV and spent extravagantly when it came to parties designed for business promotion. According to the June 6, 2004, *New York Times Magazine,* he dressed as Julius Caesar at a bash attended by thousands in Las Vegas. Attendees were given $500 to gamble at the tables after being flown in on chartered Boeing 747s.

CFS initially bought nonperforming Federal Deposit Insurance Corporation (FDIC) loans made available by the savings and loan crisis in the United States at that time and by the depressed conditions in oil-producing states due to a decline in oil prices.

In 1995, CFS started concentrating on purchasing charged-off credit card receivables. It arranged forward-flow agreements to purchase an ongoing supply of charged-off credit card receivables with top financial institutions. CFS funded most of these purchases through nonrecourse warehousing lines. It then engaged in periodic securitizations as sponsor. Securitization proceeds paid down the warehousing debt and provided revenue for CFS's operations.

CFS ultimately issued approximately $2 billion of asset-backed securities collateralized primarily by charged-off credit card receivables.

TERMINOLOGY

Credit card receivables are unsecured revolving debt obligations, meaning a minimum balance must be paid each month in order for the accounts to be considered current. If an account were delinquent for approximately six months, the lender would charge off the account and record a loss for the entire remaining account balance.

The securitized assets were held in trust for the benefit of the *noteholders* or *certificate holders,* also called the investors. Although the trusts bought and sold the assets for the securitizations, CFS was the exclusive servicer of the assets. Servicing fees were a second source of income for CFS.

At the time of these events in credit card ABS transactions, *recovery* referred to the salvage value on a defaulted nonperforming asset, an asset on which no payment had been made for a period of about 150 to 180 days, depending on the lender. The receivable was charged off, and any cash raised due to a sale was a recovery. CFS's documentation allowed for sales of assets for recovery, but industry practice generally meant defaulted, not current paying assets.

When CFS sold assets, the trust sold assets under the direction of CFS as servicer. The assets were credit card loan balances, charged-off receivables from credit card consumers from which CFS expected to collect the remaining balance of outstanding payments owed. CFS retained the residuals, the cash remaining, if any, after all of the securitizations were paid off.

Assets were either performing or nonperforming. Obligors were not making payments on many of the acquired loans, and these were referred to as *nonperforming* loans. If CFS negotiated new payment terms with an obligor, the loan was reclassified as a conversion, since a nonperforming loan had been converted to a performing loan.

Performing assets are usually defined as assets on which payments are currently being made in pre-agreed amounts. CFS sometimes used the term *performing* even if payments had not been made in several months. To avoid confusion, I will use term *current paying* to indicate that payments were being made on a performing asset.

Nonperforming assets are usually defined as assets on which no payments are being made. Among nonperforming loans, there were loans that could be collected in the future if CFS could find the obligor and make a lump-sum settlement or negotiate new payment terms. Nonperforming loans also included loans on which there was little or no expectation of future cash collections.

The assets securitized by CFS were illiquid, and there was no public market in which one could independently verify their market value. CFS represented these as *static pool securitizations*. By definition, assets cannot be sold from static pool securitizations, although limited sales of defaulted, nonpaying, or charged-off assets were sometimes allowed to recover salvage value on those assets. Furthermore, the securitizations serviced by CFS were cash flow securitizations. The only money available to pay back investors was generated by the cash flow produced by the static pool of assets. The transactions had to be self-sustaining based solely on the cash flows derived from the assets in the portfolio.

CFS needed an investment-grade rating so it could access a larger universe of investors at a lower cost for the notes and certificates issued in its securitization program. The rating that the certificates or notes received depended on the probability that the cash flow would be sufficient to meet the obligations to the investors. Since the timing and magnitude of the asset cash flows in CFS's portfolios were uncertain, the rating agencies required a cash buffer in the form of the 3 percent reserve account. The rating agencies also required overcollateralization, ranging from 30 percent to 50 percent. These seemingly high overcollateralization rates may have lulled rating agencies and investors into a false sense of security.

The securitization trusts paid CFS's servicing fees and passed through to the investors principal and interest payments generated by cash flows of the underlying collateral. For these types of securitizations to be successful, the cash flow from the collateral pool had to cover all deal liabilities, including the interest and principal obligations from the notes issued by the securitization, CFS's servicing fees, and all other deal expenses. Furthermore, to secure an investment-grade rating, there has to be a high probability cash will cover all the expenses. Theoretically, with a single A rating, investors had a very low probability of experiencing a loss due to insufficient collections from obligors. To keep its single A rating, CFS had to:

- Convert enough nonperforming loans to performing loans.
- Collect on performing loans.
- Negotiate lump-sum settlements of sufficient value.

EARLY RED FLAGS

When there is a pre-established investment banking relationship, background checks on principals of securitization transactions are not routinely done. Before its relationship with a new investment bank that became its lead underwriter, CFS had a pre-existing banking/securitization relationship with a different investment bank. For whatever reason, more than a year after meeting Mr. Bartmann, the new lead underwriter hired an outside firm to do a background check.

Many years prior, Bill Bartmann had been involved with the distribution of securities in a failed oil venture. Although he was a lawyer, he failed to register the oil venture securities and failed to get a license to sell them, which resulted in the issuance of a cease-and-desist order against him. While the lead underwriter and CFS's lawyers didn't insist this information be included in future private placement memoranda, it is a matter of good business hygiene to do so. Investors can decide whether they feel Mr. Bartmann's past track record is relevant to his new business venture.

Meanwhile, the lead underwriter arranged sales of nonperforming consumer loans from its affiliated credit card bank and also gave CFS advice on potential structures and introduced CFS to other issuers.

By the late summer of 1996, the lead underwriter's asset-backed securities (ABS) group sought credit approval for a warehouse loan from its banking/lending arm, and a senior credit officer raised concerns that CFS presented a "classic situation for fraud." Bartmann and Jones were not well known. The loans were growing at a very fast rate, and it wasn't clear how money was being collected on the loans. The securitizations were priced at huge multiples of the purchase price based on optimistic forecasts of CFS's ability to collect money from debtors who had previously failed to make payments. There was no way to verify the assumptions, and bankers were asked to rely on the unproven company's performance. The cash flow schedules seemed confusing.

CFS's cost to service its portfolio of credit card receivables was higher than CFS had projected, and CFS's financial statements did not show a servicing liability for the excess costs. CFS underestimated servicing costs, even though CFS could have immediately verified them.

Arthur Andersen (later disbanded after its problems related to Enron's accounting) was CFS's accountant; a junior partner in the Tulsa office handled CFS's books. At this point, the investment bank could have asked for a *fraud audit*. A fraud audit doesn't mean you suspect someone of fraud, only that you want a rigorous verification of the assets and cash flows of a deal.

Instead, the lead underwriter seemed to believe Bartmann's explanation of how CFS was able to collect so much more than anyone else on charged-off credit card receivables. Basically, Bartmann claimed to be able to get people to pay their long-outstanding credit card debt because CFS was more charming and diligent than previous unsuccessful collectors.

The underwriter's lending arm accepted CFS's guarantee and accepted the residual, the excess cash—if any—after all liabilities and financial obligations are met, as collateral for the warehousing agreement it later entered into with CFS. Although the lead underwriter sponsored the special purpose entity borrower (the securitization warehouse), and although the residual is a leading indicator of the cash flow health of a securitization, neither it nor its lending arm independently valued the residual.

A few potential investors balked. There were no audits, no spot checks of the underlying data, no independent verification of the model. Charged-off credit card receivables were a new asset class, and three separate collection agencies had already attempted to collect on the receivables before they were sold to CFS. CFS's data seemed biased since it only considered performing assets, not all collections, which included nonperforming assets. Furthermore, CFS did not have much of a track record, since the business was still fairly new. Added to that, Arthur Andersen had not tested CFS's model for accuracy.

The rating agencies provided no comfort, either, despite assigning investment-grade ratings. For example, S&P used data from unsecured consumer loans as a proxy for charged-off credit card receivables, even though it was unclear these assets performed in the same way, and it had no specific data. As time went on and more data became available, the rating agencies did not pursue red flags suggesting data required thorough verification and auditing. While the rating agencies do not perform this function, they could have demanded that the work be done before they continued to rate securitizations.

CFS GETS CREATIVE

Just as today's mortgage-backed securities can be put back to mortgage bankers if there are breaches of representations and warranties, CFS could put back a percentage of charged-off credit card receivables, which would be repurchased by the sellers. CFS recorded the subsequent reimbursements by sellers as "resolved collections" on credit card loans. The reality was that this was a money-losing activity, since the repurchase price was disadvantageous. CFS purchased assets at an initial price and then sold them at a high premium to the securitization trusts. When assets were put back to the originator from which CFS purchased them, the price for the resale was the initial price, not the premium price. Yet these cash flows from puts were represented as collections from obligors rather than as turnaround sales that generated an immediate loss.

CFS's cash flow problems persisted.

SELLING OUT THE FUTURE

In order to raise cash to meet its stated base-case requirements, CFS began selling assets, including performing current paying assets, to a financial entity named Cadle at the beginning of 1997. Investors were not informed of these sales. In his criminal trial, Mr. Bartmann testified that the lead underwriter was "absolutely" aware of the sales, but the lead underwriter denied having this knowledge. By selling cash generating assets, CFS seriously jeopardized the viability of the securitization trusts.

In mid-January 1997, Mitchell Vernick, an external hire and a savvy financial professional, became CFS's new CEO. After only five months, he expressed concerns about the business model, resigned, and signed a nondisclosure agreement. He also received around $10 million in severance (later returned after the cash flow deficit was exposed). Vernick thought CFS's expenses were so high that CFS needed cash raised from new securitizations to meet expenses. He also thought CFS was selling loans at prices below the projected net present value of the loans' cash flows, and even so the securitizations would not even meet stress-case requirements. He doubted the investors could be repaid in full. This is the classic description of a Ponzi scheme: raising cash from new investors to subsidize payments to existing investors; if Mr. Vernick was correct, CFS's business model was unsustainable as it stood.

At Mr. Bartmann's suggestion, Mr. Vernick met over the next few days with members of senior management at CFS and with lawyers from Mayer

Brown Rowe & Maw (predecessor to Mayer Brown), but the discussions were not shared with investors. Mayer Brown was later named as a defendant in investor lawsuits, showing that law firms also need to be wary about client behavior, since they can be legally enmeshed in problems.

Mitchell Pacelle of the *Wall Street Journal* reported on Mayer Brown's involvement on October 29, 2002. Before Vernick resigned, Mayer Brown debriefed him, but continued to represent the company.

CFS engaged in a monoline business and had relatively inexperienced financial managers. It had lost its new CEO, an experienced financial professional who questioned CFS's operating model and the value of the trusts' assets. Yet, offering documents did not make this risk information clear.

IGNORING AN AUDIT REPORT

In August 1997, the lead underwriter received an independent audit report it had commissioned on one of CFS's securitizations. The report uncovered major problems with CFS's operations. CFS had stated its collections came from either (1) settlements, negotiated lump-sum settlements of the charged-off accounts; or (2) conversions, negotiated installment payment plans. But the audit report revealed red flags about CFS's representations. The cash flow picture presented by the report was indicative of a non-investment-grade transaction.

The auditor discovered that 3 out of 20 payments sampled—15 percent—came from assets that had subsequently been sold. Since the trust was a static pool, one would expect that the sales of current paying loans from this trust should have been zero. Bulk sales in general were a red flag and, based on CFS's representations to investors, one would not have expected to see the sale of current paying assets.

CFS informed the auditor that 15 of a separate sample of 20 "resolved loans"—75 percent of the sample—were put back to the seller. The trusts lost money on puts, whereas the term *resolved loans* might lead one to believe these puts were moneymakers instead of money losers. The auditor selected another sample of 20 loans from CFS's so-called performing loans; four of these loans were behind in payments. Two obligors were more than two months behind, and the two other obligors were more than a month behind. These four loans represented 20 percent of the performing loans sampled. Loans in the performing category were failing to perform as conversions, and it was not clear if these loans had become nonperforming.

The audit painted the picture of a cash flow disaster. But the lead underwriter stumbled over the truth, picked itself up, and moved on. The investment bankers later said they hadn't looked at the audit, which they themselves had commissioned after Mr. Vernick's resignation.

Cadle stopped buying CFS's assets in the summer of 1997. CFS's securitizations were still in critical need of cash flow. Instead of having the trusts sell performing assets, some of CFS's money was diverted to a shell corporation called DIMAT. DIMAT bought assets with low or no expected cash return, essentially worthless assets, at inflated prices from the securitization trusts. Money from new investors was used to make principal and interest payments to previous investors.

The premium paid by investors was indirectly used so that the shell company could pay inflated prices for the trust's assets. This made it appear that the securitizations were generating cash when in reality, investors were getting back some of their own money as if it were an investment return.

Cash flow shortfalls in the securitizations had a direct impact on the value of the residual held by CFS. In November 1997, CFS decided to restate the value of its residual interest in the securitizations, writing it down to zero to "be conservative," but it was probably worthless, even though CFS, its lead underwriter, and the rating agencies previously estimated the value of the residual as being hundreds of millions of dollars. Yet neither the rating agencies nor the lead underwriter demanded a rigorous audit to determine a new approximate value for the residual.

After the anonymous tip-off letter became public, it was learned that Mr. Bartmann (Bartmann noted this as a shareholder advance to Jones) and Mr. Jones sold shares of CFS stock to raise cash, and Mr. Jones transferred the cash either to Calamity Jones Entertainment or directly to DIMAT. Mr. Jones or Calamity Jones Entertainment then wired funds to DIMAT just in time to cover DIMAT's purchases of the assets from the securitization trusts.

LESSONS TO BE LEARNED

Financial institutions have to follow a standard of reasonable care, and the degree of care depends on the circumstances. Obviously, less due diligence is required when buying or selling U.S. treasuries than when buying or selling asset securitizations. Since some judgment calls are always involved, a financial institution must know with whom it is doing business. For example, if an issuer or asset originator is not well-known, a background check is warranted.

A key issue that persistently comes up today is *disclosure* or, to be more specific, lack of appropriate disclosure. Financial institutions must make full and honest disclosure of the potential risks of any transaction. Even sophisticated investors capable of doing their own due diligence have a right to demand this. All material information must be disclosed. The circumstances of each transaction, including the degree of risk involved, dictate the degree of investigation and disclosure required.

The global securities industry has a reasonable expectation of trust that, among other things, you will never conceal illegal conduct or even your suspicions of it or allow false representations to go unchallenged—or worse, affirm them, distribute materially misleading information orally or in writing or via any other means, or fail to disclose red flags. Boilerplate disclaimers do not absolve a deal arranger's or an underwriter's responsibility to disclose material information or to refute misleading information about the future performance of the securities.

Yet, as we shall see later, reruns of past mistakes are run on an endless loop in the global capital markets. All of the information presented here is taken from publicly available sources. Fortune, the Wall Street Journal, the New York Times, and other major publications all published pieces of this story. Tulsa news sources covered it much better and in much more detail. Bill Bartmann's criminal trial was public, and the detailed information was eye-popping. Yet we continue to make the same mistakes over and over. Rating agencies, sophisticated investors, investment banking deal arrangers, and lawyers cannot claim they do not know better. This is a partial recap of some of the lessons to be learned:

- Heed early warning signs, particularly those from experienced senior credit officers, by doing further investigation.
- Ask to see the initial background check done by the people who introduce you to the client. If there is none, commission one. If it reveals a past securities-related irregularity, investigate it. Fully disclose it in deal documentation.
- If costs exceed fees charged for services, investigate, and tie out all cash flows.
- If a model is untested and there is not enough relevant data to verify it, raise this red flag and then go back and recheck as more data is available. Ask for specifics about the preliminary assumptions used and document potential problems in the deal documentation. Clearly state that the model is a guess at best until proven otherwise.
- Hire a special auditor to check the cash flows on the assets, and do not rely on the issuer's representations for new asset classes, particularly fast-growing asset classes. If there is very little data at the beginning, do this again later in the timeline.
- If the issuer will not cooperate with this process, walk away.
- Do not rely on the rating agencies. They do not perform due diligence. They issue opinions, and your opinion—and your model—may be much

better informed than theirs, particularly when it comes to new asset classes.

- Do not rely on the lawyers, either. After Enron collapsed, the American Bar Association Task Force on Corporate Responsibility issued ethical guidelines, but these are only guidelines: "Permit the disclosure of client confidences to prevent or rectify the consequences of a crime or fraud likely to result in substantial economic injury, when a lawyer's services have been used to further the crime [emphasis mine]. Make such disclosure mandatory, rather than just permissible. Change the standard for assessing a lawyer's obligation to report a crime or fraud by a client so that lawyers aren't permitted to 'ignore the obvious.' Set up direct lines of communication between outside lawyers and corporate general counsels, through which outside lawyers could report potential legal violations." These guidelines give scant comfort about the behavior of some lawyers. Besides, are these your lawyers or someone else's lawyers? If you have lawyers, it is important to remember that you instruct them, not the other way around. They can opine on legal issues, but the business issues are up to you.
- If investment banks, rating agencies, and investors did not independently justify the price the issuer paid for new assets or the price at which it sold assets to the securitization vehicles, ask for this to be done. If this is impossible to do, and if you do not feel the assumptions are crystal clear, consider walking away.
- If an issuer writes down the value of a residual or equity to zero, consider believing it is accurate rather than "conservative." Do not take any equity valuation as accurate, since assumptions may be faulty. If there is no independent audit of the value performed by someone you trust, ask for one. If none is forthcoming, consider walking away.
- If key officers have recently left after a short stay, question them. There are many legitimate reasons officers leave, but if you do not understand the answers, or if the answers are vague, walk away.

FALLOUT FROM CFS'S BANKRUPTCY

On December 11, 1998, CFS filed for bankruptcy protection in the U.S. Bankruptcy Court for the Northern District of Oklahoma after its unsecured creditors threatened to file an involuntary bankruptcy petition.

Jones pleaded guilty to a single count of conspiracy as part of his agreement to testify against Bartmann. He was convicted and sentenced to five years in prison for his role; he was released in January 2007.

Mr. Bartmann resigned at the end of October 1998—just weeks before CFS declared bankruptcy. He claimed that he had no relationship with DIMAT, but that Mr. Jones did. He admitted that he "purchased shares" of Mr. Jones's stock totaling tens of millions of dollars. Mr. Bartmann claimed he failed to inform CFS about Jones's sale and his purchases until October 19, 1998. Perhaps Mr. Bartmann drank his own Kool-Aid. He hadn't sold his stock to outside investors when he had the chance, and he faced personal financial difficulties. He also faced a criminal trial. Bartmann claimed he knew nothing about Jones's DIMAT involvement, but he was indicted on various counts of conspiracy, bank fraud, mail fraud, wire fraud, and money laundering. In October 1999, *Fortune* magazine's Jerry Useem reported that Bartmann claimed he gave his money to Jones to buy more shares of a "worthless" company and said: "I didn't grab the loot and scoot." In his subsequent criminal trial, Bartmann was acquitted of all counts.

In the same article, *Fortune* reported that Bartmann was a difficult boss. Employees alleged Bartmann suggested the foreheads of every third person in the room be marked to "blow [their] fucking brains out." Bartmann has reinvented himself as a motivational speaker. His web site claims he can help improve your self-esteem if it is low from, say, having a "difficult" boss.

Chapter 8

Subprime and Alt-A Mortgages: Collateral Damage

Despite Commercial Financial Services's debacle, the market made many of the same mistakes again a few years later in the subprime mortgage market. In the intervening years, there had been similar market stumbles involving manufactured housing loan–backed deals, home equity loan–backed deals and investment-grade rated corporate CDOs, but the sub-prime debacle—which also encompassed risky mortgage loans made to more creditworthy borrowers—created ripple effects in the U.S. stock market and triggered a credit tightening in the consumer credit and corporate leveraged loan markets. It also made prime brokers and other lenders to hedge funds rethink the amount of leverage they allowed these borrowers to employ.

The subprime market developed for borrowers who have lower credit scores and traditionally have had more difficulty meeting the requirements for a home mortgage. Subprime borrowers typically had FICO scores below 650. These scores were developed by the Fair Isaac Corporation to provide rough guidelines of the credit capacity of consumers. It takes into account new credit, types of credit the borrower already uses, length of credit history, amount the borrower owes, and payment history. Most of the weight is placed on the last three attributes. It was estimated that 27 percent of borrowers had scores below 650, and only 12 to 20 percent in total might be eligible for subprime loans, since borrowers with very low credit scores might not meet other hurdles.

Subprime borrowers were often approved for loans even if they had debt-to-income (DTI) ratios of 40 percent or greater, had loan-to-value (LTV) ratios greater than 80 percent, had been delinquent on previous mortgages, had been bankrupt in the past three to five years, or had their homes foreclosed in the past three to five years.

At first it appeared that Fannie Mae (FNMA) and Freddie Mac (FHLMC), the privately chartered U.S. mortgage giants which are overseen by the department of Housing and Urban Development (HUD), deserved credit for their stance on the $1.5 trillion subprime mortgage market, but even they ended up with exposure to subprime loans, and they did not speak out strongly against the abuses in mortgage lending practices.

FNMA and FHLMC have general lending standards for *conforming* loans that both meet their lending size requirements and their origination guidelines. Both entities prefer loans where the income of the borrower has been verified, the total housing cost including insurance and fees is no more than 28 percent of gross income, the borrower's total debt burden is less than 36 percent of gross income, the borrower does not have an excessive history of late payments, the borrower has his own funds for the down payments and closing costs, the borrower has two years of job stability, and the borrower has a cash cushion of at least two months of payments after all living expenses have been met. Even with all of these belts and braces, FNMA and FHLMC are concerned about this class of loans because of potential softening of the U.S. economy and a slowing and at times negative growth rate of housing prices.

But by April 2007, Richard Syron, CEO of Freddie Mac, said Freddie Mac would *no longer* buy:

- No income, no asset (NINA) loans.
- Loans not underwritten at the fully amortized rate.
- Loans that did not take into account insurance or property taxes

Syron also said Freddie Mac wanted to take care of people who are in a difficult position with more consumer-friendly loans yet have fair programs for the lender. But what if the lenders were not fair to the consumer in the first place? He claimed it was not "not fair" to call this a "bailout," since historically that means bailing out lenders. Instead, Freddie Mac would give people an opportunity—if they are in an adverse product—to refinance into a more consumer-friendly product which may be a fixed-rate product.

The most difficult vintages are the 2005, 2006, and 2007 originations. Even though the coupons had not yet reset, they were defaulting at unprecedented rates. That suggested something very odd had been occurring with these originations. Unless modification costs and associated losses were pushed onto the lenders that had originated bad products—or, if the mortgages had been sold, the investment banks and investors who bought them—the rescue would most definitely have the effect of bailing out the lenders, investment banks, and investors.

Freddie Mac has three responsibilities. It has a mission to the household public in the United States; it is responsible to its regulator, the Office of Federal Housing Enterprise Oversight (OFHEO), for safety and soundness of the mortgages; and it has a responsibility to its shareholders to handle its mission in a way that is advantageous to the shareholders, if possible.

Freddie Mac does not have a mission to protect other mortgage lenders, particularly mortgage lenders that might benefit from having damaged the U.S. mortgage market with lax underwriting standards and risky products. Freddie Mac does not have a mission to bail out sophisticated investment banks or sophisticated investors in CDOs.

Mortgage-backed securities rely on two factors: (1) the quality of the origination (i.e., the soundness of the original loan, the quality of the underlying collateral, and the equity in the home) and (2) the ongoing servicing of the loan (i.e., the procedures for the collection of payments from homeowners).

The biggest risk associated with subprime mortgages has nothing to do with the sophistication of one's model and has everything to do with common sense, specifically the type of common sense that helps us decide whether a borrower is a good credit risk or whether we are enabling the borrower into overleveraging his position. Yet even though their policies suggested FNMA and FHLMC refused to purchase loans that did not meet their standards, and that they rejected loans originated by mortgage brokers known for predatory lending practices, it seemed that they had purchased some very dodgy loans and then later got involved in an expensive bailout which they preferred to call a "rescue" lest U.S. taxpayers, the ultimate bag holders, would take notice and protest.

By summer 2007, James Lockhart of OFHEO said that FNMA and FHLMC bought $170 billion of triple-A tranches of subprime residential mortgage-backed securities. It was not clear whether these included toxic triple-A tranches of subprime-backed CDOs, which would have been a huge favor for the entity from which they purchased these securities, since these AAA tranches had substantial principal risk. Even AAA tranches of RMBSs such as deals that included more than 60 percent of loans from a mortgage lender with alleged fraud would have substantial principal risk. In addition, FNMA and FHLMC planned $40 billion of rescue mortgages, an undisputable bailout.

Among other problems with the bailout, it would not be enough. By July 2007, I estimated subprime loan losses could reach $300 billion by the time all of the coupons reset, but the Fed—apparently using numbers supplied by Wall Street—only projected $50 billion to $100 billion in losses (Credit Suisse First Boston had issued a report saying losses would be $54 billion, and Citigroup had issued a report saying losses would be $100 billion). Yet the U.S. Senate Finance Committee had stated that each foreclosure cost stakeholders $80,000, and RealtyTrac estimated defaults for the first half of 2007 at 926,000 (including delinquencies), so $54 billion would have only covered losses for the first half of 2007, and there were many more losses to come.

If only 30 percent of the $1.5 trillion subprime market defaulted, not to mention defaults on Alt-A[1] and prime mortgages, the situation could be much worse than that projected by Wall Street. In July 2007 Countrywide reported its earnings had nosedived due to losses on *prime* mortgages, due to lax underwriting and risky products. By July 2007, I felt $300 billion in losses was probable, and perhaps even too low. Furthermore, FHMLC and FNMA were achieving very low recovery rates, sometimes in the low single digits.

Purchasers of mortgage-backed securities that have not been issued by FNMA or FHLMC need to pay careful attention to what they are getting, because many mortgage lenders had engaged in a race to the bottom when it came to creating worst practices in mortgage lending. Mortgage brokers originated 70 percent of subprime loans. Some adhered to prudent self-imposed underwriting guidelines, but most did not. By March 2007, according to *The Mortgage Lender*, since the end of 2006, of the top 25 subprime lenders, 5 had been shut down, 3 no longer operated independently, 7 announced large write-downs, and 1 was up for sale. According to Implode-o-Meter, the web site started by Aaron Krowne that provides a surprisingly good chronicle of recent events in the troubled U.S. mortgage lending market (http://ml-implode.com), from late 2006 to July 2007, 100 major U.S. mortgage lenders had gone "kaput." The number continues to climb. This is an unprecedented failure rate.

Subprime and Alt-A mortgages (Alternative-A mortgages made to borrowers with the next tier up in credit scores) are being hit by a quadruple whammy: poor loan underwriting standards, creation of mortgage loan products unsuitable for lower credit score borrowers, the decline—in some areas, the *reversal*—in home price appreciation (HPA), and slower economic growth.

These failing mortgages have found their way into collateralized debt obligations (CDOs), and the normal benefits of securitization are failing to provide protection. This is partly due to the up-front lending practices, and partly due to voluntary due diligence failures, particularly in securitizations sold as private placements, 144A deals. Investors include insurance companies, foreign central banks, mutual funds, hedge funds, and pension funds.

TRUTHINESS IN LENDING AND BORROWING

Subprime borrowers tend to be less sophisticated and include a higher percentage of minorities. Unscrupulous lenders prey on the relative naiveté of these borrowers. This isn't a new problem, but like the overheated lending to hedge funds, the subprime market overheated around the beginning of

2005, and we are seeing the effects.

In the early days of this century, First Alliance Mortgage Company (FAMCO) was taken to task for fraud on borrowers, most of whom were subprime borrowers. Origination fees of 10 to 25 percent of the loan value were misrepresented as being part of the interest rate and monthly payments. Low initial teaser rates were said to be constant unless market interest rates increased, but in reality rates could climb up to one percentage point every six months irrespective of market rates. The "amount financed" should have disclosed the full amount, but did not include the high origination fees, and borrowers were not given a booklet that would explain the adjustable rate mortgages (ARMs) as required by the Truth in Lending Act (TILA).

Even if borrowers remained unscathed during origination, servicing and collection abuses abounded. Borrowers had been promised better terms in future that never materialized. Unjustified servicing fees were added to collection amounts. ARM payments calculations were inflated and difficult to interpret on statements.

To preclude class action lawsuits, the subprime mortgage documentation included language that required mandatory arbitration.

Today, purchasers of subprime mortgages complain about fraud on lenders, instead of fraud on borrowers. Some borrowers, often in collusion with unscrupulous brokers, supply phony documentation or engage in identity theft. Lenders have a right to complain about this type of fraud, even if their own due diligence standards could be tightened. If some of the mortgage loans have minimal documentation, are stated-income "liar" loans, are option ARMS, have low teaser rates, or have high loan-to-value ratios, those facts must be disclosed in the documents.

Predatory lending practices currently pose the biggest problem in the subprime market. While many of these practices are not technically illegal, they employ truthiness in lending. *Comedy Central's* Stephen Colbert defines *truthiness* as "what you want the facts to be, as opposed to what the facts are; what feels like the right answer as opposed to what reality will support." Very few states currently have predatory lending laws, but the handful include Georgia, Massachusetts, New Jersey, New Mexico, and New York. Other states have a variety of lending laws, and California, Illinois, Florida, Michigan, and Ohio are tightening standards, with many other states saying they will follow suit. Congress is considering federal legislation, and the SEC is investigating asset-backed sales practices.

In contrast to the standards required by Fannie Mae and Freddie Mac, many mortgage brokers offered no-income-verification or *stated-income* loans, making loans with very little documentation. Abuse was rife, and these loans earned the nickname "liar loans." Borrowers were often allowed to take out piggyback loans—that is, second liens—on their homes in order to fund down payments so that 100 percent of the home value was financed. Existing homeowners were targeted for refinancing so that brokers could earn more fees and to generate prepayment charges in a practice known as *rent seeking*.

Some of the loan products seemed to set up low credit score borrowers for failure. Mortgage brokers offered 40-year or 45-year ARMs in which homeowners built up virtually no equity in their homes in the early years of the mortgages.

Hybrid ARMs would have a fixed *teaser* coupon for a set period, and then would reset to a much higher rate. A 30-year maturity 2/28 ARM would have a fixed teaser rate for 2 years and then reset to an adjustable rate for the remaining 28 years. Furthermore, 3/27 and 5/25 ARMS were often common, and of course the maturities could be longer than 30 years. Teaser rates and the potential increase in payments due upon resetting to an adjustable rate were often unclear, so that homeowners were unaware how much and how quickly the coupons would increase.

Option ARMs offered the worst-case scenario. Homeowners could choose initial payments that were so low, the payments did not even cover the interest costs on the loan. The uncovered interest was added to the loan balance. These homeowners experienced *negative amortization*. As the song goes, these homeowners got "another day older and deeper in debt." But that wasn't the worst of it. In some areas, home prices declined. Homeowners now had homes that were worth less while their mortgage balances were higher and climbing.

Truthiness in borrowing in the Alt-A mortgage market has also contributed to this problem. In this market there is a greater tendency for borrowers to purchase multiple dwellings with little or no money down. Products such as option ARMs—with coupons that reset to much higher interest payments and allow for increasing balances on the loan (if payments are insufficient to cover the new interest amount owed) in areas where housing prices are flat or falling—almost guarantee that borrowers will end up in "upside-down" mortgages, in which the amount owed is more than the value of the house.

THE PREDATORS FALL

Given that Fannie Mae and Freddie Mac limited buying of subprime mortgages, and given that many banks would not extend credit without sufficient documentation, predatory lending practices thrived outside the channels of mainstream mortgage financing. Lax standards were enabled by investors' voluntary due diligence failures in the asset-backed securitization market, particularly the 144A market for securitizations and real estate investment trusts (REITs).

Mortgage lenders turned to investment banks for financing. Investment banks extended credit lines, so that mortgage lenders could originate subprime mortgages outside of traditional banking channels. Some investment banks even purchased subprime lending businesses, either in full or in part. For example, in 2006, Morgan Stanley bought subprime lender and servicer Saxon Capital for $706 million, and Merrill Lynch bought National City Corp.'s First Franklin subprime unit for $1.3 billion in 2006. Merrill also had a part interest in now bankrupt Ownit Mortgage Solutions and was a creditor—along with UBS, Bank of America, and Bear Stearns, among others—of New Century, a subprime lender that filed for Chapter 11 bankruptcy protection on April 2, 2007.

What's more, Barclays announced on April 2, 2007, that it had closed its purchase of subprime lender EquiFirst Corporation and, according to the *Wall Street Journal,* it paid "only $76 million—one third of the $225 million Barclays had agreed to pay in January."

After mortgage lenders originated mortgage loans with the help of money borrowed from investment banks, investment banks warehoused the mortgages, repacked them into mortgage-backed securitizations, and sold the repackaged and tranched risk to investors. These investors included insurance companies, foreign central banks, REITs, mutual funds, pension funds, bank portfolios, hedge funds, and others. It shouldn't be a surprise to learn that hedge funds were net buyers of the higher-yielding, riskier tranches in 2005, but by the latter part of 2006, hedge funds had become net sellers. Some hedge funds engaged in a lucrative strategy of going long the equity or first-loss tranche while shorting the mezzanine tranche and keeping the excess spread in a CDO. The savviest hedge funds, however, simply shorted the ABX index.

Securitizations tout protections for investors. Documentation usually includes reps and warranties and recourse and collateral substitution rights. For example, if housing appraisals are found to be inflated or if the borrower quickly defaults, the investment bank has the right to put the loans back to the mortgage broker from which it bought the mortgages. Credit enhancements include subordination, excess spread, overcollateralization, and credit wraps. So what could possibly go wrong with mortgage-backed securitizations?

Well, for one thing, circular credit logic began to fall apart. Investment banks that securitized deals asked mortgage lenders to buy back loans. But investment banks themselves had provided credit lines to these mortgage lenders, and during the latter part of 2006 and the first half of 2007, the investment banks slowed the gushing flow of credit to a trickle. The mortgage lenders were having a hard time coming up with the money to buy back mortgages, and often they simply could not, resulting in the wave of mortgage implosions revealed by *The Mortgage Lender.* The founders of the mortgage brokers paid themselves well, and investment banking securitization groups earned high fees.

CLASSIC PONZI SCHEME

When it became clear that mortgage lenders were not viable and needed credit lines fueled by revenues from new investors to buy loans that did not meet requirements from old deals with old investors, continued securitization of these problem loans was questionable. If one defines a classic Ponzi scheme as using money from new investors to pay obligations to existing investors, the lending relationship between investment banks and failing mortgage lenders had devolved into just that. In fact, it had devolved into the largest Ponzi scheme in the history of the capital markets, as shown in Figure 8.1.

While the business activity may not have started out as a Ponzi scheme, the business model of the mortgage lenders was shaky at best. Once the break-even Ponzi point was reached—the point at which the business model was not sustainable without borrowings whose ultimate source was the new investors in securitizations of the problem loans—investment banks knew or should have known that thorough due diligence on this business activity was

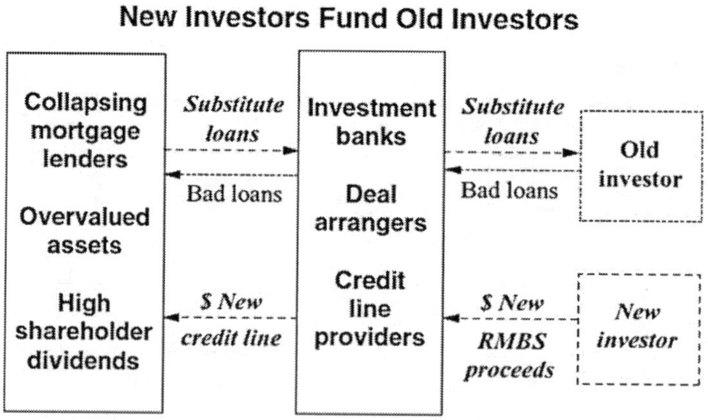

FIGURE 8.1 Largest Ponzi Scheme in Capital Markets' History

required. Many investment banks had helped mortgage lenders issue initial public offerings (IPOs) and had even made investments in mortgage lenders either through equity investments or through credit lines. Furthermore, many banks and investment banks accumulated these risky loans in warehouses awaiting securitization and sale to investors. The loans were securitized into residential mortgage-backed securities (i.e., were often subsequently used as part of collateral for portfolios backing collateralized debt obligations and CDO-squared products—resecuritizations of tranches of other CDOs. If the risk posed by the original underlying loans is underestimated, the errors are compounded and magnified with each subsequent securitization.).

Many investment banking financing arms lost money due to credit lines extended to failed mortgage lenders or pulled their credit lines to avoid losses, yet warehoused loans were securitized and sold to other investors without thorough scrutiny. Subprime mortgage borrowers became delinquent in payments and defaulted on loans in record numbers in 2007, and investors in mortgage-backed securities backed by subprime mortgages found their portfolio values plummeted.

If an investor is required to mark its portfolio to market, a lot can go wrong, and it can go wrong rapidly. Losses in the underlying mortgage portfolio do not have to cause a principal loss to cause a mark-to-market loss. As subordination and other credit protections are challenged, tranches are perceived to be higher credit risks long before the rating agencies have a chance to revise their ratings. Second-market liquidity dries up, spreads widen, and prices of even highly rated tranches drop dramatically.

Investors who bought lower-rated tranches experienced actual losses. Usually, RMBSs had only around 6 percent subordination below the triple-A level. Including other structural protections such as overcollateralization, investors in BBB– tranches could sustain cumulative losses of only 9 to 11 percent before losing principal. I estimated that subprime foreclosures would peak at 30 percent, and recoveries would fall to unprecedented lows: 30 percent and even lower in distressed zip codes. It is highly probable that principal losses will touch the BBB– tranches, and higher-rated mezzanine tranches of deals with high proportions of subprime mortgages will also probably lose principal. Many deals issued in late 2006 and 2007 experienced events of default by the end of 2007. AAA-rated tranches of poorly constructed CDOs and CDO-squared products have experienced substantial principal loss for deals that unwound and liquidated collateral, recovering as little as 25 percent of portfolio value in an illiquid market.

PORTFOLIO RISK

Not all CDOs, even CDOs with subprime collateral, are in trouble. Pre-2006 vintage deals include many that are fairly robust. A few mortgage brokers employ best practices when it comes to subprime mortgages. If you are an investor and you have the 144A documentation for your mortgage-backed securities and CDOs, check the disclosure. These documents must disclose material information. If some of the mortgage loans have minimal documentation, are stated-income "liar" loans, are option ARMS, have low teaser rates, or have high loan-to-value ratios, those facts must be disclosed in the documents. Private placements, 144A deals, are marketed to sophisticated investors who are responsible for doing their own due diligence. Since many investors competed for product, they often did not scrutinize these deals very carefully, but jumped into the market to purchase these products without demanding better documentation on the underlying loans. Investors that engaged in voluntary due diligence failures will find little sympathy. But if material information was not disclosed, that is a separate issue with potential remedies. Such investors may have thought the initially slightly higher coupons compensated them for the additional risk, even if it hasn't worked out that way.

For example, if the documents state that underwriting criteria is not available for a large percentage of the mortgage loans (one deal showed documentation was unavailable for 79 percent of the loans), it is too late to wonder why the deal was purchased in the first place. It is too late to question how the rating agencies are evaluating these deals. You very likely already own a problem, and you had the means of knowing you were at risk. Any collateral acquired through mortgage brokers and non-originators, with no information about the underwriting guidelines of the originator, is risky collateral.

THE RISK MANAGERS' DILEMMA

An investment bank's risk manager's ability to address the issues presented by subprime mortgages doesn't hinge on one's mathematical ability, the size of one's database, or the elegance of one's models. The problem is power. Risk managers usually do not have very much of it.

Even Fed Chairman Ben Bernanke has problems. Ben Bernanke has appeared on national television admonishing lenders to apply tighter standards. The problem is that the Fed regulates the investment banking arms of commercial banks like JPMorgan Chase and Bank of America, but it does not regulate investment banking/brokerage firms such as Merrill Lynch, Lehman Brothers, Morgan Stanley, and the like, and it does not regulate independent mortgage lenders.

If Ben Bernanke has problems getting the market to exercise common sense, risk managers may have an even bigger problem. According to the *New York Times,* Mike Blum, Merrill Lynch's head of global asset-backed finance, sat on the board of Ownit Mortgage Solutions. He faxed in his resignation when it imploded. Ownit made second-lien mortgages, issued 45-year ARMs, and originated no-income-verification loans. In the words of William D. Dallas, its founder and CEO: "The market is paying me to do a no-income-verification loan more than it is paying me to do the full documentation loans."

It would have been a career-cratering move for a risk manager to limit the credit line that the investment bank extended to the mortgage broker, because the bank's asset securitization group was earning high fees for securitizing the broker's subprime mortgages. Questioning the wisdom of the investment banking/mortgage broker relationship would have been career suicide.

The same could be said of many investment banks, since Merrill Lynch was not alone in continuing to securitize risky loans without stressing that the ratings provided by the rating agencies were no longer relevant for most CDOs. The other major players in subprime aggregation included Lehman Brothers; Bear, Stearns & Co.; Union Bank of Switzerland; Credit Suisse First Boston; Morgan Stanley; RBS Greenwich Capital; and Deutsche Bank.

HOW TO CREATE A SECURITIZATION DISASTER

Thinly capitalized mortgage brokers popped up across the U.S. landscape. By the end of 2006, more than 10 were in serious financial difficulty. In the period beginning in late 2006 until early July 2007, the bankruptcies accelerated until 92 mortgage bankers had either declared bankruptcy and shuttered their doors or were in serious financial difficulty.

Many mortgage lenders got the money to stay in business primarily from commercial banks and investment banks who lent them money to lend out to borrowers purchasing homes. The primary sources of income for the self-paid mortgage lenders were the fees from originating the mortgages, fees from homeowners' refinancing existing mortgages, fees from homeowners' taking out second mortgages, servicing these mortgagees, and any add-on they could earn when selling the mortgages on to investment banks and banks that had lent the mortgage lenders the money to stay in business in the first place. The more mortgages the mortgage lenders could crank into the system, the more money they made. The mortgage lenders usually worked with unregulated brokers whose commissions were based on how many mortgages they could pump into the system.

The brokers and mortgage lenders had an incentive to let underwriting standards slip, to let documentation standards slip, and to encourage homeowners to refinance their homes. They had a further incentive to introduce products that had apparently low payment rates but ramped up later. Some borrowers were lured by greed into mortgages like option ARMs and/or the purchase of multiple properties that they could not subsequently afford, especially when housing prices halted their high rates of increase. Other borrowers were deceived either by a missold mortgage or by their own lack of understanding about mortgages whose payments would unexpectedly ramp up to a level the borrower could not afford based on their foreseeable ability to pay.

Investment banks and commercial banks lent money to the mortgage lenders, usually through a warehouse line of credit. At any given time, multiple banks and investment banks were extending credit to an individual mortgage lender. The *warehouse* is simply a special purpose entity that accumulates the loans until there are enough assets to back a collateralized debt obligation. Theoretically, if loans violated their representations and warranties, were found to be fraudulent, or stopped payment within a specified time period—it varied, but 90 days is a popular time frame—the warehouse or the CDO manager/administrator could ask the mortgage lender to repurchase the loans.

But mortgage lenders were using most of the fees they earned for their expenses and to handsomely pay their officers. They usually did not have a huge reserve of working capital to buy back a lot of loans if the loans were put back to them. Many mortgage lenders relied on the fact that they had multiple credit lines so that they would have the ability to repurchase shaky loans.

If there is no source of income other than the business that got a borrower into financial difficulty in the first place, then borrowing from one lender in order to meet one's obligations to another lender is the classic formula for a Ponzi scheme.

The following example is typical of the type of problems faced by the mortgage securitization business. In 2005, Mortgage Investment Lending Associates (MILA), a 300-employee mortgage business, funded at least $4.5 billion in mortgages, which placed it among the top 30 U.S. subprime lenders. MILA had a so-called proprietary model that supposedly determined whether borrowers were good loan risks.

MODELS VERSUS COMMON SENSE

Even the Fed implied that things were sound in the mortgage market. The following is an excerpt from Alan Greenspan's address to the Federal Reserve System's Fourth Annual Community Affairs Research Conference in Washington, D.C., on April 8, 2005:

> *With these advances in technology, lenders have taken advantage of credit-scoring models and other techniques for efficiently extending credit to a broader spectrum of consumers. The widespread adoption of these models has reduced the costs of evaluating the creditworthiness of borrowers, and in competitive markets cost reductions tend to be passed through to borrowers. Where once more-marginal applicants would simply have been denied credit, lenders are now able to quite efficiently judge the risk posed by individual applicants and to price that risk appropriately. These improvements have led to rapid growth in subprime mortgage lending; indeed, today subprime mortgages account for roughly 10 percent of the number of all mortgages outstanding, up from just 1 or 2 percent in the early 1990s.*
>
> *For some consumers, however, this reliance on technology has been disconcerting. Credit-scoring models are complex algorithms designed to predict risk. Consumer advocates have raised concerns about the transparency and completeness of the information fit to the algorithm, as well as the rigidity of the types of data used to render credit decisions. Consumer advocates contend that the lack of flexibility in the models can result in the exclusion of some consumers, such as those with little or no credit history, or misrepresentation of the risk that they pose.*
>
> *To address these concerns, some firms have worked to customize credit-scoring systems to include new data and to revalue the weight of the variables employed. Also, new organizations have emerged, developing new systems for collecting alternative data, such as rent payments and other recurring payments that will enable creditors to evaluate creditworthiness of consumers who lack experience with credit.*

The Fed chairman's remarks seemed unreasonably complacent in light of consumer lending problems in the late 1990s and the early part of the twenty-first century. Just as in the CFS debacle, the rating agencies and even the Fed were prepared to rely on untested models to assess the ability of borrowers—with little credit history, poor credit history, or no credit history—to pay. Even worse, the motivations and the viability of thinly capitalized mortgage lenders was not challenged. The slippage in underwriting standards was not challenged. The emergence of loan products unprecedented in the risk they posed also remained unchallenged.

When MILA declared bankruptcy in the early summer of 2007, its Chapter 11 bankruptcy petition listed less than $8 million in assets and $174.7 million in liabilities. MILA's total contingent liabilities, the value of the loans that securitizations could put back to it within a given time period (usually 90 days) if the loans fail to perform, were not listed.

MILA's filing has more than 200 creditors and $98.7 million in secured debt. Among its creditors for its $76 million in *unsecured* debt were Bear Stearns ($21 million), GMAC/RFC ($10.5 million), Goldman Sachs Mortgage ($6.8 million), and others with multimillion-dollar claims: Wachovia Mortgage, Deutsche Bank, Countrywide Home Loans, and Indymac Bank. All of them wanted MILA to repurchase substandard mortgages, but since no one was lending money to MILA, the creditors were stuck. By the time MILA filed for bankruptcy, more than 90 other mortgage lenders were in similar trouble.

Since the rating agencies rate securitizations assuming that the mortgage bankers can repurchase problematic loans, a key link in the money chain has been broken. Obviously, MILA could not make good on the repurchases. The only way it could have stayed in business was if its circle of lenders continued to extend credit, but the lenders had finally decided that the financially explosive situation, which they themselves had enabled, had exploded.

Given the history of the securitization market, is it even remotely plausible that banks and commercial banks did not know they needed to do more due diligence on the integrity of the loans themselves and on the mortgage lenders and brokers, and that providing credit lines to thinly capitalized mortgage lenders with incentives to cut corners could lead to a classic securitization disaster? The problems in the subprime market mirrored those of CFS. This was not a new problem at all; it was simply a repeat of a classic problem. The difference here is that instead of a rogue at CFS hiding cash flow problems, there were many rogues. The securitization market had a Ponzi rash.

Since the rating agencies once again fell down on the job, the CDO arbitrage appeared to be very lucrative, but the reality is that had the rating agencies examined the situation more carefully, much of the underlying collateral would have been identified as the soon-to-default junk that it really was. The rating agencies played with models without carefully examining

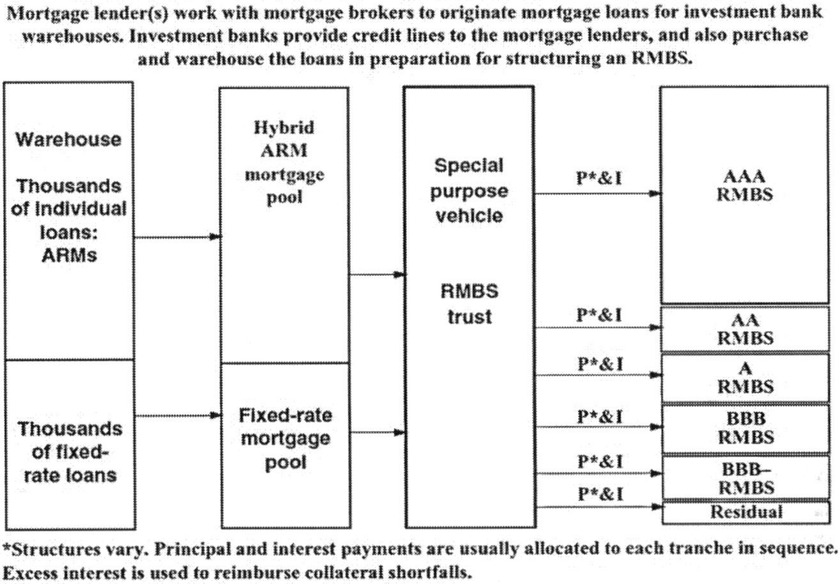

FIGURE 8.2 Residential Mortgage-Backed Securities

what it was they were modeling. Garbage in led to garbage out—to the investors, who in some cases voluntarily failed to do due diligence, and in other cases were misled. The rating agencies were broken when it came to rating most of the subprime, Alt-A, and even some of the prime mortgage market.

Securitizations came in many forms: mortgage-backed bonds, CDOs, CDOs comprised of tranches of CDOs, single-tranche (also known as bespoke) CDOs, hybrid CDOs,* and combinations based on the newly formed indexes.

Figure 8.2 illustrates a typical structure for subprime-backed residential mortgage-backed securities.

Interest is paid sequentially to the bonds but is capped at the weighted average mortgage rate (the net weighted average coupon also known as the WAC) net of deal expenses. This is the available funds cap (AFC). Excess interest can be used to make up for actual collateral losses, if any, and is only then used to make up for any shortfall if the net WAC is lower than the stated bond coupons. After that, any excess interest goes to the residual

*Hybrid CDOs are usually managed deals in which managers try to exploit relative value between the cash and synthetic markets, at least in theory.

bond holder unless some of the excess is allocated to a reserve account. Since many RMBSs are floating-rate bonds, if interest rates rise before ARMs reset, there is danger of an AFC shortfall if the stated bond coupon rises above the net WAC. If excess interest is eroded because coupons rise during the fixed payment period, there will likely be an AFC shortfall. If borrowers cannot meet higher payment requirements at the time the coupons reset, and if they begin defaulting, the AFC shortfalls will be unrecoverable.

Structured finance CDOs obtain credit enhancement from subordination, excess spread, sequential interest payments, sequential principal payments, overcollateralization, and sometimes guarantees by monolines. Customized single-tranche CDOs (bespoke tranches—see also Chapter 14) receive their credit enhancement solely from subordination based on the attachment point of the particular tranche.

Structured finance CDOs can have portfolios that are diversified among market sectors, but many structured finance CDOs concentrated in subprime-backed RMBSs in late 2005, 2006, and early 2007. The funding that the investment banks provided for the mortgage lenders was generated by this process of creating structured finance CDOs. Figure 8.3 shows

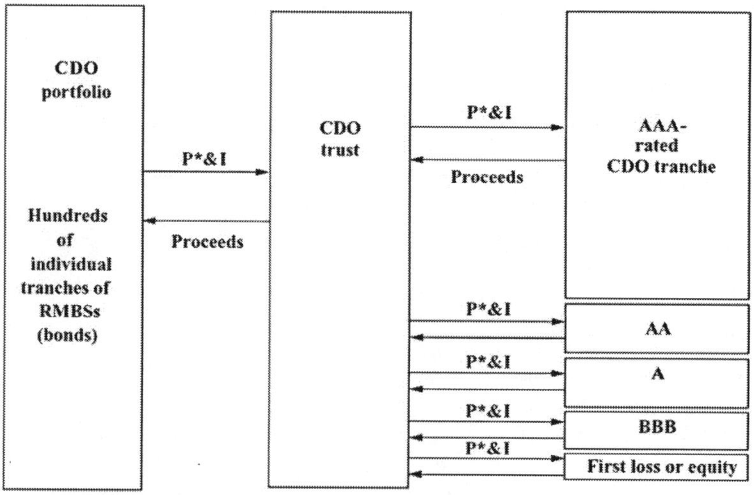

*Structures vary; deal terms vary. Principal and interest payments are allocated to each tranche in sequence. Excess interest is used to reimburse collateral shortfalls, but cash flows may be diverted, if allowed.

FIGURE 8.3 CDO Backed by Subprime-Backed RMBS

an example of a structured finance CDO backed by subprime loan-backed residential mortgage-backed bonds. This particular structure is backed by cash bonds, but later we will see bespoke and hybrid structures using credit derivatives technology to transfer risk. Bespoke structures were employed by certain hedge funds, since they could create cash flow advantages for themselves, as we will see in Chapter 14.

Static deals are usually fully ramped up when a deal closes, so principal repayments are used to amortize the senior notes, beginning with the AAA-rated notes.

Managed deals may need further purchases to accumulate collateral after the deal closes, and principal payments are usually reinvested for a specified period, usually three to six years. Managers may try to trade to maintain or improve credit quality, but if the deal deteriorates, it may become a static deal. The bank arrangers or the asset manager warehoused the bonds prior to issuing the CDO notes. When the warehouse had accumulated anywhere from 50 to 85 percent of the target portfolio, the CDO issued the notes. The portfolio was completely ramped up to its final size within six months. During the initial stages, unacceptable loans could be put back to the mortgage lender, provided the mortgage lender was still in business and provided it had the funds with which to buy back the loans. If investment banks cut off its lines of credit, the mortgage lender could not repurchase bad loans.

As the subprime crisis worsened, rating agencies attempted to rerate some securities, but even the rerating was badly flawed. The problem is that historically in supposedly good deals—and there have not been many of them in recent years—you start paying down the higher-rated tranches as the deal ages. When lower tranches start being downgraded, if your upper tranches are nearly gone, they are not downgraded, since they are almost paid down anyway.

Loans that were originated in 2006 and 2007 posed new and unique problems for the rating agencies. RMBS prospectuses disclosed that a significant number of loans included "exceptions" to underwriting "standards," but there was little detail about what that actually meant with respect to the ultimate quality of the loans. Loans began defaulting within a few months of origination, years before the dreaded coupon resets would occur. Furthermore, prepayments would drop in speed since refinancing options were limited due to falling housing prices. Subprime average delinquencies are even greater than they appeared because subprime delinquencies are usually counted one month late relative to prime mortgages.

This was and remains a mess. The deals were overrated, overpriced, and incorrectly structured at the outset. The rating agencies lacked data to make good, educated guesses, and they copped out by downgrading only the lower tranches, but this was obviously incomplete and incorrect. They hid behind their opinion to mask this sleight of hand.

The rating agencies are quick to publicly excuse themselves. *Bloomberg* reported that at a June 5, 2007, investor conference, Claire Robinson, a managing director at Moody's, said "People are surprised there haven't been more downgrades. What they don't understand about the rating process is that we don't change our ratings on speculation about what's going to happen."

Public statements by rating agencies as of this writing struck me as self-serving and irresponsible. Rating agencies claimed they were misunderstood, since investors needed to realize that ratings did not have anything to do with liquidity. It is true that ratings should have nothing to do with liquidity when interest rates rise or when there is a general credit spread widening, causing prices to fall, causing a subsequent decline in liquidity. In those cases, investors expect to sell at a loss. Investors can even expect that complex products may have less liquidity than simple products, because it will take longer for other investors to evaluate them, albeit the price may not necessarily suffer. But investors do not expect that liquidity will be impaired because the initial ratings were incorrect from the start. Failure to consider a material change in the quality of the collateral is simply a failure to correctly do the job.

LACK OF APPROPRIATE DUE DILIGENCE AND/OR DISCLOSURE

The primary key to a statistics-based model is to understand what one is modeling in the first place. The three Nationally Recognized Statistical Rating Agencies, the NRSROs most involved with rating these securitizations, failed the basics. They unabashedly repeated their past mistakes. Had the rating agencies fully understood the collateral, then they might have refused to rate certain deals. If, however, I am in error and they did indeed understand the collateral, the problem is not one of statistics. In that case the rating agencies would have to be cynical beyond belief to have rated the deals and made the public statements they made.

I fully support the fact that rating agencies issue opinions and they are not the authors of the subprime/Alt-A debacle. Although they are not the instigators, they bear responsibility for the lack of craftsmanship of their work. The consequence of issuing unreliable opinions is that no one will trust your opinion, and the reputation of the rating agencies, in my opinion, has been seriously damaged—again.

Even though they do not perform due diligence, they should have insisted on proof that rigorous due diligence on the underlying loans had been performed, particularly since there was ample news, and often disclosure that underwriting standards were lax and that the products posed unprecedented risk. Many of the products required housing prices to continuously rise in order for homeowners to refinance their homes before coupons reset.

In this case, appropriate due diligence would have included, among other things:

- A statistical sampling of the loan portfolios.
- Verification of home price appraisals of the sampled loans.
- Verification that mortgages have not been missold to homeowners.
- Verification of borrowers' total debt load.
- Income verification of sampled stated-income loans.
- Verification that the homeowner could cope with the reset when the teaser period came to an end.

The rating agencies are not alone, since our regulators are late to enter the game. Having had ample precedent, why did the Fed seem so complacent? The SEC, the Fed, and others where relevant could have questioned the wisdom of the credit lines being extended by investment banks and banks. Perhaps they did, but I could find no record of it.

INVESTORS AND RATINGS

The issue of illiquidity due to originally misrated product is important since many investors must sell if ratings drop below investment grade. Many investment-grade bond funds have a strict small limit on how much downgraded product they may keep if it falls below investment grade; then they must sell the rest. Retail investors are the primary investors in this product, and they are sold by mutual funds. Pension funds and insurance companies are large purchasers of investment-grade tranches of asset-backed securities. Bank portfolios buy the AAA and AA tranches of asset-backed CDOs.

Even highly rated tranches were in trouble. Rating agencies countered by saying that "most investors" would not suffer a loss due to default, but again, this was a self-serving statement and was no justification for having done a job that was indefensible to any beginning student of statistics.

Shoddy ratings have harmful economic consequences beyond principal loss due to default. Since most of a CDO is rated AAA, it is usually true that AAA and AA-rated tranches will not experience a principal loss due to default if held to maturity. But selling misrated tranches prior to maturity will cause an investor to realize a mark-to-market loss. Leveraged hedge funds like Bear Stearns Asset Management (BSAM) managed funds imploded due to the combination of leverage and mark-to-market losses. BSAM's managers were very savvy, and it is difficult to believe they were fooled by ratings; it is possible they were exploiting the misratings and taking advantage of the higher income offered by these tranches to be more competitive in the short run, but misrated product made this game possible in the first place. Shoddy ratings also result in an opportunity cost since illiquidity can thwart an investors' ability to exploit new opportunities. Funds investing in this product will be less competitive, since newer investors can purchase its existing assets plus more to create superior income for identical misrated risk. Furthermore, some AA tranches backed by subprime debt are at risk of principal losses due to defaults, which illustrates the extent of the rating agencies' collective failure.

The rating agencies charged first-rate prices for third-rate work, but one cannot deny that there were public problems in the subprime market that indicated the ratings were unreliable. Ratings aside, savvy investors in mortgage-backed securities knew that these products needed to be marked down, since the assumptions on which the ratings were based were faulty. Investment banks arranging these deals and sophisticated investors—including many hedge funds—knew that the ratings and prices did not reflect the reality of the risk.

Rating agencies do not perform due diligence, but the rating agencies could have asked the investment banks and banks securitizing loans such as MILA's for evidence that *they* had performed due diligence. Investors in private placements are obliged to perform their own due diligence, and barring that, they could also have asked arrangers of these deals to provide proof of due diligence on the underlying collateral. Yet all involved had the skill to stumble over the truth, pick themselves up, and scurry on as if nothing had happened. Many employees of rating agencies, investment banks, and investors claim there is no evidence of poor management. They claim the market simply turned sour as housing prices stagnated in some areas and dropped in others.

Fewer mortgages could be put back to mortgage lenders as banks and investment banks cut credit lines, and the rising rate of delinquencies and foreclosures was made worse by falling housing values. CDOs backed by this collateral experienced a permanent loss in value. Funds that leveraged positions in these assets were hit hard, as we shall see later.

HEDGE FUNDS AND ABX INDEXES: ALPHA BETS

Savvy investors knew that deals backed by subprime collateral were misrated. Rating agencies had badly underestimated the default risk. The rating agencies did not have portfolio data, including a statistical sampling of the loan portfolios, including verification of home price appraisals, verification that mortgages have not been missold to homeowners, verification of borrowers' total debt load, income verification of sampled stated-income loans, and verification that the homeowner could cope with the reset when the teaser period came to an end. Therefore, as high unprecedented defaults were reported, the rating agencies' data for rerating was also inadequate, and they had no means to get better data without paying for it out of current earnings, since they earned most of their fees up front. They literally could not competently perform their job. This was not an issue of liquidity—it was a problem of permanent destruction of underlying value, and the rating agencies had simply gotten it wrong. That is the downside of not performing due diligence on the originators of the collateral and on the integrity of the collateral.

The silver lining in this debacle was the ability to use derivatives to make money as a result of a bad situation. It is much more fun to make money off of the fact that the subprime lending process is mismanaged than it is to wage futile battles with regulators, rating agencies and investment banks. Hedge funds in particular were in a great position to exploit this situation, because they are familiar with skew. Credit derivatives provided an antidote to softening in the subprime market.

By summer 2006, hedge funds were quietly shorting the newly formed ABS index. They bought credit protection on the asset-backed index ABX-HE 06-2 BBB– referencing BBB– tranches of 20 various home equity loan asset-backed deals. There is no index as of this writing on the first-loss tranches, so the best available short was on the next most senior tranche. This index began trading its first series in January 2006, and the HE 06-2 is the second in the series. This is a price-based index. After almost no movement, it started slowly drifting downward in the late fall of 2006 and traded at 98.2 at the end of November 2006. By January 26, 2007, it had fallen to 90.34 (I continued to publicly recommend it) and by February 13, 2007, it had fallen to 80.35, when I recommended covering this short, making for a very happy Valentine's Day. Hedge funds that bought protection by shorting the index made a leveraged bet skewed in their favor and rapidly multiplied the value of their hedges.

This is a classic example of using your intelligence to resolve your frustration and get properly skewed. Given the fundamentals of the subprime lending market, the probability of the price of the index increasing was very low, and even if the price rose, the likelihood was that the rise would be very minimal and only temporary. However, the probability of a drop in price was very high, and the price drop was likely to be substantial. As the predators began falling, so did the prices of mezzanine tranches of the ABX indexes. Figure 8.4 shows the performance of the ABX.HE 06-2 BBB-Index,

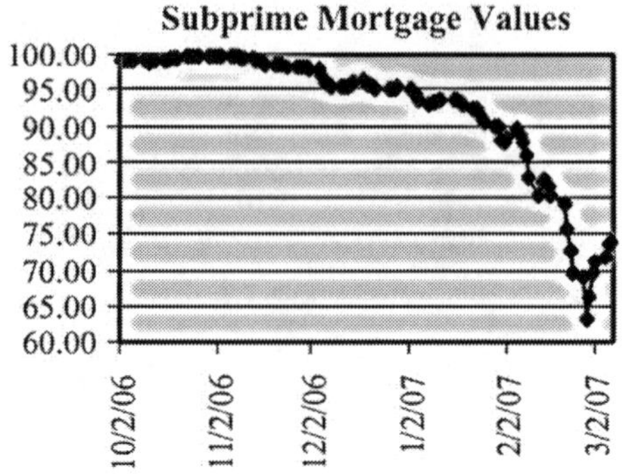

Data Source: Markit and CDS IndexCo

FIGURE 8.4 ABX.HE 06-2 BBB– Index

BBB– Index, reflecting the BBB– bonds of RMBSs backed by subprime collateral. Values plummeted during the first quarter of 2007 (the graph goes up to March 2007). The market gave a clear signal that these tranches were not worth what the ratings indicated. Values continued falling throughout 2007, and in January 2008 the value hovered at around 15.

In retrospect, this trade seems obvious, but execution is easier said than done. One has to have capital, strength of conviction, and patience. This is a brief rundown of actual events.

In summer 2006, many were appalled about the events of the previous 18 months. The mortgage market, which used to have sensible underwriting standards, seemed to have lost its mind, issuing predatory products, and throwing prudent lending guidelines out the window. My feverish frustrated mind could take no more, and I decide to look for the ray of sunshine to guide me out of this dark tunnel of madness: a suitable short. It is difficult to short CDO equity, and there was no CDO equity index. The next best thing was the ABX.HE-BBB– 06-2 linked to subprime residential mortgage loans. Notice that the *minus* after the BBB is very important, because after the equity tranche is used up from losses, losses will start munching on this tranche, the lowest-rated tranche issued in the second half of 2006. I knew this, and so did my clients, but few were gutsy enough to bet on these convictions in the summer of 2006. For one thing, there were language problems with the ABS CDS, but more on that later. After putting on these positions, hedge funds had to wait for some common sense accompanied by fear to dawn on the market.

In the language of the credit derivatives market, hedge funds *bought protection* on the index, or *shorted* the index. As the level of this index declines, it reflects a decline in the price of the underlying BBB– product, and the value of the position increases.

The hedge funds waited. Time was on their side, but they had paid money to put on this trade, and so far, there was no return. But they had seen this scenario before: charged-off credit card receivables, manufactured housing loans, and more. The bottom would fall out, but when?

Summer passed and fall began with no fall in the price of the index. October came and went.

Thanksgiving Day 2006 arrived, but no one felt particularly thankful. The mood about this trade was morose, and clients talked about pulling the plug before year-end.

On November 27, 2006, Markit, the group responsible for administering the ABX indexes, reported the first interest shortfall: two bonds underlying the ABX.HE 06-1 (not the 06-2 index) BBB and BBB– Indexes. The shortfall on the BBB index was on the M8 bond of the Structured Asset Investment Loan Trust 2005-HE3 deal and on the Long Beach Mortgage Loan Trust 2005-WL2 deal. It only amounted to $105.35 per million at the index level. The interest shortfall for the BBB– index was due to the M9 bonds of the same respective deals amounting to $142.02 per million at the index level. The available funds cap had kicked in, and that fueled hope that the general market would take more notice. At the end of November, the index blipped down a little. It was only a mild dip, not enough to lift moods or even suggest a celebration. But other hedge funds were encouraged enough to finally start shorting the index; they sensed the bottom would soon fall out of the market.

In early December, the index drifted down more for no discernable reason. Dozens of subprime mortgage brokers were in serious trouble, but nothing made big news.

A GOOD YEAR (FOR SOME)

On December 31, 2006, Aaron Krowne, entrepreneur, finance blog contributor, and head of Planet Math, started a web site called Implode-o-meter to track the number of mortgage lenders going bankrupt. He was mystified that this news wasn't making headlines. He was even more mystified that Congress, financial market regulators, and the management of financial institutions had not raised a ruckus. It continues to be a surprisingly good chronicle of recent events in the troubled U.S. mortgage lending market.

OwnIt, a California mortgage lender, filed for Chapter 11 bankruptcy protection in December 2006, and the public began taking serious notice. The *Wall Street Journal* reported on OwnIt's bankruptcy in early January. That is when the hedge funds and I learned that in mid-November, when the index began a slight downward drift, JP Morgan had pulled its credit line to OwnIt, pulling the plug on or about the time Merrill asked OwnIt to repurchase some of its substandard mortgages.

The index began dropping like a stone.

On January 20, 2007, I appeared in a CNBC interview on subprime and recommended that investors examine their documents. If their portfolios contained stated-income loans, or if the documents did not detail satisfactory underwriting standards by the mortgage lenders, the investor should sell immediately. The mark-to-market in the industry still had not caught up. Many investment banks and investors were asking for discounts on CDOs backed by subprime collateral, but not everyone was doing their due diligence.

This is a pay-as-you-go credit default swap. At the end of November, when the index was about 98.20 (the index all-time high was 100.94), for every $10 million notional amount a hedge fund shorted, it would have paid $180,000 plus accrued for protection. The coupon was 242 bps, and the hedge fund paid this monthly interest on the 25th of each month to the protection seller. If it unwound this position on February 27 at a price of about 69.97, the value of the position was $3,003,000 plus accrued.

After accounting for the accrued and your interim coupon payments, the hedge fund pocketed net profit of more than $2.7 million for every $10 million notional amount it shorted at the end of November. The payoff was lovely, but if you put the trade on in midsummer, you had to wait a long time feeling foolish about tying up your investment funds. But many hedge funds and several banks and investment banks put on this trade either as a hedge or as an outright speculation.

In February, many more investors and investment banks were asking for deep discounts on CDOs backed by subprime. By Valentine's Day, I recommended cashing out of the short ABX speculative trade, since the outlook didn't seem clear. The index subsequently headed lower, but it began seesawing, leading to mark-to-market problems for some funds, especially funds like those managed by Bear Stearns Asset Management, which used the trade as a hedge for its subprime risk.

The index was headed much lower. Many investors kept their short positions. Others who had cashed out reinitialized their short positions and began shorting "higher-rated" ABX indexes that also began to plummet in price.

Odd things were happening in the mortgage market. Homes stood vacant, and foreclosure proceedings were delayed, suggesting that crystallizing losses—and thus gaining on the short position—might be difficult.

Around this time, the *Wall Street Journal* reported that CSFB said BBB– tranches backed by subprime collateral were trading at LIBOR + 625 basis points. But among savvy investors, no one would buy BBB– tranches backed by subprime loans at that level. Depending on the deal, the level ranged to more than double, and some BBB– tranches were trading like equity since the view was that unrecognized losses had already eaten through the first-loss protection. Since delinquencies usually turned into foreclosures or mortgage restructurings, which might also subsequently fail, everyone was revising their opinions of unrealized defaults. Since there were also vacant homes on which foreclosure proceedings were mysteriously delayed, and there were allegations of fraud against some mortgage lenders, investors were nervous about additional unrecognized wild cards that could affect their portfolio value.

Bethany McLean, a *Fortune* editor at large, realized there was a problem with so-called highly rated tranches of CDOs backed by subprime debt. Along with her colleague, Peter Elkind, she co-authored *The Smartest Guys in the Room,* a best seller, and the basis of a movie of the same name in which Ms. McLean appeared, detailing the problems at Enron. She was the first reporter to question the inflated value of Enron's stock in 2001. On March 19, 2007, Ms. McLean's article entitled "The Dangers of Investing in Subprime Debt" appeared in *Fortune.* March 19 is St. Joseph's day for Catholics, the patron saint of those in need of a home. She quoted me, saying, "No one believes the ratings have any value," accompanying my observation that AA-rated tranches of CDOs backed by subprime mortgage loans were offered at much lower prices than AA-rated tranches backed by other assets.

While most AA-rated tranches would probably not be touched by defaults, depending on the portfolio collateral, there was a possibility that some AA-rated tranches could experience at least some principal loss due to defaults, especially since defaults could range from 20 to 30 percent in some areas and recovery rates in those areas would be at unprecedented lows.

Paulson & Co., an $11 billion hedge fund headed by John Paulson, a former managing director at Bear Stearns, organized a group of funds including Hayman Capital Partners and Elliott Associates to complain to regulators about the potential for "market manipulation." According to the terms of many deals—but not all—banks have the right to renegotiate and modify mortgage loans so that homeowners can avoid foreclosure. His protest was partly motivated by Bear Stearns' asking ISDA to further clarify its terms, allowing modification of mortgage loans in its ABS credit default swap documentation.

A study found that elephants in Africa have become shyer and more fearful of humans; they actually seemed nervous even paranoid. Further study revealed that braver elephants had been culled by human predators; paranoid elephants survived. Whether John Paulson's fears were founded or not, it seemed prudent to raise the question, particularly if one had an elephantine bet on the market that could be damaged by potential manipulation.

Most of the licensed dealers of the ABX index have a huge dog in the mortgage origination game through one or more of the following activities: derivatives trading in the indexes, derivatives trading in single name CDS's on mortgage lenders and others, equity stakes in mortgage lenders, credit lines to mortgage lenders, warehouse lending vehicles, securitization of mortgage product, ownership of residuals/equity in deals, mortgage servicing subsidiaries, trading positions in mortgage-backed securities, bank portfolio investments in mortgage-backed securities, hedge fund arms that invested in mortgage-backed securities, credit lines to hedge funds leveraged in mortgage-backed securities, or some other form of exposure.

The licensed dealers are ABN AMRO, Bank of America, Barclays Capital, Bear Stearns, BNP Paribas, Citigroup, Credit Suisse, Deutsche Bank, Goldman Sachs, JPMorgan, Lehman Brothers, Merrill Lynch, Morgan Stanley, RBS Greenwich Capital, UBS, and Wachovia.

The debate is not whether mortgage modifications should occur, but how they should occur. In certain areas, home values are drastically reduced due to a rash of vacant homes. In order for a mortgage to be properly renegotiated, the home should be reappraised to the new distressed market value and an affordable long-term fixed-rate mortgage should replace the old product. Perhaps points and fees should be waived if homeowners were misled into risky products. This process would cause a delay in recognition of losses, but there would be losses.

John Paulson of Paulson & Co. was concerned that something more devious could occur. Investment banks might manipulate the market by writing loans against a home's former value without recasting the mortgage in a way that would allow the homeowner to continue making payments. Instead, the clock would simply restart on a noneconomic mortgage loan.

Paulson & Co.'s concerns are not far-fetched. Unlike the S&P 500, the ABX index has only 20 underlying deals. If one purchased the first-loss and perhaps even the BBB– tranches, one could shore up the loans to avoid declaring losses and prop up the market prices on the tranches. One could probably corner the market on $20 billion worth of CDOs with an investment of only $2 billion. This was pure speculation on Paulson's part, and market manipulation of this sort is illegal, but if anyone were dark enough to consider it, Paulson's complaint probably put a halt to the idea.

In a strange twist of fate, the implosion of two of Bear Stearns Asset Managements' funds had imploded partly due to their leveraged exposure to subprime risk. That caused a further depression in the prices of the ABX indexes, and Paulson & Co.'s complaints vanished when its funds mightily benefited. Its largest credit hedge fund gained 40 percent in the month of June 2007.

Trustees complained they have difficulty finding mortgage documents to begin foreclosure proceedings and it was possible there was a game of keep-away ball going on to delay foreclosure proceedings. Unoccupied homes on which no payments are being made have multiplied in certain areas. Many have been stripped of copper pipes and other valuable fixtures. It would seem that sound business practice would demand quick resolution, yet homes languish and deteriorate. Alternatively, one could simply pay inflated prices for troubled loans to prop up the underlying collateral.

Obviously, if the losses on these homes are not recognized, it will prop up the value of the CDOs backed by these loans. That in turn would prevent protection sellers from experiencing losses from the protection they sold to hedge funds like Paulson & Co., or at the very least it would mitigate those losses.

The subprime and Alt-A mortgage market is messy. Wall Street professionals call the servicing arms in charge of adjusting the interest rate or duration of home loans for troubled borrowers the "Mod Squad." That choice is very unfortunate, because it brings to mind the acronym for the "Merchants of Death," also known as the "MOD squad," three morally challenged lobbyists for the tobacco, gun, and alcohol industries, in the movie satire *Thank You for Smoking*.

In the summer of 2007, the index dipped below 40, and the other ABX indexes, including the 2007 series, were greatly depressed. By January 2008, the ABX.HE 06-2 BBB– index was at around 15. Paulson & Co. was rumored to have made about $15 billion and Goldman Sachs reported billions in hedging gains.

Current prices can be viewed on **www.markit.com**, but it is important to note that these are average prices, not the prices one will get if one tries to execute a trade with a particular dealer.

BSAM'S HEDGE FUNDS UNDONE BY LEVERAGE

Bear Stearns Asset Management managed the Bear Stearns High Grade Structured Credit Strategies fund and, after a couple of years of apparently good performance, in August 2006 it launched the Bear Stearns High Grade Structured Credit Strategies Enhanced Leverage fund. Meanwhile, others had begun quietly shorting the ABX.HE 06-2 BBB– index to hedge against a downdraft in prices of lower-rated CDO tranches and CDO equity, which would eventually lead to a downdraft of even highly rated tranches. The funds included some CDO tranches backed by subprime debt and CLOs backed by loans and leveraged loans.

Surprisingly, both high-grade funds invested in first-loss tranches of CDOs, the unrated equity tranches. While some of the first-loss pieces were junior tranches of deals of AA-rated collateral and were very small slices, leveraged as much as 60 to 1, due to the supposedly high quality of the collateral, other first-loss tranches were very risky investments in unrated first-loss equity tranches of portfolios of lower credit quality assets.

In May 2007, Bear Stearns Asset Management posted the Everquest IPO proposal, the S-1, on the SEC web site. Everquest was purchasing some of the riskiest assets of the two funds at values provided by Bear Stearns Asset Management. It proposed to do an initial public offering, meaning the shares could eventually end up in the hands of retail investors.

If these assets were sold as private placements, the SEC would vigorously question their sale to unsophisticated investors. Among other things, the structure created a disclosed conflict of interest since the managers' fees depended on the performance of the assets, and the managers priced the assets with no ongoing third-party verification. The managers had broad substitution powers, and the managers' fees looked high. The document included a breakup fee of one to three years of management fees if the board elected to replace the managers; this was much too high a hurdle for shedding the managers if they were deemed unsatisfactory. The fees themselves seemed excessive. The charge was 1.75 percent per annum to manage assets the manager originated. Most CDOs with third-party managers charge much lower fees, usually more than 1 percent lower. Since many of the assets were first-loss equity tranches of CDOs, which were supposed to be very high-yielding assets, the 25 percent charge above a hurdle of 8 percent per annum was also very high.

There was no public market price for these assets, and even if a third party could be found, its assumptions could radically affect the price. The cost to do a competent evaluation would have cost hundreds of thousands of dollars in analyst's fees. The troubled subprime market and Everquest's exposure to it were clearly disclosed as key risks.

Since equity holders would have only a minority interest, it would be difficult for shareholders to have recourse against mismanagement, if any, of Everquest. There would be no ongoing third-party oversight of Everquest and it would be extremely difficult to assess the prices of the assets. Some of the assets included CDO tranches as collateral of new CDOs, an extremely complex product.

Parapet, a Bear Stearns CDO of CDOs, made up 53 percent of Everquest's assets. The prospectus stated that "the substantial majority" of Everquest's ABS CDOs were invested in RMBS, the majority of which were for 16.2 percent of total assets and 18.3 percent of revenue, but several of the other structured finance CDOs may have included subprime assets and seemed to be structured finance CDOs, so it was impossible to tell the exact exposure to subprime assets from the prospectus. Furthermore, 42.8 percent of Parapet's CDOs were invested in preference-share and income-note tranches of ABS CDOs, the riskiest tranches that would suffer the first losses when subprime mortgages defaulted, and some of the collateral was on the lower end of the investment grade spectrum and included tranches of other CDOs.

Brokers at the time were circulating distressed tranches. For example, an obviously distressed AA– tranche backed by second-lien subprime mortgages was offered at a price of 55 (down from an original price of 100) around the time the Everquest S-1 was made public, so pricing and analysis of each portfolio were key issues in determining the ultimate value of the portfolio. Although at the time of the IPO pricing a third party would price the deals, it was not clear whose assumptions would be used for the pricing, and it was not clear how rigorous the analysis would be. Furthermore, there would be no ongoing third-party independent pricing after the IPO came to market. Each component deal had to be considered on its own merits. Although the equity tranches did not appear to be further leveraged through borrowing (unlike the so-called high-grade assets remaining in the legacy funds), the first-loss tranches themselves were highly leveraged. On an ongoing basis, how could retail investors value Everquest, when even experienced professionals would have to perform detailed esoteric analysis?

However, Bear Stearns was attempting to raise permanent capital for its hedge funds, which in theory would give it more flexibility to execute lucrative long-term strategies. The S-1 document filed with the SEC fully disclosed the risks, even if I did not like what it was being honest about.

The Everquest IPO was set aside when the two funds suffered a triple whammy. BSAM had reportedly employed leverage of 10 to 1 on average. Some investors noted a decline in asset value in March and April 2007 and asked for their money back. Investment banks that had provided leverage (loans) noted the value of their collateral had declined and asked for more. Leverage made it difficult to raise cash without causing further downward pressure on the price of the funds' assets. Since the funds' assets had declined in value, funds with new investor money could control those assets and more for the same investment—making the funds less competitive. But that is the risk that everyone involved took, and the participants were sophisticated investors and savvy investment banks. Questions remained about the circumstances surrounding the management of the funds. Investors engaged in a legal battle with management when it became clear that investors in one of the funds would lose their entire investment and investors in the other fund would lose a substantial portion of their investment.

BEAR STEARNS' HEDGE FUND LENDERS BAILOUT

The financial press originally reported that Bear Stearns would launch a $3.2 billion bailout for the creditors of the funds managed by BSAM, but the reports quickly scaled down to $1.6 billion, half that amount. Whether that was a PR tactic, unclear reporting, or a bad miscalculation is unclear. In any case, the bailout set a precedent that could jeopardize the relatively regulatory-free environment of hedge funds.

The lenders were nervous they might lose money, but that is the problem with leverage. Even when someone else takes the first loss risk, if losses are great enough, they can eat into your position. The bulk of the risk was borne by investors, holders of the funds' first-loss risk; credit line providers had much less risk.

If a hedge fund puts up 10 percent collateral, the lender has some risk that the assets will decline more than 10 percent in price, if the hedge fund has leveraged all of its assets. It is like a homeowner borrowing to buy a house, putting up $10,000 to buy a $100,000 home and promising the bank he will keep the collateral amount at a constant 10 percent, but that the bank cannot hold him accountable for the mortgage other than by taking the house (usually a bank has recourse to the homeowner and the homeowner promises to put down a flat amount and has income and other assets to make good on his payments). If the house declines in value to $95,000, $5,000 of the collateral is erased due to the price decline, and the homeowner has to come up with another $4,500, but even if the house is sold, the lender will get back all of its money, and the borrower will have $4,500 left (ignoring fees). If the home declines in value to $89,000, however, and if the home is sold, the homeowner/borrower loses $10,000 and the bank loses $1,000. As long as the house is worth more than the loan amount plus the collateral, the lender will not lose money. It is only when assets decline in value so that the asset value plus the collateral will not cover the loan amount that the lender has a problem.

Bear Stearns initially opposed bailing out Long Term Capital Management, and I think that position was the correct one. When Bear Stearns bailed out BSAM's hedge funds' creditors, it was under no obligation to do so, despite pressure from the hedge funds' lenders. The bailout made the funds appear to be just another of the mother ship's trading desks—using outside capital and temporarily getting outside financing. Investment banks lend to each other's funds, but they earn fees and take risk. Yet the funds' investment banking lenders seemed surprised when Bear Stearns initially resisted a bailout, but they should not have been.

A bailout also creates a moral hazard. If an investment bank knows it will be called upon to rescue a hedge fund, it may feel entitled to park assets or otherwise interfere with the hedge fund. How would you feel if your money ultimately subsidized a fund's risk—wouldn't you feel entitled? I would, and I like to think I am a good person. But when my money is being used, I tend to feel very entitled.

More disturbingly, the bailout gives regulators an excuse to consider hedge funds as part of currently regulated entities. How can an investment bank claim off-shoot hedge funds are independent or off-balance-sheet? Bear Stearns acted as the lender of last resort, and it begs the question of the nature of the fees earned by the other lenders. It would be easy to say that third-party hedge funds would not be treated as well, but funds with good Wall Street connections, LTCM for example, might continue to get this sort of protective treatment.

In the end, it did not look as if the lenders would lose anything, which presumably is the reason Bear Stearns was willing to bail it out; but then again, they were reporting the losses and BSAM was marking the assets. Investors in the Bear Stearns High Grade Structured Credit Strategies fund were told their investment was worth only around 10 cents on the dollar, and investors in the Bear Stearns High Grade Structured Credit Strategies Enhanced Leverage fund were told their investments were worth almost nothing.

Of course, in prior years the first fund had earned high returns for many years, and the Enhanced Leverage fund formed in the summer of 2006 raised money from many of the investors in the previous fund. While many of the investors enjoyed the high returns that leverage can bring, they rued the losses. Many of them sued Bear Stearns Asset Management and in particular questioned the ongoing mark-to-market protocol of the funds.

BSAM's woes were not isolated. United Capital Asset Management LLC, in Key Biscayne, Florida, declared a moratorium on redemptions in July 2007 from four of its managed hedge funds. It had around $500 million in assets, many of which were backed by subprime collateral. Braddock Financial Corp. of Denver closed its subprime mortgage–loaded Galena Street Fund after losing 25 percent of its assets in a year due to redemptions. It planned to liquidate its assets and return as much as possible of the remaining $300 million in capital to investors.

By the summer of 2007, prime brokers made radical increases on the percentage margin requirements to hedge funds that had leveraged subprime-backed CDOs. Yet those percentage margin requirements did not extend to other products.

Hedge funds and prime brokers were agreeing to the larger margin requirements in exchange for partially staving off a huge markdown of the underlying assets. That meant the funds could hold off reporting large losses right away.

In many cases, neither the prime broker nor the hedge fund had a good idea of the price of the underlying assets, because it takes a lot of expensive analysis to figure it out. I estimated that the analytical work to get at the actual prices would cost *hundreds* of thousands of dollars and lots of analytical time if done by a third party. So it was a matter of give and take. We'll agree the price is X even though we both thing it is probably X minus a large amount, and we will agree to much more margin.

For so-called highly rated tranches, margin requirements doubled. Requirements varied for other mezzanine tranches. Lending against equity tranches was completely halted. That was convenient, because hedge funds would not have to mark those positions to market, and in some cases that mark would have been very low, or zero. The reality was that on a percentage basis, more margin was not actually held by the lenders. More often the higher amount reflected the fact that the underlying collateral was not properly marked down. For example, say you required 10 percent margin on an AA asset that is priced at 98, but if you have reason to know the actual price is closer to 88, asking for 20 percent collateral doesn't mean you have doubled your margin requirement—it only means you asked for the appropriate amount of margin, because you are fudging prices.

DISCLOSURE: INVESTOR FALLOUT FROM THE MORTGAGE DEBACLE

Sophisticated investors in CDOs backed by subprime collateral have little recourse if the risks were fully disclosed. They had the option to perform additional independent due diligence. But in some cases, investors will have recourse if documents were misleading or if material information was not disclosed.

For example, a prospectus for pass-through securities, seemingly targeted to foreign investors, illustrates the disclosure issue. The portfolio included first- and second-lien (piggyback) mortgages. Some loans were adjustable rate, some were not. The portfolio included negative-amortizing product and interest-only product. Stated-income loans were included in the portfolio, but they were mentioned twice in passing, and the term was not defined in the prospectus. The loans were purchased from troubled mortgage lenders. Approximately 63.16 percent of the loans were purchased from a bankrupt lender that is the target of allegations of fraud on borrowers. If the arranging investment bank knew or should have known of the predatory lending practices and alleged fraud when it brought the deal, it failed to disclose it.

Likewise, investors could have demanded a rigorous audit prior to purchase, but they may argue that the way the risks were presented, the prospectus appeared to disclose all the relevant risks when it did not.

Some of the risks the prospectus did disclose were:

- Less stringent underwriting standards and the resultant potential for delinquencies on the mortgage loans could lead to losses on your securities.
- High loan-to-value ratios increase risk of loss.
- Increased use of new mortgage loan products by borrowers may increase the risk of delinquencies and defaults.
- Some of the mortgage loans have an initial interest-only period, which may result in increased delinquencies and losses.

The prospectus does not mention that products like interest-only loans and negative amortization ARMs could potentially be deemed predatory products if made to low credit score borrowers who have not been properly informed and may even be predatory for overleveraged non-subprime borrowers. For some of these loans the interest-only period is up to 10 years, and the homeowner builds no equity in the home.

One section appears particularly difficult for a foreign investor:

> *Mortgage loans were originated consistent with and generally conform to the [now bankrupt mortgage lenders'] Underwriting Guidelines' full documentation, limited documentation and stated income documentation [emphasis mine] residential loan programs.*

The prospectus then continues on about full documentation and limited documentation and states that "the income of each applicant for a mortgage loan under the full and limited documentation programs must be verified." The prospectus also states that "all of the foregoing programs require that, with respect to salaried employees, there be a telephone verification of the applicant's employment." The phrase "all of the foregoing programs" could be misinterpreted to mean that the stated-income loans are included in the employment verification. But notice that employment—*but not income*—is verified, and even then it is with respect to salaried employees. A foreign investor might have reasonably assumed that the stated income was verified when it was not. In fact, the meaning of stated income was not clearly defined anywhere in the prospectus. The implication of the phrase was not made clear, either. Specifically it means that the borrower states his or her income, and that voluntary statement is not verified.

Taken as a whole, even though the prospectus seems to raise all of the necessary red flags, it makes it difficult for a foreign investor to understand the gravity of the situation unless it is an expert on the U.S. housing market.

Sophisticated investors purchasing private placements are required to do their own due diligence. However, investors could argue that they took the disclosed risks into consideration, but the presentation of the risks was deliberately misleading. Of course, they may not be successful in that argument.

"THE FIRST THING WE DO, LET'S KILL ALL THE LAWYERS"

A character in Shakespeare's *Henry VI* uttered the above line when thinking about eliminating opposition to a potential revolution. Lawyers were meant to be a stabilizing force in that play. But Shakespeare wrote fiction. Lawyers sometimes play a highly negative role in the securitization market. While I do not recommend killing anyone, I do recommend that qualified investors—particularly sophisticated investors (I am not including shareholders in this category)—dispense with lawyers more often. In this case, I am recommending taking effective business action instead of looking for legal solutions to business problems that are more efficiently sorted out among business managers.

The problems in the securitization market are business problems which can lead to legal problems. Nonetheless, the problems are best prevented through sound business practices and are often best solved with a business solution. Business managers should remember that they instruct their lawyers, not the other way around.

If investors have disputes, they will be probably better off negotiating directly with top managers of the deal arrangers than hiring lawyers. Lawyers have a poor understanding of these deals—although many claim to be experts after reading a few articles—and have a conflict of interest with their own clients. The legal field cries out for more effective regulation of its members, and increasingly lawyers are being named as defendants in securities fraud cases and malpractice suits. Instead of seeking speedy and effective resolution, they often drag out matters for years, charging clients high fees for inexpert work.

In many cases, lawyers want to bill their clients for work that should be done by an expert, and even try to write the expert's report for them. They want to provide outlines and do the research while withholding documents from experts, saying they will read and interpret the documents for the expert. As most business managers know, that is utter nonsense and you wouldn't tolerate it in your daily business, but when your back is turned, that is how your cases are being managed. This is not true of all lawyers, but by a very large number.

In one securities fraud case, an expert witness was being coached by the lawyers, had not read the primary documents, and was unfamiliar with the expert report he had signed, despite being a lawyer himself. Although the witness had a marquee name, the lawyers had co-opted the work, and the client ended up paying a large settlement rather than allowing the case to proceed to a trial it would have lost. The client's lawyers lost the case for the client and billed the client tens of millions of dollars.

Whether the case is handled well or handled poorly, the client pays. You wouldn't hand over important business matters to another firm to handle, so why do clients persist in handing over the resolution of weighty and expensive securitization issues to overreaching lawyers?

I have worked with very professional and ethical lawyers, but many others provide poor service to their hapless clients. Many claim expertise and abilities they do not have. Others falsely claim one has to be a lawyer to opine on various business issues, risk management issues, compliance issues—you name it. In the frothy world of securitization litigation, it is simply a legal game, and clients are themselves made pawns.

Lawyers call experts with an eye to conflicting them out—claiming the expert has had a substantive discussion regarding the case—so the opposition cannot use their skills. If they are unsuccessful in conflicting out an expert, they will claim they did anyway. Sometimes lawyers will designate the expert without permission, saying they have retained an expert when in reality, they have had no contact with him or her whatsoever. This is usually done when experts are well-known since it can intimidate the opposition into settling the case. Later they may return to the same expert in desperate need of services, but by then, they will have to be content with experts who are so in need of work that they put up with this behavior. The upshot is that clients get poorer representation, clients' time is wasted, and their ultimate case is weaker. The lawyers will get paid the same whether the client wins or loses. Yet there are few restraints on this behavior, and clients should remember that of the two of you, you are the only one who takes an oath to tell the truth.

If you are not happy with the way a law firm is handling your matters, you as the business manager can insist on changes. You instruct your lawyers, not the other way around. If you feel the lawyers are trying to act as if they are experts on matters in which they have a limited understanding, you can change that and have an outside consultant oversee that part of the work. Lawyers can handle the legal issues, if necessary, but they should not be allowed to impose their judgment over yours. A weak client is often an exploited client.

It should also be noted that in many cases, lawyers are part of the original problem. These may be the same lawyers who thought documentation is standard. Securitization professionals should rewrite documents when required, just as credit default swap language needs to be rewritten. Professionals should instruct lawyers on what the documents should include and how the securitizations should work, but it is irresponsible to leave the drafting of documents to lawyers.

Lawyers often give their employees bad legal advice, too. Employees at one investment bank, a major arranger of subprime deals, claim their general counsel told them the disclaimers he wrote and slapped on their documents will protect them in the event of investor and other disputes. It now seems clear he was incorrect in that assessment. Likewise, lawyers who drafted clever documents like the earlier mentioned prospectus may not have done their clients any favors.

In the end, how one resolves an issue is a business decision, and there is no requirement to use the formal arbitration system or the court system for what amounts to a business dispute. Often, it is not in your interest to do so. Lawyers will discourage clients from talking to their adversaries, claiming it may be used against them in a potential case. But many matters are happily resolved without lawyers. Many top managers at investment banks live to solve problems and will be delighted to agree to a solution that will avoid a contingent legal liability on their balance sheet. This will not apply to every situation, of course, but many disputes are best resolved among business managers.

MARKET FALLOUT FROM THE MORTGAGE DEBACLE

Both the United States and the United Kingdom have problems with their mortgage markets, and other venues in Europe have similar problems. The problems all seem to be related to one or more of the following: lax underwriting standards, chicanery and/or outright fraud, riskier mortgage products, ill-considered lending by banks and investment banks, somnolent regulators, shoddy practices by rating agencies, and an overly optimistic view of eternally rising housing prices. Regulators in the United Kingdom issued a statement in July 2007 expressing their very belated dismay at some of the poor underwriting practices in those countries.

The ultimate fallout from this debacle is unclear, and the total losses are still unclear. Mortgage defaults are expected to increase through 2008 as adjustable-rate mortgage loans continue to reset their coupons to higher unaffordable rates.

In the United States, regulators are not sure where to assign blame, but they are quick to avoid assigning it to themselves. Their job is made more difficult by consumer activist groups who fear that people who want homes will not be able to buy them and will be doomed to be perpetual renters.

REDLINING AND RED INK

Their fear has a historical basis. In the United States, an illegal practice called *redlining* denied sound mortgage products to eligible minorities. But recently, redlining was replaced with red ink. Some high credit score borrowers were steered into risky subprime mortgage products, and that practice needs to be stopped. In other cases, low credit score borrowers were lured to take out loans they could not afford, and that practice needs to be stopped, too. It does not disadvantage someone to deny them a mortgage they have no hope of paying off. Some advocates will argue that low credit score borrowers will be denied the possibility of stretching their funds to participate in a rising housing market, but that is not a sound mortgage practice—that is merely speculation, and no one is entitled to credit for speculation, just because they want it. Redlining was an indefensible practice, but destroying the credit records of naïve people, driving them into bankruptcy and homelessness, is a blot on the securitization industry.

If financial professionals have no sense of humility and social responsibility, then they should at least have a sense of self-preservation. Financial technology has allowed a small number of people to create a great amount of damage. In the eyes of the global financial community, financial professionals in the United States have squandered our credibility, our legitimacy, and even respect for our financial expertise. As our international customers realized this, we divided our supporters and united our critics—just the opposite of what is required to retain the United States' position as the center and global leader in finance. Our behavior in the subprime and Alt-A markets revealed aggressive arrogance. We adopted a very dangerous posture for leaders in finance. From investment banks, commercial banks, hedge funds, traditional investors, and rating agencies, there has come indefensible behavior and subsequent alternate-reality spinning. Wall Street's former standard "Your word is your bond" did not mean "Your spin is your shield."

Now we have a huge problem to fix. By insisting on sound underwriting standards and traditional mortgage products for low credit score borrowers—this would exclude most ARM products—the mortgage market would return to being a reliable asset class. No doubt this would cool the rising prices in the housing market, at least temporarily, but it will lead to a healthier housing market and a healthier economy.

Meanwhile, there will be some pain. There are a multitude of problems with mortgage loans originated in 2005, 2006, and 2007. For example, approximately 80 percent of 2006 loan originations were ARM products with resets that will occur in two, three, or five years. The 2/28 *hybrid ARMs* are fixed for the first two years and then will reset to an adjustable rate for the remaining 28 years. Other common hybrid arms are 3/27 and 5/25 ARMS, interest-only (IO) ARMS, and 40-year hybrid ARMs. After low teaser rates of around 8 percent, many reset to LIBOR plus 600 basis points, which as of this writing would be around 11.4 percent, but may be much higher by the time the actual reset occurs. Many subprime borrowers are stretched at the current rates and will not be able to make the higher payments. Note that this doesn't account for even more toxic products such as option ARMs, which allow negative amortization—that is, potentially a rising principal balance on the loan. It is unlikely home prices will appreciate to allow these borrowers to sell or to refinance when the loans reset.

I advocate a temporary moratorium on subprime foreclosures, followed by mortgage restructurings. Where appropriate, homes should be reappraised to lower values and the mortgages restructured to affordable fixed-rate mortgages. In some devastated zip codes (referred to as the zip code Katrinas), the reappraised values will be drastically lower and the mortgage terms radically different. Misled homeowners should be protected. But borrowers complicit in fraud, or borrowers who willfully overextended themselves, should not be given the same protections.

Rewriting the mortgage loans allows honest homeowners the dignity of paying for their homes in a rational way, allows investigation into mortgage practices so as not to reward borrowers who gamed the system, and does not compensate sophisticated finance professionals for risk they themselves enabled.

Fixing the problem for innocent homeowners will mean losses must be borne by lenders, including subprime mortgage bankers, investment banks that provided financing to the mortgage bankers, and the investors in subprime mortgages and CDOs backed with subprime mortgages. There is no reason for U.S. taxpayers to bail out these sophisticated financiers.

Chapter 9

Cash versus Synthetic Arbitrage CDOs

The chief cause of the phenomenal growth in the CDO market through most of 2007 was the use of synthetics in both arbitrage and balance-sheet CDO structures. Other reasons include new structures, regulatory capital arbitrage, economic effects, and organizational idiosyncrasies. Exploitation of these features also led to the downfall of the market and the rapid decline of new issuance in 2008. This technology is still in use, but usually without cash flow diversions that can deceive naïve investors. Let's examine some of the features of cash and synthetic securitizations by comparing and contrasting the peculiarities of a managed cash arbitrage CDO and a managed synthetic arbitrage CDO during every step of deal creation.

COMPARISON OF MANAGED ARBITRAGE CDO FEATURES CASH VERSUS SYNTHETIC DEALS

Both deals are cash flow deals. This means that the assets themselves, not the total return generated from active management of the portfolio, are the primary source of repayment of the liabilities. The liabilities are the deal expenses and tranche payments.

We'll discuss balance sheet CDOs and special regulatory considerations later. I start with the arbitrage CDO market since most of the key economic considerations are exemplified by this comparison. This initial comparison of cash and synthetic arbitrage CDOs uses senior unsecured bonds and generic credit derivatives as assets, respectively. I choose to use this comparison because most people are familiar with bond cash flows. Of course, a credit derivatives contract can reference any type of underlying asset, but the structural challenges of the credit derivatives contracts are most easily understood when compared with a well-understood benchmark instrument.

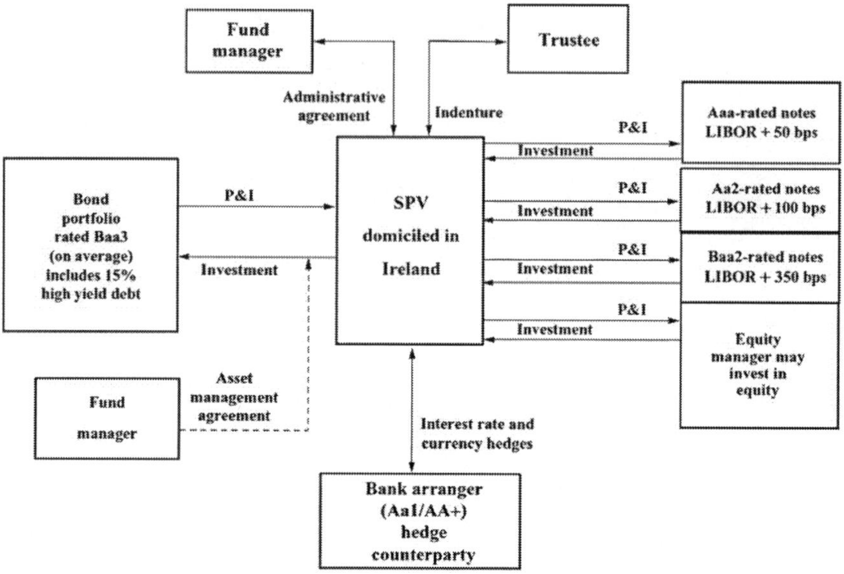

FIGURE 9.1 Managed Cash Arbitrage CDO

Figures 9.1 and 9.2 show the typical structure of a managed cash arbitrage CDO and a managed synthetic arbitrage CDO.

It is actually redundant to say the cash arbitrage CDO is managed, because that is always the case. Synthetic arbitrage CDOs can be either managed or unmanaged, and in our example it is managed.

The tranching of the cash and synthetic CDOs looks similar but has important differences. The percentages of the same rated tranches are different. The portfolio of the cash deal has an average Baa3 rating, and the synthetic portfolio has an average rating of Baa2. The synthetic deal does not have a market risk hedge counterparty. Conversely, the synthetic deal has a super senior tranche, and the cash deal doesn't.

Both deals have an overall investment-grade rating, and both are Euro 500 million in size. One key advantage of synthetic arbitrage CDOs versus cash arbitrage CDOs is that it is easier to bring a synthetic deal in larger total deal size. As we will see later when we talk about deal economics, there are economies of scale in bringing a deal to market. In this example, we're comparing deals of the same size so we can look at the relative economic effects due to differences in tranching.

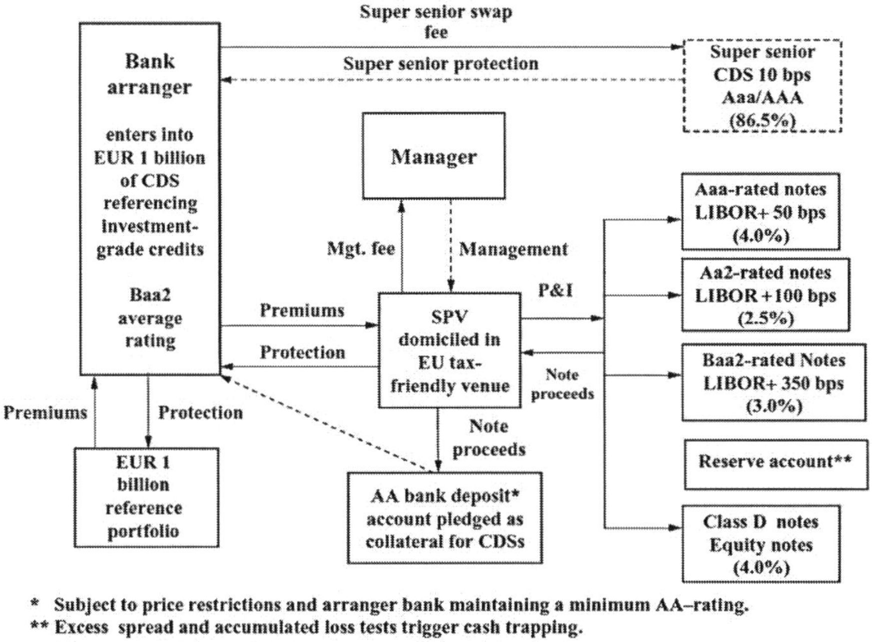

FIGURE 9.2 Managed Synthetic Arbitrage CDO

Several steps in the process of structuring a CDO will occur during overlapping time frames. The following summary of key steps is in the general order in which they occur.

THE ARRANGER AND THE MANAGER

Bank arrangers look for a good track record versus fixed-income benchmarks when choosing the manager. They also look for a name with a high degree of market recognition, and portfolio managers with longevity at the firm. A manager's willingness to retain part or all of equity and mezzanine tranches is a factor. Prior success with CDO management is an enormous plus in selection of a manager. Managers with these qualities have a long line of investment banks courting them to do deals. For synthetic securitizations, knowledge of the CDS market is a plus, especially when the rating agencies do their due diligence.

Managers have their own criteria when choosing to work with a bank arranger on an arbitrage deal. Managers will want to know the proposed management fee and will also want to know the percentage of the fee that is senior in the deal cash flow waterfall. Managers also look for other qualities from a bank arranger: (1) successful prior experience in closing and distributing managed CDOs; (2) strong distribution capability, especially for mezzanine and equity pieces; (3) strong trading capabilities; (4) willingness to absorb warehouse funding and hedge costs; (5) willingness to provide a liquidity facility for the deal; (6) ability to provide multiple hedge choices at various prices; (7) responsiveness in providing market information and mark-to-market information for the portfolio; and (8) deal modeling assistance.

Some of the better-known—not necessarily some of the better—CDO managers include AXA, CBASS, Barclays Capital, The Blackstone Group, MassMutual, Merrill Lynch, New England Asset Management, PIMCO, Prudential Investment Management, TCW, TIAA-CREF, Western Asset Management Company (WAMCO), and the ZAIS Group. But CDO managers from the ridiculous to the (rare) sublime have entered this lucrative area in droves.

Just about every fund manager, however, wants to manage CDOs to earn the 40 to 50 bps per annum fees for a cash deal or the 12 to 25 bps per annum fees for a synthetic deal. Just as the quality of fund managers varies, so does the ability to manage CDOs. The ability to manage a portfolio and the ability to manage a CDO don't always go hand in hand, but both are necessary for successful CDO management.

In our examples, the managers will both take 51 percent of the equity investment. In practice, many managers—TIAA-CREF and others—will not invest in the equity of the deals they manage going forward. Other managers claim to invest in the CDO equity but try to sell it to third parties on the quiet even while the deal is being marketed as if the manager is investing in the equity (see also Chapter 11).

MANDATE AGREEMENT

The manager and arranger will agree on broad general terms in a mandate letter. This letter includes an estimate of the deal economics and the deal timeline. At a minimum, both parties will usually agree not to engage in transactions that will create a conflict of interest for the contemplated CDO. Often the deal type is given as an exclusive for a fixed time period, especially on the part of the manager. It is not uncommon for arrangers to work on several deals at the same time. This poses no problem if the arranger has adequate staff and can handle the trading and distribution of the deals in the pipeline.

DEAL ASSEMBLY

Around the time the mandate agreement is signed, portfolio selection will begin. If it hasn't been done already, the arranger and manager will choose a law firm to draft documents. The arranger will usually propose the venue and administration for the SPE. Either the arranger or manager will nominate the trustee, custodian, and reporting accountants. If third-party credit enhancement is contemplated, the arranger may contact monoline insurance companies around this time.

The arranger may begin premarketing the deal, especially if the arranger needs to place any equity or mezzanine tranches. In our examples, the arranger will sell 49 percent of the equity and all of the mezzanine tranches. Feedback from potential investors may persuade the arranger and manager to change certain features of the structure.

The arranger will begin modeling the deal. The arranger usually provides the analytics for marketing the deal and for negotiating ratings with rating agencies. The manager will use portfolio management software to monitor the deal on an ongoing basis. The arranger and manager may share certain analytical tools so investors and trading desks can support the CDO throughout the life of the deal.

Document drafting begins now, including the warehousing agreement (not required for a synthetic deal), management agreement, and a very preliminary deal prospectus.

CDS LANGUAGE FOR THE SYNTHETIC CDO

Crafting the CDS language using state-of-the-art interdealer language gives the CDO investor the optimal advantage. In this case, *state-of-the-art* means language that gives the maximum benefit to the credit protection seller. The credit protection seller is the SPE from which the investors buy notes, so the investor ultimately benefits from better language. From the point of view of the CDO tranche investor, this language should avoid unnecessary technical defaults.

Credit events include only three triggers: bankruptcy, failure to pay (with a euro equivalent minimum of 1 million), and modified restructuring. The default trigger also includes a hurdle of a euro equivalent of USD 10 million. The language includes the supplemental successor definition.

Allowable deliverables are senior unsecured debt, except for a potential allowance of 10 percent of subordinated bank paper.

The investors take no currency risk, since the basis for recovery is calculated from an original euro amount of 10 million, and all payments are in euros.

SELECTING THE PORTFOLIO AND IMPACT ON RATING

This may be the most important part of any arbitrage CDO. A static arbitrage CDO doesn't have a manager and will be rated on diversification of the portfolio, among other criteria. Most of the early static deals were unrated, but today many static deals are rated. Managed deals are almost always rated, and that is the case for the deals in our example.

Whether or not a deal should be managed is a very controversial issue. Investors are polarized and vehement in their opinions.

Diversification is important, and rating agencies view this as a key input to the ultimate credit rating. Some investors feel this rigid thinking may obscure the value of a good manager in a deal. A competent manager may avoid obligors and entire sectors that may have systemic risk. That's what a manager is paid to do. Furthermore, a competent manager may find relative value in a sector he knows well but avoid sectors about which he knows little. This is contrary to diversification but often key to avoiding loss in value or loss due to default. Why should a manager diversify into sectors about which he knows nothing?

Moody's will penalize a deal if a manager doesn't have a good track record. Moody's will not give a deal credit, however, if the manager has a great track record. There is no way in the rating framework to factor in the possibility of a lower portfolio diversity score due to competent management choice.

However, many investors scorn managed deals. They feel managers may introduce "incompetence for a fee" or, even worse, may introduce moral hazard when the manager has a claim to equity cash flows. Even when these investors are being charitable, they sound harsh. They feel that even at their best, managers wouldn't have dodged a bullet like Enron or Railtrack. These investors feel they shouldn't pay extra for managed deals. Instead, they prefer to have input to the initial selection of the portfolio for a static deal.

If views are this polarized, one might turn to ratings to provide accurate guidance. One might think that rating agency criteria will at least be objective and will produce results that can be replicated across deals. But this would be a mistake, as we will see later when we look at rating agency criteria.

For cash deals, the arranger's trading desk provides feedback on the availability of bonds. For an investment-grade cash deal, around 25 percent non-investment-grade debt may be allowed in order to improve the arbitrage. It is difficult to find rated European high-yield debt, however, so managers will often look to the U.S. market for high-yield bonds. If the deal is euro-centric, investment-grade bonds may be difficult to find in the size desired by the manager, and diversification is often difficult. Most of the European investment-grade bond issuance for reasonably good spreads is concentrated in the telecom and automotive sectors. Bonds are sometimes difficult to find in the U.S. market, but to a much lesser degree.

Credit default swaps can reference virtually any obligation of a desired reference credit. The arranger doesn't have to scour the market for a specific bond issue that may be tied up in a reference portfolio, as often happens for a cash deal. It is much easier to source a portfolio of credits using credit default swaps than bonds.

RATING CRITERIA AND RESTRICTIONS

Structurers impose portfolio standards in an attempt to protect the integrity of the deal tranches and maintain deal ratings. Moody's, S&P, and Fitch IBCA issue long-term credit ratings for various corporate and government credits. A summary of their ratings indicators is given in Table 9.1.

Credit ratings in the lower portion are considered below investment grade: A deal with a Moody's rating below Baa3, an S&P rating below BBB−, or a Fitch IBCA rating below BBB− is considered below investment grade by each of the respective rating agencies. Ratings at or above those levels are considered investment grade by each of the respective rating agencies.

It would seem logical that the rating agency ratings can be directly mapped onto one another, but they cannot. It is important to note that the rating agencies often do not agree on the quality of a rating assigned by another rating agency. For instance, a reference entity considered to be investment grade by S&P or Fitch IBCA may not be considered investment grade by Moody's. Ratings assigned by the various agencies are almost always within a couple of notches of each other, but this isn't always the case. In addition, some entities, especially in Europe, do not have ratings by any of the rating agencies.

CDO structuring makes the rating agency issues even more interesting. Moody's and Fitch IBCA may supply ratings on cash flow structures for which S&P will refuse to provide a rating, because it doesn't fit into the S&P framework. For example, S&P will not rate raw equity cash flows, no matter how robust.

TABLE 9.1 Summary of Ratings Indications

Long-Term Credit Ratings		
Moody's	**S&P**	**Fitch IBCA**
Aaa	AAA	AAA
Aa1	AA+	AA+
Aa2	AA	AA
Aa3	AA–	AA–
A1	A+	A+
A2	A	A
A3	A–	A–
Baa1	BBB+	BBB+
Baa2	BBB	BBB
Baa3	BBB–	BBB–
Ba1	BB+	BB+
Ba2	BB	BB
Ba3	BB–	BB–
B1	B+	B+
B2	B	B
B3	B–	B–
Caa1	CCC+	CCC+
Caa2	CCC	CCC
Caa3	CCC–	CCC–
Ca	CC	CC
C	C	C
	D	D

One would think that rating agencies would at least be internally consistent. But that isn't necessarily so. Even within the same rating agency, portfolio tests and restrictions may vary by deal, and some deals are better protected than others. Different structurers within a rating agency may choose different stress scenarios when evaluating cash flows for an ultimate rating, for instance.

The rating agencies also use different modeling approaches. Each of the rating agencies publishes information about their data and models, and the magnitude of the differences from the varied approaches differs by deal type and collateral. To a limited extent, it is possible to arbitrage the rating agencies. For instance, one might tranche a synthetic corporate deal using S&P methodology because it results in less subordination to get an AAA-rated tranche than Moody's methodology.

Many investors prefer deals that are rated by at least two rating agencies, but many synthetic CDOs have been issued with a rating by only one agency or even with no rating whatsoever.

The various rating agencies have slightly different industry classifications. Moody's was the first to introduce this concept and has classifications for 33 different industries. Bloomberg lists this information, which can be found when one looks up an obligor's bond by the Committee on Uniform Securities Identification Procedures (CUSIP) number. Each obligor can be mapped to the appropriate industry classification, and the relevant rating agency may be consulted when there is doubt. Table 9.2 gives an example of the industry summary for the cash arbitrage CDO.

Now that the obligors have been mapped to an industry, one uses Table 9.3 to calculate the portfolio diversity score.

The initial diversity score for our cash arbitrage CDO is 33.8. The concentration by individual reference obligation is also important. In our cash asset portfolio, the initial concentration per obligor is 2 percent, and the maximum allowed concentration per obligor is 2 percent.

Our cash managed arbitrage CDO invests in a portfolio with an average investment grade rating of Baa2 but is allowed to have up to 15 percent high-yield assets in the portfolio and up to 10 percent asset-backed securities. Unlike synthetic CDOs, for cash arbitrage CDOs, a percentage of high yield is almost always necessary for the cash arbitrage to work. There are further restrictions. The high-yield securities must have a rating of at least BB−, and the asset-backed securities must have a rating of at least BBB−. No emerging market credits are allowed in this particular portfolio. The lower volatility of defaults for investment-grade collateral on most of the pool, combined with skilled management, should offer more stable equity (first-loss) returns relative to CDOs with only high-yield collateral. The hope is that this deal will offer good relative value for the risk versus cash managed deals that invest exclusively in high-yield collateral.

Default volatility for single-B assets is nearly *10 times* the default volatility of BBB assets. Although the cash arbitrage CDO is investment grade, it includes high-yield collateral. The manager must *barbell* the portfolio by including higher-rated investment-grade assets to get an average rating of investment grade. The lower-rated assets contribute to higher default volatility for at least a portion of the portfolio. Figure 9.3 illustrates how default volatility exponentially increases as one goes down the credit spectrum.

The cash arbitrage CDO's initial portfolio has a Moody's *weighted average rating factor* (WARF) of 319, which falls between the Baa1 and Baa2 band of 360–610. The manager must maintain a minimum average rating of Baa3 (equivalent to an S&P rating of BBB−) throughout the life of the deal. This means the maximum Moody's target WARF band is 360 to 610, with a maximum WARF of 610. Our deals are rated by Moody's only, but it is important to keep in mind that rating conventions vary by rating agency and rating factors vary between Moody's

TABLE 9.2 Industry Summary for Cash Arbitrage CDO

Moody's Industry Codes	Moody's Industry Designations	Number of Obligors	Obligors as Percent of Total
1	Aerospace and Defense	0	0
2	Automobile	1	2
3	Banking	3	6
4	Beverage, Food, and Tobacco	5	10
5	Buildings and Real Estate	5	10
6	Chemicals, Plastics, and Rubber	1	2
7	Containers, Packaging, and Glass	2	4
8	Personal and Nondurable Consumer Products (Mfg Only)	0	0
9	Diversified/Conglomerate Manufacturing	2	4
10	Diversified/Conglomerate Service	0	0
11	Diversified Natural Resources, Precious Metals and Minerals	0	0
12	Ecological	0	0
13	Electronics	1	2
14	Finance	4	8
15	Farming and Agriculture	0	0
16	Grocery	3	6
17	Healthcare, Education, and Childcare	2	4
18	Home and Office Furnishings, Housewares, and Durable Consumer Products	1	2
19	Hotels, Motels, Inns, and Gaming	0	0
20	Insurance	0	0
21	Leisure, Amusement, Motion Pictures, Entertainment	3	6
22	Machinery (Nonagriculture, Nonconstruction, Nonelectronic)	1	2
23	Mining, Steel, Iron, and Nonprecious Metals	0	0
24	Oil and Gas	2	4
25	Personal, Food, and Miscellaneous Services	0	0
26	Printing, Publishing, and Broadcasting	0	0
27	Cargo Transport	2	4
28	Retail Stores	0	0
29	Telecommunications	4	8
30	Textiles and Leather	3	6
31	Personal Transportation	0	0
32	Utilities	4	8
33	Broadcasting and Entertainment	1	2
Total		50	100 percent

TABLE 9.3 Diversity Score for Number of Obligors in the Same Industry

Number of Firms in Same Industry	Diversity Score
1	1.00
2	1.50
3	2.00
4	2.33
5	2.67
6	3.00
7	3.25
8	3.50
9	3.75
10	4.00
>10	Individually determined

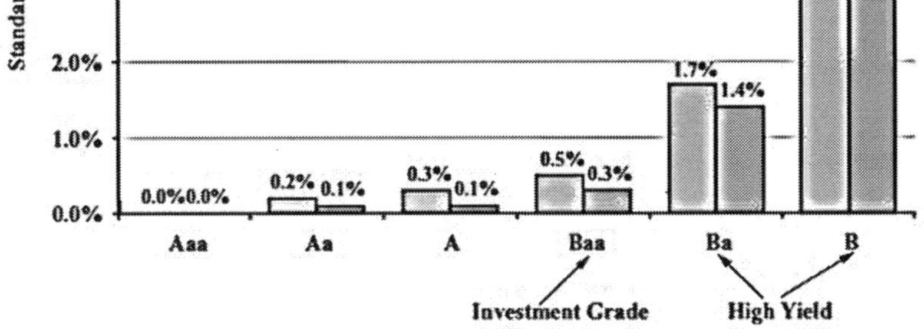

FIGURE 9.3 Moody's Historical Default Volatilities
Source: Historical Default Rates of Corporate Bond Issuers, 1920–1997, Moody's Investors Service, 2000.

and Fitch. Table 9.4 shows the rating factor conventions for Moody's and Fitch.

At purchase, the minimum allowable rating is Ba3, but only 25 percent of the assets can be rated below Baa3. Five percent of the assets can be rated below Ba3 due to downgrade. The initial portfolio rating distribution is shown in Table 9.5.

Notice that the S&P ratings are largely irrelevant, because only Moody's is rating the deal. Nonetheless, they are included here, because we allowed for 5 percent of the deal to include obligors that are not rated by Moody's but are rated by S&P. The obligor could be rated by S&P or by both S&P and Fitch and be eligible for the 5 percent inclusion. Moody's maps the rating to a Moody's rating. Usually Moody's does this by simply deducting two notches from the exogenous rating agency's rating.

The cash arbitrage portfolio must maintain a minimum weighted average spread of 150 bps over Euribor, per the minimum weighted average spread test. Investment is only allowed in entities located in the United States, Canada, or Europe. The maximum exposure to a single country risk

TABLE 9.4 Moody's and Fitch Rating Factors*

Moody's		Fitch	
Rating	Factor	Rating	Factor
Aaa	1	AAA	1.30
Aa1	10	AA+	2.00
Aa2	20	AA	2.30
Aa3	40	AA–	3.30
A1	70	A+	4.00
A2	120	A	5.00
A3	180	A–	7.50
Baa1	260	BBB+	10.00
Baa2	360	BBB	14.00
Baa3	610	BBB–	20.00
Ba1	940	BB+	37.00
Ba2	1350	BB	43.50
Ba3	1780	BB–	46.50
B1	2220	B+	50.00
B2	2720	B	52.20
B3	3490	B–	65.00
Caa	6500	CCC	90.00
Ca	10000	CC	100.00
C	10000	C	100.00

*Circa 2003. Factors change periodically.

TABLE 9.5 Cash Portfolio Ratings Summary (All Assets are Rated by Either Moody's or S&P or Both)

Moody's	Number	Notional	Percent	S&P	Number	Notional	Percent
Aaa	0	—	0	AAA	0	—	0
Aa1	0	—	0	AA+	0	—	0
Aa2	0	—	0	AA	0	—	0
Aa3	1	10,000,000	2	AA–	1	10,000,000	2
A1	2	20,000,000	4	A+	1	10,000,000	2
A2	6	60,000,000	12	A	4	40,000,000	7
A3	8	80,000,000	16	A–	7	70,000,000	13
Baa1	14	140,000,000	28	BBB+	16	160,000,000	39
Baa2	6	60,000,000	12	BBB	4	40,000,000	7
Baa3	5	50,000,000	10	BBB–	6	60,000,000	11
Ba1	2	20,000,000	4	BB+	3	30,000,000	5
Ba2	6	60,000,000	12	BB	3	30,000,000	5
Ba3	0	—	0	BB–	1	20,000,000	4
B1	0	—	0	B+	1	—	0
B2	0	—	0	B	0	—	0
B3	0	—	0	B–	0	—	0
Caa	0	—	0	CCC	0	—	0
Ca	0	—	0	D	0	—	0
NA	0	—	0	NA	3	30,000,000	5
Total	50	500,000,000	100	Total	50	500,000,000	100

is limited to 50 percent of the portfolio, and the maximum exposure to a non-euro currency (USD) is limited to 40 percent. Maximum exposure to European countries that are not members of the European Union is limited to 10 percent. There are no criteria for these limits other than the hypothetical cash manager's areas of expertise or modeling sensitivities. For instance, a high concentration of non-EU European countries might influence Moody's to give the deal a lower rating due to concentration in riskier venues. The initial country risk distribution is shown in Table 9.6.

The cash arbitrage portfolio must maintain a minimum diversity score above 30, and as we saw earlier, the initial diversity score is 33.8. The minimum weighted average life is seven years from the issue date. The maximum industry concentration is 12 percent, and only one industry may be at this level. Two obligor industries may be at the 10 percent level; all others must be at a maximum concentration of 8 percent. Maximum exposure to subordinated debt in a corporate structure is 10 percent.

Historically, investment-grade collateral has both a lower default rate and lower volatility of defaults than high-yield collateral. The synthetic

TABLE 9.6 Geographic Summary for Cash Arbitrage CDO

COUNTRY	Number	Notional	Percent
Britain	11	110,000,000	22
Finland	2	20,000,000	4
France	3	30,000,000	6
Germany	3	30,000,000	6
Italy	1	10,000,000	2
Singapore	2	20,000,000	4
Sweden	3	30,000,000	6
Netherlands	5	50,000,000	10
Spain	1	10,000,000	2
United States	19	190,000,000	38
TOTAL	50	500,000,000	100

managed arbitrage CDO uses exclusively investment-grade collateral. This should offer an advantage versus the cash deal. Idealized cumulative loss rates increase exponentially below investment grade.

Rating agencies provide data showing loss rates rising to tenths of a percent for assets rated BBB and rising to as high as 1.7 percent for assets rated BBB− before exponentially increasing for lower-rated assets. Yet this can be misleading. In 2006 Moody's owned up to the fact that loss rates from BB, non-investment-grade assets were the same as for BBB investment-grade rated assets. This was a startling revelation. Its ratings failed to distinguish between investment-grade and non-investment-grade assets. Since some funds must sell non-investment-grade assets, the distinction is important. Data showed, however, that BBB-rated assets were no safer than assets rated BB.

The synthetic arbitrage deal manager can invest in investment-grade assets but may hold up to 5 percent of the portfolio in assets rated below BBB− due to downgrades. The assets must be matched off or liquidated if the rating falls below BB−, since no assets rated below BB− are allowed in the portfolio. A maximum of only 5 percent may be nonrated by Moody's. The portfolio may take the risk of subordinated bank debt, but only up to a limit of 10 percent, and no corporate subordinated debt is allowed. No asset-backed assets are allowed, since our hypothetical manager has no expertise in ABS.

The synthetic arbitrage deal starts out with a weighted average rating factor of 236, which is between a Baa1 and an A3 rating. The minimum weighted average spread test is only 90 bps. The manager must maintain a minimum average rating of Baa1 to Baa2 throughout the life of the deal.

The Moody's minimum allowable WARF is 290 (between Baa1 and Baa2). At the deal inception, the diversity score is 45, and the minimum allowable diversity score is 40. Industry concentration is limited to a maximum of 10 percent, and only 2 industries may be at this level. All other industries have a maximum concentration limit of 8 percent. There are further restrictions on the maximum country exposure of 35 percent: No emerging market exposure—defined in this example as rated below A− and/or GDP per capita is less than 17,000 euros—is allowed. No corporate subordinated debt is allowed, but up to 10 percent subordinated bank debt is allowed. Each CDS initially has a five-year maturity from the issue date, but subsequent CDSs may be entered into to match the final maturity of the CDO.

SUBSTITUTION AND REINVESTMENT CRITERIA

Notice that the minimum weighted average spread test for the cash deal is higher than for the synthetic deal. For cash deals, there will also be a minimum spread requirement for assets that are eligible for reinvestment during the reinvestment period.

For the synthetic deal, substitution and reinvestment of recovery value is usually allowed, and the minimum spread test is equal to the average portfolio spread at the deal inception. The deal manager may substitute up to 10 percent of the portfolio per annum, but there is no limit for credit-impaired substitutions. All substitutions must be rated investment grade by Moody's or S&P (up to 5 percent total, albeit the deal itself is only rated by Moody's). Substitutions can be made to a lower-rated name if the name has a positive or stable credit watch outlook.

WAREHOUSING ASSETS

No warehousing agreement is usually needed for synthetic securitizations. No hedging or funding is normally required, and for this example, we'll use an all euro synthetic deal. The *warehouse* is the credit derivatives trading desk since the speed of assembling assets is much greater than for a cash deal. For cash deals, the warehousing period is usually two to six weeks for an investment-grade arbitrage CBO. Either the manager or the arranger must provide funding and absorb hedge costs.

Structured product–backed CDOs usually require a longer warehousing period than even high-yield transactions, often as long as two to three months, with a further ramp-up period of two to three months, since it is so difficult to assemble the necessary collateral. The overall market is smaller, and the individual issue sizes are also smaller. Analysis of structured products is also more difficult since it is deal specific. The exception to this long incubation period is when the structured products are in a bank's investment portfolio, but that isn't the case for our deal. The arranger of the cash deal sources assets from the market at the direction of the manager.

PRICING AND CLOSING

Pricing usually occurs within a week of the closing period. The closing date defines the end of the warehousing period, and the SPV is the owner of the bonds. The SPV purchases the collateral at the arranger's acquisition price.

RAMPING UP THE PORTFOLIO

Ramp-up is the period in which the remaining required portfolio assets are acquired. Some assets can be very difficult to source. For a cash deal, the ramp-up period can be four to six weeks or more. For a CDO backed by ABSs (including tranches of CBOs), the ramp-up period may last several months.

There is a danger with hard-to-find high-yield and highly leveraged loan deals in particular that full ramp-up may not be feasible in the allowed time period, or that it may not be feasible at all. Some of the early highly leveraged loan deals failed to fully ramp up in the specified deal period. The deals were scaled back. Investors agreed to the reduced size, but the portfolio characteristics (such as diversity score) did not seem to be impaired. If the portfolio diversity score or other parameters are not met, this could be a severe problem and result in a failed deal with penalties.

At a minimum, the deal must be scaled back. At the end of the ramp-up period, if the manager has been unable to purchase sufficient securities, there is a partial liquidation of the notes great enough to pass the portfolio tests as outlined in the indenture.

Synthetic arbitrage deals are fully ramped up either at closing or within a few days of closing. Trading desks often retain risk, either because they know they can quickly hedge the position, or because they have a view and are using the long protection position as a trading position. CDS traders can do this with more confidence than bond traders, because the market is more liquid than the cash markets, where it may be difficult to find a specific bond of limited issue size.

REINVESTMENT PERIOD

Cash arbitrage deals have reinvestment periods. If short-dated assets mature, they can be replaced with longer-dated assets during a reinvestment period. Recovered value from a defaulted asset is also reinvested. All principal collections from principal repayments, however they arise, are reinvested in new collateral according to the investment criteria outlined in the indenture agreement. Interest is paid as coupon to investors, and excess interest is a residual payment to equity investors.

A typical reinvestment period is five years, and that is what we will specify for our cash arbitrage CDO. This means the average life and expected final maturity may change slightly throughout the reinvestment period. Because of this feature, the deal documents will specify the acceptable average life range and acceptable expected final maturity range. The manager must stay within those guidelines.

The reinvestment period extends the average life of the deal and tends to increase equity returns. This applies to investment grade and high yield CDOs, since cash asset structured products CDOs may not have a reinvestment period.

The managed synthetic arbitrage CDO, in contrast, has no reinvestment period. It has a bullet five-year maturity. The manager trades either to avoid losses or to exploit gains.

NONCALL PERIOD

Cash CDOs usually have a noncall period, and ours will have a typical noncall period of five years. Equity investors may prefer this since it gives them a minimum time to earn a floor return on their investment. If interest rates go down, and if there is a gain in price in the underlying portfolio, they may also prefer to liquidate the portfolio and take gains. Investors in the senior tranches will have an interest in the call not being exercised. Usually the equity investors control whether a call is exercised. In our deal, a majority or more than 50 percent, of the equity investors must choose to exercise the call, or the deal cannot be called. Since in our deal the manager buys 51 percent of the equity, the manager can exercise the call without consensus from the other holders. Similarly, if the manager does not want to exercise the call, the other equity investors cannot exercise the call even if they can organize a vote to call with all of the other holders.

After the noncall period, the tranches are callable, but at a slight premium. The premium is equal to half of the annual coupon for each tranche. If the tranches are not called, they will pay par at maturity.

After the noncall period, there is an exception to the premium call for a tranche. When a tranche balance is below 10 percent of the original investment—due to bonds maturing after the reinvestment period—the tranche can be called at par. This is known as a *clean-up call.* The cost of servicing this tranche begins to outweigh the arbitrage advantage at these small principal balance amounts.

Synthetic CDOs are often structured without a call, and for our example, the CDO is not callable.

PAY-DOWN PERIOD

After the reinvestment period, the notes of the cash arbitrage CDO pay down sequentially, in order of seniority. Principal collections are no longer reinvested but are passed through to investors to pay down principal. During this period, the manager is restricted to trading to avoid losses or exploit gains within specific limits.

The synthetic arbitrage CDO requires no special pay-down period, just as it requires no reinvestment period, since it has a bullet final maturity.

WEIGHTED AVERAGE LIFE AND EXPECTED FINAL MATURITY

For the cash managed arbitrage CDO, the expected final maturity is in the range of 8 to 10 years, and the weighted average life of the deal varies between 7 and 9 years for each tranche.

For the managed synthetic arbitrage CDO, the weighted average life of the deal equals the expected final maturity. This is exactly five years, the initial maturity of the CDSs that make up the collateral of the CDO.

EARLY TERMINATION

The cash arbitrage CDO can be terminated early based on several triggers. If key prenamed members of the management team leave, and there are no acceptable substitutes, the deal can be terminated early. Failure to comply with deal covenants is another early termination trigger. Failure to make timely payments on the Aaa and Aa2 classes is an early termination trigger.

Bankruptcy of the manager or of the CDO's issuing entity is another trigger. The purpose of the triggers is to safeguard the return of principal to the Aaa and Aa2 investors. Often the class Baa2 investor is not as well protected with respect to early termination triggers.

LEGAL AND FINAL MATURITY

For cash managed arbitrage CDOs, the legal final maturity is the date on which the longest-dated asset can mature, or a prespecified date. In our example, the legal final maturity is 12 years.

For our synthetic managed arbitrage CDOs, the legal final maturity is five years and 90 days. If no defaults occur near the expected maturity date of five years, the maturity will be exactly five years. The 90 days allows for potential settlement time needed if an asset defaults just prior to the five-year mark.

TRANCHING AND THE SYNTHETIC ARBITRAGE ADVANTAGE

The portfolio is tranched into risk classes. As we observed earlier, the subordination is a form of credit enhancement for the senior notes. The *super senior* tranche, feasible only in synthetic CDOs, is a *delevered* position and bears the risk of *extreme systemic risk* to the credit markets. The *equity* tranche, or *first-to-default* risk, bears the *name risk* or the *idiosyncratic risk* of the portfolio. The *mezzanine* tranches are between these two extremes. The subordination of the equity tranche (and junior mezzanine tranches, if any) protects them from some of the name-specific risk, but these tranches are less delevered than the super senior tranche.

Table 9.7 shows the difference in the tranching of our managed cash arbitrage CDO versus our managed synthetic arbitrage CDO.

Notice the size of the equity tranche for the cash deal is larger than that of the synthetic deal. This is due to the lower average rating and the tendency for the ratings of the cash collateral to be distributed around the lower allowable rating. It is also due to more stringent stress tests required by the rating agencies for high-yield collateral. The cash manager must be more aggressive about the credit risks than the synthetic manager to make the arbitrage work. As a result, the amount of subordination required to get to the AAA level is higher than for the synthetic deal.

Synthetic deals have more highly rated assets, including more AA and A-rated assets, than do cash deals. A smaller equity tranche is sufficient,

TABLE 9.7 Managed Cash CDO versus Managed Synthetic CDO

	Cash CDO*		Synthetic CDO**	
Grade	Tranche Size	Percent of Portfolio	Tranche Size	Percent of Portfolio
Super Senior			432,500,000	86.5%
Aaa	439,500,000	87.9%	20,000,000	4.0%
Aa2	11,500,000	2.3%	12,500,000	2.5%
Baa2	14,000,000	2.8%	15,000,000	3.0%
Equity	35,000,000	7.0%	20,000,000	4.0%
	500,000,000	100.0%	500,000,000	100.0%

*Baa3 average portfolio rating. Up to 15 percent high yield and 10 percent asset-backed.

**Baa2 average portfolio rating. Exclusively investment-grade portfolio.

and the amount of subordination required to get to the AAA level is lower than for the cash deal. Structures vary. In most static deals, when the first loss occurs, the equity notional is written down by the loss amount and the recovered amount is used to write down the AAA and super senior tranches. However, managed deals may make a provision for reinvestment of recovered amounts.

WATERFALLS FOR CASH VERSUS SYNTHETIC ARBITRAGE CDOS

Interest proceeds for the cash arbitrage CDO include all interest received on the underlying assets plus interest earned on any cash in reserve accounts. They also include all amendment, waiver, and consent fees, and commissions. All payments from hedge counterparties are also considered interest proceeds. A small reserve account is maintained and replenished from future interest proceeds, if necessary. Equity cash flows can be diverted in the first year of the deal to fund this account, if required. The purpose of the reserve account is to insure that the notes above the equity tranche receive timely interest payments.

For the cash arbitrage CDO, principal proceeds include all principal prepayments from the portfolio assets, optional redemptions (due to calls, for instance), payments at maturity, mandatory sinking fund payments, exchange offers, all principal proceeds received from asset sales other than certain realized trading gains, and tender offers. Call premiums are considered principal proceeds. Realized trading gains from asset sales and recoveries on defaulted assets are also considered principal proceeds.

The interest and principal waterfalls for the cash arbitrage CDO are shown in Figures 9.4 and 9.5.

Notice that this deal incorporates interest and principal coverage tests, albeit the portfolio initially has an investment-grade rating. These tests will vary by deal and are stated in the deal prospectus. Our deal uses tests typical of cash CDOs currently in the market.

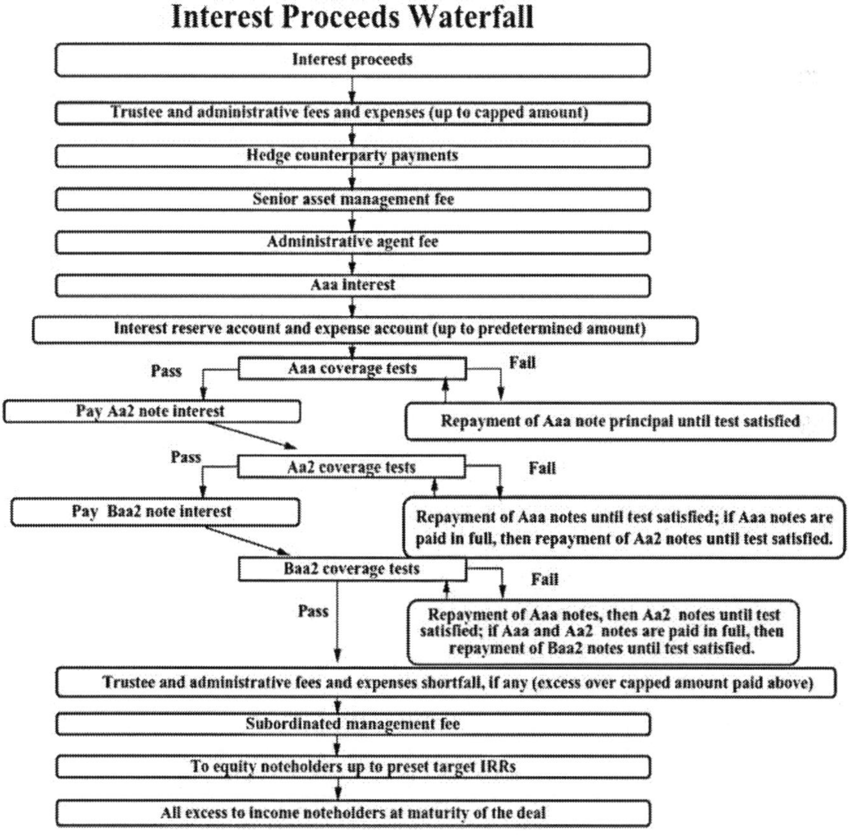

FIGURE 9.4 Managed Cash Arbitrage CDO Interest Proceeds Waterfall

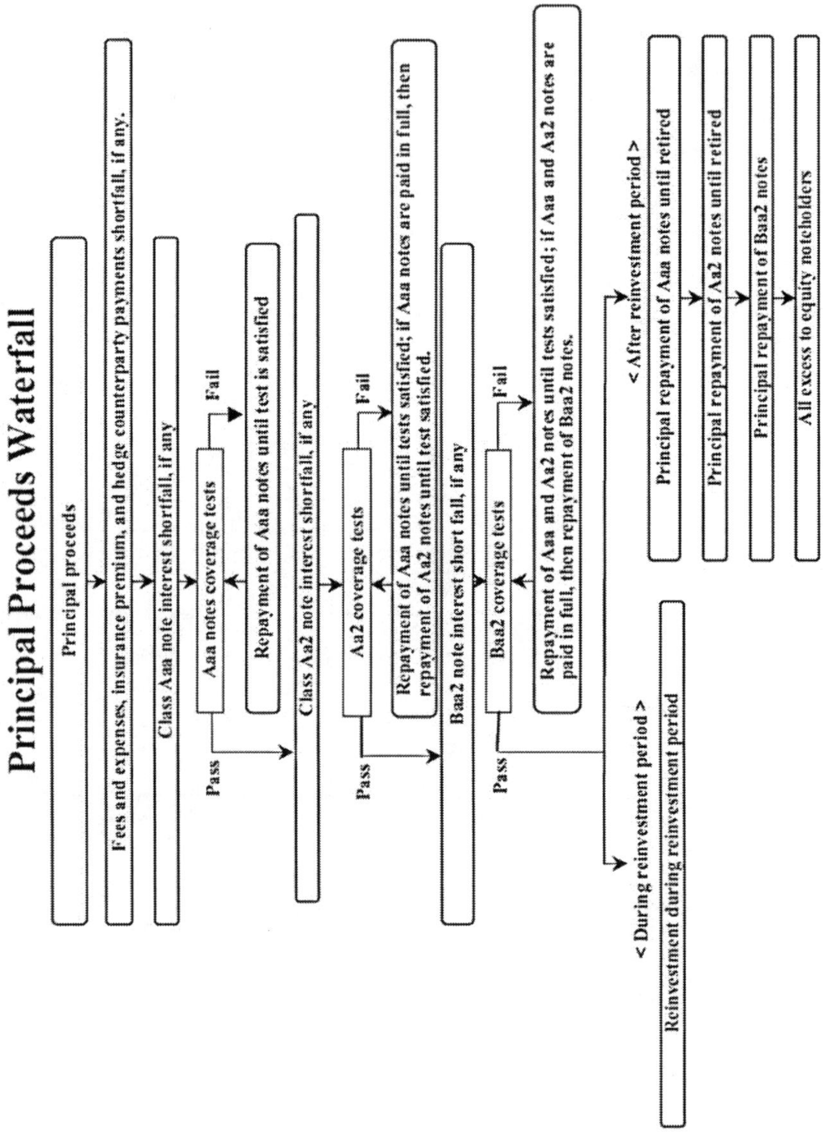

FIGURE 9.5 Managed Cash Arbitrage CDO Principal Proceeds Waterfall

The overcollateralization ratio (O/C ratio), also known as the *par value test,* for this deal is calculated as follows for tranche X:

O/C Tranche X = (Total Collateral + Cash in Reinvestment Accounts) / (Remaining Principal Amount Tranche X + Remaining Principal Amounts of Tranches Senior to X)

The principal amount for a cash flow deal is the par amount of thc bonds, irrespective of their market values. The principal amount for a market value deal is the mark-to-market principal value of the bonds.

The interest coverage ratio (I/C ratio) for this deal is calculated as follows for tranche X:

I/C Tranche X = (Collateral Interest Proceeds + Hedge Proceeds) / (Senior Expenses + Hedge Costs + Interest on Tranches Senior to X + Interest on Tranche X)

The coverage tests are lower than they would be if the portfolio consisted exclusively of high-yield collateral. The coverage tests for the various tranches are shown in Table 9.8.

For a portfolio with an average rating that is non-investment-grade, the coverage tests would be about 20 percent higher across the board.

As we can see from the interest waterfall for our cash deal, when the coverage tests are violated, interest is not paid on the subsequent tranches, and principal on the senior tranches is paid down instead. This continues until the coverage tests are satisfied. Principal is diverted to pay down senior tranches, even during the reinvestment period, if coverage tests are violated.

It is easy to see that cash flow modeling for this deal is complicated and becomes even more complicated for scenario analyses in which coverage tests are violated.

In contrast, the waterfall for the synthetic arbitrage CDO is relatively straightforward. Due to the abundant excess interest spread in the synthetic

TABLE 9.8 Coverage Tests for Various Tranches

	Overcollateralization Trigger	Interest Coverage Trigger
Aaa	106	110
Aa2	103	105
Baa2	100	102

deal, the reserve account provides the most important structural protection for the Aaa and Aa2 tranches.

The positive difference between (1) the default swap premium and the interest on the collateral security and (2) the coupons payable on the notes is excess income, which is placed in the reserve fund. The reserve fund amount is invested in eligible investments (A−1/P1 collateral). The reserve account accumulates for the benefit of netting trading losses up to 50 percent of the original class D amount, and then for the benefit of the Aaa and Aa2 noteholders, if needed to make coupon or principal payments. At the maturity of the deal, the excess reserve fund amount beyond the needs of the Aaa and Aa2 tranches, if any, reverts to the equity investor.

Losses due to (1) default and (2) trading gains and losses are netted from the class D note amount. Trading must stop when losses exceed 50 percent of the class D amount, and up to 50 percent of the original tranche D amount in trading losses can be netted from the reserve account if the original class D investment amount has been exhausted. When the original class D investment amount is exhausted, no further payments are made to the equity investors until maturity, and then a payment will occur only if excess reserve funds are available after satisfying payments due the AAA and AA investors.

If accumulated losses exceed the class D first-loss (or equity) original investment, the Baa2, Aa2, and Aaa notes will be written down in reverse order of seniority by the new loss amount. It is unlikely the AAA and AA tranches would experience any loss, since excess spread in the reserve account is available to pay any losses they would otherwise incur, and if the reserve account makes up the loss, there is no write-down of the senior notes. If any of the Baa2 tranche is written down, the average coupon payable on the notes is reduced, and the cash flow is further enhanced since all cash flow has been diverted from the equity investors at this point. An added boost to this deal is that cash settlement of the transactions allows for quicker recovery and reinvestment of recovered amounts. There are no payment-in-kind tranches in the synthetic deal.

As we compare the waterfall for the synthetic arbitrage CDO shown in Figure 9.6 with the earlier interest and principal waterfalls for the cash arbitrage CDO, we see that the waterfall for the synthetic deal is much easier to follow and model. The cash flow protection for the senior tranches of the synthetic deal structured in this fashion is also much greater than for the cash deal, as we will see later when we discuss the arbitrage advantage of synthetic CDOs. Note, however, that not all synthetic CDOs are structured in this manner. Later we discuss structures, which give no reserve account benefit to senior noteholders.

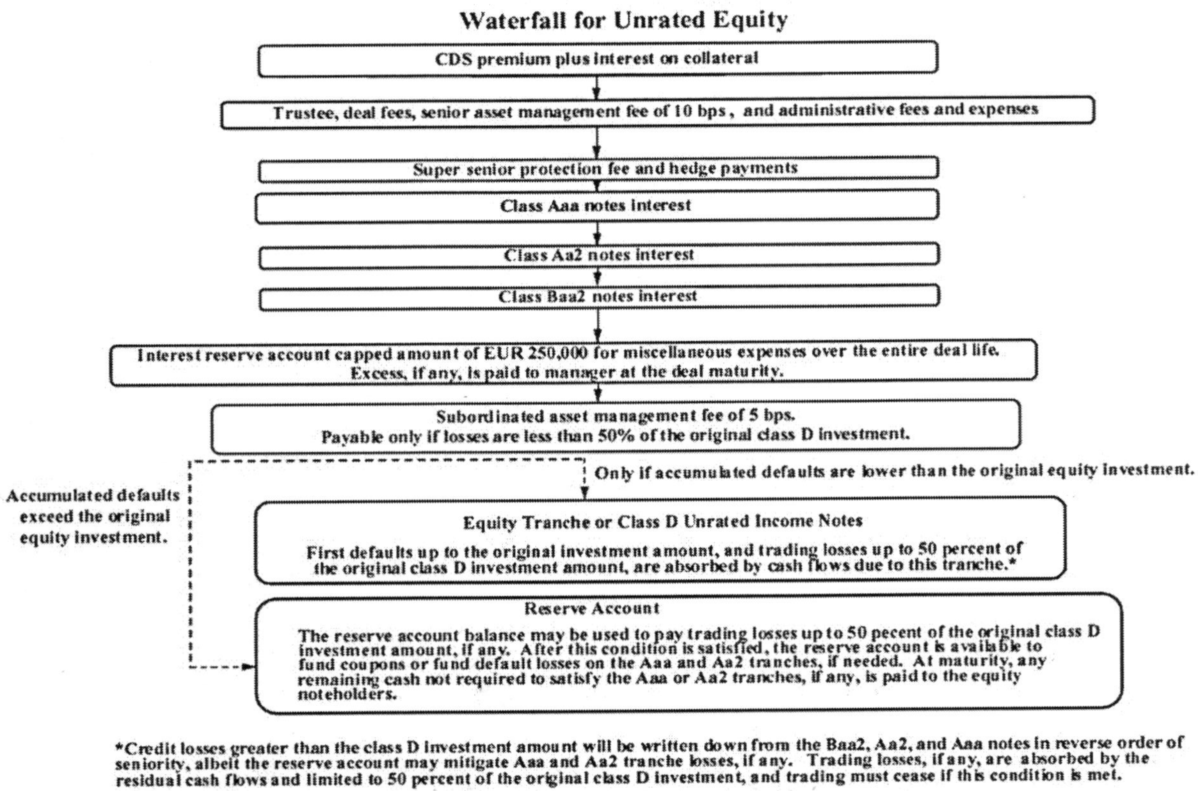

FIGURE 9.6 Managed Synthetic Arbitrage CDO

PAYMENT-IN-KIND TRANCHES

Payment-in-kind or *pay-in-kind* (PIK) corporate bonds have been in the market since the late 1980s. A corporation had the option of either paying the corporate coupon or increasing the principal amount of the bond, which was a payment in kind. Future coupon payments would be calculated off of the new principal balance, and the principal balance owed at the final maturity was increased to the new principal amount. Corporations that issued PIK bonds were lower-rated corporations. The PIK was meant to allow cash flow–strapped corporations to avoid default.

Some cash deals allow for PIK tranches, which are said to be *pickable.* Instead of making a coupon payment, the principal amount of the relevant tranche is increased by the amount of the unpaid coupon amount. The PIK tranche can either pay the current coupon calculated from the new principal balance or can pay in kind, depending on the cash flow availability in the deal. This mechanism is meant to prevent default of a tranche payment and to avoid triggering an early termination of the deal.

PIK tranches are structured primarily in high-yield bond and high-yield loan (highly leveraged transaction, or HLT) deals, especially in a high-default environment. Some investment-grade cash deals also use this device, especially those with 25 percent high-yield bonds in the collateral pool.

Notice that in comparison, the synthetic deal with reserve account support for the senior tranches is much more straightforward. Investors can more easily examine cash flows under stress tests, more easily model the CDO, and more easily determine the rating criteria.

PSYCHIC RATINGS: RATING AGENCY TREATMENT OF PIC TRANCHES

The lack of standardization among rating agencies with respect to PIK tranches can make it difficult to compare deals. Moody's uses an *expected loss approach* to rate these tranches. The expected loss approach uses the probability of loss and the potential severity of loss as the criteria for mapping a rating to a specific tranche. According to these criteria, if the tranche PIKs, but it eventually pays all accrued interest and interest on accrued interest, if applicable, there is no loss. The timely return of interest is not an issue for Moody's for purposes of this rating. Moody's will allow PIKing in all tranches, including the AAA-rated tranche. This is a recent innovation for Moody's, however. Moody's did not allow PIKing above the A2 level in deals rated before the summer of 2002, because they didn't want to treat interest on accruals the same way they treated accruals. CDO buyers may prefer deals rated prior to that time. This internal inconsistency is disturbing to many investors.

This is not true of the other rating agencies. S&P allows PIKing at the BBB level or below. S&P allows PIKing for tranches rated single-A only if there is clear disclosure that interest can be deferred. Even so, if a bond rated A−, A, or A+ PIKs for more than a year under a stress test, S&P considers it a default. This same event is not considered a default for tranches rated BBB+ or lower. S&P doesn't allow PIKing for tranches rated higher than A+. Their logic is that investors in higher-rated products expect timely payment of interest.

Fitch takes what seems to be the most reasonable approach. Fitch is specific about exactly what its rating means. If a CDO tranche pays timely principal and interest under the relevant default and recovery scenarios, Fitch will rate the tranche for timely payment of principal and interest. If the tranche only accrues coupon and eventually pays it off along with interest on accrued interest, Fitch will rate the tranche for timely payment of principal, and for *ultimate* payment of interest.

Investors focus on internal rate of return (IRR), but they also focus on timing of cash flows. In any security, timing, frequency, and certainty of cash flows are all part of determination of value from an investor's point of view. I can spend cash, but I can't spend IRR, and I can't spend yield. I can be rich in net worth but poor in cash. For instance, funds that need to make interest distributions to investors may need reliable cash flows, and for them the various rating agency approaches can be misleading. The investor bears the burden of interpreting the rating agencies' psychic ratings for PIK tranches

THE SUPER SENIOR ADVANTAGE

Notice that the super senior tranche is 86.5 percent of the synthetic deal, and the combined super senior and triple-A tranches are 90.5 percent of the deal. For the cash deal, the triple-A tranche is only 87.9 percent of the deal. In addition, the cash deal's liabilities below the triple-A level are more expensive than those of the synthetic deal. But the largest difference in cost comes from the liabilities above the triple-A attachment point. The super senior tranche of arbitrage deals backed by corporate obligors has been priced as low as 6 bps over the past few years, but I'm using 10 bps in this example. The *per annum* difference in cost due to this factor alone is 1,665,000 euros. Table 9.9 shows the cost advantage for our managed synthetic arbitrage CDO example.

TABLE 9.9 Arbitrage Advantage of Synthetic CDOs (per annum cost of liabilities at the AAA and higher levels*)

	Cash CDO*		Synthetic CDO*	
Grade	Tranche Size	Tranche Costs	Tranche Size	Percent of Portfolio
Super senior			432,500,000	432,500
Aaa	439,500,000	2,197,500	20,000,000	100,000
Total	439,500,000	2,197,500	452,500,000	532,500
Savings of synthetic versus cash			1,665,000 p.a.	

*This example assumes the Aaa-rated tranche is priced at LIBOR + 50 bps, and the super senior tranche is priced at 10 bps.

The chief arbitrage advantage of the synthetic arbitrage CDO over the cash arbitrage CDO is due to the large super senior tranche in the synthetic CDO. I believe this is the reason for the surge of synthetic CDOs issued in recent years.

CDS VERSUS CASH ASSET SPREADS

If we want to compare the cash flow of our two deals, one way to do it is to look at the CDS spreads versus asset swap spreads of the assets in the cash portfolio. For readers unfamiliar with interest rate swaps and asset swaps, the following is a simplified review of the basic concepts.

Simplified Examples of Interest Rate Swaps and Asset Swaps

It is the morning of September 14, 2008, and you are given the following term deposit rates and Eurodollar futures prices. All value dates are business days, and this is not a leap year. The initial value date is September 18, 2008. How would you determine the values shown in bold in Table 9.10?

The number of days is calculated from value date to value date for deposits with terms of three, six, and nine months. The initial value date for September 14, 2008, would be September 18. Subsequent value dates would simply be December 18, 2008; March 18, 2009; and June 18, 2009. Terminal wealth in each case is calculated as 1 + (rate/100)(days/360), and I have rounded them to five decimal places.

TABLE 9.10 Deposit rates

Term (months)	Bid (LIBID)	Ask (LIBOR)	Days in Deposit Period	Future Value Factor (at the Bid)	Future Value Factor (at the Ask)
3	7.000	7.125%	91	1.01769	1.01801
6	7.250	7.375%	181	1.03645	1.03708
9	7.500	7.600%	273	1.05688	1.05763

We need to know how to calculate forward rates if we want to bootstrap a swap curve, so I use the rates shown in Table 9.11.

I then use the well-known formula just given for calculating forward rates to fill in Table 9.12. The forward from months 3 to 6 is

$$[\{(1+(.0725 \times 181/360))\ /\ (1+(.07 \times 91/360)\} - 1] \times 360/(181-91)$$
$$= 7.372\%$$

An alternative method for calculating the forward rates is to take the ratio of the future value factors from the deposit table above and convert them to an annual rate. For example, the 3 month forward rate of 7.372 is calculated as follows:

$$[(1.03645/1.01769) - 1] \times [360/(181-91)] = 7.372.$$

Since we calculated the implied futures rates above, I'll digress for a moment to look at a classic futures analysis to determine if futures are rich or cheap relative to implied forward rates. (see Table 9.12).

The implied futures rates represent the futures markets pricing of the offer side of the forward deposit market. For the sake of simplicity, I have used the fair values of the forward offered rates calculated previously, even though the dates do not line up exactly with the value days for Eurodollar

TABLE 9.11 Three-Month Forward Deposit Rates

Months forward	Bid	Ask
0	7.000%	7.125%
3	7.372%	7.493%
6	7.711%	7.755%

TABLE 9.12 Eurodollar Futures Prices (Market Price versus Implied Prices)

Contract Month	Market Futures Price	Implied Futures Rate	Fair Futures Price	Futures Rich or Cheap? (Number of Basis Points)
Sep '08	92.87	7.125%	92.87	Fairly priced at expiry
Dec '08	92.75	7.493%	92.51	24 ticks rich
Mar '09	92.15	7.755%	92.24	9 ticks cheap
Jun '09	91.00	—	—	—

expirations. There isn't enough information to determine the fair value of the June forward rate. This analysis is useful because when we trade interest rate swaps (or forward rate agreements), we want to know whether the implied rates are telling us that futures contracts, our short-term hedge instruments, are rich or cheap.

The reason we wanted to calculate the future value factor is because this represents the terminal wealth factor for each period. A dollar invested today will have a future value in the relevant period of $1 times the terminal wealth factor (or future value). A zero-coupon bond priced today to have a terminal wealth factor of 1.00 at a future date will have a price today of 1/(terminal wealth factor) for the relevant period. Table 9.13 shows the zero-coupon prices that correspond to the terminal wealth factors (future values) for various future dates given the futures prices shown here.

From these prices, we can determine the fixed rate in September 2008 on a one-year fixed/floating interest rate swap that pays fixed and floating quarterly on International Monetary Market (IMM) value dates.

TABLE 9.13 Eurodollar Futures Summary

Contract Month	Futures Price	Implied Futures Rate	Days in Contract Period	Terminal Wealth (Future Value)	Zero-Coupon Prices (DF)
Sep '08	93.00	7.00%	91	1.00000	1.00000
Dec '08	92.50	7.50%	91	1.01769	0.98261
Mar '09	92.00	8.00%	91	1.03699	0.96433
Jun '09	91.50	8.50%	91	1.05796	0.94522
Sep '09	91.00	N/A	N/A	1.08069	0.92533

The fixed rate for a swap that pays fixed and floating quarterly would satisfy the following equation:

$$(C/4) \times (0.98261 + 0.96433 + 0.94522 + 0.92533) + (100 \times 0.92533) = 100$$

This simply sets the sum of the cash flows on a hypothetical one-year fixed-rate note equal to par. The floating side of the swap by definition is worth par if it pays an initial rate of 7.00 percent. The fixed coupon in this case would be 7.82 percent.

Using similar but much more complicated methodology, a swap trader will build a curve using appropriate benchmarks of futures and cash government bonds and will bootstrap a zero curve and calculate the fixed swap rate corresponding to a relevant benchmark floating rate (for example, USD LIBOR or Euribor).

Now that we can calculate a fixed/floating rate swap, how do we construct an asset swap? Figure 9.7 shows a schematic of a generic asset swap.

Suppose you own a five-year maturity USD-denominated corporate bond. The bond is trading at par with a semiannual coupon of 7.00 percent. You want to do a par asset swap and you want to swap the coupon to three-month LIBOR. The five-year swap is trading at 46/50 versus three-month USD LIBOR, and the five-year Treasury is trading at 6.5 percent. The swap quote means that if the interbank dealer market is going to pay a fixed rate versus receiving three-month LIBOR, they will pay the five-year Treasury rate plus 46 bps. In this case the fixed rate the swap dealer would pay versus

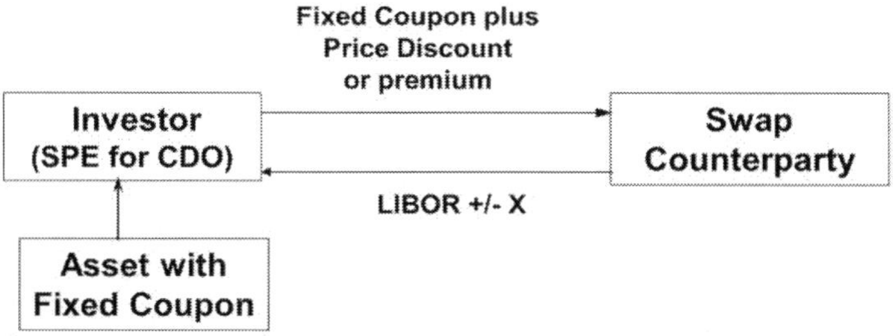

The asset may be trading at a premium or discount to par, or at par. The difference from par, if any, is amortized over the life of the swap and incorporated into the floating rate coupon.

Note that an asset swap can also swap floating coupons to fixed. The swap can be single-currency or from one currency to another currency.

FIGURE 9.7 Generic Par Asset Swap Cash Flows

receiving three-month LIBOR is 6.5 percent plus 46 bps, or 6.96 percent. This is the *bid side* of the market.

For our asset swap, we will pay a fixed rate versus receiving USD LIBOR. The trader will quote us the *offer side* of the market, which is 6.5 percent plus 50 bps or 7.0 percent. The trader wants to receive 7.0 percent versus paying three-month LIBOR. Conveniently, our bond pays a 7.0 percent semiannual BEY coupon, and this is the same way that the U.S. market quotes its interest rate swaps. Furthermore, let's assume our bond pays its coupon on the exact day the trader wants the first fixed swap payment on the swap. The cash flows are shown in Figure 9.8, where we are the investor and the owner of the bond. From the investor's point of view, this is similar to owning a par floater with a coupon of USD LIBOR flat. Notice that in this example, the swap provider faces the investor who owns the bond, so the rating on the bond is irrelevant from the point of view of the investor's swap counterparty. Only the creditworthiness of the investor matters for our example. We'll talk about asset swaps and currency swaps in more detail in a moment when we look at hedging the portfolio cash flows.

If we look at the cash portfolio swapped to a par asset swap level in euros, it is as if it is a portfolio of par floaters. We can now compare the spread level and the cash flows to a portfolio of synthetic asset swaps. Assuming for the moment that the tranches of each of the deals will trade at the same levels for same rated tranches, we can more easily see the difference in the arbitrage. Let's look at a credit like IBM. Figure 9.9 captures the five-year CDS premium versus the five-year asset swap spread for IBM for the period April 1999 to November 2000. The top line is the CDS spread. For this period, the CDS spread was close to constant while the asset swap spread

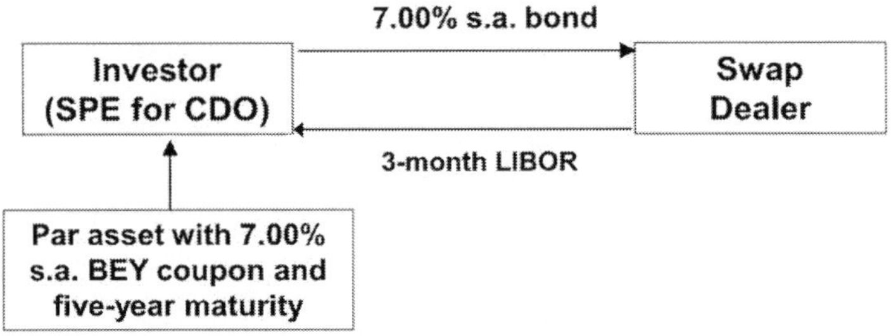

The asset is trading at par and the asset's fixed coupon matches the five-year swap fixed offer rate of 7.0% s.a. BEY. The coupon date also matches the fixed payment date in the swap.

The investor now has a par asset with a coupon equivalent 3-month LIBOR.

FIGURE 9.8 Par Asset Swap Cash Flows with Par Asset

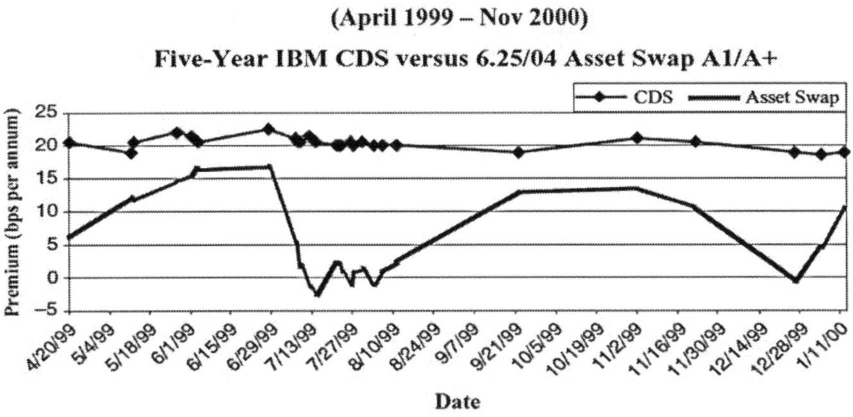

FIGURE 9.9 CDS versus Asset Swap Spreads for IBM

showed some volatility. Despite the asset swap spread's volatility, the CDS spread was always wider.

Is this typical? Do CDS spreads always trade wide relative to the cash markets? Unless a new convertible or large bond issue is involved, there is a tendency for CDS spreads to trade wider. Figure 9.10 shows typical behavior of the CDS market versus floating-rate spreads for the same credits. CDS spreads tend to be wider and more volatile than asset swap spreads or floating-rate note spreads.

Is the credit default swap market a high beta market?

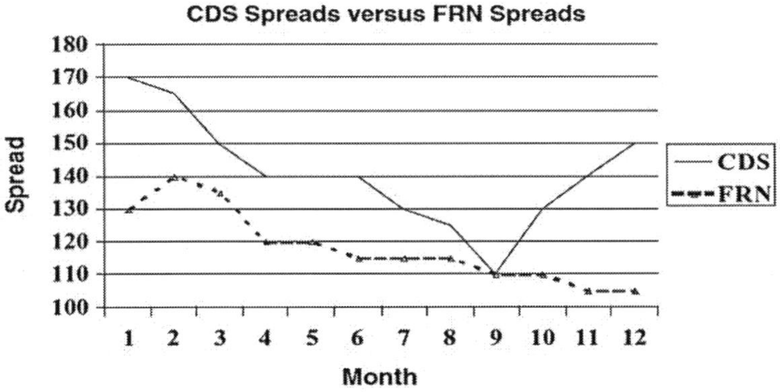

CDS spreads tend to be wider and more volatile than FRN or asset swap spreads.

FIGURE 9.10 Typical Pattern of CDS versus FRN Spreads

You beta believe it. Technical factors and faster reaction to rumors and market data often drive credit default swaps to be much more volatile than the cash market.

Even in a calm market, the credit default swap market tends to be slightly more volatile than the cash market, although the correlation between the markets is estimated to be around 90 percent for the few years in which credit default swap prices have been tracked relative to the cash markets. The difference between the spread of credit default swaps over the spreads in the cash markets, or the *basis*, is also correlated with market direction. As credit spreads widen, the basis widens. As credit spreads narrow, the basis narrows. Of course, there are exceptions in which the basis becomes negative due to supply and demand pressures, as we saw in our earlier example of convertible bond issuance.

We've already seen the advantage of the synthetic arbitrage due to the super senior tranche. The synthetic portfolio enjoys another advantage as well. For a portfolio of identical maturities with the *same weighted average rating factor*, also known as the *probability factor*, the synthetic portfolio will have a wider arbitrage spread than the cash portfolio.

Adding even more fuel to the advantage is that cash deals have a lower average portfolio quality and require more subordination, thus reducing equity leverage. For synthetic deals, not only is there more cash available for the arbitrage, but the portfolio quality also tends to be higher when comparing an investment-grade cash deal versus an investment-grade synthetic arbitrage CDO.

HEDGING THE CDO PORTFOLIO CASH FLOWS

For the cash arbitrage CDO, the challenge of hedging the portfolio cash flows is much more complicated than for the synthetic CDO. Earlier we looked at an example of a par asset swap. We would have to be incredibly lucky to find an asset in the currency we desire trading at par with the exact coupon required to meet the swap dealer's quote. Usually there is a mismatch in the cash flows that must be accounted for in a pricing model.

For a portfolio of cash assets, how much can the hedge affect value? What if a hedged asset defaults? What if the manager wants to trade a hedged asset prior to maturity? Would the potential loss on the hedge make a manager think twice about trading an asset that he thinks will deteriorate in credit? How much can this affect the value of a CDO?

Managers of cash portfolios hedge interest rate and currency risk. Let's take a simplified example where the manager purchases a fixed-rate bond in dollars and wants a par asset swap package. The following analysis is an approximation of the coupon on the bond. Even when one has a rigorous swap quote using a model and a proper swap curve, it is a good idea to have an approximation of the answer. The models are usually standard, but often users make input errors. Having a good idea of the answer enables a manager to get corrections made immediately.

The bond is trading at 101 with a semiannual coupon of 7.00 percent (7.00 percent BEY) and has a five-year maturity. You want to do a par asset swap and you want to swap the coupon to three-month LIBOR. The five-year swap is trading at 48/50 versus three-month LIBOR and the five-year fixed-rate Treasury is trading at 6.5 percent. Since you are doing a par asset swap, the swap dealer is financing the one-point premium for you, the buyer. You only pay par, and you assign the asset coupons to the swap dealer. A one-point premium is 1/100, or 0.01. One basis point is 0.0001 so a one-point premium is equal to 100 basis points.

The swap dealer will amortize the premium over the life of the swap and subtract it from the floating payment on the asset swap. You purchase the asset swap at the offer side of the swap market, or 7.00 percent. The slightly higher offer rate (versus the bid side) means that the swap dealer subtracts a higher amortized value of the premium from the coupon payment than if the dealer used the bid side rate. 100 bps amortized over five years at 7.0 percent is 22.79 bps, but these are bond basis points, so the floating coupon will be about LIBOR minus 22 bps, and this is only an approximation. Figure 9.11 illustrates the cash flows.

Similarly, if the bond were trading at 101 and had a coupon of 9 percent, the par asset swap would have a coupon of about LIBOR plus 175 bps.

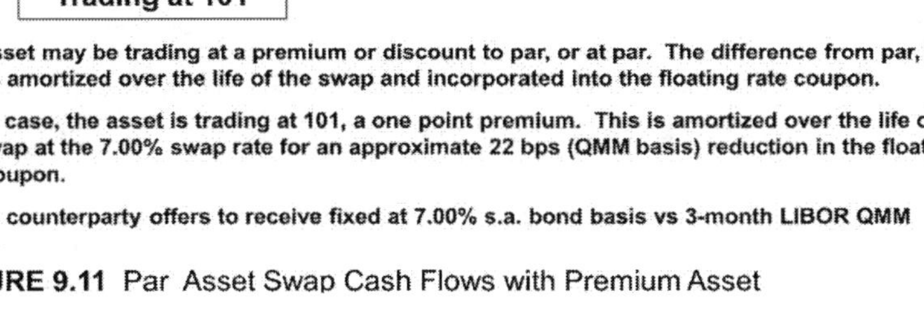

The asset may be trading at a premium or discount to par, or at par. The difference from par, if any, is amortized over the life of the swap and incorporated into the floating rate coupon.

In this case, the asset is trading at 101, a one point premium. This is amortized over the life of the swap at the 7.00% swap rate for an approximate 22 bps (QMM basis) reduction in the floating rate coupon.

*Swap counterparty offers to receive fixed at 7.00% s.a. bond basis vs 3-month LIBOR QMM basis.

FIGURE 9.11 Par Asset Swap Cash Flows with Premium Asset

If the asset defaults after one day, the manager has to pay the bid/ask spread on the hedge unwind, but that is usually only 2 to 4 basis points. Economically, the manager has lost a par asset with a coupon of LIBOR minus 23 and suffers the hedge unwind cost. If market credit spreads remain the same, and if the asset maintains its credit rating, then theoretically, changes in the hedge cost should offset potential changes in the asset price due to interest rate fluctuations. If the manager wants to sell the asset in the future, the manager must only absorb the bid/ask spread in the hedge unwind. If credit spreads change adversely or if the credit quality of the asset declines, the loss on the asset is theoretically the same as it would have been if the asset were unhedged. The hedge isn't perfect, however. Later we'll look at typical exposure due to mark-to-market differences in the swap versus the asset for interest rate moves.

When the asset is in the same currency, the analysis is fairly straightforward. When more than one currency is involved, the hedge is more complicated. Currency swaps can be structured in three ways:

1. Floating to floating
2. Fixed to fixed
3. Fixed to floating

In a currency swap there may or may not be an initial and final exchange of principal, but for our CDO, all of the currency swaps must have both an initial and a final exchange of principal. I once worked with a structurer who didn't take into account the final exchange of principal, which is the chief component of mark-to-market value. He was under the mistaken impression that if one did a par asset swap in USD to create a par floater structure, one could just swap the coupons to euros on a floating-to-floating basis and have very minimal basis risk. As a result he told a client that the hedge cost for the CDO and the ongoing unwind risk would be very low. He was unpleasantly surprised when the error was pointed out. When structurers have only a bond background and no background in the currency or swap markets, this is a common mistake.

If bond professionals have trouble with this concept, bond fund managers who are single-currency investors may have difficulty, too. A quick review of currency swaps illustrates this point.

In addition to the interest rate component, currency swaps have a foreign exchange component. The day count and payment period conventions vary for different currencies. In a euro swap, the fixed-rate basis is paid annually on a 30/360 basis (annual bond), and floating payments are on an actual/360 basis. In the sterling swap, the fixed rate is paid semiannually

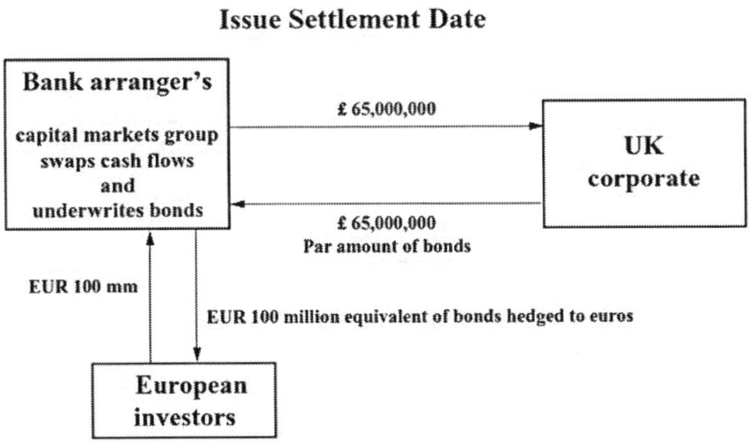

FIGURE 9.12 Initial Exchange of Cash Flows

On an actual/365 day basis,, and the floating rate is paid on an actual/365 day basis.

Suppose we are buying a five-year new issue sterling bond. The bond pays sterling LIBOR plus 25 bps. We are swapping the bond to a floating-rate euro bond so we can include it in our euro portfolio. I'm using fictitious swap rates and coupon rates for this illustration. Figures 9.12, 9.13, and 9.14 illustrate the cash flows from the perspective of the investor in the sterling asset swapped to euros.

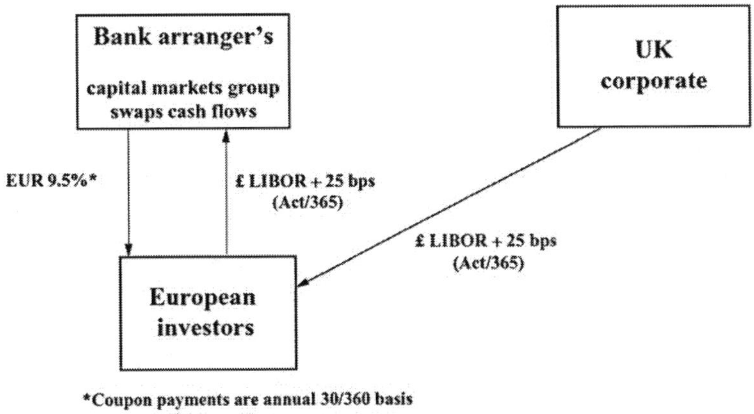

FIGURE 9.13 Coupon Payments in Euros

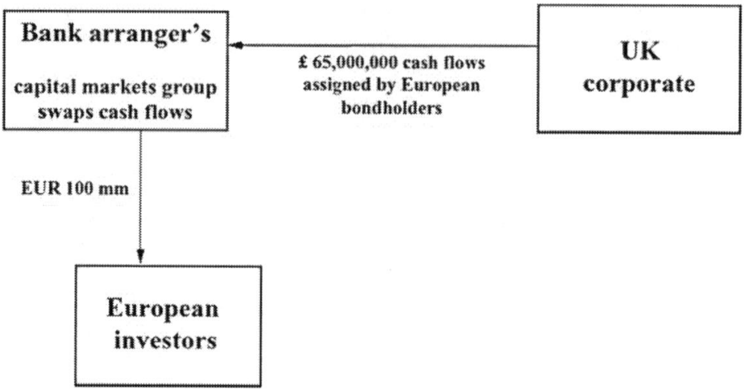

FIGURE 9.14 Final Principal Exchange at Five-Year Maturity

At issue there is an initial exchange of cash flows. The initial sterling amount owed to purchase the bonds must be swapped to euros, since our CDO will pay euros. On an ongoing basis, the coupons of the sterling bond are swapped to euros, so the CDO receives euro coupons. At the five-year maturity, the sterling payment on the bonds must be swapped back to the same amount of euros as we initially invested.

Sometimes you will hear the currency swap shown here wrongly referred to as a *dual-currency swap.* That is incorrect. It's possible that because people see two currencies involved, they think it should be called dual. A dual-currency swap is a different transaction: The counterparty receives one currency, pays coupons in another currency, and has a final exchange of principal in a third currency. Borrowers often perform this swap when they want to lower their all-in borrowing costs by taking on more currency risk.

I realize this terminology is untidy, but the only solution, if you feel there is a misunderstanding, is to have the speaker outline the cash flows. Don't assume market professionals know the correct terminology. Ask for the cash flow structure in writing so you can examine the cash flows and then see if they are consistent with the terminology as you understand it.

The value of a swap hedge changes by its mark-to-market value depending on changes both in interest rates and foreign exchange rates (if applicable). The change in value can be modeled for different exchange rate movements and interest rate movements. The mark-to-market exposure changes based on the interest rate and exchange rate scenarios one models and is a function of the volatilities the modeler assumes. Table 9.14 shows typical mark-to-market exposure patterns for a USD fixed/floating swap, and for a GBP/euro currency swap. I've highlighted the relevant exposures for our transactions for a five-year period.

TABLE 9.14 Swap Mark-to-Market Exposure Comparison

Currency	USD Fixed/Floating		Currency	Currency Swaps	
Tenor	Five Years		CDO Pays	GBP	Euro
CDO Pays	Fixed	Floating	CDO Receives	Euro	GBP
Time			Time		
0	0.00	0.00	0	0.00	0.00
2 weeks	1.85	1.79	2 weeks	3.99	4.15
1 month	2.74	2.62	1 month	5.89	6.25
2 months	3.99	3.72	2 months	8.27	9.00
3 months	4.99	4.57	3 months	9.92	10.99
4 months	5.83	5.27	4 months	11.47	12.91
5 months	6.63	5.90	5 months	12.79	14.60
6 months	7.37	6.46	6 months	14.02	16.22
9 months	9.52	7.39	9 months	17.41	18.91
1.0 year	11.24	8.51	1.0 year	20.00	22.62
1.5 years	13.22	9.18	1.5 years	24.43	27.54
2.0 years	14.23	9.24	2.0 years	27.93	31.98
2.5 years	14.44	8.88	2.5 years	30.80	36.18
3.0 years	14.20	8.23	3.0 years	33.23	40.20
3.5 years	13.15	7.19	3.5 years	35.37	44.03
4.0 years	11.11	5.77	4.0 years	37.34	47.66
4.5 years	8.04	4.06	4.5 years	39.05	51.15
5.0 years	4.27	2.05	5.0 years	40.74	54.39

From this chart, we can make some useful generalizations about single-currency and cross-currency swaps.

Notice that the single-currency fixed/floating swap exposure diminishes as we approach maturity, and in general is lower in magnitude than the currency swap. Currency swap exposure becomes greater as time passes and becomes greater in magnitude as we approach maturity. If we did a 10-year currency swap, the exposure would continue increasing in size.

This suggests that in the event of default of an asset that has been swapped from sterling to euros, there is potentially a great deal of exposure. That exposure can work to the benefit of the CDO, or it can work against it, depending on which way swap rates and currency rates have moved since the onset of the transaction.

In comparison, our managed synthetic arbitrage CDO has a much easier time of it. There is no interest rate risk or currency rate risk to hedge. For example, the CDO might earn a euro premium for selling 10 million euro of protection on a reference obligor that normally issues sterling debt. If the obligor defaults, cash settlement is based on the then 10 million euro amount of debt and the recovery is based on that benchmark amount. Notice we constructed our deal to be cash settled. In a physically settled deal, the disposition of the currency risk must be carefully outlined, especially if a long workout period is allowed. As we'll see later, balance-sheet deals referencing multicurrency portfolios also pose special problems.

For many deals, the bank arrangers will not provide hedges that have no unwind cost in the event of default. For other deals, the cost of a hedge is deemed to be too much, leaving too little excess cash for the equity investor to find investment attractive. Four common methods of lowering hedge costs are as follows:

1. The collateral is swapped based on a fixed amortization schedule set up at the start of the deal. This is usually employed for cash deals in which the tranches are to be issued as floating rate tranches, but the assets are primarily fixed rate. All or part of the portfolio that requires a hedge may be included in the swap. Sometimes managers like to keep a portion of the portfolio unhedged, since they feel they can use the extra flexibility to their advantage. In either case, as assets mature, default, or are reinvested, the hedge amount required may vary, albeit the schedule is fixed. Some investment banks may offer this swap for multicurrency assets. Other types of swaps require that the assets first be hedged to a single currency before entering into the larger portfolio swap.
2. Each asset may have its own individual currency swap; the portfolio can be hedged with currency options; or the portfolio can be completely unhedged with respect to currency. Managers may have to make a case to rating agencies about their ability to manage multicurrency portfolios if they leave a portion unhedged. Some consultants provide *currency overlays* in which they charge a hedge fee for managing the currency risk. A CDO manager essentially subcontracts the currency hedge by purchasing the currency overlay.
3. Interest rate caps are sometimes used instead of a swap to hedge interest rate risk. The cap is paid for with an up-front fee, and this cost is incorporated into the initial deal economics. If fixed rate assets are used in a floating rate deal, a cap will hedge the risk of rising Euribor rates. A cap is a series of calls on the underlying interest rate index, which is Euribor in our example. The manager specifies a strike price for the cap. The payment dates for the cap match the coupon payments on the

CDO. For example, the payment, if any, on payment date t is calculated as follows:

$$F \times N \times (\max[0, R_{t-m,t} - S])$$

where
f = payment frequency
N = notional face value/principal
S = strike or fixed cap rate
$R_{t-(\text{period})}$ = t-period floating rate set at time t – (one period)

4. Payment basis swaps account for timing mismatches in the deal. The swap desk agrees to take in deal cash flows and pay agreed coupons on the correct payment dates. Alternatively, the manager may decide to reinvest all cash flows and manage the timing of payments.

The preceding hedges are merely choices for the manager. Rating agencies do not mandate any of them, but the more certain the cash flows, the easier it is to rate a deal.

Cash asset-based CDOs, especially multicurrency deals, have a much greater degree of complexity in hedging currency and interest rate risk than synthetic CDOs.

SETTLEMENT IN THE EVENT OF DEFAULT OR CREDIT EVENT

In the event of a default in the cash CDO portfolio, the manager will try to maximize recovery on the asset. In cash deals, the manager's expertise in workout situations is one of the criteria of management selection. Investors should ask the following question. Did the manager get experience in the banking industry, and in how many workout situations has the manager participated? The workout can sometimes last up to two years. Foregoing the present value from sale of the defaulted asset might be worth it if the manager can recover more. If a default occurs near the expected final maturity of an affected tranche, the investors may want some voice in deciding whether to extend the workout process. This is particularly true of equity investors.

In the synthetic CDO, cash settlement occurs within 90 days. When a credit event occurs, the purchaser of credit protection from the CDO—usually the bank arranger—provides the CDO (the trustee) with a *credit event notice* and *notice of publicly available information*. These notifications satisfy the *conditions to payment*. The *cash settlement amount* is the difference between the relevant par value amount of the reference obligation and the market price. As soon as this occurs, coupon interest stops accruing on the cash settlement amount (the loss amount on the reference obligation). The cash settlement amount is still unknown, however, so it is estimated and retroactively adjusted, if necessary.

Several business days prior to the *valuation date*, the *calculation agent* (usually the bank arranger) gets bids on the reference obligation from five dealers that are active market makers in the CDS market. In today's market, this could include dealers such as Credit Suisse First Boston International, Morgan Stanley International, JPMorgan Chase, Citigroup/Salomon, Goldman Sachs International, Merrill Lynch, and Deutsche Bank AG, among others. The calculation agent uses the highest bid of at least two full quotations obtained on the same business day within three business days of the valuation date to calculate the cash settlement amount. The cash settlement amount is paid three business days after the valuation date.

What if the calculation agent can't get two full quotations? After all, this obligation just defaulted, and the market may be irregular. In that case, the calculation agent will attempt the process again or attempt to obtain a weighted average quotation for up to five business days after the valuation date.

After all that, in the unlikely event the calculation agent is unsuccessful, the calculation agent will request a disinterested dealer in this type of reference obligation to use this same determination method for up to an additional five business days. If the disinterested dealer is unable to obtain the *final price*, the calculation agent will determine the final price on the date following the end of the five-day period. The calculation agent will promptly notify the CDO manager and trustee of the basis for its determination. Figure 9.15 shows a typical cash settlement process.

Different dealers may have slightly different cash settlement timelines. This is based on their interpretation of the ISDA language governing physical settlement of the CDS they have written to hedge the CDS they have with the CDO. When an arbitrage deal is executed, the bank arranger hedges by buying credit default protection from the CDO and selling credit protection in a trade that is matched as much as possible. Most market transactions call for physical settlement. The bank arranger as protection buyer will not want to deliver notice until it receives notice from the counterparty to which it sold protection. The preceding timeline is based on my and Allen Overy's interpretation of ISDA documents in early 2002. These slight variations will not significantly add to or subtract from the cash settlement timeline.

This may sound more complicated than a workout situation, but it is much more streamlined. The process is much faster, and the recovery amount is available for reinvestment in another CDS or to accrue interest

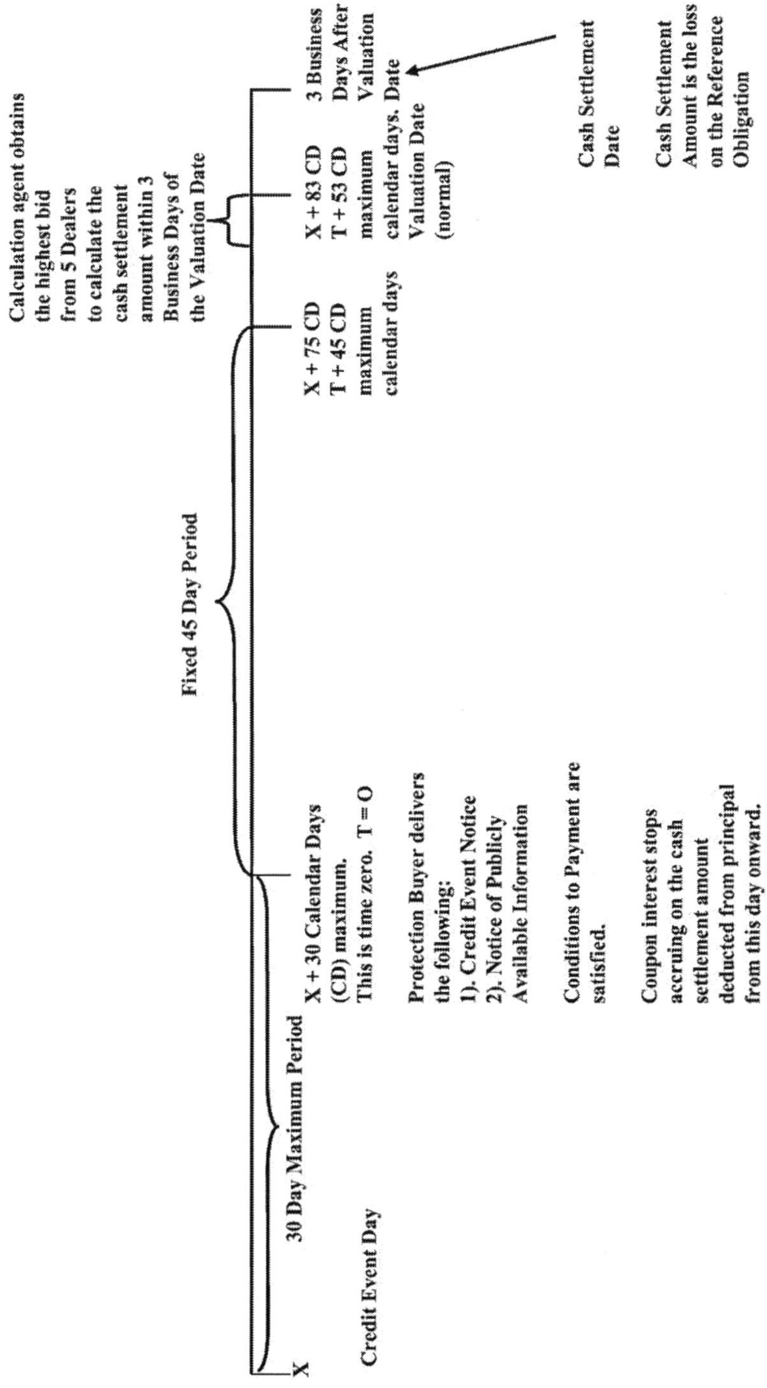

FIGURE 9.15 Typical Timeline for Cash Settlement of CDS

in the reserve account. Investors in this CDO must determine whether they feel they will get the best recovery value in the event of default. The hope is that by judiciously choosing the portfolio and manager in the first place, a default will be a rare event.

DOCUMENTATION

After all the discussion about CDS language, it would be easy to conclude that the documentation for a synthetic arbitrage CDO must be more voluminous than that for a cash synthetic arbitrage CDO. Actually the opposite is true. The cash arbitrage CDO requires much more detailed information about how the deal will be managed, triggers, and other aspects of the cash transaction. The documentation of the transaction is generally several times more massive than for a synthetic arbitrage CDO.

CASH VERSUS SYNTHETIC ARBITRAGE CDO EQUITY CASH FLOWS

The cash arbitrage CDO documentation is longer and more complicated than that of the synthetic CDOs. The hedges are much more complicated for cash arbitrage CDOs than synthetic CDOs, and in both cases, the equity investor bears the risk if hedge counterparties default. There is more risk in ramping up the portfolio for a cash arbitrage CDO than for a synthetic CDO. The portfolio of a cash arbitrage CDO includes high-yield assets, whereas the synthetic arbitrage CDO does not. It would seem to follow that greater complexity results in greater reward. It would also seem to follow that greater risk results in greater reward. But it isn't true—at least it isn't true at this time for these products.

The return on the synthetic arbitrage CDO's equity often exceeds the return on the cash arbitrage CDO. In the fall of 2002, the spreads of CDSs gapped out. They were so wide that the returns on equity exceeded the returns available in the cash market by as much as 20 percent and more. This was an anomaly, but it illustrates the point that investors can earn higher returns for comparable risks.

The type of equity structure we've used for our synthetic arbitrage CDO is very clean and advantageous to the equity investor. As we'll see later, other structures are not as advantageous, so the stated returns on those structures will offer a less favorable deal relative to cash arbitrage CDOs. As investors become more aware of the differences, they will ask for structures similar to the one we've outlined in our example, which is why I chose it.

Equity distributions are often made annually. There is usually a target objective under the no-loss and Moody's base-case historical loss scenarios. In the cash arbitrage CDO, the excess proceeds are the sum of interest collections and certain fees, less expenses (including debt expenses, asset management fees, CDO setup costs, and administrative expenses). At maturity, after repayment of all indebtedness and expenses, the equity investors receive the remainder of the CDO's assets as a final payment based on the percentage of the equity investment.

The equity payments are the obligation of the SPE that issues the CDO and are in no way the obligation of the manager. These are buy-and-hold investments, and equity investors understand that these are very illiquid investments. The only difference between the synthetic arbitrage CDO and the cash arbitrage CDO equity cash flows in our examples is that there is a possibility that when losses exceed the initial equity investment, cash flows are diverted for the benefit of triple-A and double-A noteholders, if required. This is a structural enhancement from the senior noteholder's point of view, and the likelihood this cash flow would be needed is very small. The unused accumulated cash flow reverts to the equity investors at the end of the transaction.

Figure 9.16 shows the equity IRR sensitivity analysis graph for various recovery values and default rates. The graph is representative of the returns for our managed synthetic arbitrage CDO example during an economic scenario when initial CDS spreads are relatively wide, as they were during the late fall and early winter of 2002. IRR returns are shown for the no-default scenario, the Moody's historical base-case scenario, and for defaults up to three times the base-case default scenario.

Most investors focus on the base-case default scenario. It is important to note that the base-case scenario is based on Moody's *historical* data for assets with the same WARF as our CDO portfolio. We'll examine this assumption in more detail later and make recommendations about alternative ways of looking at equity returns.

SAMPLE CASH FLOWS

A synthetic arbitrage CDO is much simpler to model than a cash arbitrage CDO. Usually direct feeds of interest rates provide data from which to build a forward curve of interest rates used to discount and amortize cash flows in the deal.

Table 9.15 shows the cash flows for the deal expenses, not including the management fees. Some of the fees and expenses occur periodically, and some occur up front. In this instance, the bank arranger pays the up-front

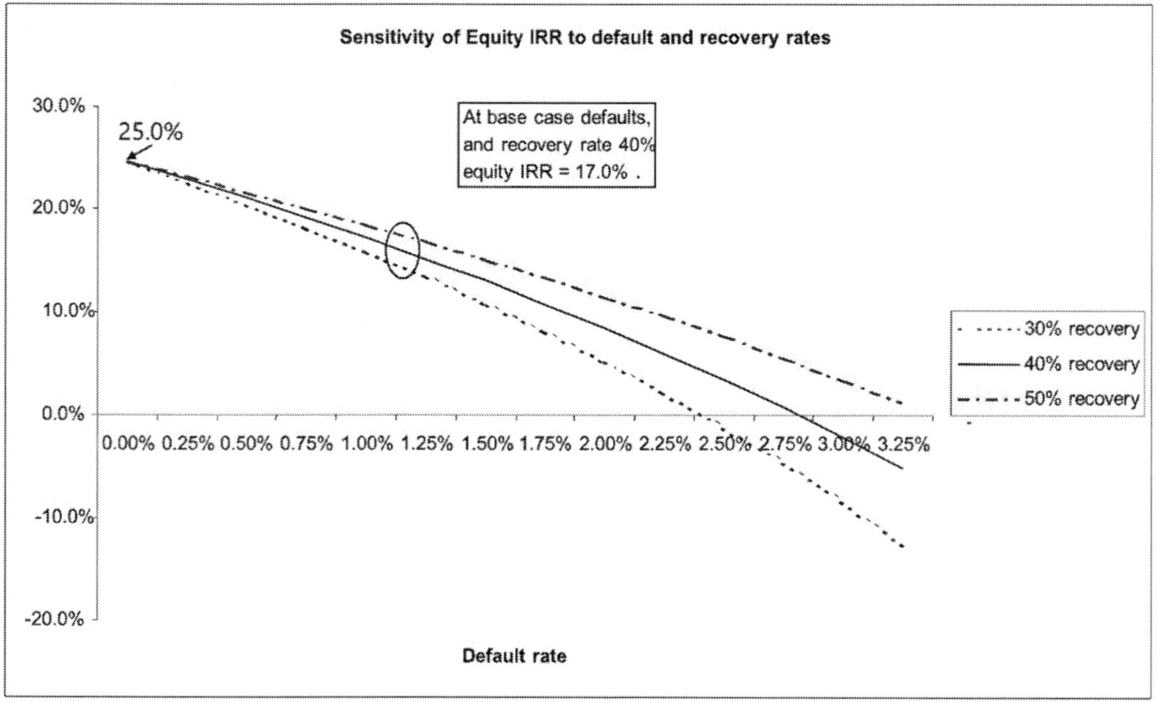

No Default Scenario IRR is 25.0%, Base Case Default scenario IRR is 17.0%.

FIGURE 9.17 Equity Returns - Sensitivity Analysis

TABLE 9.15 Typical Expenses for Synthetic Arbitrage CDO

Period Begin Date	Language Mismatch Premium	Structuring Fee 50 bps	Under-writing Fees	Bank Arranger Admin	Rating Rating Agencies	Trustee/ Collateral Ad/ Counsel	Legal Fees	Off-shore Counsel Fees	SPE Start-Up Costs	Accountant Fees	SPE Trustees 4-Tranches	SPE Admin 4-Tranches	SPE Calc. & Wire Fees	Luxem-bourg Lisitng Fee	Total Fees & Costs
	0.0005	−2,500,000	−1,022,500	−250,000	−250,000	−375,000	−520,000	−110,000	−50,000	−80,000	−77,500	−25,000	−60,000	−15,000	−7,162,814
1/2/2002															
2/2/2003	−62,500	−138,538	−56,662	−13,854	−13,854	−20,781	−28,816	−6,096	−2,771	−4,433	−4,295	−1,385	−3,325	−831	−358,141
5/2/2003	−62,500	−138,538	−56,662	−13,854	−13,854	−20,781	−28,816	−6,096	−2,771	−4,433	−4,295	−1,385	−3,325	−831	−358,141
8/2/2003	−62,500	−138,538	−56,662	−13,854	−13,854	−20,781	−28,816	−6,096	−2,771	−4,433	−4,295	−1,385	−3,325	−831	−358,141
11/2/2003	−62,500	−138,538	−56,662	−13,854	−13,854	−20,781	−28,816	−6,096	−2,771	−4,433	−4,295	−1,385	−3,325	−831	−358,141
2/2/2004	−62,500	−138,538	−56,662	−13,854	−13,854	−20,781	−28,816	−6,096	−2,771	−4,433	−4,295	−1,385	−3,325	−831	−358,141
5/2/2004	−62,500	−138,538	−56,662	−13,854	−13,854	−20,781	−28,816	−6,096	−2,771	−4,433	−4,295	−1,385	−3,325	−831	−358,141
8/2/2004	−62,500	−138,538	−56,662	−13,854	−13,854	−20,781	−28,816	−6,096	−2,771	−4,433	−4,295	−1,385	−3,325	−831	−358,141
11/2/2004	−62,500	−138,538	−56,662	−13,854	−13,854	−20,781	−28,816	−6,096	−2,771	−4,433	−4,295	−1,385	−3,325	−831	−358,141
2/2/2005	−62,500	−138,538	−56,662	−13,854	−13,854	−20,781	−28,816	−6,096	−2,771	−4,433	−4,295	−1,385	−3,325	−831	−358,141
5/2/2005	−62,500	−138,538	−56,662	−13,854	−13,854	−20,781	−28,816	−6,096	−2,771	−4,433	−4,295	−1,385	−3,325	−831	−358,141
8/2/2005	−62,500	−138,538	−56,662	−13,854	−13,854	−20,781	−28,816	−6,096	−2,771	−4,433	−4,295	−1,385	−3,325	−831	−358,141
11/2/2005	−62,500	−138,538	−56,662	−13,854	−13,854	−20,781	−28,816	−6,096	−2,771	−4,433	−4,295	−1,385	−3,325	−831	−358,141
2/2/2006	−62,500	−138,538	−56,662	−13,854	−13,854	−20,781	−28,816	−6,096	−2,771	−4,433	−4,295	−1,385	−3,325	−831	−358,141
5/2/2006	−62,500	−138,538	−56,662	−13,854	−13,854	−20,781	−28,816	−6,096	−2,771	−4,433	−4,295	−1,385	−3,325	−831	−358,141
8/2/2006	−62,500	−138,538	−56,662	−13,854	−13,854	−20,781	−28,816	−6,096	−2,771	−4,433	−4,295	−1,385	−3,325	−831	−358,141
11/2/2006	−62,500	−138,538	−56,662	−13,854	−13,854	−20,781	−28,816	−6,096	−2,771	−4,433	−4,295	−1,385	−3,325	−831	−358,141
2/2/2007	−62,500	−138,538	−56,662	−13,854	−13,854	−20,781	−28,816	−6,096	−2,771	−4,433	−4,295	−1,385	−3,325	−831	−358,141
5/2/2007	−62,500	−138,538	−56,662	−13,854	−13,854	−20,781	−28,816	−6,096	−2,771	−4,433	−4,295	−1,385	−3,325	−831	−358,141
8/2/2007	−62,500	−138,538	−56,662	−13,854	−13,854	−20,781	−28,816	−6,096	−2,771	−4,433	−4,295	−1,385	−3,325	−831	−358,141
11/2/2007	−62,500	−138,538	−56,662	−13,854	−13,854	−20,781	−28,816	−6,096	−2,771	−4,433	−4,295	−1,385	−3,325	−831	−358,141

fees and expenses, where applicable, and amortizes the cost over the life of the deal. These costs are recovered in the reduction of net CDS premium paid to the SPV for protection on the names in the portfolio and would be factored into any unwind of a CDS contract with the SPV.

The bank arranger may charge a periodic fee for making sure that the synthetic CDO uses the most favorable language for the investor. When the bank arranger hedges itself in the European market, it may not be able to get terms such as modified restructuring. This creates a language mismatch between the protection bought from the CDO and the protection sold in the market. The bank arranger will charge a small negotiable fee to hedge the language mismatch for the specific contracts involved. For the purposes of this spreadsheet, I assumed that could be all of the contracts, although in practice, I would use only the actual percentage. I arbitrarily set a mismatch fee of 5 bps, but mismatch fees as low as 2 bps are sometimes available.

Structuring fees, legal fees, and rating agency fees are paid up front, but for purposes of looking at net cash flows, I'm amortizing the fees over the life of the deal at a rate of 4.0 percent. This is arbitrary. The higher the assumed rate, the higher the costs reflected in the amortized cash flows. To be a bit perverse, I've assumed that collateral interest and reserve account interest is only 1 percent, thus penalizing the deal relative to the amortized costs. In practice, an actual rate curve can be used to determine the interest rate to use to amortize each period's costs or to calculate each period's interest.

The cash flow to the SPE before management fees is calculated for the no-loss scenario simply by multiplying the total notional amount of the deal by the premium available in the marketplace. In this example, the gross spread for the entire portfolio is 198 bps, or 1.98 percent. The net cash flow to the SPE after subtracting deal costs is shown in Table 9.16.

Of course, our synthetic arbitrage CDO has management fees of 12.5 percent, and each tranche pays interest, which is the liability cost. Notice that the AAA-rated tranche was to be offered at LIBOR plus 50 bps. In the spreadsheet, I've used 55 bps to show that in a typical deal, some room is usually allowed so that the underwriters can sell the tranches cheaper, if necessary. If the tranches are sold at 50 bps, the 5 bps may be passed on to the equity holder or may be retained by the underwriter. This is negotiated between the manager and underwriter when the fees and level at which the tranches are underwritten is discussed (see Table 9.17).

Notice that the IRR on the equity is around 30.60 percent in the no-loss scenario (see Table 9.18). One can make some base-case assumptions and recalculate. For example, using a base-case constant annual default rate (CADR) of 0.25 percent, a 35 percent recovery rate assuming the first default occurs immediately, and recovery occurs six months after default and is cash

TABLE 9.16 Cash Flows to SPE

Year Fraction	Month	Period Beg. Date	Days in Period	Notional Balance	Cumulative Notional Losses	Notional Cash Flow A/360 in arrears 1.980%	Total Fees and Costs: 7,162,814	Net Premium Paid to SPV: 174.49 bps
0	0	11/1/2002	0	500,000,000	0	0	0	
0.255556	3	2/1/2003	92	500,000,000	0	2,530,000	−358,141	2,171,859
0.247222	6	5/1/2003	89	500,000,000	0	2,447,500	−358,141	2,089,359
0.255556	9	8/1/2003	92	500,000,000	0	2,530,000	−358,141	2,171,859
0.255556	12	11/1/2003	92	500,000,000	0	2,530,000	−358,141	2,171,859
0.255556	15	2/1/2004	92	500,000,000	0	2,530,000	−358,141	2,171,859
0.250000	18	5/1/2004	90	500,000,000	0	2,475,000	−358,141	2,116,859
0.255556	21	8/1/2004	92	500,000,000	0	2,530,000	−358,141	2,171,859
0.255556	24	11/1/2004	92	500,000,000	0	2,530,000	−358,141	2,171,859
0.255556	27	2/1/2005	92	500,000,000	0	2,530,000	−358,141	2,171,859
0.247222	30	5/1/2005	89	500,000,000	0	2,447,500	−358,141	2,089,359
0.255556	33	8/1/2005	92	500,000,000	0	2,530,000	−358,141	2,171,859
0.255556	36	11/1/2005	92	500,000,000	0	2,530,000	−358,141	2,171,859
0.255556	39	2/1/2006	92	500,000,000	0	2,530,000	−358,141	2,171,859
0.247222	42	5/1/2006	89	500,000,000	0	2,447,500	−358,141	2,089,359
0.255556	45	8/1/2006	92	500,000,000	0	2,530,000	−358,141	2,171,859
0.255556	48	11/1/2006	92	500,000,000	0	2,530,000	−358,141	2,171,859
0.255556	51	2/1/2007	92	500,000,000	0	2,530,000	−358,141	2,171,859
0.247222	54	5/1/2007	89	500,000,000	0	2,447,500	−358,141	2,089,359
0.255556	57	8/1/2007	92	500,000,000	0	2,530,000	−358,141	2,171,859
0.255556	60	11/1/2007	92	500,000,000	0	2,530,000	−358,141	2,171,859

TABLE 9.17 Residual Equity Cash Flows, No-Loss Scenario

Net Premium Paid to SPV 174.49 BPS	Management Fee 0.125%	Account 1 Collateral Interest 1.00%	Account 2 Collection and Operating 1.00%	A-1 Super Senior 0.10% 432,500,000	A-2 Aaa 0.55% 20,000,000	A-3 Aa2 1.10% 12,500,000	B Baa2 3.50% 15,000,000	Cash Flow Total Ex-Equity	Interest On Equity Collateral 1.00%	Residual Cash IRR 30.60% 20,000,000 1.00%
	−625,000			0	0	0	0	−625,000		−20,000,000
2,171,859	0	118,750	2,290,609	−110,528	−28,111	−35,139	−131,250	1,627,441	48,438	1,050,878
2,089,359	0	118,750	2,208,109	−106,924	−27,194	−33,993	−131,250	1,550,607	48,438	1,599,045
2,171,859	0	118,750	2,290,609	−110,528	−28,111	−35,139	−131,250	1,627,441	48,438	1,675,878
2,171,859	−625,000	118,750	2,290,609	−110,528	−28,111	−35,139	−131,250	1,002,441	48,438	1,050,878
2,171,859	0	118,750	2,290,609	−110,528	−28,111	−35,139	−131,250	1,627,441	48,438	1,675,878
2,116,859	0	118,750	2,235,609	−108,125	−27,500	−34,375	−131,250	1,576,219	48,438	1,624,656
2,171,859	0	118,750	2,290,609	−110,528	−28,111	−35,139	−131,250	1,627,441	48,438	1,675,878
2,171,859	−625,000	118,750	2,290,609	−110,528	−28,111	−35,139	−131,250	1,002,441	48,438	1,050,878
2,171,859	0	118,750	2,290,609	−110,528	−28,111	−35,139	−131,250	1,627,441	48,438	1,675,878
2,089,359	0	118,750	2,208,109	−106,924	−27,194	−33,993	−131,250	1,550,607	48,438	1,599,045
2,171,859	0	118,750	2,290,609	−110,528	−28,111	−35,139	−131,250	1,627,441	48,438	1,675,878
2,171,859	−625,000	118,750	2,290,609	−110,528	−28,111	−35,139	−131,250	1,002,441	48,438	1,050,878
2,171,859	0	118,750	2,290,609	−110,528	−28,111	−35,139	−131,250	1,627,441	48,438	1,675,878
2,089,359	0	118,750	2,208,109	−106,924	−27,194	−33,993	−131,250	1,550,607	48,438	1,599,045
2,171,859	0	118,750	2,290,609	−110,528	−28,111	−35,139	−131,250	1,627,441	48,438	1,675,878
2,171,859	−625,000	118,750	2,290,609	−110,528	−28,111	−35,139	−131,250	1,002,441	48,438	1,050,878
2,171,859	0	118,750	2,290,609	−110,528	−28,111	−35,139	−131,250	1,627,441	48,438	1,675,878
2,089,359	0	118,750	2,208,109	−106,924	−27,194	−33,993	−131,250	1,550,607	48,438	1,599,045
2,171,859	0	118,750	2,290,609	−110,528	−28,111	−35,139	−131,250	1,627,441	48,438	1,675,878
2,171,859	0	118,750	2,290,609	−110,528	−28,111	−35,139	−131,250	1,627,441	48,438	21,675,878

settled, this base-case CADR suggests an IRR of 27.92 percent for the equity residuals.

We can also stress-test the cash flows for a 1.00 percent CADR, and the equity residuals are 16.9 percent. Notice that takes into account amounts recovered after a default, and the losses due to defaults do not yet exceed the original investment in the equity. Once accumulated losses exceeded the original equity investment of EUR 20 million, cash flows would divert to the reserve account.

Earlier we discussed economies of scale. If this deal were EUR 1 billion in size, or double the current size, the deal economics improve dramatically. The no-loss scenario equity IRR would be 37.7 percent; the base-case scenario of a CADR of 0.25 percent per annum with a 35 percent recovery rate would be 35.4 percent; and the stress case with a CADR of 1 percent per annum with a 35 percent recovery rate would be 26.4 percent.

But wait a minute—I was using a 35 percent recovery rate for these calculations. Shouldn't I use the industry standard of 40 percent? Most investment-grade deals in the European market were marketed with a 50 percent recovery rate in the first part of this decade. That was indefensible then and is indefensible now. Even 40 percent may seem too high to many buyers, albeit this is a very popular way to market these deals. In practice, I would also do sensitivity analyses over a wide range of recovery rate scenarios. Table 9.18 shows the effect of doubling the deal size as well as the effect of a 5 percent change in the recovery value assumption for this particular deal from 35 percent to 40 percent.

Sensitivities will vary by deal. One can, however, develop a feel for the order of magnitude of the effects. Spreadsheets like Table 9.18 are useful,

TABLE 9.18 Managed Synthetic Arbitrage CDO Economies of Scale: Equity IRRs

Scenario	35 percent Recovery		40 percent Recovery	
	Deal Size		Deal Size	
	500 Million	1 Billion	500 Million	1 Billion
No-loss	30.60%	37.70%	30.60%	37.7%
Base case*	27.92%	35.39%	28.1%	35.52%
Stress case**	16.90%	26.42%	17.96%	27.24%
Discrete default case***	21.22%	29.72%	22.07%	30.41%

*Base-case CADR is 0.25 percent per annum.

***Stress case CADR is 1.00 percent per annum.

***Discrete default case is one immediate obligor default and another default just before month 36.

since they can instantaneously calculate sensitivities. Many simulation models take a much longer time to calculate sensitivities. They may be more precise, but they are often not more accurate. Many sophisticated models are not transparent, making them difficult to troubleshoot. For all of these reasons, spreadsheets provide a good crosscheck of results.

Whatever the model, the structure of the CDO is the real key to the value of a CDO investment (see Table 9.18). Model refinements are wonderful, but a small error in a model is insignificant compared to accepting a structure that does not give one the proper claim to cash flows in the deal, as we discover in Chapter 10.

Since the Moody's CADR is a standard method for modeling and for showing results across a wide variety of deals, I use this for our example. The CADR assumptions shown in Table 9.18 are what investors will find in most marketing and research pieces published by the Street. The reality is that these numbers often do not capture the *granularity* of actual portfolios. You'll recall that each obligor makes up 2 percent of my portfolio. Historical probabilities indicate that a smaller percentage of my portfolio would default on a per annum basis, but in fact when a single default occurs, it will affect 2 percent of my investment portfolio. The argument is that it would be unfair to tag the portfolio with a prerecovery default of 2 percent right away, since it is unlikely this would happen. The theory is that if we show the lower CADR based on historical defaults happening right away, we should probabilistically capture this effect.

A sensitivity analysis should include tagging the portfolio with immediate discrete defaults. The last row of Table 9.18 captures this. I've inserted a scenario in which one obligor defaults immediately, and another defaults just before month 36. I used a scenario in which I didn't have to divert equity cash flows to make this easier to follow. In practice, a scenario analysis would include the case where the original equity investment is exhausted and cash flows are diverted.

Most deal presentations will not include discrete default scenarios, and it is up to the investor to review this. Given the high degree of defaults in synthetic portfolios in the past two years, it is difficult to understand why this type of sensitivity analysis is not included in standard deal presentations, for instance, showing one default per annum, but that is simply not the case. Conversely, standard marketing presentations for cash deals do not show this degree of stress testing, either.

As we mentioned before, there are economies of scale in bringing a CDO to market. Legal costs, rating agency fees, and structuring fees have a large up-front fixed component. In comparison, the ongoing maintenance fees are minimal. For the preceding analysis, I simply assumed that the initial portfolio was upsized to 1 billion, which means each obligor would have increased in value from EUR 10 million to EUR 20 million. I used this simplifying assumption so that I wouldn't have to retranche the portfolio and could compare deals in a consistent manner.

Unlike cash asset arbitrage CDOs, it is much easier to increase the size of a synthetic CDO by adding more obligors. Instead of increasing the obligor size from EUR 10 million to EUR 20 million, we could simply have increased the number of obligors from 50 to 100. This means we'd have 100 obligors with a notional size of EUR 10 million each. Now it is much easier to get a much higher diversity score for the underlying portfolio. It is also much easier to decrease the size of the equity tranche relative to the total deal.

In other words, instead of having an equity tranche that is 4 percent of the deal, we could create a smaller equity tranche on a percentage basis, as low as 2 percent to 3 percent in some transactions, and deals have come to market with even lower percentage equity tranches. This increases the leverage on the equity tranche and therefore dramatically increases the returns. For instance, for the deal just shown, if I decrease the size of the equity tranche to 2 percent of the deal, the equity IRR for the 1 billion euro deal, using the no-default scenario and a 35 percent recovery rate, increases from 37.5 percent to 78.2 percent. Of course, this isn't a strictly valid comparison. I didn't actually create a new portfolio, solve for the new tranching, calculate the new portfolio gross spread, and so forth. Nonetheless, it gives you a feel for the order of magnitude of the benefit. In this case it is more than double the IRR. The increased leverage also makes the equity tranche more vulnerable in scenario analysis, but the smaller granularity of the portfolio works to the benefit of the investor.

Another observation about creating a spreadsheet for a synthetic deal is that it is very easy to follow the cash flows, troubleshoot calculations, and observe the effects of a sensitivity analysis. It is easy to see possibilities for refinements and possibilities for further analysis.

Cash deals are much more complicated to model. A portfolio of fairly straightforward bonds may include callable bonds or sinking funds. Furthermore, each bond's principal and interest must be modelled. Each bond has a different maturity and coupon, so the cash flows aren't nice and even. Now reinvestment assumptions become more critical since the investor must be able to reinvest the proceeds of maturing bonds at a minimum spread for the deal economics to continue working. Furthermore, principal and interest coverage tests are more difficult to calculate. PIK tranches further complicate the spreadsheet. Hedges also add a degree of complexity. When the assets include asset-backed securities or MBSs, a program such as Intex might be required to model the deal's cash flows.

Dedicated, skilled quantitative analysts are required to model these deals. Often a good programmer cannot anticipate the type of analysis a

CDO structurer requires or cannot anticipate structural innovation. Each deal usually has its own dedicated program to account for its structural anomalies. It is much harder to troubleshoot the cash flow economics and sensitivity analysis.

SUMMARY OF CASH ARBITRAGE CDOS VERSUS SYNTHETICS ARBITRAGE CDOS

Table 9.19 summarizes the key issues exemplified by our comparison of cash and synthetic CDOs.

TABLE 9.19 Summary of Cash Arbitrage CDOs versus Synthetic Arbitrage CDOs

Cash Arbitrage CDOs	Synthetic Arbitrage CDOs
• Size limited to around $500 million	• Much easier to create larger size deals
• Large AAA tranche	• Large super senior above small AAA
• Long documentation	• Documentation is brief
• Higher funding cost	• Lower funding cost
• Complicated waterfall	• Relatively simple waterfall
• PIK-able tranches	• No PIK-able tranches
• Rating agency inconsistency	• Ratings more straightforward
• Substantial sourcing risk—limited European universe	• Reduced sourcing risk—wider universe
• Physical assets required	• Can securitize nontransferable assets
• Difficult execution, note placement	• Fewer notes
• Funded	• Unfunded or partially funded
• Managed	• Static or managed
• Management fees 50–75 bps p.a. typical	• Management fees 10–30 bps p.a.
• 10–15% high yield	• 100% investment grade
• Baa3/BBB– average rating	• A2/A to Baa3/BBB– typical
• Interest and currency risk	• No interest and currency risk
• 7–9 year average life; 10-year final maturity	• Five-year bullet (slightly longer legal final maturity)
• Transfers assets to trust or SPV	• No asset transfer required
• Less leverage—equity is 8 to 20% of the deal	• More leverage—equity is 1.5 to 4.5% of the deal

Chapter 10

CDO Equity Structures

If you don't understand what is going on with your cash flows, you are in serious trouble. As we saw in the previous chapter, it is important to understand under what conditions assets will pay expected cash flows. In this chapter we explore how to view cash flows in the context of a securitization.

First, let's take a step back for some caveats. We won't launch into a rigorous analysis of models. It's more useful to review some very simple examples of calculations that market practitioners routinely get wrong. These crop up again and again in various forms, and they cost both investors and capital markets groups extraordinary amounts of money.

Even when Monte Carlo engines have been well designed and sound methodology for random number generators has been used, the mistakes are made. The models are often precise, but not accurate. Incredibly, *market professionals* made all the examples of conceptual errors I highlight here. The math in the following examples is simple, but people tripped over concepts. If one can't visualize the cash flows, how does one model them?

Cash flows matter. Timing, frequency, magnitude, and probability of receipt of cash flows are the four elements that determine the value of an asset. These are also the four elements that determine the value of a structure.

Before I go further, I'd like to clarify a few points. I'm often asked why I mention both timing and frequency. Isn't this redundant? I do this for absolute clarity. It is not sufficient to state that I will get all of my cash back within the year. This is merely the timing of my ultimate receipt of cash flows. I want to know the frequency. Will I receive the cash flow in one lump sum toward year-end, in equal monthly payments, or in a varied stream of payments over the course of the year? I'm not indifferent.

Frequency of cash flows will imply different value to different investors. One reason is that different investors often have different reinvestment rates and different tax and accounting rules. One of the key factors that any investor should scout for in valuing a securitization is what assumptions are made for reinvestment of cash flows, both within a deal and in representing the deal's return to the investor. Everyone knows this—or do they?

What would the rate of interest be if you borrowed $500 million from a bank and paid it back at the rate of $46 million per month for a year? Okay, I know you don't know off the top of your head, but what would you guess it would be? You are paying back $552 million, which is 10.4 percent more than $500 million. Many smart people would guess the rate of interest is in the neighborhood of 10.4 percent.

They would be wrong.

The problem is that you don't have the full use of your money over the course of the year. The actual rate of interest is slightly more than 20.35 percent. That is very different from having full use of your money for the entire year and paying back $552 million at the *end* of the year.

You will recall from corporate finance the IRR, which on the 12-stream of monthly $46 million cash flows equals 1.55598%. This is expressed on a monthly basis, however. Annualizing this rate:

$$[(1 + .0155598)^{12} - 1] \times 100 = 20.36\%$$

Of course, you saw this immediately. No one could be fooled by this type of financial optical illusion!

Oh, but they could. Lenders to car buyers and white goods buyers perpetrated just this sort of financial optical illusion on American consumers until the law required lenders to state effective annual interest rates on loans. Many of those American consumers were bankers and Wall Street professionals.

One has to know the calculation conventions for the financial instruments one models. Ignorance can cost you money. Mistakes can cost you money. Perversely, they're rarely in your favor.

Recently, an investment banker from one of the top five U.S. banks was arranging bond issuance for a northern European bank. The deal economics were agreed, and the bond was to have a stated coupon at a set semiannual bond equivalent yield, or semiannual BEY. The U.S. bond market convention uses a 30/360 day count basis and a semiannual BEY. For instance, if the agreed rate for the bond is a semiannual BEY of 8.806 percent, the coupon is paid semiannually, or twice a year. The coupon rate is 8.806 percent divided by 2, or 4.403 percent. It doesn't need to obey rules of logic. It's just a convention.

The investment banker said that some of the investors wanted a quarterly coupon. To keep the economics the same, he told them he would pay them a quarterly coupon of 2.2015 percent, which is 4.403 percent divided by 2. I pointed out to him that the economics were not the same. This is because 2.2015 percent times four would imply a quarterly bond equivalent yield of 8.806 percent and that equated to a higher bond semiannual BEY than 8.806 percent. In fact it equated to just a bit more than 8.9029 percent.

Despite all his time in the market, he was lost. The quarterly bond rate he needed to quote was 8.71 percent, or a payment of 2.1775 percent four times per year. Rather than face the fact that he would have to call his investors and correct his earlier statement, he tried to argue why it didn't make any material difference. He persisted until I showed him the numbers. For the 12-year $250 million bond deal the error made a payment difference of $60,000 per quarter. Every quarter. For 12 years. Would he offer to personally make up the difference?

Another common error occurs when comparing fixed coupons with floating coupons. A rate of 10 percent calculated on a bond basis is not the same as 10 percent calculated on a money market basis. Similarly, the number of basis points under LIBOR calculated on a bond financing is not the same as bond basis points.

One bond basis point is not equal to a LIBOR or money market basis point.

Conventionally, conversions are done on a bond basis. If we change the frequency and go from quarterly money market (QMM) to semi bond, we must first convert QMM to a quarterly bond basis and then convert to semi bond.

Example

Three-month LIBOR is at 5 percent. You achieve a financing cost of LIBOR – 25 bps. What is the semiannual BEY?

$$5.00 - .25 = 4.75\% \text{ Q MM}$$

$$[(1 + 4.75 \times (365/360) / 4 \times 100) \wedge 2 - 1] \times 200 = 4.84\ \% \text{ s.a. bond equivalent yield.}$$

Note that 5 percent QMM = 5.10 semi-annual BEY and the difference between 5.10% and 4.84 percent is 26 bps on a semi-annual bond equivalent yield basis.

This difference is not a constant, and discrepancies are larger for higher levels of interest rates.

These are only a few examples. Structurers write programs to deal with the day count conventions of various instruments in various countries. In addition, structurers write programs to account for different ways of calculating interest rates. But not everyone gets it correct, so it is useful for investors to check the cash flows themselves. At the minimum, an occasional spot check is in order.

ACCRUING ERRORS

When asked to make the following simple calculation by hand, many people get an incorrect answer. If you don't believe me, and want to have a little fun, ask a friend to solve the following.

Refer to the following table. Using just a pencil and paper, create a two-bond portfolio using bonds A and C to duration-match and proceeds-match bond B.

Bond	Modified Duration	Full Price	Par Amount
A	4	75	$400,000
B	5	60	$1,000,000
C	6	50	$600,000

The solution is as follows:

The market value of B is $600,000. This is 0.6 x $ 1 million.

Since the duration of B is halfway between that of A and C, half of the dollars must be invested in A and half of the dollars must be invested in C. Therefore, I must purchase $300,000 of A and $300,000 of C.

The required par amount of A is	$300,000 / 0.75 = $400,000
The required par amount of C is	$300,000 / 0.5 = $600,000

The key is that I'm investing the proper amount of dollars in each bond so that I get the expected change in dollar amounts on my hedge. In order to make this work, I have to normalize the par amount I purchase by the full prices of the bonds. Of course, everyone knows how to do the math, but when attention flags, it is easy to use the wrong basis in formulating the calculation.

Mistakes in interest calculations and mistakes in forward price calculations affect CDO warehousing calculations, portfolio cash flow calculations, and structured product calculations.

Let's assume that interest rates have moved higher from the levels at year-end 2002, and the yield curve is steeper. I can borrow money for 14 days at a rate of 7 $^{7}/_{8}$ percent on an actual/360 basis. Let's also assume that I can purchase a U.S. Treasury bond with a coupon of 11 $^{1}/_{4}$ at a dollar price of 104 $_{10/32}$ (a current yield of approximately 10.8 percent).

The bond pays coupons on the 15th of the month each six-month period in May and November of every year. It is now August 1, and I am financing this bond until August 15, for 14 days. Furthermore, I do not mark to market.

On August 1, the flat price of the bond is 104 $^{10}/32$, so I would pay $1,043,125.00. The accrued interest is $23,845.11 (accrued from May 15 to August 1: 78/184 days). The full price of the bond is $1,066,970.00 (quoted as 106.6970).

I own the bond on August 15 and do not mark to market. Therefore, in 14 days, my flat price is still 1,043,125.00 and the accrued on the bond is now $28,125. My income over the 14-day period is $4,279.89

My borrowing cost is

$$\frac{(\$1{,}066{,}970.11 \times 0.07874 \times 14)}{360} = \$3{,}267.60$$

This means I have a *positive carry* of $1,012.29

In an *arbitrage-free* world, I cannot borrow to buy and earn this kind of excess cash, so the market would tell me that the forward price must be such that I have *zero positive carry.*

To satisfy the arbitrage-free condition, if I wanted to sell this bond forward, the forward price would be such that I could not make a profit. The accrued interest remains the same, so the forward flat price of the bond must change to meet the arbitrage-free condition.

The *forward flat price* would have to be as follows:

$$\$1{,}043{,}125 - \$1{,}012.29 = \$1{,}042{,}112.71 \text{ (quoted as 104.21171)}$$

Note that the forward flat price is lower than the price on August 1. This is known as the *drop.*

The forward price doesn't always have to be lower, however. Suppose interest rates have moved even higher and the yield curve is *inverted.* I can borrow money for 14 days at a rate of 15 percent on an actual/360 basis. Let's further assume that I can purchase a U.S. Treasury bond with a coupon of 12.5 percent at a dollar price of 105 $^{10}/32$. This bond pays coupons on the 15th of the month each six-month period in May and November of every year. It is now August 1, and I am financing this bond until August 15, for 14 days. Furthermore, I do not mark to market.

What is the *flat price* (the ex-interest price) of this bond on August 1? The flat price is simply 10510/32 or a dollar amount of $1,053.125.00. The *accrued interest* is $26,494.57 (accrued from May 15 to August 1: 78/184 days). The *full price* of the bond is $1,079,619.56 (quoted as 107.961956). The full price of the bond is the amount that I have to pay for the bond.

I own the bond on August 15 and do not mark to market. Therefore, in 14 days, my flat price is still $1,053.125.00, but the accrued on the bond is now $31,250.00. My income over the 14-day period is $4,755.43. My borrowing cost is

$$(\$1{,}079{,}619.56 \times .15 \times 14)/360 = \$6297.78$$

This means I have a *negative carry* of $1,542.35.

The forward price is higher than the spot price. The forward flat price would be 1,053,125.00 + 1,542.35 = 1,054,667.35 plus accrued of 31,250.00, so the full price of the bond is 1,085917.35 or 108.591735.

If you are long a forward commodity contract, you have an obligation to purchase the commodity or give its cash equivalent on the pre-agreed delivery date. The value of a long forward contract is calculated as follows:

$$f_L = (F_0 - D_L)e^{-rT}$$

Where

F_0 = the forward price of the contract today,
D_L= the delivery price on the settlement date,
r = the continuously compounded interest rate applicable for the period from the trade date to settlement date, and
T= the time from trade date to settlement date.

If you are short a forward commodity contract, you have an obligation to sell the commodity (or you will receive its cash equivalent) on the pre-agreed delivery date. The value of a short forward contract is calculated as follows:

$$f_S = (D_S - F_0)e^{-rT}$$

where F_0 = the forward price of the contract today,
D = the delivery price on the settlement date,
r = the continuously compounded interest rate applicable for the period from the trade date to settlement date, and
T = the time from trade date to settlement date.

Petroleum-related forward contracts often exhibit *normal backwardation*. This means the *future price is lower than the spot price.* The futures prices tend to decline as maturity increases, so the price curve is negatively sloped. Keynes's theory of normal backwardation is based on the premise that production is planned, and consumption is flexible. Consumers of the commodity can buy it from many sources, but producers commit to production, and sometimes consume some of the commodity in the process of production. Hedgers who produce and are long the underlying commodity tend to go short futures, and speculators tend to go long futures. Keynes theorized speculators require a positive risk premium, meaning they must earn a positive abnormal expected return to take on the risk that the hedgers are trying to avoid.

For most non-petroleum-related commodities, the forward price curve is in *contango*, meaning that the *forward price exceeds the spot price*. Keynes theory ignored long hedgers, as well as the fact that speculators can make money off of incompetent or unlucky speculators. Nonetheless, the petroleum markets tend to exhibit backwardation.

PROBABILITY OF RECEIPT

The probability of receipt of cash flows seems so simple as to not bear mentioning. Yet this is a key risk that most residual cash flow investors or CDO equity investors assess when they buy these securities. Errors in assessing this risk can be so great in order of magnitude that they swamp the cash flow risks mentioned up to now.

Much depends on tolerance for potential losses. For instance, suppose I'm asked to make a bet of $100. There is a 50 percent chance I will win $300 immediately and a 50 percent chance I will lose the entire $100 immediately. I will take the bet. I don't mind losing $100, and the expected return is $150: [(0.5 x $300) + (0.5 x $0)].

Now suppose I'm asked to make a bet of $20 million. There is an 80 percent chance I'll win $30 million and a 20 percent chance I'll lose $20 million. I will probably decline the bet, because I don't want to lose $20 million, even though the expected value is $24 million. The downside risk is too catastrophic. Expected value is another financial optical illusion. Probability of receipt or loss of cash flows is important, and so is magnitude of the cash flows.

Let's further suppose I'm a hedge fund or an investment group of a reinsurance company, and I want to buy equity that has a payoff profile similar to the previous example. I don't want to put up any money up front, but I want someone to finance the losses as they occur. I also want the transaction to be done in the form of a credit default swap, and I want a bank to provide me with financing until the maturity of the transaction. This would mean that the bank would pay any credit losses, and I would be charged a finance rate for the money paid to cover the losses. This money is essentially a loan to me, which I must repay at the maturity of the CDO. Does the bank know how many of these transactions I've engaged in already? Should the bank lend me the money to make my bets?

It gets even more interesting if we change the payoff profile. Say I bet \$20 million for a 25 percent chance of winning \$30 million; a 25 percent chance of getting back only \$15 million; a 25 percent chance of getting back only \$5 million; and a 25 percent chance of getting back nothing. Now my expected return is only \$12.5 million. I would avoid this bet even if I were asked to bet only \$100 because the expected payoff is lower than my initial bet. Yet this is what happens to people who play against house odds at a casino, albeit the odds are more in favor of the player at a casino. CDO equity investors are making a more complicated bet with a more complicated payoff profile. Yet many equity investors unwittingly set themselves up for probable returns which were lower than their original investments even at the inception of their trade. How did that happen?

THE BEST AND WORST EQUITY INVESTMENTS

All equity tranches are not created equal. Besides portfolio selection, the largest variability among deals stems from the structure of the equity cash flows. Portfolios can either be actively managed, have limited right of substitution, or be completely static. Equity can be either rated or unrated. The investment in equity can be either funded or unfunded. There is also a wide variety of ways that cash flow is made available to the equity investor and to the senior tranches.

For example, in synthetic deals, we're familiar with the loss allocation shown in Figure 10.1.

Losses are allocated first to the equity investor. That isn't the whole story, however. CDOs vary in terms of how much of the stream of residual cash flow the equity investor can claim. Another key issue is the amount of

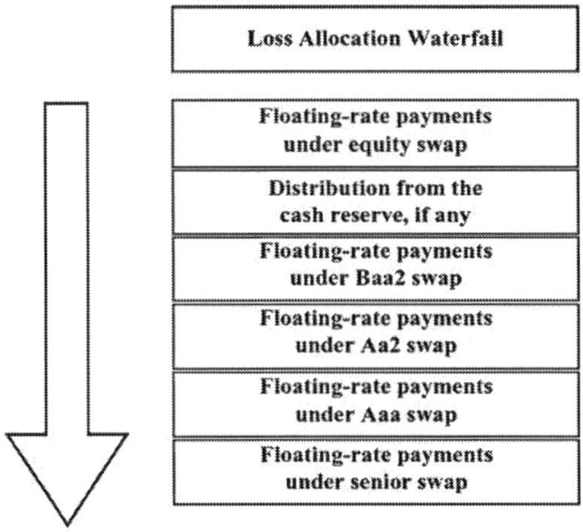

FIGURE 10.1 Loss Allocation in Reverse Order of Seniority

loss that can be allocated to the residual cash flow stream above and beyond the initial equity investment. The equity investor determines whether he is getting the best deal possible for the risk he takes, based on these structural features.

The more cash flow the equity investor gets, the less someone else gets. The following summarizes some of the common structures currently in the market:

- Best for rated tranche investors: The equity investor has the right to a return of original principal plus a fixed coupon only. One type of structure actively marketed in 2001–2002 offered fixed coupons in the neighborhood of 15 to 25 percent. The coupon is paid on the remaining equity balance only. This means that if the original equity investment is used to absorb losses due to default, the coupon is calculated only on the net balance. The remaining excess cash flows are paid to the bank arranger.
- The equity investor has the right to a return of original principal plus a fixed coupon only, but all of the residual cash flows are made available to pay the principal plus fixed coupon to the equity investor. Once this pre-agreed amount is satisfied, the remaining cash is paid to the bank arranger.
- The equity investor has the right to a portion of the equity residual cash flow, and the bank arranger retains a small strip of the residual equity cash flows.

- The equity investor has the right to the residual cash flows, but only if losses remain below a certain threshold. This threshold is usually set at 50 to 100 percent of the initial equity investment. For instance, for a 50 percent threshold, residual cash flows will be diverted to the reserve account once portfolio losses exceed $10 million, if the original equity investment is $20 million. The reserve account funds are made available to the Aaa and Aa noteholders in the unlikely event the funds are needed to meet coupon payments. Funds are also available for the unlikely event they are needed to repay principal, because losses threaten the return of principal to these highly rated tranches.
- The equity investor may invest funds that are used to purchase highly rated collateral, such as Treasuries. This highly rated collateral serves to overcollateralize the portfolio, and the equity investor earns the residual cash flows. The overcollateralization reduces the equity leverage. This device is used primarily for deals using lower-rated collateral such as highly leveraged transactions (HLTs) or high-yield bonds. The former Chase Secured Loan Trust (CSLT) deals used this type of structure.
- Best for equity investor: The equity investor gets maximum leverage and has the exclusive right to all of the residual cash flows. Loss is limited to the original investment in the equity. That is the worst type of deal from the point of view of investors in the rated tranches, but it is the best type of deal for the equity investors. As we'll discover later, if the portfolio is managed and not static, this structure has the highest degree of moral hazard.

This last structure is not exactly the same as the structure used for our earlier cash CDO deals, because cash CDO deals include structural protection for the senior investors. Overcollateralization (O/C) test, interest coverage (I/C) tests, and trading constraints work to the benefit of the senior tranches. Senior noteholders should not be indifferent to the payout structure to the equity investor.

THE BEST EQUITY EARNS ALL RESIDUALS

In many cash managed CDOs and certain synthetic managed arbitrage CDOs, the equity investor claims all of the residual cash flows. Earlier, we saw how these cash flows waterfall in a typical cash managed arbitrage CDO. The equity investor enjoys a payout of all of the residual cash flows as they occur, and the equity investor absorbs losses up to the amount of the initial equity investment only. Once the losses exceed the initial equity investment, accumulated cash flows above this amount are paid as they occur exclusively for the benefit of the equity investor. Any cash remaining at the maturity of the deal is paid out exclusively for the benefit of the equity investor.

If the equity holder manages this type of structure, the moral hazard is that once losses exceed the initial equity investment, the manager has an incentive to create a portfolio with as much spread income as possible. Any further losses are born by noteholders above the equity level. The next tranche in seniority is in peril. The only protections the other tranche investors have from this behavior are trading restrictions and cash flow triggers. If a trading desk is managing the deal and holding the equity tranche, it will attempt to pass on as many structural risks to the other tranche holders as it can.

When trading desks hold the equity of static synthetic CDOs, their first priority is to claim all of the residual cash flows.

EQUITY INVESTOR INJECTS CASH AS OVERCOLLATERALIZATION

Let's look at an example we haven't used before. In some structures, the equity investor invests a cash amount, which serves to overcollateralize a portfolio as a means of added credit enhancement for the senior investors. The equity cash flows are usually unrated, but it is possible to get a rating from Fitch or from Moody's for a segment of the equity cash flows that would have the same probability of loss as an investment-grade rated security. The entire residual cash flow stream due to the equity investor is not rated, but a probable return of a preset amount of cash flow is rated. Usually the return of principal and ultimate (not timely) return of an investment-grade equivalent coupon is rated.

Figures 10.2 and 10.3 show a funded equity tranche in which the investor gets all of the residual cash flows. The second structure shows a rated portion of the first-loss cash flows plus an unrated portion. In this structure, equity investors have varying degrees of leverage, but they both have first-loss risk.

Of course, the equity doesn't have to be rated. Both cash and synthetic arbitrage CDOs often have unrated first-loss tranches. The leveraged nature of the equity tranche means that as credit spreads widen, the equity investor receives a leveraged benefit from the widening as a new deal is assembled. Rating agency tranching is required for the rated senior tranches, and this determines the size of the unrated first-loss tranche. Rating agency tranching remains constant when credit spreads widen due to causes other than downgrades. Credit spreads may widen due to supply and demand conditions as sometimes happens in the credit default swap market.

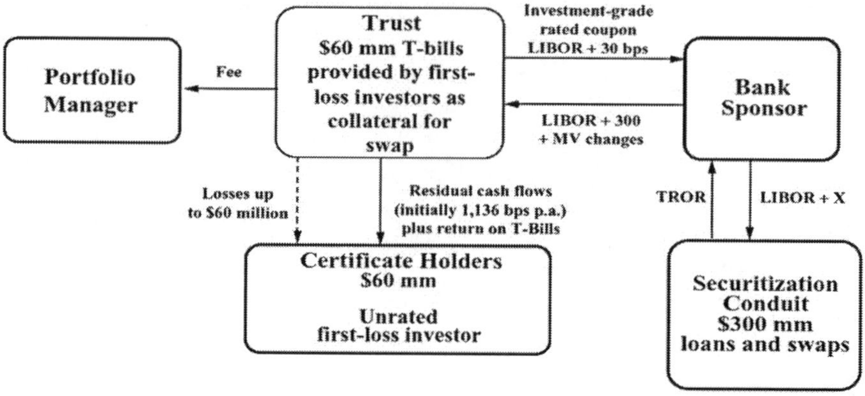

*Noteholders and certificate holders have pari passu cash flow priority. Profit and loss is magnified by leverage.

FIGURE 10.2 CDO Equity Investors Receive Unrated Residual Cash Flows

In 2002, new issue arbitrage CDOs on investment-grade corporates saw base-case equity IRRs gap out from lows of 10 to 15 percent to as high as 50 to 60 percent in the fall of 2002.

Figure 10.4 shows a principal-protected Schuldschein structured from a static synthetic arbitrage CDO with a 2.5 percent equity tranche from a

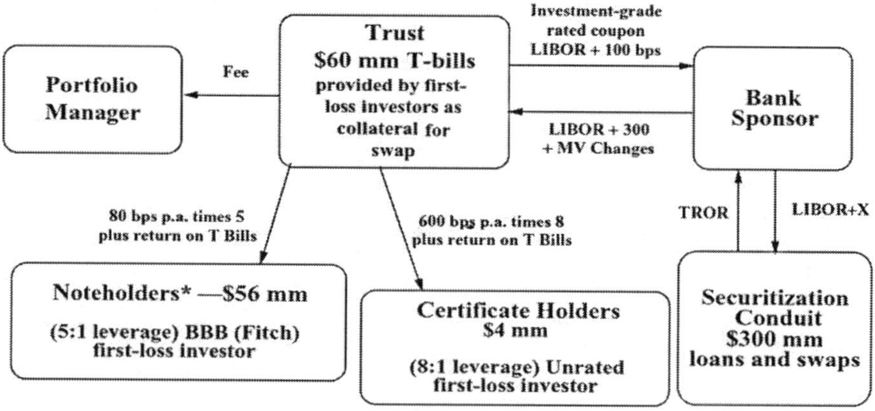

*Noteholders and certificate holders have pari passu cash flow priority. Profit and loss is magnified by leverage.

FIGURE 10.3 CDO Equity Investors Receive Residual Cash Flows: Part of Equity Cash Flow is Rated

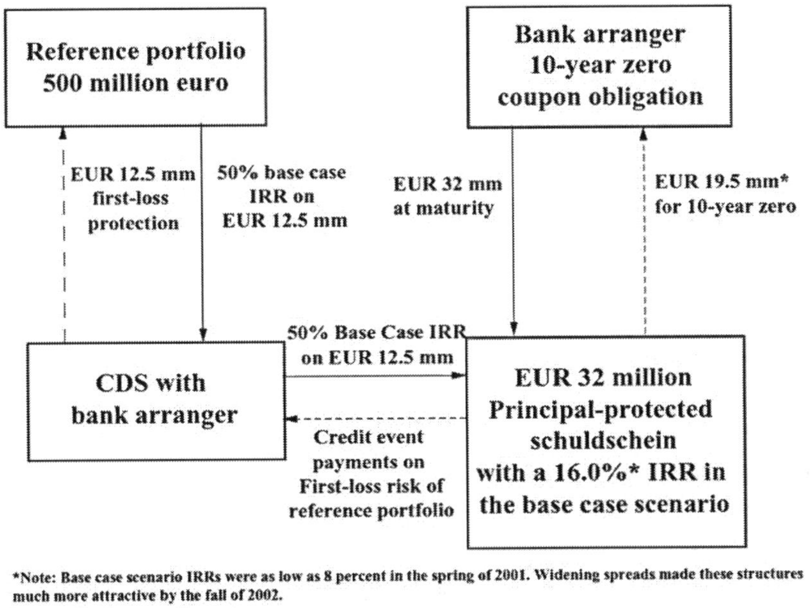

FIGURE 10.4 Unrated Equity Repackaged as 10-Year Principal-Protected Schuldschein

well-diversified portfolio 500 million euros in size. The equity base case IRR is 50 percent, and the base-case IRR on the principal-protected Schuldschein (PPS) is 16 percent. In the spring of 2001, investors were happy to receive a base-case PPS IRR of only 6.5 to 8.0 percent, depending on the underlying collateral. In the fall of 2002, 16 percent and more was achievable.

RATED EQUITY EARNS STATED COUPON APPROPRIATE TO RATING

Moody's has provided Aaa ratings for the equity of managed synthetic arbitrage CDOs. It's rare, but possible. The equity has a fixed coupon set at market levels consistent with an Aaa-rated bond. Moody's and Fitch rate the timely return of principal and the ultimate payment of the stated note coupons. S&P resisted the notion until very recently, and it has considered awarding an AAA rating to the first loss risk of a CDO, since the potential deal cash flows seemed strong enough to protect investors. Ratings to date have been private ratings.

The equity investor absorbs losses up to the entire equity investment only, but all residual cash flows are made available to absorb losses. Any accumulated cash flows remaining at maturity belong to the deal manager. The deal manager adds value to the deal by absorbing portfolio trading losses, if any, in return for potential deal upside if there are any remaining cash flows after all of the tranche holders are paid off. This type of deal gives the manager an incentive to attempt to achieve trading gains, and also an incentive to avoid losses throughout the life of the deal.

Figures 10.5 and 10.6 show the equity cash flows from the SPV and deal tranches. The waterfall shows how the deal management fee might be structured to give the manager a further performance incentive. A subordinated management fee is paid only if losses are less than 50 percent of the original equity investment. The subordinated management fee gives the manager an incentive to keep the losses to the equity investor—and therefore the rest of the investors—to a minimum.

RATED EQUITY: STATIC DEAL

Static synthetic arbitrage CDOs by definition are unmanaged. Therefore, there are no management fees to contribute to the deal costs and fees. Since there is no trading of the original portfolio, there are no potential trading losses. This means there is more cash flow available under every scenario to increase the probability of the return of the equity investor's original investment plus a stated coupon consistent with an investment-grade rated tranche.

For a well-diversified portfolio of investment-grade credits, it is much easier to get an investment-grade rating on a stated coupon first-loss note than it is for a managed deal. Rating agencies do not have to take into account trading losses and management fees when they stress-test the cash flows. The static deal equity structure and cash flow waterfall are shown in Figures 10.7 and 10.8.

In this static deal, who receives the benefit of excess cash flows, if any, once the rated notes are paid off?

Incredibly, this is negotiable. Some equity investors will agree that as long as they receive the rated cash flows, they will not ask for the potential additional upside of the remaining residual cash flows. The deal arranger will keep the excess.

Some investment banks create a rated equity note to broaden distribution of the first-loss tranche to investors who would otherwise not be able to

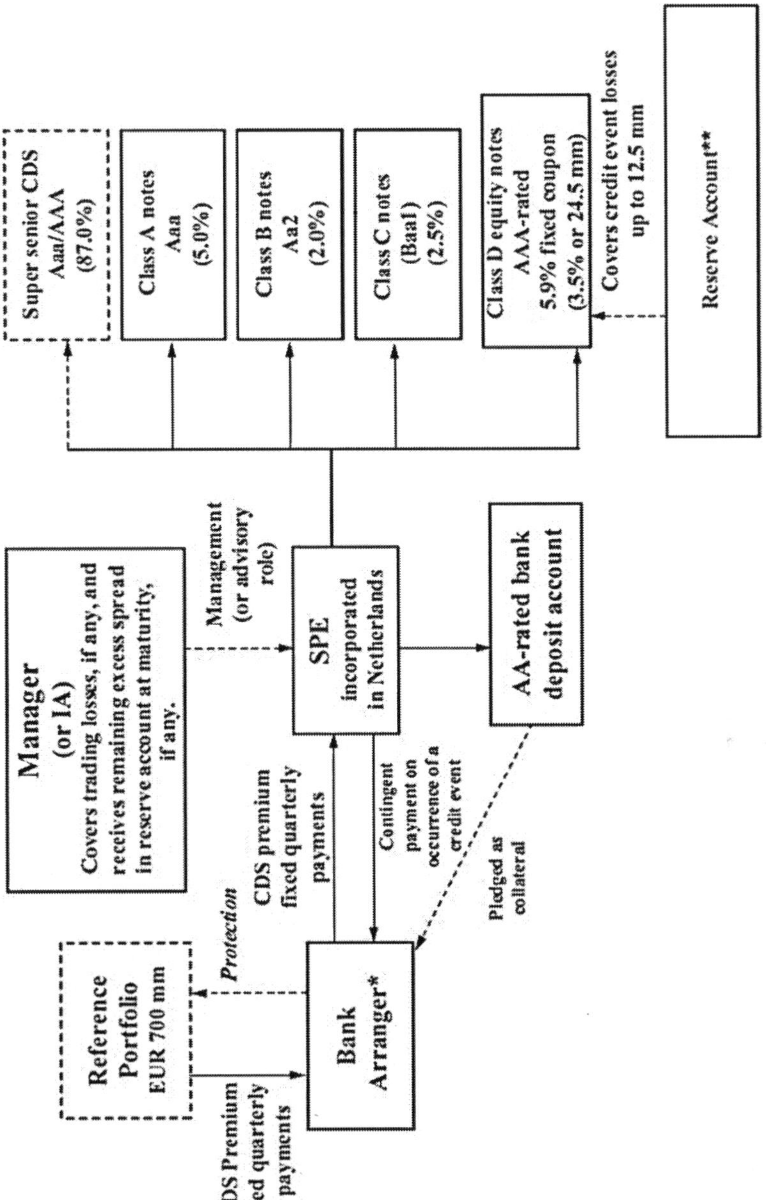

* Subject to bank arranger maintaining a minimum AA-rating.
** Covers equity credit event losses up to 24.5 mm. Remaining excess spread goes to manager at maturity.

FIGURE 10.5 Managed Synthetic Arbitrage CDO: Rated Equity Cash Flows

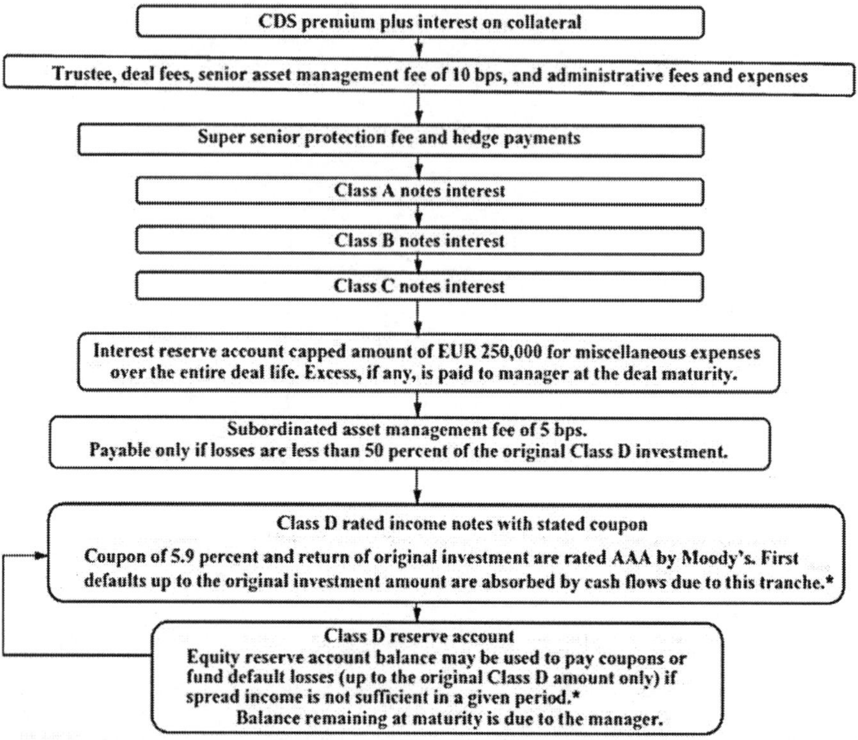

*Credit losses greater than the Class D investment amount will be written down from the Class C, B, and A notes in reverse order of seniority. Trading losses, if any, are absorbed by the deal manager and kept outside the deal.

FIGURE 10.6 Managed Synthetic Arbitrage CDO: Waterfall for Rated Equity

invest in equity. Some investors can purchase BBB rated notes but cannot buy unrated equity. By offering an AAA rated equity tranche with potential upside, they can reach new investors. All of the excess residual cash flows will be made available to these investors.

EQUITY INVESTOR EARNS A STATED COUPON ON THE REMAINING EQUITY INVESTMENT

Most of the initial static synthetic CDOs promised to pay a coupon on the remaining equity balance. The equity was unrated. Suppose the initial equity tranche size is EUR 25 million. The CDO paid a stated fixed annual coupon of 20 percent. Any cash flows in excess of the amount needed to make the liability payments for the CDO benefit the bank arranger.

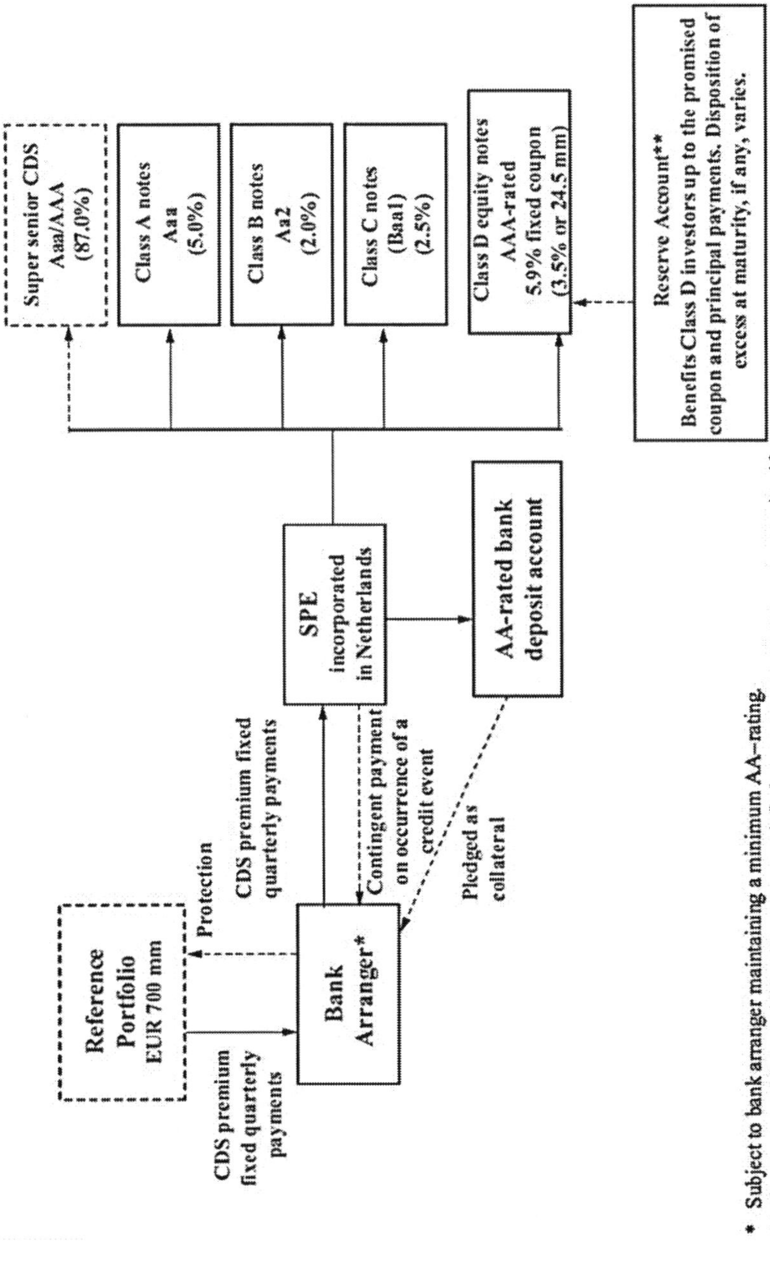

* Subject to bank arranger maintaining a minimum AA–rating.
** If payments of the rated Class D note are satisfied, reserve account excess at maturity, if any, may either be used to benefit senior noteholders, if required, or revert to the bank arranger.

FIGURE 10.7 Static Synthetic Arbitrage CDO: Rated Equity Cash Flows

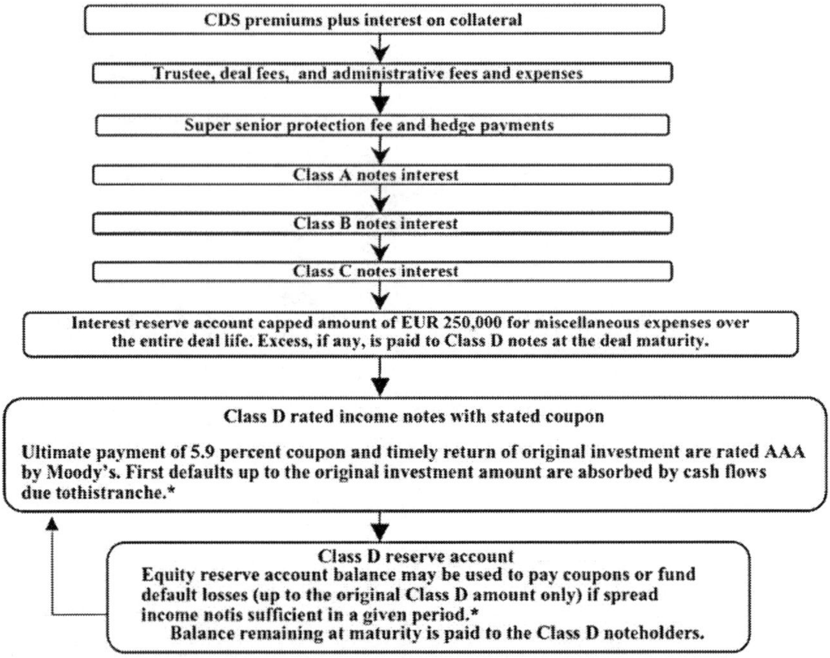

*Credit losses greater than the Class D investment amount will be written down from the Class C, B, and A notes in reverse order of seniority. The portfolio is static; no trading occurs.

FIGURE 10.8 Static Synthetic Arbitrage CDO: Waterfall for Rated Equity

This is also the structure employed in *portfolio swaps*, which is a term used to describe a product that can be as simple as a 50-name portfolio with two tranches. In general, a portfolio swap can refer to any CDS swap of any portfolio, including the reference portfolio for a CDO.

If the portfolio experiences 6 million in losses, the 20 percent coupon is paid only on the remaining balance of EUR 19 million. There is usually excess cash flow above and beyond what is needed to pay the coupon on the remaining equity balance. This excess cash flow benefits the bank arranger. Table 10.1 is adapted from our previous example.

Notice that there are significant excess cash flows that will be paid to the bank arranger at the termination of the deal if losses occur according to the historical CADR of 0.25 percent. We recall that the equity IRR stated under the no-loss scenario is 19.089 percent, but this is a semiannual bond equivalent yield. Stated on an annual basis, this is 20 percent. Likewise, the equity IRR under the 0.25 percent CADR scenario is 13.775 percent on a semiannual bond equivalent basis, which is 14.25 percent on an annual basis.

TABLE 10.1 Equity Investor Earns Stated Coupon on Remaining Balance—Equity Is Unrated

Month	Equity Remaining Balance due to Defaults	Investor's Equity Payout Residual Cash 19.089%	Net Cash Available No-Default Scenario	Equity Remaining Balance due to Defaults	Investor's Equity Payout Residual Cash 13.775%	Net Cash Available 0.25% CADR 40% Recovery
			19,375,000			19,375,000
0	20,000,000	−20,000,000	21,050,878	20,000,000	−20,000,000	21,044,866
3	20,000,000	0	22,654,113	20,000,000	0	22,642,279
6	20,000,000	0	24,338,189	20,000,000	0	23,072,718
9	20,000,000	0	17,401,475	18,750,000	0	16,629,233
12	20,000,000	4,000,000	23,082,420	18,750,000	3,750,000	22,548,002
15	20,000,000	0	24,716,345	19,250,000	0	24,171,191
18	20,000,000	0	26,405,576	19,250,000	0	24,601,845
21	20,000,000	0	19,474,031	18,000,000	0	18,458,575
24	20,000,000	4,000,000	25,160,157	18,000,000	3,600,000	24,227,935
27	20,000,000	0	26,773,665	18,500,000	0	25,826,338
30	20,000,000	0	28,468,040	18,500,000	0	26,257,523
33	20,000,000	0	21,541,651	17,250,000	0	20,414,785
36	20,000,000	4,000,000	27,232,946	17,250,000	3,450,000	26,035,052
39	20,000,000	0	28,851,635	17,750,000	0	27,634,490
42	20,000,000	0	30,551,205	17,750,000	0	28,066,587
45	20,000,000	0	23,630,024	16,500,000	0	22,524,764
48	20,000,000	4,000,000	29,326,540	16,500,000	3,300,000	27,996,325
51	20,000,000	0	30,950,464	17,000,000	0	29,597,182
54	20,000,000	0	32,655,281	17,000,000	0	30,030,578
57	20,000,000	0	6,364,360	15,750,000	0	9,665,058
60	20,000,000	24,000,000		15,750,000	18,900,000	

The equity doesn't need to be as straightforward as in this example. In fact, the cash flows as constructed here don't give the equity investor the best possible deal. The previous structures give the equity investor access to more of the cash flows of the deal and access to a larger payout. Many equity investors were unaware of this fact.

Many German insurance companies bought this type of equity structure imbedded in principal-protected Schuldscheine. Since the return of principal is supplied by a zero-coupon bond imbedded in this structure, the equity cash flows are used to pay current income on the principal-protected Schuldschein.

Because the principal is protected, if the IRRs of the combined structure look good under the no-loss and base-case CADR scenarios, it is easy to ignore the fact that the equity investor does not have a claim to all of the residual cash flows. Most investors did not question the structure of the equity tranche. It was also interesting that these investors were usually shown a scenario analysis assuming a 50 percent recovery rate.

The attraction of the principal-protected Schuldschein structure is that German insurance companies do not have to mark a Schuldschein to market. Nonetheless, there is no reason not to get the best deal possible on the cash flows imbedded in the structure.

Since the equity investor absorbs the first loss, investors should look at the likely loss experience throughout the life of the deal. Stress-testing is also a good idea. Of course, the loss calculation is affected by our assumptions about recovery. As we saw earlier, we can do some sophisticated calculations to determine equity performance under scenarios. That is always a good idea. A very simple and straightforward technique is to look at the *survival rate* of tranches for a given number of defaults. To do this, we create a table of the number of discrete obligor defaults and assume a recovery rate. Then we determine when each tranche takes its first loss and when each tranche is finally exhausted due to losses.

Tables 10.2 and 10.3 show the effect of losses on the remaining equity balance for two assumed recovery rates: 50 percent and 40 percent.

In the context of actual recoveries experienced in the period from 1999 to 2002, a recovery rate of 50 percent seems ridiculously high. The benefit of a simple chart like this is to show the sensitivity to recovery rates to number of discrete defaults.

This chart is straightforward when the equity is structured as just described (coupons are calculated from the remaining balance), and when the amount invested in each obligor is the same. This chart is more difficult to put together when equity cash flows are constructed differently and when the timing of the occurrence of defaults matters to the net equity cash flows. These charts can still be constructed for specific scenarios, however.

TABLE 10.2 Effect of Default Rate on Equity—Recovery Rate is 50 percent; Equity Tranche is 4 percent

Euro 500 Million Portfolio. Each Obligor is Euro 10 million

Class	Subordination (%)	Defaults to experience first EUR loss (50% recovery)		Defaults to experience full principal loss (50% recovery)	
		# Defaults	Cum. Default Rate	# Defaults	Cum. Default Rate
SS	16%	16	32%	50	10%
A1	11%	11	22%	16	32%
A2	8%	8	16%	11	22%
B1	4%	4	8%	8	16%
E	NA	NA	NA	4	8%

This CDO is structured so that the equity investor earns a stated coupon on the remaining initial investment less accumulated losses, if any. Accumulated losses for this calculation cannot exceed the amount of the initial equity investment.

TABLE 10.3 Effect of Default Rate on Equity—Recovery Rate is 4 percent; Equity Tranche is percent

Euro 500 Million Portfolio. Each Obligor is Euro 10 million

Class	Subordination (%)	Defaults to experience first EUR loss (40% recovery)		Defaults to experience full principal loss (40% recovery)	
		# Defaults	Cum. Default Rate	# Defaults	Cum. Default Rate
SS	14.3%	11.9	23.8%	50.0	100.0%
A1	9.3%	7.8	15.5%	11.9	23.8%
A2	7.0%	5.8	11.7%	7.8	15.5%
B1	4.0%	3.3	6.7%	5.8	11.7%
E	NA	NA	NA	3.3	6.7%

This CDO is structured so that the equity investor earns a stated coupon on the remaining initial investment less accumulated losses, if any. Accumulated losses for this calculation cannot exceed the amount of the initial equity investment.

Investors in the senior tranches also look at charts like the one just presented. Super senior investors in particular may want to know how many losses the deal can sustain before the super senior investor would experience a loss.

At first glance this structure looks as if it is the same as the previous structure, but it isn't. This equity is unrated. The stated coupon is paid from interest on the original investment amount, plus the deal cash flows. As losses occur, the equity is written down up to the amount of the original investment and the coupon amount is calculated on the lower balance.

Unlike the previous structure, once losses occur, the equity investor has no claim to further cash flows beyond the remaining balance and coupons on the remaining balance. The investor has no claim on excess residuals beyond this. The equity investor has a much lower probability of recovering the initial investment plus a coupon. The stated coupon is usually much higher than for rated structures that include all residuals, but the coupon still doesn't reflect all of the potential residual cash flows of the deal.

We recall that if the equity investor isn't entitled to all of the residual cash flows, and if the senior noteholders do not benefit from the excess residual cash flows (if required), the deal arranger keeps the remaining cash flows. The exception to this is when the manager agrees to accept potential trading losses in return for a claim to excess residual cash flows not required to satisfy a rated equity tranche. Equity investors should not give away residuals to arrangers or managers who don't have either first-loss risk or trading-loss risk.

MORAL HAZARD AND CONFLICT OF INTEREST

If a deal manager has a claim on the equity cash flows, there may be a conflict of interest between the manager and senior noteholders. Investors should be particularly wary of deals in which four structural conditions are met, which can tempt managers to behave against the interest of the noteholders.

The first is that losses are allocated in reverse order of seniority, and loss deductions are limited to the initial investment of each tranche investor. The second condition is that excess spread does not accrue to the benefit of any of the noteholders and is not available to absorb losses. The third condition is that the manager does not have adequate restraints on his ability to cause a deterioration in the quality of the underlying portfolio. The fourth condition is that the manager has a claim on the excess spread. Figure 10.9 shows an example this type of structure.

When losses exceed the initial equity investment, all of the residual cash flows are diverted to the benefit of the manager. The manager now has an

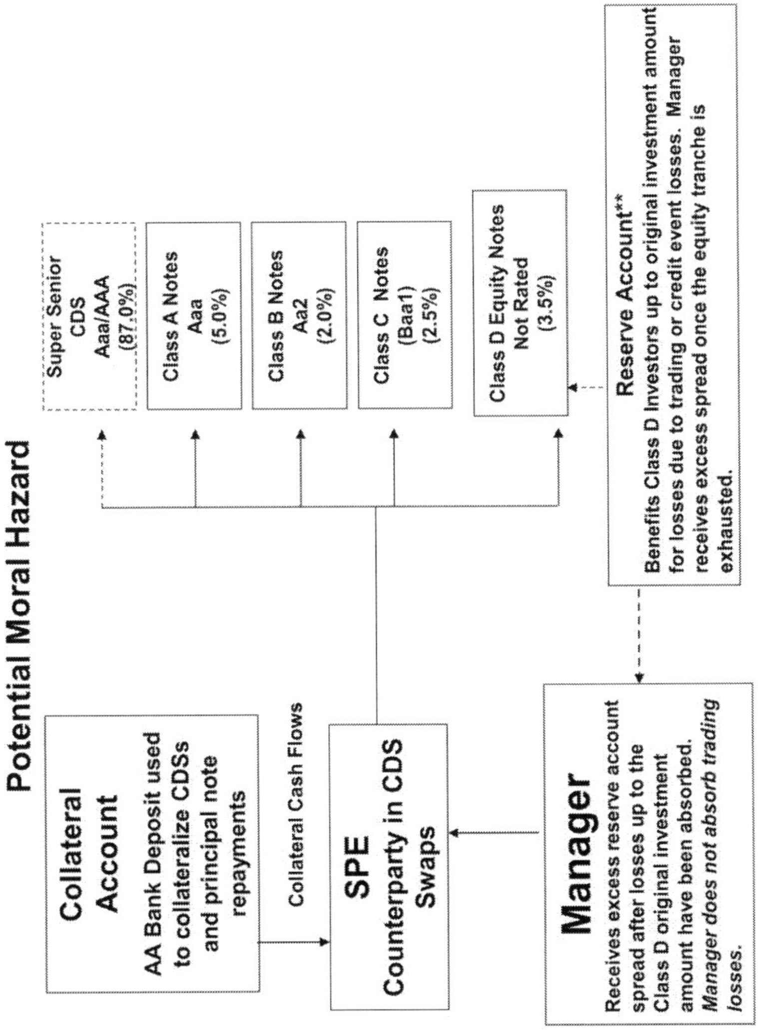

*All reference portfolio credit event losses and trading losses are allocated in reverse order of seniority and limited to the original tranche investment.

FIGURE 10.9 Potential Conflict of Interest Between Manager and Investors incentive to trade out of good credits into credits on negative credit watch or even into lower-rated but higher-spread credits, if there are no constraints prohibiting this. In any case, a manager must have some latitude to make judgment calls, but now the temptation will be to make judgment calls that result in higher spread, even if this means the portfolio will deteriorate.

Notice that once the equity is gone, the next most senior noteholder bears additional losses. If that is a BBB noteholder, any new losses reduce the BBB principal amount, and the high coupon payment is now calculated off of a lower principal amount. The deal liabilities are decreasing, and the manager earns more excess spread.

You might be thinking to yourself that this is so reprehensible that it could never happen. But it has happened. In fact, a large Yankee Bank in New York invested in a single A-rated tranche of a deal brought by a major investment banking firm, and this is exactly what happened. The deal tranches experienced multiple downgrades. The investors forcefully complained to the manager, with no result. The originally investment-grade portfolio was actively traded down in credit quality and became a non-investment-grade portfolio, a *junk* portfolio.

The Yankee Bank was in danger of losing some of its original principal investment. They brought the matter to one of the rating agencies, who said it was statistically impossible for an investment-grade portfolio to reach the junk status this deal's portfolio achieved in that period of time. The rating agency was wrong. Perhaps if you assumed a random sampling of investment-grade credits, the rating agency was correct, but the manager was working hard at investing in risky high-spread credits.

The investors at the Yankee Bank contacted their lawyers in an attempt to get the investment bank to make amends. They even considered leaking their story to the *Wall Street Journal* in an attempt to embarrass the investment bank. They didn't, and I believe that was a wise idea. It's possible that an institutional investor may embarrass himself if he attempts to paint himself as a naïve victim of a sharper bank. The Yankee Bank might have asked itself why it didn't ask for more structural protections in the first place. It was enticed by the illusion of a slightly higher original coupon but ignored the structural risk.

LEVERAGING THE BEST UNFUNDED EQUITY INVESTMENTS—ULTIMATE LEVERAGE

Equity risk can be transferred synthetically, just like any other risk. In most cases, the investor as the credit protection provider must pay the loss amount on the settlement date for credit events, if any, covered by the first-loss

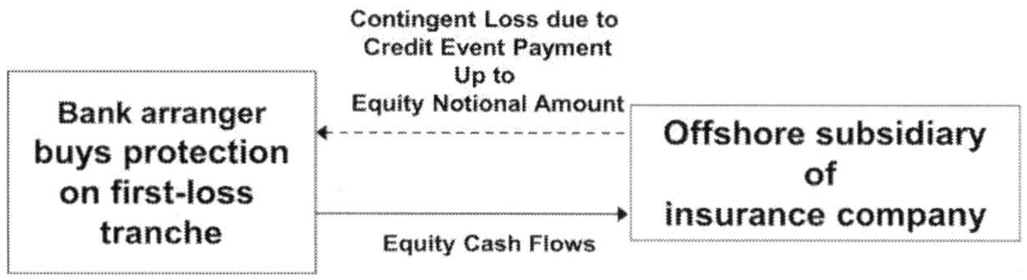

FIGURE 10.10 Unfunded Equity Risk Transfer

protection. In between the deal closing and a credit default settlement date, the only money that changes hands is the premium payment to the investor under the terms of the credit default swap, as shown Figure 10.10.

Who are the investors in unfunded equity? As you might imagine, the investors are usually hedge funds or the offshore subsidiary of a reinsurance company. Saying an investor is "an offshore subsidiary of the Reinsurance Company" sounds good to bank management and bank credit officers, but these subsidiaries that sell first-loss protection are essentially *hedge funds*. Since these are off-balance-sheet transactions, the investors usually don't want to disclose how much of this risk they have taken on. They also usually don't want to disclose the exact deals with the exact reference portfolios in which they've invested.

These investors want *leverage*. One would think that buying equity risk in unfunded form would be leverage enough. These investors ask for even more leverage. They ask the bank sponsor to *fund the losses*. This means that if the portfolio experiences a loss, the subsidiary of the Reinsurance Company (or a hedge fund) wants the CDO bank arranger to make the required payment to the CDO's SPE. The CDO bank arranger must have an open credit line to the subsidiary of the insurance company or to the hedge fund and allow this to be drawn on in the event of a default. The sponsoring bank is usually asked to charge only LIBOR plus 25 for this funding.

The problem with this is that most of the CDOs for which this has been done are synthetic CDOs with five-year maturities. The liabilities will all come due about the same time. In five years, the investors will have to come up with a big chunk of cash, and these are the investors that didn't want to put up cash in the first place. Of course, they don't have a five-year track record with this type of investment and are reluctant to disclose the degree of leverage they already have. They may have a solid investment-grade rating, but rating agencies cannot keep up with the activities of these entities.

Structurers eager to get deals done have rammed deals like this through their institutions. Often the equity investor drives the deal, and in 2001 and 2002, some investment banks and banks had trouble finding enough mainstream equity investors. They turned to these willing investors instead.

Of course these investors are interested: sky-high returns and no money up front. In fact, investors make no loss payments for five years, and earn income in the interim. The investors can use the CDS premiums to pay the interest on the loans the banks give them to fund the equity losses, if any. What a deal!

These investors hate questions. One of my favorite questions is, "How are you guys compensated?" They especially hate that question.

My point is that the personnel are usually very new. Does their contract pay them on current revenues and ignore future liabilities? How are they reporting this deal internally? Are they exploiting some internal accounting glitch to get high bonuses today and move on before the potential losses need to be paid (and thus have no bonus that year)? The usual retort is that it is none of my business. I disagree. If you are relying on this investor to make the payments, you want to understand their commitment to the survival of this business.

These investors may have a point, however. If you are a structurer, and you are compensated for current deal fee income, the long run may not matter to you, either. Most financial institutions have had rapid turnovers in personnel due to layoffs or other attrition. These departments often have rivals within the institution who want to take over their business. Everyone is under pressure to report high current fees to survive. Under such circumstances, management is spending most of its time trying to survive or to jockey for position. They won't put in the time to understand these products or these issues. It's an accident waiting to happen. If structurers want to stuff a bank trading book with risk in order to earn high current fees, they won't be too picky about their equity investors.

However, for every strategy, there is a counterstrategy. Let's say you want to do one of these deals, but you also want to survive a competent internal deal review. If you are dealing with the subsidiary of a reinsurance company, it may be possible to buy credit default protection on the subsidiary. In five years' time, when payment for the losses comes due, and if they begin defaulting on obligations, you are covered.

The premium for the CDS should be folded into the deal economics. For instance, the subsidiary of the Reinsurance Company could receive a lower net premium on the equity. This strategy may make your deal less competitive in the eyes of the subsidiary, however, because CDS premiums are usually quoted in hundreds of basis points per annum for these subsidiaries. For example, in fall 2000, one subsidiary had an AA rating, but the credit default protection on the subsidiary traded at 400 bps (4 percent) per annum. At the time, equity returns on investment-grade synthetic static portfolios were in a range of 16 to 22 percent per annum.

ACTIVELY TRADED AND LIMITED SUBSTITUTION SYNTHETIC ARBITRAGE CDOS

When bank arrangers have a claim to part of the residual cash flows, they may also have the right to actively trade the portfolio or to perform limited substitution of names in the portfolio. This is especially true for synthetic arbitrage CDOs.

Many investors do not see the point in having a manager. They dislike the fact that the manager's fee reduces overall cash flows available for the deal. They feel the manager wouldn't avoid losses due to event risk, such as Railtrack, or due to fraud, such as Enron. They also fear that if the bank arranger has the right to trade the portfolio, once losses do exceed the original equity investment, the portfolio is up for grabs. The bank arranger will have every incentive to dump deteriorating credits into the portfolio to pump up the excess cash flows. Meanwhile the tranche investors up the line will absorb any extra losses due to default.

Investors who choose to participate in these deals should take this as fair warning. The best defense is good structural protection within the documentation. Documentation may call for limited substitution only. This may limit the number of obligors that may be substituted in a given period. It may also limit the ability to substitute obligors that have not traded wider than a certain threshold amount relative to its peer group or to its historical spreads. We saw some of these restrictions earlier when we discussed the managed synthetic arbitrage CDO. These included limiting names traded to 10 percent of the portfolio per year and included rating and outlook restrictions for each substituted name.

Note that the previously mentioned manager did not have a stake in the equity cash flows. If the bank arranger acts as manager, even more severe restrictions should be included in the documentation. The senior tranche investors—particularly an outside super senior investor—may include right of refusal of names substituted in the portfolio.

INTEREST SUBPARTICIPATIONS: WHEN EQUITY ISN'T FIRST LOSS

In Europe, the interest subparticipation (ISP) structure has been used in many balance-sheet CDOs issued by many banks located in Germany and the Netherlands. Banks in these venues are exploiting a regulatory capital regulation loophole. Normally, equity attracts a one-for-one regulatory capital charge. This means that for every 10 million euro of equity, the bank must take a 10 million euro capital charge. If a bank has a return on regulatory capital target of 18 percent, the bank must get a stable return of 18 percent or 1.8 million euro on the equity to meet this target. In some venues, such as Germany, future interest does not require any capital charge at all. In other words the capital charge is *zero*. The interest subparticipation structure is meant to allow a bank sponsor to appear to be securitizing the equity risk of a portfolio of assets, but in reality, the bank retains the first loss-risk.

There is a possibility that the interest subparticipation might not get a 0 percent capital treatment but may still only attract a 100 percent times 8 percent BIS risk-weighted charge. For a EUR 10 million first-loss tranche, this amounts to 100 percent times 8 percent times EUR 10 million, or only EUR 800,000. Now to achieve an 18 percent return on capital, the bank only needs to earn EUR 144,000 (see Table 10.4).

Figures 10.11 and 10.12 show both funded and unfunded interest subparticipations of a bank balance sheet CDO.

The interest subparticipation entitles the investors to an interest subparticipation in the future interest income of the reference pool. If the CDO allocates a loss to the equity investor, the investor in the interest subparticipation receives a payment equal to the loss amount. The *issuer* makes this payment to the investor in the interest subparticipation tranche.

The available interest income is the total amount of interest payments paid on the entire reference portfolio during the interest subparticipation period. If the accumulated losses exceed the current calculation amount available, it is possible to recover the losses later as the total accumulated interest on the reference portfolio continues to build over time, up to the maturity of the interest subparticipation note.

You may be wondering about these interest payments. Aren't the other tranches of the deal higher in the waterfall, and aren't interest payments used to pay the coupons on these notes first? Yes, of course. How is it possible that the holder of the interest subparticipation tranche potentially receives a payment equal to the entire interest accrued up to the payout time?

TABLE 10.4 Equity and Potential ISP Treatment

	Equity	Potential ISP Treatment
Regulatory capital charge	1:1	100% × 8%
Size of investment (euros)	10,000,000	10,000,000
Capital charge (euros)	10,000,000	800,000
Earnings for 18% ROC*	1,800,000	144,000

*Return on Capital

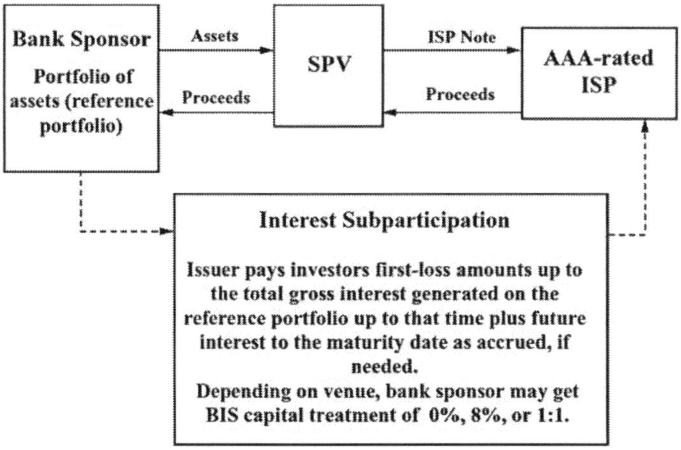

FIGURE 10.11 Interest Subparticipation (Funded)

The answer is that the payment does not come from the interest on the reference portfolio. The payment comes from the issuer's own funds, albeit the calculation amount is based on the interest earned by the reference portfolio. This is merely a calculation device to make sure there is a very high likelihood that the holder of the interest subparticipation note will get paid. It is unlikely that the accumulated losses will exceed the entire

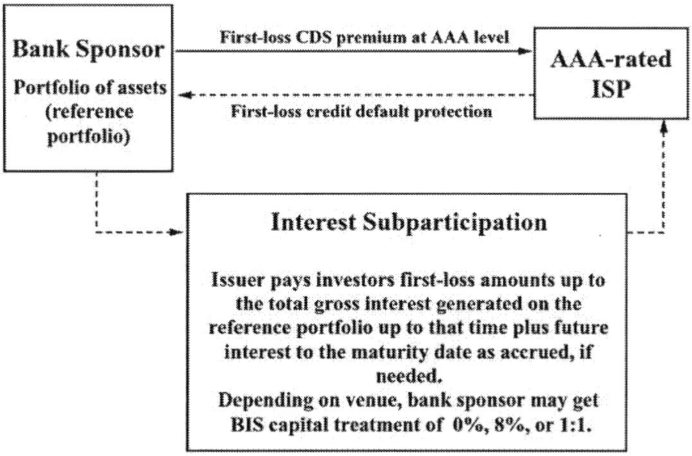

FIGURE 10.12 Interest Subparticipation (Synthetic Unfunded)

interest paid on the reference portfolio assets during the life of the interest subparticipation notes.

This means that the issuer has in effect retained first-loss risk under most probable scenarios. One could imagine an extremely high default scenario in which accumulated interest is insufficient to cover first loss on the interest subparticipation tranche, but it is very unlikely. In fact, it is so unlikely, that interest subparticipation pieces achieve private ratings as high as AAA or AA, although some have had ratings as low as single A.

The amount of the protection the issuer provides for first-loss events is usually much greater than required. The benefit will depend on the gross interest of the portfolio and the size of the equity tranche. For instance, if the portfolio gross interest is 8 percent, and the first-loss tranche is only 2 percent, the first-loss coverage is four times the amount needed.

European bank portfolio managers have invested in interest subparticipation notes as if they are rated floaters that offer enhanced coupons. The extra coupon income usually paid on the interest subparticipation note compensates the investor for the time it takes to understand the structure. When these structures first appeared a few years ago, investors could earn a premium to same-rated floaters of 20 to 40 bps. By 2002, often there was no enhanced coupon for the interest subparticipation structure since it was much better understood by a much wider investor base.

PARTICIPATION NOTES

Investors who must invest in rated notes, yet want income upside potential versus current market coupons, will consider investing in a participation note (PN). Participation notes are rated, but either with respect to return of principal only, or with respect to return of principal plus the ultimate return of a small coupon. Ratings on participation notes vary from AAA to Ba2. The rating will depend on (1) whether principal plus coupon is rated; (2) whether principal only is rated; (3) the rating of the rated tranche used in combination with the equity; and (4) the ratio of equity to the rated tranche used in combination with the equity.

Participation notes allow an investor to own a portion of, or *participate* in, the equity cash flows on a pro rata basis with the other equity investors. For example, using a single CDO, I can combine EUR 8 million of the AAA tranche and 2 million of the equity tranche. The equity return is 15.5 percent, and the AAA is priced at Euribor plus 50. The participation note will have an expected rating of Aa2, but only for return of principal and for payment of a coupon of Euribor minus 120 bps. However, the expected coupon on the note is Euribor plus 120 bps. The upside potential on the coupon is due

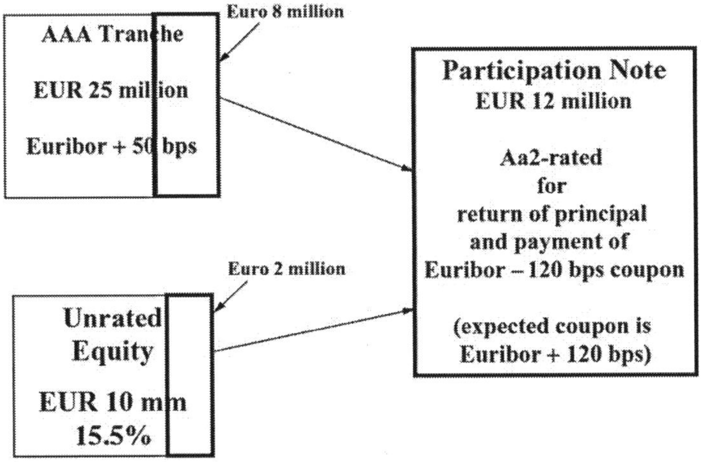

FIGURE 10.13 Participation Note

to the participation in the unrated equity tranche, most of which cannot be commingled in the rating. In the same market environment, an Aa2 trades at only Euribor plus 80 bps.

Figure 10.13 shows an example of a participation note. Note that a vertical slice of the equity tranche is used to create the participation note. This means that in terms of seniority, the equity investment is the same as the equity investment of the other equity holders. Therefore, this portion of the equity investment participates on a pro-rata basis in the equity cash flows with the other equity investors.

Participation notes can be structured at the same time as the CDO. That won't necessarily work for all investors. When the deal is being marketed, an investor may request that some of the equity be combined with an AAA tranche after the fact. In that case, the tranches can be combined in an SPV and the return of principal and a submarket coupon of the SPV-issued EMTN can be rated. It is usually slightly more expensive to create a participation note after the deal has been tranched and rated.

PARTICIPATION NOTES AND OPPORTUNITY COST

Some banks have unwittingly invested in equity risk of CDOs in their bank portfolios in the form of participation notes. One New York branch of a European bank, a Yankee Bank, learned to their dismay that the income they thought they would receive on their portfolio of CDO tranche investments was lower than anticipated. Their portfolio manager had purchased participation notes. The PNs were rated AA or better but were rated only for return of principal. The coupon payments depended on the performance of the equity tranches of various CDOs.

Apparently the portfolio manager, bank management, and risk management miscommunicated. The portfolio manager felt that as long as investments were within the wording of the bank's guidelines, he could invest in this type of security. The PNs were held on the bank book, so he didn't have to mark the PNs to market.

When the equity portion of the deals deteriorated because they had to absorb credit losses, the income on the participation notes declined. The bank managers were upset when risk management explained the dilemma.

The portfolio manager pointed out that the bank intended to hold the PNs to maturity, and therefore would not experience a principal loss. Since the bank didn't mark this portfolio to market, they wouldn't take write-down on the interim portfolio value, either.

The bank managers didn't expect to take this kind of risk in the bank portfolio on AA-rated investments. They expected that a rating of AAA or AA would apply to both the principal and interest. They didn't expect to invest money with the possibility of no income.

The bank had hidden risk, and now that the bank cannot liquidate the positions, it also has opportunity cost. The bank cannot free up the invested cash for other use before maturity without selling the securities and taking a loss.

CAPPED PARTICIPATION NOTES

Participation notes that use a senior slice of the equity tranche combined with a rated tranche from the same CDO often have a cap on the upside to the participation note holder. The equity investment is no longer pari passu with the other equity investors. The first loss is borne first by the junior equity investors and then by the equity portion of the participation note investment. The senior equity investment has a preset yield and the coupon on the participation note is therefore capped.

COMBINATION NOTES

Combination notes (CNs) or *combo* notes combine two *rated* classes of notes from the same CDO but will not include an equity tranche (even rated equity). Ratings on combination notes vary about as much as participation notes. Usually combination notes are rated BBB and above, but it is possible to have a lower rating on a combination note.

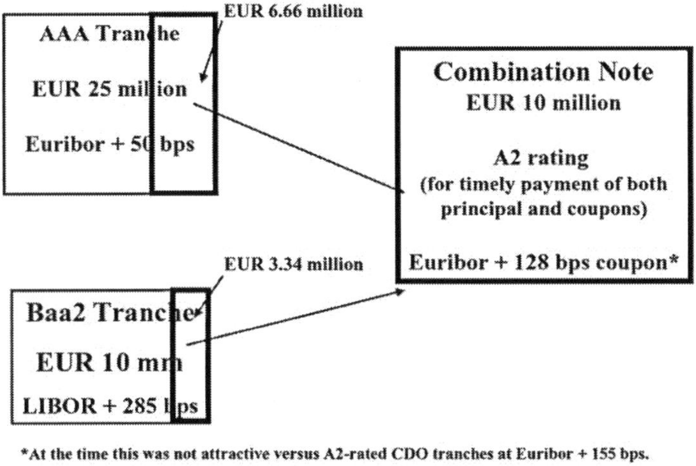

FIGURE 10.14 Comnbination Note

Not all combination notes look attractive when compared to alternatives. Figure 10.14 shows a combination note of a CDO. The CDO's AAA-rated tranche has a coupon of Euribor plus 50 bps, and the Baa2 tranche has a coupon of Euribor plus 285 bps. The combination note combines a EUR 6.66 million investment in the AAA tranche and a EUR 3.34 million investment in the Baa2-rated tranche. The resulting combination note is rated A2 for timely payment of both principal and coupons and has a coupon of LIBOR plus 128. In the same market environment, A2-rated tranches of CDOs with comparable collateral were traded at around LIBOR plus 155bps. This particular combination note does not look attractive to potential investors given the alternatives.

A combination note can be structured at the time the CDO is structured or any time before closing. If the deal has already closed and an investor is interested in a combination note from the existing rated tranches, a portion of the tranches can be combined in a multi-issuance SPV, and an EMTN combination note can be issued from the SPV.

INVESTOR MOTIVATION

Both combination notes and participation notes allow more investors to participate in a deal's cash flows in a specific way. Investors who normally cannot buy unrated equity can do so in the form of a rated participation note. In the United States, insurance companies get favorable capital treatment for notes rated above single A. This was the motivation for creation of the lower-leveraged equity tranche in the secured loan trust structure we saw earlier. The National Association of Insurance Commissioners (NAIC) rates these securities NAIC 1, their highest rating, and insurers hold less capital against these holdings. Since these securities are created as one note with one CUSIP number, they probably will not be separated out into rated and unrated components for capital purposes.

Banks and funds that require rated securities for investment portfolios are also buyers of these notes. Banks may have renewed interest in these rated securities with upside potential when Basel II comes into effect. Highly rated notes will get favorable capital treatment relative to lower-rated notes and, of course, will receive much more favorable capital treatment than equity.

PRINCIPAL-PROTECTED STRUCTURES

As we saw earlier, principal-protected structures can be issued directly by a highly rated issuer. In that case, the investor looks to the issuer for principal repayment. It is possible to get the principal rated the same rating as the highly rated issuer by a rating agency. If the issuer has a BIS risk weighting lower than 100 percent, there may be advantages to certain investors who can utilize the lower BIS risk weighting and who are able to consider the note as having the BIS risk weighting of the issuer. For instance, certain sovereigns have a 0 percent BIS risk weight, and in Europe OECD banks have a 20 percent BIS risk weight.

Equity is usually repackaged with zero coupon bonds issued by highly rated entities. An SPE issues a note with proceeds adequate to buy the zero coupon, which accretes to par at maturity to pay off the principal on the note. The remaining note proceeds are used to purchase equity, which provides cash flows for interest payments on the note.

Figure 10.15 outlines the cash flows. In this instance, the note uses the zero-coupon bond of an AA1-rated OECD bank. Although the equity has a five-year maturity, the zero-coupon bond has a 10-year maturity. The residual cash flows can be smoothed and reinvested to make a steady stream of coupon payments in the equity no-loss scenario. Alternatively, the investor may choose to receive all residual cash flows as they are paid by the underlying CDO and either liquidate the note at the five-year maturity or hold it until the 10-year maturity and receive par at maturity. Longer-dated maturities on the underlying zero allow for a lower price for the principal protection and a larger participation in the equity cash flows.

Figure 10.16 shows the expected IRR for an investment in the equity residual cash flows without principal protection. The IRR is shown for

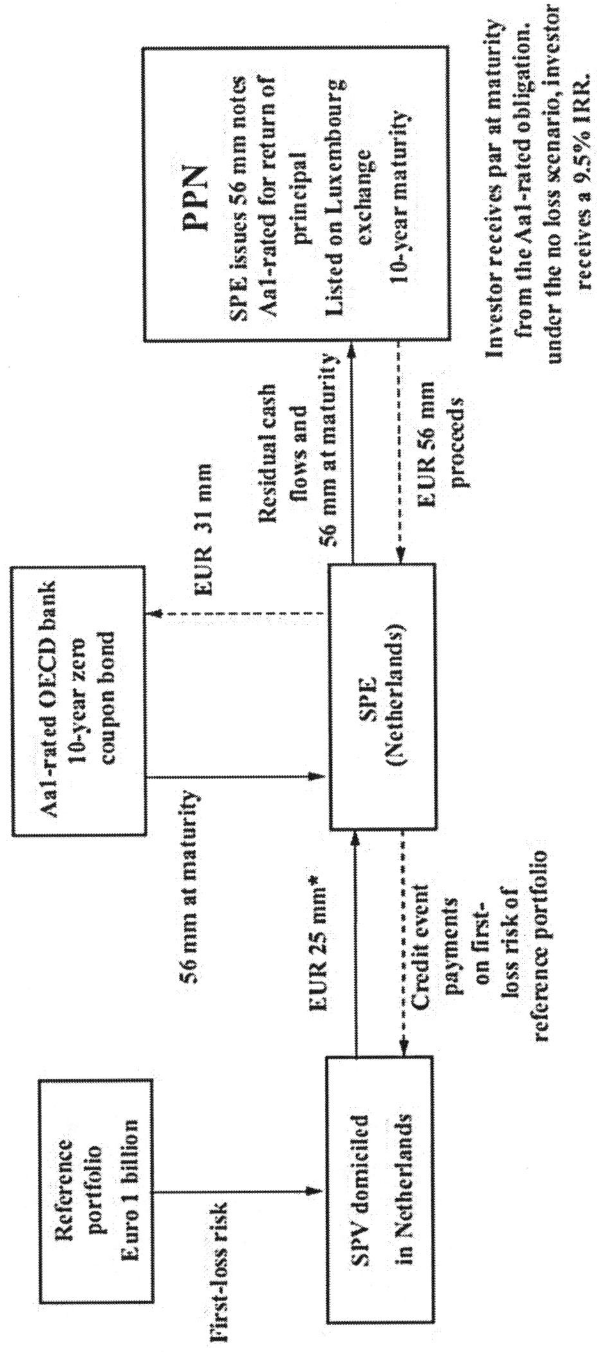

*Approximate.

FIGURE 10.15 Principal Protected Note—Equity Repackaging

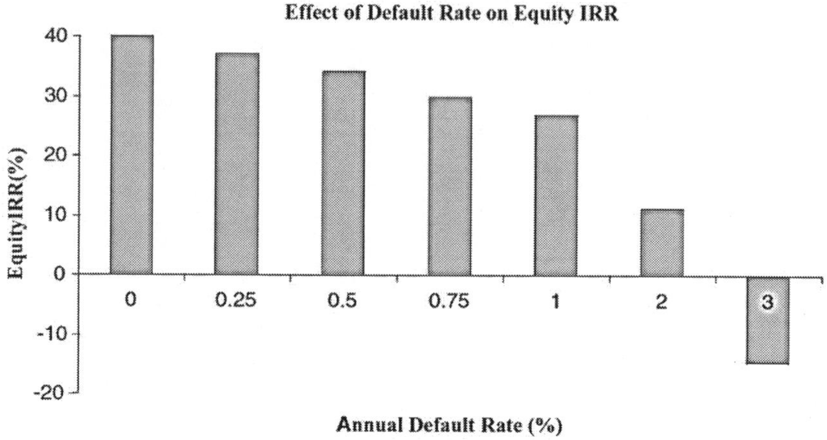

FIGURE 10.16 Effect of Default Rate on Equity IRR

various annual default rates. Notice that the IRR of the equity declines as the default rate increases. If the default rate approaches 3 percent per annum, the IRR of the equity investment becomes negative for this particular deal.

The IRR of the principal-protected note starts out lower than that of the equity investment but does not go negative due to the assumption of principal protection. The principal risk is that of the Aa1-rated issuer, and we are assuming it has not defaulted and it is not a reference credit for the CDO from which the equity has been created. A default of a reference credit of the CDO will not have an effect on the principal repayment of the note (see Figure 10.17).

As we mentioned earlier, German insurance companies prefer PPS structures since they do not have to mark a Schuldschein to market. The economics of the structure are similar to the PPN.

FIRST – (AND NTH-) TO-DEFAULT BASKET SWAPS

Some of the best financial institutions in the world disseminate pure nonsense about first-to-default protection and get the pricing wrong. *I have no confidence in any first-to-default pricing model I have ever seen.*

If you are an investor in this product, negotiate the best price possible, and be aware that you can challenge the output of any model using logical principles to make your case when negotiating.

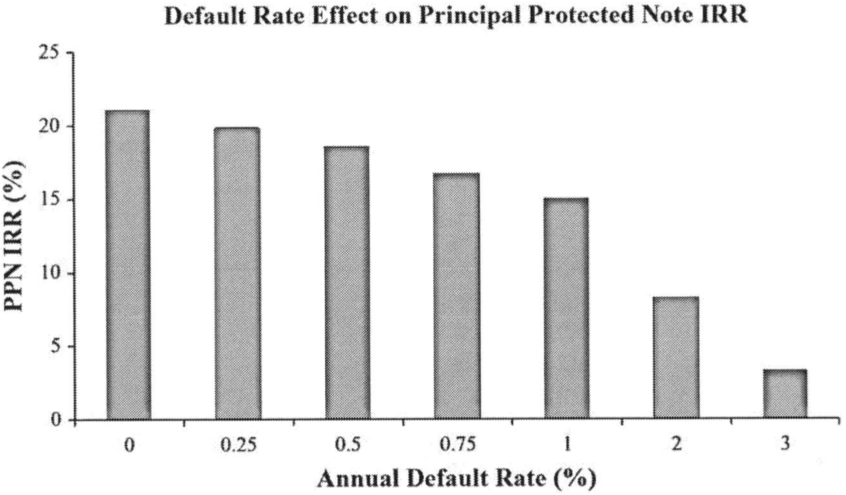

FIGURE 10.17 Effect of Default Rate on PPN IRR

If you manage first-to-default swap structurers and traders, take the model with enough salt to form an ocean from a fresh lake. It isn't possible to use single-name credit default swaps to create a static hedge for the spread and default risk of a first-to-default basket. Traders must dynamically hedge this product. They will use the valuation model to calculate the hedge ratios. The same traders who say they cannot make money trading and hedging single-name credit default swaps will claim they can dynamically hedge this product. What this really means is that they can make money if they are lucky. Many of the best firms have lost significant sums of money attempting to dynamically hedge this product, especially in our high credit default environment during the past two years. That also implies there are significant sums to be made.

If you can tolerate volatility in P&L, and if you want to make a few bets, go ahead. But don't try to claim there is more science or certainty to it than there really is. The fact of the matter is that when it comes to pricing and hedging first-to-default baskets, your informed guess is as good as mine, at least if your model is logically correct, but many are not.

In some cases, the models are simply wrong. The model price is outside the logical boundary conditions for pricing this product. One structurer asked me to look at his price, and our conversation went as follows:

"Risk management says this model is right. What do you think—is that price about right?" he nervously asked. He had worked for a couple of months on a simulation model, but still had no idea where he expected to end up.

"You may need to recalibrate your model. The answer you got is simply incorrect," I replied.

"Wait a minute," he said, trying to sound confident. "You can't possibly know that. You didn't do any calculations."

"I didn't use a model, but I know the answer your model calculated is incorrect. Have a cup of coffee while I explain," I replied again.

If you don't know where you are going, a model won't get you there.

Basket default swaps reference a small number of obligors, usually 10 to 20 or even fewer. A first-to-default swap pays a premium to the credit protection buyer to take the risk of the first default of any one of the reference obligors in the basket. The investor, or credit protection provider, in the first-to-default basket will only lose the loss amount of the first asset to default. The loss amount is simply par minus the recovery value of the first asset to default. Albeit the investor's risk is limited, the investor earns a higher spread than would otherwise be available.

The motive for the investor is leverage. The maximum loss for the investor is defined, but so is the maximum upside, the leveraged premium on the basket.

Figure 10.18 shows the mechanics of a typical first-to-default basket swap.

Most first-to-default basket swaps are cash settled. The basket is usually a well-diversified basket of investment-grade names. The diagram in Figure 10.18 shows a basket of reference obligations from diversified and relatively uncorrelated industries: electronics, finance, retail stores, and automotive. The basket has only one prespecified name from each industry, and each has an investment-grade rating of either A2 or A3.

A single-name CDS for each of these assets pays a premium of 100 to 120 bps. Notice that I chose relatively uncorrelated assets. I chose notional amounts that are the same for each asset in the basket, and I chose assets with an investment-grade rating. Each of the reference obligors/assets has a low absolute value of probability of default. Each asset is a senior unsecured obligation, meaning each asset is in the same seniority category for the respective reference obligor. The Street will price first-to-default basket swap premiums on this type of basket at around two to three times the average spread of the basket. The average spread on this basket is 100 bps, and it is common to see market prices of around 220 to 330 bps.

Theoretically, the price of a first-to-default basket depends on the default correlation of the names in the basket. In other words, we want to know how likely it is that the names in the basket will default at the same time. In this sample basket, I chose investment-grade names in industries that

Typical market premiums for investment grade baskets are two to three times the average spread ofthe reference basket.

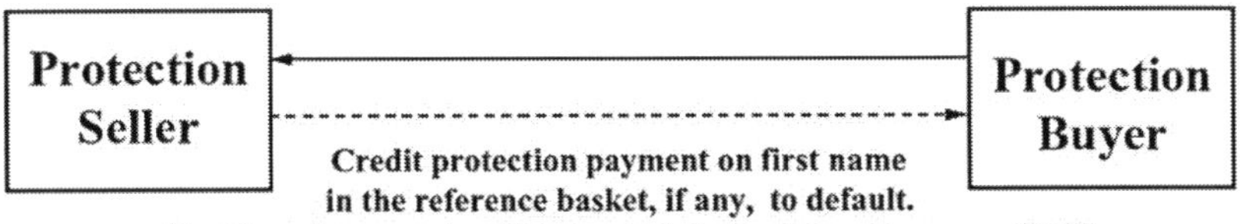

Credit protection payment on first name in the reference basket, if any, to default. Contingent payment = 10 mm x (original price – recovery value)* The protection seller's obligation terminates after the first name defaults and the protection payment is made.

Reference Basket

Rating	Industry	Size	Spread
A2	Electronics	10mm	100 bps
A3	Finance	10mm	120 bps
A2	Retail Store	10mm	100 bps
A3	Automobile	10mm	120 bps

* Most transactions are cash settled, and recovery value is market price of an allowable reference obligation for the reference obligor that is the first to default.

FIGURE 10.18 First to Default Basket Swap

are diverse, which means the names in this basket will have a low default correlation.

Several factors affect pricing: the default correlations of the names in the basket and the volatility of the assumed correlations; the absolute value of the probability of default (the potential for coincident default); the volatility of the probability of default; the ranking of potential reference assets in the reference obligors capital structure (e.g., senior unsecured debt); the dispersion of the premiums of the individual names in the basket; the notional amount of each of the assets in the basket; and the dispersion of potential recovery values.

It is possible to define the upper and lower bounds for pricing a first-to-default basket swap. I once saw an example using four credits: A, B, C, and D. The assets have the following single-name credit default swap spreads: 30, 35, 40, and 50 bps, respectively. Note that the sum of the spreads is 155 bps; the widest spread for any asset in the basket is 50 bps, while the narrowest spread is 30 bps. The example went on to say that if the credits are highly correlated, one would apply a lower percentage to the total to come up with the pricing for the first-to-default basket. The example calculated the highly correlated case as follows:

155 x 0.15 x 23 bps

What is wrong with this example?

The lower bound will never be as low as 23 basis points. The example giver knows this product well, but this was a simple case of not paying attention. *The lower bound for the basket must be higher than 30 bps, the spread of the narrowest asset in the basket.*

This was exactly the same error made by the coffee-sipping structurer.

In fact, the first-to-default basket swap premium will be higher than 50bps, the highest individual spread in the basket, which is asset D, for any correlation of the names in the basket less than 100 percent. The probability of exercise of the option is greater than just the probability of D's default,

We need to assess the probability of default of either A or B or C or D.

Let's further assume this is a two-year transaction. The individual two-year cumulative probabilities of default for assets A, B, C, and D are respectively as follows: 0.7 percent, 0.5 percent, 0.6 percent, and 0.7 percent. The probability of default for any one of those assets is not the product of the individual probabilities of default. First one must calculate the probability of no default for the basket. This is simply the product of each of the probabilities of no default. The probability of no default for each of the individual assets is simply

Probability of No Individual Default = (1 − Probability of Individual Default)

The probability of no default in the basket is:

(0.993 x 0.995 x 0.994 x 0.993) x 100 = 97.52%

The two-year probability of at least one default in the two year period is simply

(1 − 0.9752) = 0.024768

or 2.48 percent for the two-year period. Notice this is higher than the default probability of any of the individual names—0.7 percent, 0.5 percent, 0.6 percent, and 0.7 percent—and is slightly below the sum of the individual correlations. Since these are investment-grade credits, the absolute level is still very low. Remember, we assumed no correlation between the assets in this basket when we calculated the probability of at least one default in the two-year period of 2.48 percent.

The probability of no default increases with increasing correlation, meaning the probability of no default is lower for higher correlation between the names in the basket. Uncorrelated credits will have a higher spread than correlated credits because any of four different types of causes could be responsible for a default of uncorrelated assets, whereas the causes of default for correlated assets are more limited.

What, then, is the upper boundary limit of the first-to-default basket premium? Is it the sum of the individual CDS spreads, or in our case 155 bps? Some of the finest minds in the business will talk about investment-grade baskets and tell you this is the answer. They are incorrect, but they are on the right track.

The argument for the sum of the individual credit default swap premiums is that the credit default probability of the basket is almost the same as the sum of the probability of default of the individual credits. That's an error. *The protection seller will make a credit event payment on only one of the credits, not on all four.* The protection seller is compensated only for the worst-case default probability—in reality the highest single premium in the basket—plus the increased likelihood of a default occurring because there is more than one obligor in the basket. If that incremental likelihood is low, the probability of payout is low, so the incremental premium is low.

Consider a basket made up of synthetic AAA tranches of four CDOs. The underlying collateral for each of the CDOs is different. Assume for the moment that the underlying asset classes for each of the tranches are entirely uncorrelated. Each of the AAA tranches pays a spread of 55 bps. Each of the AAA tranches is 10 million in size. Would the protection seller expect to get paid a first-to-default basket swap premium close to 220 bps to take the risk of the first of the 10 million-size tranches to default? Of course not. The reason is that the absolute probability of default is still very low.

Default correlation is correlated to credit rating. Higher grade assets—that is, investment-grade assets—exhibit less default correlation than non-investment-grade assets. Non-investment-grade assets tend to be highly leveraged, and economic effects may tend to affect all leveraged companies, even those in uncorrelated industries. Furthermore, non-investment-grade assets have a higher probability of default. Even in the absence of an economic downturn, two uncorrelated assets may experience a coincident or nearby time frame default. Even if default isn't coincident, it is likely that other credits in the basket will have deteriorated so that a second-to-default or even a third-to-default is imminent.

With non-investment-grade assets, we are dealing with much higher individual probabilities of default. The individual two-year cumulative

TABLE 10.5 Comparison of Individual and Basket Default Rates for Assets of Different Credit Quality

	Investment-Grade Assets		High-Yield	
Asset	Individual Cumulative P_d Two-Year	Basket Cumulative P_d Two-Year	Individual Cumulative P_d Two-Year	Basket Cumulative P_d Two-Year
A	0.70%	2.48%	11.71%	43.78%
B	0.50%	2.48%	14.20%	43.78%
C	0.60%	2.48%	13.50%	43.78%
D	0.70%	2.48%	14.20%	43.78%

probabilities of default. The individual two-year cumulative probabilities of default for high-yield assets A, B, C, and D are respectively as follows: 11.71 percent, 14.20 percent, 13.50 percent, and 14.20 percent. The two-year probability of no default in the basket is

$$(0.8829 \times 0.8580 \times 0.8650 \times 0.8580) \times 100 = 56.22 \text{ percent}$$

The two-year probability of at least one default in the two-year period is simply

$$(1 - 0.5622) = 0.4378$$

or 43.78 percent for the two-year period. Note that this is for uncorrelated assets. The magnitude of the difference between this basket of non-investment-grade assets A, B, C, D, and our earlier example using investment-grade assets A, B, C, D is summarized in Table 10.5.

Of course, structurers can't get enough of a good thing, and they assume investors can't either. Investors who want less risk and less income can provide second-to-default credit protection. Pricing second-to-default basket risk is as much an art form as pricing first-to-default basket risk. Some firms will create nth-to-default structures, and investors can earn a premium to provide protection for the first-, second-, third-, or nth -to-default risk.

Moody's will provide ratings on the mezzanine risk of default baskets. These ratings should be viewed as a convenience for investors who require ratings. I don't believe these ratings should be taken seriously. As we've already seen, the rating agencies haven't been doing too well with ratings over the past five years. In a basket we have a very small sample, and the sampling error is likely to be huge when one tries to draw conclusions from statistical analysis, even in the best-case data scenario. But we already know

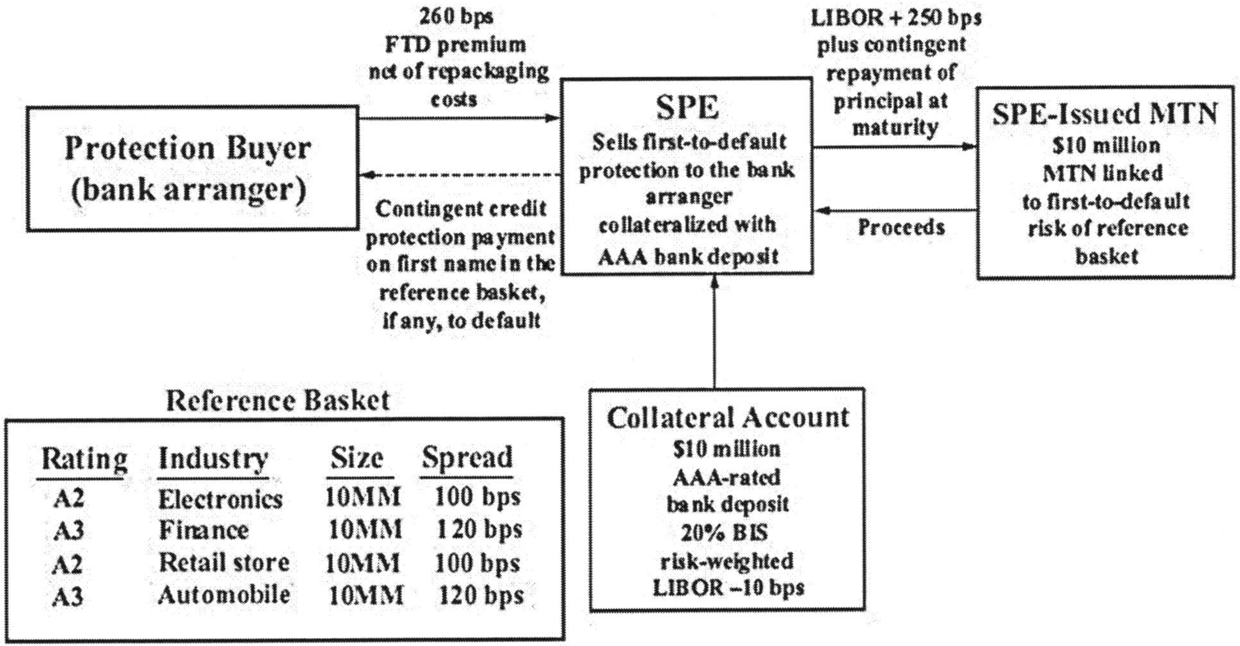

* Contingent payment = 10 MM × (Original price – recovery value). The protection seller's obligation terminates after the first name defaults and the protection payment is made. Most transactions are cash settled, and recovery value is market price of an allowable reference obligation for the reference obligor that is the first to default.

FIGURE 10.18 Repackaged First-to Default Risk

that we aren't in the best-case data scenario. Historical rating agency data has let us down in the past two years in terms of its predictive power of credit risk. Couple that with the biases introduced by using a small sample that is not necessarily representative of the credit spectrum it is meant to represent, and you are begging to be misled.

Nonetheless, if your mandate is to make market bets, if you want to diversify your market bets, and if you require pricing models and ratings in order to get permission to make those bets, the models and ratings come in handy. Consider them as guidelines. Just don't expect them to precisely or even accurately predict your outcomes.

FIRST-TO-DEFAULT NOTES

Other investors may seek leverage in the form of first-to-default baskets. A credit derivative referencing the first-to-default risk of a preselected basket is imbedded in the EMTN and purchased by the investor, as shown in Figure 10.19

THE SMARTEST EQUITY INVESTMENT: PROTECTION MONEY

The savviest clients use the synthetic market to take first-to-default risk—that is, to take equity risk. Sophisticated investors with a good grasp of corporate balance sheets form an educated opinion of the probability of default and recovery value in the event of default. They handpick the names in the portfolio on which they will write first-to-default protection. For example, on a basket of names including Collins & Aikman, investors were paid an up-front premium of 85 percent, or 85 cents on the dollar. When Collins & Aikman defaulted, they locked in a gain of 2 percent% of the notional amount of the Collins & Aikman component of the portfolio. Before the default occurred, they had use of the up-front premium cash.

The market occasionally misprices this risk, but the only way to know that is to learn the techniques of valuing corporations. This is a skill in short supply among the subset of CDO professionals who rely on correlation data—not fundamental value—for their sophisticated Monte Carlo models.

Chapter 11

CDO Managers

At their best, CDO managers can add value by monitoring CDO collateral and making sure that the trustee understands the cash flow structure of the deal so that mistakes are not made. For example, in some CDOs, reinvestments have occurred long after the reinvestment period has ended. In other deals, payments were made between special purpose entities that should not have been made. A diligent CDO manager can catch and correct these errors and can head off portfolio credit deterioration. Unfortunately, this seems to have been a utopian goal, and most collateralized debt obligation managers collected fees for little more than producing reports.

As mentioned before, if a deal manager has a claim on the equity cash flows, there is a conflict of interest between the manager and more senior noteholders. If CDO managers are affiliated with the capital markets group of an investment bank or with related hedge funds, there may be a conflict of interest with the various roles of the manager. The CDO manager may be tempted to trade deteriorating assets from the capital markets group into the CDO warehouse. There may be a temptation to trade hedge fund assets with the CDO, creating artificial mark-to-market prices for the underlying collateral.

One would think that the best way to avoid these negative consequences is to use an independent CDO manager. Independence is somewhat of a myth, however, since CDO managers rely on investment banks to award them the right to manage the deals and earn management fees. There is no easy answer to this dilemma, and for the most part, the investor has received poor service from CDO managers. The exceptions seem to be affiliated with deep-pocket, savvy non-investment-bank-related financial institutions, but that is no guarantee of competent management.

If an investor intends to pay CDO management fees, then it should ask for the manager to assure it that certain standards will be maintained. The following are best practices among CDO managers that I have observed, but I have never observed all of these characteristics in one manager.

BEST PRACTICES

- *Portfolio selection and management independence.* Selecting a good portfolio is a necessary—but not a sufficient—condition for a successful outcome. The best-practice CDO manager (BPM) takes a lead role in the selection of the original portfolio and often helps source assets. Where applicable, the BPM optimizes rating versus spread and has the clout to overrule arrangers on this issue. While superior original portfolio selection is highly indicative of subsequent performance, the BPMs joined this ability with other attributes. In other words, most of the following factors were also present, but where some of the following factors were present and good initial portfolio selection was absent, the CDO manager was not highly rated by either investors or rating agencies. In all cases, BPMs are independent asset managers, and compensation is linked only to CDO asset management. BPMs have their own warehousing capabilities, noting that managers who rely on arrangers for the warehouse are the arrangers' prisoners. BPMs take responsibility for hedging warehoused assets and mark the collateral to market until all of the debt is underwritten.
- *Surveillance.* BPMs monitor every position, including every CDO tranche, and the underlying collateral, including mortgage prepayment data and other related data. BPMs have an early warning system and primary data sources including loan tapes where applicable. BPMs have several in-house credit analysts and also purchase outside credit software.
- *Structuring.* BPMs have extensive experience with structuring, CDO documentation, asset accumulation, hedging market risk, the warehouse process, the rating process, negotiating reduced arrangers' fees, investor road shows, and the closing process.
- *Investor reporting.* BPMs have developed customized investor reporting systems. Ongoing administration includes well-developed Web-based information for investors, telephone communication with investors, and good rapport with the rating agencies.
- *Capital markets experience at an investment bank.* BPMs have diverse experience in investment banking or equivalent experience. While all BPMs have investment banking or comparable experience, not all managers with senior investment banking deal experience are BPMs, and some have been involved in legal disputes with investors. The following due diligence question may reveal past problems: "Have you ever been deposed in the Past five years? If so, please provide the case number (if applicable), a copy of the complaint, a copy of your deposition, and the resolution, if available."

- *Dedicated resources.* The BPM's sole function is CDO asset management. In other words, BPMs do not also manage hedge funds, work on structuring of other deals, or manage portfolios of other assets.
- *Tailored software.* BPMs have a clear grasp of CDO software plus ability to perform ad hoc in-house modeling with backup employees for this task.
- *Distribution.* Between the arranger and the BPM, there is the ability to place equity with long-term investors, and the BPM usually invests in a significant share of the equity. BPMs have good communication with the equity investors.

THE VALUED FEW

There is a very strong correlation between CDO managers employing best practices and ongoing high performance of the CDOs under management. Only a handful of CDO managers employ best practices, and there is a huge gap between the services provided by these managers versus all other managers.

Most CDO managers are not worth the fees being paid by investors, and do not have the expertise or resources to perform CDO management or surveillance. Many managers, even those currently managing fixed-income portfolios, do not have the in-house ability to build a CDO model. The lack of expertise is sometimes masked by good initial portfolio selection, but beyond that, investors are getting little value. Moreover, some CDO managers give little input into the initial portfolio selection process. Ongoing portfolio trading is also an issue.

Many managers rely on the bank arranger both for structuring expertise and to take a lead role with the rating agencies to secure the initial ratings. Often the key people have no structuring or CDO management/monitoring expertise but provide only the expertise for the portfolio trading decisions. These managers have no input into structuring decisions and have virtually no leverage to negotiate lower structuring fees with deal arrangers.

Rating agencies rarely do background checks on CDO managers and provide less oversight of CDO managers than of structured instrument vehicle (SIV) managers. The rating agencies' perception seems to be that "when managers failed, they had the wrong portfolio," even though many failed because managers substituted assets that accelerated portfolio deterioration. The rating agencies check systems on a black-box basis. If systems appear to produce the results the rating agencies need, the rating agencies are satisfied. They do not examine the software, but they do inquire about firewalls, capital monitoring, and controls. The rating agencies admit that managers comply to varying degrees with their ongoing requirements. In cases where legal disputes have arisen between managers and investors, rating agencies have claimed journalist-like privileges to avoid turning over notes and analyses produced during the rating process.

Many CDO managers do not understand the mechanics of ramping up assets and negotiation of warehousing agreements. This has resulted in behind-the-scenes legal disputes after investors felt they lost value due to asset repricing, credit losses prior to closing, market hedging losses prior to closing, or defaults prior to closing. Several inexperienced managers complained about insufficient flow of information from arrangers prior to deal closing.

BPMs monitor trustee performance as part of their surveillance activities. There has been litigation related to trustees making payments and allowing sales of assets that should never have been authorized, because trustees were not aware agreements in deal documents were being violated. Trustees point out they do not have the time to read deal documents, complain they are underpaid, and state they cannot always tell if payments are authorized. Yet most managers take a hands-off approach to trustee monitoring. This seems to be an unresolved risk in the management of most CDOs.

Another unresolved risk is that while management agreements usually seek to keep key people in place, it is usually much more difficult to change managers and/or key people without incurring fees. Yet the language of these agreements is still highly variable. Since arrangers usually negotiate this documentation with managers, investors must become more proactive to protect their interests.

BPMs instruct their lawyers—instead of relying on their lawyers to handle documentation—and take responsibility for negotiating the deal documents. Several non-BPM managers said they do not handle deal documents; they send them to their legal departments.

CDO managers are unregulated, and only a handful of managers provide good value for the fees charged, even though the least competent manager usually charges the same fees as BPMs. The key areas in which BPMs distinguish themselves are in portfolio selection, warehouse management, negotiating structuring fees, negotiating documentation, and surveillance.

Chapter 12

Balance Sheet CLOs and CDOs

Consumer loan securitizations are balance-sheet CDOs. As we saw earlier, the technology for these deals originated in the United States in the 1980s. New product development has centered on applying the lessons learned to nonconsumer loans.

The introduction of synthetics allowed new product development in the dollar market. The introduction of the euro gave an added boost to balance-sheet securitization, since euro-denominated assets found a new, broader investment base than was possible with the currency Tower of Babel that existed pre-1999. A critical mass of technology, assets, and currency acceptability contributed to innovations in the U.S. market and product development in the European market. While new products appeared in 2002, the full menu of the following products is currently in use in the CDO markets.

TRUE SALE (FULLY FUNDED) DELINKED STRUCTURE

The first rated collateralized loan obligation (CLO) backed by U.S. bank loans was brought in 1990. The first deals were arbitrage CLOs and were mainly securitizations of smaller-size loans. The return on the equity tranche is the sole driver of an arbitrage CLO. The collateral manager's goal is to maximize the return on the equity tranche, the difference between the spread on the investment assets and the deal liabilities (coupons on the non-equity tranches and deal expenses). Arbitrage CLOs sometimes use sponsor collateral. Arbitrage CLOs also commonly use collateral purchased in the secondary market. The deal arranger might not have an underwriting or servicing relationship with many of the loan obligors.

The bank originator/seller/sponsor is usually not motivated by a potential arbitrage. The bank originator that has assets on balance sheet is motivated by regulatory capital relief and wants to fund the assets off balance sheet, similar to the motives for a traditional consumer loan ABS transaction. The bank originator has an underwriting and servicing relationship with the borrowers. The bank originator in a fully funded CLO has intimate knowledge of the credit characteristics of the underlying borrowers.

The following characteristics are typical of these cash flow CLOs. Cash flow from interest on the underlying collateral services the deal liabilities including coupons on the various CLO tranches and fees. Excess spread is diverted to a reserve account to service the deal.

These transactions have a two- to four-year revolving period called the *lockout* period. During the lockout period, the deal doesn't amortize. The deal manager invests principal from maturing loans in additional loans according to criteria set out in the deal prospectus. Although defined reinvestment is allowed during the lockout period, cash flow balance-sheet deals usually restrict trading throughout the life of the deal.

The lockout period is followed by an amortization period. Both principal and interest are repaid on a sequential basis. The payment priority is based on tranche seniority, and tranches have a predetermined target amortization schedule.

The CLO will amortize early if one of several unwind triggers is breached. There are several types of possible unwind triggers that can cause the early termination of a fixed-level structure or that can cause early amortization of an amortizing structure. These triggers include insolvency of the issuer, breaching a boundary condition for collateral maintenance, or reaching a certain level of defaults on the underlying reference obligors, among others.

Note that commercial and industrial (C&I) loans can be either *bilateral* or *multilateral*. A bilateral loan means that the sponsor bank is the sole lender or *underwriter* to the borrower or *obligor* for that particular loan. Many loans are syndicated among several bank underwriters to reduce total obligor exposure. These multi-underwriter loans are multilateral loans.

Since the loans are sold, this transaction reduces the size of the bank's balance sheet. One would normally think this would be an advantage and allow the bank to originate new business.

Incredibly, some financial institutions reject this structure because this efficient transfer of risk combined with funding doesn't appeal to them; they don't want to reduce the size of their balance sheets. For instance, officers of savings banks in Germany are compensated based on the size of their balance sheet. The last thing they want is a major reduction in balance sheet size.

In the United States, C&I loans may be either fixed rate or floating rate. The tranches of balance-sheet CLOs normally pay a floating-rate coupon indexed to LIBOR. Floating-rate C&I loans can be indexed to a number of floating-rate indexes. Many loans allow the credit spread of the loan versus the index to increase or decrease as the borrower's financial condition deteriorates or strengthens, respectively. This basis risk and spread risk of the underlying loan coupons versus the ultimate note coupons is hedged by entering into an interest rate swap with a hedge provider.

CLOs have varied in size from $300 million to $5 billion, albeit larger sizes are usually synthetic, non-true-sale structures. By selling the interests in the loans to an SPV, the seller/originator/sponsor is *delinked* from the investor. For U.S. FDIC institutions, this step is usually not required to achieve a bankruptcy-remote structure. Figure 12.1 shows how traditional ABS technology employing an intermediate SPV and a master trust structure can be applied to a true sale CLO.

As shown in Figure 12.2, it is possible to have an AAA-rated tranche in a delinked structure, since the rating is based on having the appropriate degree of subordination for a given CDO structure and for a given portfolio of loans.

As we saw earlier in our discussion of SPVs, the experience and credit rating of the servicer is important to rating agencies, as is the ability to substitute servicers. The credit rating of the hedge provider is also important. (See also the section in Chapter 2 titled "Bankruptcy-Remote?")

As we saw earlier, some investors are concerned with the moral hazard imbedded in balance-sheet CLOs. One school of thought is that the reputation of the seller bank is bound up with the CLO issuance. Another school of thought is that the bank may let the loan portfolio deteriorate once the loans are sold. Theoretically, if the bank retains servicing rights and if the bank retains an equity interest, the bank has an interest in solid performance of the loan portfolio. If things go wrong, however, some investors fear the bank may use the revolving period to dump shaky loans by selling them to the SPV. Subsequent events have shown that both schools of thought have merit. Structural protections can mitigate this risk but can never completely eliminate it. One can protect against the moral hazard, but it is difficult to protect against incompetence or fraud. Fortunately, this is rare.

The documentation for true sale structures is more intensive than for synthetic structures. The key documents are as follows: (1) the purchase agreements for the various note classes; (2) documentation for Reg S and Rule 144A global notes; (3) the paying agency agreement; (4) the trust deed; (5) the cash bond administration agreement; (6) asset sale agreements; and (7) the servicer agreement. Deals that employ an interest subparticipation tranche have additional documentation outlining this agreement.

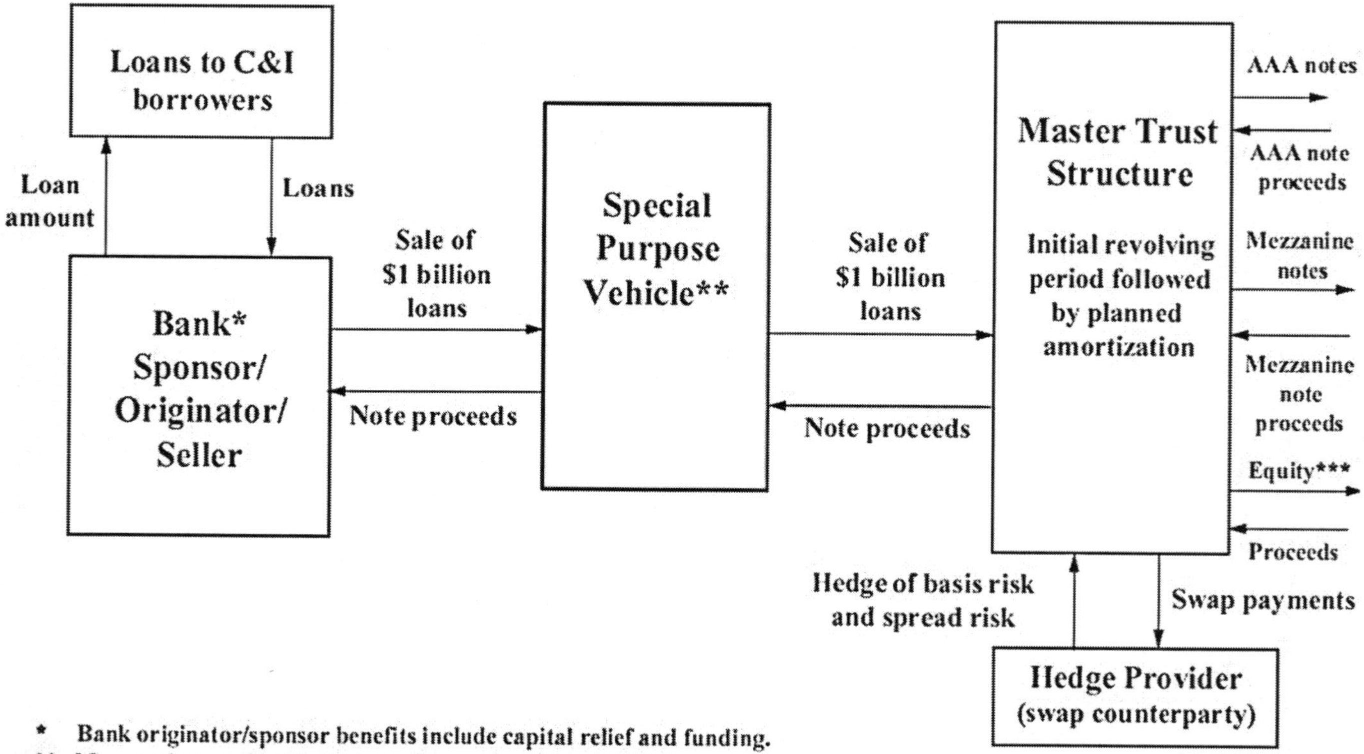

* Bank originator/sponsor benefits include capital relief and funding.
** May not be required for U.S. banks regulatedby the FCIC.
*** Equity is usually retained by the bank sponsor.

FIGURE 12.1 True Sale (Fully Funded) Balance Sheet, C&I Loan Cash Flow CLO

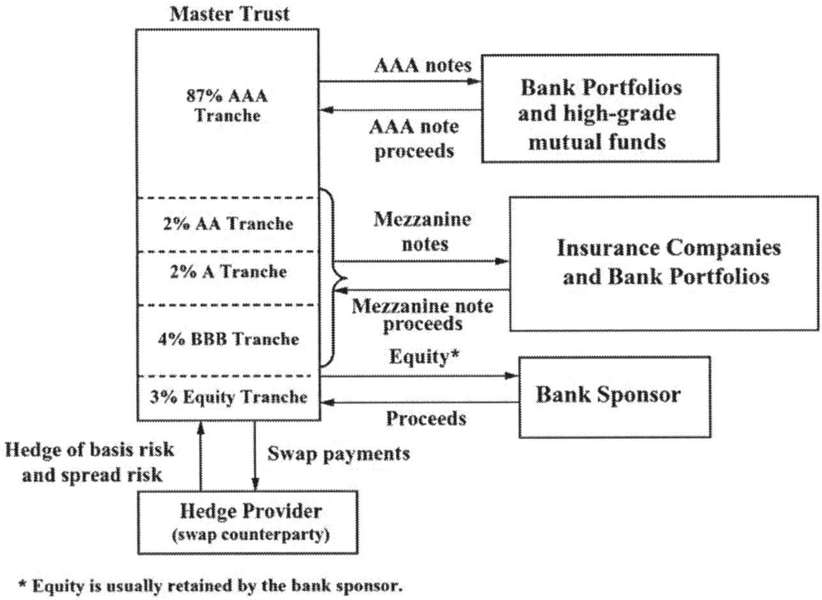

FIGURE 12.2 True Sale CLO, Investor Perspective

LINKED NONSYNTHETIC STRUCTURES

In 1996, National Westminster Bank (NatWest, now part of Bank of Scotland) brought the $5 billion Repeat Offering Securitization Entity Funding No. 1 (R.O.S.E.) CDO to market. National Westminster retained legal ownership of the loans but transferred the loan risk in the form of subparticipation interests in the loans. Subparticipation interests do not have loan voting rights, so deciding how to administer those rights in the context of the structure wasn't an issue. The collateral consisted of revolving corporate loan facilities. This was a *linked* transaction since the deal was linked to NatWest's credit risk. The collateral consisted of C&I loans. This deal was the first large-scale non-arbitrage CLO. This deal had no AAA-rated tranche, because the highest rating possible for any tranche was NatWest's rating, which was below AAA. This is a significant drawback of linked transactions. Figure 12.3 shows the generic structure.

The benefit to NatWest was that it got funding and regulatory capital relief under BIS I guidelines. The collateral was investment-grade rated, and the equity tranche size was only 2 percent of the CDO, which meant that NatWest held only $100 million in capital against the equity tranche

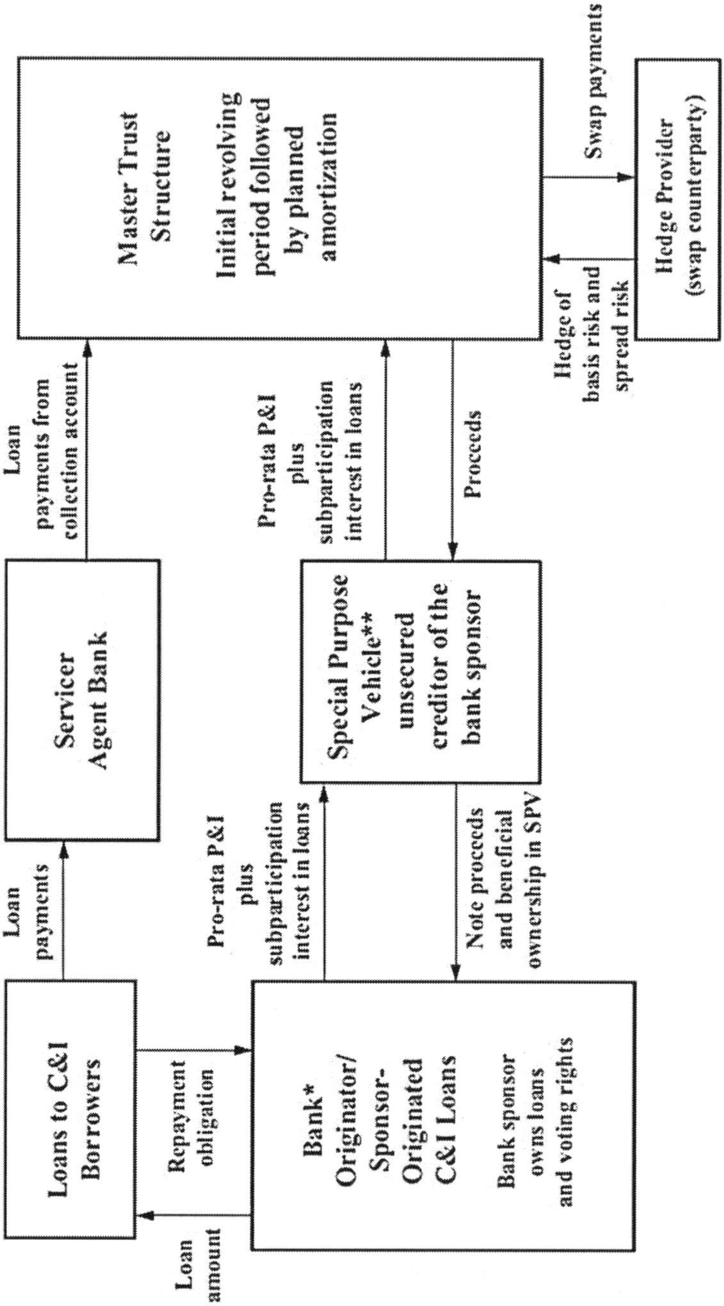

* Bank originator/sponsor benefits include capital relief and funding.
** May not be required for U.S. banks regulated by the FCIC.

FIGURE 12.3 Generic Funded CLO Linked to the Bank Sponsor versus $400 million required before the securitization. This was a 4:1 capital reduction at the time.

While this was a seminal deal at the time, from the investor point of view, the recent rash of bank credit rating downgrades makes a delinked structure desirable. From NatWest's point of view, the CLO wasn't cost efficient. This deal had no AAA tranche. At the time, NatWest's rating was Aa2/AA, and that was the highest rating possible for any tranche in this CDO. The Aa2/AA tranche size was about 95.9 percent of the transaction. If this deal were delinked and tranched, the Aa2/AA tranche would probably have been about 2 percent of the deal, and the AAA tranche would have made up about 94 percent of the deal. This means that the liability cost of the largest tranche increased by the difference in per annum spread between an AAA tranche and an AA2 tranche! A R.O.S.E. by any other name would still stink from the point of view of cost efficiency.

As we look at more recent structures, we'll see the objective is to find a balance between capital efficiency and all-in deal costs to the bank sponsor.

LINKED BLACK BOX CLN CDOS

While CLOs up to 1997 could transfer credit risk of a bank's loan portfolio, what if a bank wanted to transfer credit risk on an enterprise wide basis? For instance, what if you had swap counterparty exposure and wanted to transfer this credit risk? SBC made the first attempt to do this using CLNs. On September 10, 1997, the then Swiss Bank Corporation (SBC), rated AA+/AA1 at the time, launched Glacier. This first-of-its-kind deal proved so popular that SBC upsized the deal from $1.5 billion to $1.75 billion at its launch. It is, however, another linked structure.

Glacier Finance is a master trust structure special purpose entity domiciled in the Grand Caymans. The portfolio consists of SBC-issued credit-linked notes. At the time of issue, the maximum achievable rating on the senior notes was AA+/AA1, capped at SBC's rating, but the amount of subordination was only 8.25 percent to get to the AA+/AA1 rating threshold. This suggests that the AAA tranche, if it had been feasible, would have been very large, probably around 90 percent of the total deal size.

SBC gave a lot of thought to international issues in the deal structure. While the CDO appears cost inefficient, there were added economic benefits to SBC. SBC issued the medium-term notes (MTNs) from its New York branch since funding is an expense item for tax purposes in New York.

Glacier uses a blind pool, also known as a *black box*. Investors do not know the composition of the risks to which the CLNs are linked. Swiss banking laws require high client confidentiality standards. Penalties include a 15-year prison term for violation of client confidentiality. To preserve this confidentiality, SBC imbedded the client credit risk in credit-linked notes, medium-term notes issued by Swiss Bank's New York branch. Figure 12.4 outlines the structure.

Credit risk is transferred on an enterprise wide basis from investment and commercial banking businesses: loans, derivatives, securities, and project loans. The maturity of the underlying credit risks does not need to match the maturity of the notes issued by the SPV. The CLNs also vary in maturity and do not necessarily match the maturity of the notes issued by the Glacier entity. The CLNs are callable by SBC on any interest payment date, and SBC can revolve credits imbedded in the CLNs into and out of the SPV. As CLNs in the SPV mature, the SPV uses the cash to purchase other CLNs. Unlike the CLOs issued previous to this deal, the Glacier senior notes are bullet notes with bullet maturities of five years and seven years for each credit tranche. At the time of issue, the senior five-year tranche was priced at LIBOR plus16, and the senior seven-year tranche was priced at LIBOR plus 19.

The investors invested in a black-box structure, but the structure is also a black box for SBC's (and UBS's) relationship managers and line credit officers. They do not know whether their client's credit is imbedded in CLNs used as collateral for the SPV. Only a few key credit officers have this information.

SBC mapped its internal bank rating system to the ratings of Moody's and S&P. This allows SBC to continually revolve collateral in the SPV. SBC can call its CLNs and substitute others. This vehicle allows SBC's trading department to manage credit exposures. The rating agencies do not see the individual obligors.

SBC defines the credit events for the MTNs it issues. The investors have recourse to the CLN, not to the underlying credit risks. If there is no credit event, SBC pays par at the maturity of the CLN. If there is a credit event, SBC calls the CLN and redeems it at the recovery value. The recovery value is determined by the senior unsecured debt obligation of the underlying reference credit. The SPV would receive a payment after 18 days of the determined recovery value. If there is no reference security, the payout is preset at 51 percent, the average recovery value for senior unsecured obligations according to Moody's data at the time the deal closed.

SBC achieved its goal of regulatory capital relief since the regulators look at the resulting credit protection as cash-collateralized exposure. CLNs, which imbed full loan risk, are eligible for full regulatory capital relief. For the CLNs that reference a 51 percent recovery rate, 51 percent is cash-collateralized, and that portion requires no regulatory capital. SBC estimated that it achieved about a 5:1 regulatory capital reduction.

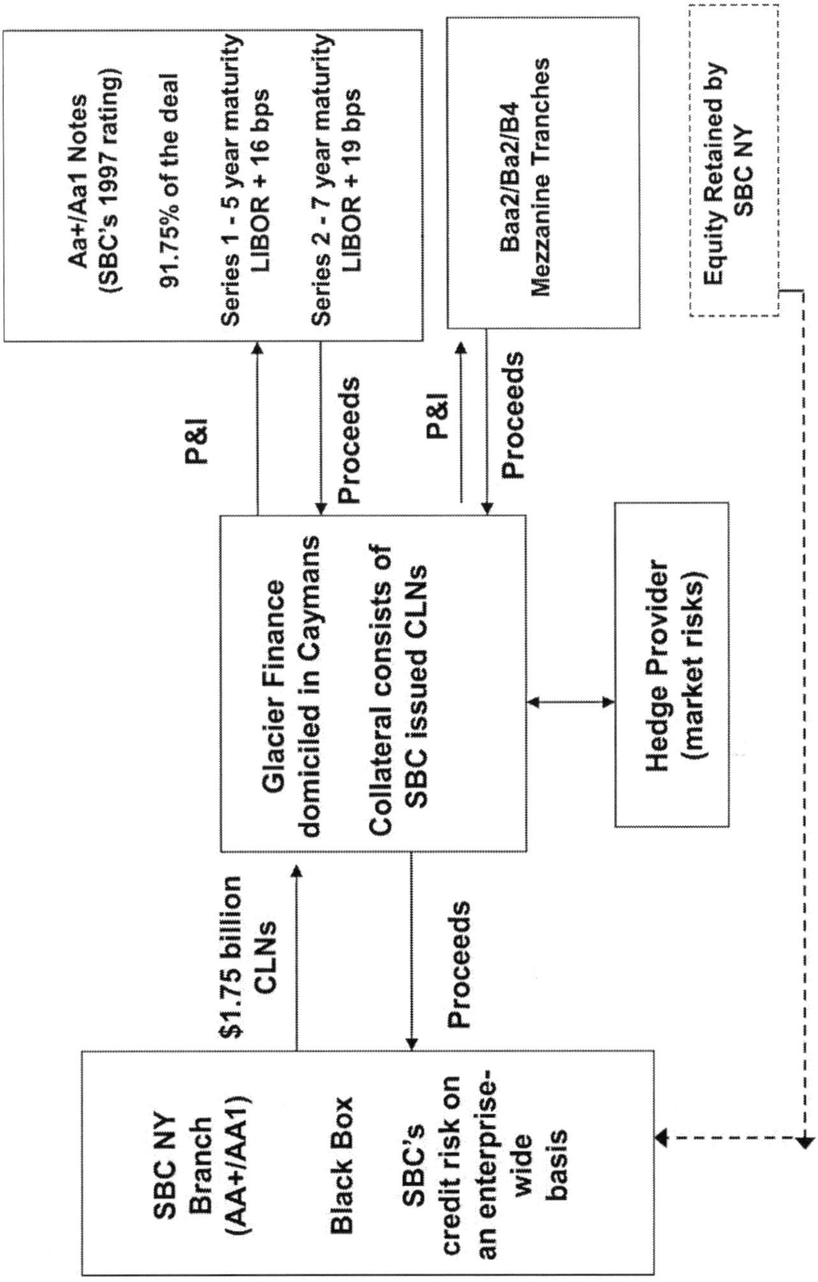

FIGURE 12.4 Glacier CLN CDO - Black Box

This deal sold well because at the time, there was a dearth of product on the market. This deal was followed by the Triangle I deals, which had a very similar structure. For the first time, via the R.O.S.E., and via Glacier and Triangle CDOs, investors had access to investments in huge, diversified pools of bank portfolio loans. Like the R.O.S.E. deal, the linked nature of the Glacier and first Triangle deals has its drawbacks, as investors have seen in the current bank credit rating downgrade environment. Another drawback is the black-box nature of the portfolio. Today, very few investors would accept either a linked structure or a black-box structure.

SYNTHETIC STRUCTURE WITH SPE

Portfolio managers use single-name credit default swaps to lay off risk to individual obligors but laying off the risk of a major portion of the portfolio requires a different strategy. Synthetic CLOs or synthetic CBOs are the tools managers use to mitigate the credit risk of a diversified portfolio of assets. These are cash flow deals. These balance-sheet deals may have revolving periods and lockouts, just as we saw earlier in the true sale structure.

The issuer usually retains the first-loss risk. In the United States, the originating bank almost always explicitly retains the equity tranche. In Europe, the ISP structure often makes it appear as if this risk has been sold to an investor, but the first-loss risk is actually retained by the originator.

It is possible to directly sell equity risk to an investor or a fund. As we'll see later, a modification of the secured loan trust structure may enable the transfer of equity risk. While this is a very good idea, most banks don't put in the required effort to accomplish it.

A synthetic structure can be partially funded using an SPE. Since the bank sponsor doesn't issue notes as collateral, the structure is *delinked* from the bank originator's risk. JPMorgan brought the first of many Broad Index Secured Trust Offerings (BISTROs) to market in December 1997. It was the first CDO to exploit this type of synthetic structure. The transaction was both leveraged and delinked from JPMorgan.

For the first time, default risk of a pool of loans was transferred using credit default swaps. The super senior risk could be transferred purely in synthetic form, but JPMorgan liked to keep this tranche. The mezzanine risks were purchased by senior and junior noteholders in the form of credit-linked notes. The mezzanine risk CDSs were repackaged in the BISTRO SPE, and BISTRO issued the notes. The note proceeds were used to purchase AAA collateral.

Today, this is a widely used structure. Figure 12.5 outlines the generic structure.

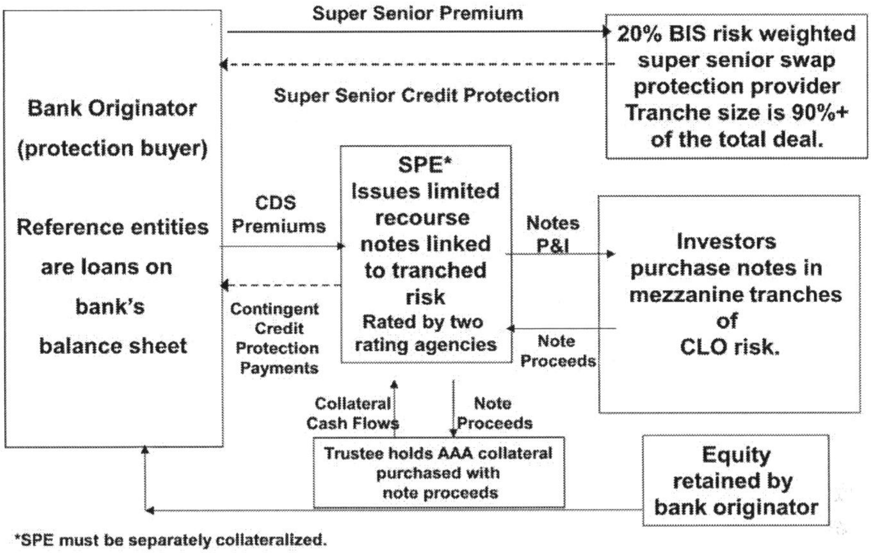

FIGURE 12.5 Synthetic Structure with SPE: Delinked Structure (BISTRO - type Structure)

The super senior swap counterparty is almost always a 20 percent BIS risk-weighted entity. Depending on the venue, the counterparty may be an OECD bank or a 20 percent BIS risk-weighted financial institution or agency. The 20 percent BIS risk-weighted counterparty may retain the risk in its trading book, or it may in turn lay off the risk with a monoline insurance company, a reinsurer, or a financial guarantor. Given the nervousness in the marketplace about non-monoline insurance, protection bought from reinsurers will be closely scrutinized.

The equity is usually retained by bank originators.

Many balance-sheet transactions allow for revolving periods and substitution of credits. The earlier deals are written with old credit default swap language.

Although this is the core structure, there are many variations, especially in the treatment of the equity tranche and transference of mezzanine risk from the SPE. Furthermore, this structure has now been adapted to synthetic arbitrage deals. Earlier we saw an example of a managed synthetic arbitrage CDO. Static synthetic arbitrage CDOs also use a variation of this structure.

Most balance-sheet deals are rated by at least two rating agencies. Although the approaches of the agencies differ somewhat, in general they will look at the bank originator and assets very closely.

For the bank originator and, to a more limited extent, for the bank arranger, the rating agencies consider the following: (1) the administration and organization of the bank, (2) credit policies and controls, (3) technology systems, (4) decision making processes for adding assets, and (5) internal reporting procedures.

The rating agencies evaluate the asset pool using most of their standard criteria: (1) diversification of obligors including industry and regional diversification, (2) liquidation profiles, (3) delinquency and default data, and (4) recovery value data.

This structure allows only partial regulatory capital relief, and the equity is held on the bank's balance sheet and requires dollar-for-dollar capital. If 20 percent BIS risk-weighted counterparties are used for the super senior, and if the collateral is 0 percent risk weighted, the capital will be calculated for these tranches accordingly based on the size of each tranche.

European variations on this structure include marketing equity as an interest subparticipation tranche. Figure 12.6 shows how this tranche is incorporated into the overall structure.

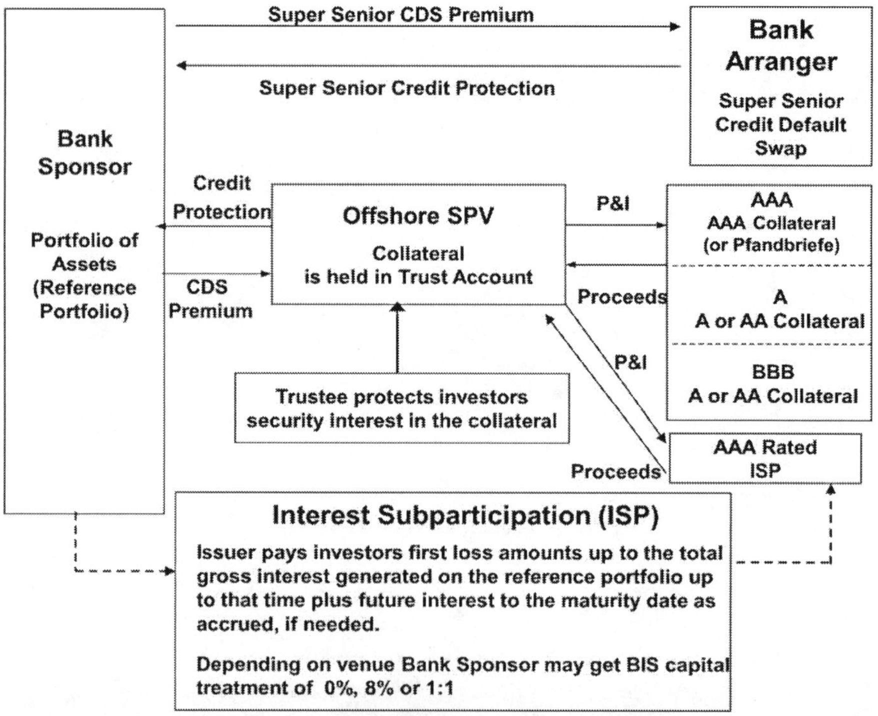

FIGURE 12.6 Partially Funded CDO with SPV and ISP

Funding is limited to the tranches for which notes are issued, but the cost of bringing this deal to market is much lower than the cost of a true sale structure. These deals require much less documentation than true sale CLOs. The three key documents are (1) the terms and conditions of each of the note classes, (2) the credit default swap confirmations, and (3) the trust agreement. Deals that employ an interest subparticipation tranche have additional documentation outlining this agreement. In contrast to the documentation for the true sale structure discussed earlier, this documentation is minimal.

PARTIALLY SYNTHETIC LINKED CDOS

Landesbank Kiel (LB Kiel) brought a EUR 1 billion balance-sheet CDO to market in 2001. The underlying collateral consists of first and second residential mortgage loans. The deal is named F ¨ORDE 2000-1 and is rated by Moody's and Fitch. At the time, LB Kiel was rated Aa1 by Moody's, A1+ by S&P, and AAA by Fitch. Figure 12.7 shows that LB Kiel used

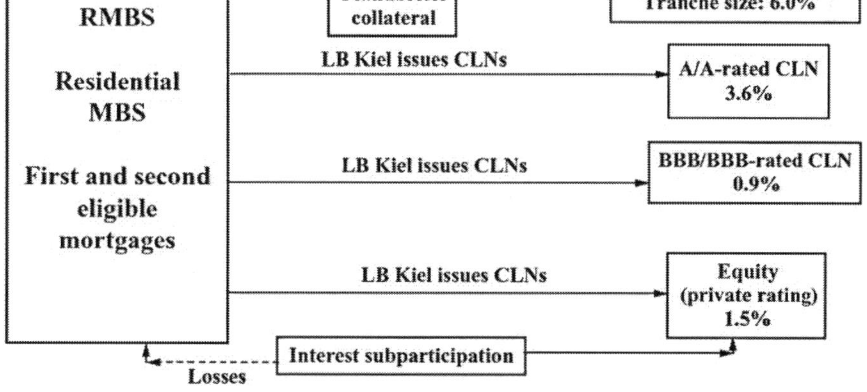

*Notes are rated by Moody's and Fitch and listed on the Luxembourg Stock Exchange.

FIGURE 12.7 Partially Synthetic CDO: Förde 2000-1

many of the innovative elements of partially synthetic structures available at the time.

LB Kiel transferred the super senior risk in the form of a super senior swap and acted as issuer of CLNs for the other tranches. The equity tranche was sold in the form of a privately rated interest subparticipation. In order to get an AAA/AAA rating for the relevant CLN, LB Kiel had to use AAA Pfandbriefe collateral to back the principal repayment of the note.

FULLY SYNTHETIC CDOS

The SPV isn't necessary if other counterparties can be found for each of the credit default swaps. The bank originator, as protection buyer of the credit default protection, may require AAA collateral for the AAA-rated tranche swap.

Figure 12.8 is a schematic of a fully synthetic balance-sheet CLO.

Many arbitrage CDOs are fully synthetic, albeit mezzanine tranches may be repackaged. In this instance, the bank arranger's credit default swap trading desk, rather than a bank's balance sheet, provides the reference assets for the CDO. Figure 12.9 shows the reference portfolio.

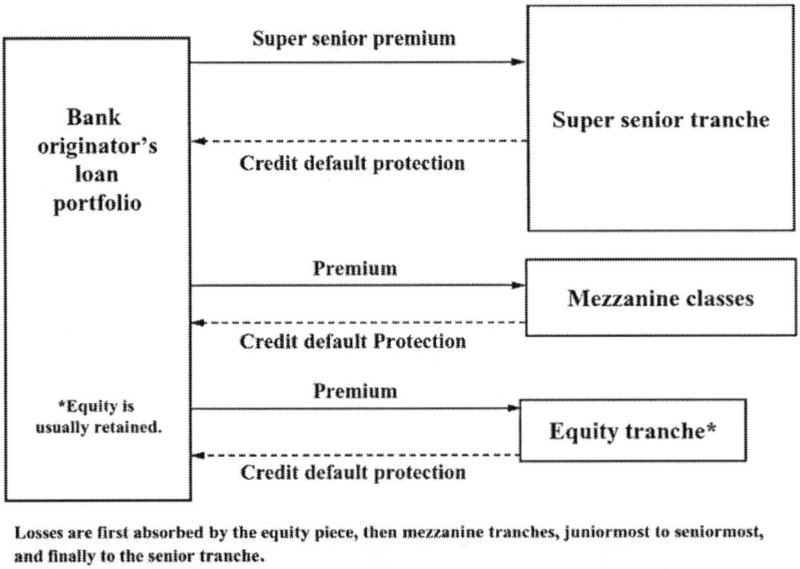

FIGURE 12.8 Fully Synthetic CLO

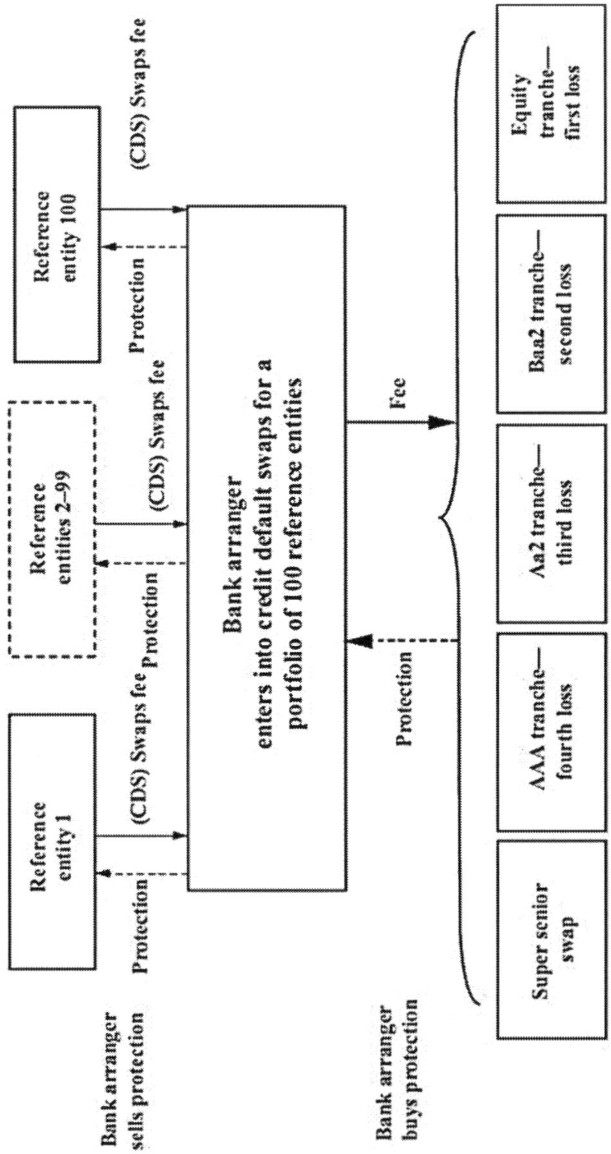

FIGURE 12.9 Synthetic Static Arbitrage CDO

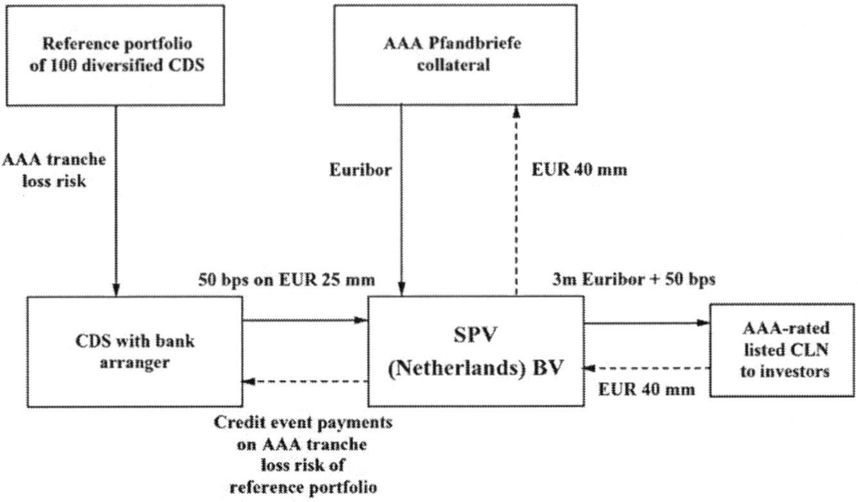

FIGURE 12.10 AAA Repacked CDS Note Structure

Many investors are willing to take the tranched risk of a diversified portfolio of synthetic credits, but need the risk repackaged in note form. This is usually done in one of two types of vehicles. A dedicated SPE can be set up for each deal. The SPE is prefunded with the purchases of limited recourse notes. We examined this structure previously when we compared managed synthetic and managed cash arbitrage CDOs.

Alternatively, the CDSs can be repackaged in a rated multi-issuance SPE that can accommodate any number of deals, albeit each tranche is ring-fenced. The SPV usually requires AAA-rated collateral, such as Pfandbriefe, for a AAA-rated credit-linked note, linked to the AAA CDS tranche of the reference portfolio. Investors often want the notes both listed and rated. Figure 12.10 shows the repackaged note structure.

SMALL TO MEDIUM SIZE ENTERPRISES—EUROPE

Small to medium-size enterprises (SMEs) are often defined as companies with annual sales of less than EUR 250 million, but this definition varies by program. SME CDOs are backed by claims against SMEs. These claims comprise all types of debt instruments including loans, receivables, undrawn revolvers, and undrawn guarantees.

Most of these claims are unrated. Usually implied ratings vary from as low as BB+ to as high as single A. To get an idea of the rating agency implied rating on the underlying reference portfolio, an originating bank may map its internal rating criteria to rating agency criteria. If the originator doesn't have a good internal rating system with a track record, the rating agencies may not accept this analysis. In that case, it is important for the originator to produce good records of historical default and loss data on the SME portfolio. When all else fails, a rating agency may apply an internal corporate rating model.

The key issue with SMEs is the quality of the data and the stability of the portfolio characteristics so that conclusions based on good historical data are likely to apply to the future performance of the SME portfolio. Confidence in the stability of future SME loan character is particularly important for revolving portfolios. These rating challenges contribute to a longer lead time in bringing a rated SME CDO to market.

The first SME CDOs were funded transactions. Currently both funded and synthetic SME CDOs are brought to market, but synthetic CDOs dominate the market. SME CDOs can be either static or revolving. SME CDOs have been issued as part of promotional programs designed to stimulate economic growth, but they have also been issued as nonpromotional SME CDOs. The European Investment Fund and other organizations in Europe sponsor promotional programs that often include guaranteeing tranches of CDOs backed by SMEs. The programs and protection offered vary by sponsor.

In Germany, the Kreditanstalt für Wiederaufbau (KfW) initiated a promotional program for SMEs. The Federal Republic of Germany guarantees KfW's obligations. Therefore all of KfW's primary obligations have a 0 percent BIS risk weighting and an AAA rating. KfW issues CDOs through the Program for Mittelstand-loan Securitization (PROMISE). KfW also has a sister program, PROVIDE, that has been used for non-Pfandbriefe eligible residential mortgages to support the housing industry. KfW, often with the help of another arranger bank, consolidates loans from more than one German bank originator in order to increase the size of the transaction, if necessary. The reference portfolio is a revolving reference portfolio of SMEs.

KfW acts as the credit protection provider in a credit default swap with the banks that originated the loans. From the point of view of the originating banks, they are laying off credit risk, which currently has a 100 percent BIS risk weight, and getting credit protection from a 0 percent risk-weighted provider. They not only receive the credit protection, but they free up regulatory capital for additional bank business.

KfW transfers the credit risk in one of two ways. The first method transfers mezzanine risk to the SPV via KfW-issued CLNs in the form of KfW certificates of indebtedness linked to the tranched mezzanine credit risk of the reference portfolio of SMEs (see Figure 12.11). If there are no defaults at the relevant mezzanine level in the reference portfolio, the certificates repay principal with an AAA certainty. Therefore the AAA tranched risk

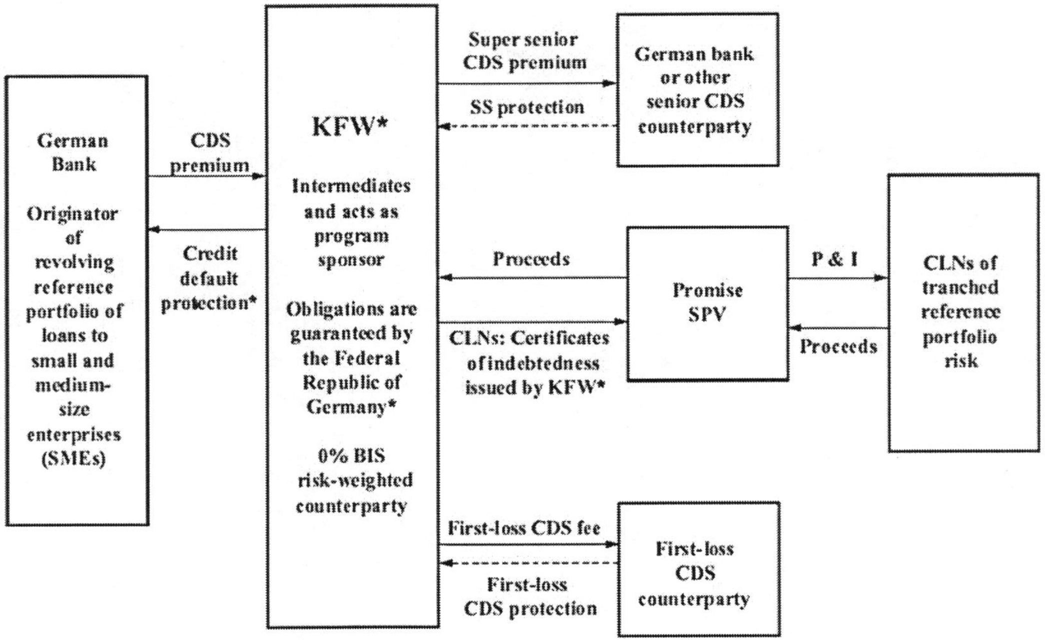

*The Federal Republic of Germany guarantees the obligations of the Kreditanstalt für Wiederaufbau (KFW). KFW as swap counterparty has a 0 percent BIS percent weight from the point of view of the German bank originator. The collateral for the SPV are KFW's certificates of indebtedness linked to the tranched mezzanine credit risk of the reference portfolio. If there are no defaults at the mezzanine level, there is an AAA certainty of payment of principal at maturity on the CLNs.

FIGURE 12.11 PROMISE SME CDO with CLNs

can get an AAA rating. The super senior risk is transferred with a super senior credit default swap. The first-loss risk is also transferred via a credit default swap. The second method differs from the first in that the mezzanine risk is transferred to the PROMISE SPV using credit default swaps for the mezzanine tranches (see Figure 12.12). The proceeds of the sales of the mezzanine notes are invested in KfW-issued medium-term notes (MTNs). The KfW MTNs are used as collateral for the credit default swaps. Since the MTNs are AAA-rated, the AAA tranched risk can achieve an AAA rating.

Bank Austria Creditanstalt (BaCa), an Austrian subsidiary of HypoVereinsbank, became the first non-German user of KfW's PROMISE platform in December 2002. The deal was called PROMISE Austria-2002 Plc. and was rated by Moody's and Fitch. The EUR 1 billion synthetic CDO securitized Austrian SMEs. The EUR 90.7 million AAA/AAA-rated tranche sold at three-month Euribor plus 38 bps, and has a 2.4-year average life, an expected maturity in 2011, and a legal final maturity in 2013.

In March 2002, the European Commission approved the use of KfW's state-aid guarantees for specialized promotional activities and SME financing. KfW's securitization activities under the PROMISE and PROVIDE platforms are promotional activities, and KfW may soon play a large role in European securitization. Credit default swaps smooth over many of the difficulties of bringing deals in venues other than Germany. It is much simpler to handle the legal and practical issues of asset risk transfer with credit default swaps, and this is evidenced in the greater speed and diminished documentation requirements of these deals.

In Spain, the Instituto de Credito Oficial (ICO) sponsors another promotional loan program with different structural features to other programs in Europe. For instance, unlike KfW, ICO does not act as an intermediary, albeit ICO acts as paying agent. The portfolio of SMEs usually includes a number of ICO-sponsored loans, which have higher recovery rates than unrestricted Spanish SME loans. The Spanish treasury acted as a credit wrap provider for CLO transactions prior to 2002. The Kingdom of Spain guaranteed timely payment of interest and principal on the senior notes and gave a partial guarantee to notes rated Aa and below on a sliding scale. In 2002 the Kingdom of Spain eliminated guarantees to the lower tranches, but it continues to guarantee the senior tranche. The Kingdom of Spain was upgraded to Aaa from Aa2 by Moody's in 2001.

Deutsche Bank's CORE and CAST deals are examples of nonpromotional SME CDOs. Deutsche Bank used a true sale structure and a static SME reference portfolio for the CORE deal. For the CAST deal, Deutsche Bank issued credit-linked notes linked to the tranches of SME risk on its balance sheet. Like the Glacier deal, the credit risk of the CLNs included Deutsche Bank's credit risk (as of this writing AA−) and the relevant tranched credit risk of the SME reference portfolio.

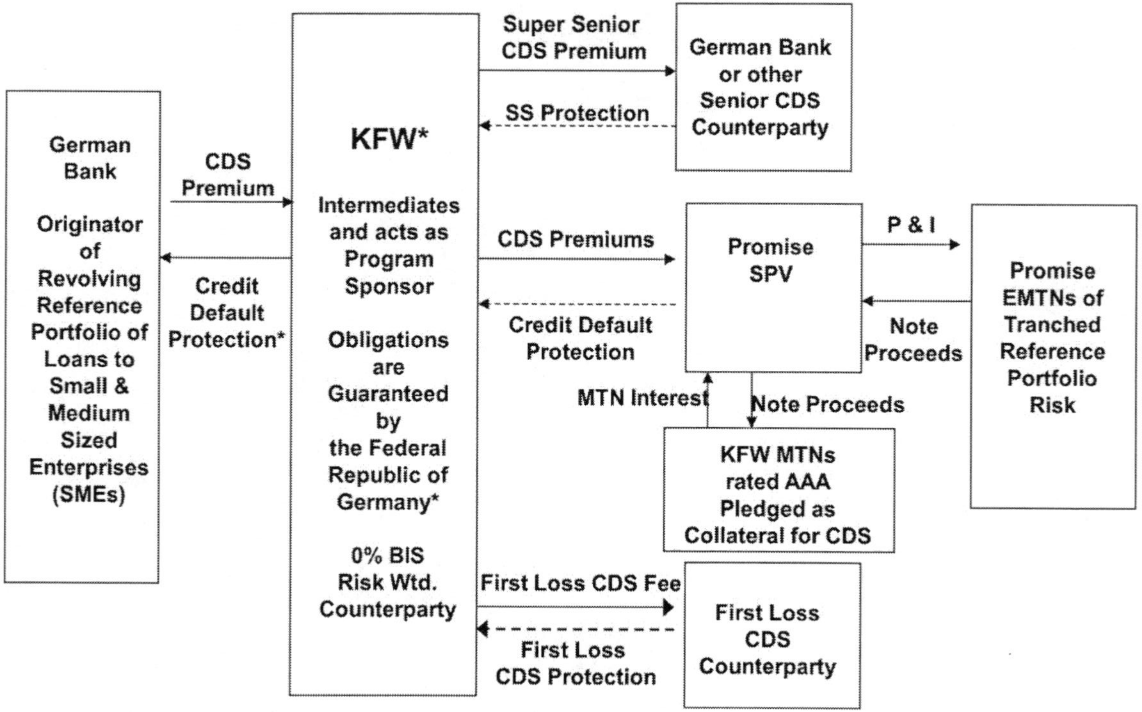

*The Federal Republic of Germany guarantees the obligations of the Kreditanstalt für Wiederaufbau (KFW). KFW as swap counterparty has a 0% BIS risk weight from the point of view of the German Bank Originator.

The collateral for the SPV are MTNs issued by KFW and pledged as collateral for the CDSs.

FIGURE 12.12 PROMISE SME CDO with CDSs

Banco Bilbao Vizcaya Argentaria S.A.'s (BBVA) SME CDO is another example of a nonpromotional SME CDO. BBVA referenced a revolving portfolio of SMEs and used a synthetic structure.

A few reinsurers have helped this market by seeking to invest in a diversified pool of European loans. They seek to avoid overconcentration in the actively traded names, and usually invest in medium-size enterprises, many of which do not have explicit ratings.

As an example, one French reinsurer guarantees the first-loss risk of diversified pools of European loans. They have individual size constraints and portfolio concentration limits within a single deal. They also have single obligor concentration limits in their macro portfolio. Since this reinsurer is single A rated and guarantees a first-loss tranche that is 30 percent of the deal, the credit rating of the senior tranches is investment-grade for the grade of collateral they have accepted so far. As we shall see later, this structure may become very popular with banks after Basel II becomes official.

SMES: UNITED STATES VERSUS EUROPE

In Europe, most loans are issued on a floating-rate basis. Loans securitized by countries in the European Community have floating-rate coupons paying at a spread to Euribor. The January 1, 1999, introduction of the euro as a multicountry currency has given a boost to the securitization of small and medium-size loans in the European Community countries for consumption in the European market.

Prior to 2000, the U.S. Small Business Administration (SBA) securitized SBA loans into Guaranteed Loan Pools Certificates (GLPCs). Pooling was similar to the device used in the mortgage market. Capped loans were pooled separately from uncapped loans. A pool of 50 loans might make up a $5 million GLPC. It was possible to sell GLPCs in the Eurodollar (European U.S. dollar) market.

These loans are guaranteed by the full faith and credit of the U.S. government, currently rated AAA. The guarantee gives these securities a 0 percent BIS risk weighting. The U.S. government guarantees *timely* payment of both principal and interest. Unlike most asset-backed securities, these CDOs are undercollateralized, because the loans trade at a premium to par due to their high credit rating and relatively high coupons.

GLPCs have maturities that range from 5 to 25 years. The coupons are variable rate coupons that adjust monthly or quarterly. The coupons can be either capped or uncapped. In a securitization, capped loans would not be securitized with uncapped loans, so that the pools are homogenous with respect to coupon cap character. This would normally be a plus in the

European market which often shuns U.S. fixed-rate loans, but the GLPC coupons are indexed to the U.S. prime rate, not USD LIBOR. Prime is the consumer lending rate used solely in the United States. USD LIBOR is usually acceptable to European banks that match funds on a floating-rate basis and often have USD floating-rate liabilities. The prime index is not as well correlated with their liabilities, however. This difference in the indexing, or basis, of the coupons versus the European market is a source of basis risk for many European investors.

In the U.S. market, these securities have many advantages. These investments can be held in a U.S. bank's portfolio. The index is well understood in the U.S. market. Since many U.S. banks lend at prime, albeit they do not fund at prime, the assets provide a hedge for potential liabilities. However, since the pools have a 55-day delay, it is not usually possible to match assets and liabilities. In most cases, these assets can be pledged as collateral for public funds at the Federal Reserve.

The negatives for both the U.S. and European markets are that the loans may default or prepay, in which case the premium is prepaid at par (the par amount is guaranteed by the U.S. government, as we saw earlier). Most loans amortize at a scheduled principal repayment rate, but there is no penalty for prepayment of a loan. The prepayment risk due to default is minimized by securitizing a large pool of diversified loans. If one loan prepays, only the premium on that particular loan is lost.

The SBA International program eliminated the prime/LIBOR basis risk for investors. SBA International uses a grantor trust to securitize the loans and issues AAA-rated "A" trust certificates, and the proceeds are used to purchase the premium GLPCs. The trust also has a subordinated tranche that takes most of the prepayment risk if constant prepayment rates (CPR) increase. The protection is usually up to the 95 percent confidence band based on historical CPR data up to the time of issuance. Since the SBA International program warehouses loans it eliminates the 55 delay days, which is an additional benefit to investors.

The coupons can be either hedged or unhedged for basis risk. If investors don't hedge, they receive the difference between the spot prime/LIBOR spread and the swap strike price. These investors may initially get a higher coupon than investors that hedge, but they accept that in future the spread between prime and LIBOR can either move wider (in their favor) or narrower (against them).

Many European venues look through the grantor trust structure (unlike the SPC structure) to the underlying collateral. An SPC would attract a 100 percent BIS risk weighting from European banks. The grantor trust with 0 percent risk weighted collateral will attract zero regulatory capital requirement from most European banks (see Figure 12.13).

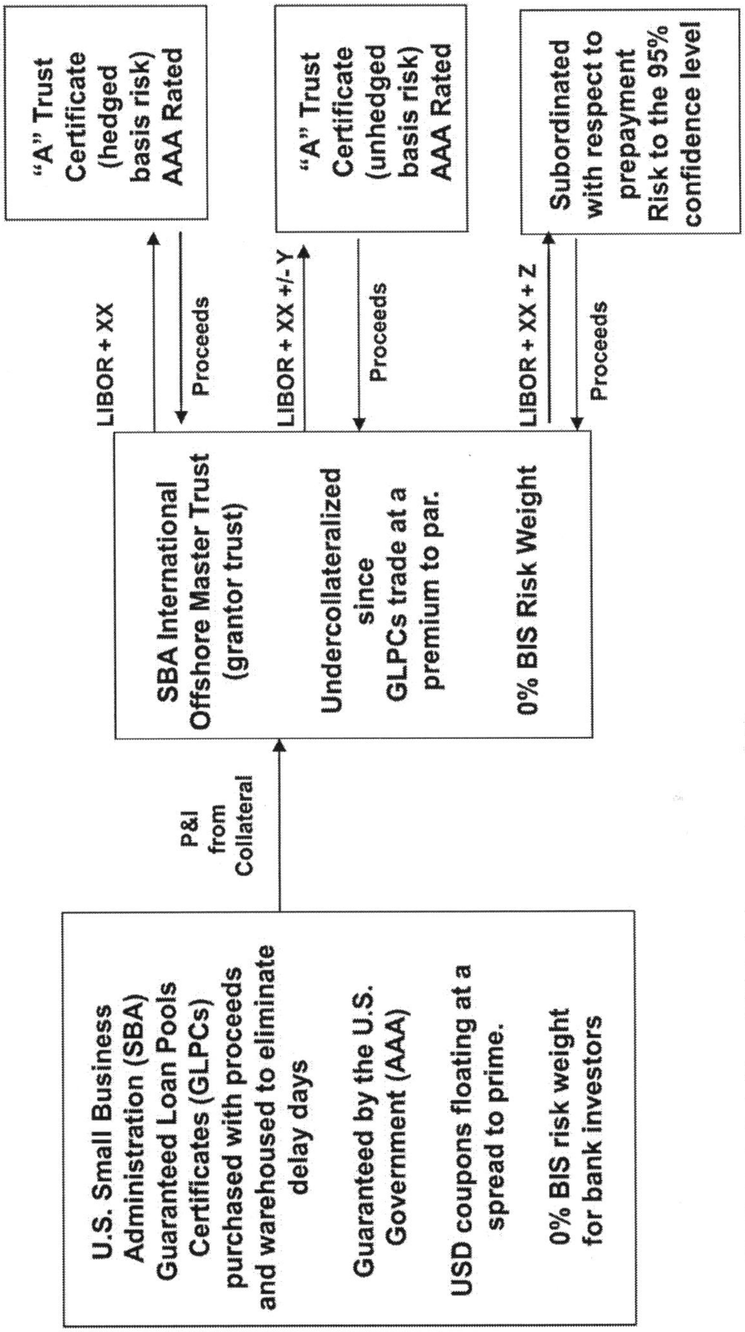

FIGURE 12.13 SBA International Program

SECURED LOAN TRUSTS

The first CLOs to use synthetics were the former Chase Manhattan Bank's secured loan trust structures. The maturity of these deals was around three years. These arbitrage CLOs sometimes used loans from Chase's balance sheet, but additional loans were purchased in the secondary market to add diversity. For the most part, the loans were highly leveraged transactions (HLTs), with implied ratings of B to BBB. The coupons on these loans were at a spread of the low hundreds to LIBOR.

Secured loan trusts use total rate of return swaps (TRORS) to transfer first-loss risk. The first-loss risk is bifurcated for two types of investors. The bifurcated risks are pari passu, but one of them is more leveraged than the other. In Chase's structures, the less leveraged tranche often received a single A rating. Some structures had a BBB-rated note, rated by Duff & Phelps (now Fitch). The investor in the rated tranche is called the *noteholder*. The investor in the more highly leveraged tranche is called the *certificate holder*. Although they both have first-loss risk, the certificate holder is deemed to be the equity investor. Figure 12.14 outlines the basic cash flows of this structure.

In this structure, the noteholder and certificate holder are pari passu with respect to first-loss risk, but the noteholder is only leveraged 5:1, whereas the certificate holder is leveraged 8:1. The leverage depends on the portfolio and the structure, and in this example, the note is only rated BBB. This investment-grade rating is based on the return of the initial cash investment plus the return of a nominal coupon, not the return of the potentially high leveraged coupon.

U.S. insurance companies were the investors who originally drove these transactions. The insurance companies acted as portfolio manager and investor in part of the first-loss risk. U.S. insurance companies are regulated by the National Association of Insurance Commissioners (NAIC), and theoretically cannot invest in high-yield loans. If the less leveraged first-loss tranche receives a single A rating, it achieves a NAIC 1 classification. This is the highest asset classification and attracts the lowest asset capital charge. If the less leveraged first-loss tranche receives a BBB rating, it achieves a NAIC 2 classification, the second highest asset classification, and attracts the second lowest asset capital charge. The insurance companies receive the leveraged return of an equity tranche while enjoying the reduced capital charge of an investment-grade rated asset.

Hedge funds are willing certificate buyers. For this customer base, a rating is irrelevant. Ironically, hedge funds, while reluctant to disclose their own balance sheets, prudently ask for full disclosure of the current portfolio.

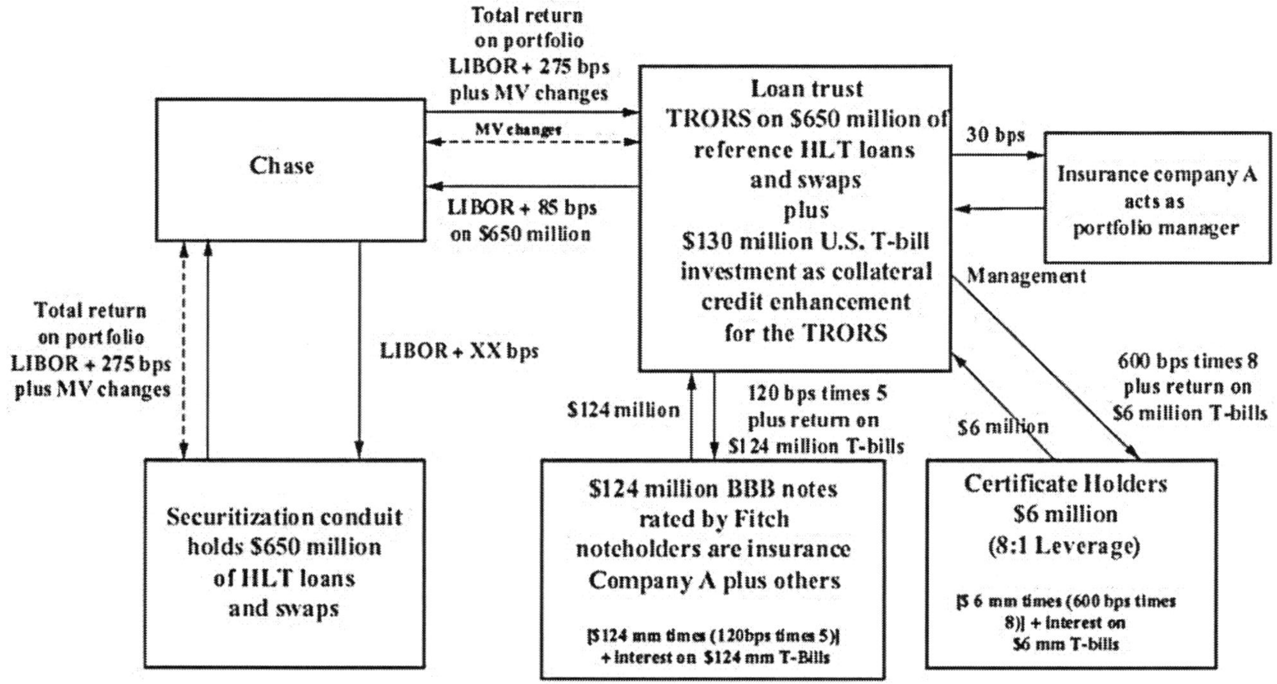

Chase and the portfolio manger have the option to unwind at any point. Payment of LIBOR + 85 bps is subordinate to management fees and to noteholder and certificate holder interest payments. The noteholders and certificate holders are pari passu, albeit with different amounts of leverage.

FIGURE 12.14 Secured Loan Trust circa 1996

They also ask for models so they can perform stress tests to determine that the potential net reward will achieve their targets under their most important stress scenarios.

If possible, the hedge funds will try to get even more leverage. They may ask to receive the certificate cash flows in the form of a TRORS. A sponsor bank for a secured loan trust usually won't want to fund the hedge finance purchasing the certificate, so hedge funds ask yet another bank for the financing. From a U.S. tax perspective, it is often easier to net interest income and funding expenses in a swap form. Swap income is usually viewed as ordinary income. Equity income can be deemed to be either interest income or capital loss. There are other itemized deduction and state tax implications for equity income that can usually be avoided when recognizing swap income.

The bank sponsor receives a stream of floating-rate payments from a TRORS backed by a significant amount of risk-free collateral. With 30 percent collateral, this stream of cash flows would have an investment-grade rating, even as high as AAA or super senior risk, depending on the collateral and unwind triggers. The bank sponsor is usually the primary structurer and has control over diversification criteria for the portfolio, the triggers, the amount of the initial collateral, and the structural features of the CLO. The bank sponsor books the TRORS in the bank's trading book and has a back-to-back TRORS with the securitization conduit. The securitization conduit pays the TRORS on the loans and the bank sponsor pays a funding cost. The bank sponsor pays the TRORS to the loan trust, which is collateralized with AAA collateral. The bank sponsor charges the trust a higher funding cost than the funding rate it pays to the securitization conduit, thus earning annual income.

Counterparty risk is mitigated by frequently marking the TRORS to market. The bank sponsor is most concerned with its exposure to the loan trust. If the assets depreciate in value, the bank sponsor receives a make-whole payment from the loan trust, which matches the make-whole payment the bank sponsor must make to the securitization conduit. If there is a systemic rapid deterioration in the value of the HLTs, the TRORS will behave more like equity than debt. Unwind triggers can mitigate this risk. Since the loan trust is 30 percent overcollateralized, the SLT structure calls for the entire structure to unwind once the overcollateralization falls to the trigger threshold. The trigger level will depend on hedge exposures, diversification and credit quality of the portfolio, and the seniority of the bank sponsor in the event of unwind.

For regulatory capital purposes, the bank sponsor adds the mark-to-market value of the assets to the counterparty risk factor from a regulatory look-up table. This is a small fraction of the capital required to hold the loans on balance sheet. Economic capital required for the long position (receiving the TRORS from the securitization conduit) is offset by the short position (paying the TRORS to the loan trust). The true sale of the assets combined with the low remaining capital charge makes this an efficient way to reduce risk, and the transaction also reduces the size of the bank's balance sheet.

BANK REGULATORY CAPITAL AND BASEL II

In July 1988, the Bank for International Settlements (BIS) issued the Basel Capital Accord (Basel I). This accord defined the capital requirement for credit risk in all the world's major banking communities. It may even have worked for a picosecond. As soon as the rules were issued, each country set up its own capital guidelines for banks, often applying inconsistent interpretations of the BIS guidelines. As soon as that happened, banks began looking for ways to arbitrage the inconsistencies.

Examples of venue-specific regulatory bodies that can interpret guidelines to fit into their respective regulatory frameworks are the Federal Reserve Bank (the Fed) in the United States, the Financial Service Authority (SFA) in the United Kingdom, the Office of the Superintendent of Financial Institutions (OSFI) in Canada, the French Commission Bancaire, the Bundesanstalt für Finanzdienstleistungsaufsicht (BAFin) in Germany, and the Ministry of Finance (MOF) in Japan.

When new products such as credit derivatives and synthetic CDO products were developed, the Basel I regulatory capital framework couldn't readily accommodate the new products. That left them fair game for regulatory capital arbitrage. Even worse, Basel I created arbitrary non-credit-related capital distinctions, such as a 0 percent risk weight for OECD sovereign risk. In a system meant to dole out credit-related regulatory capital, this was a major flaw.

Basel II is an attempt to fix all of that. The new rules were due to come into effect in 2005, but special-interest groups disputed BIS decisions and there were delays. In November 2005, the Basel Committee issued revisions to the proposed framework. It also issued a paper called "Guidelines for Computing Capital for Incremental Default Risk in the Trading Book." The United States agreed to adopt Basel II in November 2007, but some global banks may not fully implement it until 2015.

After December 31, 1992, all banks were expected to meet a minimum ratio of qualifying total capital to BIS risk-weighted assets of 8 percent. The amount of capital reserved against a risk-weighted asset is not necessarily 8 percent, however. The amount of capital reserved against an asset will depend upon its BIS risk weighting. But the risk weight of a reference asset may vary by jurisdiction. This further complicates matters because central banks and ministries of finance have the right to set local standards for assets, which aren't clearly addressed by BIS.

For bank books with no value-at-risk (VAR) models, a default swap that is hedging a loan must meet the criteria for hedge accounting, which means that the seniority and legal entity of the reference asset must match the loan held in the portfolio, and the reference asset and loan must have cross default provisions. If these criteria are met, then the regulatory risk-based capital rules treat the default swap as a guarantee, so the counterparty risk replaces the obligor.

Since 1998, many venues, led by the U.S. Federal Reserve, decided to treat credit derivatives like derivatives transactions. This meant they could be booked either in the bank book or in the trading book. Credit derivatives can used model-based capital treatment or can use regulatory look-up tables in most venues. Under these new market risk proposal, there are three components of risk:

1. *Counterparty risk* is the mark-to-market exposure for the credit derivative (a function of the underlying asset value) due to the possibility that the counterparty may default on its obligation or potential obligation under the terms of the credit derivative transaction.
2. *General market risk* arises from changes in the reference asset's value caused by broad market movements. It is the net exposure to interest rates, foreign exchange rates, commodity prices, and equity prices.
3. *Specific risk* arises from the changes in the reference asset's value *specific* to that asset, such as credit quality. This is the risk of an adverse change in price from factors related to the issuer of the reference asset due to nonmarket movements. One example would be changes in the credit risk of the reference asset. This can be accounted for by BIS's prespecified scaled risk weightings. Banks have the alternative of using standard, specific risk add-on factors.

Bank that can calculate exposures in a reproducible and consistent manner can use this model-based approach for capital treatment for credit derivatives. The whole point of purchasing credit default protection is to take advantage of the effect of the benefit of the reduction of default probability as evidenced by a reduced joint probability of default. Hence the extremely beneficial reduction in the required economic capital factors for low-correlation obligor/counterparty transactions. The potential reduction in regulatory capital is enormous and return on capital usually jumps threefold or more when model-based capital is applied to transactions.

TABLE 12.1 Risks for Type of Trading Position

Position	Definition	Risk Type Market	Specific	Counterparty
Open	No offset	VAR	Reference asset	Credit risk
Matched	Longs and shorts must reference identical assets	N/A	N/A	Credit risk
Offsetting	Longs and shorts with different maturities or legs (i.e., total return versus default instruments)	VAR Residual risk*	Reference asset residual risk*	Credit risk

*Residual risk depends on the degree of mismatch of maturity, reference asset basis, or type of credit protection

Whether each of the three risk types requires regulatory risk-based capital depends on the combination of long and short positions housed in the trading portfolio. These are summarized in Table 12.1.

General market risk capital is determined by a bank's internal value-at-risk model and follows the same procedures as for cash instruments. The bank's internal model must use certain parameters set by Basel II. These, too, are sometimes arbitrary values depending on the specific asset, as we'll see later when we discuss Basel II in more detail.

Specific risk capital depends on the credit risk of the derivative's reference asset, as shown in Table 12.2. The factor is applied to the greater

TABLE 12.2 Specific Risk Capital Factors for Government Counterparties

Asset Category	External Credit Assessment	Specific Risk Capital Charge
Government	AAA to AA–	0%
	A+ to BBB–	0.25% (6 mos. or less maturity) 1.00% ≤ 6 months ≤ 24 mo 1.6% > 24 mo
	BB+ to B–	8.00%
	Below B–	12.00%
	Unrated	8.00%

of the derivative notional or the market value of any cash asset hedging the derivative. The standardized approach is not available to some banks. When it is available, there is a specific table look-up in the Basel II guidelines, as there was with Basel I for the standardized approach within the trading book, similar to the changes made for the banking book capital requirements. Table 12.2 is an excerpt from the new guidelines detailing government counterparty changes.

Determining *counterparty credit risk* capital begins by computing the swap's risk-weighted asset, which may be the sum of two components if add-ons are regionally applicable.. The first is the current, positive mark-to-market (MTM) of the derivative. The second is an add-on for potential future MTM and is determined by multiplying the swap's notional principal times a factor such as shown in Table 12.3.

The resulting risk-weighted asset is then (1) multiplied by the appropriate counterparty risk weight and then (2) multiplied by 8 percent to arrive at the risk-based capital for counterparty credit risk. Credit exposure is broken down by deal, maturity, counterparty, obligor, and reference asset type. Trading groups must send exposure reports to the bank's credit department.

Different VAR models will come up with different end results, depending on their sophistication and degree to which regulators will ratify them and allow banks to move away from arbitrary add-on factors. Let's take a simple example. The trading book sells and buys a credit default option. The trading book assumes credit risk and purchases a hedge in the form of *matching credit default protection* (or shorts the reference asset). Matched positions encompass long and short positions in *identical* credit derivative structures over *identical* maturities referencing *identical* assets.

In the absence of a model, the bank must calculate the regulatory capital as follows:

Notional of the Credit Default Protection x Counterparty Risk Weight x 8%.

TABLE 12.3 Example of Regional Counterparty Add-On Factors

	Reference Asset	
Remaining Maturity	Investment Grade (Equity Factors)	Below Investment Grade (Commodity Factors)
≤ 1 year	6%	10%
> 1 year to ≤ 5 years	8%	12%
> 5 years	10%	15%

The bank sells protection on a reference asset for 30 bps and simultaneously purchases credit default protection from an OECD bank selling protection for 20 bps. The net profit is 10 bps. Regulatory capital required is

100 x 20% (for OECD bank counterparty) x 8% risk capital x 1.6

or 160 bps. The return on regulatory capital is 3.12 percent.

But if our counterparty, the credit default protection seller, is a non-OECD bank, the return on regulatory capital decreases by a factor of 5. (Economic capital would remain the same, but economic calculations will also be unaffected by the change to Basel II.) The regulatory capital required is simply calculated as follows:

100 x 100%(for non-OECD bank counterparty) x 8% risk capital x 8.0

or 800 bps. The return on regulatory capital is now only 0.63%, or there is a five-fold reduction in return on regulatory capital.

Under market risk guidelines, the calculation is different. This is a matched position and is captured under the market risk capital guidelines. Capital is held on the counterparty protection provider risk created by the purchased option. Each bank will have its own unique model. Most banks start out with a model that does not include a means of evaluating specific risk—that is, reference asset risk. These banks use the VAR model with the add-on number provided in Table 12.3. This is a type of modified VAR model and is an interim step to a simulation model that can accommodate all of the risks, including specific risk. Table 12.4 shows the reduction in regulatory capital with the use of a modified VAR model.

First we calculate the on-balance-sheet asset equivalent according to regulatory guidelines. This is then multiplied by the relevant risk weight of the counterparty protection seller to determine the counterparty risk capital.

The balance sheet asset equivalent is $1.16 million. We add the market value of the purchased option ($360,000) to the notional amount of the option ($10 million), and multiply by the percentage derived from Fed table for the credit risk factor for the reference asset, in this case 8 percent for an investment-grade asset with a maturity between one and five years.

This is then multiplied by the relevant category risk weight. In the case of the triple-A bank, this is 20 percent to get the adjusted-risk asset value of $232,000. This is further multiplied by the regulatory capital percentage of 8 percent to get the required regulatory capital for the counterparty risk of $18,560.

TABLE 12.4 Market Risk Treatment for Regulatory Capital (with Matched Credit Default Protection and a Nonsovereign Bank Counterparty)

"Triple-A" Bank Counterparty		"Triple-B" Bank Counterparty	
Counterparty Risk*		Counterparty Risk*	
Notional Amount of Option	$10,000,000	Notional Amount of Option	$10,000,000
Reg. Credit %age	8.00%	Reg. Credit %age	8.00%
M-T-M Purchased Option BP	$360,000	M-T-M Purchased Option BP	$360,000
Original Price of Option $	$300,000	Original Price of Option $	$300,000
Orignal Price of Option bps	30.00	Orignal Price of Option bps	30.00
On-Bal Sheet Asset	$1,160,000	On-Bal Sheet Asset	$1,160,000
Category Risk Weight	20%	Category Risk Weight	50%
Adj. Risk Asset Value	$232,000	Adj. Risk Asset Value	$580,000
Percent of Notional	2.32%	Percent of Notional	5.80%
× Reg Capital 8% =	0.19%	× Reg Capital 8% =	0.46%
Total Regulatory Capital	$18,560	Total Regulatory Capital	$46,400
Notional	$10,000,000	Notional	10,000,000
Net Income (bps)	5	Net Income (bps)	5
Net Income in Dollars	$5,000	Net Income in Dollars	$5,000
Capital:	$18,560	Capital:	$46,400
Return on Capital:	26.94%	Return on Capital:	10.78%

* Counterparty Risk = *f* (Counterparty type, market value of buy option, notional amount of the option, investment grade/non investment grade status of reference obligation, maturity of the option)

While every bank will see a different degree of benefit, Table 12.5 shows the potential benefit of using just a crude first-generation VAR model for matched trades under Basel I regulations.

I deliberately used a small transaction of $10 million with a small net profit of only $5,000. This transaction makes little economic sense but makes sense on a return on regulatory capital basis.

Notice that it still matters whether our counterparty is a nonsovereign AAA-rated bank, but the magnitude of the difference is less. The return on capital jumped fivefold after we switched from a nonsovereign BBB-rated bank to a AAA-rated bank counterparty pre-model, but with the model, it jumps around 2.5 times. This result is specific to the type of model. There is still an enormous benefit for using the lower BIS risk-weighted counterparty, however.

The major overall advantage comes from using the model. For the nonsovereign BBB-rated bank counterparty, return on regulatory capital jumps 17 times. For the nonsovereign AAA-rated bank counterparty, return on regulatory capital jumps 8.6 times.

This model-based capital benefit encouraged banks to set up trading desks for CDSs, which in turn allowed banks to structure synthetic CDOs for other banks which had no models or had less sophisticated models. It also allowed banks to trade CDSs in a regulatory capital efficient manner for the sole purpose of creating synthetic arbitrage CDOs.

Some bank arrangers with poor capital markets distribution entered the synthetic CDO business knowing their only advantage was that they could reduce balance sheet regulatory capital for a customer, earn a fee, and park the assets in their trading books where the assets attracted much less regulatory capital. Many of the original transactions simply involved creating a structure to earn fees for the convenience of exploiting the regulatory capital arbitrage.

TABLE 12.5 Regulatory Capital and Return on Capital Calculated without and with VAR Model

Hedge Counterparty Type	Regulatory Capital without VAR Model	Regulatory Capital with VAR Model	Return on Regulatory Capital without VAR	Return on Regulatory Capital VAR Model
AAA Bank	1.60%	0.19%	3.12%	26.94%
BBB Bank	8.00%	0.46%	0.63%	10.78%

The most recent updates—hundreds of pages long—on the Basel II framework can be found on its web site, www .bis.org. One should expect the regulatory framework to change further. Total regulatory capital will be calculated according to the following formula:

$$\text{Total} = \text{Capital Requirements for (Credit Risk + Market Risk} \\ \text{+ Operational Risk)}$$

We'll focus on the credit risk capital requirement since changes in this capital requirement are the ones most relevant to ABS and CDO transactions. Banks can use any one of the following approaches, which incorporate both expected and unexpected losses:

- The standardized approach (U.S. banks cannot use this approach).
- A foundation model internal ratings-based approach (IRB).
- An advanced model internal ratings-based approach.

Under Basel II, the International Monetary Fund (IMF), the European Community (EC), and the European Central Bank (ECB) will continue to have 0 percent risk weights. All other credits will have a risk weight that depends on their external ratings. Under Basel I, all OECD sovereigns had a 0 percent risk weight, while all OECD banks had a 20 percent risk weight. The risk weights will now reflect their creditworthiness—or at least, that is the intent.

Basel II will attempt to design a regulatory capital framework for asset-backed securities, CDOs, and other securitized products. The standardized approach will result in the worst-case BIS risk capital charge. No one will develop a model that results in a larger capital charge if they are paying attention.

For most structures, an internal ratings-based approach will offer more regulatory capital relief than the standardized approach. Tables 12.6 and 12.7 gives the ratings-based approach risk weight to be applied for ABS tranches with various external ratings. Notice that BIS introduces new terms, *granularity* of pools and *thickness* of tranches, as defined in the guidelines. These guidelines have changed since the original proposal, and one should always check for further changes. The ongoing global mortgage securitization debacle may inspire further changes.

The new rules are meant to encourage actual risk transfer, and to discourage banks from bailing out failing deals. The deal should be *true sale* or meet certain tests for synthetic deals. Banks can only provide credit enhancement at the outset of the transaction.

TABLE 12.6 RBA Approach for ABS Tranches with Long-Term Rating

External Ratings	Risk Weights		
Long-Term Rating	Risk Weights for Senior Positions and Eligible Senior IAA Exposures	Base Case	Nongranular Pools
Aaa	7%	12%	20%
AA	8%	15%	25%
A+	10%	18%	35%
A	12%	20%	35%
A−	20%	35%	35%
Baa1	35%	50%	50%
Baa2	60%	75%	75%
Baa3	100%	100%	100%
Ba1	250%	250%	250%
Ba2	425%	425%	425%
Ba3	650%	650%	650%
Below Ba3 (or Unrated)	Deduction	Deduction	Deduction

Basel II is an attempt to fix the problems of Basel I, but it heavily relies on rating agency ratings, flawed models, and arbitrary work-arounds. Table 12.7 changed from the original proposal, and the risk weightings mainly went down. Fiddling with these numbers was an arbitrary exercise, since Basel II failed to account for much greater risks presented by misrated products and insufficiently vetted portfolios. In other words, arbitrary methods once again are often used as a crutch for crippled thought.

TABLE 12.7 RBA Approach for ABS Tranches with Short-Term Rating

External Ratings	Risk Weights		
Short-Term Rating	Risk Weights for Senior Positions and Eligible Senior IAA Exposures	Base Case	Nongranular Pools
A1/P1	7%	12%	20%
A2/P2	12%	20%	35%
A3/P3	60%	75%	75%
Lower (or Unrated)	Deduction	Deduction	Deduction

Basel II is part of a series of failures by various financial regulators to capture the most fundamental risk in the banking system: lending money to someone who may not pay you back. If you do not properly measure that risk at the outset, no amount of securitization or credit derivatives technology will correct the problem for you. If you work hard to ignore the risk or cover it up, no amount of paperwork issued by Basel II will solve that problem. Basel II has been ineffective in heading off problems such as the global securitization crisis due to securitizing risky product that was improperly rated.

As securitizations began to come back on bank balance sheets in 2007, it was clear that BIS had no idea of the problems that leverage, synthetics, and securitizations could pose. By default, many bank underwriters became investors, and Citigroup was a notable example among many. It took back on balance sheet tens of billions of dollars of assets, including the assets of its off-balance-sheet structured investment vehicles. It also took back on balance sheet tranches of CDOs it underwrote and sold, since it had supplied full liquidity lines for asset-backed commercial paper tranches of those deals (see also Chapter 17).

Chapter 13

Super Senior Sophistry

Synthetics are a key driver of the CDO market, and super senior tranches are a key driver of the synthetic CDO arbitrage. When banks wanted to reduce the credit risk of their loan portfolios, they realized they had a problem. Loans were put on the books for very little income. For investment-grade loans, the so-called CDO arbitrage didn't work. Bankers invented a creative and somewhat deceptive solution. Bank regulators, including the Bank for International Settlements (BIS), allowed banks to get away with it. The solution was the super senior tranche.

Super seniors were created to hide some unpleasant problems. Synthetics made super seniors possible, but the low margins on investment-grade loans made them necessary. It was just too expensive to issue an AAA tranche, so the market created a cheaper tranche.

Super seniors first appeared in JPMorgan's BISTRO bank balance-sheet deals. As we saw earlier, BISTRO stands for Broad Index Secured Trust Offering, but in some circles it stands for "BIS total rip-off." Who is getting ripped off? Let's take a closer look at deals with super senior tranches to make sure it isn't you.

Originally, all venues considered the super senior tranche as 100 percent BIS risk-weighted. This meant that if the super senior were \$1 billion in size, the capital charge would have been \$80 million. If I'm earning 10 bps on the super senior, my return on regulatory capital is only 1.25 percent. This is still the case for most non-U.S. venues, and that is why non-U.S. banks seek government-guaranteed entities or OECD banks as counterparties. With the 20 percent risk-weighted OECD bank as counterparty, the capital required is only \$16 million, and the return on regulatory capital for a 10 bps super senior is 6.25 percent. In the United States, the Federal Reserve already recognizes a 20 percent risk weight for super senior risk, and recently switched over to Basel II guidelines to allow AAAs to get 20 percent BIS risk-weighted treatment. Even so, 6.25 percent is nothing to shout about. But that isn't the end of the story. For banks that can use model-based capital treatment, the return dramatically improves, since the regulatory capital requirement is usually very small according to the models.

That's fine as far as regulatory capital goes, but that treatment merely allowed the deals to go forward. It wasn't the total driving force. We're aware the huge low-cost super senior tranche dramatically lowers the all-in cost of a CDO. This is really convenient if you need to securitize low-margin loans to alleviate balance sheet risk. Issuing a large AAA would drive up your all-in cost. It would be very unpleasant to have to explain that you booked loans at such tight levels that you will lose lots of cash if you securitize them. The super senior was the answer. Banks created a new artificial low-cost tranche. It erased some questions about the tight lending levels.

But even with the huge economic boost from the super senior tranche, several U.S. banks realized that economically they were often breakeven or worse on a balance-sheet CDO. That suggests that a review of bank loan activity is probably in order.

Super seniors spilled over into arbitrage deals driven from capital markets trading books. And why not? Everyone was saying this was free money. The market had magically created extra value in deals and created an enormous arbitrage where none had existed before!

How do you define super senior risk? Notice the exact definition hasn't come up until now. Were you even suspicious?

The reason is *there is no market standard definition of super senior risk. There is no standard means of pricing super senior risk.* The super senior is the most important driving force in synthetic deals and the super senior is the largest chunk of a synthetic deal. In fact, super senior tranches make up the major percentage of total CDO issuance, being 80 to 90 percent of most synthetic deals, which comprise the largest part of the CDO market. Yet the mark-to-market is open to wide interpretation. How can it be there is no standard pricing method and no standard definition?

It's incredible, but true. For instance, I can create two CDOs, each using exactly the same underlying risks, rate them by the same rating agencies, and create different super senior tranches. Table 13.1 shows two different ways of tranching an identical portfolio.

Which tranching is correct? The disturbing answer is that they are *both* correct. The AAA attachment point is the same for both deals. By *attachment point*, I mean the amount of subordination that is required to achieve a rating of AAA by a rating agency. This super senior phenomenon is true no matter which rating agency or combination of rating agencies rates the CDO.

Once we have the AAA attachment point, the question is, how much subordination is required to deem the tranche above it a super senior?

TABLE 13.1 Synthetic Static Arbitrage CDO Tranching

Expected Rating	Principal	Percent Structure	Subordination
Super Senior	420.00 MM	84.0%	16.0%
Aaa	25.0 MM	5.0%	11.0%
Aa2	15.0 MM	3.0%	8.0%
Baa2	20.0 MM	4.0%	4.0%
NR	20.0 MM	4.0%	NA
Super Senior	432.5 MM	86.5%	13.5
Aaa	12.5 MM	2.5%	11.0%
Aa2	15.0 MM	3.0%	8.0%
Baa2	20.0 MM	4.0%	4.0%
NR	20.0 MM	4.0%	NA

I've seen several presentations in which the super senior tranche was labeled the AAAA tranche. Quadruple A. I wish it were true. Unfortunately, it is not.

I asked people at Moody's, S&P, and Fitch how to determine the super senior attachment point. From the rating agency point of view, it is completely irrelevant. The rating agencies do not rate a super senior tranche. In fact, *the rating agencies do not acknowledge the existence of a super senior tranche.* The super senior tranche is a convention created by structurers. All the rating agencies care about is whether you have solved for the AAA attachment point in a manner consistent with their methodology. That methodology will be the same regardless of whether a structurer later creates a super senior tranche in the deal. As far as the rating agencies are concerned, the super senior is a retrofit that has nothing to do with them.

Except that it does.

CASH FLOW MAGIC TRICK

If the investment-grade deal were a cash deal, the AAA tranche would make up more than 85 percent of the CDO. That meant banks would have to pay out LIBOR plus 50 bps on more than 85 percent of the deal (85 percent for the purposes of this paper). Since synthetic deals are unfunded, an AAA tranche investor would receive 50 bps on the notional amount of 85 percent of the deal. This was unworkable, until the creation of the super senior tranche.

The synthetic deal just described, with a 5 percent AAA tranche under the super senior tranche, would now have a super senior tranche as 80 percent of the notional amount of the deal. Banks claimed this tranche had virtually no risk, and therefore one shouldn't have to pay much of a premium to hedge the risk. Instead of paying 50 bps, banks could now pay around 6 bps to an outside protection provider, or the bank could simply retain the risk.

Monolines have become the protection provider of choice. Standard and Poor's assesses one such financial guarantor a capital charge of 10 bps against AAA tranches. Even though the monolines' internal economic capital assessments are considerably higher than the rating agency's charge, super senior deals clear return on capital hurdles. Super senior tranches on corporate underlyings have traded as low as 6 bps, especially on early CDO deals. This was a savings of 44 bps per annum. For a $5 billion five-year transaction, the savings amounted to $17.6 million per annum for five years.

Ironically, credit derivatives professionals have long criticized bank loan officers for putting on loans at ridiculously low levels. One credit derivative professional criticized bank loan practices: "We're in the business of taking on risk for the wrong fee for future business we're never going to get." The necessary improvement in the CLO arbitrage is what prompted creation of the super senior tranche in the first place. Banks squeezed cash out of the AAA tranche to make up for the low-income loans' cash shortfall so that the arbitrage for collateralized loan obligations would artificially appear more attractive. This was the only way to get the bulk of the credit risk off of the bank balance sheet.

The greatest triumph of illusion in twentieth-century finance is perfectly legal. Now that it suits banks and investment banks to put super senior risk in trading books at much lower levels than the payment they formerly received for the same risk from the top tier of the AAA tranche, bank managers have been persuaded it is a great deal. Banks used the super senior to facilitate moving risk off the bank balance sheet, but banks later used the super senior to facilitate putting risk in trading books.

RATING AGENCIES—MOODY'S TRANCHING

The rating agencies are overlooking the effect on the AAA-rated tranches. When I asked a Moody's analyst about this, he said Moody's would think about this and get back to me. I'm still waiting. I got similar nonresponses from the rest of the rating agencies. Several analysts did not see how there could be any impact. The rating agencies might want to reconsider their position.

There is a compelling reason why the rating agencies might wish to take a point of view on super seniors in the context of their rating on Aaa (or AAA) tranches. I hear many arguments about rating agency models and how many angels can dance on the head of a pin. Oddly, I hear no arguments about AAA tranches. Getting distracted by models often makes us miss a huge problem that is right before our eyes.

Let's take a look at how we can create an AAA on the cash Baa3 portfolio we tranched in Chapter 5. For the moment, let's assume this portfolio is on a bank's balance sheet. Let's assume we can either do a true sale structure and create an all-cash deal, or we can do a synthetic structure and create a large super senior tranche along with some mezzanine tranches. The tranching comparison is shown in Table 13.2.

The same portfolio can be tranched two different ways. The AAA attachment point is the same for both CDOs, as the rating agency models would predict. The amount of subordination required to get an AAA rating for a tranche of this portfolio is 12.1 percent. For the synthetic CDO, we add an extra step. After solving for the 12.1 percent AAA attachment point, we create a super senior tranche. The synthetic CDO has a super senior tranche that makes up 82.9 percent (17.1 percent subordination) of the portfolio. As we've already seen, we could just as easily have created a super senior tranche with a smaller or even a slightly larger size and still be correct.

Both CDOs have a AAA tranche. Are you indifferent to owning the AAA from the fully funded deal versus the deal with the super senior?

The rating says you should be happy to buy either one. But you shouldn't be. Let's look only at the AAA level and up and compare an investment of EUR 25 million in the AAA tranche of both of these CDOs. Figure 13.1 shows the two investments.

TABLE 13.2 Portfolio Tranching with and without Super Senior Tranche

GRADE	Fully Funded CDO* Tranche Size	Percent of port	Synthetic CDP* Tranche Size	Percent of port
Super Senior			414,500,000	82.9%
Aaa	439,500,000	87.9%	25,000,000	5.0%
Aa2	11,500,000	2.3%	11,500,000	2.3%
Baa2	14,000,000	2.8%	14,000,000	2.8%
Equity	35,000,000	7.0%	35,000,000	7.0%
	500,000,000	100.0%	500,000,000	100.0%

*Baa3 average portfolio rating. Includes up to 15 percent high yield and 10 percent asset backed.

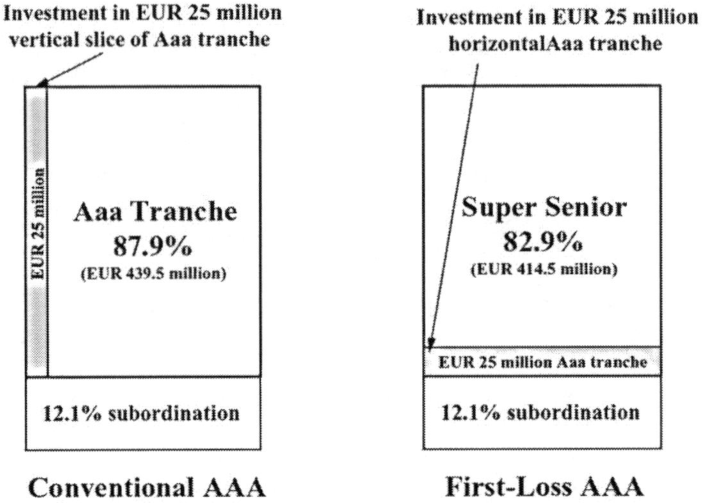

FIGURE 13.1 Two Different AAA Tranches of the Same Portfolio

The second AAA is a first-loss tranche supporting the super senior tranche, or a *first-loss AAA tranche*. You may be asking yourself if it really makes all that much difference. Let's see. Suppose you were unlucky enough to have bought one of the deals that had WorldCom and Enron, each 1 percent of the deal, so that 2 percent of the total names in the portfolio defaulted. Chances are that other names in the portfolio were downgraded, so that the amount of subordination to maintain an AAA rating would have to increase by more than 2 percent. But you know for sure that it would have to increase by at least 2 percent. Using this knowledge, let's take a look at the effect on our two AAA investments (see Figure 13.2).

The two AAA tranches are not equivalent in a nonstatic world. If everything else remained the same, but 2 percent of the portfolio defaulted, about 0.57 million or about 2.27 percent of the EUR 25 million first AAA tranche would not be deemed AAA. If we restructured to add 2 percent more subordination to the total deal, about 24.43 million of this tranche would still be deemed AAA. The AAA of the synthetic CDO presents a different picture. Forty percent or EUR 10 million of this tranche would not be deemed AAA.

Almost all of the AAA tranches of static synthetic arbitrage deals initially brought to market traded close to levels of cash AAA tranches. None of them had added structural protections to benefit the senior noteholders. This is still the case with many of the deals brought to market today. The excess spread generated by the cheap super senior tranche was siphoned off for

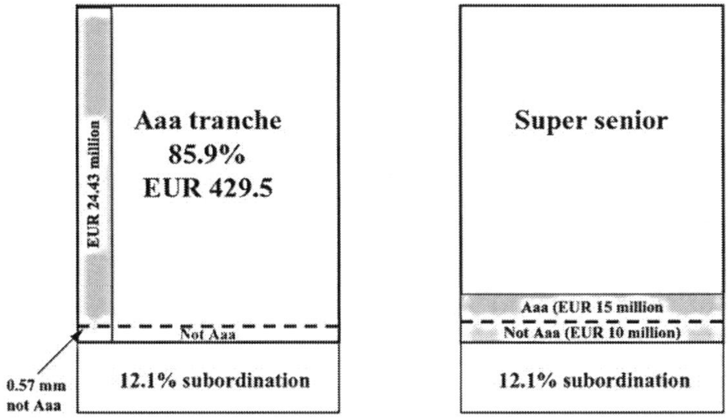

FIGURE 13.2 Effect of Default of 2 percent of the Portfolio on AAAs

the benefit of the bank arranger, and most of the excess spread was not even passed through to the equity investor, who accepted a maximum fixed coupon for the equity investment. The coupons looked good relative to a cash arbitrage CDO, but the clear benefit was to the bank arranger.

THE AAA DISAPPEARING ACT

The rating agencies do not quite know what to make of it. In the simple example just given, I made up the numbers for the size of the AAA tranche and the super senior tranche. Everyone else in the market makes up the numbers, too. There is no standard for the size of the AAA tranche required below the super senior tranche. Even more disturbing, Standard and Poor's (S&P) insists that they do not recognize the super senior tranche. S&P does not recognize anything above AAA. According to S&Ps definition, if the AAA is subordinated to anything else, it is no longer AAA. Figure 13.2 shows an example of the AAA tranche as a horizontal slice of a tranched portfolio and as the vertical slice of a synthetic deal using the same portfolio of underlying credits. The new AAA tranche of the synthetic deal is the first-loss tranche of a formerly AAA tranche, and if defaults occur in the portfolio, it is more vulnerable to downgrade than the vertically sliced AAA tranche.

Investors should be aware that if they are sold the AAA tranche of a synthetic CDO, they should ask for more coupon income. They do not own an AAA tranche. What they own is the first-loss position of what was formerly the AAA tranche. Yet these first-loss AAA tranches are being sold as legitimate AAA-rated tranches. Investors should demand higher compensation for these AAA-rated tranches.

To add to the confusion, an identical CDO tranche may earn the AAA rating from S&P but only an AA rating from Moody's. If an investor will accept the S&P rating, then it should ask for even more coupon income to compensate for the subsequent liquidity risk. This is the perfect investment for a fund seeking a tranche that is nominally rated AAA but provides the coupon income as if it were rated AA. Less experienced investors will be at a disadvantage if they don't negotiate for more income.

This is also true of cash asset-backed CDO products, but the ratings and risk waters are particularly muddied for synthetic CDOs. Investors aren't alone in their potential confusion. Rating agencies and bank managers are also challenged by synthetic CDO products.

It seems that investors who bought AAA tranche structures like the one described here didn't get the best deal possible, because they didn't know what to ask for at the time. As we saw in the discussion about equity tranches, there are several structural protections for senior tranche investors. As we saw in the section on equity, there are many structural features that can be built into a CDO to protect senior noteholders. For instance, once losses exceed a certain threshold, excess spread can be trapped in a reserve account and used for the benefit of the AAA and super senior noteholders, if required. If the equity holder is promised a fixed coupon, excess spread can be trapped for the benefit of the senior noteholders and revert to the bank arranger, only if they are not needed to cover losses to the AAA and super senior investors. Other structural protections can be employed as well.

It isn't possible to determine the relative value of AAA tranches without knowing the entire deal structure. The way we price first-loss AAA tranches is due for a shake-up. It is darkly amusing just to combine the words *first-loss* and *AAA tranche* into a phrase that accurately describes a tranche of a CDO. For the most part, these risks and rewards have not been accurately represented to AAA tranche investors. As more of these investors become conversant with synthetic structures, they will become more demanding. It is logical they'll ask for some of the spread stripped off of the super senior tranche and will reject deals that do not trap sufficient excess spread in a reserve account.

RATING AGENCIES AND RATINGS SHOPPING

Even so, many firms will act as if all AAAs are the same. The AAA tranche of a proposed CDO restructuring exemplifies this point. The original CDO had several dogs in the portfolio, and the small degree of subordination was aggressive to begin with. Due to defaults, the underwriter decided to restructure several deals to crystallize losses at the lower tranche levels and remarket the deals. The underwriter's marketer showed me the portfolio and told me the amount of subordination they were using to get to the AAA attachment point. The amount of subordination for the restructured tranche was insufficient to merit an AAA rating using a Moody's model. I explained this to the salesman. The salesman said the underwriter was tranching the restructuring using the S&P model.

This highlights another CDO challenge. Different rating agency models produce different results. When I pointed out to S&P that for every arbitrage deal I had time to look at using both a Moody's and S&P tranching methodology, S&P was always insufficient relative to Moody's. They weren't aware of this and hadn't done comparisons of their model versus Moody's.

Most market professionals and many investors feel that for corporate portfolios, Moody's used to dominate this field, but S&P grabbed market share, because many market professionals perceived them to be more lenient, and less subordination helps the CDO arbitrage. Fitch benefited along with the other rating agencies from the overall growth in the market through most of 2007. When a deal is rated by more than one agency, the worst-case tranching is the one that dominates, and that is generally Moody's. Furthermore, Moody's tranching is used as the benchmark tranching in almost all of the unrated static arbitrage CDOs. It's true that some investors require an S&P rating. Nonetheless, investors would be remiss in not asking for Moody's benchmark tranching if it gives them more subordination.

I told the salesman that he may find people to buy the tranche, but I wouldn't be one of them. Furthermore, a KMV analysis showed that the portfolio was worse than portfolios I was being shown from his competitors.

"Don't be afraid to make a bid at a much wider spread," he said. I couldn't imagine why he thought I'd be shy.

"Okay," I said, "did you want me to give you a bid at a double-A level? I would, except I'm not in the market for a double-A tranche. I need triple-A."

"Well, how much subordination does the Moody's model say you need?" he asked.

I told him. But that wasn't the entire point.

The underwriter was restructuring the deal to increase protection, presumably so investors could avoid getting burned the second time around. Their deals were suffering from a downgrade epidemic. Yet they were showing relatively lousy portfolios using S&P benchmark tranching and no structural protections at a time when many others were building these features into their deals.

The marketer called me a few weeks later to tell me the underwriter had sold the AAAs at much wider spreads than he offered me originally, but he didn't have the details of the exact spread. Neither of those facts surprised me.

Another marketer sent me a portfolio in response to my request for AAA tranches. A few days later he began sending me e-mails asking me what I thought. I responded that after a KMV analysis, the portfolio looked promising, but I was awaiting details on the CDO structure.

After a few more days passed, I received more e-mails asking what I thought. I again asked for the deal structure. He responded telling me the degree of subordination on the AAA tranche. I pointed out that the degree of tranching seemed insufficient relative to Moody's model. After a few days, he said they were hearing that from other customers, too, and had decided to tranche using Moody's as their benchmark.

He again asked what I thought. I responded that I needed to see the entire structure of the deal before I could comment. I said I needed to see each of the tranches and the structure of the cash flows for starters.

"How do you think they should be structured?" he asked. That investment bank had an interesting approach. Were they actually asking me to structure their deals?

"With as many structural protections for the AAA tranche as possible," I responded.

TRIPLE-A BASKET WITH 2 PERCENT FIRST-LOSS TRANCHE

Let's compare the pricing of 55 bps, common throughout most of 2001 and 2002, for the first-loss triple-A tranche shown earlier, with pricing of a similar product. Baskets of triple-A tranches of various CDOs are sometimes credit-enhanced with a small first-loss tranche. The early deals securitized triple-A tranches of CDOs backed by residential mortgages. At the time, the triple-A tranches were trading around LIBOR plus 30 to LIBOR plus 35 bps, or 30 to 35 basis points on a synthetic basis. The SPE bought protection on the first-loss risk of the basket through a first-to-default basket swap. The first-loss piece was around 2 percent of the basket. Figure 13.3 shows this first-loss tranche.

The protection sellers received 100 bps for this risk. Since we know the residential mortgage collateral had a very high correlation across tranches, one could view it as being similar to a large triple-A tranche of one deal.

Returning to our previous discussion, some first-loss triple-A tranches of synthetic arbitrage CDOs are only 2 percent in size (albeit I used an example

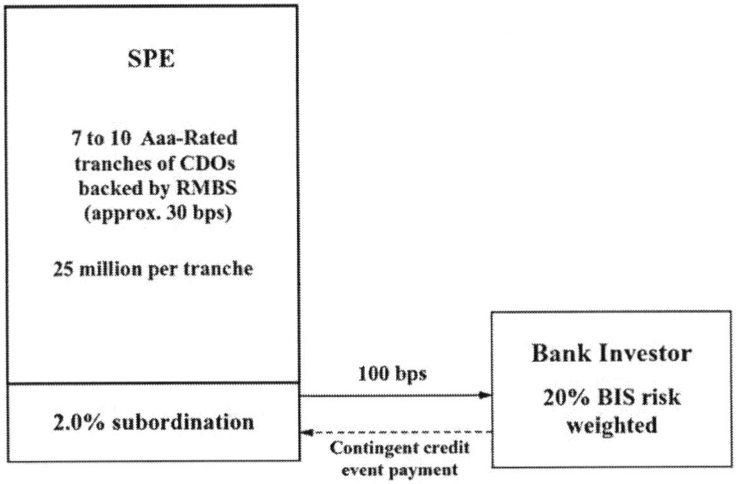

FIGURE 13.3 First Loss on Basket of Triple-A Tranches

of a triple-A tranche that was 5 percent of the CDO). The triple-A tranches of those deals traded at only 50 to 55 bps at same time the protection providers of the first-loss basket transactions received 100bps. This suggests these investors were getting a bad deal.

These prices fluctuate. By the end of 2002, triple-A tranches of synthetic investment grade arbitrage CDOs had widened to around 75 bps, but the triple-As of residential MBS-backed CDOs had also widened, which suggests that investors in these first-loss triple-As are still getting underpaid.

SUPER SENIOR ATTACHMENT POINT

Structurers and rating agencies don't always agree on the AAA attachment point, but rating agency model results serve as benchmarks to frame the debate. There is no rating agency model for super seniors, however. How can we agree on a super senior attachment point when there are no benchmark models?

One bank uses the Moody's model to solve for the attachment point at the 10^{-6} probability of default and calls the amount above that super senior. The trouble is, no two analysts can agree on the 10^{-6} attachment point, even if they could agree that should be the criteria in the first place. If we examine historical data for corporates, different time series of data result in different values for volatility, recovery rates, and default rates. Correlation data is even more difficult to produce.

Another bank solves for the Moody's AAA attachment point and arbitrarily asks for at least a 5 percent AAA tranche underneath the super senior.

Other financial institutions have shown CDO structures with no AAA tranche whatsoever. They go from an AA tranche directly to a super senior tranche. In my view, they failed to meet the basic requirement for a super senior, which is to have AAA tranche subordination.

Ambac recently reviewed a 150-name corporate portfolio, and each of the names was of equal size. They liked the portfolio and were willing to bid on the super senior tranche. They asked for 10 percent subordination for the super senior, which would have been 90 percent of the CDO. In other words, they wanted the deal to be able to sustain the default of 15 names before the super senior tranche would be affected. The arranger found someone else to provide super senior protection. The alternate counterparty only required default protection for 12 names before the super senior would be affected. The definition of a super senior tranche is arbitrary.

SUPER SENIOR PRICING

Several factors influence super senior pricing. Bank arrangers who retain super senior risk in their trading books are often pressured by structurers to accept narrower spreads on the super senior tranche. The lower all-in CDO cost achieved by a lower spread on the super senior tranche can be the deciding factor in winning a mandate with an outside bank customer that wants to securitize balance-sheet risk. The bank arranger's structurers earn fee income for structuring the deal. The super senior book is asked to "take one for the team." There's nothing logical about this pricing, other than a desire to win deal mandates. Since the mark-to-market on the super senior is rarely rigorously performed, this moral hazard is invisible to bank managers.

Trading books that retain the equity portion of CDOs use the cash they hived off the super senior tranche and incorporate it into equity returns. This extra cash is part of a slush fund that can hide a myriad of mistakes. Managers of banks have accepted this without much question. This ruse is about as sophisticated as the schoolyard prank of saying, "Look, your shoelace is untied!" And it works.

Some banks use model-based capital pricing. They have an internal benchmark for the super senior attachment point for a given set of data and volatility assumptions. They solve for the premium that gives them a target return on model-based capital. The results vary by financial institution. Since this is merely a target, and since the data can be manipulated, there is a lot of room for latitude in super senior pricing.

The monoline insurers have internal capital models that allow them to bid super seniors at tighter levels than most banks. In 2002, when many banks required super senior premiums of 8 to 12 bps for the super senior tranche of corporate deals, the reinsurance companies were willing to take this risk at around 6 bps. For residential mortgage deals, they would be willing to go as low as 4 bps. Sometimes it was cheaper for a bank arranger to intermediate (or to find an OECD intermediary) between the originating bank and the reinsurance company than for an OECD bank to take the super senior risk outright. Banks require much less capital for intermediations than for outright positions and can usually intermediate for 1 to 2 bps.

By the end of 2002, MBIA and FSA had pulled back from being super senior protection providers for corporate deals, due to corporate defaults in the portfolios in which they had already invested. Ambac entered the market but asked for wider premiums of around 12 bps and asked for well-diversified portfolios with good levels of subordination. Due to the widening of corporate spreads, it was able to get what it asked for in many instances.

Many banks pulled back from the super senior market by the end of 2002. JPMorgan Chase had a large super senior portfolio and curtailed its super senior activities beginning in late 2001. Other banks instituted a policy that they would only retain super seniors on deals they were arranging and would not invest in outside super seniors.

New banks entered the market. Banks doing arbitrage deals decided to keep the super senior and the equity tranches and go short the mezzanine tranche. We discussed that earlier, but there is a feature worth reiterating. Since bank arrangers own the equity, which is itself subject to investor acceptance pricing, they can set the level of the super senior and the equity at will. The tranches are kept on the trading book, and there is moral hazard in the ultimate pricing as well as the structuring and ongoing deal management.

Monolines continued to guarantee Super Senior and AAA- rated tranches through 2007. In addition, they guaranteed other structured finance deals. By the end of 2007 through 2008, many of their deals began to unravel, and the monolines found themselves capital constrained, with their ratings either drastically downgraded or in jeopardy (see Chapter 17).

SUPER SENIORS OR SENILE SENIORS?

The rating agencies have downgraded the AAA tranches of many synthetic CDOs in 2007 and 2008. What does that mean for super senior tranches? We can use our earlier corporate debt-backed CDO example to examine the effect of defaults of 2 percent of a synthetic corporate portfolio. For purposes of this example, we'll assume that the super senior and AAA are not written down by recovered amounts. We have to solve for the new super senior attachment point, just as we did for the AAA tranche. The new attachment point is shown in Figure 13.4.

Let's assume we mark the 2 percent strip of the former super senior to AAA levels of 55 bps versus 10 bps for the super senior tranche. The 45 bps difference is a loss of EUR 45,000 per annum. That doesn't seem too bad. Of course, we neglected the fact that many of the corporate names have been downgraded, and the overall subordination should probably increase more than 2 percent. The larger difference in the mark-to-market is from the portion that is still super senior. If Ambac is taking on board super senior risk at around 12 bps, banks will usually be about 4 bps wider. That suggests 16 bps might be a good benchmark level for the remainder of the tranche. That means there is a 6 bps loss in the mark-to-market of the remaining EUR 404.5 million. That's an additional EUR 242,700 per annum mark-to-market loss. The total mark-to-market loss on the super senior tranche is 287,700 per annum. Since volatility has increased, our internal model might suggest an even higher price, and even greater loss.

Notice that this calculation was for a small deal, only EUR 500 million in size. Most financial institutions have super senior portfolios of at least

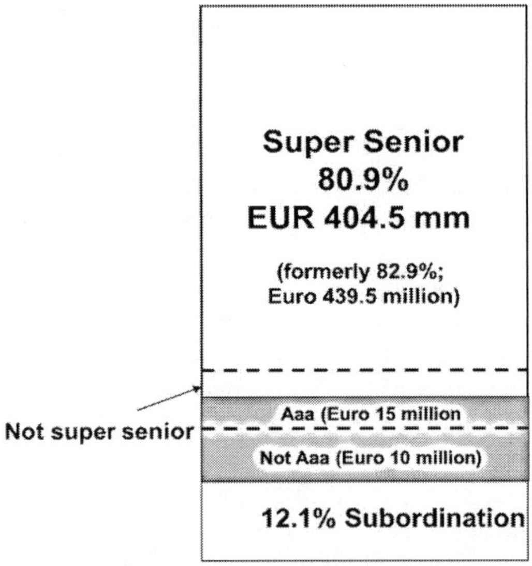

FIGURE 13.4 Effect of Default of 2% of the Portfolio on the Super Senior Tranche

the equivalent of $10 billion, and for institutions like JPMorgan Chase, it is in the triple digits. A $10 billion corporate-backed portfolio might have experienced mark-to-market losses on the order of EUR 5.75 million per annum, and that is a kind estimate. But this mark-to-market loss won't show up on the P&L of most trading books.

Since there is no visible market in super seniors, and since the definition is fluid, how can anyone say what the mark-to-market should be with complete conviction? Trading desks are counting on this ambiguity to obscure potential mark-to-market losses. One bank provided super senior protection for an early Deutsche Repon deal that had several defaults in the portfolio. Many of the remaining names had been downgraded. The AAA tranche was downgraded to AA. Nonetheless, the mark-to-market on the super senior didn't budge.

The example above was for a corporate-backed deal. Mortgage-backed CDOs brought to market from the latter part of 2005 through 2007 were in much worse shape. Some were constructed out of tranches of other CDOs that the lowest possible investment grade rating, and even those ratings were overstated. The subordination and overcollateralization protection was so meager that the principal of these tranches was at risk. Therefore, a significant portion of the principal of the Super Senior tranche was also at risk (see Chapter 17).

WHERE ARE THE REGULATORS?

Risk managers will have difficulty verifying mark-to-market losses they cannot observe. Super seniors aren't actually marked to market. They are marked to perception. There is a strong incentive for super senior providers to put low bids in the market or reference the low bid of a reinsurance company and declare victory. It is unlikely risk managers or senior bank managers will see those unpleasant mark-to-market losses show up on their desks in the magnitude I've previously described.

It's unlikely bank regulators will see it, either, but then they aren't asking the question in the first place. In the fourth quarter of 2002, I discussed this topic with a senior bank regulator. He was unaware of the issue, although he is a considered a structured products expert. As we discussed the pricing of super seniors and the economics of synthetic deals, his brow furrowed in unaccustomed thought. If he thought about this hard enough, he might actually have to take a position. This was dangerous. New ideas and drive are not valued qualities in the regulatory network. Team players are highly valued. *Team player* is a code for toeing the party line. This means not rocking the boat and never introducing a new idea that may have political ramifications. Fortunately, the moment of thought morphed into a familiar lifetime of inertia. The regulator persuaded himself that it wasn't his problem. In fact, it isn't a problem at all.

"I've read that the market figures out all new products in around eighteen months, so this will soon be generally known." The official struck the precise tone of pompous complacency that resonates in bureaucracies the world over. Once again, he was relaxed and calm. All was right with his world.

As of the time of our conversation, BISTROs had been around for 5 years.

It is an interesting theory that the markets are efficient. It is one I subscribe to myself, in theory. The difficulty is that information distribution is not always efficient. Another difficulty is that humans only have so much time and life to analyze complex ideas.

In the long run, markets are efficient, but in the short run they are not. That is why arbitrage desks are often very successful. Many of the lucrative jobs in the capital markets exist because information distribution is not efficient in the short run. Sometimes it even seems inefficient in the long run.

Even if markets are efficient in the long run, bureaucracies are not. We can't take comfort in a notion that regulation makes our banking system safer. Countries that make bureaucracy an art form such as Japan and Germany are currently seeing the worst consequences of incompetent bank management, and the regulators are miles away from being part of the solution.

The responsibility for sound bank management lies with bank managers. A handful of banks have looked at the game of putting super seniors in the trading book for better capital treatment and have declined to play the game. They rightly point out that they can't mark the super seniors to market, and the economics are a shell game. They expect that structures should add value other than providing a way to manipulate cash flows and siphon off fees for structurers. These managers didn't need to wait for risk managers or regulators to catch up; they studied the business and made their own decision. In the end, they will probably end up the winners in the shell game.

JUNIOR SUPER SENIORS

When banks and investment banks realized that monoline insurance companies would take super senior risk for much lower spreads than most banks, they were overjoyed. Occasionally, however, monolines didn't want the entire super senior tranche, only a portion of it. Furthermore, it was difficult to find additional buyers of the remaining vertical slice of the super senior tranche anywhere near the low levels to be had from the monolines.

Structurers could have created a smaller super senior tranche and a larger triple-A tranche, but this would have raised the cost of the securitization. Instead, many banks and investment banks offer a *junior super senior tranche*. They created another horizontal tranche in between the triple-A tranche and the super senior tranche.

The junior super senior is more likely to become a senile senior since a need for increased subordination to maintain an AAA rating will affect the mark-to-market of this tranche before the super senior (super-super senior?) is affected.

Many of the original junior super senior tranches were priced from 8 to 12 basis points, but recently super senior tranches traded at 12 bps. What does that say about the mark-to-market on those junior super seniors? We can see that the percentage mark-to-market loss will be greater than for an original super senior tranche, but there is no standard pricing for a junior super senior. The mark-to-market challenges for this tranche are the same challenges we faced for the super senior tranche.

Earlier we discovered that there is no standard definition of a super senior tranche. The junior super senior tranche adds more mud to the already muddy waters. There are no guidelines for the creation of this tranche. It is a distribution gimmick and an attempt to keep the costs of the liabilities to a minimum in the absence of buyers of the full super senior tranche.

The term *junior super senior* makes a mockery of the entire concept of the super senior tranche. Why stop at two super senior tranches? Why not have senior, junior, sophomore and freshman super seniors?

SUPER SENIOR INVESTORS

If you think about super seniors in the context of AAAs, you could ask yourself the following question: "Would I rather own a triple-A and earn a spread over LIBOR of 55 bps, or would I prefer to split the AAA into a small first-loss piece and earn 55 bps and a second large piece that pays me only 10 bps?"

No one needs a model to figure that out. This is exactly what banks have done with their balance-sheet risk, but purely in response to regulatory capital pressure and cost pressures. Only the unfunded nature of the synthetic AAA allowed us to split it into two pieces and create one piece with such a low premium.

Many people remark that a repackaged super senior tranche (repackaged in note form which would require funding) should be ideal for "credit arbitrage" funds, structured investment vehicles (SIVs) that can lever the fund based on the quality of credit risk in the portfolio. Actually, super seniors would be a disaster.

These funds would get no benefit of additional leverage from a super senior tranche paying 10 bps than for an AAA tranche paying 55 bps, because the rating agencies consider the super senior and the AAA as having the same risk. The SIV would earn 45 bps per annum less relative to the funding cost and have no additional leverage. The SIV can buy an AAA tranche of a nonsynthetic deal and earn investors much more spread income than they would get if they purchased the AAA plus super senior of a synthetic deal, even if the underlying collateral was the same for both deals. Leveraged super senior products and constant proportion portfolio insurance products are exceptions to that rule.

Who then are the investors in super seniors? Financial guarantors (monoline insurance companies), reinsurance companies, and banks are the primary investors. Both are looking for off-balance-sheet, unfunded, high-quality credit risk. Both can exploit model-based capital treatment or some variation to show a reasonable return even with the low premium.

The other investor is the bank originator that is eligible for a 20 percent BIS risk weight on super seniors and retains the tranche. There is still a regulatory capital reduction for laying off mezzanine risk. If the bank originator retains the equity, it still captures excess spread, but for investment-grade bank loans, that spread is minimal due to the narrow spreads at which the loans were originated.

Another investor is the bank arranger that wants to earn fee income and has a trading book willing to take on the risk. Super seniors are illiquid, never trade, and do not have a transparent mark-to-market. The capital markets trading book has become an investment portfolio for super senior tranches.

The excess cash hived off the super senior tranche covers up a multitude of problems in the trading books. The synthetic income created from the low pricing of the super senior tranche creates a huge slush fund of apparent new revenue for the trading book, which is partially reflected in the equity (first-loss) cash flows but is often reflected in larger fees retained by deal arrangers.

NEGATIVE BASIS TRADES

The negative basis trade is a new innovation designed to mitigate the risk of these large low-risk positions. These are not so much trades as the buildup of a huge bank-financed high-quality credit investment portfolio. In a *negative basis trade* at the super-senior level, the bank or investment bank trading book retains the very senior level in the CDO capital structure and buys protection from a monoline at a low cost in the form of a wrap. *Negative basis trade* is just a fancy name for "I want a big bonus for an old-fashioned low-tech carry trade." The trading book becomes a parking lot for a huge carry trade investment.

For example, Standard & Poor's required one of the major monoline insurance companies to reserve 10 bps in capital against an AAA-rated asset. The monoline's internal capital model required a little bit more, but the monoline wrote protection on junior super senior tranches (the tranche below the highest super senior tranche) and was paid enough over its internal capital charges to earn a 6 to 7 basis point premium, at least temporarily. Meanwhile, investment banks held the junior super senior tranches on their books combined with the monoline's guarantee. The investment bank counterparties were able to buy protection at a cheaper lever than they were getting paid to take risk, locking in a positive spread, but again, this was a temporary state of affairs for most deals.

These are called negative basis trades. Theoretically one should not be able to buy an asset, pay for AAA-rated protection, and lock in a positive spread, at least not unless there are supply and demand anomalies driving the trade. This trade was purely capital model driven, instead of being driven by fundamental value. Many of these trades done on subprime-backed CDOs quickly unraveled when it transpired that the super senior tranches often had material principal risk, and the monolines had drastically underpriced the true risk.

LEVERAGED SUPER SENIORS AND CONSTANT PROPORTION PORTFOLIO INSURANCE

Each super senior tranche can be $1 billion or more in size, depending on the deal size, since it is usually such a large percentage of a deal that is supposed to be backed by investment-grade collateral. In a leveraged super senior (LSS) transaction, investors put up a small amount of cash in the form of the par investment in a note. The investment is much less than the notional amount of the super senior tranche. Usually the leverage amount is 10 times, so if one invested in a notional amount of EUR 100 million, one would only have to put up EUR 10 million in actual cash. The investment bank has purchased credit protection from the investor, but it is capped at the investors' investment which is one-tenth of the actual notional amount of the super senior. If portfolio losses were much greater than expected, say, due to a large concentration of subprime-related risk in the portfolio, the investment bank protection buyer could have losses that exceed the protection provided by the investor's cash amount. The investment bank protection buyer would be able to unwind the trade prior to exhausting the full amount of the investor's cash, because of the existence of the unwind triggers.

These deals are exposed to market value risk, and rating agencies are not as well qualified to assess this type of risk. LSS deals have early unwind triggers of various types: (1) a trigger when a certain level of realized losses is reached; (2) a trigger when the portfolio weighted average spread widens to a certain level; and (3) a trigger for a market value or price change in the underlying super senior tranche. If the LSS unwinds and delevers, the investor can have significant losses due to market value risk, similar to the way hedge funds have losses due to leverage, as we saw earlier.

For example, in the 10 times leveraged LSS transaction mentioned previously, a 10 percent change in the value of the underlying super senior tranche would result in a 100 percent change in the market value of the underlying investment and it would be wiped out.

Note that the value of super senior tranches in CDOs backed by mezzanine subprime collateral fluctuated more than this in market value. LSS deals were all the rage in 2004–2006. They have recently fallen out of favor for obvious reasons, but they will reappear in another form once market participants forget today's lessons about leverage and hubris.

Some of this product found its way into Constant Proportion Portfolio Insurance (CPPI), a product that is a capital guarantee derivative security embedding a dynamic trading strategy. This way, the investor did not lose capital, just yield, but the product was still obviously flawed, even though CPPI was often highly rated.

FINAL THOUGHTS ON SUPER SENIORS

It may seem as if I'm saying don't ever invest in super seniors, but I'm not advocating that. What I'm pointing out is that there are irrational dislocations in the current market. The way we tranche and accumulate super senior risk requires examination.

The lack of definition for super seniors and junior super seniors is a problem waiting to be solved. Earlier we discussed Basel II. It addresses super senior risk in an oblique way. Under Basel II, one of the ratings-based approach classifications for AAA-rated thick tranches from highly granular portfolios might serve as the definition of a super senior tranche. The Basel II current proposed risk weight for tranches that meet the classification criteria is 7 percent, lower than the 20 percent risk weight already adopted in the United States for super senior risk that isn't accounted for using model-based treatment. To qualify, the triple-A rated risk must have 35 percent subordination and at least 100 obligors in the portfolio. Most super seniors today would only partially meet this test, and the rest might then be considered a lesser tranche. While this would at least be a consistent definition, it is arbitrary, but no more arbitrary than definitions currently in the market.

Basel II begs the question. Who got to BIS? If the rating agencies don't allow additional leverage—beyond that of an AAA tranche—for super senior risk in a credit arbitrage fund, why does BIS allow a reduction in regulatory capital beyond that of AAA risk?

If a bank has to create a new tranche that pays less that what it received earlier for taking the same slice of risk, just to make the economics look better, has any value been created?

I don't believe BIS came up with the idea of reduced regulatory capital for thick, highly granular tranches on its own. I believe it responded to the requests of banks that had already created super senior risk. If the most recent working paper is adopted, Basel II will create some new arbitrary rules ripe for arbitrage.

It's convenient to have super senior tranches in the trading book to take advantage of model-based capital treatment. It's convenient that super seniors are derivatives and are off-balance-sheet. It's convenient to think of super seniors as having virtually no risk, yet the owner still gets paid to take it. One bank remarked it felt that super seniors were *free money*, but one must ask whether instruments that never trade belong in a trading book in the first place.

One head of structuring at a U.S. investment bank justified holding large stagnant positions of super senior positions in the trading book by asking "Has a super senior ever experienced a default?"

At the time, they had not. (That changed, however, as CDOs unwound in 2007 and investors got back only one-quarter of the initial portfolio value.) But neither had most other publicly rated tranches, and none at the Aaa or Aa level. Since the risk of owning publicly rated CDO tranches (with non-moral hazard with respect to the manager) is downgrade and mark-to-market risk, why not apply this fuzzy logic to the other tranches of CDOs and earn a greater spread?

The answer is that holding stagnant positions isn't what the trading book was designed to do in the first place, and creating structures to obscure that fact did not help in the long run as super senior tranches experienced huge mark-to-market losses and started experiencing actual losses.

Chapter 14

Synthetics and Mark-to-Market Issues

SYNTHETIC CASH WINDFALL

Bank managers were persuaded that the super senior tranche was virtually risk free. With respect to actual losses at this level, it was a pretty good assumption, until the poorly crafted CDOs of the 2005–2007 vintages hit the market. Furthermore, the assumption is not useful when one considers mark-to-market risk at the trading book level. The defaults of Worldcom, Kmart, Enron, Adelphia, and others left arrangers' books with portions of former super senior tranches that would only merit an AA rating. The actual and anticipated defaults due to abusive mortgage lending practices, combined with insane structured finance techniques, resulted in principal losses at the super senior level.

An honest mark-to-market would require the arrangers to show a loss. But fortunately for traders, senior bank managers did not control the mark-to-market process. The traders who put the super senior on the books worked out the mark-to-market methodology with the risk managers or colluded to get supposed market evidence of the trading level. Since super senior tranches rarely traded, there was no way to independently verify prices. Creative trading book managers traded small slices of super senior tranches at pre-agreed prices as evidence that the levels at which they marked their own positions was correct.

In an exception to FASB's policy on guarantees, monoline wraps on synthetic CDO tranches—or any products that must be marked to market—require mark-to-market treatment. Some feel that monoline pricing is one method for marking super senior risk to market.

At the first-loss level, synthetic CDOs have created other valuation challenges. When credit spreads were wide, the first-loss or equity tranche of an investment-grade CDO generated cash flow that provided more than a

60 percent internal rate of return (IRR)—assuming Moody's base-case losses. This was such a good deal that arrangers often kept a portion of the excess spread for themselves and sold the equity at the lowest feasible IRR to unwary investors. This still happens today to investors in the equity tranches of index CDOs and customized first-loss CDOs.

It would have been ideal to retain the entire first-loss risk on the arrangers' books, and some arrangers did this, instead. At those levels, the risk was a good bet.

Or so it seemed.

A large chunk of the excess income was simply the found money from the super senior tranche. Arrangers were keeping the super senior tranche and taking the income from this former AAA tranche (remember the 44 bps) and applying it to their so-called equity investment. The arrangers robbed themselves of income at the AAA level to pay themselves at the equity tranche level. At 60 percent IRR, the equity still looked great, but a large chunk of that IRR was due to synthetic income.

It is fine to agree to report income that way, but it is not fine to deceive ourselves about fundamental value. What had originally been a device to remove credit risk was now a device to put credit risk on the trading book and claim high real revenues. In reality, much of this cash flow stream should have been considered either credit risk reserves or synthetic income and not applied as trading desk real revenues. But that would have been no fun at bonus time. Since senior bank managers didn't question the practice, arrangers and other participants now declare revenue victory when the reality is the cash flows have simply been reshuffled.

SYNTHETIC EQUITY

As they say in poker, if you don't know how to spot the sucker at the table, it is you. If you bought a bespoke tranche, also known as a single-tranche collateralized debt obligation (STCDO), without first running an independent cash flow analysis, the probability is very high that you are the sucker at the table. This is particularly true if you bought the equity tranche.

Notice that the internal rate of return using Moody's base case assumptions was 60 percent in the previous example. Yet in recent years the same deals have been getting done even though credit spreads collapsed, and only *single digit* returns were achievable for the identical portfolio, and one would be lucky to even achieve that. How can this possibly be a good deal for the arranging banks?

Bank arrangers have been doing economically unfavorable deals under very tight credit spread conditions. That isn't immediately obvious when one sells a single tranche and then hedges it with insufficient income. Credit spreads have often been very tight in the past couple of years. The return on the implied equity has been under 10 percent versus 60 percent and higher when credit spreads have been very wide. For single-tranche hedges, this means that the income on the credit default swaps used to hedge the position is too low for the risk. If one considers the full notional amount of the CDO, it is easy to see that arrangers took on too much risk for too little reward. Senior bank managers and investors have been fooled by the lack of transparency in these deals into thinking that they are doing quality business.

For example, the CDX4, an investment-grade CDS index, was used as the underlying portfolio of an STCDO tailored to the desired tranche requirements of an investor. In a rational world, the investor would use a rating agency model to tranche a CDO using the underlying reference credits in the index. Then the investor would run the cash flows of the deal to make sure it is getting fair value in the deal. This is particularly important if the investor wants to buy the equity tranche. But this rarely happens.

Initially, the indexes were touted by everyone—including me—as a giant step forward in transparency for the CDS market in general and for synthetic CDOs in particular. We have managed to turn transparency to mud, because transparency meant that arrangers could not retain some of an unwary investor's cash flow value for themselves.

Instead of showing investors the potential internal rate of returns—along with clearly articulated assumptions and scenario cash flows—under different scenarios, arrangers quote correlation values and sell equity risk by offering an up-front cash payment and ongoing fixed payments, provided no defaults occur.

Unwary investors think this is a great deal. They are investing in a portfolio of investment-grade names that they believe are unlikely to default. They receive upfront cash and ongoing payments. For the CDX4, as of the end of August 2005, for every $10 million pledged to cover losses of the equity tranche, the horizontal 3 percent notional slice, an investor would have received an up-front payment of $3.9 million plus 500 bps per annum. Many investors looked at this as free money, but the cash payments were too low relative to the risk and relative to what they should have asked for.

In early November 2005, investors could get paid an up-front premium of 80 percent-plus (*Note:* This is not IRR) of the notional amount of first-loss risk on the bottom 0 to 3 percent tranche of the investment-grade index. It may appear like a good deal until one runs the implied cash flows, but this tranche actually provides the worst value of all of the tranches in the deal.

The mezzanine investor should also be wary. It is easy to fiddle around with the tranching of the mezzanine tranche. The way that index CDOs are quoted obscures the implied rating of the various slices offered to investors. Investors should always independently run a rating agency model and determine the amount of subordination required for the rating quality one wants. The investor should then do a price comparison. I recommend Moody's since it usually requires more subordination or protection for the investor. S&P uses a black box called The Evaluator. The assumptions used in The Evaluator are not transparent, so it is difficult to trust the ratings produced by this model.

If you are willing to take the equity risk of a deal, you should arrange your own deal and earn the excess spread on the entire notional amount of the deal. You should always choose your own portfolio, and this won't necessarily include all of the names in a predetermined index. Eliminating restructuring as a credit event should be standard, however. The cash flow return for the risk will be much greater than that offered to you by any other arranger.

One very savvy hedge fund retains all of the equity and shorts the mezzanine tranche without using a bank arranger. The hedge fund realizes it can play with the mezzanine subordination levels. It also realizes that retaining all of the excess spread for its own benefit is a much better deal than the fixed payments offered for equity risk by bank arrangers.

As a general rule, never accept fixed payments from an arranger if you are the buyer of equity risk.

There are no hard and fast rules for how much implied IRR is enough, but here are some suggestions based on the past three years of credit spread fluctuations. If one isn't getting more than a 25 percent base-case IRR, it is a good idea to wait for a wider credit spread environment. If you see a base case higher than that, examine the IRR under different scenarios. You may wish to assign probabilities to the various scenarios to calculate a probable return, and also examine the IRRs under the various scenarios to make sure it is always acceptable under every scenario that concerns you. In recent history, base case IRRs of more than 50 percent have been feasible and have held up well under stress scenarios. Notice that a wider credit spread does not necessarily mean more intrinsic credit risk.

PORTFOLIO SWAPS

As we saw earlier, any synthetic balance-sheet CDO or trading book arbitrage CDO could be classified as a portfolio swap. The Bank for International Settlements' (BIS) Basel II distinguishes portfolios by granularity, so first-to-default baskets and any portfolio with 32 reference obligors or fewer would be considered nongranular pools. Portfolios with 100 or more obligors would be considered highly granular. As the size of the pool becomes larger, a synthetic swap is often referred to as a *portfolio swap*. The terminology is very ambiguous, so it is best to get clarification from the speaker.

Evaluation of the loss distribution or of the probability of default and the recovery rate become key. Some portfolio swaps simply have only two tranches: a senior tranche and a subordinated tranche. During the period 2001–2003, SCOR, the French insurer, liked to issue guarantees on a 30 percent first-loss tranche for a diversified pool of around 30 to 50 investment-grade corporate names. SCOR was rated A+ by S&P, so the first-loss tranche is eligible for this rating. Since the first-loss tranche was so large, the senior tranche would be considered super senior risk by today's standards. Under the proposed Basel II treatment, it would not make the senior most tier, however. By 2005 SCOR was rumored to have large losses as a result of losses on these positions.

For most portfolio swaps, a 90 percent senior tranche to a 10 percent subordinated tranche is more common. The structure for the subordinated tranche is usually the least advantageous to the investor. As losses occur, the notional amortizes down. The spread paid remains a constant percentage of the remaining notional. The portfolios are usually static, and the notional on the senior tranche steps down by the amount recovered.

Investors weren't sensitive to the disadvantage of this structure versus alternatives in the cash market and seemed to willingly accept these structures. Nonetheless, most of these early structures were a clear disadvantage to the investor. If a structuring group were to retain the first-loss risk, they wouldn't accept this type of structure. Instead, they would insist on receiving the residual cash flows of the deal. Investors should compare the offered spread on this type of structure with the IRR had the investor received the residual cash flows instead. Except in cases where they are being offered an extraordinary spread relative to the residuals, stress test analysis will show that receiving the residual cash flows is the better deal.

BESPOKE TRANCHES: SINGLE-TRANCHE CDOS

Regulatory capital arbitrage was the indirect precursor to bespoke tranches (STCDOs). Many banks are eager to enter the securitization business, but few have the distribution reach to support it. As a result, structurers and traders will create convoluted justifications to get the bank to take risk in its trading books in order for structuring groups to earn fee income. Earlier we saw how risk ballooned on bank books, but when the risk is in a trading book, it can be virtually invisible to bank board members.

Let's take another look at the fully synthetic balance-sheet trade we discussed earlier (see Figure 14.1). Up until now, we focused on getting the risk off of the bank balance sheet of the originating bank. We assumed the

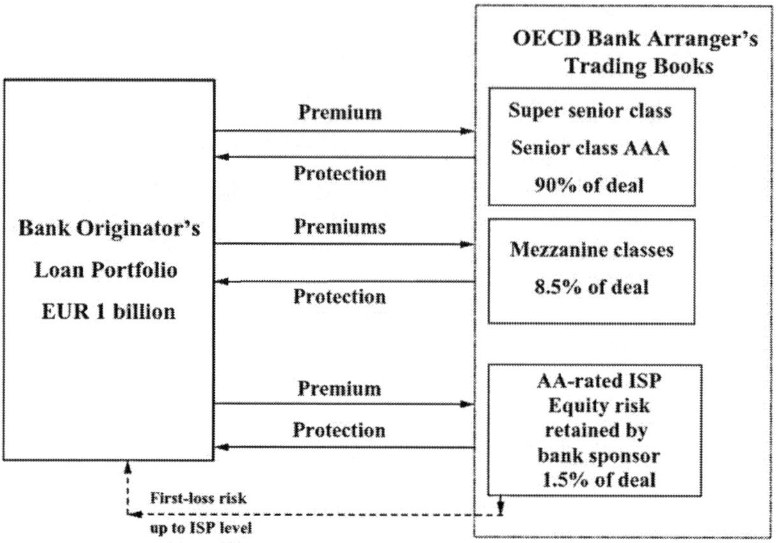

FIGURE 14.1 Fully Synthetic Balance Sheet CLO

originating bank found an acceptable OECD bank counterparty to get a 20 percent BIS risk weighting (or better if the counterparty is a government-guaranteed entity). We also looked at the total reduction of regulatory capital in certain venues for the interest subparticipation (ISP) structure.

In the example illustrated by Figure 14.1, the originating bank's original regulatory capital charge is calculated as follows, assuming all of the assets are nonsovereign loans:

EUR 1 billion x 100% x 8% x = EUR 80 billion.

where 100% = BIS risk weighting for the assets
8% = regulatory capital charge

After=the entering into the synthetic CDO with the OECD bank counterparty, the capital charge is calculated as follows:

EUR 1 billion x 20% x 8% x EUR = 16 million

where 20% = BIS risk weight
8% = regulatory capital charge

This assumes the originating bank gets an alternative favorable treatment on the equity risk of a 100 percent risk weighting and an 8 percent capital charge, due to taking advantage of ISP regulatory loopholes.

In rare cases, an aggressive interpretation gives a 0 percent charge for the equity for a total charge of EUR 15.76 million, but that treatment won't be supportable for long. If the bank is not in a favorable venue, the relevant regulatory capital charge is EUR 1.5 million for the equity. There is no advantage to an interest subparticipation, so the bank can retain the equity without structuring this feature and the total regulatory capital charge is EUR 17.26 million (985 million x 20% x 8% + 1.5).

What is the position of the OECD bank arranger? The OECD bank arranger now has the synthetic tranches in its trading book. If it has counterparties for the synthetic risk, it can lay off the risk in back-to-back transactions. The OECD bank may enjoy model-based capital treatment in its trading book and have a very much reduced regulatory capital charge versus a bank book. Several OECD banks have earned a fee simply for taking the risk off of the balance sheet of a customer bank's bank book and putting the risk into their own trading books. The net value added to the banking system is only the exploitation of a regulatory capital arbitrage and a little paperwork. There is no net economic benefit.

I'm familiar with one bank that held the risk of every tranche of every synthetic deal it had ever arranged sitting in it CDS trading books. It had no model to mark its deals to market. It didn't even have model-based capital treatment for regulatory capital purposes. Eventually, it set up repackaging SPVs to repackage the mezzanine risk so it could be sold to the bank's cash bond investors.

Since the super senior tranches weren't funded, however, the bank retained this risk in its trading books. Since it didn't have model-based capital treatment, the return on regulatory capital was dismal. Over each quarter-end, it did bed-and-breakfast trades to lay off the risk for one day with an OECD bank counterparty to reduce its overall regulatory capital charge. Even so, the small premiums earned on the super seniors left it with tepid returns on a regulatory capital basis, but at least it was a high single digit. Meanwhile, it continued to earn income on the large super senior positions. This was reported as accrual income (an anomaly in a trading book).

SHORT MEZZANINE AND LONG EQUITY

The next evolutionary change was the single-tranche CDO, and these products started catching on around the year 2000. These trading books grew in size, because arrangers didn't invest in the resources to effectively market all

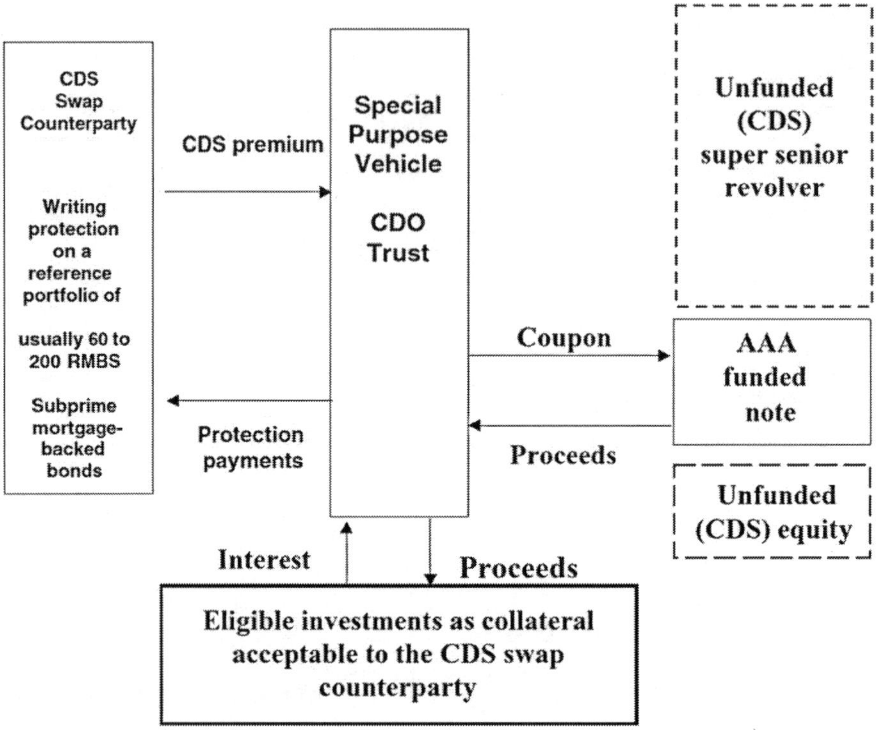

FIGURE 14.2 Bespoke Subprime-Backed CDO Mezzanine Tranche

of the CDO tranches. Instead, arrangers typically sold only the mezzanine risk. As a result, arrangers often unwittingly held equity risk—as well as the risk of the higher-rated tranches—in their trading books. Figure 14.2 shows an example of a bespoke mezzanine tranche of a subprime RMBS-backed CDO. The retained first-loss tranche of this deal poses significant risk that is difficult to hedge even by shorting the ABX index.

If one looks at the analogy with a cash CDO, it is easy to see the flaw in the hedge practices. If this were a cash deal, the arranger would sell the mezzanine tranche of the CDO and delta-hedge by buying each bond named in the portfolio, but only a fractional amount of the total original reference portfolio. If the deal were $5 billion in size (difficult to achieve in the bond market), the mezzanine tranche might be only $250 million in size, and the corresponding hedge would be to buy around $1 billion in bonds, assuming the market risk was already perfectly hedged, typical of recent delta-hedge ratios for investment-grade CDOs calculated using correlation models.

Investment bank arrangers often do not know how to quantify the value of synthetic single-tranche CDO trading books. Arrangers wish to report the size of the synthetic CDO market by only counting the sold tranches. But the risk of the arranger's position is equivalent to that of the remaining tranches of the full notional amount of the synthetic CDO. For instance, if the arranger sells a $250 million mezzanine tranche of a $5 billion CDO, the remaining risk position has the impact of the remaining $4.75 billion synthetic CDO in terms of value at risk.

When deal arrangers sold each tranche of the synthetic CDO and then sold protection in the credit derivatives market on each portfolio position, they were fully hedged. Since single tranche trading books usually sell only the mezzanine (the middle) tranche and then delta-hedge, they are riskier than fully hedged positions. Theoretically, one should make more money than the fully hedged position because one has more risk. That hasn't been the market experience very often, however. The single tranche books often make even less money for greater risk, because traders make additional credit bets or make a bet on hedge ratios.

When traders lose money on the bets relative to a fully hedged position, the trading book is making insufficient income relative to the risk. That should show up in lower bonuses. It should, but it often does not, because senior management has no idea what is happening in the trading book relative to customary CDO business.

Risk is measured as value at risk (in simplified terms). The sold tranches of synthetic CDOs are notional slices of a much larger CDO, and the equivalent risk of the unsold CDO tranches remains on the arranger's books. The sold tranche only bears a horizontal slice of the risk of the entire CDO. The typical hedge for the sold tranche is to sell credit default swaps that are a vertical slice of the risk of the notional amount sold. The hedge ratio is a best guess.

It is very easy for traders to obscure the risk/reward economics of these deals. These are the single most gamed transactions both from the investor's and, ironically, from the investment bank/arranger's point of view.

The cleanest and most conservative hedge (from a risk perspective) for a synthetic CDO is to sell protection in the credit default swap market on the full notional amount of the deal while simultaneously buying protection from the CDO investors by selling every tranche of the deal. In contrast, the STCDO always leaves the investment bank/arranger's trading book with residual credit risk and a huge position to hedge.

One would think that greater risk means greater reward. One might reason that fully hedging the deal cuts into the deal profitability. Often just the opposite is true, given the state of the art of hedging STCDO deals.

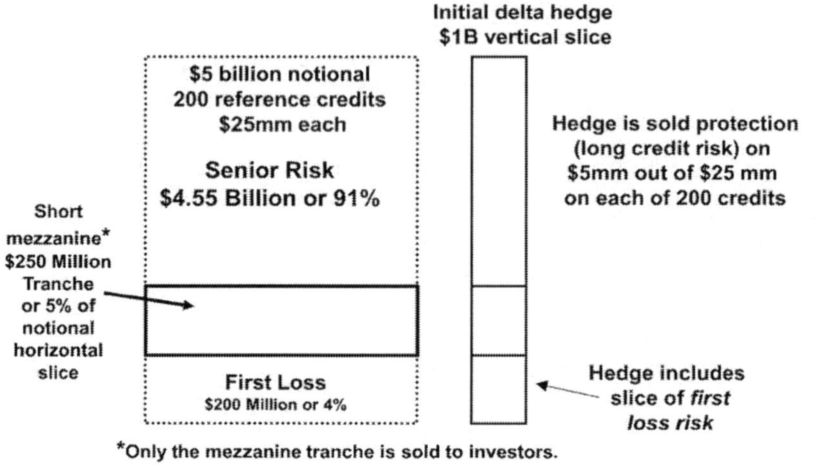

FIGURE 14.3 Initial Delta Hedge for $5 Billion Notional STCDO

If this is true, why do banks do STCDOs? One of the main reasons is that arrangers have difficulty finding investors for all of the tranches. Arrangers created STCDOs so they could still do business without developing a deeper investor base for these transactions.

The following is an example of an STCDO brought to market when credit spreads were wider than today's levels. If this deal, using the same reference portfolio and notional amount, had been brought to market as a fully hedged CDO, the locked-in revenue of the deal would have been approximately $11.3 million. For example, if the deal arranger locks in the bid/offer spread on 200 names, and if the bid/offer spread is 5 bps*, the arranger can lock in $2.5 million per annum, for a typical deal with a five-year maturity. In the no-default scenario, this has a present value of about $11.3 million using a 4 percent discount rate over the life of the deal.

For our mezzanine STCDO, the arranger sold the mezzanine tranche, but now the arranger was long the credit risk of the credit default protection sold to delta-hedge the short mezzanine position. The arranger is long the credit risk of a large slice of the equity tranche (often unbeknownst to its own management), long the credit risk of the tranches that are senior to the particular mezzanine class being shorted, as illustrated in Figure 14.3.

* For many off-the-run names, the bid/offer spread is greater than 5 bps, and some well-traded names may have a tighter bid/ask spread

For a \$5 billion notional CDO, the arranger created a mezzanine risk STCDO for an investor with a notional size of \$250 million, and an approximate credit risk equivalent to a tranche rated AA. The STCDO arranger needed to pay the stated coupon on the mezzanine tranche. Instead of selling protection on the entire \$5 billion notional amount, the arranger initially only sold protection on a notional amount of \$1 billion. Note that the hedge amount must be recalculated over time, but this is the initial delta hedge amount.

The average offer spread on the portfolio was 80 bps. The stated coupon on the \$250 million mezzanine tranche is 120 bps per annum. The arranger earned the following:

$$\$1 \text{ billion} \times 0.0080 \times \$8 \text{ million per annum.}$$

After tranche expenses, the net amount was

$$(\$1 \text{ billion} \times 80 \text{ bps}) - (\$250 \text{ million} \times 120) \text{ bps} = \$5 \text{ million per annum}$$

or \$22.3 million over the five-year life of the deal, assuming a 4 percent discount rate.

Note that if there are no defaults, the arranger does better than it otherwise would have done with the fully hedged deal. At first glance, one might think the arranger is making more money doing the STCDO than doing a fully hedged deal, but this isn't necessarily the case. This revenue must cover other deal expenses plus reserves for potential losses. In other words, the higher apparent revenue comes with greater risk.

For instance, if one of the 200 names, or reference entities, in the reference portfolio defaulted immediately, the arranger must settle on the protection it sold. Let's assume a potentially generous recovery rate of 40 percent in the event of default. The original notional amount was \$5 billion, and the arranger sold protection on approximately one-fifth (20 percent) of that amount, or \$1 billion. In the event of default of one of the \$25 million notional reference entities, the arranger would have to pay a cash amount of

$$(0.20 \times \$25 \text{ million}) \times (1 - 0.4) = \$3 \text{ million}$$

When the STCDO comes to market, it isn't obvious that the arranger has the first-loss risk. If losses are tracked by the individual deal, however, it is easy to see that the arranger has underwritten the equity of the entire CDO, albeit losses will be limited to the notional amounts of the individual names on which the arranger has sold credit default protection. Risk-adjusted income is a key metric, but there is a lot of confusion in how to quantify the risk.

In this case, the arranger has the first-loss risk on the $1 billion in credit default protection it sold, but it also has the income on only the $1 billion it sold; the risk/reward is theoretically equivalent to the entire equity tranche. Note that $1 billion is only the initial hedge amount. Over time the hedge ratio will have to be readjusted.

But you ask, what about the short mezzanine position? Doesn't correlation trading ensure that the short position will change in value similar to the long credit risk position? No, not by a long shot. Correlation trading is a guess. The delta of the price of the mezzanine tranche with respect to credit spread changes is largely an unknown, despite what arrangers claim. Often credit spreads on underlying names can gap out, but the mezzanine pricing for rated tranches can remain constant. This has often happened in the market. The models that try to quantify this relationship are fairly useless.

One of the key problems is that the short mezzanine position has different risk characteristics than the long position of sold protection. If credits are downgraded or if defaults occur that do not threaten the principal of the mezzanine tranche, it is difficult to monetize the increase in value of this short position.

In May 2005, S&P's downgrades of GM and Ford to below investment-grade highlighted the weaknesses of the models. Traders blamed losses on unanticipated changes in correlation, but this excuse just obscures the fact that the trading books are making one-sided credit bets.

When Treasury books take losses, traders own up that their hedges reflected a view on the direction of interest rate moves, and they lost their bet. In the credit markets, we want to blame correlation or correlation smiles, as correlation laughs at our efforts to model it. Later in this chapter, I comment on the false analogy of the *correlation smile*, sometimes called *correlation convexity*, which arrangers employ to avoid owning up to the fact that these trading books are covertly accumulating income by piling on credit risk, often at the wrong prices—the same behavior for which we formerly criticized loan officers.

The advantage to all of this smoke and mirrors is that one can fiddle around with the model assumptions. One can change the hedge ratio and create a lot of synthetic income at will. Senior managers and risk managers will rarely successfully challenge this sleight of hand. We explore this in more detail later.

INVISIBLE HEDGE FUNDS

In our example, whether arrangers make more money over time than they would have done if they had fully hedged their position is a matter of how well they manage their residual risk. Whether it was a good deal in the first place depends on the implied pricing of the equity risk.

Notice that the initial retained equity risk on the $1 billion hedge position is virtually invisible. For banks this is problematic. If reported, this equity exposure should attract a dollar-for-dollar deduction against regulatory capital. This equity risk is not always reported, however. As the head of structuring at a Canadian bank said, "If my boss knew what I was really doing, he'd fire me."

To add to the confusion, traders tend to make additional lopsided bets to exploit a particular viewpoint on the way they hedge the risk. The traders don't have a lot of downside in making a bet, but they have quite a bit of upside.

If they aren't rigorously tracked, STCDO cash flows effectively obscure the effect of bets. If credit bets win, the traders have a call on the upside in the form of a higher bonus related to the higher profitability (the bet payoff). Anyone who owns such a call option has an affinity for greater volatility, so the interests of the arranger's managers and traders are misaligned. This isn't intentional—it is the nature of this business, and managers must fully understand this natural tension.

If the arranger isn't making more on STCDOs than the arranger would have made on a fully hedged CDO, then the positions weren't managed in a way that compensated the arranger for the additional risk. That means their traders were unsuccessful in exploiting the risk/reward potential (or they made unsuccessful bets), and the arranger would have been better off fully hedging the positions.

EXTRAORDINARY POPULAR DELUSIONS AND THE MADNESS OF CORRELATION

The twenty-first century has started off with a spectacular mass financial delusion in the fastest-growing segment of the financial markets. One generally considers three stochastic variables when calculating credit losses: default probability, recovery rates, and correlation. Of these three, correlation is the *least* important. Yet correlation trading has spread through the psyche of the financial markets like a highly infectious thought virus. So far, there have been few fatalities, but several victims have fallen ill, and the disease is rapidly spreading. Financial engineers who have built a career around market default correlation assumptions are likely to add cardiac arrest to their list of symptoms.

To illustrate the madness, consider the following problem. Suppose I told you that I ran a single-name CDS trading book and had sold credit default protection on $1 billion notional of 200 diversified investment-grade corporate names. How would you suggest that I hedge the risk? One might suggest various approaches: Leave the position unhedged (like an old-fashioned bank loan portfolio); short the riskiest credits as indicated by a Moody's KMV model or CreditSights (or buy credit default protection for the riskiest names); short an investment-grade credit index in a calculated ratio. These are only a few examples among several possibilities.

The possibility that would probably come to your mind dead last is to create a $5 billion notional CDO using the 200 names as the underlying collateral, and then short the mezzanine tranche to hedge the risk. As time goes on, change the notional amount of the $1 billion sold credit default swap position to adjust for new market conditions.

The reason this would be the last to leap to mind is because the hedge is nonsense. Yet when we create and sell the mezzanine tranche of a $5 billion notional deal, the hedge of choice is a delta hedge that requires us to sell credit default protection on a pro rata amount of each of the underlying 200 names, amounting to $1 billion notional of sold credit default protection.

Correlation traders have adopted the language of the conventional options markets. This is a false analogy. For conventional option pricing, the volatility of the underlying is a function of the price of the underlying, the strike price of the option, the time to option expiration, interest rates, and the price of the option. If we consider an interest rate option, the price of the underlying instruments can be calculated with certainty for various interest rate environments.

Market implied default correlation is much more nebulous. Market implied default correlation is a function of the tranche being considered (the hard-to-pinpoint-price and the attachment points), the loss given default assumptions (as usually estimated from flawed averages of CDS premiums and historical loss given default), and asset default correlation assumptions (equal pairwise default correlations and a form of copula model—Gaussian, Student's t, or Archimedean).

All of this effort is a waste of time and resources. In the first place, the market is estimating *asset* correlations instead of the necessary *default* correlations. The overwhelming flaw in the methodology, however, is that the only reason default correlation exists at all is if we pretend that default probability does not vary—but of course, it does.

This suggests that hedging should focus on default probability and recovery rates. Instead of hiring quantitative analysts to write inaccurate models that solve the wrong problem, a fundamental corporate balance sheet analysis that reveals better information about the probability of default and loss given default is a more sensible approach. That requires a different skill set and a different focus than is currently in use on the majority of trading desks today.

A major improvement in the financial markets would be to spend zero time, money, and resources on correlation and spend all of one's time, money, and resources on better estimates of default probabilities and recovery rates.

DELTA HEDGES, CORRELATION MODELS AND JUNK SCIENCE

I recommended taking down the equity risk on the entire notional amount and skipping the part about delta hedging, but that is just a recommendation. If you want to delta hedge, go right ahead. Knock yourself out. Just don't call it science, unless you call it junk science.

Since the data used by the models is so debatable, it is no surprise that the results are often ridiculous. The delta hedge ratio is defined as the change in the mark-to-market of a tranche for the change in mark-to-market of credit.

Arrangers typically calculate the delta by shifting the spreads on each individual name in the CDO by 1 to 10 bps and then calculating the mark-to-market change of the tranche. It is a nice theory but, as mentioned previously, it doesn't work that way in the market.

Arrangers use the term *spread convexity* to explain departures from the model for large spread moves. This requires an adjustment to the hedge ratio.

The term *spread convexity* implies the predictability is as good as in the Treasury market in which we define duration and convexity. The terms are similar, but the dynamics of these two markets are very different. In the Treasury market one can precisely recalculate the price of a Treasury bond for a change in yields. The duration and convexity of the price curve for different bonds vary in precisely predictable ways. Treasury models are reliable and the results are quantifiable in advance. In contrast, delta hedging models for STCDOs are not reliable, and a back of the envelope guess of the hedge ratio is as good as a model.

In the case of coins and dice, you can learn a lot about them by flipping and throwing them thousands of times and recording the results. A Monte Carlo simulation uses a computer to throw a whole lot of random inputs into a model. It is like shaking a newly made chair to see how stable it is.

Correlation models appear clever but have little to do with reality. The result is a chair that collapses beneath you as soon as you sit on it. The models are highly unstable. Small changes to model inputs result in huge hedge ratio changes.

This is very bad news for correlation models. In the credit markets we are guessing at the relationships, and we are guessing about most of the data. One huge guess is about the relative spread movements. We also guess somewhat about the subordination required to get the credit quality we desire. Then we guess about the correlations. Even the rating agencies do not agree on how to treat correlation. Finally, we guess on the recovery rate assumptions.

The experts at one investment bank agree that the delta of the entire CDO should be 100 percent of the deal's notional. Over time, if there are no defaults, the delta of the equity tranche will increase to 100 percent and the delta of the tranches above it will decrease to 0 percent. But when they calculate the individual deltas of the tranches in a synthetic CDO using their model, the deltas do not add up to 100 percent unless they force the model to give them that result. By that I mean they have to fudge (i.e., fake) the results.

Table 14.1 shows a summary of their results. Note that the deltas add up to 118 percent of the notional of the hypothetical $1 billion notional CDO.

What is the correct delta on the mezzanine tranche, the 4 to 8 percent horizontal slice of this custom-tailored synthetic single-tranche CDO? Who can say for certain? We could use 7.7□ leverage, but would 7.3□ be more accurate? If I fiddle with the model, I may be able to get a hedge ratio of 7.9 or even 8.1. Notice that for the same trade, I can fiddle around quite a bit, and boost my income while claiming the identical risk profile.

Tranche	Delta as % of Notional	Notional Size of Delta Hedge	Tranche Notional	Leverage Delta / Tranche Notional	Tranche Size (% Total)
Super Senior	22.36%	223,600,000	880,000,000	0.3	88.00%
Senior	18.88%	188,840,040	40,000,000	4.7	4.00%
Mezzanine	30.62%	306,200,000	40,000,000	7.7	4.00%
Equity	46.37%	463,700,000	40,000,000	11.6	4.00%
Total	**118.23%**	**1,182,340,040**	1,000,000,000	NA	100.00%

TABLE 14.1 Synthetic CDO Delta Hedge Summary

Increasing the hedge ratio creates an income slush fund for the same reported risk. Risk managers often rely on the recommendations of the much more highly paid traders for bonuses and future jobs. This tends to make risk managers open to suggestion and very accommodating. Senior managers are often oblivious to the nuances of these models. At bonus time, there is an incentive to create synthetic income to aid in the negotiation for real bonus dollars.

SYNTHETIC NOTIONAL AND ACTUAL RISK

When the first STCDOs appeared, the market practice was to report the full notional amount of the CDO reference portfolio. The reported notional amounts soon ballooned beyond what had been reported for fully hedged deals.

The huge notional amounts created a potential problem. Senior bank managers and bank regulators could become uncomfortable with the huge reported notionals. Even more important, they might become uncomfortable with the huge increase in risk taken on by traders who formerly claimed they couldn't make much money trading single-tranche CDOs. Instead of reporting the entire deal notional amounts, arrangers only reported the amount of the tranches they actually sold.

This new method of reporting provides little meaningful content. Notice that if one adds up the notional amounts, it doesn't reveal anything about the degree of tranching, the relative risk taken on given the underlying portfolio, or the potential risk as credit conditions change. The amount could refer to the equity tranche, the BBB tranche, the AA tranche, or a blend of the CDO tranches. These are very different risks and reporting the notional amounts this way isn't very useful.

The only way to back out the risk of these deals is to start with the full notional amount. The only reliable benchmark is the fully hedged risk/reward of a hypothetical fully hedged deal. Furthermore, subsequent tranches of the entire deal can be issued, leaving no tranches on the trading book. I believe the only sensible way to report the statistics of synthetic CDOs is to report the entire notional amounts of the deals based on the entire notional amounts of the reference portfolios.

If the single-tranche notional amounts aggregated from dealers and reported by *CreditFlux* are correct, then the underlying notional amounts of the CDOs are very large. As of the end of July 2005, bespoke tranches were reported to be $169 billion. If this represents tranches ranging approximately, on average, from 5 to 10 percent of the total notional amount, then the full notional of the deals ranged from approximately $1.7 trillion to $3.4 trillion. Activity waned for corporate-backed CDOs but surged for mortgage-backed CDOs. No one knows the current market size of bespoke tranches, but my estimate of the market size is around $400 billion. The corresponding full notional size is impossible to estimate since the size and subordination level of more recent bespoke tranches were often not linked to a specific index and were more variable than earlier deals.

I've heard disagreement and dissatisfaction from arrangers about my position on this issue. I've heard arguments involving implied correlations, dynamic hedging, spread convexity, and other obfuscating jargon. Can you spend implied correlation? Can you spend hedge ratios? Can you spend spread convexity? No. But you can spend cash.

Insist on a cash flow analysis that shows the timing, the magnitude, and the probability of receipt of the cash flows. The only way to do this is to start with a first principles analysis of the deal, which requires knowledge of the full notional amount of the CDO. I haven't heard any sensible alternatives to reporting full notional amounts, but I would be delighted if someone could provide an alternative that didn't involve magical thinking.

EXPLOSIVE GROWTH, UNCERTAIN FUTURE

Investment-grade synthetic CDOs gained market share through 2007 because of the tremendous boost credit derivatives give to the CDO arbitrage. Now they have come under suspicion because of their opacity and wide-ranging abuse, particularly in the mortgage-backed CDO market. Credit derivatives add flexibility, but investors must invest time in education, or they will invest for less relative value than they enjoy when they invest in more conventional instruments.

Historically, most stand-alone credit derivatives trading desks could not generate much revenue for the banks that housed them. This was because much of the trading inquiry was for protection, the products were illiquid, there were a limited number of trading partners, the trading desks had limited credit lines, and the trading desks had difficulty matching off or hedging the positions.

Yet the same trading desks that couldn't make money trading single-name credit default swaps (CDS) have experienced explosive growth until the end of 2007. There are several reasons, but in my view the main ones are as follows:

- Trading desks were unlikely to experience short-term losses despite massive net long positions in credit risk.

- Senior investment banks and bank managers, confused by misleading jargon, are unaware they had large one-sided positions in credit risk.
- The way structured credit products were presented and quoted obscured the cash flows for both senior bank managers and investors.

FOUND MONEY AND MORAL HAZARD

If I had a large bonus in my sights and mischief on my mind, it would be very easy to manipulate the hedge ratio so that I would sell more credit default protection and increase my income without a perceived increase in risk. This is the source of the extreme moral hazard of the delta hedging strategy.

It would be even simpler if one could do away with the inconvenient sold single tranche and simply sell credit default protection outright. But most investment managers would not allow this type of one-sided bet. The bet would simply be a use of the bank's credit line to generate risky income. Yet by manipulating my hedge ratios, I can create a large net long position in credit risk that is virtually invisible.

The easiest way for an arranger to do this is to sell the mezzanine tranche of a synthetic CDO and then delta-hedge. Given the arguments about correlation data and given the dissimilar nature of the hedge to the risk being hedged, the outcome is a coin flip. In this case, the coin is biased, because the hedger has control of the hedge ratio and therefore control of the income and of the perceived risk. The bet is that credit spreads will not gap out and that defaults will not touch the trading book until after bonus time, or even better, until one has a big contract at another investment bank.

•

Chapter 15

Comments on Selected Structured Finance Products

MULTISECTOR CDOS: $CDOS^N$

Multisector CDOs are also known as *ABS CDOs*, *ABS of ABS*, *CDOs squared* (or *CDOs^2*), or *CDOs cubed* (*CDOs^3*). These products appeared in 1999 in response to investors' desire to securitize their own positions of structured product. Both balance-sheet and off-balance-sheet arbitrage deals have been done.

The spectrum of collateral for this product is more varied than for other CDOs. By that I mean that some multisector CDOs have been structured backed by AAA-rated tranches of other CDOs, and some have been structured using BBB-rated tranches of other CDOs. All types of CDO and non-CDO collateral have been added to the multisector collateral mix, including nonperforming loans, mezzanine tranches of other CDOs, and the result is an indigestible collateral stew.

Since it is possible to do a synthetic deal with highly rated collateral, as we saw earlier, banks and insurance companies that need regulatory capital relief are happy to provide collateral for these CDOs, at least under the current regulatory capital regime.

Motives may change in the future. As more investors become aware of the structural risks of older deals on their balance sheets, they may seek to reduce the risk of poorly structured mezzanine tranches. For example, BBB tranches that are at risk of moral hazard trading of the underlying asset portfolio are likely securitization candidates. Two large UK banks recently completed synthetic securitizations of BBB tranches of various CDOs they had accumulated in their investment portfolios. The arbitrage was one motivation, but another may have been to reduce legacy structural risk.

Multisector CDOs include exclusively cash and exclusively synthetic collateral as well as a mix of both cash and synthetic collateral.

In one instance, a UK bank did an all-synthetic deal referencing a multicurrency portfolio of BBB-rated tranches of CDOs. The diversified portfolio consisted of positions of the euro equivalent of approximately 10 million each.

These deals pose a currency problem unique to other synthetic deals. For instance, in many synthetic arbitrage deals, the deal may be brought in euros or USD and each name referenced will only offer protection on the prestated notional amount of the deal at the time the credit event occurs.

In a synthetic balance-sheet multisector CDO, the bank is trying to hedge a physical or notional position in the exact amount of the relevant currency. The amount of deliverable is referenced from the start of the transaction, not at the time of the credit event. The currency mismatch risk must be borne either by the bank sponsor holding the assets or by the bank arranger, if any, helping the bank sponsor to bring the deal. Unwary investors may end up bearing this risk.

An American investment bank showed me the AAA tranche of a multisector balance-sheet CDO and stated that the investor had no currency risk. I asked the investment bank how they were hedging the risk. Did they have a model to quantify the credit default protection which they (as bank arranger) were selling the bank originator? They said they didn't.

In many cases, bank arrangers will charge a currency mismatch fee, usually arbitrarily set at 2 to 5 bps, and take the currency risk in their trading books. This risk is very difficult for auditors and risk managers to find, and once found it is difficult for them to quantify. This could probably be modeled using gross assumptions with a currency option model adjusted for the contingent credit event, but many firms do not take this extra step. This is probably an area where more general modeling will be done in future.

Multisector CDO technology has also been abused, and the complexity masked the risk. In multisector CDOs that include subprime collateral, one can find subprime mortgage loans, subprime auto loans, credit card receivables, and mezzanine corporate loans backing mezzanine tranches of CDOs used as collateral in a CDO-squared. These deals are nearly impossible for sophisticated investors to fairly value, and they are not worth the work. Many of these deals seem to have been constructed solely to offload the risky CDO tranches.

FUTURE FLOWS: PAYMENT RIGHTS SECURITIZATIONS

How can a transaction get a rating higher than its sovereign rating? How can a structurer accomplish this without using a credit derivative or a financial guarantee?

A key concern for emerging market transactions is that a deal normally has a rating ceiling the same as the sovereign rating. Nonetheless, it is possible for a deal to get an investment-grade rating even if the sovereign rating is below investment-grade.

One structure that makes this possible is securitization of payment rights. For instance, if a bank generates payment rights sourced from export business and other foreign currency payments made offshore, there is a possibility of securitizing these receivables and getting a rating higher than that of the sponsor bank or of the sovereign rating of the country in which the sponsor bank is located. Vakif Bank is rated only B by Fitch. It is located in Turkey, which is also rated only B by Fitch. However, securitization of Vakif Bank's payment rights is rated BBB by Fitch. Other banks in Turkey and North Africa are keen to do these transactions. These transactions can be done for any bank which has rating issues, if it securitizes foreign currency payments originated abroad.

The Society for Worldwide Interbank Financial Telecommunications (SWIFT) is the automated communication network that facilitates the transfer of currencies and financial information. Via SWIFT, the sponsor bank located in an emerging market country can divert offshore foreign currency payments to highly rated specified correspondent banks (SCBs) located in highly rated countries such as the United States, the United Kingdom, or Switzerland. Asian banks located in Japan or other highly rated countries are also a possibility but have not been used as frequently since most of the payments have not originated in Asia on deals done to date.

Foreign currency payments to banks in emerging market countries arise from various sources. One source is export business. Cash against goods transactions (CAGs), letter of credit transactions (LOCs), and cash against documents transactions (CADs) all result in foreign currency payments that normally transfer through the SWIFT system. SWIFT also handles check transactions. SCB accounts take in other foreign currency receivables from individuals and banks that are also transferred to banks in emerging market countries. These present and future foreign currency receivables are called *future flows* and the payment rights to these flows can be bought and sold.

The key to a successful future flow transaction is to capture the rights to the foreign currency deposits offshore, in highly rated SCBs in highly rated countries. The sponsor bank located in the emerging market country sells these rights to an offshore, bankruptcy-remote, special purpose trust incorporated in a tax-friendly venue. Figure 15.1 shows a general schematic of a transaction for a Turkish bank. Note that the special purpose trust is located in Jersey, a tax-friendly venue that is one of the United Kingdom's Channel Islands.

Although the payment rights originate in Turkey, the rights are sold and the SCBs are instructed to make payments to collection accounts offshore.

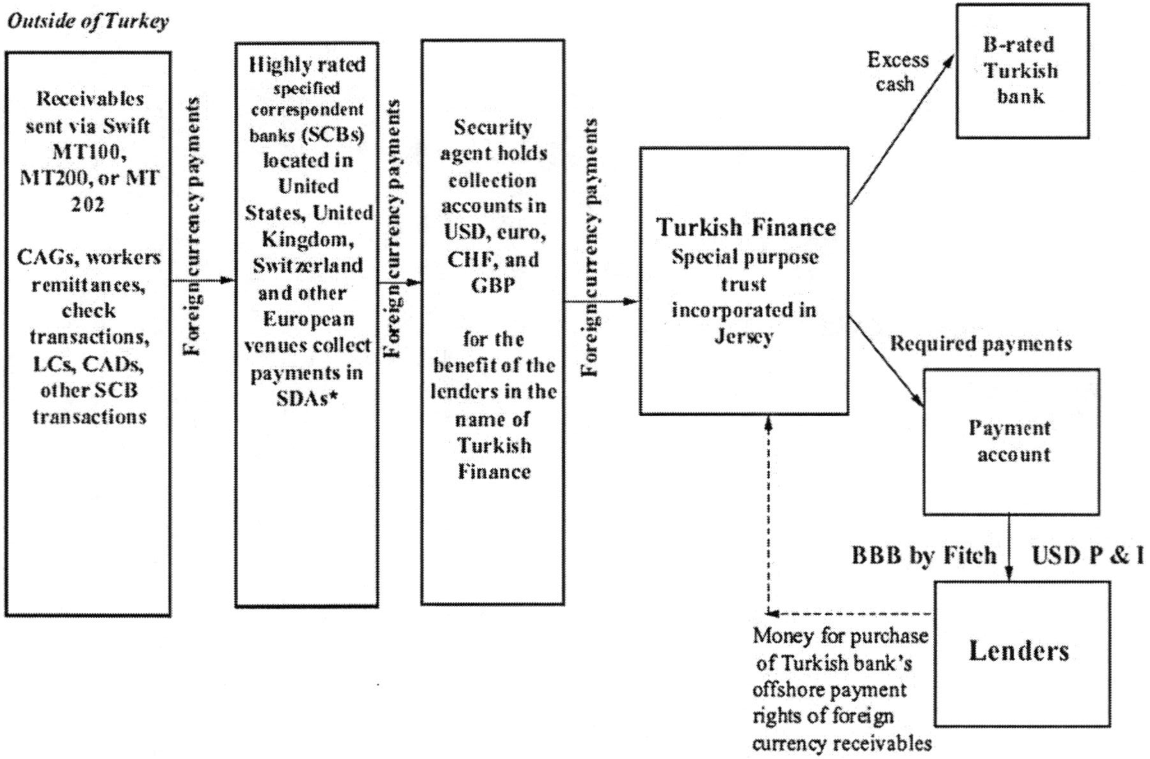

*Turkish Finance purchases Turkish bank payment rights and SCB transfers balance of SDAs to currency collection accounts.

FIGURE 15.1 Future Flows—Payment Rights Securitization

The payments never pass through Turkey or through a foreign branch of the sponsor bank located in Turkey.

The tranches of the loan facility agreement receive an investment-grade rating of BBB and are denominated in a single hard currency. In our example, the tranche payments are denominated in U.S. dollars.

The money paid for the tranches is used to buy the sponsor bank's payment rights. The sponsor bank notifies obligors of LOC, CAD, and check transactions that the payment rights have been sold to the special purpose trust, Turkish Finance, and instructs them to remit funds to an SCB. The special correspondent bank signs an acknowledgment that it will receive the funds in a specified deposit account (SDA). Since CAG transactions are completed between exporters and importers, the Turkish bank only promises to use best efforts to ask exporters to notify importers to remit payments through SCBs. This works in most of the transactions, but not all. Cash against goods transactions may require special due diligence to ensure that payments are properly remitted. Fraud is always a potential issue, especially if there is no ongoing due diligence to check on importers, exporters, and instructions made to banks from the sponsor bank. It's not clear that the rating agencies take into account the full measure of this potential risk.

My personal view is that the rating agency assessment of the political risk of deals like this should be viewed with extreme skepticism. Since rating agencies rate deals, turnabout is fair play, and investors are free to rate the rating agencies' expertise. How qualified are they to assess this risk? How secure are cash flows when payment instructions to exporters can be changed to divert cash flows to accounts other than the ones previously specified at the SCBs?

Fitch relies on three major assessments to determine the rating of these transactions.

The first consideration is whether the sponsor bank located in the emerging market country will continue to operate. Depth and breadth of management expertise is a consideration.

A second assessment is the sovereign-related risk. If there is a war, coup d'état, major law change, or other sovereign-related problem, will the structure insulate the foreign currency receivables from the reach of foreign intervention? Could a sovereign prohibit the foreign currency deposits from being transferred by the SCBs to the foreign currency collection accounts? Could the sovereign nullify the sale of the payment rights? Could the legality of the transaction be challenged in each of the foreign venues? These are questions for specialists in international law, and investors should invest some time and money to satisfy themselves on these issues. Investors should rightly demand a premium over more generic BBB tranches due to this extra documentation risk.

The third assessment is the debt service coverage ratio (DSCR). Fitch looks at the historical and potential generation of foreign currency receivables of the sponsor bank's payment rights processing business. The DSCR is calculated as follows:

DSCR = (Diversified Payment Rights Cash Flows for Time Period X) / (Single Largest Loan Debt Service Payment for Time Period X over the Deal Life)

In other words, for the time period in which the largest debt service must be made over the life of the deal, Fitch looks at the receivables and calculates the DSCR. The DSCR may vary by deal, but a DSCR of around a minimum of 15 is expected for an investment-grade rating of BBB, among other conditions.

Fitch looks for added structural protection with respect to the magnitude of the payment rights in the form of early amortization triggers. The following triggers are often included in a single securitization:

- Fall of monthly DSCR below a prespecified level.
- Fall of quarterly DSCR below a prespecified level (higher than the monthly DSCR trigger).
- Collection trigger based on a monthly rolling average.
- Annual collection trigger event.
- Audit test in which quarterly collections fall more than a prespecified percentage of the prior quarterly period or a lower preset percentage from the same quarter in the previous year.
- Specified correspondent bank events such as monthly collections from SCBs falling below a prespecified percentage of the total purchased payment rights.
- Fall of ratio of pre-export loans to the combined outstanding principal balance of the tranches, below a prespecified level.

Since future flows transactions are paper transactions, there should be some sensitivity to the possibility that documents can be falsified. If it were discovered that fraud was involved in the representation of receivables, for instance, that should be a trigger event in these deals. The type of fraud that should be of a concern is where inventories are not where they are expected to be, or paperwork has been forged.

With the caveat that investors should satisfy themselves that (1) the documentation is well-crafted, (2) international law will support the transaction, and (3) they are adequately compensated for the extra documentation risk, these deals may present opportunities for investors in the business of taking these risks. These deals tend to have short average lives. Investors with some experience in import/export businesses and in analyzing bank foreign currency receivables may find these transactions an attractive way to capture hard-currency receivables and essentially offer a collateralized loan for high spreads to emerging market banks to which they otherwise could not lend.

EMERGING MARKET CAVEATS

All of the caveats previously mentioned apply to emerging markets CDOs. How much should an investor rely upon the rating agency rating? Can a rating agency rate an emerging markets deal as competently as a corporate deal or an MBS deal? Does the BBB rating for an emerging markets CDO tranche reflect the same cash flow certainty as the BBB rating of an investment-grade rated corporate deal?

A BBB-rated tranche backed by corporate bonds will be downgraded if corporates in general are downgraded. Is ratings migration for a BBB-rated tranche backed by corporate bonds comparable to the ratings migration risk of emerging market debt?

The answer to all of these questions is no. Even if the initial BBB rating reflected exactly the same cash flow certainty, which it doesn't, the historical corporate ratings transition matrix shouldn't be used to attempt to predict ratings transitions for emerging market debt.

View these deals as separate types of risk, and let common sense and documentation be more of a guide than the rating assigned by the rating agencies.

The lack of experience and expertise with economic or political instability in a given country is a serious disadvantage to rating agencies. While Fitch feels they are taking this into account when assigning a rating for future flows deals such as the example in the previous section, the simple truth is they are guessing how severe sovereign reaction will be in times of economic or political crisis.

In the past few decades, we've seen governments turn sour fast. Some governments rise and fall based on whose gangs are more powerful. Educated people like bank managers are sometimes forced to flee for their lives. Documents are lost. Deals made before the government collapse can be nullified.

I don't mean to pick on the Republic of Turkey, but—hold on. Yes, I do, because it is a good example of how easy it is to lull ourselves into a belief that appearance is reality. Turkey has a lot going for it. Most people travel to Istanbul, and some even venture to Ankara. Bankers stay in the best hotels. The interior of a luxury hotel makes it difficult to tell what country one is staying in. Of course a country like Turkey looks well developed when viewed from the bottom of a crystal wine glass!

To its credit, parts of Turkey are better developed than many of its neighbors. Turkey is a political ally of the west. Turkish citizens elect their leaders. Turkey is progressive compared to many of its neighbors and near-neighbors. The bloody territorial disputes with Greece in the Aegean Sea and Cyprus seem to have calmed down.

It's true that the economy has been rocky in Turkey, but the International Monetary Fund (IMF) stepped in within the past year with financial support, and Turkey adopted a tighter fiscal policy and a major bank restructuring program. This was deemed necessary to maintain Turkey as a stabilizing force in this region of the world. Turkey is the global poster child for a liberal Islamic state that works.

Or is it?

Further east, some Turkish people feel they can be incarcerated without due process. The eastern road connecting Turkey to Iran is called "blood alley" because so many motorists were assaulted by roving bands of armed Turkish mountain men.

Let's not forget those friendly neighbors out east. Turkey squabbles with those even-tempered rationalists in Syria and Iraq over water development plans for the Tigris and Euphrates rivers. The skulls of 10,000 Christian-Armenian Turkish residents are decades old but attest to lingering religious and ethnic intolerance. Armenians still claim this was attempted genocide, and that the actual death toll was much higher. Today the border with Armenia remains closed over the Nagorno-Karabakh dispute.

Religious tolerance is mere lip service, but there is little to be intolerant about. The CIA estimates 99.8 percent of Turks are Sunni Moslems, and only 0.2 percent of the population are Christians or Jews. There have been rumblings among fundamentalist Islamic groups that Turkish society and government is much too liberal for their taste, and there are attempts at political reorganization which could change the character of the government if they are successful. Sitting in a luxury hotel in Ankara, life is just as sweet as it was in Iran about six months before the Shah was overthrown. It's a very western-friendly atmosphere, but the true stability is anybody's guess.

Not all governments are equal, just as some families are more functional than others. Governments that tend to concentrate power in favored factions, favored families, one favored family, or—even worse—one man, are inherently unstable, even if they aren't currently challenged. The cliché "Poor men want to be rich; rich men want to be kings; kings want to be gods," reflects a truism about human nature.

Good constitutions limit the power of monarchs. For instance, the United Kingdom is still the only European country in which its citizens are subjects of the crown as opposed to citizens of their country. Nonetheless, people in the United Kingdom have a high degree of confidence in their constitutional monarchy. The system of government has a strong system of checks and balances. Governments that administer according to rule of law are better governments for the people than governments that do not administer according to the rule of law.

But don't all governments administer by the rule of law, however unpalatable some of us may find the laws? No, of course they don't. Many governments administer by the rule of law when the law is convenient, but rule by executive fiat when the law is inconvenient.

When a government appears to administer by rule of law, one must ask how committed the government will be to the rule of law in times of stress. A key factor in the stability of a government in times of stress is the system of internal checks and balances within the government, and that means power can't be concentrated in a single branch of government.

Inequity breeds hostility.

Even in a stable constitutional republic like the United States, there was recently nonviolent spirited disagreement about the legality of a presidential election. The stabilizing factor seems to be ultimate faith in rule of law, ultimate faith in checks and balances, ultimate faith in a well-crafted constitution, and ultimate faith that the government is for the people.

U.S. citizens can laugh out loud when Michael Moore lampoons stupid white men, they can laugh in public, and they can laugh without getting incarcerated or shot. Michael Moore doesn't grow old in prison; he grows rich in freedom.

Another feature of a stable government is the separation of church and state. A feature of unhealthy government is the claim of its leaders to know the will of God. (Not true! She only talks to me!) While the SEC may not be able to arrest anyone for using this kind of inside information, the citizens of these countries don't seem to benefit. The separation of church and state is required, not to protect religion from the grasp of government; it is required to protect government from the grasp of religious fanaticism.

Nothing can ruin your investment portfolio faster than a government takeover by religious zealots, except perhaps the zealots of Long Term Capital Management. Armed with the claim that they have superior inspiration, zealots are universally crummy at managing risk.

If it sounds as if I'm encouraging you to be irreverent when evaluating ratings assigned by rating agencies, I am. Reverence has its place, and I encourage it, too. A show of reverence inspires people to explain themselves. Reverence is useful when one is attempting to gather information, attempting to understand the methodology, and attempting to better appreciate a point of view. The right time for *irreverence* is when you are evaluating the information you gathered, evaluating the methodology you understand, and evaluating the point of view you appreciate.

CONSTANT PROPORTION DEBT OBLIGATIONS AND RATING AGENCIES

During the summer of 2006, ABN AMRO's investment bank launched the Constant Proportion Debt Obligation (CPDO). This was soon followed by many look-alike products from Lehman, Calyon, and others. Early deals were targeted to yield LIBOR plus 200 bps, but no one should have been buying them, in my view. Later, the rating agencies felt they had been too aggressive, and targets were lowered to LIBOR plus 100 bps, but again, no one should have been buying them in my opinion. (Later this proved correct as it became obvious that principal losses would likely occur in the latter part of 2007.) The products were supposed to pay junk bond yields but be as safe as U.S. Treasuries. They were rated AAA by Standard & Poor's and later by Moody's. Fitch and DBRS, another rival rating agency, said these deals deserved a single-A rating at best, but this seemed to be empty contrarian posturing, because in my mind these deals did not even deserve that rating.

The CPDO was simply a leveraged bet on credit derivative indexes—a leveraged bet on credit spreads. Again, rating agencies are not well suited to assessing leveraged market risks, so the triple-A rating conveyed almost no information. Under many likely scenarios, this product had substantial principal risk.

In a February 2007 letter to the SEC, I pointed out that CPDOs generate cash by taking in premiums for selling protection on investment-grade U.S. and European credit default swap indexes, the iTraxx Europe and the Dow Jones CDX. CPDOs employ leverage, usually a maximum of 15 times, in order to boost their income. A $100 million notional initial investment would allow a CDO to make an investment up to $1.5 billion in a credit default swap index. Without these products, around $50 billion of contracts were traded in the early part of 2007. Demand created by CPDOs would more than double that volume.

These products typically invest in the Dow Jones CDX North America Investment Grade Index comprised of credit-default swaps on 125 investment-grade U.S. and Canadian companies, or in the ITraxx European index of 125 investment-grade companies. The product is not limited to these indexes, and there are a plethora of indexes that have sprung up. Some are riskier than others.

There are several challenges with this product since excess spread above what is needed to pay the promised coupon is needed to support the triple A rating. This excess reserve has to absorb defaults, if any. Default risk is mitigated, since deteriorating credits are kicked out of the indexes and the exposure is rolled over every six months. But there is also the potential of mark-to-market losses when the sold protection is rolled over into a new index series every six months. Furthermore, many investment banks charge around 2 bps each time this roll occurs. Since many CPDO managers will need to roll their trades at specific times, there is the potential for front-running by hedge funds and investment banks.

Potential losses are due to defaults or market value changes (when spreads widen). The high leverage puts investors' principal at risk since it acts as first-loss protection on the leveraged exposure to the indices. CPDOs have an extreme amount of mark-to-market and liquidity risk. The ratings volatility is likely to be very high. Potentially, investors may hold a 10-year maturity bond levered fifteen times to a five-year index. If a reference credit were to default prior to being replaced (recall the fast deterioration of names like Enron and Worldcom), however, the recovery value on CPDO would probably be much lower than the recovery value on a traditional "triple-A" rated bond, and therefore it presents more risk.

During 2006 and early 2007, these products played a significant role in driving spreads on credit derivative indices to levels so low that it is often possible to put on a profitable negative basis trade: for example, buy a bond and pay a premium on a credit derivative protecting against default while locking in a profit.

An unintended consequence of CPDOs was that fixed income pension funds that used bought protection on CDS (credit default swap) index products in 2006 were harmed. Many funds shorted a CDS index (bought credit protection) and took a long position in swap spreads to hedge their bond portfolio credit risk. Huge inflows from protection sellers, CPDO investors, who don't have to account for mark-to-market caused these spreads to narrow, and at times caused the basis to go negative, thus destroying the utility of this hedge for pension funds. CDS indexes were originally hyped as hedge instruments for credit risk, but this new development turned that theory on its head.

The SEC solicited comments on its proposed rules for oversight of the rating agencies, and my letter was the first one posted on its web site in mid-February 2007. In it I pointed out the folly of, among other things, awarding a "triple-A" rating to products like Constant Proportion Debt Obligations. I recommended the SEC revoke the Nationally Recognized Statistical Rating Organization (NRSRO) designation from the credit rating agencies with respect to structured financial products.

CONSTANT PROPORTION PORTFOLIO INSURANCE

As noted before, zero-coupon bonds embedded in financial products often lull investors into thinking they are getting a good investment because their principal appears safe. For example, if an investor has a five-year time horizon and there is a zero-coupon bond trading at 75 percent of par, the other 25 percent can be invested in very risky products. A leveraged super senior investment, for example, may be doomed to lose all or a substantial amount of its principal, but once it is embedded in a constant proportion portfolio insurance (CPPI) product and combined with a zero-coupon bond, that loss—and the inherent risk in the leveraged super senior—is not obvious.

My objection to most of these CPPI investments is lack of transparency. Most seem like parking lots for risky products designed in such a way so as to lull investors into a false sense of security. If an investor wishes to liquidate prior to maturity, there is usually a substantial principal loss involved.

Managers claim CPPI is "dynamically hedged," code words for "death by one thousand cuts." The death referred to is death of an investor's liquidity prior to maturity and death of an investor's interest earnings. Managers trotted out sophisticated models and spouted catch phrases like Geometric Brownian Motion (GBM), and other even more sophisticated models, to describe the performance of the risky portion of the investment and a constant interest for the so-called risk-free asset. The overwhelming flaw in the structures is due to the lack of common sense among the structurers, rating agencies, and sellers.

While the investor may receive the original par amount at maturity, the investor has an opportunity cost. It could have invested in T-bills and done better during that five-year time horizon, and the investor would have had liquidity, too.

MULTILINE INSURANCE PRODUCTS: DISAPPOINTMENT AND PROMISE

The market is accustomed to the timely payment of credit-enhanced cash flows by the AAA-rated monoline insurers such as Ambac, FSA, and MBIA. As we discussed earlier, JPMorgan's disappointment with the performance of surety bonds is an indication that contracts with multiline insurance companies are often not equivalent to the financial guarantees with monoline insurers, upon which structurers and investors traditionally rely. The recent disputes over claims for payment will inspire structurers to avoid using multiline insurance companies. We discuss one of the most famous, Hollywood Funding, in this chapter.

When we discussed credit derivatives, we contrasted them with insurance contracts, which are contracts of indemnity. Under a credit derivatives contract—in contrast to an insurance contract—the protection buyer does not have to sustain an actual loss in order to receive the credit protection payment once a predefined credit event has occurred. Guarantees, such as financial guarantees provided by monolines, are just that. Monoline credit enhancement has satisfied both investors and structurers with timely payment of credit-enhanced cash flows.

An insurance policy issued by a multiline insurance company, by contrast, may not assure timely or even ultimate payment of cash flows. Insurance contracts require a loss on the part of the insured, and also have several defenses against payment. Even when it appears defenses against payment are waived, disputes occur. The assurances of rating agencies and investment bankers carry no weight when investors cannot get their claims honored by the insurance providers.

Future flows deals will probably not successfully close if multiline insurance contracts are used to credit-enhance the cash flows. Recent disputes may have soured the market's appetite for this type of multiline insurance product.

Insurance companies have a variety of other structured finance products. Catastrophe-linked issuance in the property market has not lived up to its initial promise. There has been virtually no volume growth in the past five years; the annual issuance is flat at around $1 billion.

Other products such as mergers and acquisitions (M&A) enhancement and contingent capital show some potential but have yet to show they can become significant factors in the market place.

M&A enhancement is a form of transaction insurance. Insurance companies mitigate a wide variety of risks such as tax liability, successor liability, reps and warranties, and other risks that may occur. Given recent payment disputes by insurance companies, investment bankers may question whether insurance companies will challenge their obligation to pay in the event that a deal doesn't go as planned. For instance, if reps and warranties were misrepresented, would the insurance company be able to defend against payment due to fraud?

Contingent capital transactions enable investors to earn interest—enhanced by premiums—and principal for prefunding an SPE that provides contingent event protection to an insurer. If the event occurs, the insurance company gains liquidity in the form of the SPE's cash, and investors agree to accept a debt instrument that will pay them back over time. The structure may or may not be reinsured with respect to interest, principal, or both.

HOLLYWOOD FUNDING

Lexington Insurance Co., an AAA-rated insurer and wholly owned subsidiary of American International Group Inc. (AIG), issued an insurance policy to provide credit enhancement to a deal issued by an SPE named Flashpoint Inc. Flashpoint securitized future receivables from Hollywood film productions. The CDO proceeds would provide financing for the movies to be made. The SPE issued series of notes called Hollywood 1, 2, 3, 4, 5, 6, and 7. Each series was linked to specific movie projects. The receivables were supposed to be the future revenues from future movies made by Hollywood film productions. Lexington credit enhanced Hollywood Funding 4, 5, and 6 with insurance contracts. The Hollywood 4, 5, and 6 transactions were rated AAA by S&P due to Lexington's credit enhancement. Figure 15.2 is a schematic of Hollywood Funding No. 5 Ltd.

But it looks as if these films won't be made, and Lexington Capital and AIG take the view that the credit enhancement was an insurance contract, not a guarantee of timely payment of principal and interest. Since the films

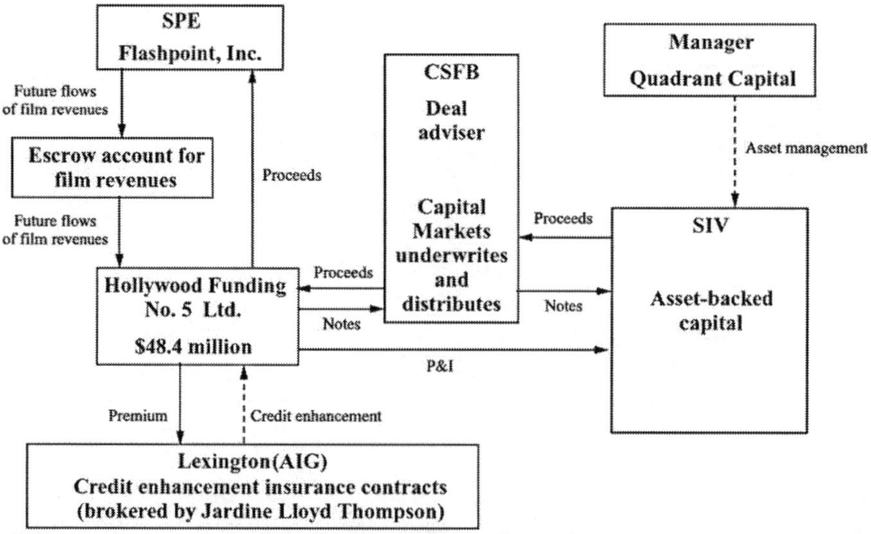

FIGURE 15.2 Hollywood Funding No. 5 Ltd.

were never made, no payment of claims is due under their interpretation of the contract.

HIH Casualty and General Insurance Ltd. provided credit enhancement for Hollywood Funding 1, 2, and 3, and they reinsured their risk—or so they thought—with AXA Re, New Hampshire Insurance, and others. These deals are the center of UK litigation. The case is *HIH Casualty and General Insurance Ltd. v. New Hampshire Insurance Company and others*. The reinsurance companies disputed HIH Casualty's and General Insurance's claims. The court ruled that breach of warranty issues, coverage issues, and fraud can properly be raised as defenses to payment. The decision is being appealed.

Lexington's case seems virtually identical. Therefore, Lexington feels confident that it has defenses to payment in its Hollywood Funding deals 4, 5, and 6. Disputes concerning Hollywood Funding 4, 5, and 6 are being litigated in the United Kingdom.

Asset-Backed Capital, managed by Quadrant Capital, is suing Credit Suisse First Boston, Jardine Lloyd Thompson, and Weil, Gotshal & Manges (the legal adviser). Asset-Backed Capital bought all of Hollywood Funding 4 and 5, and most of 6. The bond trustee is suing AIG and Lexington.

Standard & Poor's said it believes the policies are absolute and unconditional, that there are no conditions or warranties that need to be satisfied in order to draw on the policies (other than the money in the escrow account being insufficient). They believe Lexington has waived all of its defenses to payment on the policies. They further believe the policies meet the standards of the capital market for credit enhancement of financial market instruments. Nonetheless, they downgraded these deals from AAA to BB.

We've already seen several instances where a deal's rating may be a convenience, but it isn't necessarily an accurate representation of the quality of the cash flows. If there is a dispute, the rating agency will never step in to make an investor whole, no matter what rating they have placed on a security. Ratings are a convenient way to evidence that steps were taken to evaluate the cash flows, but they are entirely irrelevant when an investor is attempting to interpret whether the documentation assures he will get paid. An investor should never rely on a rating agency rating as assurance that documentation is in order. Rating agencies don't take losses; investors do.

One can't rely on the structurer or marketer to assure you that your cash flows are properly protected, either. We'll revisit this point in the next section when we look at a *transformer*.

The reasons I focused on AIG's involvement with Hollywood Funding are twofold. The key reason is that the investor is suing Lexington, and the investor is suffering the consequences of nonpayment. In the HIH case, HIH protected the investors, but reinsurance failed HIH. Since a high-profile investor has been burned in the later Hollywood deals, insurance protection will come under closer scrutiny by other investors.

A secondary reason is that it appears Lexington/AIG's defense is having repercussions for AIG's ability to bring other structured finance deals with insurance contract protection to market. In the summer of 2002, AIG postponed AIG Credit Premium Finance Master Trust Series 2002–1. The deal was backed by premium finance loans to AIG's customers—so they could spread their insurance premiums over a year—from AIG's subsidiaries. AIG had tried and failed to bring the same deal to market in April 2001.

There is tremendous confidence in the creditworthiness of AIG, but investor confidence in the specific business of credit enhancement in the form of insurance contracts is at an all-time low.

TRANSFORMERS

While monoline insurance companies such as Ambac, FSA, and MBIA seem to have mastered the art of credit wrapping to make structured finance investors feel as comfortable as if they'd bought credit default protection, the same statement isn't true for multiline insurance companies.

Many multiline insurance companies and reinsurance companies also want to participate in the credit default swap market. Several have created special purposes corporations called *transformers* to act as counterparties in credit default swap contracts. The claim is that the SPEs should pay off under the terms of the credit default swap contract in a similar fashion to credit default swaps. This product has not taken off for multiline insurance companies, however.

One well-known, well-respected American investment bank asked me to consider protection from one of their transformer vehicles. They asked if the bank I worked for would intermediate a credit default swap transaction. Requests for intermediation are common. Many banks need an OECD bank counterparty for regulatory capital purposes. If the structure is right, the intermediation fee can allow the intermediary bank to earn a reasonable return on the minimal capital required, and all parties are satisfied.

The investment bank sent over their documentation. It was a paltry two-page document, whereas monolines will send a small booklet and make their lawyers available to discuss language details. When I looked at the document, I realized that the transaction was unsuitable. Figure 15.3 shows the gist of the proposal, without embarrassing those who should be.

The investment bank assured me they would give me proper credit default swap documentation incorporating whatever language I wanted. If

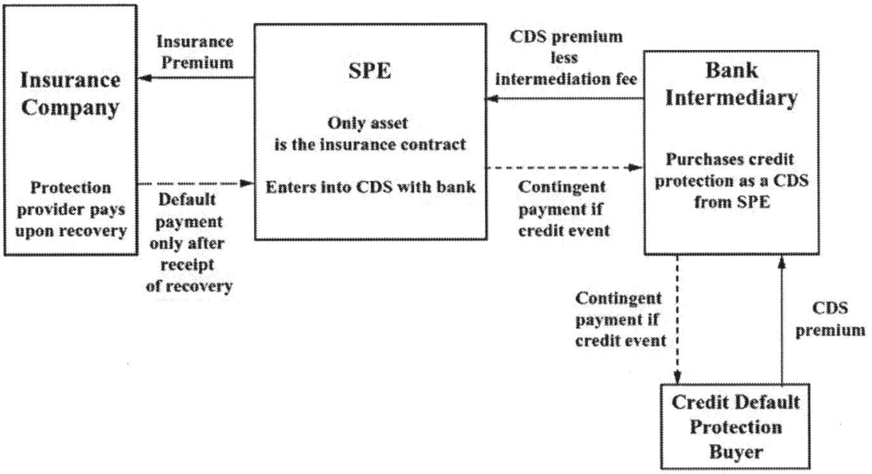

FIGURE 15.3 Transformers

a credit event occurred, the bank would look to the SPE to make payment under the terms of the credit default swap, and I could design the terms.

I declined.

The investment bank invited me to a meeting at their offices. Four tailored Armani suits or better appeared at the meeting. If life were a fashion war, the investment bankers would be winning. They were confident and took victory postures. They attempted to persuade me to do the transaction. I continued to decline. I could sense their building frustration. They couldn't understand why they weren't getting my agreement. After all, they were taller, they were louder, and they were in the majority.

So what was the problem?

I picked up a cookie—the meeting didn't have to be a total loss—and explained. I didn't want to play their shell game. The problem was that my counterparty for the credit default swap protection would have been the SPE, a shell corporation. The only asset of the SPE was an insurance contract. The SPE would only receive a credit default payment after the insurance company determined its actual recovery after taking the matter through bankruptcy proceedings. The SPE had no way of assuring timely payment under the terms of the credit default swap confirmation.

The transformer wasn't even worth the price of the child's toy of the same name for the purpose they were suggesting. Sure, the SPE would have ultimately gotten paid, and the bank would ultimately have received payment, but that wasn't the point. The point was that the SPE did not

have the
resources to perform under the terms of its transaction with the bank. It could not pay on a timely basis, no matter how cleverly crafted the credit default swap confirmation. If a credit event occurred, the bank would have to fund the credit default payment to the ultimate protection buyer until the SPE finally received its payment from the insurance company. The investment bank only offered the usual credit default swap intermediation fee, but the bank had additional risk beyond the credit default swap agreement.

It's possible that the well-dressed guys weren't aware of this until I pointed it out. The implications of that are ugly enough. But if they were aware, the implications are even uglier. I couldn't help wondering how many other counterparties they had already approached or were planning to approach. Would their counterparties look through the SPE to the ultimate obligor, the insurance company?

It is possible that other multiline insurance companies have put together sound transformer structures allowing them to provide credit default protection that stands up to the acid test of default, but the lack of growth in this product suggests otherwise.

SEC GASLIGHT ON LIFE SETTLEMENTS

On June 21, 2006, Eleanor Laise's article, "Wall Street Pushes Complex 'Structured Products,' Long Aimed at Institutions to Individuals," appeared in the *Wall Street Journal*. Laise noted how structured products were ending up in retirement portfolios and that individual investors were at a huge disadvantage when dealing with the banks and investment banks flogging these products.

Investors could not pull apart the structure into its components, price the components, and then put it back together to figure out how much they were really being charged in markup fees, which added to usually high commissions. Ms. Laise quoted me: "When I was on the sell side I loved these products because of the fees I could stuff in" them. But I was dealing only with institutional investors at the time.

Some of these products were being marketed to unsuspecting retail buyers. Sometimes financial analysts were offered large fees to recommend very risky products as holdings in retirement portfolios.

Some of these products made sense, if one didn't mind the fees, and sometimes the fees were reasonable for the convenience provided by the particular structure. For instance, an investor could have his principal protected and make a bet that the Standard & Poor's stock index would go up. The investor would get his principal back at maturity, and if the stock market went up, he would also get a payout based on how much it increased.

But there were other features that dampened the appeal. Since these structured products were often customized, it was difficult to get prices from anyone except the investment bank that originally put together the deal. The investor would have to pay commissions in addition to the fees imbedded when the note was created. The investor would have to hold on to the note until maturity or very likely suffer loss of principal. The investor had to fully understand the product, and even then, the fees could be very high.

The problem was that most financial advisers and almost all individual investors were not in a position to figure out the actual fees on these notes. Fees above and beyond commissions were easily imbedded in these notes. For instance, if the note had an imbedded option, say a call option, it gave the investor the upside of a stock index; the markup on the option could be huge, and it would be invisible to the investor. The investor might be offered a percentage point increase in value for every percent increase in the Standard and Poor's index; fair value, however, might indicate that the investor should get two percentage points increase for every percentage point increase in the Standard and Poor's index. How would an investor or a financial adviser know?

Liquidity was another potential problem. Once an individual investor bought one of these products, it was hard to resell it for a reasonable price. Even principal-protected products have unprotected principal risk when they are sold before the maturity date. Usually only the investment bank that sold it in the first place would buy it back, and it would do so only at a greatly reduced price. Other investment banks might not buy it at all, and if they did it would be at an even greater price reduction. If an investor wanted to avoid this problem, he had to be prepared to hold the note until the maturity date. But other products were not nearly as benign; some structured products were so risky and had fees so enormous that they did not belong in investors' retirement portfolios.

One proposed product using life settlements as collateral struck me as particularly problematic. In the summer of 2004, I was contacted by a purveyor of "life settlement" products. He wanted help finding a $100 million line of credit for up to three months so that he could accumulate product for a fund. He claimed a Wall Street background and that he and his boss had worked at Morgan Stanley. I checked. They had—in the early 1980s. He failed to mention their more recent exploits, however.

The salesman's last place of employment was being investigated by the Securities and Exchange Commission (SEC) for being a "Ponzi-like Scheme."

The SEC does not conduct criminal investigations; it only has civil authority in securities cases. As a result, some of the SEC's work is not widely reported in the financial press. The investigation would not hit most financial advisers' or investors' radar screens.

The salesman said his current fund was regulated by the Securities and Exchange Commission (SEC), and it was eligible for sale in all 50 states, Holland, the United Kingdom, Germany, Denmark, Sweden, Austria, Italy, and Spain. He used an investment bank's name to add credibility to his pitch. He claimed Bear Stearns had agreed to help distribute the fund to high net worth accredited investors in exchange for high fees.

The salesman claimed to be selling the rights to death benefits. Investors in the fund would get the right to the benefits from the life insurance policies taken over from terminally ill or very elderly people. He presented this as a public service: Terminally ill people and the very old often needed money, and the fund would pay cash up front to these people. The fund would also continue paying the premiums on the policies. And when the original policyholders died, the fund would collect the death benefits. In the meantime, investors would get a coupon payment of 8 percent. Or so the salesman claimed.

These deals were called *viaticals* or life settlements, and they were originally popularized years ago as a way for AIDS sufferers to raise much-needed cash near the end of their lives. For a fraction of the ultimate payout, viatical buyers bought the right to collect on the AIDS patient's life insurance policy, and AIDS patients got instant cash to pay their bills. This was a way for AIDS patients to monetize policies for more money than they otherwise could have gotten, and for investors to access a lucrative new asset class. It was a win-win for everyone.

But predicting when someone is going to die, or even whether the life insurance policy was legitimate in the first place, is very tricky. If you buy the life insurance benefit, it is in your interest for the original policyholder to die sooner rather than later.

What if people stubbornly refused to die? What if they recovered or enjoyed an extraordinarily long life? Not only would the investor have to hand over the up-front cash payment; he would also have to continue the policy premiums. Juan Espina, lead senior risk analyst at the Federal Home Loan Bank in Chicago, joked: "I wonder if the buyers of these securities get the disclosure of the policyholder's address as collateral. Sounds like a business model to be run by the Sopranos."

On top of this risk, the fund managers were charging extraordinarily high fees and commissions. Investors could find that not only would their entire investment be quickly exhausted, they might be asked for even more money to continue the premium payments.

If the life insurance policies were in any way problematic or even worse, falsified, there might not even be a payout on the policies. While life settlements were growing in popularity, their reputation was tarnished. Scam artists sold fake insurance policies. Fraudsters faked illnesses. And there was the potential for cash flow manipulation to make faked life settlements appear to be a profitable investment when they were not. The entire fund could devolve into a "Ponzi-like Scheme."

The persistent salesman pointed out that the life settlements were securitized into a fund that was registered with the SEC, and the documents for his product were on the SEC web site. Unfortunately, statements like this could lead an investor to believe that the SEC has conferred some credibility to a product. This simply isn't true. Almost anyone can get their documents placed on the SEC web site, since there is very little fact checking done by the SEC before posting them. It is incredibly easy to exploit the appearance that the SEC has in some way sponsored a deal: One can be lulled into a false sense of security just because a salesman or financial adviser invokes the name of the Securities and Exchange Commission.

The SEC does not opine on whether an investment is too risky for a high net worth individual who meets the test of being an accredited investor. As long as appropriate disclosure has been made, the investor has to decide how much risk to take. The SEC steps in only if it can allege an actual violation of securities laws.

The proposed product was extremely risky. The fees for were around 12.5 percent up front. The CEO had no prior experience with these products, and the prior experience he did have included a former fund now under the cloud of an SEC investigation.

There were conflicts between the fund, the manager, the life settlements provider, and the underwriter. These conflicts included non-arm's-length agreements and payments of substantial fees and expenses. The manager had a fee incentive that could result in the recommendation of more risky investments, and the investment strategies could be changed at any time without the investors' consent. If that weren't enough risk, the investors would also have to pay premiums once the fund's money was exhausted. This meant investors could lose their entire investment and still owe more money. Investors had a lot of principal risk if they sold before maturity, but if the insurance policies could not cover fees and returns, the picture was even bleaker. *Investors could lose more than their initial investment.*

Although the stated target was for an 8% return, there was no limit to an investor's risk. Not only could investors have zero income; they could lose all of the money they invested. Worse than that, they could be called on for even more money.

The documents stated that only accredited investors as defined by Regulation D of the Securities Act of 1933 would be offered these securities, and they should not invest money that they needed to live on. Accredited investors are not hard to find. Banks, savings and loans, and most investment companies qualify. Most trusts with more than $5 million in assets and partnerships also qualify as accredited investors. Anyone with a net worth, including the value of real estate, in excess of $1 million qualified. If one's net worth were not that high, but one had income greater than $200,000 for the past two years and expected the same this year, one could qualify as an accredited investor. Many retirement plans, including employee benefit plans, Keogh plans, and IRAs met the test of an accredited investor.

I shared my concerns with the president of the investment bank the salesman mentioned. My concerns were bad news to the investment bank's president, too. Contrary to the salesman's representations, the investment bank's president said: "There are lots of people peddling this idea and it's extremely unlikely that we will do anything with any of them, so I appreciate knowing who's dropping our name."

The technique employed by the salesman—selectively mentioning that his background was Wall Street, the posting of his fund's prospectus on the SEC web site—is known as *gaslighting* (probably after *Gaslight,* the psycho-thriller movie starring Ingrid Bergman and a conniving Charles Boyer). The trick is to attempt to put the target at a psychological disadvantage to make them more pliable and easily controlled.

Many people fall for this ruse, and Matt Goldstein later wrote about a series of subsequent life settlement scams in a detailed cover story for *BusinessWeek* ("Death Bonds: Profiting from Mortality," July 30, 2007).

SPECIAL PURPOSE ACQUISITION COMPANIES

Special purpose acquisition companies (SPACs) are investment vehicles in which investors put in cash and allow managers to employ the money as they see fit for acquisitions. This term usually applies to private equity investments, but the lines are blurry. The character of the manager is paramount since investors are giving the manager a blank check without knowing in advance the target companies.

Many corporations have an element of being a SPAC in that shareholders trust management to have the company's best interests at heart when contemplating an acquisition (or a merger). In some cases that trust is well placed and in others it is not.

Even when management is trustworthy, the investment may be very risky. Chrysler is an example of a conventional corporation that received a huge injection of private equity investment after Cerberus bought it out. Payment-in-kind (PIK) bonds allow the principal balance to increase rather than forcing the company to make interest payments. The only thing between Chrysler and technical bankruptcy at the end of 2007 was a $10 billion investment, because Chrysler said it was operationally bankrupt.

If management's interests are not aligned with investors due to lopsided compensation structures, for example, that trust may not be well placed. But if management's interests are obviously aligned with those of its shareholders—Berkshire Hathaway is the gold standard in that category—that trust is warranted. (Disclosure: I own shares of Berkshire Hathaway, BRKA.)

Chapter 16

Credit Funds

CREDIT HEDGE FUNDS

Limited purpose finance corporations (LPFCs) and convertible bond funds have been in existence for decades. While these funds deal with credit, for the purposes of this section, I do not consider them credit hedge funds and focus instead on more recent funds that aggressively make bets on credit across many sectors. Aggressive credit hedge funds are a more recent product having sprung into existence a few years into this century. As of this writing, these funds are based in London, the United States, and Switzerland: venues that are friendlier to this activity.

Funds that trade only in correlation are also viewed as credit hedge funds. Funds that invest in tranches of CDOs levering the position are also viewed as credit hedge funds. I would not consider convertible arbitrage funds as credit hedge funds for the purposes of this section, but Magnetar, a leveraged structured credit fund, would be viewed as a credit hedge fund.

Many funds have limited mandates, employ little leverage, and invest cash in high-yield and emerging market debt. Other credit hedge funds often have a broad mandate ranging from cross-currency transactions on credits to credit plays within the same sector—for example, trading Citibank versus JPMorgan Chase. Often these funds use total return swaps to engage in leveraged structured credit transactions. As we saw with single-tranche transactions, hedge funds may engage in correlation trades, going long the equity of a CDO while shorting the mezzanine tranche. Likewise, credit derivatives or total return swaps may be used to make leveraged bets on leveraged loans.

One of the attractions of the credit derivatives market on slices of risk linked to an index of corporate credits is that often hedge funds could generate fast income while the payment for risks is largely deferred.

While most of these funds use a multitude of strategies, what this usually means is they will make bets wherever they are allowed to use leverage and get access to a fast stream of cash flows. Skill is not an overriding requirement.

Hedge funds specializing in structured credit fueled the recent credit bubble and, along with investment banks that allowed them to use leverage against these products, became participants in the credit crunch as unwitting investors on the other side of hedge fund trades lost money.

HEDGE FUNDS AND STRUCTURED CREDIT

For example, at the latter part of 2005, a hedge fund could participate in the risk of a 100-name investment-grade corporate index when the market believed that implied correlation was relatively low at 20 to 30 percent, so that income was distributed more to the upper tranches than to the first-loss piece.

These structures do not pretend to follow any type of ratings or subordination guidelines. Synthetic indexes serve as reference portfolios and are cut up as percentages. Investment banks often created their own customized index of names, presumably because they badly needed to offload the risk of a few of the names imbedded in the index. If one accepted the risk of the first 0 to 3 percent of the index to default, one did not get paid much up front, but if one accepted the risk of the first 0 to 10 percent of the deal to default, one could get paid a premium as high as 90 percent of the notional amount for high-yield debt if one took on risk for a five-year time horizon. Investment-grade names would pay 85 to 88 percent. Often funds did this transaction with very little fundamental credit analysis of the underlying names. The up-front premium was a huge cash injection that was extremely attractive to hedge funds.

Other bespoke structures allowed hedge funds to receive "two times recovery," so if recovery were 50 percent or greater, the hedge fund would have no loss. An investment bank would include 80 to 100 unequally weighted names. The hedge fund would post the up-front premium as collateral and get paid LIBOR plus a spread as interest on the collateral.

Some hedge funds claimed to invest in "highly rated" structured credit products and employed leverage to boost returns, at least temporarily. The ill-fated funds managed by Bear Stearns Asset Management discussed in Chapter 8 are two examples.

Hedge funds started talking about the difference between default risk and spread risk and created models to try to capture the difference between what was essentially market risk and ultimate default risk. Using very little fundamental credit analysis, hedge funds created new tea leaves to read the market and felt safe as long as enough of them believed in the tea leaves.

Most of these funds called themselves correlation funds, and investment banks seemed happy to pay them up-front premiums and to extend credit so the hedge funds could leverage their positions.

IO AND PO TRANCHES: JUNIOR TRANCHES AND EQUITY OIDS

In 2006 and 2007, investment banks had a difficult time selling the first-loss risk of CDOs backed by subprime and other risky mortgage collateral. Hedge funds received an added inducement. An interest-only/principal-only (IO/PO) structure for the junior tranches was developed. A hedge fund could put up only 5 percent of the value of the preferred shares, which were issued as an original issue discount (OID). This meant that the bond would accrue to par (or a pre-agreed discount from par), and defaults would be deducted from the final payment. Since the collateral was very risky, the hedge fund was almost certain not to receive a further payment.

The inducement for agreeing to lose the 5 percent up-front payment was the right to purchase the IO tranche. The hedge fund made a small up-front payment of 5 percent for the right to excess interest spread on the deal. There was an incentive to stuff the portfolio with risky collateral that threw off a lot of interest. There were many variations on this theme. Sometimes the IO tranche had a double-digit cap of, say, 12 percent, which made it appear to investors that the IO tranche had a limited benefit. Elsewhere in the prospectus, an alert investor might find that both the IO and PO tranches would begin receiving principal payments a few months after the deal closed. In this way a hedge fund could receive a very fast payout on a small initial investment, since both the IO and PO tranches were largely unfunded.

Specialized hedge funds also rushed into bespoke CDO-squared tranches. When backed by mezzanine tranches of subprime-backed CDOs, the portfolios are high yielding, risky, and overrated. In other words, this is only a good deal for a hedge fund going long the equity, short the mezzanine tranches, and grabbing rights to as much excess spread as possible. It is a lousy deal for every other investor in the CDO-squared. These deals are private placements that should only be sold to sophisticated investors.

LIMITED PURPOSE FINANCE CORPORATIONS

As of January 2008, only the Sigma and Theta funds managed by Gordian Knot had been designated as limited purpose finance corporations (LPFCs). The rating agencies created this classification in 2007 to distinguish them from structured investment vehicles (see the next section). The Sigma and Theta funds have zero subprime, zero Alt-A, and zero home equity loan investment. Predictably, these well-managed funds had zero exposure to the subprime mortgage market, and for years the managers of these funds turned down overrated deals.

Limited purpose finance corporations are offshore special purpose entities set up to invest in assets and issue notes at a funding cost low enough to enable the manager of the vehicle to earn an arbitrage. The first credit arbitrage fund of this type was Alpha Finance, established in the 1980s by the founders of Gordian Knot, who worked for Citibank at the time. Initially many banks confused them with hedge funds and were reluctant to extend credit lines. Once the credit and investment constraints were better understood, these vehicles were able to issue AAA-rated paper, and a downgrade would trigger a program unwind. These vehicles have produced triple-digit spreads over LIBOR for their equity investors, and equity investors have never experienced a loss.

After the demise of Long Term Capital Management, it was clear that selling impaired assets into a distressed market could be punitive, and sound assets could also trade poorly due to temporary lack of demand. Gordian Knot improved on the original structure by eliminating market value unwind triggers for the Sigma and Theta funds, recognizing that a forced liquidation into a nervous market could force a well-structured fund to sell sound assets at disadvantageous prices.

The emergence of structured investment vehicles (SIVs) has jeopardized the ability of these funds to raise money as easily as they did in the past. This is not because of any change in strategy of these LPFCs but is due to market nervousness over SIVs that promised safety but did not produce it. It is a case of mistaken identity.

The idea is that the diversity of the LPFC's portfolio of assets makes this a very low-risk strategy for the equity investors yet allows them to benefit from a carefully controlled leveraged investment. At least, this is the conventional understanding of LPFC used in the marketplace.

An LPFC is an SPE that is a limited liability corporation incorporated in the Cayman Islands. The SPE engages in the activities of an investment company within proscribed parameters. Gordian Knot conducts the investment activities of the SPE.

Program credit enhancement is provided by capital raised in the market. The SPE's capital (commonly understood as equity) consists of pari passu A shares and B shares (preferred shares) and capital notes denominated in a variety of currencies. The ratio of issued and paid-up capital to investments under management is on the order of 1 to 10 ($2 billion for $20 billion under management). Prime-1 rated bank liquidity facilities and liquid investment assets provide the necessary liquidity.

Optimization programs define the investment criteria. The LPFC has constraints on credit quality, maturity, portfolio diversification, asset-to-liability maturity gap, and liquidity eligibility. The LPFC purchases a portfolio of high-grade assets, vetted by the managers, generally with an average AA credit quality, and is allowed to lever AA-rated investments up to around eight times. The gearing is adjusted for the rating of specific assets.

There is a material difference between LPFC management that reviews the underlying credit quality of its assets, irrespective of ratings, and SIV management that has little understanding of credit. An SIV sometimes employs leverage for the sake of leverage up to the maximum amount allowed based on a nominal credit rating. An LPFC poses little risk in a normal market environment, while the SIV structure poses significant risk. In fact, SIVs helped destabilize the credit markets during the recent credit bubble and almost derailed LPFCs.

STRUCTURED INVESTMENT VEHICLES

Like LPFCs, structured investment vehicles are offshore SPEs set up to invest in assets and issue notes at a low funding cost. Some SIVs are well-run, but all of them experienced a credit crunch as investors shunned debt issued by all structured investment vehicles. Well-run entities scrambled to educate investors on the quality of their assets.

The first synthetic SIV was launched in 2002, but earlier SIVs often allowed the use of credit derivatives. The attraction of credit derivatives is to allow the SIV to take advantage of the fact that CDS spreads are often wider for the same credit risk than those in the capital markets. An added attraction is that there are often periods of high volatility and extraordinary widening, such as in the fall of 2002. Capitalizing on spread widening is a matter of luck and timing.

So-called SIV-lites sprang up beginning around 2005. These vehicles issued short-term asset-backed commercial paper while investing in longer-dated triple-A paper. The problem for many of them is that many of the assets were overrated. Therefore, the triple-A ratings assigned to the SIV-lites were also incorrect. Many of the assets backing the SIVs' commercial paper issuance were subprime CDO tranches. In July 2007, Henry Tabe of Moody's wrote that SIVs were "an oasis of calm" just as the CDO market began to panic and mark down subprime-backed assets. Moody's said it expected SIV ratings to remain stable. After all, he reasoned, they invested in triple-A and double-A rated debt. Yet the rating agencies were starting to downgrade the underpinnings of many of the assets in which the SIVs invested.

The market gradually lost faith in the ratings of the underlying assets, and the SIV-lites were unable to find enough new investors when their asset-backed commercial paper matured. Unable to roll their liabilities, they had to draw on liquidity lines provided by various financial institutions. Affiliated banks began bringing SIVs and SIV-lite assets on balance sheet.

CREDIT DERIVATIVE PRODUCT COMPANIES

Unlike an SIV, a credit derivative product company (CDPC) does not use a funding arbitrage and does not have to post collateral or meet a mark-to-market test. A CDPC typically limits itself to triple-A product. The risk to a CDPC is chiefly that its portfolio may experience a downward migration of credit ratings. Since they can employ leverage as high as 85×, the triple-A rating of these entities can quickly erode when ratings decline.

Primus Financial Products, LLC (2004), an independent subsidiary of Primus Guaranty Ltd., and Athilon (2005) were the first credit derivative product companies. They were set up as structured finance companies intending to sell protection on highly rated underlying credits. Babson Capital Management was the second-largest manager of CDOs and part of Massachusetts Mutual Life Insurance, followed by Invicta Credit LLC, intending to write protection on collateralized debt obligations. Deutsche Bank and Axa Investment Managers created NewLands Financial CDPC, also intending to write protection on CDOs. Aladdin Financial Products and Deerfield Capital also started entities.

Key to the early success of these entities was securing triple-A ratings from two of the top rating agencies. For example, Primus Financial is rated Aaa/AAA by Moody's and S&P. Many of them sought to write protection on low-spread, low-risk, highly-rated tranches of CDOs via the credit derivatives market. Higher spreads for junior were attainable in the cash market, but that required funding. If it were not for the creation of super senior tranches and various grades of synthetic junior triple-A tranches, these entities might not exist. In many ways, they compete with the monoline financial guarantors. CDPCs also write single-name credit default protection.

Incredibly, by late 2005, Primus Guaranty said it was interested in reference entities that were not actively traded, viewing this as an opportunity. It intended to sell protection in subinvestment-grade credits and subinvestment-grade tranches. It declared it had sold protection on two tranches that offered very attractive premiums and risk-adjusted returns.

This probably related to either up-front premium structures or partially funded excess spread structures, but Primus did not elaborate.

Primus Financial Products said it would also begin selling credit swaps on ABSs, identifying it as a high-growth sector. Primus also intended to get into the synthetic CDO management business. Primus thought CDSs of ABSs offer very good risk-adjusted returns, yet hedge funds such as Paulson and Co. shorted that market as soon as the indexes became available to easily do so in the early part of 2006. However, most of Primus Financial Products' business was writing protection on highly rated single name corporate credits.

By early 2007, Moody's had proposals for 24 CDPCs awaiting ratings. Some of those who did not get ratings might feel relieved they did not. By the end of 2007, Primus had $20.4 billion in credit default swaps, of which $3.7 billion were against tranches of AA-rated non-mortgage-related products. Primus had only $80 million in contracts tied to mortgage securities, but 19 percent of the underlying ABSs had been downgraded to non-investment-grade. Primus was having difficulty selling new debt, and it shut down a newly launched hedge fund. Primus also said that further downgrades could trigger a technical default. Primus joined a list of insurers having difficulty raising capital, but as of the end of 2007, it still had sufficient capital to do future business with its ratings intact.

HEDGE FUNDS AND COLLATERALIZED FUND OBLIGATIONS

How does one evaluate investments in hedge funds as collateral for a CDO? How does one tranche and rate the CDO?

Fund of funds managers are issuers of collateralized fund obligations (CFOs). A fund of funds is a pool of hedge fund interests chosen by the manager. The collateral is a diversified portfolio of hedge fund securities. CFOs are actively managed, market-value CDOs. Obviously, the experience and track record of the manager is key to a successful launch of a CFO.

Moody's and Fitch rate these deals. Since the hedge fund strategies vary so much, the key to the ratings is the CFO's structural protections. That makes sense, but a key issue is the degree of structural protection required to make the ratings pari passu with more conventionally understood CDO structures. It's a guess, but the rating agencies are attempting to make it a more informed guess. CFOs incorporate many of the structural features of other CDOs, but the following are uniquely characteristic of CFOs.

The unrated equity tranches of these deals tend to be much greater in size than even the equity tranches of high-yield-backed CBOs. Equity subordination is often 30 percent and higher, and AAA tranches make up only about 40 to 45 percent of the deal.

CFOs must maintain a specified advance rate, which is expressed as the percentage of debt versus the market value of the underlying assets. The CFO will also have a volatility test. If the volatility on a rolling 12-month calculation exceeds a preset threshold, or if volatility exceeds a preset threshold for three consecutive months, the CFO must pass overcollateralization tests based on a second set of advance rates. CFO assets are marked to market monthly, and the advance rate is recalculated to see if the deal is in compliance. Just as one might expect, the cure is either to inject more cash collateral, redeem hedge funds, or reduce leverage by paying down tranches in order of seniority.

CFOs also have collateral quality tests (CQTs) with cures similar to that of the advance rate. Losses in excess of around 15 percent will usually start triggering CQTs. The overcollateralization test is a deleveraging trigger and requires the net asset value (NAV) times the advance rate to be greater than the remaining principal amount plus accrued and certain other senior liabilities (for instance, hedge costs, if applicable). If the overcollateralization test fails, the manager will have to switch some investments to cash (if possible at a profit to increase NAV), add capital, or delever until the deal passes the CQT.

The minimum net worth test is an unwind trigger in the extreme scenario. The CFO must exceed the prespecified minimum net worth requirement or else it must inject additional capital. If additional capital injection sufficient to pass the test isn't possible, the deal must be liquidated.

The manager is usually happy to retain the leveraged equity portion. Leverage and the cheaper funding available in the CDO market (versus prime brokers) make this a very interesting investment. Outright hedge funds might also be interested in the equity tranche, particularly if they could find a friendly bank arranger to finance the purchase. It would be the ideal hedge fund product: leverage upon leverage with financing to create further leverage.

Chapter 17

The Credit Crunch and CDOs

RATING AGENCIES, REGULATORS, AND JUNK SCIENCE

NRSRO stands for Nationally Recognized Statistical Rating Organization. Moody's, Standard and Poor's, and Fitch were the key rating agencies participating in rating collateralized debt obligations, yet they failed to follow basic statistical principals. When the SEC solicited comments for its proposed rules for the Credit Rating Agencies, mine was the first letter it posted on its web site in February 2007. I recommended the SEC revoke the NRSRO designation for the rating agencies with respect to rating structured finance transactions.

Statistics is the mathematical study of the probability and likelihood of events. Known information can be taken into account, and likelihoods and probabilities are inferred by taking a statistical sampling.

One would expect that the rating agencies can be relied upon to apply generally recognized statistical concepts when assigning ratings based on the data presented to them, but that is not always the case. *Notching*—arbitrarily lowering the rating of securities rated by other rating agencies in pools of securitized assets—is one example. The NRSROs do not wish to recognize each other's ratings. Far from an attempt to employ nationally recognized statistical methods, notching is simply arbitrary junk science. There is little accountability or independent outside auditing of the soundness or consistency of rating agency methodologies with respect to statistical principles.

Considering subprime mortgage loans, for example, a statistical sampling of the underlying loans should be taken and key characteristics should be verified: integrity of the documentation, verification of the identity of the borrower, existence of and verification of the appraisal of the property, ability of the borrower to repay the loan, and so on (see also Chapter 8). Yet rating agencies were content to rate securitizations containing risky mortgage loans without making sure they had the proper data to do it. Given their rich history of failures, they can hardly claim they did not have reason to rethink their processes.

Ratings of CDOs employed financial junk science: a combination of financial astrology, financial alchemy, and financial phrenology. Using old data for new risky mortgage products amounted to astrology; subordination and credit enhancement requirements were alchemists' guesses; and evaluating no-name managers without asking for evidence of thorough background checks was the equivalent of financial phrenology.

In defending their practices, rating agencies oddly claim for themselves exemptions from scientific testing. Past failures such as the Commercial Financial Services debacle are waved aside, even though it provided evidence of flawed methodologies. Moody's went so far as to attempt to convince me of the "validity" of its notching methodology by admitting to no higher authority than itself for the validity of its assertions. The analysis it provided in no way proved its assertions, as if it expected unquestioning agreement of its nonsense essentially because "Moody's says so." Standard and Poor's and Fitch essentially take the same approach when they are challenged. Dogma has replaced science as the prerogative of the ratings cartel.

The Bank for International Settlements (BIS), the Federal Reserve Bank, the Securities and Exchange Commission, and many investors have created what Arturo Cifuentes, a ratings guru, calls "a dangerous regulatory environment." They rely on ratings labels instead of fundamental credit analysis of value to replace informed decision making. The financial markets pose enough risk factors without making up new ones. (See also Chapter 5.)

Part of the reason that the BIS, the Fed, and the SEC have been so quick to hang their hats on flawed methodologies is that these institutions are chiefly made up of economists and, in the case of the SEC, of lawyers. I do not expect lawyers to be rigorous in their analysis, but one could expect more of the BIS and the SEC. While there is such a thing as *junk economics*, economics itself is not considered a science. That does not mean, however, that economists can allow the lack of rigor that pervades their field to seep into other fields. Yet, by relying on the lax standards set by the rating agencies, this is what they have allowed to happen. The rating agencies have created a junk science out of their process and have abandoned the rigors of statistical principles.

Rating agencies insist they do not perform due diligence for investors; they merely provide an opinion. In legal battles involving ratings on asset-backed securitizations, rating agencies have successfully claimed journalist-like privileges to avoid turning over notes and analyses produced during the rating process. Independent organizations exist that will perform rigorous reviews and audit tests for placement agents, and their reviews go well beyond what rating agencies will do. However, even they must be instructed by underwriters and investors as to the extent of appropriate due diligence.

My own view is that for structured products, the NRSRO designation should be revoked since the rating agencies have failed to adhere to basic statistical principles. For example, in the mortgage debacle, the rating agencies are part of the problem, but demonizing the rating agencies deflects attention from other culprits in the mortgage market, and it ignores the fact that the rating agencies issue opinions, albeit those opinions are often ill-informed.

It sometimes seems to me that the rating agencies charge a quarter for a nickel's worth of work. I believe they were lax in not sufficiently adjusting data applicable to saner underwriting standards and sounder mortgage products to newly lowered underwriting standards and risky products. For instance, it is difficult to ignore the negative potential of a product like stated-income loans—for which borrowers disclose their income with no verification. While I find the rating agencies' shortcomings exasperating, they did not instigate the subprime problem.

While rating agencies fees' for rating structured products are high relative to the quality of their work, they are now forced to rerate products for very little compensation. Their original fees are much less than those charged by investment banks (which are often more than 20 times what the rating agencies make) for structuring and selling the securitizations. Investment banks and banks that extended credit lines to irresponsible, undercapitalized mortgage bankers bear much more responsibility for the debacle. The underwriters and sophisticated investors are obliged to perform due diligence appropriate to the circumstances, and they were in a good position to question the ratings. Many credible people were public about their dissatisfaction with the mortgage loan market and the ratings. Historical problems with ratings were well publicized.

SAVVY INVESTORS IGNORE RATINGS

The savviest investors, especially those managing their own money, were quick to discard ratings, except when they wanted to short a sector due to distortions partially fueled by misrated products.

John Calamos Sr., chairman and CEO of Calamos Investments, addressed the University of Chicago's Finance Roundtable in March 2007. Mr. Calamos mortgaged his house to start his eponymous funds and did not seek outside money. The funds have won 30 Lipper awards for excellence. The funds' initial focus was convertible bond arbitrage, and he is one of the world's largest convertible bond managers. If an interesting company is not issuing convertibles, it will synthesize its own.

Initially, Mr. Calamos tried using Moody's and S&P ratings as benchmarks, and according to him, they "got smoked" a couple of quarters. After that unpleasant experience, they set up their own credit models and use their own models to the exclusion of ratings. His experience is not unique. Some of the most skilled investors in the world ignore the rating agencies, and, as we saw in Chapter 8, hedge funds actively shorted misrated products using synthetic indexes.

In Chapter 13, I mentioned the rating agencies' failure to address the pseudo AAA tranches created in deals that have super senior tranches. I also mentioned a deal in which Standard & Poor's (S&P) required less subordination than Moody's to award an AAA rating. Naturally, the arranger preferred to rate the deal with S&P. Many securitization professionals pay careful attention to the rating agencies, but not for a wholesome reason; it is because they find it useful to shop the rating agencies.

The rating agencies' role with respect to rating securitizations has become a necessary tick on a checklist and serves to facilitate the investment banking process of bringing deals to market. The robustness of securitization ratings from an investor's point of view is unreliable across asset classes and at times even across deals. Furthermore, ratings of synthetic securitizations employing leverage are nearly meaningless due to the fact that the primary risks are market risks influenced by supply and demand forces, and credit ratings are wholly insufficient to evaluate that risk. Investment-grade ratings, even AAA investment-grade ratings, should not lull the SEC, investors, and other financial industry professionals into an unwarranted sense of safety.

MISFORTUNE'S FORMULA: STRUCTURED CREDIT RATINGS

The rating agencies protest they are misunderstood rather than miscalculating when it comes to rating structured products. They claim the market misapplies ratings by expecting ratings to indicate market price and liquidity, but the former are merely symptoms of the real problem. When it comes to structured products—in particular those involving asset-backed securitizations and collateralized debt obligations (CDOs)—the rating agencies have failed to apply the most basic of statistical principals: One must take reasonable steps to understand the character of the risk one is modeling.

Rating agencies point out that the deal sponsors and investment bank underwriters are responsible for due diligence. Although the rating agencies do not perform due diligence for investors, they can demand evidence that proper due diligence has been performed before attempting to apply their respective ratings methodologies. In fact, sound practice of statistics requires them to do so.

For example, with respect to securitizations of mortgage loans, the consequences of the unwholesome mix of lax underwriting standards and new risky loan products combined with varying degrees of overreaching, predatory lending, real estate speculation, and outright fraud were easily foreseeable. As stated earlier, the negative potential of a product like stated-income loans, in which no verification is made of the income the borrower claims, should be obvious. The ratings agencies should not have accepted broad information about the collateral underlying these securities, especially as this is provided by the issuers and investment banks, both interested parties in ensuring that the ratings across the CDO structure are as high as possible.

Figure 17.1 shows how quickly a securitization of simple collateral like residential mortgage-backed securities can become opaque. In Chapter 8, we saw how residential mortgage loans were securitized into residential mortgage-backed securities. These securities were then sold as different rated

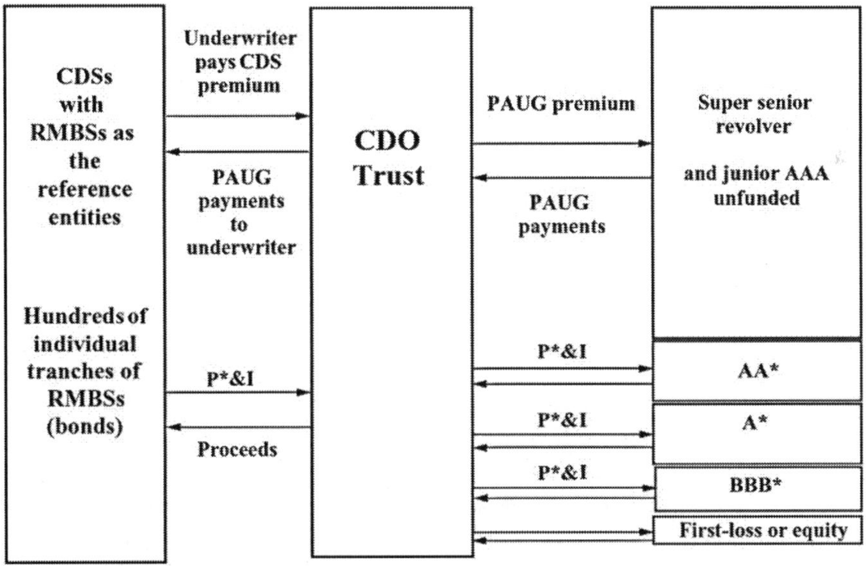

*These are usually funded notes, but the first-loss tranche and some junior tranches may be unfunded.

FIGURE 17.1 Typical Hybrid CDO Backed by Subprime RMBSs

tranches based on the cash waterfall of the capital structure. That may have seemed like more than enough complication for even sophisticated investors. Securitization did not stop there, however. Tranches of these residential mortgage-backed securities were then further securitized as cash assets or as reference assets for credit default swaps used as collateral for mortgage-backed collateralized debt obligations called hybrid CDOs.

The rating agencies could have—and should have—asked issuers and investment bank underwriters to demonstrate that they had performed a statistical sampling and verification of underlying loans in the proposed portfolios. This includes independent checks of appraisals, checks that mortgages have not been missold, background checks of mortgage brokers, background checks on mortgage lenders, background checks of CDO managers, verification that the homeowner can cope with the reset when a teaser period comes to an end, and income verification on stated-income loans.

The rating agencies underestimated default probabilities, underestimated loss given default, and overly relied on historical data when assigning ratings. In a repeat of past mistakes, the basis of the analysis was flawed, and the amount of protection required to award the various ratings was insufficient at the outset.

These errors compound when tranches of securitizations with flawed ratings are used as collateral in other CDOs. From the start, AAA-rated tranches of these deals showed the possibility of significant principal loss.

Figure 17.2 shows an example of a synthetic CDO-squared. Tranches of CDOs and sometimes CDO-squared tranches are used as reference assets for credit default swaps. In some cases, the underwriter of the CDOs is also the sole buyer of the credit default protection. The credit default swaps can be custom-made contracts using nonstandard language. This is an extremely risky and illiquid product that holds the investor hostage to the original underwriter of the CDO collateral used in the portfolio. Moral hazard and conflicts of interest abound. This is so opaque that it is impossible for a third party to accurately price tranches of these deals. The ratings on these deals are virtually meaningless, except for the clear indication that these deals were overrated and overpriced. These are troubled deals. It is difficult to understand how rating agencies defended their initial ratings. They pointed to their flawed models, asking to be excused for flawed common sense.

The problem is magnified further when hedge funds apply leverage to these products, virtually guaranteeing eventual disaster. Flawed products purchased at par with the use of leverage are on a one-way trip down net asset value's slippery slope. Yet rating agencies handed out AAA ratings on vehicles like structured investment vehicle lites, also known as SIV-lites. These vehicles employed short-term financing on long-dated assets that had flawed ratings.

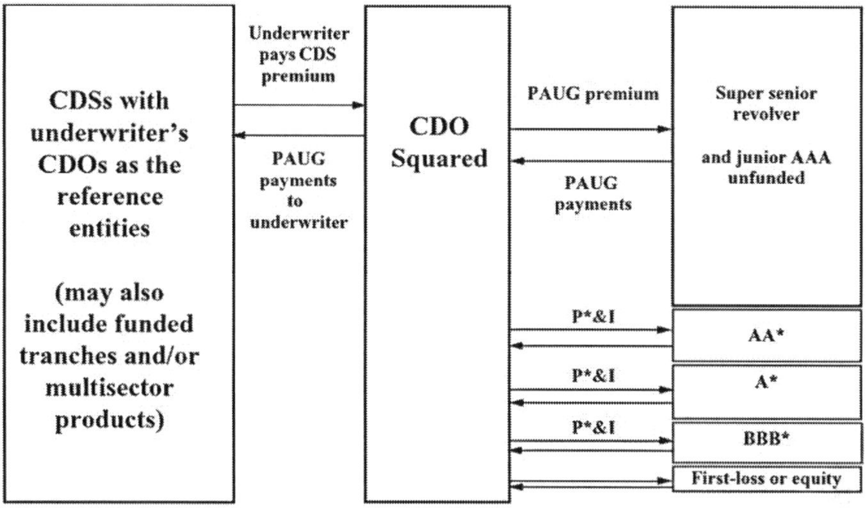

*These are usually funded notes, but the first-loss tranche and some junior tranches may be unfunded.

FIGURE 17.2 Synthetic CDO-Squared

Furthermore, ratings on leveraged synthetic credit products are often misleading. A recent example is the AAA rating achieved by products like the constant proportion debt obligation (CPDO), which is largely a leveraged bet on the credit quality and market spreads of indexes based on U.S. and European investment-grade companies. Besides credit risk, there is a substantial amount of financial engineering risk. Potential losses are due to defaults or market value changes (when spreads widen). The high leverage puts investors' principal at risk since it acts as first-loss protection on the leveraged exposure to the indexes.

Throughout the first three quarters of 2006, the rating agencies continued to make excuses for their poor performance, saying the overwhelming majority of ratings actions have been directed at the weakest-quality subprime securities. They pointed out that few AAA-rated tranches had been downgraded. The rating agencies claimed that AAA-rated tranches were unlikely to experience a loss. But that is true of any investment-grade product, and it is the distinction between grades that is of real importance. Even the rating agencies' assertion that AAA tranches were unlikely to experience losses was proved incorrect for several types of structures by the end of 2007.

The rating agencies' assertion that it did not matter much if only BBB-rated and lower tranches were downgraded was risible. In the past, when

BBB and below tranches were downgraded, AAA-rated tranches were not downgraded because the deals were usually older deals, and the higher-rated tranches were largely amortized with only a small principal balance remaining. There was very little risk to the higher-rated tranches. But many of the subprime-backed deals had been downgraded and/or placed on negative watch, particularly the 2006–2007 vintages. No reasonable financial professional accepted that the AAA-rated tranches of such deals were as creditworthy as the AAA-rated tranches of nonmortgage and nonleveraged loan deals in which the lower tranches had not been downgraded.

If this were not bad enough, liquidity dried up due to oversupply of misrated product and too little demand for hard-to-value securities. The market not only penalized CDOs with wider credit spreads to account for the greater credit risk, but also penalized these tranches for their opacity. Prices can decouple from fundamental value, causing even further price drops. The rating agencies assert that the entire price drop was due to lack of demand and illiquidity, but the cause of the lack of demand was the fact that many structured products were incorrectly rated at creation.

Products including CPDOs and AAA tranches of CDO-squared deals with portfolios consisting of BBB-rated tranches of deals backed by subprime collateral started to unwind and experienced substantial principal loss. It became clear that even if CDOs did not liquidate, other AAA-rated products would ultimately experience substantial principal loss due to defaults. The senior debt of many SIV-lites was downgraded to CCC from AAA almost overnight.

ABCP CRISIS AND MLEC

By August, the asset-backed commercial paper (ABCP) market showed signs of strain. Investors did not want to reinvest in commercial paper issued by SIVs. In response, Treasury Secretary Hank Paulson announced the possibility of a super-SIV, called the Master Liquidity Enhancement Fund (MLEC), but details had not been sorted out. The premature announcement froze the ABCP market as investors waited and did nothing. No one, including competent managers of successful SIVs, had any confidence that the MLEC assets would not be contaminated with low-quality (albeit highly rated) CDO product. The quality of SIVs was extremely variable.

The rating agencies quickly made up a new category for funds like the Sigma and Theta funds managed by Gordian Knot, calling them limited purpose finance corporations (LPFCs) to distinguish them from SIV-lites and other shaky investment vehicles. As mentioned before, the Sigma and Theta funds have zero subprime, zero Alt-A, and zero home equity loan paper.

They also do not have market value triggers that would cause a mandatory sale during a market liquidity crunch—unlike many other investment vehicles in the market. A few years ago, Fitch liked the idea of mandatory sales, and put the Gordian Knot's funds on negative watch for a couple of weeks, before conceding. Yet the rating agencies did not ask other funds to remove the triggers that can unintentionally force an otherwise sound investment vehicle into bankruptcy during a liquidity crunch.

MLEC could not assure the market it would be as careful when allowing assets into the fund. By November, SIV affiliates took matters into their own hands and began extending substitute financing when they could. This admission of failure to attract investors at viable interest rates meant that financial institutions took off-balance-sheet entities onto their balance sheets. This created capital constraints for banks that did not have enough surplus capital to cover this contingency.

Shortly after Citigroup rescued its SIV investments, Citigroup, Bank of America, and JPMorgan Chase, originally sponsors of the MLEC idea, shelved plans to launch the $75 billion MLEC.

CONSTELLATION CDOS: FALLING STARS

By October 2007, a CDO called Carina CDO unwound. It was one of several CDOs that became known as the *constellation CDOs*. Like falling stars, these deals began experiencing events of default (EOD). A large hedge fund drove most of these deals. It did the classic long equity, short mezzanine trade, described in earlier chapters, and the seniormost tranches were wrapped by the monoline insurers.

Losses mounted on Sagittarius CDO I, another constellation CDO. LaCrosse Financial Products LLC, an MBIA affiliate, fought with other investors for cash flows, even though it was ostensibly the senior noteholder.

The unnecessarily complicated prospectus language made it difficult for the trustee to determine which investor had payment priority. As was typical of these deals, there was an interest-only class. Disputes over cash flows due to poorly written prospectuses for CDOs experiencing mounting losses was distressing enough. Liquidation provided certainty but based on the experience of other subprime CDO liquidations, it provided the certainty of crystallized losses.

For example, Adams Square Funding I, a CDO underwritten by Credit Suisse, closed December 15, 2006. It was an asset-backed deal, a collateralized deal, rated by both Moody's and S&P. In March 2007, the rating agencies had defended their ratings of subprime-backed CDOs saying they had "scrubbed the numbers, and slices of debt that are rated investment-grade will mostly stay that way. . ..” (Bethany McClean, “The Dangers of Investing in Subprime Debt,” *Fortune* 2, April 2007). Yet in December 2007, less than one year after the deal closed, it unwound. According to S&P, investors in Adams Square Funding I got *less than 25 percent of par value—more than a 75 percent loss*—on average.

By the end of December 2007, 33 CDOs had issued event of default notices, and the list was climbing. The CDO debacle was reminiscent of the opening scenes of the movie *Cliffhanger,* in which a climber’s supports snap one by one, ending in a spectacular steep fall. That last plastic buckle was AAA-rated, and investors such as SIVs, monolines, money market funds, pension funds, banks, investment banks, CPPI, and CDPCs experienced losses on AAA-rated tranches, including super senior tranches.

Constellation CDOs seemed designed to fail and were largely synthetic. Figure 17.3 shows a schematic of typical buyers in different parts of the capital structure of a synthetic CDO. As deals such as the constellation CDOs crumbled, AAA-rated monolines that had wrapped the deals realized they had insufficient capital to maintain their AAA ratings, and A-rated ACA Capital had to give itself over to a regulatory workout. Mezzanine tranches of these CDOs that could not be sold were themselves used as collateral for other CDOs. This was simply a way to get rid of undesirable

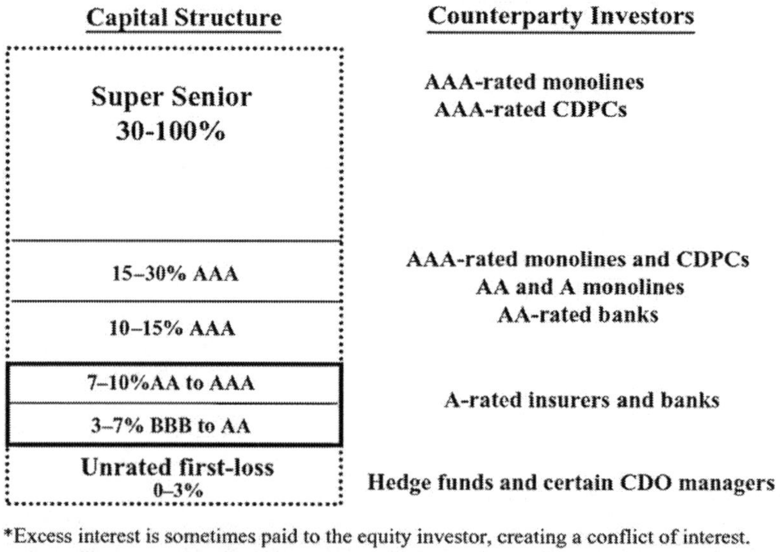

FIGURE 17.3 Synthetic CDO Investors

product in a way that would be opaque to investors. Those subsequent CDOs received wraps from monolines, and the undesirable mezzanine paper was alchemically changed to an apparently smaller residual risk. But there was risk to investors in the senior tranches as the underlying collateral began disappearing due to losses.

NEW FLAWED MODELS REPLACE OLD FLAWED MODELS

Potential losses are deal-specific. Many financial institutions are building new models, and most of them are as worthless as the old model. One must evaluate deal-specific risks. The senior noteholders of some CDOs will experience no losses if they hold to maturity—not the normal mandate of a trading book. Other deals seem fine on a hold-to-maturity basis at first glance, but a pessimistic scenario of not-yet-downgraded tranches may show a loss potential of 50 percent of principal on a hold-to-maturity basis.

There is wide variability in potential for loss, and selling distressed assets in any distressed market will exacerbate it. Part of the loss will be due to credit impairment, and part will be due to the fact that investors are shunning opaque products.

Adams Square Funding I had collateral consisting of both cash and synthetic (pay-as-you-go credit default swaps) of ABS CDOs on mezzanine subprime loans, among other items. The conflicts of interest between the collateral manager, Credit Suisse Alternative Capital (CSAC), and other affiliated entities, including the Leveraged Investment Group (LIG) of Credit Suisse Securities (CSS), were apparent and disclosed in the prospectus. This is the kind of moral hazard—or to be more accurate, conflict of interest—from which I stated investors should walk briskly away. Rating agencies' models do not capture the risks of moral hazard and conflicts of interest, and the rating agencies even failed to capture the obvious magnitude of the collateral risks.

Adams Square Funding I is not an isolated example, just a handy one, because it unwound. It was not even close to being the funkiest deal I had seen, and the conflicts of interest were disclosed, whereas in many other deals the conflicts were more obscure.

RATING AGENCIES IN CRISIS

By the end of 2007 and through 2008, rating agencies scrambled to keep up. Moody's kept changing its models and correlation assumptions. At one point it announced that "new correlation" would equal three times "old correlation." In December 2007, Standard and Poor's announced an increase in capital requirements in order for certain financial guarantors to maintain triple-A ratings, only to materially increase its loss assumptions in January 2008. Fitch announced it might issue one-notch downgrades for Ambac and MBIA in December 2007, only to downgrade Ambac two notches in January 2008 when Ambac announced larger than expected losses in its credit derivatives portfolio. The rating agencies were inconsistent, ill-informed, and floundering.

Executives at New York–based S&P, Moody's, and Fitch say they are waiting until foreclosure sales before recognizing losses, but they did not comment on the rising number of vacant homes on which foreclosures had not occurred, the complaints of trustees who could not foreclose because they could not find the required documentation to prove they had the right to foreclose, or on the possibility of noneconomic mortgage restructuring which would simply delay foreclosure. They also did not comment on the rising delinquencies which most often led to inevitable foreclosure.

Monolines (financial guarantor providing bond guarantees) rated AAA and ACA Capital (rated A) wrote guarantees on super senior tranches. This seemed fine according to generic models and capital economic models, but many of these tranches have substantial principal risk. A competent risk evaluation would have required substantial capital increases. Finding a reinsurer may be very time consuming and costly. When ACA Capital failed, its counterparties, including Merrill Lynch, Credit Agricole (Calyon), and CIBC, wrote off billions of dollars due to their having to take risky exposure back on balance sheet at depressed market prices. The super senior tranches turned out to have substantial principal risk; they were not the super-safe tranches indicated by Basel II or by investment banking models.

Analysts seemed to have just noticed details like unwind triggers, including market value triggers for shaky SIVs that issued short-term debt to fund longer-term higher-yielding assets. In November 2007, MBIA Inc., the largest bond insurer, sold assets to bondholders of its Hudson Thames Capital SIV. It wound down from $2 billion to $400 million after announcing that it had failed to find investors since August in the asset-backed commercial debt issued by this vehicle.

MBIA reported an "impairment" on its $15.8 million equity stake. But that problem seemed insignificant in the wake of the mark-to-market losses and real projected losses in its credit derivative/financial guaranty book.

The rating agencies were finally forced to own up to the magnitude of their miscalculations, putting into question their competence to maintain the designation of Nationally Recognized Statistical Ratings Organizations. The rating agencies started to announce steps that would lead to downgrades of the monolines.

In early December 2007, Barclays Capital—apparently oblivious to the irony of its having helped many entities set up SIV-lites—pointed out that there would be steep losses in unwinding CDOs, observing the substantial principal risk to the super senior holders in an unwind scenario. Loss estimates were *30 to 65 percent* of par value for high-grade super senior CDO tranches, and *20 to 30 percent* of par for mezzanine super senior (usually called mezzanine triple-A) tranches.

By December 2007, HSBC Holdings provided financing for its SIVs, essentially taking the assets on balance sheet. Even Citibank, with relatively robust SIVs containing minimal subprime exposure, financed its SIVs. Barclays provided liquidity for an off-balance-sheet SIV. Societe Generale (SocGen) moved its SIV, Pace, on balance sheet. It had a credit line of $4.3 billion. Other banks also followed suit. By January 2008, Banque AIG, a banking unit owned by the insurer, got financing for its Nightingale SIV from AIG Financial Products Corp., another unit of the insurer, after asset prices declined and demand for the SIVs' senior debt waned.

By January 2008, New York State prosecutors obtained the cooperation of Clayton Holdings, a due diligence firm, to provide the reports it had prepared for investment banks underwriting mortgage loans. Investigators seek to determine whether material information concerning the risks of mortgage loans was adequately disclosed. They also want to determine whether rating agencies asked enough questions about the loans used as collateral in CDOs.

MONOLINE MELTDOWN: FINANCIAL GUARANTORS IN CRISIS

Note: This section was written in January 2008, and the monolines are in a state of crisis and flux. By the time this book is printed (usually 10 months after the manuscript is submitted), the landscape of this industry will have changed. This section explains how and why it is changing.

On December 14, 2007, Moody's expressed its concerns about the monoline financial guarantors ("Moody's Announces Rating Actions on Financial Guarantors"). To achieve the triple-A (Aaa) rating, Moody's looks for an insurer with capital equal to 130 percent times base-case losses and 100 percent times stress-case losses. Using my base-case assumptions for subprime losses and Moody's base-case capital criteria, five of the seven financial guarantors rated triple A did not merit their high ratings. If they were downgraded, investors would have to mark down assets to reflect the greater of the financial guarantor's downgraded rating or the credit rating of the underlying asset. For the public finance market—including $1 trillion of U.S. municipal bonds guaranteed by these financial guarantors—it would mean massive confusion. Given 2008 is a U.S. election year, the political implications were massive.

Financial Guaranty Insurance Corporation (FGIC), MBIA Inc., and Security Capital Assurance (XL Capital Assurance Inc. and XL Financial Assurance Ltd.) merited immediate multinotch—in some cases multigrade—downgrades. (ACA Financial Guaranty Corp. was already downgraded to CCC by S&P.) Ambac Financial Group Inc. and CIFG were stronger, yet not sufficiently strong to merit the triple-A rating, and only Financial Security Assurance Inc. (FSA) and Assured Guaranty Corp. (AGC) would retain a triple-A rating (based on subprime exposure). Unfortunately, the latter two were relatively small (with FSA being the larger), so the problems of the larger players will have a huge market impact. Stress-test scenarios are even worse. If one considered that an increase in capital cushion may also be required to support other business lines, the situation was desperate.

Since more than $2 trillion in securities were insured by Ambac and MBIA, and another $315 billion insured by FGIC, massive downgrades can be expected on all of those insured bonds. Downgrades would affect CDOs and, to a much greater extent, public finance securities. Investment banks would have massive mark-to-market write-downs of collateralized debt obligation positions insured by any of the downgraded entities, and other investors would have similar problems.

In December 2007, S&P affirmed the ratings of Financial Security Assurance Inc. (FSA is AAA rated), Assured Guaranty Corp (AGC is AAA rated), and Radian Asset Assurance, Inc. (AA rated). Moody's also affirmed FSA's and AGC's Aaa ratings and Radian's Aa3 rating with stable outlooks.

Of the AAA-rated entities, only AGC and FSA have minimal exposure to subprime-backed CDOs, and both have recently provided bond wraps for other triple-A entities. Radian (double-A rated) also has minimal subprime exposure, but it has other mortgage exposure and may or may not be out of the woods.

RATING AGENCIES IN DENIAL

In December 2007, S&P affirmed the ratings for Ambac Assurance Corp, CFIG's entities, MBIA Insurance Corp., and Security Capital Assurance (XL Capital Assurance Inc. and XL Financial Assurance Ltd.) with negative outlook. FGIC was rated AAA but was on negative watch. But all had varying degrees of exposure to subprime loans and subprime-related CDOs, including in some cases CDO-squared products.

ACA Financial Guaranty Corp. had been recently downgraded from A to CCC with CreditWatch Developing, but the downgrade was long overdue. It had strong ties to Bear Stearns, Merrill Lynch, and Canadian Imperial Bank of Commerce (CIBC); all of those investment banks replaced senior personnel, including their CEOs, due to the subprime crisis.

Moody's put the Aaa ratings of FGIC and XL on review for possible downgrade. It affirmed the Aaa ratings of MBIA and CIFG, but with negative outlook. Moody's had a stable outlook when it affirmed the ratings of Ambac (Aaa).

In late December 2007, Fitch placed the AAA ratings of Ambac, MBIA, and FGIC on review for possible downgrade, giving them more than a month to raise only an additional $1 billion in capital—insufficient, in my view, to retain a genuine triple-A rating; but perhaps the rating agencies were happy to lower their former standards. XL Capital Assurance was put under review, and Fitch said it needed to raise $2 billion (this was higher than my estimate—see the next section). Fitch indicated Ambac and MBIA would be cut to only to AA+ (higher than I thought they deserved); in MBIA's case in particular, it is unclear how it justified that indication.

OVERWHELMING LOSSES

In its December 19, 2007, report ("Detailed Results of Subprime Stress Test of Financial Guarantors"), Standard & Poor's estimated that monoline financial guarantors would have $10.7 billion in aggregate losses under S&P's subprime loan stress tests for residential mortgage-backed securities (RMBSs) and collateralized debt obligations. S&P acknowledged that from the six-year period beginning 2001 to the end of 2006, the industry had losses of only $2.5 billion, representing only 0.14 percent of a lower average par base outstanding.

S&P's assumptions seemed much too optimistic and may have failed to take into account important data. S&P's stress case for losses was below my base case. For example, for 2006 vintage first-lien subprime loans, I was assuming a 30 percent default rate and a 70 percent loss rate for net base-case losses of 21 percent. S&P assumed stress case losses of only 15.5 percent. Moody's base-case assumption for 2006 vintage first-lien sub-prime loans was 11 percent average losses across securitizations. Moody's stress-case loss of 19 percent for subprime loans was near my base-case of 21 percent and well below my stress case of 30 percent for 2006-originated subprime loans.

POOR ACTUAL RECOVERIES

One major servicer asserted that the rating agencies' subprime recovery rates were much too optimistic and had noted that modifying a mortgage was highly preferable to recovering zero or negative value after foreclosure fees and depressed asset prices take their toll on recovery of relatively low loan balances. One major servicer told me that my recovery rate assumption of 30 percent (70 percent loss rate) is too high, and my recovery rate is already much more pessimistic than that of the rating agencies. Furthermore, loan scrubbing firms have reported current bad loans as high as 20 percent in 2006 vintage subprime portfolios, and increased interest payment resets on adjustable rate mortgages have not yet occurred. When that happens, the default rates will increase.

My ultimate subprime principal loss projections prepared at the beginning of 2007 are unchanged at $270 billion to $340 billion for the approximately $1.5 trillion subprime market (depending on what one includes in this cohort), a 30 percent ultimate default rate on recent multi-year originations beginning in late 2004 and ending in early 2007, and a 30 percent average recovery rate. When I include all risky product— subprime, Alt-A, and prime—the ultimate loss figure for this cohort of loans is projected to be around $450 billion to $560 billion. The latter figures include another $1 billion of loans at risk including Alt-A ARMs, Alt-A IOs, option ARMs to higher credit quality borrowers, and piggyback loans—capped-out second liens—to higher credit quality borrowers.

On August 3, 2007, I appeared on a CNBC *Squawk Box* segment with Joe Kernan and discussed my estimates. At the time, Fed Chairman Ben Bernanke said subprime losses would amount to $50 to $100 billion; CSFB said $50 billion, and Citigroup said $100 billion. I pointed out that the Fed had to stop letting Wall Street do its homework. My loss projections were higher than anything coming out of the U.S. government or Wall Street.

In the fall of 2007, a major mortgage servicer of geographically diverse U.S. subprime loans was working 13-hour days frantically trying to salvage what it could of its subprime mortgage loan portfolio. They were desperate to avoid having to report a delinquency or foreclosure. They disclosed disturbing information. The servicer asserted the rating agencies were incorrect in their optimism; recovery rates of 60 percent were unattainable. My average recovery rate assumption of 30 percent was also unattainable as far as the servicer was concerned.

At times, the servicer has been selling loans for pennies (three to six cents) on the dollar. The servicer aggressively re-aged mortgages—restructuring loans doomed to fail in the future. They allowed skipped payments and did not report them as delinquencies. They were doing everything possible to avoid foreclosure because the recovery rates were dismal.

A contributing factor to the dismal recovery rates is the fact that legal costs relative to the relatively low loan balances are huge, and delays are long. Some of the assets include trailers, mobile homes, and houses in areas where prices have plummeted. While average housing prices fell nationwide, in specific subprime areas the fall in housing prices was much greater. Some of the loans had negative equity at the time of delinquency.

The day a homeowner missed a payment, the servicer got on the phone, trying to work out a new deal. The servicer discovered that if homeowners missed two payments, the loan was virtually doomed to default, because most homeowners gave up after that. The servicer tried not to report delinquencies, which were usually reported one month behind prime mortgages already. If this practice was typical, the scope of the subprime problem was underreported.

Most of the early post-signing defaults in loans originated through the early months of 2007 had been on stated-income loans—also known as liar loans—especially with loan-to-value ratios approaching 100 percent, whether they were subprime or not. This suggested that the stated income had been overstated. Future defaults would kick in as resets on coupons occurred in a soft housing market.

In the early years of a typical long-dated mortgage loan, little equity buildup occurs, and some of the subprime mortgage products have even less equity accumulation, or worse, negative equity. Some ARM products are 40-year loans with very little equity buildup in the early years. Some of the option ARMs have *increasing* principal balances. With housing prices stagnating and falling, the homeowner often has negative equity.

As ARM coupons reset to much higher rates, we can expect a wave of defaults combined with dismal recovery rates.

Most models have relied on purchased prepayment data and trustees' reports. They had limited utility for marking portfolios to market or projecting ultimate losses. The models grossly underestimated potential losses. As market participants caught on, inventory stagnated, and wasting assets caused further write-downs at financial institutions with remaining subprime inventories, including the monolines.

By the end of 2007, it was painfully clear that the losses would be much higher than the Fed's earlier highest projections and that my numbers were closer to reality. By January 2008, the *Wall Street Journal* summed up the subprime-related losses of major financial institutions, and the losses had already reached more than $130 billion. Some of these were mark-to-market losses, but some losses that were off-balance-sheet looked as if they might come on balance sheet, and most resets of 2006 and 2007 loans had not yet occurred. Furthermore, these losses were only those of investment banks and did not include hedge funds, mainstream sophisticated investors, insurance companies, mortgage lenders, and many others.

It is important to note that percentage changes in default and recovery assumptions are now very important, since the moat has been crossed and the fortress walls have been breached. For many deals, support tranches will be consumed by losses, so incremental losses will be a dollar-for-dollar hit against wrapped tranches.

UNDERCAPITALIZED FINANCIAL GUARANTORS

Standard & Poor's points out that a reduction in future business volume and lower risk would free up capital. The irony is that lower future business volume—not actually a good thing, unless risk premiums are too low to justify participation—is the only guarantee on which the monolines can rely. The key problem facing financial guarantors is lack of faith in their ratings.

By late 2007, five of the seven monolines with a nominal triple-A rating no longer merited those ratings, since they were undercapitalized. Even if these entities raised capital to meet rating agencies' requirements, they would still be undercapitalized in the eyes of many investors who no longer trusted rating agency guidelines. My own initial estimates for additional capital far exceeded those of the rating agencies (with the exception of Fitch's estimate for XL). Many former low-risk customers would not be repeat customers.

While the financial guarantors—other than ACA—do not have to post collateral and seem to have done pay-as-you go credit enhancement structures, they could experience death by one thousand cuts, so it is critical to view the overall picture and not near-term survival when evaluating the ratings. If unwind triggers are hit and financial guarantors elect to unwind deals as opposed to trying to work out loan recoveries—possibly a futile exercise—both the CDOs and the inevitable losses will be accelerated.

DICEY DEALS DONE DIRT CHEAP

Contrary to S&P's assertions, underwriting quality for several of the financial guarantors was not high and was actually naïve. Rigorous statistical sampling of the underlying portfolios was not performed, and they overly relied on faulty models. S&P seems to be the most optimistic of the three major rating agencies (including Moody's and Fitch). The *Wall Street Journal* also made S&P famous for refusing to rate securitizations using loans originated in Georgia and New Jersey, after these states enacted restrictive consumer protection laws designed to raise underwriting standards, albeit somewhat ambiguously ("Lender Lobbying Blitz Abetted Mortgage Mess,"

December 31, 2007). Yet S&P was content to rate securitizations containing stated-income loans.

Standard & Poor's notes that the financial guarantors have offered credit enhancement for deals that include inner collateralized debt obligations (CDOs used as collateral within a CDO), and the financial guarantors have no control over whether these inner CDOs can be liquidated if they hit rating unwind triggers. My larger concern is that some of the CDOs for which financial guarantors offered credit enhancement have other features that are included in the worst practices playbook from the point of view of senior noteholders.

A publicly available prospectus from a deal brought in the last quarter of 2006 revealed poor underwriting practices on the part of a particular monoline. It was a subprime mezzanine deal, a CDO-squared, among the worst-performing of all CDOs. The underlying portfolio includes tranches of CDOs with the lowest available investment-grade rating of BBB when the tranches were initially brought to market. The interest cash flows are diverted to the benefit of lower class tranches. If the deal hits an unwind trigger enabling the financial guarantor to liquidate the portfolio, the prospectus language is ambiguous enough that the financial guarantor may have to fight with other investors for cash flows. Furthermore, it is virtually guaranteed that the illiquid overrated tranches used as collateral will fetch poor market prices.

The CDO-squared was rated by both Moody's and S&P, and it is inexplicable how the rating agencies justified their opinions. The prospectus states: "Reliable sources of statistical information do not exist with respect to the default rates for all of the type of securities represented by the Collateral Debt Securities." In fact, reliable performance data was sparse for *most* of the securities in the portfolio. The underwriter should have stated that given the lack of data, the ratings were no more than paid-for labels and should not be relied upon to make investment decisions.

Within a year of coming to market, both rating agencies downgraded the CDO's tranches several notches with negative outlook, and more downgrades are inevitable. The deal was overrated before it closed.

As noted before, S&P's stress case in December 2007 was more optimistic than my base case, and the financial guarantors look stretched when one considers only the subprime-related credit enhancements. The following comparisons are roughly in order of worst to best case at the time:

- *ACA*. According to S&P's stress tests, ACA's stress case after-tax loss would be around $2.1 billion, but ACA has only $650 to $700 million of capital cushion. My estimate was it would take roughly $3.5 billion in capital to reclaim a single-A rating, and the prospects for future business would be poor. ACA had close ties to CDO underwriters, and Canadian Imperial Bank of Commerce (CIBC) was the first to announce $2 billion in losses related to its ACA guarantees. All of ACA's projected losses were due to credit enhancement of CDOs. The Maryland Insurance Commissioner signed a December 19 consent order saying ACA could be placed under conservation, rehabilitation, or liquidation. This seemed not merely possible but inevitable.

- *FGIC.* Standard & Poor's stress tests showed estimated after-tax losses due to subprime RMBSs and CDOs combined of $2.2 billion, of which around 40 percent is due to CDOs. FGIC's capital cushion was only around $300 to $350 million. I estimated FGIC would need $4 billion in capital to maintain a triple-A rating. Some of its private equity owners including PMI Group Inc., Blackstone Group LP, and Cypress Group LLC were trying to raise capital, but rating agencies express skepticism about whether their efforts will succeed in time. One of the other private equity owners is CIVC, which was part owner of Ownit, the mortgage lender that went bankrupt in December 2006. CIVC's Dan Helle was on Ownit's board, so subprime distress should not be a surprise to these owners. It had just engaged Blackrock to model its positions, and it was not a good sign that it is depending on outside resources and doing this late in the game. FGIC insured $315 billion in bonds, and its outlook was problematic. FSA had recently rewrapped bonds already wrapped by FGIC. FGIC should have been downgraded not merely several notches, but several grades.
- *MBIA.* Standard & Poor's estimated after-tax subprime-related stress-case losses at $3.2 billion, of which 47 percent is CDO-related. The capital cushion was only $1.75 to $1.8 billion prior to a $1 billion additional capital infusion. I estimated MBIA would need an additional $3.5 billion in capital—even after its proposed additional cash infusion of $1 billion from Warburg Pincus—to maintain its triple-A rating.
- *XL (SCA).* Standard & Poor's estimated after-tax subprime-related stress-case losses at $884 billion and the capital cushion was only $600 to $650 million. I estimated XL would need an additional $1.2 billion capital infusion beyond that estimate to maintain its triple-A rating.
- *Ambac.* Standard & Poor's estimated after-tax subprime-related stress-case losses at $1.85 billion, of which approximately 50 percent will be due to CDOs, and the capital cushion is only $1.55 billion to $1.6 billion. I estimated Ambac would require an additional $2.1 billion in capital beyond that. It reinsured $29 billion in other debt with Assured Guaranty, but that only freed up $255 million of capital, a small fraction of what it needed according to my estimates. FSA had also rewrapped bonds already wrapped by Ambac.

- *CIFG.* Natixis transferred CIFG to its two major shareholders: Caisse Nationale des Caisses d'Epargne and Banque Fédérale des Banques Populaires. They provided $1.5 billion in additional capital for maintenance of the triple-A credit rating. There was some indication that the shareholders are trying to shore up expertise and may provide additional support, viewing this as a business opportunity. CIFG's shareholders may be switching to a Berkshire Hathaway Assurance–type strategy (see the next section) in anticipation of the effective demise of other triple-A financial guarantors, but CIFG's intentions are not yet clear.

Furthermore, Alt/A and prime loans that originated in late 2005 to early 2007 included negative amortization loans and other risky products that would become delinquent as the soft housing market persists and interest payments reset upwards.

COMPETITIVE PRESSURE

Berkshire Hathaway Assurance's announced that it will enter the municipal bond business, and it may become a litmus test for other insurers. Berkshire Hathaway is clear that it is happy to do zero business when the risk premiums make no sense. Its triple-A rating is viewed as a genuine rating. Its stated intention of doing premium business at premium prices may leave the largest of the legacy financial guarantors scrambling for scraps.

UNCERTAIN FUTURE

In the late 1990s, when CapMAC Holdings Inc. was in trouble (CapMAC merged with MBIA in 1998), it was given a minimal grace period; there was no kidding around. The rating agencies' recent actions reek of desperation, since several financial guarantors have been given more than a month to raise capital.

Why were the rating agencies being so indulgent in 2007–2008? There may be several reasons. In its previously mentioned report, Moody's revealed that 90,549 securities—of which 89,709 are politically charged public finance deals—are on negative watch due to the potential downgrades of FGIC and XL (SCA) alone. Including all of the financial guarantors, more than $2.4 trillion in insured securities will be affected, most of which are public finance deals. Of those, $1 trillion were U.S. municipal bonds, and 2008 is a U.S. presidential election year.

By the spring of 2008, FGIC and XL (SCA) not only officially lost their AAA ratings, but they were also downgraded below investment grade by one or more rating agencies. Both were in legal disputes with investment bank counter-parties. CIFG had been downgraded several notches and other monoline insurers were under review.

Investment banks that bought protection from financial guarantor counterparties had large mark-to-market losses Other investors would have to acknowledge mark-to-market losses when the monolines were downgraded. Finally, the rating agencies' lack of vigilance in awarding initial ratings on structured finance deals has drawn criticism from many quarters, and I continue to assert that the NRSRO designation of Moody's, S&P, and Fitch should be withdrawn with respect to structured finance ratings.

The situation of many of the financial guarantors is much more desperate than the ratings reflect, and once again, I am at odds with the slow response time and artificially high ratings of the rating agencies.

By January 2008, the New York insurance regulator called a meeting of investment banks to discuss the way forward for the monoline insurers. He brought up the fact that there was an extraordinary amount of fraud associated with the origination of the underlying mortgage loan collateral in deals wrapped by the monolines. It is uncertain whether this will be used as an argument to reverse or nullify transactions. There may be some other accommodation between the financial guarantors and their counterparties as a result of these unusual circumstances.

COUNTRYWIDE'S BAILOUT AND MORAL HAZARD

Countrywide is regulated by the Office of Thrift Supervision, and it is a primary dealer, authorized to trade U.S. government and other select securities with the Federal Reserve System.

On September 24, 2003, Countrywide posted its expanded interest-only programs. The program included 80/20, NINA (no documentation—no income verification, no asset verification), no-ratio (no income information, so no debt-to-income ratio is calculated, allowing the borrower to assume a greater debt load than would be allowed with a traditional mortgage), and SISA (stated income, stated assets) loans. FNMA and FHLMC were the chief buyers of Countrywide's loans, but many of these loans were problematic.

By the end of 2006, Countrywide's loans were showing signs of trouble. They hired a team to securitize assets and fired them shortly thereafter. By the end of 2006, Countrywide tried securitization with a new team pricing its first ABS CDO. It was also interested in doing more in derivatives and synthetics.

The week of August 13, the ABCP market showed serious strain. Investors began questioning the quality of the loans and other assets backing commercial paper. They asked for higher interest rates.

Countrywide let its bankers know it wanted to draw down its liquidity lines; it wanted $11.5 billion from a 40-bank syndicate. On Thursday, August 16, the stock market (Dow) tanked more than 340 points. Countrywide announced it tapped into the $11.5 billion in liquidity lines. The Fed agreed to extend the overnight discount window borrowings to 30 days and allow borrowings to be extended; the Fed also agreed to accept asset-backed collateral with a triple-A rating. In effect this would allow banks extending credit lines to post Countrywide collateral. The Fed effectively became a buyer of Countrywide 30-day extendable ABCP. This was effectively a liquidity bailout. The Fed news seemed to be leaked by one or more of the banks involved and the stock market popped up before the close on August 16 to finish down only 15 points.

On Friday, August 17, the stock market continued marching upward. The Fed announced a cut of 50 bps in the discount rate to 5.75 percent from 6.25 percent and also announced its new and longer borrowing terms. The *Wall Street Journal* reported "Countrywide has shifted its focus to only those that meet its criteria for being retained as investments and those that can be sold to government-sponsored investors Fannie Mae and Freddie Mac."

While the Fed denied this was a specific bailout of Countrywide, it seemed that way to many market participants. Countrywide, the largest U.S. mortgage lender, was deemed too big to fail.

In January 2008, Bank of America announced it would acquire Countrywide in an all-stock transaction worth $4 billion as the troubled mortgage lender continued to bleed. Countrywide also faces allegations of sloppy accounting and abusive lending and foreclosure practices. Bank of America plans to modify the loan practices and drop the Countrywide name after the purchase—targeted to be completed at the end of 2008—is closed.

Chapter 18

Future Developments in Structured Finance

The post-Enron global credit crunch provides ample evidence of the complete failure of the bloated global network of regulators. Institutional investors are obliged to do their own due diligence, but there have been voluntary due diligence failures. Complex structured finance products have introduced systemic risk into the financial system. Many investors rely on rating agencies to assess risk of the products they purchase. Rating agencies are often overwhelmed by pressure from Wall Street to rate complex products and have an incentive to be quick and lenient due to the lucrative fees for rating new products. This has been a failure in assessing default risk and even more of a failure in assessing liquidity risk for many new asset classes.

Regulators have relied on supervisory bodies that lack the knowledge and resources to keep up with new complex structured finance products. Often regulatory changes have political rather than economic motivations. The money and clout of investment banks can influence regulators. Former senior SEC personnel can expect lucrative work after they leave the SEC. They become senior investment bankers, become expert witnesses for law firms defending investment banks, garner arbitration work, and even become the beneficiaries of Wall Street fund-raising assistance if they start an investment fund.

Basel II is a useless paperwork exercise when it comes to the challenges posed by structured products.

Accounting disclosures have proven inadequate to provide sufficient transparency for structured financial products. Forensic accountants call me often, because they have no idea how to properly value CDOs, yet they take the client work anyway, representing that their expertise is up to the task when it is not. They ask that I anonymously subcontract my services, and I refuse. The so-called expertise of accountants is on par with that of rating agencies.

Hedge funds have made massive leveraged credit bets, knowing that their upside is billions in fees and their downside is millions in fees.

In the credit derivatives markets, many investors—encouraged by their credit derivatives counterparties and ISDA—have relied on ISDA documentation, without fully understanding the implications of those documents.

One would have thought that in a post-Enron world, all of these problems would have been solved. So what happened?

REGULATORY FAILURE: INVESTORS ARE ON THEIR OWN

Post-Enron, the U.S. Congress seems to be fed up with the various excuses of corporate officers: "I'm responsible, but I'm not guilty. I'm guilty, but I'm not responsible. I'm not responsible, and I'm not guilty." Individual corporate managers grew wealthy, but somehow that elusive combination of guilt and responsibility belonged to someone else in corporate management. It seemed those quickest to claim credit are also the most adept at denying liability. Congress's ire now seems to have been nothing more than a photo opportunity.

President George W. Bush signed into law the Sarbanes-Oxley Act of 2002, which was passed by the U.S. Congress on July 30, 2002. The bill was named for Senator Paul Sarbanes (Democrat from Maryland) and Representative Michael Oxley (Republican from Ohio), who were instrumental in drafting the necessary compromises to get it passed. The Act addresses issues of accounting oversight and corporate responsibility. The Act applies to companies that must file Form 10-K, 10-Q, and 8-K reports required by the Securities Exchange Act of 1934.

The part that seems to most affect structured finance is that the 10-K and 10-Q must disclose off-balance-sheet transactions, contingent obligations, and relationships with unconsolidated entities. In other words, the financial reports should tell the entire story, and tell it accurately. Yet accounting disclosures have proven inadequate to address the challenges posed by the opacity of complex structured financial products.

In each 10-Q and 10-K, CEOs and CFOs should certify the following:

- The signing officer has reviewed the report.
- To the officer's knowledge, the report doesn't contain any lies or misleading omissions.
- To the officer's knowledge, the financial statements actually represent the financial condition of the firm.

- The officers who provide signatures are responsible for establishing and maintaining internal controls. The officers have designed such internal controls to ensure that the people reporting to them are actually doing it, are doing it on time, and are doing it honestly.
- The signing officers have to report whether or not they have a grip on the situation to their company's auditors and the audit committee of the board of directors. They have to report any fraud involving management or other employees with a significant role.
- The signing officers have to come clean about whether there are any changes in internal controls or whether they had to correct weakness.

Financial statements must include correcting adjustments identified by a registered public accounting firm in accordance with generally accepted accounting principles and the rules and regulations of the SEC.

The 10-K and 10-Q has to disclose off-balance-sheet transactions, arrangements, obligations (including contingent obligations), and other relationships of the company with unconsolidated entities or other persons.

The pro forma financial information must reconcile with the financial condition and results of operations of the company under generally accepted accounting principles (GAAP).

Executive officers and directors must report their purchase or sale of company stock within two business days following the day they did it, and within the year, they'll have to file this electronically.

The SEC will make companies say whether they have a code of ethics (and if not, why not) for their principal financial officers and comptrollers or principal accounting officers or persons performing similar functions.

There are newly created criminal penalties for tampering with records in federal investigations and bankruptcy. Destroying audit records or work papers within five years will get a criminal penalty, too. Certain securities fraud will also get criminal penalties. If CEOs and CFOs fail to perform the certifications the Act mandates, they'll get a criminal penalty. If the company retaliates against a whistleblower, there will be a criminal penalty.

The corporation has to hire a public accounting firm registered with the Public Company Accounting Oversight Board (called simply "the Oversight Board").

Audit committees now have more responsibility by statute. Audit committees will be directly responsible for choosing, paying, and overseeing the auditor, and for resolving financial reporting disagreements. No member of the audit committee can have a conflict of interest or take anything other than a director's fee. *No hidden payoffs are allowed.* Audit commit-tees must handle complaints about accounting, controls, or audits, even anonymous ones.

The SEC will adopt rules for companies to disclose whether the audit committee of the company has at least one member who is a "financial expert," and if not, why not. This expert has to understand generally accepted accounting principles (GAAP) and audit committee functions. The expert must also have experience preparing or auditing financial statements and with internal accounting controls.

How hard can it be to put together a credible audit committee? Apparently it can be pretty difficult. It seems even the former head of the SEC had difficulty putting together a new national board to oversee the accounting industry, as illustrated by the following events.

In late December 2002, the SEC filed a lawsuit charging C. Gregory Earls, chief executive officer of US Technologies Inc. (UST), with one count of securities fraud, one count of mail fraud, and eight counts of wire fraud, alleging that Earls used USV Partners LLC, an SPE that was a limited liability company, to misappropriate around $13.8 million that investors gave him to purchase UST's preferred stock and warrants. Although Earls said he'd get no management fees, he paid himself $4.7 million in management fees plus $9.1 million that he disguised as legal and accounting expenses. The SEC's complaint further says that Earls and UST covered up Earls' misdeeds. UST knew that Earls had previously been accused of misappropriating investors' funds in relation to other companies, but publicly praised his business acumen. UST failed to disclose its auditor's concerns about its controls. UST also forgot to mention that half of its board of directors resigned in the spring of 2002.

US Technologies had an impressive sounding audit committee; after all, it was headed by William Webster, a former FBI director. Webster was chosen by the head of the SEC to head a new national board, the Public Company Accounting Oversight Board (PCAOB), created to police the accounting industry, until he resigned in November 2002. He was to serve on the committee with Harvey L. Pitt, the then chairman of the SEC, who also resigned. The SEC and Congress questioned why Pitt chose Webster in the first place, given Webster's involvement with US Technologies.

In 2005, Earls was sentenced to 10 years and fined $21.9 million for defrauding investors.

The incident reminded me of a World War I joke. A man stood on a corner in Berlin and yelled, "The Kaiser is an idiot!" Two policemen came to arrest him for treason. The man said, "You can't arrest me, I meant the Austrian Kaiser." The policemen retorted, "You cannot fool us, we know who the idiot is."

It seems corporate malfeasance is a matter of risk and reward. For the most part, vast rewards come with limited downside.

More benignly, senior officers often sit on the top of large corporations when things are going badly wrong. The credit crunch is a glaring example. The extraordinary payments that corporate executives earn for their services should also come with extraordinary consequences when things go badly wrong. The Sarbanes-Oxley Act has little impact on executive behavior when the risk isn't commensurate with the rewards.

Wall Street management has often failed to reign in its investment bankers and has turned a blind eye to the risks of leverage combined with risky new asset classes. Yet CEOs have retired with packages of more than $100 million in some cases, in the wake of reporting tens of billions in losses due to subprime exposure.

Citigroup's Chuck Prince, Merrill Lynch's Stan O'Neal (now a chairman on the board of Alcoa), Bear Stearns' Warren Spector, and Barclays Capital's Grant Kvalheim are just a few senior officers to lose their positions in the wake of huge write-downs. As of this writing, Societe Generale's Chairman Daniel Bouton is on shaky ground after reporting billions in losses, including losses related to an equity derivatives rogue trader, and UBS's Marcel Ospel is fighting for corporate survival after writing down $14.5 billion (SFr 15.9 billion).

The Sarbanes-Oxley Act requires CEOs and CFOs to give up their bonuses for a year after the publication of a financial statement that needs to be redone because of misconduct. Boards confidently passed out attractive exit packages for most CEOs involved in the subprime crisis.

The future of finance is unclear. It is not as if finance needs more regulation. Bloated and ineffective global regulatory bodies abound. What is needed is effective regulation. Until that occurs, investors will have to fend for themselves and practice the fundamentals of prudent lending and investing.

Appendix

Interesting Web Sites

(All are prefixed by http://www.)

bafin.de — Bundesanstalt für Finanzdienst-leistungsaufsicht (BaFin), Bundesbank Regulations and Guidance.

bba.org.uk — British Banker's Association.

bloomberg.com — Bloomberg.

bis.org — Bank for International Settlements.

boj.or.jp/en — Bank of Japan (in English).

defaultrisk.com — a credit risk modeling resource.

fdic.gov/bank - Federal Deposit Insurance Corporation.

frbservices.org — U.S. Federal Reserve Regulations and Guidance.

garp.com — Global Association of Risk Professionals.

gloriamundi.org — VaR resources and risk professionals.

isda.org — International Swap and Derivatives Association, Inc.

loanpricing.com — Loan Pricing Corp.

markit.com — Markit Partners.

ml-implode.com — Implode-o-Meter.

mof.go.jp/english — Japanese Ministry of Finance (in English).

moodys.com — Moody's Investors Service.

occ.treas.gov — U.S. Office of the Comptroller of the Currency.

sec.gov — U.S. Securities and Exchange Commission.

Bibliography

Basel Committee on Banking Supervision. *Basel II: Revised international Capital Framework.* Bank for International Settlements, June 2006.

Brealey, Richard, and Stewart Myers. *Principles of Corporate Finance.* McGraw-Hill, 2006, 2003, 2000, 1996, 1988, 1984, 1981

Brooks, Brady, Roger J. Vos, and Diane Vazza. "Corporate Defaults Peak in 2002 Amid Record Amounts of Defaults and Declining Credit Quality—Hazards Remain." Standard & Poor's Ratings Direct, January 23, 2003.

Camerer, Colin, George Loewenstein, and Drazen Prelec. "Neuroeconomics: How Neuroscience Can Inform Economics." *Journal of Economic Literature,* March 2005.

Carty, Lea, Dana Lieberman, and Jerome S Fons. *Corporate Bond Defaults and Default Rates 1970–1994.* Moody's Investors Service Global Credit Research. New York, January 1995.

Caouette, John B., Edward I. Altman, and Paul Narayanan. *Managing Credit Risk: The Next Great Financial Challenge.* John Wiley & Sons, 1998.

Cialdini, Robert B., Ph.D. *Influence: How and Why People Agree to Things.* William Morrow and Company, 1984.

Cifuentes, Arturo, and Brian P. Lancaster. *Collateralized Debt Obligations: Structures, Strategies, and Innovations.* 2nd ed. Wachovia Capital Markets, LLC, 2004.

Dowd, Kevin. *Beyond Value at Risk: The New Science of Risk Management.* John Wiley & Sons, 1998.

Efrat, Isaac, Ph.D., Jeremy Gluck, Ph.D., and David Powar. *Moody's Refines Its Approach to Rating Structured Notes.* Moody's Investors Service, July 3, 1997.

Fabozzi, Frank J. *Handbook of Structured Financial Products, Pa.* Frank J. Fabozzi Associates, 1998.

"Global Market for Derivatives." *Wall Street Journal*, December 19, 1995, 1.

Goodman, Laurie. *Collateralized Debt Obligations.* John Wiley & Sons, 2002.

Gordy, Michael. *A Risk-Factor Model Foundation for Ratings-Based Bank Capital Rules.* Washington, DC: Board of Governors, Federal Reserve System, November 2002.

Gordy, Michael, and David James. *Capital Allocation for Securitization with Uncertainty in Loss Prioritizations.* Washington, DC: Federal Reserve Board, December 6, 2002.

Hessol, Gail I., Francis Parisi, Mark Puccia, and Joanne W. Rose. *Credit Comments.* Standard & Poor's Structured Finance, November 1995.

Hosking, Patrick, "Amaranth Collapse Was 'Easily Foreseeable'." *The Times,* October 13, 2006.

Hull, John C., *Options, Futures, and Other Derivatives.* 4th ed. Prentice-Hall, 2000.

International Swap Dealers Association. "Confirmation of OTC Credit Swap Transaction Single Reference Entity Non-Sovereign." ISDA, 1999.

Jorion, Phillipe. *Value at Risk.* McGraw-Hill, 1997.

Lee, Peter. "Masters of Credit or Hype?" *Euromoney*, July 1997, 44–49.

Nasar, Sylvia. *A Beautiful Mind.* Touchstone, 2001.

Natenberg, Sheldon. *Option Volatility and Pricing.* Richard D. Irwin, 1994.

Nelken, Israel, ed., *Option Embedded Bonds.* Times Mirror, 1997.

Pacelle, Mitchell. "A Debt Collector Implodes and the Lawyer Gets Sued." *Wall Street Journal,* October 29, 2002.

Porter, Bruce. "A Long Way Down." *New York Times,* June 6, 2004.

Poundstone, William. *The Prisoner's Dilemma.* Doubleday, 1992.

———. *Fortune's Formula.* Hill and Wang, 2005.

Rosen, Dr. Dan. *Effectively Measuring and Integrating Market Risk and Credit Risk.* New York: Algorithmics Inc. January 29, 1997.

Savage, Sam, Ph.D., "The Flaw of Averages," *San Jose Mercury News*, October 8, 2000.

Southern District of New York. *J.P. Morgan Chase Bank v. Liberty Mutual Insurance Company*, 01-CV-11523. March 5, 2002.

Smith, Randall, and Susan Pulliam. "As Funds Leverage Up, Fears of Reckoning Rise," *Wall Street Journal,* April 30, 2007.

Taleb, Nassim. *Fooled by Randomness.* 2nd updated ed. Random House, 2005.

Tavakoli, Janet. *Credit Derivatives and Synthetic Structures: A Guide to Instruments and Applications.* 2nd ed. John Wiley & Sons, 2001.

The New Palgrave Dictionary of Money & Finance. Macmillan Press, 1992.

Till, Hilary. "Inferences about the Amaranth Case and the Emerging Maturity of the Hedge Fund Industry." *Hedge Funds Review,* January 2007.

Tobias, Andrew. *Money Angles.* Avon Books, 1984

United States of America v. William R. Bartmann, 02-CR-163-H

Useem, Jerry. "How to Lose a Billion: Bill Bartmann Amassed a Huge Personal Fortune Building a Wildly Profitable Company. Too Bad It Was All on Paper." *Fortune,* October 25, 1999.

Westlake, Melvyn. "The Credit Crucible." *Emerging Market Investor* 2 (February 1997): 10–14.

Winkler, Robert L., and William L. Hays. *Statistics Probability, Inference, and Decision.* Holt, Rinehart, and Winston, 1975.

Index

Made in the USA
Monee, IL
13 November 2026

2efba7d0-a8d1-4a63-9bc0-2ff6d2ac7719R02